Doug Earle
ETSSW
9-82

A LINGUISTIC KEY TO THE GREEK NEW TESTAMENT

VOLUME 2

COMPANION TEXTS FOR NEW TESTAMENT STUDIES

A Critical Lexicon and Concordance to the English-Greek New Testament (Bullinger)
A Dictionary of New Testament Greek Synonyms (Berry)
A Grammar of Septuagint Greek (Conybeare and Stock)
A Greek-English Lexicon of the New Testament and Other Early Christian Literature (Bauer, Arndt, Gingrich, and Danker)
A Greek Grammar of the New Testament and Other Early Christian Literature (Blass and Debrunner, Funk)
A Linguistic Key to the Greek New Testament (Rienecker, Rogers)
A Reader's Greek-English Lexicon of the New Testament (Kubo)
A Shorter Lexicon of the Greek New Testament (Gingrich)
Do It Yourself Hebrew and Greek (Goodrick)
Greek-English Lexicon to the New Testament (Greenfield, Green)
Greek-English Lexicon of the New Testament (Thayer)
New Testament Greek Primer (Marshall)
The Analytical Greek Lexicon Revised (Moulton)
The Englishman's Greek Concordance of the New Testament (Wigram)
The Englishman's Greek New Testament (Newberry)
The Greek New Testament Slidaverb Conjugation Chart (Peterson)
The Interlinear Greek-English New Testament (Berry)
The Interlinear Greek-English New Testament (Marshall)
The New International Dictionary of New Testament Theology (Brown)
The NIV Interlinear Greek-English New Testament (Marshall)
The RSV Interlinear Greek-English New Testament (Marshall)
The Zondervan Parallel New Testament in Greek and English (Marshall)

A LINGUISTIC KEY TO THE GREEK NEW TESTAMENT

VOLUME 2
ROMANS-REVELATION

FRITZ RIENECKER

Translated and revised by Cleon L. Rogers, Jr.

ZONDERVAN
PUBLISHING HOUSE
OF THE ZONDERVAN CORPORATION
GRAND RAPIDS, MICHIGAN 49506

Second printing 1981

ISBN 0-310-32030-5

This book was first published in Germany under the title SPRACHLICHER SCHLUESSEL ZUM GRIECHISCHEN NEUEN TESTAMENT © 1970 by Brunnen-Verlag, Giessen

The Greek text used in this book is that of *The Greek New Testament* edited by Kurt Aland, Matthew Black, Carlo M. Martini, Bruce M. Metzger and Allen Wikgren. Copyright © 1966, 1968 by the American Bible Society, British and Foreign Bible Society, National Bible Society of Scotland, Netherlands Bible Society, Wurttemberg Bible Society. This text was checked against *Novum Testamentum Graece* edited by Eberhard Nestle.

Library of Congress Cataloging in Publication Data

Rienecker, Fritz.
A linguistic key to the Greek New Testament.
CONTENTS: v. 1. Matthew through Acts.—
v. 2. Romans through Revelation.
1. Bible. N.T.—Criticism, Textual. 2. Bible.
N.T. Greek-Versions. I. Rogers, Cleon L.
II. Title.
BS1938.R513 225.4'8 75-45486
ISBN 0-310-32030-5 (v. 2)
Edited by Edward Viening

Printed in the United States of America

CONTENTS

FOREWORD TO THE ENGLISH REVISION

The *Sprachlicher Schlussel* has undergone numerous German editions and has proven to be a real help to students of God's holy Word. All who have used it with immense profit are deeply indebted to the scholar and man of God, Fritz Rienecker.

On August 15, 1965, the earthly work of Fritz Rienecker came to an end. The Lord whom he so loved called him home after a fruitful ministry here on earth. His many literary works live on and continue to be used by those seeking to study the Bible.

Mr. Rienecker had intended to write two other books which were to supplement the *Linguistic Key*. One was to cover the theological concepts of the Scriptures and the other was to provide a historical background explaining the world of the New Testament. The realization of this vision was cut short by his death.

The translation and revision of the *Linguistic Key* has attempted in a limited way to achieve the purpose intended by the two proposed works of Rienecker. Explanations have been given not only regarding the grammatical forms, but there are also numerous new references to other works where the background material may be found. The revision includes a wider range of references to grammatical works, commentaries, journal articles, and historical works, and these are especially adapted to the English reader. The citation of a work does not mean that the theological position of its author is endorsed, but only that the particular quote was deemed valuable in reference to its historical or grammatical insight.

A word of thanks is due to my relatives and friends for their patient endurance during the long hours of work with Rienecker. A special word of thanks is due to Dr. Robert De Vries of The Zondervan Corporation and also to the senior editor of the project, Mr. Ed Viening, for his untiring work. The faithful work of the typists, Mrs. Linda Hutchinson, Mrs. Barbara Capps and Miss Aileen Dunn has also been deeply appreciated. Above all I would like to again formally express my deepest appreciation to my dear wife, Gail, for her patience, and to our children Cleon III, Charles, Sharon, and Suzanne for their constant encouragement. Cleon spent many hours in copying the Greek words and proofreading the manuscript.

May the Spirit of God use these efforts to increase an interest in and an understanding of His Holy Word.

Cleon Rogers,
Seeheim, Germany

FROM THE FOREWORD OF THE FIRST EDITION

A renewed struggle for a deeper understanding of God's Word is present in the ranks of all who earnestly want to live as Christians. There is a stronger desire to be clothed with the "whole armor of God." Where do we find the whole armor of God? It is not in the polemic, not in the apologetic, not in speculations, not in the mystical, and not in philosophy, but rather in the Word, the Holy Scriptures alone. This is where God has revealed Himself. This is where we must be at home. This is what matters, to grasp and learn the Word in all its weight and reality.

In order for this to be accomplished three tools are designed to help us. These are "Keys" which are to open the door of the New Testament for us, especially the door of the original text. Three "Keys" are designed to be our servants: *A Linguistic Key; A Key to the Concepts of the New Testament; A Key to the Background of the New Testament.*

Exactly what these three "Keys" mean, and the special duty of each will be presented in an introduction to each and references will be made to each of these three keys.

However, above everything else, this thesis remains absolute and certain: the Holy Spirit is the only true Key to the Word of God. Nevertheless, the petition for the Holy Spirit does not exclude earnest and energetic study.

Introduction to the *Linguistic Key to the New Testament.*

In 1524 Luther wrote this concerning the value of the Greek language: "In the measure that we love the Gospel, so let us place a strong emphasis on the languages. For it was not without reason that God wrote the Scriptures in two languages, the Old Testament in Hebrew and the New Testament in Greek. That language which God did not despise but rather chose above all others for His Word is the language which we also should honor above all others. It is a sin and shame that we do not learn this language of our Book, especially since God has now provided us people and books, and gives us all kinds of things which both help us with this task and at the same time stimulates us to do this." There is nothing more to add to these words of Luther.

The user of the *Linguistic Key* will find in this work an exact explanation of the verb forms. The substantives and adjectives are given in the nominative. When it is necessary, the root of both the verbs and substantives will be presented; that is when it appears important to the author that it serves a practical purpose, but not however as an extra philological burden just for the sake of philology. The results of the newest commentaries will conscientiously be considered. The concern is that the reader and the exegete will be given an abundance of points of contact which the scientific student can only receive from the original text. Every chapter is complete in itself and even every section is understandable in itself.

It will often be seen in the *Linguistic Key* how important it is for the seeking reader and the practical exegete to take into consideration the grammatical side of the text investigation. He must do this through the exact examination of what may perhaps appear to be an unimportant "but" or "for." It is intended to sharpen his vision for the world of the little and the least. By this careful detail work it can, under circumstances, happen that a totally unimportant appearing word turns out to have a decisive meaning. It can even be that without this, a true understanding of the text is not possible. The *Linguistic Key* is intended also to be an initial and quick introduction to the understanding of the original text. Born out of the practical need, the *Key* is to serve the practical. It is intended to make possible a constant and living relation to the original text, to encourage a reflective reading of the text, to produce joy in the study of the Bible, both in family and private devotions, and to provide a personal adherence and careful attention to the Word. May the *Linguistic Key* often give new light through the grammatical usage to many a well-worn and threadbare word. May many words regain new life and new love.

In regard to the external feature, the *Linguistic Key* is further intended to be an aid in learning the New Testament vocabulary. Then, it is to build a first bridge to the use of the scholarly New Testament Greek grammar of Blass and Debrunner and to make reference to the great and valuable *Lexica* of Menge-Güthling, Bauer, and above all to Kittel's great *Theological Dictionary*. May the *Key* give a greater incentive to the useful study of the commentaries.

Fritz Rienecker

FOREWORD TO THE 7TH EDITION

No one would ever have thought that with the first edition of the *Linguistic Key* there would have been such a surprisingly large demand for it and that this demand would have continued. From 1938 to the first years of the war there were already 17,000 copies in 6 editions sold. The growing distress of war and the ever-increasing pressure of anti-Christian tendencies which were opposed to everything biblical made another new edition impossible. Since the end of the war the request for a new edition has been continually present. The interest for the *Linguistic Key* has started and continues so strongly that is has put the earlier demands in the shadows. The Brunnen Publishers, Giessen, have graciously undertaken the new edition. May God's goodness guide this new edition and may He use the 7th edition to deepen the study of the original text of the New Testament!

FOREWORD TO THE 8TH EDITION

The editors and the publishers thankfully rejoice that already, nine months after the appearance of the 7th edition, a new printing of the *Linguistic Key* is necessary. The fact that this edition is printed on India paper is welcomed with joy. May the Lord of the Word grant through His Spirit His blessed presence to this aid to the study of the Scriptures!

FOREWORD TO THE 9TH EDITION

In this edition of the *Linguistic Key* there are a few corrections. They have to do with corrections of some grammatical explanations (in the earlier editions there were always some typographical errors which kept creeping in). There are also some better styled expressions related to matters found in the latest commentaries.

The fact that 45,000 copies have been printed has filled our hearts with joy, especially since this is a work which is not designed to edify, but rather to give a purely linguistic help. It is a new proof showing how strong the desire is among earnest students of the Word and energetic readers to penetrate to a deeper understanding of God's Word with the help of the original text. May the Lord of the Word bless all of these dear friends and students of our faithful Bible!

Fritz Rienecker

ABBREVIATIONS

BOOKS AND JOURNALS

Abbott	Edwin A. Abbott, *Johannine Grammar* (London: Adam and Charles Black, 1906).
Abbott	T.K. Abbott, *A Critical and Exegetical Commentary on the Epistles to the Ephesians and the Colossians. The International Critical Commentary* (Edinburgh: T. & T. Clark, 1956).
Adamson	James Adamson, *The Epistle of James. The New International Commentary on the New Testament* (Grand Rapids: Eerdmans, 1977).
Alford	Henry Alford, *The Greek Testament,* 5 Vols. (London: Rivingtons, 1855).
APC	Leon Morris, *The Apostolic Preaching of the Cross* (Grand Rapids: Eerdmans, 1956).
AS	G. Abbott-Smith, *A Manual Greek Lexicon of the New Testament* (Edinburgh: T. & T. Clark, 1936).
BA	*Biblical Archaeologist*
BAG	Walter Bauer, *A Greek-English Lexicon of the New Testament*. Translated by William F. Arndt and F. Wilbur Gingrich (Chicago: University of Chicago Press, 1957).
Bakker	W. F. Bakker, *The Greek Imperative* (Amsterdam: Adolf M. Hakkert, 1966).
Barrett	C. K. Barrett, *The Epistle to the Romans* (New York: Harper, 1957).
Barrett	C. K. Barrett, *A Commentary on the First Epistle to the Corinthians* (London: Adam & Charles Black, 1968).
Barrett	C. K. Barrett, *The Second Epistle to the Corinthians* (London: Adam and Charles Black, 1973).
Barth	Marcus Barth, *The Anchor Bible: Ephesians,* 2 vols. (Garden City, N.Y.: Doubleday, 1974).
BC	F. J. Foakes Jackson and Kirsopp Lake, *The Beginnings of Christianity,* 5 Vols. (London: Macmillan, 1920).
BD	F. Blass and A. Debrunner, *A Greek Grammar of the New Testament*. Translated and Revised by R. W. Funk (Chicago: University of Chicago Press, 1957).

BE — Richard Longenecker, *Biblical Exegesis in the Apostolic Period* (Grand Rapids: Eerdmans, 1975).

Beare — F. W. Beare, The *Epistles to the Philippians* (London: Adam and Charles Black, 1969).

Beare — F. W. Beare, *The First Epistle of Peter* (Oxford: Basil Blackwell, 1958).

Bengel — John Albert Bengel, *Gnomon of the New Testament,* 5 Vols. (Edinburgh: T.& T. Clark, 1857).

Best — Ernest Best, *A Commentary on the First and Second Epistles to the Thessalonians* (London: Adam and Charles Black, 1972).

Best — Ernest Best, *First Peter. The New Century Bible* (London: Oliphants, 1971).

Beyer — Klaus Beyer, *Semitische Syntax im Neuen Testament* (Gottingen: Vandenhoeck & Ruprecht, 1968).

BG — Maximillian Zerwick, *Biblica Greek* (Rome: Scripta Pontificii Instituti Biblici, 1963).

BHS — James D. G. Dunn, *Baptism in the Holy Spirit* (London: SCM Press, 1974).

Bib Sac — *Bibliotheca Sacra*

Bigg — Charles Bigg, *A Critical and Exegetical Commentary on the Epistles of St. Peter and St. Jude. The International Critical Commentary* (Edinburgh: T. & T. Clark, 1902).

Blomqvist — Jerker Blomqvist, *Greek Particles in Hellenistic Prose* (Lund, Sweden: C. W. K. Gleerup, 1969).

Bousset — Wilhelm Bousset, *Die Offenbarung Johannis* (Gottingen: Vandenhoeck and Ruprecht, 1906).

Brooke — A. E. Brooke, *A Critical and Exegetical Commentary on the Johannine Epistles. The International Critical Commentary* (Edinburgh: T. & T. Clark, 1912).

Bruce — F. F. Bruce, *I and II Corinthians: The New Century Bible* (London: Oliphants, 1971).

Bruce — F. F. Bruce, *Commentary on the Epistle to the Hebrews* (Grand Rapids: Eerdmans, 1977).

BS — Adolph Deissmann, *Bible Studies,* 2nd edition. Translated by Alexander Grieve (Edinburgh: T. & T. Clark, 1903).

Buchanan	George Wesley Buchanan, *The Anchor Bible: To the Hebrews* (Garden City, N. Y.: Doubleday, 1972).
Buckland	W. W. Buckland, *A Textbook of Roman Law* (Cambridge: Cambridge University Press, 1932).
Bultmann	Rudolf Bultmann, *Der zweite Brief an die Korinther; Meyers Kritschexegetischer Kommentar über das Neue Testament* (Gottingen: Vandenhoeck and Ruprecht, 1976).
Bultmann	Rudolf Bultmann, *Die drei Johannesbriefe. Kritsch-exegetischer Kommentar über das Neue Testament* (Gottingen: Vandenhoeck & Ruprecht, 1967).
Burton	Ernest DeWitt Burton, *A Critical and Exegetical Commentary to the Galatians: The International Critical Commentary* (Edinburgh: T. & T. Clark, 1956).
CAC	Fred O. Francis and Wayne A. Meeks (Editors), *Conflicts at Colossae: A Problem in the Interpretation of Early Christianity Illustrated by Selected Modern Studies*. Revised Edition (Missoula, Mont.: Scholars Press, 1975).
CAH	*The Cambridge Ancient History,* 12 vols. (Cambridge: At the University Press, 1927-1975).
Caird	G. B. Caird, *The Revelation of St. John the Divine. Black's New Testament Commentaries* (London: Adam and Charles Black, 1966).
CBB	L. Coenen, E. Beyreuther, H. Bietenhard, *Theologisches Begriffs-lexicon zum Neuen Testament,* 2 vols. (Wuppertal: Brockhaus, 1971).
CC	Stephen Benko and John J. O'Rouke (Editors), *The Catacombs and The Colisseum* (Valley Forge: Judson Press, 1971).
CD	*Cairo Damascus Document*
CEJC	Richard N. Longenecker, *The Christology of Early Jewish Christianity. Studies in Biblical Theology* (London: SMC Press Ltd., 1970).
CH	W. J. Conybeare and J. S. Howson, *The Life and Epistles of St. Paul* (Grand Rapids: Eerdmans, 1953).
Charles	R. H. Charles, *A Critical and Exegetical Commentary on the Revelation of St. John. The International Critical Commentary,* 2 Vols. (Edinburgh: T. & T. Clark, 1920).
CNT	Leon Morris, *The Cross in the New Testament* (Grand Rapids: Eerdmans, 1965).

Conzelmann — Hans Conzelmann, *Der erste Brief an die Korinther. Kritschexegetischer Kommentar über das Neue Testament,* von H. A. W. Meyer (Gottingen: Vandenhoeck & Ruprecht, 1969).

CPJ — Victor A. Tcherikover and Alexander Fuks (Editors), *Corpus Papyrorum Judaicarum* (Cambridge, Mass.: Harvard University Press, 1957-1964).

Cranfield — Charles E. Cranfield, *Epistle to the Romans* (Naperville, Ill.: Allenson, 1979).

Cremer — Hermann Cremer, *Biblico-Theological Lexicon of the New Testament Greek,* Translated by William Urwick (Edinburgh: T. & T. Clark, 1954).

Crouch — James E. Crouch, *The Origin and Intention of the Colossian Haustafel* (Gottingen: Vandenhoeck and Ruprecht, 1972).

DC — Dio Chrysostom

DCNT — G. Mussies, *Dio Chrysostom and the New Testament* (Leiden: E. J. Brill, 1972).

DSS — *Dead Sea Scrolls*

Delitzsch — Franz Delitzsch, *Commentary on the Epistle to the Hebrews.* Translated from the German by Thomas L. Kingsbury, 2 Vols. (Grand Rapids: Eerdmans, 1952).

DGRA — William Smith, *A Dictionary of Greek & Roman Antiquities* (London: John Murray, 1872).

Dibelius — Martin Dibelius, *An Die Kolosser Epheser An Philemon. Handbuch zum Neuen Testament. Dritte Auflage; Neu Bearbeitet vow Heinrich Greeven* (Tubingen: J. C. B. Mohr, 1953).

Dibelius — Martin Dibelius, *Die Pastoralbriefe; Handbuch zum Neuen Testament* Vierte, ergäntze Auflage von Hans Conzelmann (Tübingen: J. C. B. Mohr, 1966).

Dibelius — Martin Dibelius and Heinrich Greeven, *A Commentary on the Epistle of James. Hermeneia.* Translated by Michael A. Williams (Philadelphia: Fortress Press, 1976).

DM — H. E. Dana and J. R. Mantey, *A Manual Grammar of the Greek New Testament* (New York: Macmillan, 1950).

Dodd — C. H. Dodd, *The Epistle of Paul to the Romans* (London: Hodder & Stoughton, 1932).

Eadie	John Eadie, *Commentary on the Epistle of Paul to the Galatians* (Minneapolis: James and Klock Christian Publishing Co., 1977).
Eadie	John Eadie, *Commentary on the Epistle to the Ephesians* (Grand Rapids: Zondervan, 1956).
Eadie	John Eadie, *Commentary on the Epistle of Paul to the Colossians* (Minneapolis: James and Klock Christian Publishing Co., 1977).
EBC	Frank E. Gaebelein (Gen. Editor), *The Expositor's Bible Commentary* (Grand Rapids: Zondervan, 1976).
ECC	Vernon H. Neufeld, *The Earliest Christian Confessions* (Grand Rapids: Eerdmans, 1963).
EGT	W. Robertson Nicoll (ed.), *The Expositor's Greek Testament,* 5 Vols. (Grand Rapids: Eerdmans, 1956).
Ellicott	Charles J. Ellicott, *A Critical and Grammatical Commentary on St. Paul's Epistle to the Galatians* (Boston: Draper and Halliday, 1867).
Ellicott	Charles J. Ellicott, *St. Paul's Epistle to the Ephesians:* With a Critical and Grammatical Commentary, and a Revised Translation, 4th Edition (London: Longman, Green, Reader and Dyer, 1868).
Ellicott	Charles J. Ellicott, *St. Paul's Epistle to the Philippians, the Colossians and Philemon* (London: Longman, Green, Longman, Roberts and Green, 1865).
Ellicott	Charles J. Ellicott, *A Critical and Grammatical Commentary on St. Paul's Epistles to the Thessalonians* (Andover: Warren F. Draper, 1865).
Ellicott	Charles J. Ellicott, *The Pastoral Epistles of St. Paul.* The 5th Edition Corrected (London: Longmans, Green and Co., 1883).
EWNT	Horst Balz and Gerhard Schneider, *Exegetisches Werterbuch Zum Neuen Testament* (Stuttgart: Kohlhammer, 1978).
ELR	H. A. Trebel and K. M. King, *Everyday Life in Rome* (Oxford, 1958).
Fairbairn	Patrick Fairbairn, *Commentary on the Pastoral Epistles, First and Second Timothy, Titus* (Grand Rapids: Zondervan, 1956).
Fascher	Erich Fascher, *Der Erste Brief des Paulus An die Korinther* (Berlin: Evangelische Verlagsanstalt, 1975).

FCS	S. Scott Bartchy, *First Century Slavery & First Corinthians 7:21* (Missoula, Mont.: The Society of Biblical Literature, 1973).
FFB	*Fauna and Flora of the Bible. Helps for Translators,* Vol. XI (United Bible Societies, 1972).
Fitzmyer	Joseph A. Fitzmyer, *Essays on the Semitic Background of the New Testament* (Missoula, Montana: Scholars Press, 1974).
Ford	J. Massynberde Ford, *Revelation. The Anchor Bible* (Garden City, N.Y.: Doubleday and Company, 1975).
Frame	James Everett Frame, *A Critical and Exegetical Commentary on the Epistles of St. Paul to the Thessalonians. The International Critical Commentary* (Edinburgh: T. & T. Clark, 1953).
Funk	Robert W. Funk, *A Beginning-Intermediate Grammar of Hellenistic Greek,* 3 vols. (Missoula, Mont.: Society of Biblical Literature, 1973).
GAM	William M. Ramsey, *The Historical Geography of Asia Minor* (Amsterdam: Adolf M. Hakkert, 1962).
Gaugler	Ernst Gaugler, *Der Epheserbrief: Auslegung Neutestamentlicher Schriften* (Zurich: EVZ—Verlag, 1966).
Gaugler	Ernst Gaugler, *Die Johannesbriefe. Auslegung Neutestamentlicher Schriften* (Zurich: EVZ—Verlag, 1964).
GELS	H. G. Liddell, Robert Scott, H. Stuart Jones, *A Greek-English Lexicon. A Supplement.* Edited by E. A. Barber with the assistance of P. Maas, M. Scheller and M. L. West (Oxford: At the Clarendon Press, 1968).
GEW	Hjalmar Frisk, *Griechisches Etymologisches Wöterbuch* (Heidelberg: Carl Winter, 1973).
GI	Nigel Turner, *Grammatical Insights Into the New Testament* (Edinburgh: T. & T. Clark, 1965).
Gifford	E. H. Gifford, *The Epistle of St. Paul to the Romans* (London: John Murray, 1886).
Gnilka	Joachim Gnilka, *Der Epheserbrief. Herders theologischer Kommentar zum Neuen Testament* (Basel: Herder, 1971).
Gnilka	Joachim Gnilka, *Der Philipperbrief. Herders theologischer Kommentar zum Neuen Testament* (Freiburg: Herder, 1976).

GNT	James Moffatt, *Grace in the New Testament* (New York: Ray Long and Richard R. Smith, Inc., 1932).
Godet	Frederick L Godet, *The Commentary on the Epistle to the Romans,* Translated by A. Cusin and Talbot W. Chambers (Grand Rapids: Zondervan, 1956).
Godet	Frederick L. Godet, *Commentary on the First Epistle of St. Paul to the Corinthians,* translated by A. Cusin, 2 vols. (Grand Rapids: Zondervan, 1957).
Goppelt	Leonhard Goppelt, *Der erste Petrusbrief. Kritschexegetischer Kommentar Uber das Neue Testament.* Herausgegeben von Ferdinand Han (Gottingen: Vandenhoeck and Ruprecht, 1977).
Govett	Robert Govett, *The Apocalypse Expounded by Scripture,* abridged from the 4 vol. ed. 1864 (London: Charles J. Thynne, 1920).
GPT	F. E. Peters, *Greek Philosophical Terms: A Historical Lexicon* (New York: New York University Press, 1967).
Green	Michael Green, *The Second Epistle General of Peter and the General Epistle of Jude. Tyndale New Testament Commentaries* (London: The Tyndale Press, 1970).
Grosheide	Frederick Grosheide, *Commentary on First Corinthians,* NICNT (Grand Rapids: Eerdmans, 1953).
Guthrie	Donald Guthrie, *Galatians; The New Century Bible* (London: Oliphants, 1969).
Guthrie	Donald Guthrie, *The Pastoral Epistles* (London: The Tyndale Press, 1969).
GW	David Hill, *Greek Words and Hebrew Meanings: Studies in the Semantics of Soteriological Terms* (Cambridge: University Press, 1967).
HDB	James Hastings (ed.), *A Dictionary of the Bible,* 5 Vols. (Edinburgh: T. & T. Clark, 1901).
Hendriksen	William Hendriksen, *New Testament Commentary: Colossians and Philemon* (Edinburgh: The Banner of Truth Trust, 1974).
Hering	Jean Hering, *The First Epistle of St. Paul to the Corinthians,* translated by A. W. Heathcote & P. J. Allcock (London: Epworth Press, 1969).

Hering — Jean Hering, *The Second Epistle of St. Paul to the Corinthians,* translated by A. W. Heathcote and P. J. Allcock (London: Epworth Press, 1967).

Hewitt — Thomas Hewitt, *The Epistle to the Hebrews. An Introduction and Commentary. Tyndale New Testament Commentary* (Grand Rapids: Eerdmans, 1960).

HJP — Emil Schürer, *A History of the Jewish People in the Time of Jesus Christ,* two divisions, translated by John Macpherson (Edinburgh: T. & T. Clark, 1910).

Hodge — Charles Hodge, *Commentary on the Epistle to the Romans* (Grand Rapids: Eerdmans, 1953).

Hodge — Charles Hodge, *Commentary of the Second Epistle to the Corinthians* (Grand Rapids: Eerdmans, 1953).

Hodge — Charles Hodge, *Commentary of the First Epistle to the Corinthians* (Grand Rapids: Eerdmans, 1953).

Hodge — Charles Hodge, *A Commentary on the Epistle to the Ephesians* (Grand Rapids: Eerdmans, 1950).

Hofius — Otfried Hofius, *Der Christushymnus Philipper 2, 6-11* (Tübingen: J. C. B. Mohr, 1977).

Hort — F. J. A. Hort, *The First Epistle of St. Peter I.1-II.17* (London: Macmillan, 1898; reprint Minneapolis: James and Klock Publishing Company, 1976).

Hort — F. J. A. Hort, *The Apocalypse of St. John I–III* (London: Macmillan, 1908; reprint by James and Klock Publishing Co., 1976).

Houlden — J. L. Houlden, *A Commentary on the Johannine Epistles. Black's New Testament Commentary* (London: Adam and Charles Black, 1973).

Hughes — Philip E. Hughes, *Commentary on the Second Epistle to the Corinthians* (Grand Rapids, Eerdmans, 1971).

Hughes — Philip Edgcumbe Hughes, *A Commentary on the Epistle to the Hebrews* (Grand Rapids: Eerdmans, 1977).

Huther — Joh. Ed. Huther, *Critical and Exegetical Handbook to the Epistles of St. Paul to Timothy and Titus. Critical and Exegetical Commentary on the New Testament.* H. A. W. Meyer (Edinburgh: T. & T. Clark, 1881).

Huther — J. E. Huther, *Critical and Exegetical Handbook to the General Epistles of Peter and Jude. Meyer's Critical and*

	Exegetical Commentary on the New Testament (Edinburgh: T. & T. Clark, 1881).
IB	George Arthur Buttrick (ed.). The *Interpreter's Bible,* vol. 10 (Nashville: Abingdon Press, 1952).
IBG	C. F. D. Moule, *An Idiom Book of New Testament Greek* (Cambridge: University Press, 1959).
IDB	George Arthur Buttrick (ed.), *The Interpreter's Dictionary of the Bible,* 4 Vols. (Nashville: Abingdon Press, 1962).
Jastrow	Marcus Jastrow, *Dictionary of the Targumim, The Talmud Babli and Yerushalmi, and the Midrashic Literature,* 2 Vols. (New York: Pardes, 1950).
JBL	*Journal of Biblical Literature.*
Jeremias	Joachim Jeremias, *Die Briefe an Timotheus und Titus: Das Neue Testament* Deutsch (Gottingen: Vandenhoeck and Ruprecht, 1963).
JETS	*The Journal of the Evangelical Theological Society*
JNP	G. N. Stanton, *Jesus of Nazareth in the New Testament Preaching* (Cambridge: Cambridge University Press, 1974).
Johnson	Alan F. Johnson, *The Freedom Letter* (Chicago: Moody Press, 1974).
Jones	A. H. M. Jones, *The Roman Economy.* Studies in Ancient Economy and Administrative History. Edited by P. A. Brunt (Oxford: Blackwell, 1974).
JPF	S. Safrai and M. Stern (eds.), *The Jewish People in the First Century: Historical Geography, Political History, Social, Cultural and Religious Life and Institutions,* Vol. 1 (Assen, Holland: Van Gorcum & Comp. B. V., 1974).
JS	Otto Betz, Klaus Haacker, Martin Hengel (Editors) *Josephus-Studien. Untersechenven zu Josephus, dem antiqun Judentum und den Neuen Testament.* Sustschrift sur Otto Michel (Gottingen: Vandenhoeck and Ruprecht, 1974).
JTJ	Joachim Jeremias, *Jerusalem in the Times of Jesus* (London: SCM Press, 1969).
JTS	*Journal of Theological Studies.* N.S. (New Series).
Käsemann	Ernst Käsemann, *An Die Römer Handbuch Zum Neuen Testament* (Tübingen: J. C. B. Mohn, 1974).

Kelly — J. N. D. Kelly, *A Commentary on the Pastoral Epistles* (London: Adam and Charles Black, 1972).

Kelly — J. N. D. Kelly, *A Commentary on the Epistles of Peter and of Jude. Black's New Testament Commentaries* (London: Adam and Charles Black, 1969).

Kent — Homer A. Kent, Jr., *The Epistle to the Hebrews: A Commentary* (Winona Lake, Ind.: B. M. H. Books, 1974).

Knowling — R. J. Knowling, *The Epistle of St. James. Westminster Commentaries* (London: Methuen and Co., 1904).

KP — Konrat Ziegler & Walther Sontheimer (Editors), *Der Kleine Pauly: Lexikon der Antike* (Munich: Alfred Druckenmüller, 1975).

Kuss — Otto Kuss, *Der Romer Brief* (Regensburg: Friedrick Pustet, 1963).

Ladd — George Eldon Ladd, *A Theology of the New Testament* (Grand Rapids: Eerdmans, 1974).

LAE — Adolf Deissmann, *Light From the Ancient East,* translated by Lionel R. M. Strachan (London: Hodder and Stoughton, 1927).

Lenski — R. C. H. Lenski, *The Interpretation of the Epistle to the Hebrews and the Epistle of James* (Minneapolis: Augsburg Publishing House, 1966).

Lenski — R. C. H. Lenski, *The Interpretation of St. Paul's I & II Epistles to the Corinthians* (Columbus, Ohio: Wartburg Press, 1946).

Lenski — R. C. H. Lenski, *The Interpretation of the Epistle to the Hebrews and the Epistle of James* (Minneapolis: Augsburg Publishing House, 1966).

Lietzmann — Hans Lietzmann, *An die Korinther I-II: Handbuch zum Neuen Testament* (Tübingen: J. C. B. Mohr, 1969).

Lightfoot — J. B. Lightfoot, *St. Paul's Epistle to the Colossians and to Philemon* (Grand Rapids: Zondervan, Reprint of 1879 edition).

Lightfoot — Joseph Barber Lightfoot, *The Epistle of St. Paul to the Galatians* (Grand Rapids: Zondervan, 1956).

Lightfoot — J. B. Lightfoot, *St. Paul's Epistle to the Philippians* (Grand Rapids: Zondervan, 1953).

Lightfoot, *Notes* — J. B. Lightfoot, *Notes on the Epistles of St. Paul* (I & II

	Thessalonians, I Corinthians 1-7, Romans 1-7, Ephesians 1:1-14) (Grand Rapids: Zondervan, 1957).
N. Lightfoot	Neil R. Lightfoot, *Jesus Christ Today, A Commentary on the Book to the Hebrews* (Grand Rapids: Baker Book House, 1976).
Lock	Walter Lock, *A Critical and Exegetical Commentary on the Pastoral Epistles. The International Critical Commentary* (Edinburgh: T. & T. Clark, 1966).
Lohmeyer	Ernst Lohmeyer, *Die Briefe an die Philipper, an die Kolosser und an Philemon. Kritischexegetischer Kommentar über das Neue Testament* (Gottingen: Vandenhoeck & Ruprecht, 1964).
Lohse	Eduard Lohse, *Die Offenbarung Des Johannes. Das Neue Testament Deutsch* (Gottingen: Vandenhoeck and Ruprecht, 1971).
Lohse	Eduard Lohse, *Hermeneia. A Critical and Historical Commentary on the Bible: Colossians and Philemon* (Philadelphia: Fortress Press, 1976).
LP	William M. Ramsay, *Luke the Physician and Other Studies in the History of Religion* (Grand Rapids: Baker Book House, 1956).
LS	Henry George Liddell and Robert Scott, *A Greek English Lexicon,* A new edition revised and augmented throughout by Henry Stewart Jones and Roderick McKenzie (Oxford: Oxford University Press, 1953).
LSC	William M. Ramsey, *The Letters to the Seven Churches of Asia* (London: Hodder and Stoughton, 1904).
Lünemann	Gottlieb Lünemann, *Critical and Exegetical Commentary on the New Testament*. Edited by H. A. W. Meyer (Edinburgh: T. & T. Clark, 1880).
M	James Hope Moulton, *A Grammar of New Testament Greek: Prolegomena,* I (Edinburgh: T. & T. Clark, 1957).
M	(f. by the name of the tractate) *The Mishnah,* translated by Herbert Danby (London: Oxford University Press, 1967).
Marshall	I. Howard Marshall, *The Epistles of John. The New International Commentary on the New Testament* (Grand Rapids: Eerdmans, 1978).
Martin	Ralph Martin, *Colossians: The Church's Lord and the Christian's Liberty* (Grand Rapids: Zondervan, 1973).

Martin	R. P. Martin, *Carmen Christi. Philippians 2.5-11.* In recent interpretation and in the setting of early Christian worship (Cambridge: At the University Press, 1967).
Martin, NCB	Ralph Martin, *Colossians and Philemon. New Century Bible* (London: Oliphants, 1974).
Mayor	Joseph B. Mayor, *The Epistles of St. James* (Grand Rapids: Zondervan, 1954).
Mayor	Joseph B. Mayor, *The Epistle of St. Jude and the Second Epistle of St. Peter* (Grand Rapids: Baker Book House, 1965).
McKay	K. L. McKay, "The Use of the Perfect Down to the 2nd Century A.D.," *Bulletin of the Institute of Classical Studies of the University of London,* 12 (1965), 1-21.
Meyer	Heinrich August Wilhelm Meyer, *Critical and Exegetical Commentary on the New Testament,* translation revised and edited by William P. Dickson and Frederick Crombie, 20 Vols. (Edinburgh: T. & T. Clark, 1891).
MH	James Hope Moulton and William Francis Howard, *A Grammar of New Testament Greek: Accidence and Word Formation,* II (Edinburgh: T. & T. Clark, 1956).
Michel	Otto Michel, *Der Brief an die Romer, Kritschexegetischer Kommentar über das Neue Testament* (Gottingen: Vandenhoeck & Ruprecht, 1966).
Michel	Otto Michel, *Der Brief an die Hebräer. Kritschexegetischer Kommentar über das Neue Testament* (Gottingen: Vandenhoeck & Ruprecht, 1966).
Milligan	George Milligan, *St. Paul's Epistles to the Thessalonians* (Grand Rapids: Eerdmans, 1953).
MKG	G. Mussies, *The Morphology of Koine Greek, As Used in The Apocalypse of St. John: A Study in Bilingualism* (Leiden: E. J. Brill, 1971).
MM	James Hope Moulton and George Milligan, *The Vocabulary of the Greek Testament* (London: Hodder & Stoughton, 1952).
MNTW	William Barclay, *More New Testament Words* (London: SCM Press, 1958).
Moffatt	James Moffatt, *A Critical and Exegetical Commentary on the Epistle to the Hebrews. The International Critical Commentary* (Edinburgh: T. & T. Clark, 1968).

Montefiore	Claude Joseph Goldsmith Montefiore and Herbert Martin James Loewe, *A Rabbinic Anthology* (New York: Meridian Books, Inc. [n.d.]).
Montefiore	Hugh Montefiore, *A Commentary on the Epistle to the Hebrews* (London: Adam & Charles Black, 1964).
Moore	A. L. Moore, *The First and Second Thessalonians. The Century Bible* (London: Thomas Nelson and Sons, 1969).
Moore, Judaism	George Foot Moore, *Judaism in the First Centuries of the Christian Era the Age of Tannaim,* 3 Vols. (Cambridge: Harvard University Press, 1958).
Moorhouse	A. C. Moorhouse, *Studies in the Greek Negatives* (Cardiff: University of Wales Press, 1959).
Morris	Leon Morris, *The First and Second Epistles to the Thessalonians. The New International Commentary on the New Testament* (Grand Rapids: Eerdmans, 1959).
Morris	Leon Morris, *The First Epistle of Paul to the Corinthians* (Grand Rapids: Eerdmans, 1958).
Moule	C. F. D. Moule, *The Epistles to the Colossians and to Philemon. The Cambridge Greek Testament Commentary* (Cambridge: At the University Press, 1958).
Mounce	Robert H. Mounce, *The Book of Revelation, The New International Commentary on the New Testament* (Grand Rapids: Eerdmans, 1977).
MRP	J. A. Ziesler, *The Meaning of Righteousness in Paul* (Cambridge: Cambridge University Press, 1972).
MS	C. H. Dodd, *More New Testament Studies* (Grand Rapids: Eerdmans, 1968).
MT	James Hope Moulton and Nigel Turner, *A Grammar of New Testament Greek:* Vol. III *Syntax* (Edinburgh: T. & T. Clark, 1963).
MT Style	James Holt Moulton and Nigel Turner, *A Grammar of New Testament Greek,* Vol. 4, Style (Edinburgh: T. & T. Clark, 1976).
Munck	Johannes Munck, *Christ and Israel,* An Interpretation of Romans 9-11 (Philadelphia: Fortress Press, 1967).
Murray	John Murray, *The Epistle to the Romans,* 2 vol. (Grand Rapids: Eerdmans, 1971).

Mussner	Franz Mussner, *Der Galaterbrief; Herders Theoloqischer Kommentar zum Neuen Testament* (Basel: Herder, 1974).
Mussner	Franz Mussner, *Der Jakobusbrief. Herders Theologischer Kommentar zum Neuen Testament* (Freiburg: Herder, 1975).
NBD	J. D. Douglas (ed.), *The New Bible Dictionary* (Grand Rapids: Eerdmans, 1962).
ND	Richard N. Longenecker and Merrill C. Tenny (Editors), *New Dimensions in New Testament Study* (Grand Rapids: Zondervan, 1974).
Nov T	*Novum Testamentum*.
NTCW	Allison A. Trites, *The New Testament Concept of Witness* (Cambridge: Cambridge University Press, 1977).
NTRJ	David Daube, *The New Testament and Rabbinic Judaism* (New York: Arno Press, 1973).
NTS	*New Testament Studies*.
NTW	William Barclay, *A New Testament Wordbook* (London: SCM Press, 1955).
Nygren	Anders Nygren, *Commentary on Romans,* Translated by Carl C. Rasmussen (Philadelphia: Fortress Press, 1949).
OCD	H. G. L. Hammond and H. H. Scullard (eds.), *Oxford Classical Dictionary,* 2nd. ed. (Oxford: University Press, 1972).
PAA	John Howard Schütz, *Paul and the Anatomy of Apostolic Authority* (Cambridge: Cambridge University Press, 1975).
PAM	Victor C. Pfitzner, *Paul and the Agon Motif. Traditional Athletic Imagery in the Pauline Literature*. (Leiden: E. J. Brill, 1967).
PAT	Robert Jewett, *Paul's Anthropological Terms* (Leiden: E. J. Brill, 1971).
PCG	Edwin M. Yamauchi, *Pre-Christian Gnosticism* (London: Tyndale Press, 1973).
Pearson	Birger Albert Pearson, *The Pneumatikos-Psychikos Terminology* (Missoula, Mont.: The Society of Biblical Literature, 1973).
PGL	G. W. H. Lampe, *A Patristic Greek Lexicon* (Oxford: Clarendon Press, 1968).

PIP — Gordon P. Wiles, *Paul's Intercessory Prayers: The Significance of the Intercessory Prayer Passages in the Letters of Paul* (Cambridge: Cambridge University Press, 1974).

Plummer — Alfred Plummer, *The Epistles of St. John. The Cambridge Bible for Schools and Colleges* (Cambridge: At the University Press, 1894).

Plummer — Alfred Plummer, *A Critical and Exegetical Commentary on the Second Epistle of St. Paul to the Corinthians. The International Critical Commentary* (Edinburgh: T. & T. Clark, 1956).

Preisigke — Friedrich Preisigke, *Wörterbuch der griechischen Papyrusurkunden* (Heidelberg-Berlin, 1924-31).

PRJ — W. D. Davies, *Paul and Rabbinic Judiasm: Some Rabbinic Elements in Pauline Theology* (London: SPCK, 1965).

PS — J. N. Sevenster, *Paul and Seneca* (Leiden: E. J. Brill, 1961).

PTW — Hans Dieter Betz, *Plutarch's Theological Writings and Early Christian Literature* (Leiden: E. J. Brill, 1975).

PW — R. G. Hamerton-Kelly, *Pre-existence Wisdom and the Son of Man* (Cambridge: Cambridge University Press, 1973).

PWC — Charles Caldwell Ryrie, *The Place of Women in the Church* (New York: Macmillan, 1958).

1QS — *The Manual of Discipline.*

1QH — *Hymns of Thanksgiving.*

1QM — War of the Sons of Light Against the Sons of Darkness.

1 Q Gen Ap — *The Genesis Apocryphon.*

R — Johannes Friedrich, Wolfgang Pöhlmann, Peter Stuhlmacher (Editors) *Rechtfertigung: Festschrift für Ernst Käsemann* (Tubingen: J. C. B. Mohr, 1976).

RAC — Theodor Klauser (Editor), *Reallexikon Fur Antike und Christentum* (Stuttgart: Anton Hierseman, 1950-76).

Ramsey — William M. Ramsey, *A Historical Commentary of St. Paul's Epsitle to the Galatians* (Grand Rapids: Baker Book House, 1965).

Ramsey, LP — William M. Ramsey, *Luke the Physician and other Studies in the History of Religion* (Grand Rapids: Baker Book House, 1956).

Reicke	Bo Ivar Reicke, *The Anchor Bible. The Epistles of James, Peter, and Jude* (Garden City, N. Y.: Doubleday & Co., 1964).
RG	A. T. Robertson, *A Grammar of the Greek New Testament in the Light of Historical Research* (Nashville: Broadman, 1934).
RH	Robert Banks (Editor), *Reconciliation and Hope: New Testament Essays on Atonement and Eschatology* (Grand Rapids: Eerdmans, 1974).
Ridderbos	Herman N. Ridderbos, *The Epistle of Paul to the Churches of Galatia; The New International Commentary of the New Testament* (Grand Rapids: Eerdmans, 1970).
Riggenbach	Edward Riggenbach, *Der Brief an die Hebräer* (Leipzig: A. Deichert, 1913).
Robinson	J. Armitage Robinson, *St. Paul's Epistle to the Ephesians* (London: Macmillan & Co., 1914).
Ropes	James Hardy Ropes, *A Critical and Exegetical Commentary on the Epistle of St. James. The International Critical Commentary* (Edinburgh: T. & T. Clark, 1916).
RP	Archibald Robertson and Alfred Plummer, *A Critical and Exegetical Commentary on the First Epistle of St. Paul to the Corinthians: The International Critical Commentary,* 2nd edition (Edinburgh: T. & T. Clark, 1955).
RWP	A. T. Robertson, *Word Pictures in the New Testament,* 6 Vols. (New York: Harper & Brothers, 1930).
SB	H. L. Strack and P. Billerbeck, *Kommetar zum Neuen Testament aus Talmud und Midrasch,* 6 Vols. (Munich: C. H. Beck, 1965).
SBT	Robert H. Gundry, *Soma in Biblical Theology With An Emphasis on Pauline Anthropology* (Cambridge: Cambridge University Press, 1976).
SCA	Richard C. Trench, *Commentary on the Epistles to the Seven Churches in Asia–Revelation II–III,* 6th ed. (Minneapolis, Minn.: Klock and Klock, 1978, originally published 1897).
Schelkle	Karl Hermann Schelkle, *Die Petursbriefe, Der Judasbrief. Herders Theologischer Kommentar zum Neuen Testament.* Dritte Auflage (Freiburg: Herder, 1970).

Schlatter	Adolf Schlatter, *Die Kirche der Griechen im Urteil des Paulus. Eine Auslegung seiner Briefe an Timotheus und Titus* (Stuttgart: Calwer Verlag, 1958).
Schlier	Heinrich Schlier, *Der Brief an die Galater; Kritsch-exegetischer Kommentar Uber Das Neue Testament* (Gottingen: Vandenhoeck and Ruprecht, 1965).
Schlier	Heinrich Schlier, *Der Brief an die Epheser* (Düsseldorf: Patmosverlag, 1968).
Schnackenburg	Rudolf Schnackenburg, *Das Johannesevangelium: Herder's Theologischer Kommentar zum Neuen Testament,* 2 vols. (Joh. 1–12) (Freiburg: Herder, 1971).
Schnackenburg	Rudolf Schnackenburg, *Die Johannesbriefe. Herders Theologischer Kommentar zum Neuen Testament* (Basil: Herder, 1965).
Schweizer	Eduard Schweizer, *Der Brief an die Kolosser: Evangelisch-Katholischer Kommentar zum Neuen Testament* (Zürich: Benziger Verlag, 1976).
Scott	Walter Scott, *Exposition of the Revelation of Jesus Christ* (London: Pickering and Inglis [n.d.]).
SEH	M. Rosteovtzeff, *The Social & Economic History of the Roman Empire,* 2nd ed. 2 vols. (Oxford: Oxford University Press, 1960, 1963).
Seiss	Joseph Augustus Seiss, *The Apocalypse. Lectures on the Book of Revelation* (Grand Rapids: Zondervan, 1957).
Selwyn	Edward Gordon Selwyn, *The First Epistle of St. Peter* (London: Macmillan, 1958).
SH	William Sanday and Arthur C. Headlam, *A Critical and Exegetical Commentary on the Epistle to the Romans,* The International Critical Commentary (Edinburgh: T. & T. Clark, 1955).
Simpson	E. K. Simpson and F. F. Bruce, *Commentary on Ephesians and Colossians. The New International Commentary on the New Testament* (Grand Rapids: Eerdmans, 1975).
SL	Robert A. Kraft, *Septuagintal Lexicography* (Missoula, Mont.: Scholars Press, 1975).
SMT	Ernest DeWitt Burton, *Syntax of the Moods and Tenses in New Testament Greek,* 3rd. ed. (Edinburgh: T. & T. Clark, 1955).

SP	A. S. Hunt and C. C. Edgar (Editors) *Select Papyri* 2 vols. *The Loeb Classical Library* (Cambridge, Mass.: Harvard University Press, 1932).
Spicq	C. Spicq, *L, Épitre Aux Hebreux,* 2 Vols. (Paris: J. Gabalda, 1952-53).
Stibbs	Alan M. Stibbs and Andrew F. Walls, *The First Epistle General of Peter. Tyndale New Testament Commentaries* (London: The Tyndale Press, 1971).
Stott	John R. W. Stott, *The Epistles of John. Tyndale New Testament Commentaries* (London: The Tyndale Press, 1969).
Stuhlmacher	Peter Stuhlmacher, *Der Brief an Phelemon: Evangelisch-Katholisher Kommentar zum Neuen Testament* (Zürich: Benziger Verlag, 1975).
Swete	Henry Barclay Swete, *The Apocalypse of St. John* (London: Macmillan, 1907).
T	Joseph Henry Thayer, *A Greek-English Lexicon of the New Testament* (New York: American Book Company, 1889).
Tasker	R. V. G. Tasker, *The General Epistle of James. The Tyndale New Testament Commentaries* (Grand Rapids: Eerdmans, 1956).
TB	*Tyndale Bulletin.*
TC	Bruce M. Metzger, *A Textual Commentary on the Greek New Testament* (London: United Bible Societies, 1971).
TDNT	Gerhard Kittel and Gerhard Friedrich (eds.), *Theological Dictionary of the New Testament,* 9 Vols. (Grand Rapids: Eerdmans, 1973).
TDOT	G. J. Botterweck and Helmer Ringgren, *Theological Dictionary of the Old Testament* (Grand Rapids: Eerdmans, 1973).
Thrall	Margaret E. Thrall, *Greek Particles in the New Testament* (Leiden: E. J. Brill, 1962).
Trench, Synonym	R. C. Trench, *Synonyms of the New Testament* (Grand Rapids: Eerdmans, 1953).
TT	Martin McNamara, *Targum and Testament, Aramaic Paraphrases of the Hebrew Bible: A Light on the New Testament* (Grand Rapids: Eerdmans, 1972).
Vincent	Marvin R. Vincent, *A Critical and Exegetical Commentary on the Epistles to the Philippians and to Philemon. The*

	International Critical Commentary (Edinburgh: T. & T. Clark, 1955).
von Dobschütz	Ernst von Dobschütz, *Die Thessalonickerbriefe* (Gottingen; Vandenhoeck & Ruprecht, 1974).
Walvoord	John F. Walvoord, The *Revelation of Jesus Christ* (Chicago: Moody Press, 1966).
Weiss	Johannes Weiss, *Der erste Korinther Brief* (Gottingen: Vandenhoeck and Rup律cht, 1910).
Westcott	Brooke Foss Westcott, *The Epistles of John* (Cambridge: Macmillan, 1892).
Westcott	Brooke Foss Westcott, *The Epistle to the Hebrews* (Grand Rapids: Eerdmans, n.d.).
Westcott	Brooke Foss Westcott, *St. Paul's Epistle to the Ephesians* (Grand Rapids; Eerdmans, 1952).
Wiesinger	August Wiesinger, *Biblical Commentary on St. Paul's Epistles to the Philippians, to Titus, and the First to Timothy* (In Continuation of the work of Olshausen) (Edinburgh: T. & T. Clark, 1861).
Windisch	Hans Windisch, *Der zweite Korintherbrief Meyers Kritschexegetischer Kommentar über das Neue Testament* (Goettingen: Vandenhoeck and Ruprecht, 1970).
Wuest	Kenneth S. Wuest, *Galatians in the Greek New Testament* (Grand Rapids: Eerdmans, 1951).
ZNW	*Zeitschrift fur die Neutestamentliche Wissenschaft*.
ZPEB	Merrill C. Tenney (General Editor), *The Zondervan Pictorial Encyclopedia of the Bible* (Grand Rapids: Zondervan, 1975).

GENERAL ABBREVIATIONS

abs	absolute	n	neuter
acc	accusative	neg	negative
adj	adjective	nom	nominative
aor	aorist	obj	object
adv	adverb	obj. gen	objective genitive
cf	confer (compare)	opt	optative
comp	comparative	org	original
conj	conjunctive	p. pp	page (s)
dat	dative	part	participle
dep	deponent	pass	passive
dimin	diminutive	perf	perfect
e.g.	exempli gratia (for example)	pers	person
		pl	plural
esp	especially	plperf	pluperfect
f, ff	following	poss	possessive
fem	feminine	pred	predicate
fig	figuratively	pref	prefix
fut	future	prep	preposition
gen	genitive	pres	present
Gr	Greek	pron	pronoun
imp	imperative	refl	reflexive
Heb	Hebrew	rel	relative
impf	imperfect	s	see
indef	indefinite	sing	singular
ind	indicative	subj	subjunctive
indir	indirect	subst	substantive
inf	infinitive	suf	suffix
instr	instrumental	superl	superlative
intr	intransitive	synon	synonymous
interat	interative	t.t.	technical term
masc	masculine	temp	temporal
mid	middle	trans	transitive
Lat	Latin	voc	vocative
lit	literally	Vulg	Vulgate
LXX	Septuagint	w	with

ROMANS

Ch. 1

δοῦλος slave, bondservant. The term emphasizes the bond- 1
age and the belonging to another (CBB; TDNT). (For the concept of slavery in the ancient world, s. Philemon 21f.) The following genitives show possession. **κλητὸς** called. The verbal adj.
w. this ending usually has a pass. sense (BG, 47; s. also M, 221).
ἀφωρισμένος perf. pass. part. ἀφορίζω to mark off, to separate
by a boundary. The absence of the article w. the words in v.1
indicate the nature or quality (BG, 55). ■ **προεπηγγείλατο** aor. 2
mid. προεπαγγέλλω to promise before, to promise previously
or in advance. **γραφή** writing, Scripture. The absence of the
article throws the stress on "holy" (SH). ■ **περὶ τοῦ υἱοῦ αὐτοῦ** 3
to be connected closely w. the word "gospel" (Lightfoot, *Notes*).
γενομένου aor. mid. part. γίνομαι. ■ **ὁρισθέντος** aor. pass. 4
part. ὁρίζω to mark out the boundary, to decree, to appoint (s.
S. Lewis Johnson, Jr., "The Jesus that Paul Preached," Bib Sac,
128 [April, 1971], 129f.; L.C. Allen, "The Old Testament Background of [προ] ὁρίζειν in the New Testament," NTS, 17 [Oc-
tober, 1970], 104–108; TDNT). **ἁγιωσύνη** holiness. Here it
indicates a spirit or disposition of holiness which characterized
Christ spiritually (Johnson, 132). ■ **ἐλάβομεν** aor. λαμβάνω. 5
The pl. refers only to Paul and his stylistic method avoiding the
emphasis on "I" (Kuss). **ἀποστολή** apostleship, the office of an
apostle. **ὑπακοή** obedience. ■ **οὖσιν** pres. part. εἰμί. **ἀγαπητός** 7
beloved. (For verbal adjectives w. this ending, s.v.1.)

■ **καταγγέλλεται** pres. pass. καταγγέλλω to proclaim, to 8
report, to publicly report (Barrett). ■ **λατρεύω** to serve, to serve 9
for pay then to do service for a deity (TDNT). **ἐν τῷ πνεύματί
μου** "with (in) my spirit." It is by using his spirit that Paul
renders God service (Barrett). **ἐν τῷ εὐαγγελίῳ** "in the gospel."
The prep. here denotes the external sphere (Lightfoot, *Notes*).
ἀδιαλείπτως adv. without ceasing, constantly. **μνεία** remembrance, mention. ■ **δεόμενος** pres. mid. part. δέομαι to pray, to 10
make a request. **εἴ πως** "if perhaps." By omitting the apodosis
of the conditional sentence, the first clause may be taken as a
wish (MT, 91). **εὐοδωθήσομαι** fut. pass. εὐοδόω to cause one

to journey prosperously, to make one succeed (Godet). **ἐλθεῖν**
11 aor. act. inf. ἔρχομαι. ■ **ἐπιποθέω** to long for. The prep. compound marks the direction of the desire (SH). **ἰδεῖν** aor. inf.
ὁράω. **μεταδῶ** aor. subj. μεταδίδωμι to share w. someone.
χάρισμα a gift (freely and graciously given), a favor bestowed
(BAG). **πνευματικός** spiritually, pertaining to the spirit. The
suffix indicates a dynamic relation to the idea involved in the
root (MH, 378). **στηριχθῆναι** aor. pass. inf. στηρίζω to
strengthen. The pass. indicates it is God who will strengthen
(Godet). The inf. is used w. prep. to express purpose (s. MT,
12 143). ■ **συμπαρακληθῆναι** aor. pass. inf. συμπαρακαλέω to
encourage together, to encourage mutually. Here it signifies "I
w. you, Christians of Rome" (Godet). Infinitive used to express
13 purpose. ■ **προεθέμην** aor. mid προτίθημι to place before, to
purpose, to intend. **ἐκωλύθην** aor. pass. κωλύω to hinder.
δεῦρο adv. here, until now. **σχῶ** aor. subj. ἔχω to have, to get.
14 The idea expressed is that of gathering fruit (Murray). ■
βάρβαρος one who does not speak Gr. properly; one who
speaks an unintelligible language then applied to people who did
not familiarly use Gr., and so were regarded as uncultured
(Dodd). **σοφός** wise. **ἀνόητος** ignorant, not understanding.
ὀφειλέτης one who owes a debt. (For the binding obligation
15 placed upon debtors in the ancient world, s. SEH I, 382f.) ■ **τὸ
κατ' ἐμέ** either to be taken as the subject w. the next word as
the predicate, "for my part, I am all readiness" (EGT) or the
prep. is to be taken as a circumlocution for the poss. gen., "my
readiness" (BD, 120). **πρόθυμος** ready, willing eager.
εὐαγγελίσασθαι aor. mid. inf. εὐαγγελίζομαι to evangelize,
to proclaim the good news.
16 ■ **ἐπαισχύνομαι** to be ashamed. **πιστεύοντι** pres. act.
part. **Ἕλλην** Gr. Here it refers to anyone who is not a Jew
17 (Gifford). ■ **δικαιοσύνη** the phrase could mean "the righteous
standing which God gives" or "the righteous character which
God is" or "the righteous activity which comes from God." (For
a review of these meanings, s. MRP, 9–14; Cranfield). **ἐν αὐτῷ**
"in it," that is, in the gospel. **ἀποκαλύπτεται** pres. pass.
ἀποκαλύπτω to reveal. **ἐκ** "out of." The prep. here may indicate the source of the righteousness. (For the various interpretations of this phrase, s. S. Lewis Johnson, Jr., "The Gospel that
Paul Preached," Bib Sac, 128 [October, 1971], 336f.)
γέγραπται perf. pass. The perf. emphasizes the permanent and
authoritative character of that which was written (s. MM).
ζήσεται fut. mid. ζάω to live.
18 ■ **ἀποκαλύπτεται** pres. pass. The word need not be totally

eschatological but has the sense of God's displeasure at sin, the sense that God will not overlook sin (Lightfoot, *Notes*). **ὀργή** wrath. The word indicates the deep-seated anger of God against sin. This anger arises from His holiness and righteousness (s. TDNT; CBB; Trench, *Synonyms*, 130–134; Cranfield). **ἀσέβεια** ungodliness. **ἀδικία** unrighteousness. The first represents impiety toward God and the second injustice toward men (Hodge). **ἀλήθεια** truth. The knowledge of God as communicated to the human conscience (Godet). **κατεχόντων** pres. part. κατέχω to
hold down, to suppress, to hold fast or firmly. ■ **διότι** because. 19
It gives the reason of that which precedes (Godet). **γνωστός** known or knowable. **ἐφανέρωσεν** aor. φανερόω to make clear,
to manifest. ■ **ἀόρατος** unseen, invisible. (For the use of the 20
prefix as a neg., s. Moorhouse, 41–66.) **κτίσις** creation. **ποίημα** that which is made. It refers to the source from which our perception of the invisible things is derived (Murray). **νοούμενα** pres. pass. part. νοέω to perceive, to gain an insight into (s. TDNT). **καθορᾶται** pres. pass. καθοράω to see, to see clearly or plainly, distinctly (LS). The force of the prep. compound is intensive or it may relate to the direction of sight, "contemplated" (SH). **τε** " and," "both." It joins words closely which have between themselves a close or logical affinity (MT, 339). **ἀΐδιος** eternal. **θειότης** divinity, divine nature, a summary term for the attributes which constitute deity (SH). (For this term and its contrast with the word "deity" as used in Colossians 2:9, s. TDNT; Cranfield; Trench, *Synonyms*, 7–10.) **εἶναι** pres. inf. used w. prep. to express purpose or result (MT, 143). **ἀναπολόγητος** without excuse, without legal defense (Lightfoot, *Notes*). ■ **γνόντες** aor. act. part. γινώσκω. (For the Jewish 21
teaching regarding the Gentiles knowing God's demands, s. SB III, 36–46.) **ἐδόξασαν** aor. δοξάζω to form an opinion about, to glorify. **ηὐχαρίστησαν** aor. εὐχαριστέω to give thanks, to be thankful. **ἐματαιώθησαν** aor. pass. ματαιόω to render futile, worthless, pass. to be given over to worthlessness, think about worthless things, to be foolish (BAG). **διαλογισμός** reason, here "inward questionings" (Lightfoot, *Notes*). **ἐσκοτίσθη** aor. pass. σκοτίζω to darken, ingressive aor. to become darkened. **ἀσύνετος** unintelligible, without insight. ■ **φάσκοντες** 22
pres. act. part. φάσκω to affirm, to assert. **ἐμωράνθησαν** aor.
pass. μωραίνω to make foolish, pass. to become foolish. ■ 23
ἤλλαξαν aor. ἀλλάσσω to exchange. They exchanged one thing for another (Hodge). **ἄφθαρτος** incorruptible. **ὁμοίωμα** likeness, implies a resemblance which may be accidental. **εἰκών** image, presupposes an archetype of which it is a copy. The gen.

is gen. of apposition or explanation. (For this word and the
preceding, s. Lightfoot, *Notes*.) **φθαρτός** corruptible. **πετεινά**
(pl.) birds. **τετράπους** four-footed. **ἑρπετά** (pl.) creeping
things, snakes.
24 ■ **διό** "therefore." **παρέδωκεν** aor. παραδίδωμι to deliver
over, to hand over. (For the judicial aspect, s. Gifford; SB III,
62f.) **ἐπιθυμία** lust, desire. **ἀκαθαρσία** uncleanness. It refers
to sexual aberration (Murray). **ἀτιμάζεσθαι** pres. pass. inf.
25 ἀτιμάζω to dishonor. The inf. is epexegetic (Barrett). ■
μετήλλαξαν aor. μεταλλάσσω to change w., to exchange.
ἐσεβάσθησαν aor. pass. σεβάζομαι to worship, to show reverence to. **ἐλάτρευσαν** aor., s.v.9. **παρά** w. acc. "more than."
Used to express the comp. and here means virtually "instead of"
(BD, 123f.). **κτίσαντα** aor. part. κτίζω to create. **εὐλογητός**
26 blessed. ■ **πάθος** passion or a passionate desire. It represents the
pass., ungoverned aspect of evil desire (AS). **ἀτιμία** dishonor,
disgrace. (For the prefix as a neg., s.v.20.) **θῆλυς** female.
φυσικός natural, that which pertains to nature. (For the meaning of the suffix, s. MH, 378.) **χρῆσις** use, function, esp. of
27 sexual intercourse (BAG). ■ **ὁμοίως** likewise. **ἄρσην** male.
ἀφέντες aor. act. part. ἀφίημι to leave, to forsake.
ἐξεκαύθησαν aor. pass. ἐκκαίω to set on fire, pass. to be consumed, to be inflamed. **ὄρεξις** desire. It is always the reaching
out after and toward an object, w. the purpose of drawing that
after which it reaches to itself, and making it its own (Trench,
Synonyms, 326). **ἀσχημοσύνη** shameless, disgraceful, obsceni-
ty (Barrett). **κατεργαζόμενοι** pres. mid. part. **κατεργάζομαι**
to work, to accomplish. (For the perfectivizing force of the prep.
compound, s. M, 112f.) **ἀντιμισθία** reward, penalty. The prep.
compound emphasizes the reciprocal nature of the transaction
(BAG). **ἔδει** impf. δεῖ it is necessary. **πλάνη** error. (For the
Jewish view on sexual perversion of the heathen, s. SB III, 64–
74.) **ἀπολαμβάνοντες** pres. act. part. ἀπολαμβάνω to re-
28 ceive, to receive back, to receive one's due (SH). ■ **ἐδοκίμασαν**
aor. δοκιμάζω to test, to put to the test, to make a decision after
a trial. They tested God at first and turned aside from Him
(RWP). **ἐπίγνωσις** cognizance, knowledge. **ἀδόκιμος** rejected,
rejected after a trial, failing the test, disqualified, useless (Cranfield). **νοῦς** mind, the reasoning faculty, esp. as concerned w.
moral action, the intellectual part of conscience (SH).
καθήκοντα pres. act. part., that which is proper, or fitting,
moral. The word w. a technical term of Stoic philosophy (s.
29 TDNT; Barrett). ■ **πεπληρωμένους** perf. pass. part. πληρόω
to fill. **πλεονεξία** greediness, the insatiable desire to have more

even at the expense of harming others (s. Lightfoot, *Notes;* NTW, 97ff.; TDNT). **μεστός** full. **φθόνος** envy. **φόνος** murder. **ἔρις** strife, wrangling. **δόλος** deceit, cunning, treachery. **κακοήθεια** malice, the tendency to put the worst construction upon everything (SH; Trench, *Synonyms*, 38–40). **ψιθυριστής** whisperer, the man who pours his poison against his neighbor by
whispering in the ear (Godet). ■ **κατάλαλος** speaking evil 30
against others, slanderous, slanderer. The prep. compound indicates the action of the word is unfavorable to its object (MH, 316). **θεοστυγής** "hated of God" (pass.) or "haters of God" (active) (s. Gifford; Kuss). **ὑβριστής** a man of arrogant insolence. The word contains a mixture of cruelty and pride. The proud insolence and contempt for others displays itself in cruelty for the mere enjoyment of seeing others suffer (s. Trench, *Synonyms*, 202–205; Cranfield; MNTW, 77–85; TDNT). **ὑπερήφανος** proud, arrogant, one who shows himself above others. It is the proud, insolent, self-sufficient person who in his heart sets himself upon a pedestal above all others, even above God (s. Trench, *Synonyms*, 101f.; MNTW, 85–89; TDNT). **ἀλάζων** boastful, bragger, one who makes empty boasts and false promises often for the purpose of gain (s. Trench, *Synonyms*, 98–101; MNTW, 38–42; TDNT). **ἐφευρετής** inventor.
γονεύς parents. **ἀπειθής** disobedient. ■ **ἀσύνθετος** covenant- 31
breaker, faithless to an agreement. **ἄστοργος** unloving, without tenderness. It refers to the lack of the feelings of natural tenderness, as seen in a mother who exposes or kills her child, a father who abandons his family, or children who neglect their aged
parents (Godet). **ἀνελεήμων** unmerciful, without pity. ■ 32
δικαίωμα that which is declared right, judgment, ordinance (TDNT; MRP, 209). **ἐπιγνόντες** aor. part. **ἐπιγινώσκω** to know. **συνευδοκέω** to heartily approve (SH).

Ch. 2

■ **διό** therefore. It refers either to the preceding section 1
(1:18–32) or only to v. 32, or to that which follows in Ch. 2 (Murray). **ἀναπολόγητος** without excuse, without defense. **κρίνων** pres. part. **κρίνω** to judge. **κατακρίνω** pres. ind. to
judge against, to condemn. ■ **κρίμα** judgment, decision, either 2
good or bad (RWP). **τοιοῦτος** such as this, of such a kind.
πράσσοντας pres. act. part. ■ **λογίζομαι** pres. ind. mid. 2nd 3
per. sing. to reckon, to consider, to suppose. ■ **χρηστότης** kind- 4
ness, kindness in general, as expressed in giving favors (Hodge; TDNT). **ἀνοχή** patience. It is that forbearance or suspense of wrath, that truce w. the sinner, which by no means implies that

the wrath will not be executed at the last (Trench, *Synonyms*,
200). **μακροθυμία** longsuffering, a long holding out of the mind
before it gives room to action or passion (Trench, *Synonyms*,
196; TDNT). **καταφρονέω** pres. ind. act. to think down on, to
despise. **ἀγνοῶν** pres. part. ἀγνοέω to be ignorant, to ignore
(Barrett). **ἄγειν** pres. act. inf. conative pres. "to try to lead"
5 (Käsemann) ■ **σκληρότης** hardness. **ἀμετανόητος** unrepent-
ant. **θησαυρίζω** to store up, to treasure up. The idea is gradual
accumulation (Lightfoot, *Notes*). **δικαιοκρισία** just judgment,
judgment according to that which is right. It denotes God's
6 justice in the narrow, even distributive sense (MRP, 189). ■
ἀποδώσει fut. ἀποδίδωμι to give back, to recompense. Used
in the papyri for the paying of a debt or restoring of a due of any
7 kind (MM). ■ **ὑπομονή** patience, endurance, bearing up under.
ἀφθαρσία incorruptible, immortality. **ζητοῦσιν** pres. part.
8 ζητέω to seek. ■ **ἐριθεία** selfish ambition (BAG; s. also Barrett;
Phil. 2:3). **ἀπειθοῦσι** pres. act. part. ἀπειθέω to be disobedient.
πειθομένοις pres. mid. part. πείθομαι to obey, to be obedient.
ἀδικία unrighteousness. **θυμός** anger, rage. (For this and the
9 following word, s. Trench, *Synonyms*, 130–134; TDNT.) ■
θλῖψις pressure, tribulation. **στενοχωρία** anguish, torturing
confinement (SH). **κατεργαζομένου** pres. mid. part.
10 κατεργάζομαι to do, to accomplish (s. Rom. 1:27). ■
11 **ἐργαζομένῳ** pres. mid. part. ■ **προσωπολημψία** partial, the
accepting of the appearance of a pers. A Hebraic term for partiality. The Oriental custom of greeting was to bow one's face to the
ground. If the one greeted accepted the pers., he was allowed to
12 lift his head again (TDNT; s. also, SB III, 79–83). ■ **ὅσοι** as
many as, "all alike, whether under the law or not under the law"
(Lightfoot, *Notes*). **ἀνόμως** adv. without law, lawless. **ἥμαρτον**
aor. ἁμαρτάνω to send. A timeless aor. (RWP). **ἀπολοῦνται**
fut. ind. mid. ἀπόλλυμι to perish. **κριθήσονται** fut. ind. pass.
13 ■ **ἀκροατής** one who hears. **ποιητής** one who does. (For the
ending of these two nouns indicating the agent who performs the
action, s. MH, 364f.) **δικαιωθήσονται** fut. ind. pass. δικαιόω
to justify, to declare righteous, to declare in the right. (For this
important term, s. TDNT; APC, 224–280; GW, 82–162; MRP.)
14 ■ **ὅταν** w. subj. "whenever." **ἔχοντα** pres. part. **φύσις** nature,
15 instrumental dat. **ποιῶσιν** pres. subj. ■ **ἐνδείκνυνται** pres. ind.
mid. to demonstrate, to show. The word implies an appeal to
facts (SH). **γραπτός** written. **συμμαρτυρούσης** pres. act. part.
f. sing. συμμαρτυρέω to testify w., to confirm, to testify in
support of someone or something (BAG). **συνείδησις** conscience. Paul regarded conscience as performing in the gentile

world roughly the same function as was performed by the law
among the Jews (s. Margaret E. Thrall, "The Pauline Use of
Συνείδησις," NTS, 14 [Oct. 1967], 124). **μεταξύ** between.
κατηγορούντων pres. act. part. κατηγορέω to speak against,
to accuse, to bring a legal accusation against someone, gen. abs.
ἀπολογουμένων pres. mid. part. ἀπολογέομαι to excuse, to
defend, to offer a legal defense, gen. abs. ■ **κρυπτός** hidden. 16
■ **ἐπονομάζῃ** pres. ind. pass. 2nd per. sing. ἐπονομάζω to 17
put a name upon, pass. to have a name imposed, to bear the name
(SH). **ἐπαναπαύῃ** pres. ind. mid. 2nd per. sing. to rest upon, to
rely upon, to lean upon (Michel). **καυχᾶσαι** pres. ind. mid. 2nd
per. sing. to boast, to pride one's self in. ■ **δοκιμάζω** pres. ind. 18
act. to test, to examine, to approve after testing. **διαφέροντα**
pres. part. διαφέρω. The part. could mean either "the things
which excel" or "the things which differ." Here it refers to the
most delicate shades of the moral life alluding to the legal casuis-
try in which the Jewish schools excelled (Godet).
κατηχούμενος pres. pass. part. κατηχέω to instruct. ■ 19
πέποιθα perf. ind. act. πείθω to persuade, to be persuaded, to
put one's trust in. **ὁδηγός** guide, one who leads the way (RWP).
■ **παιδευτής** educator, teacher, schoolmaster. The word has the 20
idea of discipline, correction, as well as teaching (SH). **ἄφρων**
unthinking, foolish, ignorant, obj. gen. **νήπιος** infant.
μόρφωσις form, the rough sketch, penciling of the form, the
outline or framework without the substance (Lightfoot, *Notes*).
■ **διδάσκων** pres. act. part. **κηρύσσων** pres. act. part. ■ 21/22
βδελυσσόμενος pres. mid. part. βδελύσσομαι to abhor, to
detest. **εἴδωλον** idol. **ἱεροσυλέω** to rob a temple. Perhaps a
reference to the robbing of heathen temples (Kuss; SB III, 113).
(For the Jewish opposition against heathen idolatry, s. Moore,
Judaism I, 362f.; SB III, 111f.) ■ **βλασφημεῖται** pres. pass. 24
βλασφημέω to blaspheme. **γέγραπται** perf. pass. ■ **ὠφελεῖ** 25
pres. ind. act. gnomic pres. Used to express customary action
and general truths (SMT, 8). **πράσσῃς** pres. subj. The pres.
would emphasize the continual doing of the law. **παραβάτης**
trangressor, one who steps across a line (RWP). **ᾖς** pres. subj.
εἰμί. **ἀκροβυστία** uncircumcision. (For the importance of circumcision in Judaism, s. Moore, *Judaism* II, 16–21; TDNT; SB
IV, 23–40; Gal. 2:3.) **γέγονεν** perf. ind. act. γίνομαι. The perf.
emphasizes the continuing state or results. ■ **δικαίωμα** ordi- 26
nance, righteous to man (s. Rom. 1:32). **φυλάσσῃ** pres. subj.
φυλάσσω to guard, to observe. **λογισθήσεται** fut. pass. ■ 27
κρινεῖ fut. **τελοῦσα** pres. part. τελέω to bring to an end, to
complete, to fulfill. **διά** w. gen. "with." Used to describe the

attendant circumstances; that is, w. all your advantages of cir-
28 cumcision and the possession of a written law (SH). ■ **φανερός**
29 visible, open to sight, manifest. ■ **οὗ** rel. pron. gen. sing., the
antecedent is Ἰουδαῖος. **ἔπαινος** praise.

Ch. 3

1 ■ **περισσός** advantage, that which encircles a thing, that
which is in excess, over and above (SH). **ὠφέλεια** benefit, usefulness. (For the use of the rhetorical question to express clarity,
s. BD, 262.) **περιτομή** circumcision. The article and the pl. verb
in v.2 shows that it refers to the nation. Paul is thinking of the
promises of the Abrahamic Covenant as the superiority that
Israel had (s. Lewis Johnson, Jr., "Studies in Romans: The Jews
2 and the Oracles of God," Bib Sac, 130 [July, 1973], 239). ■
πρῶτον first, in the first place. **ἐπιστεύθησαν** aor. pass.
πιστεύομαι to entrust, pass. to be entrusted w. **λόγιον** saying,
oracle. Here it is a reference to the O.T. promises. The acc. is
used after a pass. verb (s. Johnson, "The Jews and the Oracles
3 of God," 240–246). ■ **ἠπίστησαν** aor. ἀπιστέω to disbelieve,
to refuse to believe or w. the meaning to be unfaithful (s. SH).
(For the prefix as a neg., s. Rom. 1:20.) **ἀπιστία** unbelief, unfaithfulness. **καταργήσει** fut. καταργέω to render inactive, to
4 render invalid (SH). ■ **γένοιτο** aor. opt. mid. γίνομαι in this
phrase "let it not be." It expresses the abhorrence of an inference
which may be falsely drawn from the argument (SMT, 79).
γινέσθω pres. mid. imp. Here "be found"; that is, become,
relatively to our apprehension (Lightfoot, *Notes*). **δέ** "but." The
contrast really means "though every man be found a liar"
(RWP). **ἀληθής** true. **καθάπερ** just as. **γέγραπται** perf. pass.
The perf. emphasizing the completed state and the continual
authority of that which is written. **δικαιωθῇς** aor. pass. subj.
δικαιόω to declare right, to justify, pass. to be declared to be in
the right (s. Rom. 2:13). **νικήσεις** fut. νικάω to be victorious,
to conquer. **κρίνεσθαι** pres. inf. mid. or pass. κρίνω to judge.
(For the use of the inf. w. the prep. to express contemporary
5 action, s. MT, 144f.) ■ **ἀδικία** unrighteousness. **συνίστησιν**
pres. ind. act. συνίστημι to bring together, to commend, to
demonstrate, to bring out something (BAG). Used in a first-class
conditional clause where the condition is assumed for the sake
of argument to be true (s. BG, 103). **ἐροῦμεν** fut. λέγω.
ἐπιφέρων pres. part. ἐπιφέρω to inflict. The sentence expects
6 the answer no (Barrett). ■ **γένοιτο** aor. opt. mid., s.v.4. **ἐπεί**
since, if that were so; that is, "if the inflicting of punishment
7 necessarily implied injustice" (SH). **κρινεῖ** fut. ■ **ἐν** "by,"

"through." (For the instrumental use of the prep., s. MT, 252f.)
ψεῦσμα lie. **ἐπερίσσευσεν** aor. περισσεύω to be in abundance, to increase. **κἀγώ** = καὶ ἐγώ. The word καί "then" is
used to introduce the main clause of a conditional sentence and
connotes a previously expressed circumstance (BG, 155).
ἁμαρτωλός sinful, sinner. **κρίνομαι** pres. ind. pass. ■ **μή** used 8
in a question expecting the answer no. (For the construction of
this v., s. RWP.) **βλασφημούμεθα** pres. pass. βλασφημέω to
slander. **ὅτι** recitative; that is, equivalent to quotation marks (s.
RG, 951f.). **ποιήσωμεν** aor. subj., deliberative subj. "let us do."
ἔλθῃ aor. subj. ἔρχομαι. **ὧν** rel. pron. gen. pl. "whose." It refers
to all who draw these antinomian inferences (Lightfoot, *Notes*).
κρίμα judgment. **ἔνδικος** just. (For this passage, s. S. Lewis
Johnson, Jr., "Studies in Romans: Divine Faithfulness, Divine
Judgment, and the Problem of Antinomianism," Bib Sac, 130
[Oct. 1973], 329–337.)

■ **προεχόμεθα** pres. mid. or pass. προέχω to excel, to be 9
first, or mid. to have an advantage or to hold something before
one's self for protection, or pass. to be excelled, to be in a worse
position (BAG; s. also SH; Käsemann). **οὐ πάντως** "not all
together," "only in a limited sense" (s. Barrett; S. Lewis Johnson, Jr., "Studies in Romans: The Universality of Sin," Bib Sac,
131 [April, 1974], 166). **προῃτιασάμεθα** aor. mid
προαιτιάομαι to make a previous accusation, to accuse previously, to incriminate previously. It belongs to the language of the
bar (Godet). ■ **γέγραπται** perf. pass. The perf. indicates the 10
permanent and authoritative character of that which was written
(s. MM). (For the composite character of the following quotation, s. Fitzmyer, *Essays*, 66f.) ■ **συνίων** pres. part. συνίω to 11
understand. **ἐκζητῶν** pres. part. ἐκζητέω to seek out. ■ 12
ἐξέκλιναν aor. ἐκκλίνω to turn away from, to turn aside from.
ἅμα together. **ἠχρεώθησαν** aor. pass. ἀχρέομαι to be worthless, to be useless, ingressive aor. "to become worthless." The
idea of the Heb. word is "to go bad or sour" like milk (Lightfoot,
Notes). **χρηστότης** goodness, the widest sense, w. the idea of
utility (SH). ■ **τάφος** grave. **ἀνεῳγμένος** perf. pass. part. 13
ἀνοίγω to open. **λάρυγξ** throat. **ἐδολιοῦσαν** impf. act. δολιόω
to deceive, to practice or use deceit. (For the impf. of contract
verbs w. the aor. ending, s. MH, 195.) **ἰός** poison. **ἀσπίς** asps,
the Egyptian cobra (RWP). **χεῖλος** lip. ■ **ἀρά** curse (s. TDNT). 14
πικρία bitterness. ■ **ὀξύς** swift, fast. **ἐκχέαι** aor. act. inf. ἐκχέω 15
to pour out, to shed. ■ **σύντριμμα** destruction, ruin, fracture (s. 16
MM). **ταλαιπωρία** misery. ■ **ἔγνωσαν** aor. γινώσκω. ■ 17/18
ἀπέναντι before, in the presence of. ■ **ὅσος** "whatever things." 19

λέγει pres. ind. act. **λαλεῖ** pres. ind. act. The first verb calls attention to the substance of what is spoken, the second to the outward utterance (SH). **ἵνα** used to express purpose or result (s. BD, 198). **φραγῇ** aor. subj. pass. φράσσω to shut, to stop, to close or stop the mouth, so that the man must remain silent (BAG). **ὑπόδικος** liable to judgment or to punishment, a legal term meaning "to answer to," "to bring under the cognizance of." Used in the papyri of officials who are held answerable
20 (MM). **γένηται** aor. subj. mid. γίνομαι. ■ **διότι** because. **δικαιωθήσεται** fut. pass. The fut. may indicate that this will never be the case. The whole context has reference to a judicial trial and verdict (SH; s. also Rom. 2:13). **ἐπίγνωσις** recognition, knowledge. The prep. w. the gen. indicates "through," "by means of" (IBG).
21 ■ **πεφανέρωται** perf. pass. φανερόω to make manifest, to make clear. The perf. emphasizes the state or condition. (For a study of the perf., s. K.L. McKay, "The Use of the Ancient Greek Perfect Down to the Second Century A.D.," *Bulletin of the Institute of Classical Studies of the University of London*, 12 [1965], 1–21.) **μαρτυρουμένη** pres. pass. μαρτυρέω to testify,
22 to bear witness. ■ **εἰς πάντας** "unto all," "for all." **πιστεύοντας** pres. act. part. **διαστολή** difference, distinction.
23 ■ **ἥμαρτον** aor. ἁμαρτάνω to sin, to miss the mark (s. CBB). **ὑστεροῦνται** pres. mid. ὑστερέω to come too late, to miss, to fail to reach, to be lacking, to come short of, followed by the gen. (BAG; TDNT). **δόξα** glory. The following gen. could be obj.; that is, failing to give God glory, or subj., failing to receive the glory God gives, or poss.; that is, failing to conform to His image
24 (s. Murray). ■ **δικαιούμενοι** pres. pass. part. The pres. tense is iterat. and emphasizes the repeated action in each case (RWP). (For the grammatical connection and use of the part., s. SH; Murray; Cranfield.) **δωρεάν** freely, as a gift without payment. (For the adverbial use of the acc. in the papyri, s. MM.) **ἀπολύτρωσις** redemption, release, or deliverance of the pay-
25 ment of a price (s. APC, 37–48; GW, 71f.; TDNT). ■ **προέθετο** aor. mid. προτίθημι to place before, mid. to purpose, to design or to set forth publicly (SH). **ἱλαστήριον** that which expiates or propitiates, the means of expiation or the place of propitiation (for example mercy seat) (s. APC, 167–174; GW, 38–47; TDNT). **ἔνδειξις** demonstration, sign, proof. **διά** w. acc. because of. **πάρεσις** passing over; Christ died and thereby manifested God's righteousness because in the past God had merely overlooked man's sins (Barrett; s. also MRT, 210). **προγεγονότων** perf. act. part. προγίνομαι to happen before,

to happen previously. The prep. compound is temporal. ■ **ἀνοχή** 26
patience, forbearing (s. Rom. 2:4). **δικαιοῦντα** pres. act. part.
■ **καύχησις** boasting. **ἐξεκλείσθη** aor. pass. ἐκκλείω to 27
shut out, to exclude. **ποῖος** what sort of? ■ **δικαιοῦσθαι** pres. 28
pass. inf. ■ **εἴπερ** if, if on the whole. Used of a thing which is 30
assumed to be (T). **δικαιώσει** fut. **ἀκροβυστία** uncircumcision. ■ **καταργοῦμεν** pres. ind. act., s.v.3. **γένοιτο** aor. opt. 31
mid., s.v.4. **ἱστάνω** to establish.

Ch. 4

■ **ἐροῦμεν** fut. λέγω. **εὑρηκέναι** perf. act. inf. Infinitive 1
used in indirect discourse (s. BD, 203,204). **προπάτωρ** forefather, ancestor. ■ **ἐδικαιώθη** aor. pass. δικαιόω to justify, to 2
declare righteous (s. Rom. 2:13). **καύχημα** boasting, ground of
boasting (SH). (For the righteousness of Abraham in Jewish
thinking, s. SB III, 186–201.) ■ **γάρ** for. To be taken as an 3
argumentative particle showing why Abraham has no ground of
boasting (Barrett). **ἐλογίσθη** aor. pass. λογίζομαι to reckon to
one's account. In the language of an accountant the word means
"to enter in the account book" (s. Ramsey; LP, 286f.). ■ 4
ἐργαζομένῳ pres. mid. part. ἐργάζομαι to work. **μισθός** pay,
wage, salary (s. MM). **λογίζεται** pres. pass. **ὀφείλημα** debt,
that which is owed (s. Rom. 1:14). ■ **πιστεύοντι** pres. part dat. 5
sing. **δικαιοῦντα** pres. part. **ἀσεβής** ungodly. A very strong
word used to place the gratuity of the gift in the strongest light
(Lightfoot, *Notes*). ■ **καθάπερ** even as. (For Paul's use of the 6
rabbinical exegetical principle of comparing the same word used
in two passages, s. Barrett.) **μακαρισμός** declaration of blessedness (T). The ending of the word indicates a state or condition
(MH, 355). ■ **μακάριος** blessed, happy. **ἀφέθησαν** aor. pass. 7
ἀφίημι to forgive. **ἀνομία** lawlessness. **ἐπεκαλύφθησαν** aor.
pass. ἐπικαλύπτω to cover over. ■ **οὐ μή** "not ever." (For this 8
emphatic neg. use, s. M, 188f.; BG, 149f.) **λογίσηται** aor. mid.
subj. ■ **περιτομή** circumcision. **ἀκροβυστία** uncircumcision. 9
The prep. used here w. acc. primarily designates movement
toward. In this sense "for" (s. IBG, 49). ■ **ὄντι** pres. part. εἰμί. 10
■ **σημεῖον** sign. **ἔλαβεν** aor. λαμβάνω. **σφραγίς** seal. That 11
which confirms a test or authenticates. Used w. gen. The sign of
circumcision simply confirms righteousness through faith that
was already pres. (BAG; s. also TDNT). **λογισθῆναι** aor. pass.
inf. Infinitive used to show purpose (contemplated result) or
actual result (RWP). ■ **στοιχοῦσιν** pres. act. part στοιχέω to 12
walk. A well-known military term meaning strictly "to march in
file" (SH). **ἴχνος** footstep, track.

13 ■ **νόμου** "in the context of law." The prep. w. gen. indicates
attendant circumstances (Barrett). The word law without the
article refers to law as commandment demanding obedience and
applies to all law which falls into this category (Murray).
ἐπαγγελία promise. **κληρονόμος** heir. (For the Jewish view of
Abraham as heir of the world and that this was achieved through
14 his law righteousness, s. SB III, 204–209.) ■ **κεκένωται** perf.
pass. κενόω to empty. The perf. emphasizes a state or condition
brought about by a previous result (s. Rom 3:21). **κατήργεται**
perf. pass. καταργέω to render inoperative (s. Rom. 3:3). The
conditional sentence of this v. could be classified as a second-
class conditional sentence where the condition is not true (s.
15 IBG, 148f.). ■ **ὀργή** wrath (s. Rom. 1:18). **παράβασις** trans-
16 gression, stepping over the mark. ■ **βέβαιος** ratified (Lightfoot,
17 *Notes*). **σπέρμα** seed. ■ **γέγραπται** perf. pass. **ὅτι** recitative,
equal to quotation marks. **τέθεικα** perf. act. **τίθημι** to place, to
appoint. **κατέναντι** opposite to, in the presence of. (For this
prep., s. MH, 129.) **ζωοποιοῦντος** pres. act. part. ζῳοποιέω to
make alive. Refers to God's ability to give a child to Abraham
18 and Sarah in their old age (Godet). **καλοῦντος** pres. part. ■
ἐλπίς hope. Here lit. "against (or, beyond) hope, in hope," that
is, "hoping against hope" (Barrett). **γενέσθαι** aor. mid. inf. used
w. prep. to express purpose. **εἰρημένον** perf. pass. part. λέγω.
19 **ἔσται** fut. εἰμί. ■ **ἀσθενήσας** aor. act. part. ἀσθενέω to be
weak, ingressive aor. w. neg., "without showing weakness,"
"without becoming weak" (SH). **κατενόησεν** aor. κατανοέω to
see clearly, to discern. (For the prep. compound, s. M, 117.)
νενεκρωμένον perf. pass. part. νεκρόω to kill, pass. to die. The
perf. emphasizes the completed state or condition (s. Rom. 3:-
21). **ἑκατονταέτης** a hundred years. **που** about. **ὑπάρχων** pres.
part. ὑπάρχω to exist, to be. **νέκρωσις** death, deadness. (For
20 nouns w. this suffix, s. MH, 373f.) ■ **διεκρίθη** aor. pass.
διακρίνω to separate, to divide into, to be divided in one's own
mind, to waiver (RWP). **ἐνεδυναμώθη** aor. pass. ἐνδυναμόω to
strengthen, pass. to be strengthened, to be empowered. **δούς** aor.
21 act. part. δίδωμι. ■ **πληροφορηθείς** aor. pass. part.
πληροφορέω to fill completely, to convince fully, pass. to be
fully convinced, assured (BAG; TDNT). **ἐπήγγελται** perf. pass.
23 ἐπαγγέλλω to promise. **ποιῆσαι** aor. inf. ■ **ἐγράφη** aor. pass.
24 ■ **μέλλει** pres. ind. act. to be about to. Used w. inf. to express
fut. (s. MKG, 307). **ἐγείραντα** aor. act. part. **ἐγείρω** to raise.
25 ■ **παρεδόθη** aor. pass. παραδίδωμι to deliver up. Perhaps a
reference to Isaiah 53:12 (Lightfoot, *Notes*). **διά** w. acc. because
of. The first prep. here could be causal and the second final

(MRP, 196) or both prep. could have a prospective reference (Murray). **παράπτωμα** transgression, a falling along side, a false step, transgression (TDNT; Cremer, 498f.). **ἠγέρθη** aor. pass. ἐγείρω. **δικαίωσις** justification, the judicial vindication and justification (TDNT; MRP, 196).

Ch. 5

■ **δικαιωθέντες** aor. pass. part. δικαιόω to justify, to de- 1
clare to be in the right (s. Rom. 2:13). The aor. part. expresses
time before the main verb and could be here either temporal or
causal. **πρός** w. ■ **καί** "also" (Godet). **προσαγωγή** access, 2
introduction (SH). **ἐσχήκαμεν** perf. ind. act. ἔχομεν. The perf.
emphasizes the state "to have received and still possess" (M,
238). **ἑστήκαμεν** perf. ἵστημι, perf. to stand. **καυχώμεθα**
pres. ind. or subj. It means a triumphant, rejoicing confidence in
God (Barrett). ■ **καί** also. **ἐν ταῖς θλίψεσιν** "in the tribula- 3
tion." The word refers to pressures, hardships, and sufferings
(SH; TDNT; Trench, *Synonyms*, 202f.). **εἰδότες** perf. part. of the
defective verb οἶδα. **ὑπομονή** patient endurance, patiently
waiting in hope (TDNT; CBB). **κατεργάζεται** pres. ind. mid. to
produce. The prep. compound is perfective carrying the action
of the main verb to its conclusion (s. M, 112f.). ■ **δοκιμή** ap- 4
proved character, the quality of being approved as a result of test
and trials (BAG; SH). ■ **καταισχύνει** pres. ind. act. to put to 5
shame. **ἐκκέχυται** perf. pass. ἐκχέω to pour out. The word
denotes both abundance and diffusion (Lightfoot, *Notes*). The
idea of spiritual refreshment and encouragement is conveyed
through the metaphor of watering (SH). The perf. emphasizes
the completed state (s. Rom. 3:21). **δοθέντος** aor. pass. part.
δίδωμι. ■ **εἴ γε** "if indeed." The combination is used to in- 6
troduce a fact of which one was absolutely certain (Thrall, 89f.).
ὄντων pres. part. εἰμί gen. abs. **ἀσθενής** weak. **ἀσεβής** ungodly. **ἀπέθανεν** aor. ἀποθνήσκω to die. ■ **μόλις** w. difficulty, 7
scarcely, hardly. **ὑπὲρ δικαίου** "for a righteous (man)." (For a
discussion of the structure of this v., s. Frederik Wisse, "The
Righteous Man and the Good Man in Romans 5:7," NTS, 19
[October, 1972], 91–93.) **ἀποθανεῖται** fut. mid. ἀποθνήσκω.
τάχα perhaps, possibly, probably. **τολμᾷ** pres. ind. act. to dare.
ἀποθανεῖν aor. act. inf. ἀποθνήσκω. ■ **συνίστησιν** pres. ind. 8
act. to bring together, to demonstrate. **ὄντων** pres. part. gen. pl.,
gen. abs. expressing contemporaneous time. ■ **μᾶλλον** more, 9
here "much more," argument from the greater to the less
(RWP). (For examples of this method of argument among the
rabbis, s. SB III, 223–226.) **σωθησόμεθα** fut. pass. σῴζω to

save, to rescue, to deliver. Here it means the consummation of
that work of which justification is the commencement. It is a
preservation from all causes of destruction (Hodge; TDNT;
10 CBB). ■ **ἐχθροί** enemies. **κατηλλάγημεν** aor. pass.
καταλλάσσω to exchange, to make other a state of enmity, to
exchange enmity for friendship (APC, 187f.; s. also TDNT;
MNTW, 102–106). The prep. compound is perfective and means
"to effect a thorough change back, reconciled" (MH, 298).
11 **καταλλαγέντες** aor. pass. part. ■ **καυχώμενοι** pres. mid. part.
καταλλαγή reconciliation. **ἐλάβομεν** aor. λαμβάνω.
12 ■ **εἰσῆλθεν** aor. εἰσέρχομαι to come into. **διῆλθεν** aor.
διέρχομαι to pass through. It contains the force of distribution
"made its way to each individual member of the race" (SH). **ἐφ'**
ᾧ perhaps best understood as causal, "because" (s. F.W. Danker,
"Romans 5:12: Sin Under Law," NTS, 14 [April, 1968], 424–
439; but s. also GI, 116f.). **ἥμαρτον** aor. ἁμαρτάνω to sin.
13 ■ **ἐλλογεῖται** pres. pass. ἐλλογέω to charge to one's account
14 (s. MM). **ὄντος** pres. act. part. gen. sing. ■ **ἐβασίλευσεν** aor.
βασιλεύω to be king, to rule as king. **ἁμαρτήσαντας** aor. act.
part. **ὁμοίωμα** likeness. It denotes a resemblance which may
however be purely accidental (AS). **παράβασις** transgression.
τύπος type. The word means a visible mark left by some object.
Then the mark left in history or nature by the antitype (Barrett;
TDNT). **μέλλοντος** pres. act. part. μέλλω to be about to, here
"the one who is coming."
15 ■ **παράπτωμα** transgression (s. Rom. 4:25; Trench, *Synonyms*, 239f.). **χάρισμα** grace gift, an act of grace (Godet; s.
TDNT; CBB). **ἀπέθανον** aor., s.v.6. **πολλῷ μᾶλλον** "how
much more" (s.v.9.). **δωρεά** gift, the act of giving (Godet).
ὑπερίσσευσεν aor. περισσεύω to be more than enough, to
16 abound. ■ **δώρημα** gift. It denotes the concrete gift, the blessing
bestowed (Godet). **κρίμα** judgment, decision. **κατάκριμα** condemnation, judgment against someone. (For the force of the
prep. compound, s. MH, 316.) **δικαίωμα** justification, acquittal
17 (s. MRP, 198f.). ■ **περισσεία** more than enough, abundance.
λαμβάνοντες pres. act. part. It is the gift which man receives,
it is imputed, not infused (SH). **βασιλεύσουσιν** fut. to be king,
18 to rule as king. ■ **ἄρα** therefore. It gives a summation of the
doctrine set forth in the whole passage from v.12 onward (Murray). **δικαίωσις** justification. ■ **παρακοή** disobedience.
19 **κατεστάθησαν** aor. pass. καθίστημι to set down, to constitute, to establish. ■ **παρεισῆλθεν** aor. παρεισέρχομαι to
20 come in along side, to come into the side of a state of things
already existing (SH). **πλεονάσῃ** aor. subj. πλεονάζω to be, or

to become more, to be pres. in abundance. Here it is probably
intr. (Lightfoot, *Notes*). The subj. is used to express purpose.
ἐπλεόνασεν aor. **ὑπερεπερίσσευσεν** aor. ὑπερπερισσεύω
to abound more exceedingly. The prep. compound magnifies
(MH, 326). ■ **βασιλεύσῃ** aor. subj. Subjunctive used to express 21
purpose. **αἰώνιος** eternal. Eternal life is not only related to the
fut., but is organically related to the actual life lived and is a pres.
possession of the believer (GW, 189f.).

Ch. 6

■ **ἐροῦμεν** fut. λέγω. **ἐπιμένωμεν** pres. subj. ἐπιμένω to 1
stay, to remain, to reside in. The pres. tense indicates the practice of sin as a habit. The subj. is deliberative (RWP). **πλεονάσῃ**
aor. subj. πλεονάζω to be in abundance, to abound, to cause to
increase. Subjunctive used to express purpose. ■ **γένοιτο** aor. 2
opt. mid. γίνομαι (s. Rom. 3:4). **ἀπεθάνομεν** aor.
ἀποθνῄσκω to die. **τῇ ἁμαρτίᾳ** "w. respect to sin," dat. of
reference or respect (s. BD, 105f.). **ζήσομεν** fut. ζάω to live;
that is, at any fut. time whatever after the occurrence of our
dying (Meyer). ■ **ἀγνοεῖτε** pres. ind. act. not to know, to be 3
ignorant. **ὅσοι** as many as, "all of us who" (BAG).
ἐβαπτίσθημεν aor. pass. βαπτίζω to baptize. ■ **συνετάφημεν** 4
aor. pass. συνθάπτω to bury together. **εἰς θάνατον** "into the
death." The prep. conveys the notation of incorporation into
(Lightfoot, *Notes*). **ὥσπερ** just as, even so. **ἠγέρθη** aor. pass.
ἐγείρω pass. to be raised, to rise. **καινότης** freshness, newness,
"in a new state, which is life." The idea of the word is "strange-
ness," and therefore a change (Lightfoot, *Notes*).
περιπατήσωμεν aor. subj. περιπατέω to walk, to walk about,
to conduct one's life (s. TDNT). The subj. is used to express
purpose. ■ **σύμφυτος** grown together w. The process of grafting 5
may be in mind (Barrett). **γεγόναμεν** perf. γίνομαι. **ὁμοίωμα**
likeness (s. Rom. 5:14). **ἐσόμεθα** fut. εἰμί. ■ **γινώσκοντες** 6
pres. part. **παλαιός** old. **συνεσταυρώθη** aor. pass.
συσταυρόω to crucify together. **καταργηθῇ** aor. pass. subj.
καταργέω to render inoperative, to make inactive (s. Rom.
3:13). **μηκέτι** no longer. ■ **ἀποθανών** aor. act. part. 7
δεδικαίωται perf. pass. δικαιόω to justify, to declare to be in
the right. Here the word means either to be declared to be free
from sin or to be acquitted from sin (s. MRP, 200f.). ■ 8
συζήσομεν fut. συζάω to live together. ■ **εἰδότες** perf. part. of 9
defective verb οἶδα to know. **ἐγερθείς** aor. pass. part. **κυριεύω**
w. gen. to be lord over, to rule over, the idea of master and slave
is pres. (SH). ■ **ἐφάπαξ** once for all. ■ **λογίζεσθε** pres. mid. 10/11

imp. λογίζομαι to consider, to reckon. The pres. imp. could
mean "do this continually," or "continue doing this" (MKG,
272). **ζῶντας** pres. part. ζάω. The dat. w. part. could be dat. of
respect or dat. of personal interest or advantage (s. DM, 84f.).
12 ■ **βασιλευέτω** pres. imp. βασιλεύω to be king, to rule as
king. The pres. imp. w. neg. means either "do not always," or "do
not continue" (MKG, 272). **θνητός** mortal, subject to death.
ὑπακούειν pres. act. inf. to listen to, to obey. The inf. used w.
prep. expresses either purpose or result (MT, 143). **ἐπιθυμία.**
The prep. compound is directive. The basic meaning "drive,"
13 "passion," is directed to an object (s. TDNT; Godet). ■
παριστάνετε pres. imp. παρίστημι to place beside, to put at
one's disposal, to present. The word could be used in a military
sense (Käsemann). (For the meaning of the pres. imp. w. neg.,
s.v.12.) **μέλη** acc. pl. members. **ὅπλον** tool, weapon. Sin is
regarded as a sovereign (v. 12), who demands the military service of its subjects, levys their quota of arms (v. 13), and gives
them their soldier's-pay of death (v. 23) (Lightfoot, *Notes*).
ἀδικία unrighteousness. **παραστήσατε** aor. imp. παρίστημι.
The previous pres. imp. calls for the discontinuation of an action.
The aor. imp. calls for an immediate decisive new action as a
break from the past (Johnson; Bakker, 65). **ζῶντας** pres. act.
part. "alive, after being dead," a common classical expression
14 (Lightfoot, *Notes*). ■ **κυριεύσει** fut.
15 ■ **ἁμαρτήσωμεν** aor. subj. ἁμαρτάνω to sin, deliberative
16 subj. ■ **ἤτοι** "either." It has the notion of restriction (RG, 1154).
17 ■ **ἦτε** impf. εἰμί. **ὑπηκούσατε** aor. ὑπακούω. **παρεδόθητε**
aor. pass. παραδίδωμι to deliver over to. **τύπος** a type. Incorporation of the antecedant into the rel. clause, "to which form
18 of doctrine ye were delivered" (RWP). ■ **ἐλευθερωθέντες** aor.
pass. part. ἐλευθερόω to free, to make free. The part. could be
19 temporal "after" or causal. **ἐδουλώθητε** aor. pass. ■
ἀνθρώπινος human, here "to speak in human terms" (BAG).
ἀσθένεια weakness; that is, "because of the difficulties of apprehension" (SH). **παρεστήσατε** aor. παρίστημι. **δοῦλα** acc. pl.
predicative acc. in a double acc. construction "as servants" (s.
MT, 246; RG, 480f.). **ἀκαθαρσία** uncleanness. **ἀνομία** lawlessness. **ἁγιασμός** sanctification, holiness, consecration. It refers to the process or state (Murray) of being set apart for God's
service and the development and display of His characteristics
20/22 (s. Cremer; TDNT). ■ **ἐλεύθερος** free. ■ **δουλωθέντες** aor.
23 pass. part. ■ **ὀψώνιον** provisions, wages of a soldier (s. C.C.
Caragounis, "Ὀψώνιον: A Reconsideration of its Meaning,"
Nov T 16 [January, 1974], 35–57; TDNT). (For a description of

soldier's pay, s. Lightfoot, *Notes*; CC, 206–209; BC V, 428.) **χάρισμα** free gift, grace gift (s. Rom. 5:14).

Ch. 7

■ **γινώσκουσιν** pres. act. part. dat. pl. He speaks to those 1
who have a knowledge of a general principle of all law (SH).
κυριεύω pres. ind. act. to be lord over, to rule (w. gen.). **ζῇ** pres.
ind. act. to live, to be alive. ■ **ὕπανδρος** under (subjected to) a 2
husband, married. The word may itself include the idea of subordination (Barrett). **ζῶντι** pres. act. part. dat. sing. ζάω. The part.
used as an adj. "living husband" (s. Lightfoot, *Notes*). **δέδεται**
perf. pass. δέω to bind. The perf. emphasizes the state or condition. (For the perf., s. Rom. 3:21.) **ἀποθάνῃ** aor. subj.
ἀποθνῄσκω to die. Subjunctive used in a third-class conditional sentence where the condition is probable. **κατήργηται** perf.
pass. καταργέω to render inoperative, to nullify, to annul. The
perf. emphasizes she is completely absolved or discharged (SH).
■ **ἄρα** then. **μοιχαλίς** adulteress. **χρηματίσει** fut. 3
χρηματίζω. The basic meaning is to do business, to negotiate.
Then to be called, to bear the name or title of. Then in a special
sense of giving answers or communications as an oracle (SH).
The fut. is gnomic used to state what will customarily happen
when occasion offers (SMT, 36). **γένηται** aor. mid. subj.
γίνομαι. **γενομένην** aor. mid. part. ■ **ὥστε** therefore, conse- 4
quently. It draws an inference from the preceding and introduces
the actual relation w. respect to Christians who are in a position
corresponding w. that of the wife (Meyer). **ἐθανατώθητε** aor.
pass. θανατόω to put to death. **τῷ νόμῳ** dat. of respect or
reference (BD, 105). **γενέσθαι** aor. mid. inf. γίνομαι. Infinitive
used w. prep. to express purpose. **ἐγερθέντι** aor. pass. part.
ἐγείρω to rise, pass. to be raised. **καρποφορήσωμεν** aor. subj.
καρποφορέω to bear fruit. Subjunctive used to express purpose.
■ **σάρξ** flesh, human nature as controlled and directed by sin 5
(Murray; s. TDNT; CBB; Kuss). **πάθημα** passion. **ἁμαρτία** pl.
sins. **ἐνηργεῖτο** impf. mid. ἐνεργέω to work within. The pricks
and stings of passion were active in our members (SH). The impf.
pictures the continual action. **καρποφορῆσαι** aor. act. inf. Infinitive used to express purpose. ■ **κατηργήθημεν** aor. pass. 6
καταργέω s.v.2. **ἀποθανόντες** aor. act. part. ἀποθνῄσκω.
κατειχόμεθα impf. pass. κατέχω to hold down, to suppress, to
hold fast, to confine. **καινότης** newness. **παλαιότης** obsolete-
ness, oldness. The genitives following these two words are genitives of apposition denoting that in which the newness or oldness
consists (SH).

7 ■ **ἐροῦμεν** fut. λέγω. **γένοιτο** aor. mid. opt. γίνομαι (s.
Rom. 3:4). **ἔγνων** aor. γινώσκω. **εἰ μή** used to introduce a
contrary to fact conditional clause. **τε γάρ** "and in fact" denotes
a second fact of the same kind as the preceding (τέ, also); and
the second fact serves as a proof or explanation to the first (γάρ,
for) (Godet). **ἐπιθυμία** desire, lust. **ᾔδειν** plperf. οἶδα.
ἐπιθυμήσεις fut. ἐπιθυμέω to desire, to long for, to covet. It
8 includes every kind of illicit desire (SH). ■ **ἀφορμή** occasion,
pretext, opportunity for something, lit., the starting point or base
of operations for an expedition, then generally the resources
needed to carry through an undertaking (BAG). **λαβοῦσα** aor.
act. part. λαμβάνω. **ἐντολή** commandment. **κατειργάσατο**
aor. mid. κατεργάζομαι to achieve, to work out, to bring about
9 (s. Rom. 5:3). ■ **ἔζων** impf., s.v.1. He had no dread of punishment, no painful conscientiousness of sin (Hodge). **ἐλθούσης**
aor. part. ἔρχομαι gen. abs. **ἀνέζησεν** aor. ἀναζάω to revive,
10 to live again, to regain life. ■ **ἀπέθανον** aor. ἀποθνῄσκω to
11 die. **εὑρέθη** aor. pass. ■ **ἐξηπάτηαεν** aor. ἐξαπατάω to deceive
completely, to make someone lose the way (RWP). The prep.
compound may be intensive ("completely") or perfective ("successfully") (s. MH, 309f.). **ἀπέκτεινεν** aor. ἀποκτείνω to kill.
12 ■ **μέν** "undoubtedly." This is intended to guard beforehand the
unassailable character of the law (Godet).
13 ■ **ἐγένετο** aor. mid. γίνομαι. **φανῇ** aor. pass. subj.
φαίνομαι to appear. Used to express purpose. **κατεργαζομένη**
pres. mid. part. **γένηται** aor. mid. subj. **ὑπερβολήν** beyond
14 measure, exceedingly. **ἁμαρτωλός** sinful. ■ **σάρκινος** fleshly.
It denotes the material of which human nature is composed
(SH). (For adj. w. this suffix indicating the material of which
something is made, s. MH, 359, 378.) **πεπραμένος** perf. pass.
part. πιπράσκω to sell. The perf. emphasizes the state or condi-
15 tion "sold" and therefore its bondslave (Lightfoot, *Notes*). ■
16 **πράσσω** to do, to practice. ■ **σύμφημι** to speak w., to agree,
to consent. **οὐκέτι** no longer. **ἐνοικοῦσα** pres. part. ἐνοικέω to
18 indwell. ■ **παράκειμαι** pres. ind. mid. to lie along side, to lie
20/21 at hand, to be within reach (SH). ■ **οἰκοῦσα** pres. part. ■
22 **θέλοντι** pres. act. part. dat. sing. ■ **συνήδομαι** pres. ind. mid.
23 to rejoice w. someone, to joyfully agree. **ἔσω** inner. ■
ἀντιστρατευόμενον pres. mid. part. ἀντιστρατεύομαι to
make a military expedition or take the field against anyone, to
oppose, to war against (T). **νοῦς** mind, the reflective intelligence
(RWP). **αἰχμαλωτίζοντα** pres. act. part. αἰχμαλωτίζω lit. to
capture w. a spear, to take a prisoner of war, to subdue (s. LS).
24 **ὄντι** pres. part. εἰμί. ■ **ταλαίπωρος** miserable, wretched, dis-

tressed. **ῥύσεται** fut. mid. ῥύομαι to rescue. The word is used
to denote the act of the soldier who runs at his comrade's cry to
rescue him from the hands of the enemy (Godet). ■ **αὐτὸς ἐγώ** 25
I, myself. **τῷ νοΐ, τῇ σαρκί** dat. of reference (s. BD, 105).

Ch. 8

■ **ἄρα** so, therefore, consequently, an inference drawn from 1
that which precedes (s. Murray). **κατάκριμα** condemnation, a
judgment against someone. ■ **ζωή** life. The gen. expresses the 2
effect wrought. The Spirit is the author and giver of life (Gifford). **ἠλευθέρωσεν** aor. ἐλευθερόω to liberate, to make free.
■ **ἀδύνατος** impossible. **ἐν** "in which," "wherein" defining the 3
point in which the impossibility of the law consisted (SH).
ἠσθένει impf. ἀσθενέω to be weak. **διὰ τῆς σαρκός** "through
the flesh," through the reacting influence of the flesh (Meyer).
πέμψας aor. act. part. πέμπω to send. **ὁμοίωμα** likeness (s.
Rom. 5:14). **κατέκρινεν** aor. ind. act. κατακρίνω to condemn.
It refers both to the pronouncement of judgment and the carrying out of the sentence (TDNT). ■ **δικαίωμα** righteous demand, 4
ordinance (s. Rom. 1:32). **πληρωθῇ** aor. pass. subj. πληρόω to
fill, to fulfill. **περιπατοῦσιν** pres. act. part. περιπατέω to walk
about, to conduct one's life (s. TDNT). ■ **ὄντες** pres. part. εἰμί. 5
φρονοῦσιν pres. ind. act. to think, to set one's mind or heart
upon something. It denotes the whole action of the affections
and will as well as of the reason (SH). ■ **διότι** because. **ἔχθρα** 7
hatred, hostility, enmity. **ὑποτάσσεται** pres. ind. pass.
ὑποτάσσω pass. to be in subjection, to place one's self under.
■ **ἀρέσαι** aor. act inf. ἀρέσκω to please. ■ **ἐν πνεύματι** "to be 8/9
under the domination of the Spirit" (SH). **εἴπερ** "if indeed" (s.
Rom 3:3). **οἰκεῖ** pres. ind. to dwell. ■ **σῶμα** body, the physical 10
body (Meyer). ■ **ἐγείραντος** aor. part. ἐγείρω to raise, to resur- 11
rect. **ζωοποιήσει** fut. ζωοποιέω to make alive. **θνητός** mortal,
subject to death. **ἐνοικοῦντος** pres. part. ἐνοικέω to dwell in.

■ **ὀφειλέτης** one who owes a moral debt, debtor (s. Rom. 12
1:14). **ζῆν** pres. act. inf. to live. Infinitive used to explain the
debt. ■ **ἀποθνῄσκειν** pres. act. inf. **πρᾶξις** deed, act. 13
θανατοῦτε pres. ind. act. to put to death **ζήσεσθε** fut. mid.
ζάω. ■ **ὅσοι** as many as. **ἄγονται** pres. ind. pass. ἄγω to lead. 14
■ **ἐλάβετε** aor. λαμβάνω. **δουλεία** servitude, slavery. **υἱοθεσία** 15
adoption. The word indicates a new family relation with all the
rights, privileges, and responsibilities. (For the custom of adoption, s. TDNT; OCD, 8f.; Francis Lyall, "Roman Law in the
Writings of Paul—Adoption," JBL, 88 [December, 1969], 458–
466.) **ἀββά** abba (Aramaic) father. An Aramaic expression used

16 in prayer and in the family circle (BAG; CBB). ■ **αὐτό** "himself." (For this use of the pron., s. MT, 40f.) **συμμαρτυεῖ** pres. act. to bear witness w. someone, to confirm, to testify in support of someone. Used in the papyri where the signature of each attesting witness is accompanied by the words "I bear witness w. and I seal w" (MM). **τέκνον** child. It expresses the relation of
17 nature and indicates community of life (Godet). ■ **κληρονόμος** heir. Paul is still concerned to demonstrate the certainty of fut. salvation, and argues that if we are heirs of God our inheritance is secure (Barrett). **συγκληρονόμος** fellow heir, co-heir. **εἴπερ** "if indeed" (s. Rom. 3:30). **συνδοξασθῶμεν** aor. pass. subj. συνδοξάζω to glorify together.
18 ■ **λογίζομαι** to consider, to reckon. **ἄξιος** that which balances the scales, comparable, worthy (TDNT). **πάθημα** suffering. **πρός**. The basic meaning is "near" w. acc. "toward," "against." Here "in comparison w." (RG, 622f.; DB, 124f.). **μέλλουσαν** pres. part. "coming," "about to be."
19 **ἀποκαλυφθῆναι** aor. pass. inf. ἀποκαλύπτω to reveal. ■ **ἀποκαραδοκία** watching eagerly w. outstretched head, eager waiting. The sense is strengthened by the prep. in compound which denotes diversion from all other things and concentration on a single object (SH). **κτίσις** creation. **ἀποκάλυψις** uncovering, unveiling, revelation. **ἀπεκδέχεται** pres. mid. to await expectantly but patiently. The prep. in compound are perfective w. the idea of readiness and preparedness and the pres. tense indi-
20 cates the going on of the act until he comes (MH, 310). ■ **ματαιότης** vanity, aimlessness, the inability to reach a goal or achieve results (Trench, *Synonyms*, 180–184; TDNT). **ὑπετάγη** aor. ind. pass. ὑποτάσσω s.v.7. **ἑκών** willing, unconstrained, gladly. It usually stands opposed to violence or compulsion
21 (Cremer, 246). **ὑποτάξαντα** aor. part. ■ **ἐλευθερωθήσεται** fut.
22 pass., s.v.2. **φθορά** corruption, deterioration. ■ **συστενάζω** pres. ind. to groan together. **συνωδίνω** to suffer birth pains together. The prep. in these two words indicates in all the parts of which creation is made up (SH). The pres. tense indicates the
23 continual action. ■ **ἀπαρχή** firstfruits. The first portion of the harvest, regarded both as a first installment and as a pledge of the final delivery of the whole (Barrett). The following gen. is gen. of apposition. The Holy Spirit is regarded as an anticipation of final salvation, and a pledge that we who have the Spirit shall in the end be saved (Barrett). **ἔχοντες** pres. part. **υἱοθεσίαν** adoption (s.v.15). **ἀπεκδεχόμενοι** pres. mid. part. (s.v.19). **ἀπολύτρωσις** redemption, release, a deliverence from the "ills
24 that the flesh is heir to" (SH). ■ **τῇ ἐλπίδι** "in hope." The dat.

is not instrumental but is modal referring to the fact that salvation bestowed in the past is characterized by hope (Murray). **ἐσώθημεν** aor. pass. σῴζω to save, to rescue. **βλεπομένη** pres.
pass. part. ■ **ὑπομονή** patience, patient endurance. 25
■ **συναντιλαμβάνεται** pres. ind. mid. to lend a hand to- 26
gether w., at the same time w. one (RWP), to help, to come to the aid of someone (BAG). **ἀσθένεια** weakness. **προσευξώμεθα** aor. mid. subj. προσεύχομαι to pray. **δεῖ** it is necessary. **αὐτὸ τὸ πνεῦμα** "the Spirit Himself" (s.v.16). **ὑπερεντυγχάνω** pres. ind. act. to plead or intercede on behalf of someone. It is a picturesque word of rescue by one who "happens on" one who is in trouble and "in his behalf" pleads w. "unuttered groanings" or w. "sighs that baffle words" (RWP).
ἀλάλητος unable to be spoken. ■ **ἐρευνῶν** pres. part. ἐρευνάω 27
to search, to examine. **κατὰ θεόν** "according to God." The prep.
denotes the standard (Godet). ■ **οἴδαμεν** perf. of the defective 28
verb w. pres. meaning to know. **ἀγαπῶσιν** pres. act. part. gen. pl. ἀγαπάω to love. **συνεργεῖ** pres. ind. to cooperate, to work together, to work w. one another (Gifford). **πρόθεσις** "according to His purpose." Setting before, purpose (s. TDNT). **κλητός** dat. pl. called, dat. of advantage. Used to designate the person whose interest is affected (BD, 101). **οὖσιν** pres. part. εἰμί.
■ **ὅτι** because. **προέγνω** aor. ind. act. 3rd per. sing. 29
προγινώσκω to know before, to take note of, to fix the regard upon (SH). **προώρισεν** aor. προορίζω to mark out w. a boundary beforehand, to predestine. **συμμορφος** conformed, having the same form w. It denotes an inward and not merely superficial conformity (RWP; s. TDNT). **εἰκών** image (s. TDNT; CBB). **πρωτότοκος** firstborn. The term reflects on the priority and the
supremacy of Christ (Murray, s. Col. 1:15). ■ **ἐκάλεσεν** aor. 30
ἐδικαίωσεν aor. δικαιόω to declare to be in the right, to justify. **ἐδόξασεν** aor. δοξάζω to glorify. The aor. speaks of God who sees the end from the beginning and in whose decree and purpose all fut. events are comprehended and fixed (Hodge).
■ **ἐροῦμεν** fut. λέγω. ■ **γε** an intensive particle here magni- 31/32
fying the deed (RWP). **ἐφείσατο** aor. mid. φείδομαι to spare. **παρέδωκεν** aor. παραδίδωμι to deliver over. **χαρίσεται** fut. mid. χαρίζομαι to give graciously, to give out of grace (s. Rom.
5:15). ■ **ἐγκαλέσει** fut. ἐγκαλέω to call in, to bring a legal 33
charge against someone. **δικαιῶν** pres. part. ■ **κατακρινῶν** 34
pres. part., s.v.3. **ἀποθανών** aor. part. ἀποθνῄσκω. **ἐγερθείς**
aor. pass. part. **ἐντυγχάνει** pres. s.v.27. ■ **χωρίσει** fut. χωρίζω 35
to separate. **θλῖψις** pressure, tribulation. **στενοχωρία** narrowness, distress. (For these two words, s. Rom. 2:9.) **διωγμός**

persecution. **λιμός** hunger. **γυμνότης** nakedness. **κίνδυνος**
36 danger. **μάχαιρα** sword. ■ **γέγραπται** perf. pass.
θανατούμεθα pres. pass. **ἐλογίσθημεν** aor. pass. **σφαγή**
37 slaughter. ■ **ὑπερνικῶμεν** pres. act. to conquer, to win a victory. The prep. compound intensifies the verb, "we are winning a most glorious victory" (BAG). **ἀγαπήσαντος** aor. act. part.
38 ■ **πέπεισμαι** perf. pass. πείθω to persuade, pass. to be persuaded. **ἐνεστῶτα** perf. pass. part. ἐνίστημι to place in, perf. to be at hand, to be pres. It signifies present events and circumstances
39 (Cranfield). **δυνάμεις** potentate. ■ **ὕψωμα** height, exaltation. **βάθος** depth. **δυνήσεται** fut. mid. **χωρίσαι** aor. act. inf.

Ch. 9

1 ■ **συμμαρτυρούσης** pres. part. συμμαρτυρέω to witness together (s. Rom. 8:16) gen. abs. **συνείδησις** conscience (s.
2 Rom. 2:15). ■ **λύπη** sorrow, grief as a state of mind (SH). **ἀδιάλειπτος** continually, unceasing. **ὀδύνη** pain. It implies the anguish or smart of the heart which is the result of sorrow (SH).
3 ■ **ηὐχόμην** impf. mid. εὔχομαι to pray, to wish, idiomatic impf. "I was on the point of wishing" (RWP; for the desiderative impf., s. IBG, 9). **ἀνάθεμα** a thing or per. devoted to destruction,
4 accursed (Barrett; TDNT). **συγγενής** relative, kinsman. ■ **υἱοθεσία** adoption (s. Rom. 8:15). **διαθήκη** agreement, covenant, treaty (s. TDNT). **νομοθεσία** giving of the law. **λατρεία** religious service. The sum total of the Levitical services institut-
5 ed by the law (Godet). **ἐπαγγελία** promise. ■ **πατέρες** fathers. **ὤν** pres. part. εἰμί. **εὐλογητός** blessed.
6 ■ **οὐχ οἷον** rel. pron. qualitative what sort or manner of, such as. Used here as an idiom "but it is not as though" (AS). **ἐκπέπτωκεν** perf. ἐκπίπτω to fall out, to fall from its place;
7 that is, perished and become of no effect (SH). ■ **κληθήσεται**
8 fut. pass. καλέω. ■ **λογίζομαι** pres. ind. pass. to be counted as.
9/10 ■ **ἐλεύσομαι** fut. mid. ἔρχομαι. **ἔσται** fut. εἰμί. ■ **Ῥεβέκκα** perhaps best to be taken as a nom. abs. providing the introduction to what is stated in verses 11 and 12 (Murray). **κοίτη** bed, sexual intercourse. Used w. pres. part. **ἔχουσα** "having" as an
11 idiom meaning "to conceive" (BAG). ■ **μήπω** not yet. **γεννηθέντων** aor. pass. part. γεννάω to bear, pass. to be born. **πραξάντων** aor. act. part. πράσσω to do. **φαῦλος** bad, foul. Worthlessness is the central notion (Trench, *Synonyms*, 317f.). **ἐκλογή** election, choice. **πρόθεσις** purpose. **μένῃ** pres. subj. μένω to remain. The pres. tense emphasizes the continual re-
12 maining. ■ **καλοῦντος** pres. part. **ἐρρέθη** aor. pass. part. λέγω. **μείζων** comp. μέγας. **δουλεύσει** fut. δουλεύω to serve as a

slave. **ἐλάσσων** comp. ὀλίγος. ■ **γέγραπται** perf. pass. The 13
perf. emphasizes the lasting and binding authority of that which
was written (s. M). **ἠγάπησα** aor. ἀγαπάω to love. **ἐμίσησα**
aor. μισέω to hate. The Heb. idiom means, "I prefer Jacob to
Esau"; but Paul may again have taken the word literally (Barrett). ■ **ἐροῦμεν** fut. λέγω. **μή** used in questions expecting the 14
answer no. **γένοιτο** aor. mid. opt. γίνομαι (s. Rom. 3:4). ■ 15
ἐλεήσω fut. ἐλεέω to show mercy. **οἰκτιρήσω** fut. οἰκτίρω to
show compassion. The first of these words expresses the compassion of the heart, the second the manifestion of that feeling
(Godet). ■ **θέλοντος** pres. part. **τρέχοντος** pres. part. τρέχω to 16
run. The two words indicate human striving and may reflect the
symbol of an athletic contest (Michel). **ἐλεῶντος** pres. part.
■ **ἐξήγειρα** aor. ἐξεγείρω to raise out, to raise up. It is used of 17
God calling up the actors on the stage of history (SH).
ἐνδείξωμαι aor. mid. subj. ἐνδείκνυμι to show, to demonstrate.
διαγγελῇ aor. pass. subj. διαγγέλλω to proclaim. ■ **σκληρύνω** 18
to harden.

■ **μέμφεται** pres. mid. to blame, to find fault. **ἀνθέστηκεν** 19
perf. ἀνθίστημι to stand up against, to resist. ■ **μενοῦν γε** on 20
the contrary. (For the use of this particle, s. Thrall, 34f.)
ἀνταποκρινόμενος pres. mid. part. ἀνταποκρίνομαι to answer back, to talk back, to reply. Reciprocal action is expressed
by the prep. compound (MH, 297). **πλάσμα** that which is mold-
ed or formed (AS). **πλάσαντι** aor. part. πλάσσω to form, to
mold. **ἐποίησας** aor. ind. act. ■ **κεραμεύς** potter. **πηλός** clay. 21
The gen. is used w. the word "authority," that is, "authority over
the clay." **φύραμα** lump of clay. **ποιῆσαι** aor. inf. Infinitive
used epexegetically to explain the authority. **σκεῦος** vessel.
ἀτιμία dishonor. That is one vessel designed for noble, one for
ignoble use (Barrett). ■ **θέλων** pres. part. **ἐνδείξασθαι** aor. mid. 22
inf. **γνωρίσαι** aor. inf. γνωρίζω to make known. **ἤνεγκεν** aor.
φέρω to carry, to bear. **μακροθυμία** longsuffering (s. Rom.
2:4). **κατηρτισμένα** perf. pass. part. καταρτίζω to make
ready, to prepare. The perf. emphasizes the state or condition (s.
Rom. 3:21). **ἀπώλεια** ruin, destruction. ■ **γνωρίσῃ** aor. subj. 23
Subjunctive used to express purpose. **δόξα** honor, glory. **ἔλεος**
mercy. **προητοίμασεν** aor. προετοιμάζω to prepare before.
The prep. compound is temporal. ■ **οὓς** whom (pl.) "even us 24
whom He has called." The rel. pron. is attracted to the gender
of the personal pron. (SH). **ἐκάλεσεν** aor. ■ **καλέσω** fut. 25
ἠγαπημένην perf. pass. part., s.v.13. ■ **ἔσται** fut. εἰμί. **ἐρρέθη** 26
aor. pass. part., s.v.12. **κληθήσονται** fut. pass., s.v.7. **ζῶντος**
pres. part. ζάω to live. ■ **ἀριθμός** number. **ἄμμος** sand. 27

ὑπόλειμμα rest, remnant. **σωθήσεται** fut. pass. σῴζω to res-
28 cue, to save. ■ **συντελῶν** pres. part. συντελέω to bring to an
end, to complete, to finish, to consummate. The prep. compound
29 is perfective (s. MH, 325). **ποιήσει** fut. ■ **προείρηκεν** perf.
προλέγω to say before. **ἐγκατέλιπεν** aor. ἐγκαταλείπω to
leave behind. Used in a second-class conditional clause which is
contrary to fact. **ἐγενήθημεν** aor. pass. γίνομαι. **ὡμοιώθημεν**
aor. pass. ὁμοιόω to be like.
30 ■ **ἐροῦμεν** s.v.14. **διώκοντα** pres. part. διώκω to hunt, to
pursue, to persecute. **κατέλαβεν** aor. καταλαμβάνω to lay
31/32 hold on, to obtain. ■ **ἔφθασεν** aor. φθάνω to arrive at. ■
προσέκοψαν aor. προσκόπτω to cut against, to stumble on or
33 at. **πρόσκομμα** stumbling, offense. ■ **γέγραπται** perf. pass.
σκάνδαλον a stumbling block, that which gives offense. (For
this word, s. TDNT; NTW, 111–114.) **πιστεύων** pres. part.
καταισχυνθήσεται fut. pass. καταισχύνομαι to be ashamed.

Ch. 10

1 ■ **εὐδοκία** good will, good pleasure, wish or desire inasmuch as a desire is usually directed toward something that
2 causes satisfaction or favor (BAG; s. also TDNT). ■ **ζῆλος** zeal,
followed by the obj. gen. "zeal for God." **ἐπίγνωσις** knowledge,
accurate knowledge. The prep. compound is directive (MH,
3 314). ■ **ἀγνοοῦντες** pres. part. ἀγνοέω to be ignorant, not to
know. (For the suffix as a neg., s. Rom. 1:20.) **ζητοῦντες** pres.
part. ζητέω to seek. The pres. part. emphasizes the continuing
search. **στῆσαι** aor. inf. ἵστημι to cause to stand, to establish.
It means to cause to stand erect as a monument raised, not to
the glory of God, but to their own (Godet). **ὑπετάγησαν** aor.
pass. ὑποτάσσω to put one's self under orders, to obey, pass.
4 to be in subjection (RWP). ■ **τέλος** end, goal, completion.
πιστεύοντι pres. act. part.
5/6 ■ **ποιήσας** aor. part. **ζήσεται** fut. mid. ζάω to live. ■
εἴπῃς aor. subj. λέγω. The aor. subj. w. neg. as a prohibition
forbids the beginning of an action (s. Rom. 6:12). **ἀναβήσεται**
fut. mid. ἀναβαίνω to go up, to ascend. **καταγαγεῖν** aor. inf.
κατάγω to lead down. Infinitive used to express purpose. The
thought here is to precipitate the Incarnation. The Messiah has
appeared, and it is therefore impossible to hasten His coming by
perf. obedience to the law and penitence for its transgression
7 (Barrett). ■ **καταβήσεται** fut. mid. καταβαίνω to go down.
ἄβυσσος abyss, depth, underworld (s. SH; TDNT). **ἀναγαγεῖν**
aor. inf. ἀνάγω to lead up. Infinitive used to express purpose.
This also is sheer impossibility, since the Resurrection has al-

ready happened (Barrett). ■ **ἐγγύς** near (used w. dat.) **τῆς** 8
πίστεως obj. gen. gospel message concerning faith (RWP). ■ 9
ὁμολογήσῃς aor. subj. ὁμολογέω to agree, to confess, to proclaim. As a judicial term, the word indicates the binding and
public declaration which settles a relationship w. legal force
(Käsemann; TDNT). **πιστεύσῃς** aor. subj. **ἤγειρεν** aor. ἐγείρω
to raise. **σωθήσῃ** fut. pass. σῴζω to rescue, to save. ■ 10
πιστεύεται pres. pass. **ὁμολογεῖται** pres. pass. Both pass. are
the impersonal pass. "it is believed"; that is, "one believes" (s.
RG, 820). ■ **καταισχυνθήσεται** fut. pass. καταισχύνω to put 11
to shame. ■ **διαστολή** division, difference. **πλουτῶν** pres. part. 12
πλουτέω to be rich. **ἐπικαλουμένους** pres. mid. part.
ἐπικαλέω to call upon. ■ **ἐπικαλέσηται** aor. mid. subj. 13
■ **ἐπίστευσαν** aor. **πιστεύσωσιν** aor. subj., deliberative 14
subj. used in a rhetorical deliberative question (SMT, 77).
ἤκουσαν aor. ἀκούω. **ἀκούσωσιν** aor. subj., deliberative subj.
κηρύσσοντος pres. part. ■ **κηρύξωσιν** aor. subj. deliberative 15
subj. **ἀποσταλῶσιν** aor. pass. subj. ἀποστέλλω to send, deliberative subj. **γέγραπται** perf. pass. **ὡραῖος** originally, seasona-
ble, ripe, beautiful, fair, lovely, pleasant (BAG).
εὐαγγελιζομένων pres. mid. part. εὐαγγελίζομαι to proclaim
good news (TDNT; CBB). ■ **ὑπήκουσαν** aor. ὑπακούω to 16
listen to, to obey, in the sense of give credence to. The word
implies the idea of voluntary submission (SH). **ἀκοή** hearing,
that which is heard; that is, message report (s. SH). ■ **ἄρα** then, 17
it follows. ■ **μή** Used in questions expecting the answer no. 18
μενοῦν γε s. Rom. 9:20. **ἐξῆλθεν** aor. ἐξέρχομαι to go out.
φθόγγος sound, vibration of a musical string (RWP). **πέρας**
boundary, limit. **οἰκουμένη** earth, the inhabited earth. ■ **ἔγνω** 19
aor. act. 3rd per. sing. γινώσκω. **παραζηλώσω** fut.
παραζηλόω to provoke to jealousy, to make jealous. **ἀσύνετος**
senseless, not understanding. **παροργιῶ** fut. παροργίζω to
provoke to anger. ■ **ἀποτολμᾷ** pres. ind. act. to be bold of one's 20
self; that is, to assume boldness, to make bold (T). The prep.
compound is perfective; that is, "carry daring to its limit" (MH,
298). **εὑρέθην** aor. pass. **ἐμφανής** visible, manifest. **ἐγενόμην**
aor. mid. γίνομαι. **ἐπερωτῶσιν** pres. part. dat. pl. ἐπερωτάω
to ask for, to inquire. ■ **ἐξεπέτασα** aor. ἐκπετάννυμι to spread 21
out, to stretch out. **ἀπειθοῦντα** pres. part. ἀπειθέω to con-
tradict, to speak against.

Ch. 11

■ **μή** Used in questions expecting the answer no. **ἀπώσατο** 1
aor. mid. ἀπωθέω to push away, to repel, mid. to push away

from one's self, to reject, to repudiate. ***γένοιτο*** aor. mid. opt.
2 *γίνομαι* (s. Rom. 3:4). ***φυλή*** tribe. ■ ***προέγνω*** aor. ind. act. 3rd
per. sing. *προγινώσκω* to foreknow, to know beforehand (s.
Murray at Rom. 8:29). ***ἐν Ἠλίᾳ*** "in Elijah," a rabbinic method
of quotation denoting "in the passage of Scripture which contains the history of Elijah" (Godet). ***ἐντυγχάνει*** pres. ind. act.
to intercede, to plead w. (w. dat.). The verb means to meet w.,
then to meet w. for the purposes of conversation, to have an
3 interview w., to plead w. or to accuse (SH). ■ ***ἀπέκτειναν*** aor.
ἀποκτείνω to kill. ***θυσιαστήριον*** altar, place of sacrifice.
κατέσκαψαν aor. *κατασκάπτω* to dig under or down, to tear
4 down. ***ὑπελείφθην*** aor. pass. *ὑπολείπω* to leave behind. ■
χρηματισμός oracle. The word is used here to emphasize the
localization; the awesomeness is probably the indirectness of the
divine communication (Anthony Hanson, "The Oracle in Romans 11:4," NTS, 19 [April, 1973], 301). ***κατέλιπον*** aor.
καταλείπω to leave behind, to reserve. ***ἐμαυτῷ*** "for myself,"
refl. pron. It emphasizes the thought that the remnant is preserved by God Himself for His own gracious purpose (Gifford).
5 ***ἔκαμψαν*** aor. *κάμπτω* to bend, to bow. ***γόνυ*** knee. ■ ***οὕτως***
so. It refers to the internal resemblance of the two facts, for the
same principle is realized in both (Godet). ***οὖν*** then, also. The
words refer to the moral necessity which the one follows the
other and indicates the addition of a new example to the former
(Godet). ***λεῖμμα*** rest, remnant. ***ἐκλογή*** selection, election.
6 ***γέγονεν*** perf. *γίνομαι*. ■ ***οὐκέτι*** no longer. ***γίνεται*** pres. ind.
mid. Grace ceases to show itself as that which according to its
nature it is. It becomes what according to its essence it is not;
7 it gives up its specific character (Meyer). ■ ***ἐπιζητέω*** pres. ind.
act. to seek for. ***ἐπέτυχεν*** aor. *ἐπιτυγχάνω* to obtain, to reach,
to hit upon. ***ἐπωρώθησαν*** aor. pass. *πωρόω* to harden, to cover
w. a thick skin, to harden by covering w. a callous (T; s. also SH).
8 ■ ***γέγραπται*** perf. pass. ***ἔδωκεν*** aor. *δίδωμι*. ***κατάνυξις***
stupefacation. Derived from the verb meaning to strike or prick
9 violently, to stun (SH). ■ ***γενηθήτω*** aor. imp. pass. *γίνομαι*.
παγίς trap, snare. ***θήρα*** a net used in hunting as a trap.
ἀνταπόδομα a recompense, a paying back, that which is paid
10 back. ■ ***σκοτισθήτωσαν*** aor. pass. imp. *σκοτίζω* to darken.
νῶτος back. ***διὰ παντός*** continually, constantly (BAG).
σύγκαμψον aor. imp. *συγκάμπτω* to bend together, to bow
down, as of captives whose backs were bent under burdens
(RWP).
11 ■ ***μή*** s.v.1. ***ἔπταισαν*** aor. *πταίω* to stumble. ***πέσωσιν***
aor. subj. *πίπτω* to fall. A man who stumbles may recover

himself, or he may fall completely. Hence, the word is used here
of a complete irrevocable fall (SH). **γένοιτο** aor. opt. mid. (s.
Rom. 3:4). **παράπτωμα** transgression, false step (s. TDNT).
παραζηλῶσαι aor. act. inf. παραζηλόω to make jealous, to
provoke to jealousy. Infinitive used w. prep. to express purpose.
■ **ἥττημα** defeat. **πόσῳ μᾶλλον** by how much more. (For this 12
type of argument, s. Rom. 5:9.) **πλήρωμα** fullness.

■ **ἐφ᾽ὅσον** "inasmuch as," "insofar as" (RWP). **δοξάζω** to 13
glorify. ■ **εἰ** "if by any means." The use of the particle w. purpose 14
or aim is a kind of indirect discourse (RWP). **παραζηλώσω** aor.
subj. or fut. **σώσω** aor. subj. or fut. **σῴζω** to rescue, to save.
■ **ἀποβολή** casting away. **καταλλαγή** reconciling (s. APC, 15
186–223; TDNT). **πρόσλημψις** receiving. ■ **ἀπαρχή** firstfruit 16
(s. Rom. 8:23). **φύραμα** dough, lump. (For the rabbinical practice based on Num. 15:18, s. SB IV, 665f.) **ῥίζα** root. **κλάδος**
branch.

■ **ἐξεκλάσθησαν** aor. pass. ἐκκλάω to break off. 17
ἀγριέλαιος wild olive tree. **ὤν** pres. part. **εἰμί**. **ἐνεκεντρίσθης**
aor. pass. **ἐγκεντρίζω** to graft in. **συγκοινωνός** participant,
partner, one who shares something w. someone (BAG; s.
TDNT). **πιότης** fatness. **ἐλαία** olive tree. **ἐγένου** aor. mid. 2nd
per. sing. γίνομαι. ■ **κατακαυχῶ** pres. mid. imp. 2nd per. sing. 18
κατακαυχάομαι to boast against, to brag. The prep. compound
indicates an action unfavorable to its object (MH, 316). The
pres. imp. w. neg. indicates either to stop an action in progress
or do not make the action a habit (MKG, 272). ■ **ἐρεῖς** fut. 19
λέγω. **κλάδοι** branches. Without the article, the character is
emphasized, "beings who had the character of branches" (Godet). **ἐγκεντρισθῶ** aor. pass. subj. (For the process of grafting
and its relation to the figure of the olive tree, s. Munck, 128–
130.) ■ **καλῶς** adv. well, "true enough" (Barrett). **ἕστηκας** 20
perf. ἵστημι to stand. **ὑψηλός** high. **φρόνει** pres. imp. φρονέω
to think, to set one's mind upon. **φοβοῦ** pres. mid. imp.
φοβέομαι to be afraid, to fear. ■ **φύσις** nature. **ἐφείσατο** aor. 21
mid. φείδομαι (w. gen.) to spare. The verb is used in a first-class
conditional clause which accepts the condition as a reality.
φείσεται fut. mid. ■ **ἴδε** aor. imp. ὁράω. **χρηστότης** goodness, 22
kindness (s. Rom. 2:4). **ἀποτομία** severity. The word comes
from a verb meaning "to cut right off, to cut short" and emphasizes a rigor which does not bend (Godet). **πεσόντας** aor. part.
πίπτω to fall, s.v.11. **ἐπιμένῃς** pres. subj. ἐπιμένω to remain,
to continue. **ἐπεί** since, otherwise. **ἐκκοπήσῃ** fut. pass.
ἐκκόπτω to cut out. ■ **ἐγκεντρισθήσονται** fut. pass. 23
ἐγκεντρίσαι aor. inf. ■ **ἐξεκόπης** aor. pass. ἐκκόπτω. 24

καλλιέλαιος a cultivated olive tree as opposed to a wild olive
tree (BAG). **πόσῳ μᾶλλον** "by how much more" (s. Rom. 5:9).
25 ■ **ἀγνοεῖν** pres. act. inf. to be ignorant, not to know.
μυστήριον mystery, the plan and purpose of God which was
hidden in the past and impossible for human beings to discover
but which is now made known by God (s. TDNT; CBB; Cremer,
424f.). **ἦτε** pres. subj. εἰμί. **φρόνιμος** wise. **πώρωσις** the covering w. a callous, dulled perception, hardness (T; s. also v.7).
μέρος a part. **γέγονεν** perf., s.v.5. **ἄχρι οὗ** w. aor. subj. "until,"
"until that" (s. Godet). **εἰσέλθῃ** aor. subj. εἰσέρχομαι to come
26 into, to come in. ■ **οὕτως** so, accordingly. It continues the
thought of what precedes or draws out its implications (Murray).
πᾶς Ἰσραήλ "all Israel." It refers to the forgiveness of the
whole Jewish people or nation, the whole ethnic group in contrast to the saved remnant of Jews in Paul's day and ours (Johnson). **σωθήσεται** fut. pass. σῴζω. **γέγραπται** perf. pass. **ἥξει**
fut. ἥκω to come. **ῥυόμενος** pres. mid. part. ῥύομαι to rescue,
to deliver, Jesus as the Messiah (SH). **ἀποστρέψει** fut.
27 ἀποστρέφω to turn. **ἀσέβεια** ungodliness (s. Rom. 1:18). ■
διαθήκη treaty, covenant. **ἀφέλωμαι** aor. mid. subj.
28 ἀφαιρέομαι to take away, to remove. ■ **κατὰ τὸ εὐαγγέλιον**
"according to the gospel." The relation is thereby designated
according to which they are enemies (Meyer). **ἐχθροί** enemies.
It points to the rejection of Israel w. which Paul is dealing
throughout this chapter (Murray). **δι᾽ ὑμᾶς** "because of you,"
"for your advantage" (Barrett). The prep w. acc. is extended to
29 the final cause (BG, 37). **ἀγαπητός** beloved. ■ **ἀμεταμέλητος**
not to be sorry afterward, not to be regretted, without regret,
irrevocable of something one does not take back (BAG).
χάρισμα a gift of grace. God does not go back on His acts of
30 grace (Barrett, s. Rom. 5:15). ■ **ἠπειθήσατε** aor. ἀπειθέω to
be disobedient. **ἠλεήθητε** aor. pass. ἐλεέω to have mercy or
31 pity, pass. to obtain mercy or pity. **ἀπείθεια** disobedience. ■
32 **ἐλεηθῶσιν** aor. pass. subj. ■ **συνέκλεισεν** aor. συγκλείω to
shut together, to shut together like a net (RWP). **ἐλεήσῃ** aor.
33 subj. ■ **βάθος** depth. **ἀνεξερεύνητος** unsearchable. (For the
prefix used w. the neg., s. Rom. 1:20; for the use of verbal
adjectives w. this ending, s. M, 221f.; MH, 188, 370f.) **κρίμα**
literally, not to be tracked out, incomprehensible, inscrutable
34 (BAG). ■ **ἔγνω** aor. γινώσκω. **σύμβουλος** fellow counselor,
35 advisor. **ἐγένετο** aor. mid., s.v.17. ■ **προέδωκεν** aor.
προδίδωμι to give before, to give beforehand, to give in advance. If man could really be the first to do something for God,
he would make God his debtor (Godet). **ἀνταποδοθήσετει** fut.

pass. ἀνταποδίδωμι to recompense, to give back, to repay.
■ **ἐξ** from, out of. It refers to God as Creator (Godet). **διά** 36
through. It refers to the government of mankind. Everything is
executed only through Him (Godet). **εἰς** for. It refers to a final
goal (Godet).

Ch. 12

■ **παρακαλέω** to admonish, to encourage, to exhort. The 1
word was used in classical Gr. of exhorting troops who were
about to go into battle. Here it is a request based on the apostolic
authority of Paul (MNTW, 134; Michel; s. also TDNT). **οὖν**
therefore. It refers to the result of the whole previous argument
(SH). **οἰκτιρμός** mercy, compassion, compassion and pity arising from the miserable state of one in need (s. TDNT; Cremer).
The prep. w. gen. ("by") gives the reader to understand that the
divine mercies are the power by means of which this exhortation
should take possession of his will (Godet). **παραστῆσαι** aor.
inf. παρίστημι to present, a technical term for presenting a
sacrifice, literally meaning "to place beside" for any purpose
(SH). **θυσία** offering, sacrifice. **ζῶσαν** pres. part. ζάω to live.
εὐάρεστος well-pleasing. **λογικός** pertaining to reason, rational, spiritual. The use of our bodies is characterized by conscience, intelligent, consecrated devotion to the service of God
(Murray). (For adjectives w. this suffix having the idea of
"belonging to," "pertaining to," "w. the characteristics of," s.
MH, 378.) **λατρεία** service, worship, acc. in apposition to the
object (SH). ■ **συσχηματίζεσθε** pres. pass. imp. 2
συσχηματίζομαι to form or mold after something. The verb
indicates the adoption or imitation of a pose or received mode
of conduct (Godet). The pres. imp. w. neg. indicates the discontinuance of an action in progress or means that the action is not
to be continually done (MKG, 272f.). **μεταμορφοῦσθε** pres.
imp. pass. μεταμορφόω to transform, "but be ye transformed in
your inmost nature" (SH). The prep. compound indicates
change; that is, change in form (MH, 318). **ἀνακαίνωσις**
renewing. **νοῦς** mind, the thinking power, reason in its moral
quality and activity (Meyer). **δοκιμάζειν** pres. inf. to prove by
testing, to accept as approved after testing. The inf. w. prep.
expresses the purpose or result (MT, 143).

■ **δοθείσης** aor. pass. part. δίδωμι. **ὄντι** pres. part. εἰμί. 3
ὑπερφρονεῖν pres. act. inf. to think over, above or beyond, to
think highly of one's self, to be haughty. Infinitive used in indirect discourse, here indirect neg. command (RWP). **δεῖ** it is
necessary. **φρονεῖν** to think, to set the mind or attention on

something (CBB). **σωφρονεῖν** pres. act. inf. to be of sound mind,
to be reasonable, sensible, to keep the proper measure, not going
beyond the set boundaries, "to turn the energy of the mind to
recognize its limits and respect them" (Godet; TDNT).
4 **ἐμέρισεν** aor. μερίζω to measure. **μέτρον** measure. ■
καθάπερ just as. **μέλος** member. **πρᾶξις** practice, function.
5 ■ **καθ'εἷς** "as to each one." A late idiom w. prep. is treated
6 adverbially (RWP). **ἀλλήλων** one another. ■ **διάφορος** differing. **ἀναλογία** proportion, proportionate allowance. (For the
7 use in the papyri, s. MM.) ■ **διακονία** ministry. The word
indicates a personal ministry done in service of another (s.
TDNT). Here it probably refers to the administration of alms
and attendance to bodily wants (SH). It may also refer to the
8 ministry of the Word (Murray). **διδάσκων** pres. part. ■
παρακαλῶν pres. part., s.v.1. **μεταδιδούς** pres. part.
μεταδίδωμι to give, to share w. someone. **ἁπλότης** sincerity,
generously, liberally. It refers to open-handed and open-hearted
giving out of compassion and a singleness of purpose, not from
ambition (SH). **προϊστάμενος** pres. part. προΐστημι to stand
on the first place, to preside. **σπουδῇ** zeal. **ἐλεῶν** pres. part.
ἐλεέω to show mercy. **ἱλαρότης** cheerfulness, gladness, gra-
ciousness.
9 ■ **ἀνυπόκριτος** without hypocrisy. (For the prefix used as
a neg., s. Rom. 1:20.) **ἀποστυγοῦντες** pres. part. ἀποστυγέω
to despise, to hate bitterly. It expresses a strong feeling of horror
and the prep. compound emphasizes the idea of separation (SH).
κολλώμενοι pres. mid. part. κολλάομαι to glue or cement
together, to join firmly, to join one's self to (AS). Our attachment
to the good is to be that of the devotion illustrated by the bond
10 of marriage (Murray). ■ **φιλόστοργος** full of tenderness. It
denotes the delicate affections mutually rendered by those who
cherish one another w. natural affection, as parents and children,
brothers and sisters (Godet). **τῇ τιμῇ** "in or w. honor." The
result of true affection is that no one seeks his own honor or
position, and everyone is willing to give honor to others (SH).
προηγούμενοι pres. mid. part. προηγέομαι to go before and
show the way, to consider, to esteem. It either means to try to
outdo one another in showing respect or to consider better, to
11 esteem more highly (BAG). ■ **ὀκνηρός** idle, lazy, irksome, troublesome, not irked by the demands of (Murray). **ζέοντες** pres.
part. ζέω to boil, to be fervent. **δουλεύοντες** pres. part. δουλεύω
12 to serve as a slave. ■ **τῇ ἐλπίδι** in hope. The dat. is voc. in the
point of hope (EGT). **χαίροντες** pres. part. **θλῖψις** pressure,
tribulation (s. Rom. 2:9). **ὑπομένοντες** pres. part. ὑπομένω to

remain under, to endure w. patience. ***προσκαρτεροῦντες*** pres.
part. *προσκαρτερέω* to hold fast to, to persevere, to give attention to, to be faithful in (s. TDNT). ■ ***χρεία*** need. 13
κοινωνοῦντες pres. part. *κοινωνέω* to share in, to have fellowship w. (TDNT). ***φιλοξενία*** hospitality, fond of strangers.
διώκοντες pres. part. *διώκω* to hunt, to pursue. ■ ***εὐλογεῖτε*** 14
pres. imp. *εὐλογέω* to bless, to invoke God's blessings upon
them (Murray). The pres. imp. could be iterat. and calls for
habitual action (s. Rom. 6:11). ***καταρᾶσθε*** pres. mid. imp.
καταράομαι to curse, to invoke a curse. The pres. imp. w. neg.
forbids the habitual action. ■ ***κλαίειν*** pres. act. inf. to weep. The 15
inf. expresses the force of an imp. (s. RG, 1092f.; IBG, 126).
κλαιόντων pres. act. part. ■ ***φρονοῦντες*** pres. act. part. 16
ὑψηλός high, exalted. ***ταπεινός*** low, humble. ***συναπαγόμενοι***
pres. mid. part. *συναπάγομαι* to lead along w. one, pass. to be
carried along w., as by a flood which sweeps everything along w.
it and then to give one's self up to (SH). ***γίνεσθε*** pres. mid. imp.
φρόνιμος wise. ■ ***ἀποδιδόντες*** pres. act. part. *ἀποδίδωμι* to 17
render, to give back, to pay back. ***προνοούμενοι*** pres. mid. part.
προνοέω to think before, to have regard for, to be preoccupied
w. (Godet). ■ ***εἰρηνεύοντες*** pres. part. *εἰρηνεύω* to practice 18
peace, to live in peace. (For verbs ending w. this suffix which
expresses the notion of "being or behaving, or acting as," s. MH,
400.) ■ ***ἐκδικοῦντες*** pres. part. *ἐκδικέω* to secure someone's 19
right, to avenge, to revenge. (For the use of the part. in vv. 9–19
w. an imp. sense in a series of exhortations, s. BG, 129f.) ***δότε***
aor. imp. *δίδωμι*. ***γέγραπται*** perf. pass. ***ἐκδίκησις*** revenge.
ἀνταποδώσω fut. *ἀνταποδίδωμι* to pay back, to recompense.
The prep. compound expresses a reciprocal idea (MH, 297).
■ ***πεινᾷ*** pres. subj. *πεινάω* to be hungry. ***ψώμιζε*** pres. imp. 20
ψωμίζω to feed w. morsels, then generally to feed (AS). ***διψᾷ***
pres. subj. *διψάω* to be thirsty. ***πότιζε*** pres. imp. *ποτίζω* to give
to drink. ***ποιῶν*** pres. part. ***ἄνθραξ*** coal. ***σωρεύσεις*** fut.
σωρεύω to pile up, to heap. ■ ***νικῶ*** pres. pass. imp. *νικάω* to 21
conquer, to overcome. *νίκα* pres. act. imp.

Ch. 13

■ ***ἐξουσία*** authority. Here a reference to governmental 1
authorities rather than invisible angelic powers (s. Murray, Ap-
pendix C). ***ὑπερεχούσαις*** pres. part. f. pl. *ὑπερέχω* to have or
hold over, to be above or supreme. ***ὑποτασσέσθω*** pres. pass.
imp. *ὑποτάσσω* to place or rank under, to subject, to obey.
οὖσαι pres. part. *εἰμί*. ***τεταγμέναι*** perf. pass. part. *τάσσω* to
draw up an order, to arrange in place, to assign, to appoint (AS).

The part. is used in a periphrastic construction and the perf.
emphasizes the state or condition, "stand ordained by God"
2 (RWP). ■ **ὥστε** therefore. It presents the logical result (SH).
ἀντιτασσόμενος pres. mid. part. ἀντιτάσσω to arrange one's
self opposite or against, to resist. **διαταγή** ordinance.
ἀνθέστηκεν perf. ἀνθίστημι to take one's stand against, to
withstand. **ἀνθεστηκότες** perf. act. part. **λήμψονται** fut. mid.
3 λαμβάνω. ■ **φόβος** fear, terror. **φοβεῖσθαι** pres. mid. inf. to be
4 afraid, to fear. **ποίει** pres. imp. **ἕξεις** fut. ἔχω. ■ **σοί** dat. sing.
"for you," "to you," the ethical dat. (RWP). **ποιῇς** pres. subj.
φοβοῦ pres. mid. imp. **εἰκῇ** without a cause, purposeless, in vain.
μάχαιρα sword. The sword is the symbol of the executive and
criminal jurisdiction of a magistrate and is therefore used of the
power of punishing inherent in the government (SH). **φορεῖ**
pres. act. to bear, to carry. **ἔκδικος** avenging. The adj. is used
as a substitutive the avenger, the one who punishes (BAG).
5 **πράσσοντι** pres. part. πράσσω to do, to practice. ■ **ἀνάγκη**
necessity, imposed either by the external condition of things, or
by the law of duty, regard to one's advantage, custom, argument
(T). **ὑποτάσσεσθαι** pres. pass. inf. **συνείδησις** conscience (s.
6 Rom. 2:15). ■ **φόρος** tax. **τελεῖτε** pres. ind. act. to fulfill, to pay.
(For taxation in the Roman Empire, s. CC, 183f.; A.H.M. Jones,
The Roman Economy, 151–158.) **προσκαρτεροῦντες** pres.
part. προσκαρτερέω to attend constantly, to adhere to (s. Rom.
7 12:12). ■ **ἀπόδοτε** aor. imp. ἀποδίδωμι to pay back. **ὀφειλή**
obligation, debt. Here it is the obligations we owe to those in
authority in the state (Murray). **τέλος** duty, toll, custom.
8 ■ **ὀφείλετε** pres. imp. ὀφείλω to owe, to be indebted to
someone. **ἀγαπᾶν** pres. inf. to love. **ἀγαπῶν** pres. part.
9 **πεπλήρωκεν** perf. ind. πληρόω to fill, to fulfill. ■ **μοιχεύσεις**
fut. μοιχεύω to commit adultery. **φονεύσεις** fut. φονεύω to
murder. **κλέψεις** fut. κλέπτω to steal. **ἐπιθυμήσεις** fut.
ἐπιθυμέω to desire, to covet. (For the use of the fut. under
Semitic influence to express a categorical imp., s. BG, 94f.)
ἀνακεφαλαιοῦται pres. pass. ἀνακεφαλαιόω to summarize,
to sum up. A rhetorical term used of the summing up of a speech
or argument and hence of including a large number of separate
10 details under one head (SH). **ἀγαπήσεις** fut. ■ **πλήρωμα** fulfillment, a complete fulfillment (Barrett).
11 ■ **εἰδότες** perf. part. οἶδα. **ὕπνος** sleep. **ἐγερθῆναι** aor.
pass. inf. ἐγείρω to raise, pass. to rise. **ἐγγύτερον** comp. ἐγγύς
12 near, close. **ἐπιστευσαμεν** aor. ■ **προέκοψεν** aor. προκόπτω
to put forward, to advance. **ἤγγικεν** perf. ἐγγίζω to draw near,
to come close. **ἀποθώμεθα** aor. mid. subj. ἀποτίθημι to put

off, hortatory subj. **ἐνδυσώμεθα** aor. mid. subj. **ἐνδύω** to put on,
to clothe one's self, hortatory subj. **ὅπλον** weapon. ■ 13
εὐσχημόνως adv. decently, becomingly. **περιπατήσωμεν** aor.
subj. περιπατέω to walk about, to conduct one's life. **κῶμος** carousing, reveling. It was used of a nocturnal, riotous procession of half-drunken and frolicsome fellows who paraded through the streets w. torches and music in honor of Bacchus or some other deity. Then it was used generally of feasts and drinking parties that were protracted till late at night and indulged in revelry (T). **μέθη** drunkenness (s. TDNT; Philo, *De Ebrietate*). **κοίτη** bed, sexual intercourse, here unlawful intercourse (SH). **ἀσέλγεια** debauchery. The word contains the idea of shameless greed, animal lust, sheer self-indulgence which is such a slave to its so-called pleasures that it is lost to shame. It is one who acknowledges no restraints, who dares whatsoever his caprice and wanton petulance may suggest (NTW, 26f.; Trench, *Synonyms*, 56). **ἔρις** strife. **ζῆλος** envy. ■ **ἐνδύσασθε** aor. mid. imp. 14
πρόνοια forethought, thought in advance, provision. **ποιεῖσθε** pres. mid. inf. **ἐπιθυμία** desire, lust (s. Rom. 7:7).

Ch. 14

■ **ἀσθενοῦντα** pres. part. ἀσθενέω to be weak. The part. 1
denotes one whose faith falters (becomes weak) at a given moment and in a special case (Godet). **προσλαμβάνεσθε** pres. mid. imp. προσλαμβάνω to take to one's self, to receive. The word is used of God receiving or helping man and of men receiving others into fellowship or companionship (SH). **διάκρισις** distinguishing, quarrel, "welcome, but not for the purpose of getting into quarrels about opinions" (BAG). **διαλογισμός**
thought, reasoning, questioning. ■ **πιστεύει** to believe, to have 2
faith; that is, he is completely uninhibited by relics of a pagan or a Jewish past, expressing itself in religious scruples (Barrett).
φαγεῖν aor. inf. ἐσθίω to eat. **λάχανον** vegetable. ■ **ἐσθίων** 3
pres. part. **ἐξουθενείτω** pres. imp. 3rd per. sing. ἐξουθενέω to consider as nothing, to treat w. contempt. **κρινέτω** pres. imp. 3rd per. sing. κρίνω to judge. **προσελάβετο** aor. mid.
προσλαμβάνω. ■ **κρίνων** pres. part. **ἀλλότριος** belonging to 4
another, not one's own. **οἰκέτης** servant, household slave. **ἴδιος** "to his own master," dat. of reference. It is to his own master that he is responsible (SH). **σταθήσεται** fut. pass. ἵστημι pass. to stand. (For the pass. deponent, s. RG, 817.) **δυνατεῖ** pres. act.
to be able. **στῆσαι** aor. inf. ἵστημι to cause to stand. ■ **παρά** 5
more than. **πληροφορείσθω** pres. pass. imp. πληροφορέω to fill completely, to convince fully, pass. to be fully convinced,

6 assured, certain (BAG). ■ **φρονῶν** pres. part. φρονέω to think
7/8 of, to esteem, to regard. ■ **ζῇ** pres. ind. act. to live. ■ **ζῶμεν** and
9 **ἀποθνῄσκωμεν** pres. subj. ■ **ἀπέθανεν** aor. ἀποθνῄσκω to
die. **ἔζησεν** aor. **ζώντων** pres. part. **κυριεύσῃ** aor. subj.
10 κυριεύω to be lord, to rule. ■ **παραστησόμεθα** fut. mid.
11 παρίστημι to stand, to stand beside, to stand before. ■
γέγραπται perf. pass. **κάμψει** fut. κάμπτω to bend.
ἐξομολογήσεται fut. mid. ἐξομολογέομαι to confess, to ac-
12 knowledge, to give praise. ■ **δώσει** fut. λόγον δίδωμι to give
an account.
13 ■ **κρίνωμεν** pres. subj. to judge, hortatory subj. **κρίνατε**
aor. imp. **τιθέναι** pres. act. inf. to place. **πρόσκομμα** stumbling, the opportunity to take offense or to make a misstep (BAG). **σκάνδαλον** snare, the stick which caused the trap to fall, cause of offense, it is that which trips us up or that which
14 lures us into sin (NTW, 111–114; s. also TDNT). ■ **πέπεισμαι**
perf. pass. πείθω to persuade, pass. to be persuaded, to have confidence. **κοινός** common, unclean, defiled. It is a technical term to express those customs and habits which, although "common" to the world, were forbidden to the pious Jew (SH). **εἰ μή** except. **λογιζομένῳ** pres. mid. part. λογίζομαι to consider, to
15 suppose. ■ **βρῶμα** food. **λυπεῖται** pres. pass. λυπέω to cause
sorrow, to hurt. It expresses the painful and bitter feeling produced in the heart of the weak (Godet). **ἀπόλλυε** pres. imp.
16 ἀπόλλυμι to ruin, to destroy. **ἀπέθανεν** aor., s.v.9. ■
βλασφημείσθω pres. imp. pass. βλασφημέω to slander, to
17/18 speak evil of. ■ **βρῶσις** eating. **πόσις** drinking. ■ **ἐν τούτῳ** "in
this," that is, by recognizing that food and drink are secondary matters (Barrett). **δουλεύων** pres. part. δουλεύω to serve as a slave. **εὐάρεστος** pleasing. **δόκιμος** approved, approved after
19 examination. ■ **διώκωμεν** pres. subj. διώκω to pursue, hortato-
ry subj. "let us pursue." **οἰκοδομή** building as a process, figura-
20 tive of spiritual strengthening, edifying, building up (BAG). ■
κατάλυε pres. imp. καταλύω to tear down, to overthrow. It is the opposite of the building up involved in the word of v. 19 (Murray). The pres. imp. w. the neg. indicates the discontinuing of an action in progress or that the action should not be a habit
21 (s. Rom. 6:12). **ἐσθίοντι** pres. part. dat. sing., s.v.3. ■ **φαγεῖν**
aor. inf., s.v.2. **κρέας** meat. **πιεῖν** aor. inf. πίνω to drink. **προσκόπτω** pres. act. to strike against, to stumble. Used of those who strike against a stone or other obstacle in the path.
22 Here it indicates to be induced to sin (T). ■ **ἔχε** pres. imp.
κρίνων pres. part. **δοκιμάζει** pres. ind. to approve of after test-
23 ing and examining (SH). ■ **διακρινόμενος** pres. mid. part.

διακρίνω to judge between, to hesitate, to waiver.

Ch. 15

■ **ὀφείλομεν** pres. ind. act. to owe someone, to be a debtor 1
(s. Rom. 1:14). **ἀσθένημα** weak. **ἀδύνατος** powerless, without
strength. **βαστάζειν** pres. act. inf. to bear. **ἀρέσκειν** pres. act.
inf. to please. ■ **πλησίον** neighbor, dat. used w. verb. **ἀρεσκέτω** 2
pres. imp. 3rd per. sing. **τὸ ἀγαθόν** "for the good," "for his
benefit" (Meyer). The end or purpose of pleasing must be the
promotion of what is absolutely to their good, further defined by
"their edification" (SH). ■ **ἤρεσεν** aor. ἀρέσκω. **γέγραπται** 3
perf. pass. **ὀνειδισμός** reproach, reviling, insult. **ὀνειδιζόντων**
pres. part. ὀνειδίζω to reproach, to heap insults upon.
ἐπέπεσαν aor. ἐπιπίπτω to fall upon. ■ **ὅσος** as great, how 4
great, whatever. **προεγράφη** aor. pass. προγράφω to write
beforehand. The prep. "before" is in contrast w. "today" (SH).
παράκλησις consolation, encouragement (s. TDNT). **ἔχωμεν**
pres. subj. Subjunctive used w. particle to express purpose. ■ 5
δῴη aor. act. opt. δίδωμι. The opt. is used to express a wish (s.
MT, 120f.; s. also J. Gonda, *The Character of the Indo-European
Moods* [Wiesbaden; Otto Harrassowitz, 1956]). **φρονεῖν** pres.
act. inf. to have in mind, to think of, to set one's mind upon.
κατὰ Χρ. "according to Christ's example" (Murray). ■ 6
ὁμοθυμαδόν of one accord, w. unity of mind (SH). **δοξάζητε**
pres. subj. δοξάζω to glorify, to cause a good opinion about
someone.

■ **προσλαμβάνεσθε** pres. mid. imp. προσλαμβάνω to 7
receive, to welcome (s. Rom 14:1). **προσελάβετο** aor. mid.
προσλαμβάνω. ■ **γεγενῆσθαι** perf. pass. inf. γίνομαι. Infini- 8
tive used in indirect discourse after a verb of "saying" (s. BD,
203f.). **βεβαιῶσαι** aor. inf. βεβαιόω to confirm, to make firm,
to establish, to establish a promise is to confirm by fulfilling it
(Godet). ■ **δοξάσαι** aor. inf. The inf. is used to express purpose 9
and is to be related to the εἰς τό of v.8 (Michel). **γέγραπται**
perf. pass. **ἐξομολογήσομαι** fut. mid. ἐξομολογέω to confess,
to praise. **ψαλῶ** fut. ψάλλω to play a stringed instrument w. the
fingers, to sing to a harp, to sing a hymn, to sing praise (AS).
■ **εὐφράνθητε** aor. pass. imp. εὐφραίνομαι to rejoice. ■ 10/11
αἰνεῖτε pres. imp. αἰνέω to praise. **ἐπαινεσάτωσαν** aor. imp.
3rd per. pl. ἐπαινέω to approve, to praise. The prep. compound
is directive (MH, 312). ■ **ἔσται** fut. εἰμί. **ῥίζα** root. 12
ἀνιστάμενος pres. part. ἀνίσταμαι to arise, to rise up in the
sense appear, come (BAG). **ἄρχειν** pres. inf. to rule. **ἐλπιοῦσιν**
fut. ἐλπίζω. (For the use of composite quotations by Paul, s.

13 Rom. 3:10.) ■ **πληρώσαι** aor. opt. πληρόω to fill, to fulfill. (For
the opt. expressing a wish, s.v.5.) **περισσεύειν** pres. inf. to
abound. Infinitive used to express purpose.
14 ■ **πέπεισμαι** perf. pass. πείθω to persuade, pass. to be
persuaded, perf. to have confidence. **μεστός** full. **ἀγαθωσύνη**
goodness. **πεπληρωμένοι** perf. pass. part., s.v.13. **δυνάμενοι**
pres. mid. part. **νουθετεῖν** pres. act. inf. to admonish, to warn.
It is an appeal to the mind where opposition is present. The
person is lead away from a false way through warning, instruction, reminding, teaching, and encouraging and his conduct is to
15 be corrected (CBB; s. also TDNT). ■ **τολμηροτέρως** adv.
comp. τολμηρός bold, daring. **ἔγραψα** aor. **μέρος** part, measure, "in some measure," "in part of the epistle" (SH).
ἐπαναμιμνήσκων pres. part. ἐπαναμιμνήσκω to call back to
mind again, to remind again (RWP). **δοθεῖσαν** aor. pass. part.
16 δίδωμι. ■ **λειτουργός** minister, one who performs a public
service, particularly a religious service (s. BAG; TDNT; NTW,
74–76). **ἱερουργοῦντα** pres. part. ἱερουργέω to serve as a
priest, to perform a sacred function, especially to sacrifice (SH).
γένηται aor. mid. subj. γίνομαι. **προσφορὰ** offering.
εὐπρόσδεκτος pleasing, acceptable. **ἡγιασμένη** perf. pass.
17 part. ἁγιάζω to sanctify, to set apart for divine purposes. ■
18 **καύχησις** boasting, glorying. ■ **τολμήσω** fut. τολμάω to be
bold, to dare. **κατειργάσατο** aor. mid. κατεργάζομαι to ac-
19 complish, to produce. **ὑπακοή** obedience. ■ **τέρας** wonder.
κύκλῳ in a circle, round about. The idea in the word is that of
a complete circle and Paul describes the territory already evan-
gelized in Palestine, Syria, Asia Minor and Greece as lying within a circle; that is, within the circle of the nations around the
Mediterranean Sea (John Knox, "Romans 15:14–33 and Paul's
Conception of His Apostolic Mission," JBL, 83 [March, 1964],
11). **πεπληρωκέναι** perf. inf. to fulfill, to fill up. To fill up the
space lacking in preaching the gospel where others have not
20 (Knox, 10). ■ **φιλοτιμούμενον** pres. mid. part. φιλοτιμέομαι
to be fond of honor, to have as one's ambition, to aspire (BAG).
εὐαγγελίζεσθαι pres. mid. inf. to proclaim the good news, to
preach the gospel. **ὠνομάσθη** aor. pass. ὀνομάζω to name, here
"so named as to be worshipped" (SH). **οἰκοδομῶ** pres. subj. to
21 build. ■ **γέγραπται** perf. pass. **ὄψονται** fut. mid. ὁράω.
ἀνηγγέλη aor. pass. ἀναγγέλλω to proclaim. **ἀκηκόασιν** perf.
ἀκούω. **συνήσουσιν** fut. συνίημι to comprehend, to understand.
22 ■ **ἐνεκοπτόμην** impf. pass. ἐγκόπτω to cut in, to hinder.
The impf. pictures the repeated action. **ἐλθεῖν** aor. inf. ἔρχομαι.

■ **ἔχων** pres. part. **κλῖμα** territory, region, district. **ἐπιποθία** 23
longing. ■ **πορεύωμαι** pres. mid. subj. πορεύομαι to travel. 24
διαπορευόμενος pres. mid. part. διαπορεύομαι to travel
through. **θεάσασθαι** aor. mid. inf. θεάομαι to see.
προπεμφθῆναι aor. pass. inf. προπέμπω to send forth, to help
on one's journey w. food, money by arranging for companions,
means of travel, etc., to send on one's way (BAG). Infinitive
used to express purpose. **ἐμπλησθῶ** aor. pass. subj.
ἐμπίμπλημι to fill. ■ **διακονῶν** pres. part. ■ **ηὐδόκησαν** aor. 25/26
εὐδοκέω to be well pleased, to think it good. **κοινωνία** fellowship, sharing, contribution (s. TDNT). **ποιήσασθαι** aor. mid.
inf. ■ **ὀφειλέτης** debtor (s. Rom. 1:14). **πνευματικός** spiritual. 27
ἐκοινώνησαν aor. κοινωνέω to have a share in. **σαρκικός**
fleshly, carnal. Here it has no evil associations. It is used with
reference to tangible, material possessions (Murray).
λειτουργῆσαι aor. inf. λειτουργέω to minister, to do a service
(s. v.16). ■ **ἐπιτελέσας** aor. part. ἐπιτελέω to complete, to 28
bring to completion. **σφραγισάμενος** aor. mid. part.
σφραγίζω to seal, to seal w. a sign of ownership and a guarantee
of the correctness of the contents (Deissmann; BS, 238f.;
TDNT). **ἀπελεύσομαι** fut. mid. ἀπέρχομαι to go away, to
depart. ■ **ἐρχόμενος** pres. mid. part. **ἐλεύσομαι** fut. mid. 29
ἔρχομαι. ■ **παρακαλῶ** pres. ind. to urge, to exhort, to encour- 30
age (s. Rom. 12:1). **συναγωνίσασθαι** aor. mid. inf.
συναγωνίζομαι to fight or contend along w. someone, to strive
together. It is the picture of wrestling in prayer (Michel). ■ 31
ῥυσθῶ aor. pass. subj. ῥύομαι to rescue, to deliver.
ἀπειθούντων pres. part. ἀπειθέω to be disobedient, to be unbelieving. ■ **ἐλθὼν** aor. part. ἔρχομαι. **συναναπαύσωμαι** aor. 32
mid. subj. συναναπαύομαι to rest together w., to refresh together, "I may rest and refresh my spirit w. you" (SH).

Ch. 16

■ **συνίστημι** to commend, to introduce, commendatory 1
letters were well known in the ancient world (Barrett). **οὖσαν**
pres. part. εἰμί. ■ **προσδέξησθε** aor. mid. subj. προσδέχομαι 2
to receive, to welcome. **ἀξίως** worthily. **παραστῆτε** aor. subj.
παρίσταμι to stand beside, to help, to assist, to stand beside in
order to hold up (Godet). **χρῄζῃ** pres. subj. χρῄζω to need, to
have a need. **προστάτις** helper. The masc. form of the word was
used by the Romans for the legal representative of a foreigner.
In Jewish communities it meant the legal representative or
wealthy patron. Here it indicates the personal help given to Paul
(SH; Michel). **ἐγενήθη** aor. pass. γίνομαι. ■ **ἀσπάσασθε** aor. 3

mid. imp. ἀσπάζομαι to greet. (For a study of greetings sent
in letters, s. T.Y. Mullins, "Greeting as a New Testament Form,"
JBL, 87 [December, 1968], 418–426.) **συνεργός** fellow worker.
4 ■ **οἵτινες** qualitive pron. signifying "as people who," "who, as
such" (Godet; BG, 69). **τράχηλος** neck. **ὑπέθηκαν** aor.
ὑποτίθημι to place under (the axe of the executioner), to risk
5 one's life for another (s. RWP). ■ **ἀπαρχή** first fruit (s. Rom.
8:23). **εἰς** "for." The prep. makes Christ the person to whom the
6 first fruits are offered (Godet). ■ **ἐκοπίασεν** aor. κοπιάω to
7 grow weary, to work w. effort. ■ **συγγενής** kinsman. Probably
a reference to fellow Jews (Barrett). **συναιχμάλωτος** fellow
prisoner, fellow captive (s. Rom. 7:23). **ἐπίσημος** splendid, out-
10 standing. **γέγοναν** perf. γίνομαι. ■ **δόκιμος** approved, ap-
12/13 proved after trial. ■ **κοπιῶσας** aor. part. ■ **ἐκλεκτός** elect.
16 ■ **φίλημα** kiss. (For this custom, s. TDNT.)
17 ■ **σκοπεῖν** pres. inf. to observe, to mark, to scrutinize (T);
"to mark and avoid" (SH). **διχοστασία** division. **σκάνδαλον**
offense, cause of stumbling (s. Rom. 14:13). **ἐμάθετε** aor.
μανθάνω to teach. **ποιοῦντας** pres. part. "causing." **ἐκκλίνετε**
pres. imp. ἐκκλίνω to come away from someone, to shun, to
18 avoid. ■ **τοιοῦτος** such a one. **χρηστολογία** smooth, plausible
speech, fair and insinuating speech (MM). **εὐλογία** praise, fine
speaking, well-chosen (but untrue) words, false eloquency, or
flattery (BAG). **ἐξαπατῶσιν** pres. ind. act. to deceive (s. Rom.
19 7:11). **ἄκακος** without evil, innocent. ■ **ἀφίκετο** aor. mid.
ἀφικνέομαι to reach, to come from, then to arrive at (RWP).
20 **ἀκέραιος** unmixed, simple, unsophisticated, innocent. ■
συντρίψει fut. συντρίβω to rub together, to crush, "will throw
him under your feet, that you may trample upon him" (SH).
21/22 **τάχος** quickly. ■ **ἀσπάζομαι** pres. mid. s.v.3. ■ **γράψας** aor.
23 part. ■ **ξένος** host, one who extends hospitality. **οἰκονόμος**
steward, manager, city treasurer (s. TDNT).
25 ■ **δυναμένῳ** pres. mid. part. **στηρίξαι** aor. inf. στηρίζω
to make firm, to make stable, to establish. **ἀποκάλυψις** unveiling, revelation. **σεσιγημένου** perf. pass. part. σιγάω to be silent. The perf. part. emphasizes the state or condition, "a state
26 of silence" (RWP). ■ **φανερωθέντος** aor. pass. part. φανερόω
to make clear, to manifest, to reveal. **προφητικός** prophetical.
ἐπιταγή command, commandment. **γνωρισθέντος** aor. pass.
part. γνωρίζω to make known.

1 CORINTHIANS

Ch. 1

κλητός called. Verbal adj. here w. a pass. meaning (s. BG, 1
47f.). **ἀπόστολος** apostle, one who is called by the Lord, commissioned by Him, carrying His authority (s. TDNT; J. Andrew
Kirk, "Apostleship Since Rengstorf: Towards a Synthesis,"
NTS, 21 [January, 1975], 249–264). **Σωσθένης** "Sosthenes, the
brother." Probably the Sosthenes of Acts 18:17. The term brother is here probably more than the common bond of brotherhood
true of all believers and refers to a colleague in the Christian
mission; that is, one who makes the ministry his primary occupation (s. E. Earle Ellis, "Paul and His Co-Workers," NTS 17
[July, 1971], 445–452). ■ **τῇ ἐκκλησίᾳ** "to the church." Here 2
the Christian community in Corinth (Hering; s. also TDNT).
The gen. is poss. and is at once a protest against party spirit; "the
church of God" not of any one individual (RP). **οὔσῃ** pres. part.
εἰμί. **ἡγιασμένοις** perf. pass. part. ἁγιάζω to sanctify, to
consecrate, to separate from the secular for sacred use and purposes (s. TDNT; CBB). The perf. emphasizes the state or condition resulting from a previous action (s. Rom 3:21). **κλητοί**
called, s.v.1. **ἐπικαλουμένοις** pres. mid. part. ἐπικαλέω to call
upon, to invoke. The pres. tense emphasizes the habitual act
which characterizes their life (s. Hodge). **αὐτῶν καὶ ἡμῶν**
"theirs and ours." The words could refer to "place" but better
"Lord." Christians share in a common holiness because they
share a common Lord (Barrett). ■ **χάρις** grace (s. Rom. 5:15). 3
εἰρήνη peace. The Heb. word as used in greetings emphasizes
holiness and prosperity of life and personality (s. TDNT; CBB).
■ **πάντοτε** always. **περὶ** w. gen. for, concerning. The mean- 4
ing often overlaps w. **ὑπέρ** (BD, 121). **ἐπὶ** "because of." It
indicates the reason (Hering). **δοθείσῃ** aor. pass. part. δίδωμι.
■ **παντί** "in everything," "in every respect" (Barrett). 5
ἐπλουτίσθητε aor. pass. πλουτίζω to make rich. **λόγῳ** speech,
utterance. **γνῶσις** knowledge. The first is the outward expression and the second the inward conviction (Lightfoot,
Notes). ■ **καθὼς** just as, inasmuch as. Produces not a mere 6
parallel but rather an explanation of what precedes (RP). **τὸ**

μαρτύπιον τοῦ Χρ. "the witness of Christ." The gen. could be either objective or subj. **ἐβεβαιώθη** aor. pass. *βεβαιόω* to make firm, to make stable, to confirm. It was used in the papyri in the sense of a legally guaranteed security (BS, 104–109). The mystery of Christ was given legal force through the apostle (TDNT).
7 ■ **ὑστερεῖσθαι** pres. mid. inf. *ὑστερέω* to come short, to lack. Infinitive used to express contemplated result. It was what was to be looked for in the Corinthians (RP). **χάρισμα** gift, that which was given out of grace, empowerments given to the church from God or from the risen Lord (E.E. Ellis, " 'Spiritual' Gifts in the Pauline Community," NTS, 20 [January, 1974], 128–144; TDNT). **ἀπεκδεχομένους** pres. mid. part. *ἀπεκδέχομαι* to wait eagerly but patiently for something. The double prep. in compound implies a degree of earnestness and intensity of expectation (Lightfoot; s. also MH, 298, 310). The pres. tense emphasizes the continuous action and the part. expresses an attendant circumstance (Grosheide). **ἀποκάλυψις** unveiling, revelation. It is here followed by the objective gen.
8 ■ **βεβαιώσει** future *βεβαιόω* to establish, to confirm (s.v.6). **ἕως** unto, until. **τέλος** end, goal. The phrase moves easily from a temporal meaning to the meaning "completely" (Barrett). **ἀνέγκλητος** without accusation, blameless (s. MM; for the pref.
9 expressing a neg. idea, s. Moorhouse, 42–68). ■ **δι' οὗ** "through whom." The prep. is used of the principal cause and expresses the indirect calling of God through the gospel and not by a voice from heaven (Grosheide). **ἐκλήθητε** aor. pass. *καλέω* to call. **κοινωνία** fellowship, communion, participation. It expresses the blending of two wills into one common cause (s. TDNT; CBB; RAC). **Ἰησοῦ Χριστοῦ**. The name reoccurs in every phrase of this preface (Godet).
10 ■ **παρακαλέω** to entreat, to encourage. Used in the sense of a polite command (Conzelmann; s. Rom. 12:1). **διά** w. gen. "through," the instrument of the appeal (RWP). **τὸ αὐτὸ λέγειν** "that you speak the same thing," pres. subj., subj. used after a verb of command. **ᾖ** pres. subj. *εἰμί*. **σχίσμα** split, division. The word pictures the destruction of the unity through force (Weiss). **ἦτε** pres. subj. *εἰμί*. **κατηρτισμένοι** perf. pass. part. *καταρτίζω* to put in order, to restore, to restore to its former condition, to put into proper condition. The word is used by Herodotus (V, 28) for composing civil disorder (Barrett), periphrastic perf. pass. subj. (RWP). The perf. emphasizes the completed state or condition. **νοῦς** mind, the intellect in its judging faculty (Grosheide). **γνώμη** opinion, judgment. It indicates the expressed opinion, the conviction (Grosheide). The former

denotes the general principles, the latter the special application
of those principles (Lightfoot). ■ **ἐδηλώθη** aor. pass. δηλόω to 11
make clear, to make known. **περί** w. gen. concerning. **ὑπό** w.
gen. by. **τῶν Χλόης** This probably means "by slaves belonging
to Chloe's household" (RP). **ἔρις** here pl. "strifes," "conten-
tions." The word points to quarrels (Morris). ■ **δὲ** and, now, 12
"now this is what I mean." **ἕκαστος** each. ■ **μεμέρισται** perf. 13
pass. μερίζω to divide, to separate, to divide up and distribute
(Barrett). The perf. pictures the completed action or state. The
tense means "he has already been divided up and distributed"
(s. Lenski). This sentence could be a question or a statement. **μή**
introduces a question expecting the answer "no." **ἐσταυρώθη**
aor. pass. σταυρόω to crucify. **ἐβαπτίσθητε** aor. pass.
βαπτίζω to baptize. ■ **ἐβάπτισα** aor. **εἰ μὴ** except, only (s. BD, 14
221). ■ **ἵνα** w. subj. in order that, expresses purpose. **εἴπῃ** aor. 15
subj. λέγω to say. **ἐμὸν** "my," placed before the noun for the
sake of emphasis. ■ **καὶ** "also." **λοιπὸς** otherwise, besides that, 16
acc. of general reference "as for anything else" (RWP). **οἶδα**
defective perf. w. pres. meaning to know. **εἰ** "if." Used in an
indir. question. ■ **ἀπέστειλέν** aor. ἀποστέλλω to send, to 17
commission, to commission someone to a special task and to
empower him w. the authority of the one sending (s. TDNT;
CBB; s.v.1). **βαπτίζειν** pres. inf. The inf. expresses either purpose or explains the idea of sending. **εὐαγγελίζεσθαι** pres. mid. inf. εὐαγγελίζομαι to bring good news, to preach the gospel. (For this word, s. TDNT; RAC VI, 1107–1160.) **σοφία** wisdom. What is prohibited is the transformation of words into wisdom. Paul does not use worldly wisdom (Grosheide). **ἵνα** that. It introduces a neg. purpose "lest." **κενωθῇ** aor. pass. subj. κενόω to make enmity, "dwindle to nothing, vanish under the weight of rhetorical ornament and dialectic subtlety" (Lightfoot). **σταυρὸς** cross (s. CNT 180–269; Martin Hengel, *Crucifixion* [London: SMC, 1977]).

■ **λόγος τοῦ σταυροῦ** "the word of that cross." The re- 18
peated article is almost demonstrative (RWP). The cross occupies a central place in proclaiming the gospel. It is both the crowning point of a life of self-renunciation and also the ordained instrument of salvation (Lightfoot). **ἀπολλυμένοις** pres. mid. part. ἀπόλλυμι to ruin, to be lost. The prep. in compound is perfective and the pres. tense indicates that the goal is ideally reached. A complete transformation of its subjects is required to bring them out of the ruin implicit in their state (M, 114f.). **μωρία** foolishness, nonsense. **σῳζομένοις** pres. pass. part. σῴζω to save. The dat. of the first part. is a simple subj. ap-

preciation. The dat. of this part. includes an effective relation and the idea of an effect produced (Godet; s. also Conzelmann).
19 ■ **γέγραπται** perf. pass. The form expresses the authoritative character of the document, "it stands written" (s. MM). **ἀπολῶ** fut. ἀπόλλυμι to ruin, to be lost. **σύνεσις** understanding, a bringing together. The faculty of putting two and two together (MNTW, 148f.; TDNT). (For the DSS, s. I QS III, 15; IV, 22; I QH I, 8.) **ἀθετήσω** fut. ἀθετέω to do away w. that which has been laid down, to set aside, to disregard, to make void (AS).
20 ■ **ποῦ** where? **συζητητής** debator. **οὐχί** a strengthened form of οὐ used in a question which expects the answer yes. **ἐμώρανεν**
21 aor. μωραίνω to regard as foolish, to make foolish. ■ **ἐπειδὴ** since, since then, because. **σοφίᾳ τοῦ θεοῦ** the wisdom of God. **ἔγνω** aor. γινώσκω. **διὰ τῆς σοφίας** "through wisdom." **εὐδόκησεν** aor. εὐδοκέω to please, to have pleasure in. **κήρυγμα** proclamation, preaching. **σῶσαι** aor. inf. σῴζω to save, to rescue. The inf. explains what is pleasing to God.
22 **πιστεύοντας** pres. part. ■ **ἐπειδὴ** since, because. The conj. is causal but only loosely subordinating (BD, 238). **σημεῖον** sign. To ask for a sign implies a refusal to take God on trust (Barrett). (For the Jews demanding a sign, s. SB I, 640, 726f.; for signs in the DSS, s. 1 QS 10:4; 1 QH 12:8; 15:20.) **αἰτοῦσιν**; **ζητοῦσιν** pres. act. The pres. tense shows the habitual action and describes what is always done. (For the Greeks seeking after knowledge,
23 s. DC XII, 39; XXXVII, 26.) ■ **ἡμεῖς δὲ** "but we," for emphasis and contrast. **ἐσταυρωμένον** perf. pass. part. σταυρόω to crucify. The perf. emphasizes the state or condition (s. Rom. 3:21). It refers primarily to the exalted Lord who, in His exaltation, remains the crucified One (E.E. Ellis, " 'Christ Crucified'," RH, 70). **σκάνδαλον** the stick which an animal stumbled over causing the trap to shut, stumbling block, cause of stumbling, something that trips men up (Barrett; s. also TDNT; NTW, 111–114). **μωρία** foolishness, nonsense, that which displays a senseless act or thinking or speaking (CBB). The two acc. are in
24 apposition to the object. ■ **αὐτοῖς** "to them," or "to the called
25 themselves" (Weiss). **τε καὶ** "both . . . and." ■ **μωρός** foolish, "the foolish thing of God," is that work of God which the world considers foolishness (Grosheide). **σοφώτερος** comp. of σοφός followed by the gen. of comparison, wiser than men w. all their strength (Godet). **ἀσθενής** weak, without strength. **ἰσχυρότερος** comp. ἰσχυρός strong.
26 ■ **βλέπετε** pres. indic. act. **γάρ** for. It is explanatory "you can see what I mean" (Barrett). **κλῆσις** calling. **κατὰ** according, according to the standard of. It speaks of wisdom gained

according to the flesh; that is, according to natural and human
abilities (Weiss). **δυνατός** powerful. **εὐγενής** noble, well-born.
The social structure of the church at Corinth included those
from all levels of society. There were those from the lower levels
of society as well as some from the upper levels (s. Gerd Theiss-
en, "Soziale Schichtung in der korinthischen Gemeinde. Ein
Beitrag zur Soziologie des hellenistischen Urchristentums,"
ZNW, 65 [1974], 232–272). ■ **ἐξελέξατο** aor. mid. ἐκλέγομαι 27
to pick out, to select, to choose for one's self. **καταισχύνῃ** pres.
subj. καταισχύνω to put to shame. The prep. in compound is
perfective (RWP). ■ **ἀγενής** not of noble birth, low, insignifi- 28
cant. (For the neg. force of the pref., s. Rom. 1:20.)
ἐξουθενημένα perf. pass. part. ἐξουθενέω to despise, to consider as nothing. (For the force of the prep. in compound and the
development of this word, s. MH, 310.) The perf. denotes not
only quality but also indicates that that which was once despised
will continue to be despised (Grosheide). **τὰ μὴ ὄντα** pres. part.
εἰμί "the things which are not," "things which do not exist." A
more contemptible expression in Greek thinking was not possible. Being was everything (Weiss). **καταργήσῃ** aor. subj.
καταργέω to put out of action, to make inactive. The prep. in
compound indicates an action unfavorable to its object (MH,
316). ■ **ὅπως** w. subj. used to express intended results (BD, 196). 29
Here it expresses neg. results. **καυχήσηται** aor. mid. subj.
καυχάομαι to boast, to glory. **μὴ πᾶσα σὰρξ** no flesh; that is,
"no one" an OT expression (Barrett). ■ **ἐξ αὐτοῦ** "from him" 30
that is, you are born of him in Christ Jesus (Lightfoot). **ἐστέ**
pres. ind. εἰμί. **ἐγενήθη** aor. pass. γίνομαι. **σοφία** wisdom,
Christ is the true wisdom and union w. Him makes the believer
truly wise (Hodge; for Christ as the wisdom of God, s. PW; PRJ,
147–176). **ἡμῖν** "for us" dat. of advantage. **δικαιοσύνη** righteousness, the status of being in the right before God (GW, 147;
for the view that it means God's loving, gracious, loyal action
which believers share in, s. MRP, 155). **ἁγιασμὸς** holiness,
sanctification. **ἀπολύτρωσις** redemption, release through the
payment of a ransom price. Perhaps here pointing to the last
great day, the consummation of redemption (Morris). The last
three terms are an explanation of the word "wisdom" (Lightfoot). ■ **ἵνα** w. subj. Used here in an elliptical expression "in 31
order that it might come to pass, work out just as" (BD, 255).
γέγραπται perf. pass. s.v.19. **καυχώμενος** pres. mid. part.
s.v.29. The conditional part. used as the subject of the clause is
due to Semitic influence (Barrett). **καυχάσθω** pres. mid. imp.
3rd per. sing.

Ch. 2

1 ■ **κἀγὼ** "and I, accordingly." It emphasizes the apostle's
consistency w. the principles laid down in the preceding verses
(RP). **ἐλθὼν** aor. act. part. ἔρχομαι to come, temporal use of
the part. **καθ'**= κατά w. acc. according to. It can indicate the
nature or characteristic of a thing or manner (BAG). **ὑπεροχή**
prominence, superiority, excellency. **λόγος** word, speech.
σοφία wisdom. The two nouns are close together in meaning,
"eloquence" is rational talk and "wisdom" is wordy cleverness
(Barrett). (For the emphasis on oratory in education and the
importance of a skilled speaker in the ancient world, s. CC,
151ff.; KP IV, 1396–1414.) **καταγγέλλων** pres. part.
καταγγέλλω to proclaim, to make a solemn proclamation
(CBB). The pres. tense emphasizes the continual action and the
part. is a part. of manner. In his proclamation Paul placed no
reliance upon eloquence or wisdom but it does not mean that he
did not employ any kind of speech or wisdom. It is just that these
were not prominent in his evangelism (Barrett). **μυστήριον τοῦ**
θεοῦ "the mystery of God," the counsel of God, unknown to
man except by revelation, especially concerning His saving work
and ultimate purposes in history (ZPEB IV, 327). The gen. is
subj. gen. (Lightfoot, *Notes.*) (For the variant reading
2 μαρτύριον "testimony," s. TC, 545.) ■ **ἔκρινά** aor. κρίνω to
judge, to decide. It emphasizes a deliberate act of the will (Lietzmann). The aor. states a fact which had come to its conclusion
when Paul arrived at Corinth. He had to go on preaching Christ
(Grosheide). **εἰδέναι** perf. inf. οἶδα to know, "to exhibit the
knowledge of, recognize" (Lightfoot). **ἐν ὑμῖν** "in your midst."
εἰ μὴ except. **καὶ** "and this one" specifies the point on which
stress was laid, the effect being that of a climax (RP).
ἐσταυρωμένον perf. pass. part. σταυρόω to crucify (s. 1 Cor.
3 1:23). ■ **κἀγὼ** s.v.1. Here it points again to Paul's arrival at
Corinth (Weiss). **ἀσθένεια** weakness. **τρόμος** trembling. The
words point to the anxiety or solicitude of mind arising out of
a sense of his insufficiency, and of the infinite importance of his
work (Hodge). **ἐγενόμην** aor. mid. γίνομαι to become. Used w.
4 **πρὸς** to come to someone, to be w. someone. ■ **πειθός** persuasive. (For the formation of this word, s. RG, 157.) Paul may be
referring to the halakic and haggadic discussions current in
Jewish Corinth rather than sophistic rhetoric in Hellenistic Corinth (Wilhelm Wuellner, "Haggadic Homily Genre in I Corinthians 1–3," JBL, 89 [June, 1970], 203). **ἀπόδειξις** demonstration,
proof. The word indicates a compelling decision demanded by
the presupposition (s. Fascher). The following genitives are both

obj. (spirit and power are manifested) and subj. (the spirit and
power bring proof and conviction) (Barrett). ■ **ᾖ** pres. subj. εἰμί 5
to be. Used to express purpose. **ἐν** "in." The prep. marks the
medium or sphere in which faith has its root (RP).
■ **δέ** "but." Paul contrasted the wisdom which he speaks w. 6
that of his opponents (Pearson). **αἰών** age, the course and current of this world's affairs (Trench; *Synonyms*, 217). **ἄρχων** pres. part. ἄρχω to rule. The part. "ruler" refers to the human rulers of this world, the great men of authority (s. A.W. Carr, "The Rulers of this Age—I Cor. ii. 6–8," NTS, 23 [October, 1976], 20–35; Gene Miller, "ΑΡΧΟΝΤΩΝ ΤΟΥ ΑΙΩΝΟΣ ΤΟΥΤΟΥ—A New Look at I Corinthians 2:6–8," JBL, 91 [December, 1972], 522–528). **καταργουμένων** pres. pass. part. καταργέω to make idle, to put out of commission, to remove
from power (s. 1 Cor. 1:28). ■ **ἀλλά** "but." It introduces the 7
positive side again and at the same time gives a strong neg. emphasis (Grosheide). **θεοῦ** the gen. is placed before the noun for strong emphasis. The wisdom of God is the work of Christ in His crucifixion, as God's secret plan of redemption and the exalted Christ who presently mediates God's hidden wisdom to His people (E.E. Ellis, " 'Wisdom' and 'Knowledge' in I Corinthians," TB, 25 [1974], 95). **ἐν μυστηρίῳ** "in a mystery" (s.v.1.). **ἀποκεκρυμμένην** perf. pass. part. ἀποκρύπτω to veil, to hide. **προώρισεν** aor. προορίζω to mark off w. boundaries beforehand, to predetermine, to predestinate. **πρὸ δόξαν ἡμῶν** "for our glory." The word indicates our complete salvation (RP).
■ **ἔγνωκεν** perf. γινώσκω to know, to recognize, to discern. **εἰ** 8
Used in the ind. w. a contrary to fact conditional clause (s. BD,
182). **ἔγνωσαν** aor. γινώσκω. **ἐσταύρωσαν** aor. s.v.2. ■ 9
καθὼς just as, in accordance w. **γέγραπται** perf. pass. γράφω. The source of Paul's quotation is not known. It may be from a Jewish liturgy, or be based on Isaiah 64:4, or be from an "Apocalypse of Elijah" (Pearson, 35). **εἶδεν** aor. ὁράω. **οὖς** ear. **ἤκουσεν** aor. ἀκούω to hear. **καρδία** heart. The whole man is viewed from his intentionality; it is the source of the will, emotion, thoughts, and affections (PAT, 448). **ἀνέβη** aor. ἀναβαίνω to go up, to arise, here "to enter into." **ἡτοίμασεν** aor. ἑτοιμάζω to prepare. **ἀγαπῶσιν** pres. part. ἀγαπάω to
love. ■ **ἀπεκάλυψεν** aor. ἀποκαλύπτω to unveil, to reveal. **διὰ** 10
w. gen. "through." **πνεῦμα** spirit. Paul denies the views of Philo that the human spirit can know the divine and asserts that only the divine spirit can make known the things of God (PW, 122). **ἐραυνᾷ** pres. ind. act. to search, to penetrate, to examine, to investigate. The pres. tense indicates that which is always true,

the gnomic pres. (s. IBG, 8). **βάθος** depth. The deep things of God designates God's essence, then His attributes, volitions, and
11 plans (Godet). ■ **οἶδεν** defective perf. w. pres. meaning *οἶδα* to know. **τοῦ ἀνθρώπου** "the things belonging to man," the personal memories, reflections, motives of any human being; all the thoughts of which he is conscience (RP). **τά τοῦ θεοῦ** "the things belonging to God." Used as parallel to the preceding. **ἔγνωκεν** perf. ind. act. *γινώσκω* to know, to recognize, to
12 discern. The perf. emphasizes the continuing knowledge. ■ **τὸ πνεῦμα τοῦ κόσμου** "the spirit of the world," the spirit which animates the world. The gen. is qualitative gen. (Lenski). **ἐλάβομεν** aor. *λαμβάνω* to receive. **εἰδῶμεν** perf. subj. of the defective perf. *οἶδα*. **χαρισθέντα** aor. pass. part. *χαρίζομαι* to give as a gift of grace, to give graciously as a favor (BAG). The aor. tense indicates that Paul is not speaking only of the future
13 but also of the pres. life of Christians (Barrett). ■ **διδακτός** taught. A substantivized verbal adj. w. a pass. meaning followed by the gen. designating the agent (MT, 234). "Not in words taught by human wisdom, but in words taught by the Spirit" (IBG, 40). **ἀνθρώπινος** human. (For adj. w. this ending signifying material, origin, or kind, s. MH, 359.) **πνευματικοῖς** spiritual, pertaining to the Spirit. (For adj. w. this ending, s. MH, 378.) The word can be n. "spiritual things" or masc. "spiritual persons" (s. RP; Barrett). **συγκρίνοντες** pres. part. *συγκρίνω*. The verb has various meanings which are possible in this passage: to bring together, to combine or to compare or to explain,
14 to interpret (BAG; RP). ■ **ψυχικός** pertaining to the soul or life, soulish. It describes the natural man who does not possess the Holy Spirit (s. TDNT; PAT, 334–346; for strong arguments rejecting the gnostic influence on Paul's use of this term, s. Pearson, 7–14). **δέχεται** pres. mid. to receive. The pres. tense indicates the habitual action. **μωρία** foolishness, nonsense. **γνῶναι** aor. act. inf. *γινώσκω*. **πνευματικῶς** adv. spiritually. Paul rejects Philo's view that man has within him—breathed into him by God—the capacity for knowing God and the higher truths of the universe. The wisdom of God comes only through the Holy Spirit (Pearson, 39). **ἀνακρίνεται** pres. pass. *ἀνακρίνω* to examine, used of judicial hearings, to conduct an examination, to examine and judge, to call to account, to discern
15 (BAG). The pres. tense indicates that which is always true. ■ **πάντα** "all things." The spiritual man is able to consider and appraise all things because he is not only inspired to understand what he sees; he is also furnished w. a moral standard by which
16 all things may be measured (Barrett). ■ **ἔγνω** aor. ind. act. s.v.8.

νοῦς mind, thought, plan. A comprehensive name for the thoughts existing in the conscientious (Schlatter). **ὅς** rel. pron. used to express purpose and followed by the fut. (s. BG, 118). **συμβιβάσει** fut. συμβιβάζω to put together so as to draw an inference from, to conclude, here to instruct (Lightfoot). **νοῦς Χριστοῦ** "the mind of Christ," the thoughts, counsels, plans and knowledge of Christ known through the agency of the Holy Spirit (s. RP).

Ch. 3

■ **κἀγώ** "and I," emphatic w. a slight contrast to the preced- 1
ing (Grosheide). **ἠδυνήθην** aor. pass. δύναμαι to be able.
λαλῆσαι aor. act. inf. λαλέω to speak. **σάρκινος** fleshly, made
of flesh. (For nouns w. this ending denoting the material relation,
s. RP.) **νήπιος** infant, baby. ■ **γάλα** milk. **ἐπότισα** aor. ind. act. 2
ποτίζω to give to drink. **βρῶμα** food, solid food. (For similar
terminology appearing in Philo, s. Pearson, 29f.) **οὔπω** not yet.
γὰρ "and indeed." The word has an intensifying effect (Barrett).
ἔτι νῦν "even now." ■ **σαρκικός** fleshly, pertaining to the flesh, 3
controlled by the flesh. Words w. this ending denote an ethical
or dynamic relation (RP). Flesh is the outlook orientated toward
the self, that which pursues its own ends in self-sufficient independence of God (CBB; s. also TDNT; PRJ, 17–35; PAT, 49–
95). **ὅπου** where, insofar as. (For the causal use, s. BD, 238.)
ζῆλος envy. **ἔρις** strife. It is the outward result of envious feeling
(RP). **οὐχὶ** A strengthened form of οὐ used to introduce a question which expects the answer yes. **κατὰ** according to, "w.
merely human motives or feelings." Your walk in life conforms
to a merely human standard. The prep. denotes the measure or
standard (Lightfoot, *Notes*). **περιπατεῖτε** pres. ind. act. to walk,
to conduct one's life. The pres. tense points to an action which
was taking place. ■ **ὅταν** "whenever." **οὐκ** used in questions 4
expecting the answer yes. **ἄνθρωποι** human beings. ■ **δι** = διά 5
w. gen. through. **ἐπιστεύσατε** aor. ind. act. πιστεύω to believe, ingressive aor. to become a believer, to come to belief.
ἑκάστῳ dat. of attraction for the abbreviated form "each as the
Lord gave to him" (Grosheide). ■ **ἐφύτευσα** aor. φυτεύω to 6
plant. **ἐπότισεν** aor. to give to drink, to water. **ηὔξανεν** impf.
αὐξάνω to cause to grow. The impf. indicates the continuous
blessing of God on the work of both Paul and Apollos (RWP).
■ **ὥστε** "therefore." Used w. ind. to draw an inference from the 7
previous sentence (RG, 999; IBG, 144). **οὔτε . . . οὔτε** neither
. . . nor. **φυτεύων** pres. part. **ποτίζων** pres. part. **αὐξάνων** pres.
part. emphasized by its position in the sentence. ■ **ἕν** one, n. 8

"one thing." The aim, result, and motivating power of their work
are identical (Barrett). **μισθὸς** reward, wage, salary. (For the
idea of receiving rewards for work, s. SB IV, 484–500; TDNT.)
9 **λήμψεται** fut. mid. λαμβάνω to receive. ■ **συνεργός** fellow
worker. The word w. gen. could mean "fellow workers *w.* God"
or "fellow workers in God's service." The context indicates that
Paul is speaking of the equal relation of God's workers w. one
another (s. Victor Paul Furnish, " 'Fellow Workers, in God's
Service'," JBL, 80 [December, 1961], 364–370). **γεώργιον**
working field, cultivated land, field. (For the agricultural picture,
s. ZPEB I, 71–78; IDB I, 56–59; OCD, 29–30.) **οἰκοδομή** building. Perhaps Paul could be referring to the many buildings and
temples in Corinth. (For architecture and buildings, s. TDNT;
ZPEB I, 287–297; RAC I, 1265–1278.)
10 ■ **δοθεῖσαν** aor. pass. part. δίδωμι to give. **ἀρχιτέκτων**
architect, master worker, skilled craftsman (s. Philo, *On Dreams*
II, 8). **θεμέλιος** foundation. **ἔθηκα** aor. **τίθημι** to lay.
ἐποικοδομεῖ pres. ind. act. to build upon. The pres. tense pictures the continual action and is to be contrasted w. the previous
11 aor. ■ **θεῖναι** aor. act. inf. **τίθημι**. **παρὰ** w. acc. beside, along,
beyond. In comparisons the sense is "than," "more than," "rather than" (DM, 108; IBG, 51). **κείμενον** pres. mid. part. **κεῖμαι**
12 to lie, of a foundation "be laid" (BAG). ■ **ἀργύριον** silver.
τίμιος precious, expensive. Here it means valuable stones for
building such as granite and marble (Hodge). (For the use of
precious metals and stone in building, s. RAC VI, 451–457; SB
III, 333f.) **ξύλον** wood. **χόρτος** grass, hay. **καλάμη** stalk, straw,
13 used as a building material for thatching roofs (BAG). ■
γενήσεται fut. mid. γίνομαι. **ἡ ἡμέρα** "the day." The article
refers to a day which is well-known (Schlatter). **δηλώσει** fut.
δηλόω to make visible, to make plain, to make clear. **ὅτι** because. **ἐν** dat. **πῦρ** fire. **ἀποκαλύπτεται** pres. pass. to unveil,
to reveal. The word "day" is the subject of the verb. The pres.
tense is used to express the fut. It is a confident assertion regarding the fut. (BD, 168). **ὁποῖος** what kind of, what sort of.
δοκιμάσει fut. δοκιμάζω to approve after testing, used particu-
14 larly of metals which are tried by fire (s. Weiss; TDNT). ■ **εἰ**
"if," a first-class conditional sentence where the condition is
assumed to be true. **μενεῖ** fut. μένω to remain. **λήμψεται** fut.
15 mid. λαμβάνω. ■ **κατακαήσεται** fut. pass. κατακαίω to burn
up completely. The prep. in compound is perfective (s. MH,
316). **ζημιωθήσεται** fut. pass. ζημιόω pass. to suffer loss; that
is, he will lose his reward (Hodge). **σωθήσεται** fut. pass. σῴζω
to rescue, to save. **ὡς διὰ πυρός** "as through fire." The prep. is

to be taken in a local sense; that is, "as one who dashes through
the flames safe, but w. the smell of fire upon him" (Barrett).
■ **οἴδατε** perf. act. w. pres. meaning to know. The neg. introduc- 16
ing the question expects the answer yes. **ναὸς** temple, dwelling
place of a deity, the inward shrine or sanctuary. The reference
is to the one temple of Jerusalem and there may be an allusion
to the dissensions which are corrupting God's temple (Lightfoot,
Notes). **οἰκεῖ** pres. ind. act. to dwell. ■ **φθείρει** pres. ind. act. to 17
corrupt, to ruin, to spoil. **φθερεῖ** fut. ind. act. **οἵτινές** who,
whoever, ones of such a nature (BG, 68).

■ **ἐξαπατάτω** pres. imp. ἐξαπατάω to deceive, to cheat. 18
The prep. in compound is perfective "to successfully deceive"
(MH, 311). (For the pres. imp. in the neg., s. Rom. 6:12.) **εἴ** "if."
It introduces a first-class conditional clause in which the condition is assumed to be true. **γενέσθω** pres. mid. imp. γίνομαι.
γένηται aor. mid. subj. ■ **παρὰ** w. dat. "beside," "with," "in the 19
presence of" (DM, 108). **γέγραπται** perf. pass. γράφω.
δρασσόμενος pres. mid. part. δράσσομαι to catch, to seize.
πανουργίᾳ cunning, craftiness, trickery, literally, "readiness to
do anything" (BAG). ■ **διαλογισμός** thought, reasoning. 20
μάταιος empty, vain, useless. It expresses the aimlessness, the
leading to no object or end (s. Trench; *Synonyms*, 180–184).
(For God destroying the wisdom of the wise as seen in the DSS,
s. 1 QS 5:19f.) ■ **ὥστε** therefore. It draws a conclusion or infer- 21
ence from the preceding (s.v.7.). **καυχάσθω** pres. mid. imp.
καυχάομαι to boast, to glory in something or someone. **πάντα**
"all things." He puts no limit to their possessions in Christ
(Morris). ■ **ἐνεστῶτα** perf. act. part. ἐνίστημι to be pres. 22
μέλλοντα pres. part. μέλλω to be about to, here "things that are
coming." **πάντα ὑμῶν** "all things are yours," "all things belong
to you," pred. gen. (RWP).

Ch. 4

■ **λογιζέσθω** pres. mid. imp. λογίζομαι to reckon, to 1
count, to consider. **ἄνθρωπος** man, used in the indef. sense
"one" or "a man," "a person" (Meyer; MM). **ὑπηρέτης** minister, helper, one who is in the service of another (s. TDNT; Acts
13:5). **οἰκονόμος** steward, manager of a household, often a
trusted slave was put in charge of the whole household. The
word emphasizes that one is entrusted w. great responsibility
and accountability (s. TDNT; CBB). **μυστηρίων θεοῦ** (s. 1 Cor.
2:1). The gen. expresses that which the steward was entrusted w.
and what he is to administer. ■ **ὧδε** "in that case," "on that 2
showing," used here to draw an inference "therefore." **λοιπός**

used here either to strengthen the inference or to introduce a fresh point "now" and would be the progressive use (s. Thrall, 26f.; Blomqvist, 100–103). **ζητεῖται** pres. ind. pass. to seek, to look for. The pres. tense indicates that which is always true. **ἵνα** "that." It introduces the clause which is the object of the verb. **πιστός** faithful, dependable. **εὑρεθῇ** aor. pass. subj. **εὑρίσκω** to
3 find. ■ **ἐλάχιστος** "it amounts to very little," "it counts for a very small matter" (RP). The adj. is the superl. of **μικρός** and is elative (RWP). (For the use of the prep. after the verb "to be," s. RG, 595f.) **ἵνα** "that," s.v.2. **ὑφ'** = **ὑπό** w. gen. "by" used w. a pass. verb to show the agent. **ἀνακριθῶ** aor. pass. subj. **ἀνακρίνω** question, to examine, to interrogate, used of a judicial examination before the final verdict is given (Weiss; 1 Cor. 2:14).
4 ■ **σύνοιδα** defective perf. w. a pres. meaning to share knowledge, here "to know about one's self," what is unknown to others (RP). **δεδικαίωμαι** perf. ind. pass. δικαιόω to justify, to declare to be in the right. The form could also be perf. mid. "I have not
5 justified myself." ■ **ὥστε** "therefore." It draws an inference from the preceding (s. 1 Cor. 3:7). **ἕως ἄν** w. subj. "until." **ἔλθῃ** aor. act. subj. ἔρχομαι. **φωτίσει** fut. φωτίζω to illumine, to bring to light. **φανερώσει** fut. φανερόω to make visible, to reveal. **γενήσεται** fut. mid. γίνομαι. **ἕκαστος** dat. of advantage "for each one."
6 ■ **ταῦτα** "these things," n. pl. and refers to the figures of gardeners, builders, and stewards. (For a discussion of this verse, s. M.D. Hooker, " 'Beyond the Things Which Are Written': An Examination of I Cor. 4:6," NTS, 10 [October, 1963], 127–132.) **μετεσχημάτισα** aor. μετασχηματίζω to change the form of, to transform. Here the meaning seems to be "I have applied these figures of speech to myself and Apollos" (Hooker, 131). **μάθητε** aor. subj. μανθάνω to teach, to instruct. **ὑπὲρ** beyond. **γέγραπται** perf. pass. γράφω to write. It was used to refer to the authoritative character of that which stands written (s. MM). Paul may be referring to the Scripture passages which he has quoted or to his own teaching (s. Hooker, 128ff.). **εἷς ὑπὲρ τοῦ ἑνός . . . κατὰ τοῦ ἑτέρου** "each on behalf of one and against another" (Barrett). **φυσιοῦσθε** either pres. ind. pass. or pres. subj. pass. by irregular contraction (RWP). φυσιόω to puff up,
7 to inflate, to blow up. ■ **διακρίνει** pres. ind. to judge between two, to make a distinction, to make different (s. Weiss; MH, 302). This is probably best taken as a rhetorical question (s. Barrett). **ἔλαβες** aor. ind. act. λαμβάνω to receive. **καὶ.** It throws emphasis on the verb and w. the conditional particle
8 represents the insistence on what is fact (RP). ■ **κεκορεσμένοι**

perf. pass. part. κορέννυμι to satisfy w. food, to fill, pass. to be
satisfied w. food, to have enough of. Used ironically "you think
you already have all the spiritual food you need" (BAG). The
perf. emphasizes the completed state or condition.
ἐπλουτήσατε aor. πλουτέω to be rich, ingressive aor. to
become rich. **χωρὶς** without. **ὄφελον** pres. part. n. ὀφείλω to
owe. The part. is used in a construction to express an impossible
wish; that is, the speaker himself considers the fulfillment of
the wish impossible (s. MKG, 252; RG, 1003f.).
συμβασιλεύσωμεν aor. subj. συμβασιλεύω to rule together,
to be a co-ruler. ■ **ἔσχατος** last. **ἀπέδειξεν** aor. ind. 9
ἀποδείκνυμι to show, to expose to view, to exhibit. A technical
word of bringing a pers. into the arena. The apostles were
brought out to make the grand finale (Lightfoot, *Notes*).
ἐπιθανάτιος condemned to die, used of criminals sentenced to
death in the arena (PAM, 189). **θέατρον** theater, play, spectacle
(Lightfoot). **ἐγενήθημεν** aor. pass. γίνομαι to become, to be
made. Paul uses the picture to illustrate the humility and indig-
nity to which the apostles are subjected. God is the one who set
up this spectacle and He uses the weakness of His servants in
order to demonstrate His power and strength (PAM, 189). ■ 10
μωρός foolish, ridiculous. **διά** w. acc. because, on account of.
φρόνιμος sensible, smart. **ἔνδοξος** honored, distinguished, emi-
nent. ■ **πεινῶμεν** pres. ind. act. πεινάω to be hungry. **διψῶμεν** 11
pres. ind. act. διψάω to be thirsty. **γυμνιτεύομεν** pres. ind. act.
γυμνιτεύω to be naked, to be scantily clothed, to be poorly
clothed. **κολαφιζόμεθα** pres. pass. ind. κολαφίζω to hit w. the
fist, to beat w. the fist, not simply struck, but in an insulting
manner (like slaves or a condemned man) (Barrett).
ἀστατοῦμεν pres. ind. act. ἀστατέω to be homeless, to be
without a roof over one's head. ■ **κοπιῶμεν** pres. ind. κοπιάω 12
to toil, to labor, to do hard work, to work to weariness or exhaustion. **ἐργαζόμενοι** pres. mid. part. ἐργάζομαι to work. Greeks
despised manual labor; St. Paul glories in it (RP).
λοιδορούμενοι pres. pass. part. λοιδορέω to abuse w. words. It
was a common practice of speakers and politicians to insult and
abuse the opponents (TDNT). **διωκόμενοι** pres. pass. part.
διώκω to pursue, to hunt, to persecute. **ἀνεχόμεθα** pres. mid.
ἀνέχομαι to endure, to forbear. ■ **δυσφημούμενοι** pres. mid. 13
part. δυσφημέω to defame, to slander. **περικάθαρμα** that
which is cleansed all around, that which is removed as a result
of a thorough cleansing; that is, dirt, filth. The word was also
used of condemned criminals of the lowest class who were sacrificed as offerings for the cleansing of a city (s. TDNT; Lightfoot;

EGT). **ἐγενήθημεν** aor. pass. s.v.9. **περίψημα** that which is
removed by the process of cleaning dirt off, scouring, scum. The
previous word indicates a "rinsing," this word indicates a "scrap-
ing" of a dirty vessel. It was used in the papyri in a letter greeting
conveying the idea "your humble and devoted servant" (MM).
14 ■ **ἐντρέπων** pres. act. part. ἐντρέπω to shame, to make
ashamed. The pres. part. expresses purpose (MT, 157). The pres.
tense may also be viewed as conative "I am not trying to shame
you" (Barrett). **νουθετῶν** pres. act. part. νουθετέω to admonish, to correct through admonition (s. TDNT). The pres. part.
15 expresses purpose. ■ **ἐάν** w. subj. introduces a third-class conditional sentence in which the assumption is left undetermined,
but there is some expectation of realization (Funk II, 683).
μύριοι ten thousand. **παιδαγωγός** child trainer, instructor (s.
Gal. 3:24). **ἔχητε** pres. subj. ἔχω to have. **ἐγέννησα** aor.
γεννάω to bear, to produce. Paul describes himself as their
father. The instructor acts as representative of the father but can
16 never take his place (Schlatter). ■ **μιμητής** imitator, one who
copies or mimics another. **γίνεσθε** pres. mid. imp. γίνομαι.
17 ■ **ἔπεμψα** aor. πέμπω. Not the epistolary aor. because Timothy
had not yet reached Corinth and was not the one who delivered
this letter (s. 1 Cor. 16:10) (Lietzmann). **ἀναμνήσει** fut.
ἀναμιμνῄσκω to bring to memory, to remind. The fut. is used
in a rel. clause which expresses purpose (s. RG, 960). **ὁδούς**
masc. acc. pl. "ways." Here it probably refers to Paul's teachings
18 (s. Weiss). **πανταχοῦ** everywhere. ■ **ἐρχομένου** pres. mid. part.
ἔρχομαι to come, gen. abs. expressing a neg. condition "as if I
were not coming." **ἐφυσιώθησαν** aor. pass. φυσιόω s.v.6.
19 **τινές** "certain ones." ■ **ἐλεύσομαι** fut. mid. ἔρχομαι. **ταχέως**
adv. quickly, soon. **θελήσῃ** aor. subj. θέλω to wish, to desire.
γνώσομαι fut. mid. γινώσκω. **πεφυσιωμένων** perf. pass. part.
φυσιόω s.v.6. The perf. emphasizes the completed state or con-
20 dition (s. Rom. 3:21). ■ **βασιλεία τοῦ θεοῦ** "the kingdom of
God"; that is, God's rule. The verb to be supplied is either "is"
21 or "does not operate" (Barrett). ■ **ἐν** "with," instrumental use
of the prep. similar to the Hebraic use (s. BD, 117f.; Lietzmann;
Hering). **ῥάβδος** rod, staff, stick. The figure indicates severity
and is intended as a warning (Lenski). **ἔλθω** aor. subj. ἔρχομαι,
deliberative subj. "should I come?" **πραΰτης** meekness, gentleness, restrained patience (s. Matt. 5:5).

Ch. 5

1 ■ **ὅλως** actually (Barrett), universally, everywhere (Hering). **ἀκούεται** pres. pass. "is reported"; that is, commonly

known to exist (Lightfoot, *Notes*). **πορνεία** fornication. It refers
to general sexual acts outside of legal marriage (TDNT). **καί**
"even." **τοιαύτη** of such a kind, such as this. **ἥτις** which, in the
consecutive sense "such as" (s. BG, 68f.). **ἔθνεσιν** Gentile,
those who were not Jews. **ὥστε** used w. acc. of the inf. to express
results "so that." **γυναῖκα** fem. acc. sing. "his father's wife," the
woman was probably the stepmother of the offender and the
father had probably died (Barrett). The separation of the gen.
from its noun emphasizes both parts of speech (BD, 249). **ἔχειν**
pres. act. inf. The pres. tense emphasizes the continual possession. They were living as man and wife without being married.
Both the OT (Lev. 18:7, 8; 20:11) and the rabbis (M Sanhedrin
VII, 4) as well as Roman law prohibited such marriages (s. Lietzmann; RAC IV, 685f.; Buckland, 115f.). ■ **πεφυσιωμένοι** perf. 2
pass. part. φυσιόω to blow up, to puff up, a term used to express
pride. The perf. emphasizes the state or condition. **οὐχί**
strengthened form of οὐ. Used in a question expecting the answer yes. **μᾶλλον** rather. **ἐπενθήσατε** aor. πενθέω to mourn,
to express deep sorrow as one mourning for the dead. **ἵνα** "that."
Used to express desired result (RWP) or a consequence resulting
from some quality, "such that" (BD, 192). **ἀρθῇ** aor. pass. subj.
αἴρω to lift up, to take away, to remove. **πράξας** aor. act. part.
πράσσω to do, to practice (variant reading **ποιήσας** aor. part.
ποιέω to do). ■ **τῷ σώματι** dat. of reference. The word "body" 3
refers to Paul's physical presence or absence (PAT, 268; for a
study showing the emphasis on the material aspect of the word,
s. SBT). **κέκρικα** perf. ind. act. κρίνω to judge, to pass judgment. The perf. emphasizes the continuing results of the decision
reached. **τὸν οὕτως** "the one who has so acted," "under circumstances such as these" (Lightfoot, *Notes*). **κατεργασάμενον**
aor. mid. part. κατεργάζομαι to do, to accomplish, to bring an
action to fruition. ■ **συναχθέντων** aor. pass. part. συνάγω to 4
gather together, pass. to be assembled. ■ **παραδοῦναι** aor. act. 5
inf. παραδίδωμι to deliver over, to turn over, used in a judicial
sense. This appears to be a curse of execration w. special reference to satanic affliction of the body (SBT, 143). **τὸν τοιοῦτον**
"such a one." **εἰς ὄλεθρον** "for destruction." The word refers to
destruction and death, often in connection w. God's judgment
against sin (s. TDNT; s. also SB III, 358). **σωθῇ** aor. pass. subj.
σῴζω to rescue, to save. ■ **καύχημα** boasting, boasting uttered 6
(RP). **οἴδατε** defective perf. w. a pres. meaning οἶδα to know.
ζύμη leaven, yeast (s. Matt. 13:33; TDNT). **φύραμα** that which
is mixed or kneaded, a lump or batch of dough (BAG). **ζυμοῖ**
pres. ind. act. to leaven. (For the use of the proverbial saying, s.

7 Barrett.) ■ **ἐκκαθάρατε** aor. imp. ἐκκαθαίρω to clean out, to purge thoroughly. (For the Jewish regulations regarding the removal of all leaven from the house before celebrating the Passover, s. SB III, 359f.) The prep. in compound is perfective (MH, 309f.). **παλαιός** old; that is, the leaven used in the period before Passover (Barrett). **ἦτε** pres. subj. εἰμί. **νέον** new, fresh. **ἄζυμοι** unleaven. **καὶ γάρ** "for also." The "also" introduces the obj. relation of things corresponding to the exhortation (Meyer). **πάσχα** Passover, Passover lamb (s. ZPEB IV, 605–611; M Pesahim). **ἐτύθη** aor. pass. θύω to kill, to slay, to kill a sacrifice, to
8 slaughter. **χριστός** in apposition w. the subject. ■ **ὥστε** therefore, it draws a conclusion from the preceding. **ἑορτάζωμεν** pres. subj. ἑορτάζω to celebrate the feast, hortatory subj. "let us celebrate." **κακίας** malice. This is the vicious disposition and the next word is the act. exercise of it (Lightfoot, *Notes*). **ἀζύμοις** unleavened loaf. The pl. may be a reference to the unleavened cakes eaten at the Passover or is indefinite "unleavened elements" (RP). **εἰλικρίνειας** sincerity, purity of motive. Perhaps the literal meaning is "checked by sunlight" (s. TDNT; NTW, 32f.).
9 ■ **ἔγραψα** aor. not an epistolary aor. but refers to another letter (RP). **ἐν τῇ ἐπιστολῇ** "in the letter." The article points to a well-known specific letter written by Paul. **συναναμίγνυσθαι** pres. mid. inf. to mix together, to mix up w., to associate w., inf. used to express purpose. The pres. tense points to a regular association (Grosheide). **πόρνος** one who engages in illicit sexual activities, a sexually immoral pers. Corinth was well-known to the ancient world for this type of activ-
10 ity. ■ **πάντως** at all, in general. The meaning here is "not in the abs. sense" (Barrett; s. also BD, 224). **πλεονέκτης** a covetous pers., one who seeks to fulfill his unsatisfiable desires at all cost and at the expense of others (s. Rom. 1:29). **ἅρπαξ** robber, extortioner, joined to the previous word w. one article indicating that both words form a single class of those who are absolutely selfish, who covet and sometimes see more than their just share of things (RP). **εἰδωλολάτρης** idol worshiper, idolator. **ἐπεί** since, used to introduce the conclusion of a suppressed conditional clause which is contrary to fact (s. RG, 965; BD, 181). **ὠφείλετε** impf. ὀφείλω to be under obligation to pay a debt, should, must, ought. **ἄρα** "in that case" (RWP). **ἐξελθεῖν** aor.
11 act. inf. ἐξέρχομαι to go out from, to depart. ■ **ὀνομαζόμενος** pres. pass. part. ὀνομάζω to name, to bear the name of. His behavior shows that in truth he is not a Christian (Barrett). **ᾖ** pres. subj. εἰμί. **λοίδορος** an abusive pers., one who attacks

another w. abusive language (s. TDNT). **μέθυσος** drunkard.
τοιούτῳ such a one. **συνεσθίειν** pres. inf. to eat together. The
prohibition evidently includes the church's common meal as
well as private entertainment (Barrett). ■ **τί γάρ μοι** "for what 12
is it to me," "for what business of mine is it." **ἔξω** outside, "those
who are outside." An expression used by the rabbis to indicate
those who belong to another religion (SB III, 362). ■ **κρινεῖ** fut. 13
κρίνω to judge. **ἐξάρατε** aor. imp. ἐξαίρω to exclude, to
remove, to drive away. The prep. in compound makes the verb
effective, "to put out completely." **τὸν πονηρόν** the evil one or
the article is used in a generic sense referring to the wicked in
general (s. BD, 138). **ἐξ ὑμῶν αὐτῶν** "from yourselves." Perhaps here not reflex (MT, 194; s. BD, 150).

Ch. 6

■ **τολμᾷ** pres. ind. τολμάω to dare. The pres. tense indi- 1
cates that the action was in process. **πρᾶγμα** matter, lawsuit.
κρίνεσθαι pres. mid. or pass. inf., the permissive mid. or pass.
"allow yourselves to be judged" (s. BD, 165, 166). The pres.
tense indicates that the trial was being held and no decision had
yet been reached. **ἐπί** w. gen. before, in the presence of (s.
RWP). **τῶν ἀδίκων** the unrighteous ones. These were either
pagan judges or, perhaps better, Paul is referring to Jewish judges
who tried cases in the synagogue (s. Albert Stein, "Wo trugen
die korinthischen Christen ihre Rechtshändel aus?," ZNW, 59
[1968], 86–90; SB III, 364). ■ **οὐκ οἴδατε** defective perf. w. pres. 2
meaning to know. **κρινοῦσιν** fut. κρίνω to judge (s. Dan 7:22;
SB III, 363). **ἀνάξιος** unworthy, not equal to the task. (For the
neg. pref., s. Rom. 1:20.) **κριτήριον** law court, tribunal, lawsuit,
cause, law preceding (s. Weiss). (For the suf. and its meaning, s.
MH, 343.) Genitive used w. the adj. "unworthy" which express
value (s. BD, 98). **ἐλάχιστος** superl. μικρός small, insignificant. ■ **κρινοῦμεν** fut. **μήτιγε** "not to speak of" (BD, 220). 3
βιωτικός that which pertains to daily living. It means questions
related to our life on earth or to the resources of life such as food,
clothing, property, etc. (RP). ■ **μὲν οὖν** "no but" or "no rather" 4
(RP). **ἐξουθενημένους** perf. pass. part. ἐξουθενέω to consider
as nothing, to despise, to reject w. contempt. It refers either to
those in the church who are a little esteemed (Grosheide) or to
those outside of the church. **καθίζετε** pres. ind. or imp. καθίζω
to cause to sit, to appoint. ■ **ἐντροπήν** shame. **οὕτως** "so," "has 5
it come to this that," "is it to such a degree true that?" (Lightfoot, *Notes*). **ἔνι** shortened form for ἔνεστιν to be, to exist, to
be found (s. BD, 49). **οὐδείς** no one, not even one. **δυνήσεται**

fut. mid. δύναμαι. The fut. is used to designate a sort of consequence resulting from some quality, "such that" (BD, 192).
διακρῖναι aor. act. inf. διακρίνω to judge between two, to
decide. (For the force of the prep. in compound, s. MH, 302f.)
ἀνὰ μέσον between. **τοῦ ἀδελφοῦ ἀυτοῦ** an abridged sentence
conveying a reproach "must his brothers go before strangers?"
6 (Lightfoot, *Notes*) ■ **ἀλλά** but in reality. **κρίνεται** pres. mid. or
pass., s.v.1 **καὶ τοῦτο** "and that," climactic force of the particle
used w. acc. of general reference (RWP). **ἄπιστος** unbeliever.
7 (For the neg. force of the pref., s. Rom. 1:20.) ■ **ὅλως** adv.
altogether, assuredly, actually. **ἥττημα** defeat. The word was
used of a judicial defeat in court (Schlatter), here used of the
moral and spiritual defeat (Weiss). **κρίμα** law suit. **μεθ' ἑαυτῶν**
"w. yourselves." The reflex. pron. emphasizes the idea of corporate unity (Lightfoot, *Notes*). **μᾶλλον** adv. rather. **ἀδικεῖσθε**
pres. ind. mid. or pass. ἀδικέω to wrong someone, to treat
someone unjustly. **ἀποστερεῖσθε** pres. ind. mid. or pass.
ἀποστερέω to defraud, to steal, to deprive. The two forms here
8 are permissive mid. or pass. (s. MT, 56f.; BD, 165). ■ **ὑμεῖς** you
9 (emphatic). **καὶ τοῦτο** "and that," s.v.6. ■ **θεοῦ** emphatic by its
position. **κληρονομήσουσιν** fut. κληρονομέω to inherit, to
enter into full possession of (Morris). **πλανᾶσθε** pres. imp. mid.
or pass. πλανάω to lead astray, to mislead, to deceive, permissive mid. or pass. (s.v.7). The pres. imp. w. the neg. is used to
stop an action in progress "do not continue" (MKG, 272).
εἰδωλολάτρης one who serves idols, idolator. **μοιχός** adul-
terer. **μαλακός** soft, effeminate, a technical term for the pass.
partner in homosexual relations (Barrett; Conzelmann; s. also
RAC IV, 620–650; LAE, 164). **ἀρσενοκοίτης** a male who has
sexual relations w. a male, homosexual. The Jewish punishment
10 for the sin of homosexuality was stoning (s. SB III, 70f.). ■
πλεονέκτης one desirous of having more and seeks to fulfill his
desires through all means (s. 1 Cor. 5:10). **μέθυσος** drunkard.
λοίδορος one who uses abusive language (s. 1 Cor. 5:11).
ἅρπαξ robber, one who uses force and violence in stealing. (For
similar lists which were used in the ancient world in a popular
11 game, s. LAE, 316.) ■ **καί** "and," "and it is true" (Godet).
ταῦτα "these things." The n. is contemptous "such abominations!" (EGT). **τινες** some. Paul narrows the picture to some,
not all (RWP). **ἦτε** impf. εἰμί. **ἀλλά** but, emphasizes strongly
the contrast between their pres. state and their past and the
consequent demand which their changed moral condition makes
upon them (RP). **ἀπελούσασθε** aor. mid. ἀπολούω to wash,
to wash thoroughly. The prep. in compound points to the com-

plete washing away and the aor. refers to a decisive action (Morris), permissive mid. **ἡγιάσθητε** aor. pass. *ἁγιάζω* to sanctify, to make holy. It does not refer to the process of ethical development but means "you were claimed by God as His own and made a member of His holy people" (Barrett). **ἐδικαιώθητε** aor. pass. *δικαιόω* to justify, to declare righteous, to declare to be in the right (s. Rom. 2:13).

■ **ἔξεστιν** it is allowed, it is permitted. Paul is evidently 12
quoting a common saying in Corinth (s. Weiss; Barrett).
συμφέρει pres. ind. act. to bring together, to confer a benefit,
to be advantageous or profitable or useful (BAG).
ἐξουσιασθήσομαι fut. pass. *ἐξουσιάζω* to bring under the
power of someone, to put under the authority of someone. ■ 13
βρῶμα food. **κοιλίᾳ** stomach, dat. of advantage. **καταργήσει**
fut. *καταργέω* to make ineffective, to do away w. The organs
of digestion will be changed at the resurrection and the physical
constitution of the resurrected body will be different from that
of the mortal body (SBT, 54). **σῶμα** body, the physical body,
not a reference to the whole pers. w. his personality but rather
the physical body (s. SBT, 51–80). ■ **ἤγειρεν** aor. *ἐγείρω* to 14
raise up. **ἐξεγερεῖ** fut. *ἐξεγείρω* to raise up out of. ■ **μέλος** 15
member, used in an ecclesiastical and figurative meaning but the
figure rests on a strictly physical definition (SBT, 61). **ἄρας** aor.
act. part. *αἴρω* to take away, to take. **ποιήσω** aor. subj., deliberative subj. The form could also be fut. ind. act. (s. RWP).
πόρνη prostitute. **μὴ γένοιτο** aor. opt. mid. *γίνομαι* "let it not
be" (s. Rom 3:4). ■ **κολλώμενος** pres. mid. part. *κολλάω* to join 16
together, to unite. **ἔσονται** fut. mid. *εἰμί*. **φησίν** pres. ind. *φημί*
to say. **εἰς σάρκα μίαν** "one flesh." The prep. in place of the
pred. nom. is due to Semitic influence (s. MH, 462). The becoming "one flesh" refers to physical union through sexual intercourse (SBT, 62). ■ **ἓν πνεῦμα** "one spirit." Illicit union w. a 17
harlot effects a oneness of physical relationship which con-
tradicts the Lord's claim over the body and creates a disparity
between the body and the spirit (still united to the Lord) (SBT,
69). ■ **φεύγετε** pres. imp. *φεύγω* to flee. The pres. imp. indicates 18
it is to be a continual and habitual fleeing. **ἁμάρτημα** sin, sin
as the act or result of the principle of sin. (For the suf. indicating
the result of an action, s. MH, 355.) **ἐάν** used after a rel. pron.
giving a generalization "whatever." **ποιήσῃ** aor. subj. *ποιέω*.
ἐκτός w. gen. outside, without. **εἰς** w. acc. against. Immorality
arises within the body and has as its sole purpose the gratification of the body (Grosheide). ■ **ναός** temple, the dwelling place 19
of God, the inner sanctuary itself (Lenski). An illusion either to

the temple in Jerusalem or to the temple of Aphrodite near Corinth (s. SBT, 78). **οὗ** rel. pron. gen. sing. gen. by attraction. **ἐστέ** pres. ind. εἰμί used w. gen. in the sense of "belonging to"
20 (s. MT, 231). ■ **ἠγοράσθητε** aor. pass. ἀγοράζω to buy, to buy at the market place. (For the purchasing of slaves in the ancient world, s. FCS, 37ff.). **τιμῆς** "w. a price," gen. of price. **δοξάσατε** aor. imp. δοξάζω to cause one to have a good opinion of someone, to glorify. **δή** then, certainly. Used as an intensive particle and commands an exhortation and indicates that the point at last is clear and may be assumed as true (RG, 1149; BD, 285). **ἐν** "with." The physical body is man's means of concrete service for God (SBT, 244).

Ch. 7

1 ■ **περί** w. gen. concerning. (For the elliptical expression w. the gen. of the personal pron., gen. by attraction, s. RP.) **ἐγράψατε** aor. γράφω to write. Paul now gives his opinion to questions the Corinthians had asked him (Grosheide). **καλόν** good, that which is useful or pleasing, that which is suitable or appropriate for a situation (T; CBB; TDNT). (For an analysis of the formula "better . . . than," s. G.F. Snyder, "The *Tobspruch* in the New Testament," NTS, 23 [October, 1976], 117–120.) **ἅπτεσθαι** pres. mid. inf. ἅπτομαι to touch, followed by the
2 gen. ■ **πορνεία** fornication, illicit sex. **ἐχέτω** pres. imp. ἔχω to have. The imp. is hortatory, not merely permissive (RP). (For a study showing that consecrated virginity was not a customary way of life in the most primitive communities, s. J. Massingberd Ford, "St. Paul, The Philogamist (I Corinthians VII in Early
3 Patristic Exegesis)," NTS, 11 [July, 1965], 326–348.) ■ **ὀφειλή** obligation, debt, due. The specific obligation involved in the marital union (Lenski). **ἀποδιδότω** pres. imp. ἀποδίδωμι to pay back, to pay one's dues, to render. The pres. imp. indicates habitual duty (Morris). The rabbis required that the marriage partners have regular relations w. one another (s. SB III, 368–
4 371). ■ **ἐξουσιάζει** pres. ind. act. to exercise authority over, used w. gen. The pres. tense emphasizes a general statement
5 which is always true. ■ **ἀποστερεῖτε** pres. act. imp. ἀποστερέω to rob, to deprive. **εἰ μήτι** except, unless in a given case, unless perhaps (s. M 169; BS, 204). **σύμφωνος** agreement, consent. **πρὸς καιρὸν** "for a time," "for a period" (no longer) (BD, 124). The rabbis taught that abstinence from intercourse was allowable for generally one to two weeks but disciples of the law may continue abstinence for thirty days against the will of their wives while they occupy themselves in the study of the law

(M Ketuboth V, 6). **ἵνα** w. subj. that. Either used to express purpose or could be viewed as an imperatival use (s. MT, 94f.). **σχολάσητε** aor. subj. σχολάζω to have leisure time for, to devote one's self to something (Lightfoot, *Notes*). **πάλιν** again. **τὸ αὐτό** "for the same thing," "be together." It refers to being sexually together as before (Lenski). **ἦτε** pres. subj. εἰμί. **πειράζῃ** pres. subj. πειράζω to tempt, to try to bring someone to a fall. The subj. is used to express purpose and the pres. tense indicates that Satan may not keep on tempting you (RWP). **ἀκρασία** lack of self-control, incontinence. Here in the sense of
irrepressible desire for sexual relations (Barrett). ■ **συγγνώμη** 6
concession, allowance, "I do not give this as a binding rule. I
state it as what is allowable" (Lightfoot, *Notes*). ■ **θέλω** to wish, 7
to desire followed by the inf. His desire is not only that they be unmarried, but that they also be able to control themselves (Weiss). At this time Paul may have been unmarried or a widower or his wife may have left him and returned to her family because of his conversion to Christianity (Bruce). **χάρισμα** gift, gracious gift, a gift given out of grace. **ἐκ** "from." It gives the source of the gift.

■ **ἄγαμος** unmarried. (For the neg. pref., s. Rom. 1:21.) 8
χήρα widow. The article may suggest that Paul has in mind the members of the Corinthian church who are widows, but it may also be a generalization (Barrett). **καλόν** good, s.v.1. **μείνωσιν**
aor. subj. μένω to remain. ■ **εἰ** w. ind. introduces a condition 9
which is assumed to be true. **ἐγκρατεύονται** pres. ind. mid. to exercise self-control, to have power over one's self. **γαμησάτωσαν** aor. imp. γαμέω to marry. Perhaps ingressive aor. "let them seek marriage" (Grosheide). **κρεῖττον** comp. ἀγαθός better. **πυροῦσθαι** pres. pass. inf. πυρόω to set afire, pass. to be inflamed. It may mean "to burn w. passion," but may possibly mean "to burn in Gehenna," because of falling into
fornication (Bruce). ■ **γεγαμηκόσιν** perf. act. part. γαμέω to 10
marry. The perf. emphasizes a state or condition (s. Rom. 3:21). **παραγγέλλω** to give orders, to command, to instruct. Both Paul and the church at Corinth knew the words of Jesus and Paul gives an additional command and expects obedience because he receives revelations from the Lord which he can communicate to the churches (Grosheide). **χωρισθῆναι** aor. pass. inf. χωρίζω to separate, to divide. The wife is separated, the husband puts away. Then in the converse point of view the believing wife is said to put away and the unbelieving husband is to be
separated (Bengel). Infinitive used in indirect discourse. ■ **καί** 11
even, actually, "if a separation *does* take place" (Barrett).

χωρισθῇ aor. subj. pass. *χωρίζω* ingressive aor. "she gets separated" (RWP). ***μενέτω*** pres. imp. 3rd sing. *μένω*. ***τῷ ἀνδρί*** "to the husband." The definite article is used to denote previous reference; that is, "to her husband" (s. DM, 141; Funk, 556). ***καταλλαγήτω*** aor. imp. pass. *καταλλάσσω* to reconcile, pass. to be reconciled. The prep. in compound is perfective "to effect a thorough change back, to reconcile" (APC, 187ff.). In Judaism it was possible for the wife to return to the husband before the bill of divorcement had been received (SB III, 374).

12 ***ἀφιένατ*** pres. inf. *ἀφίημι* to send away, to divorce. ■ ***λοιπός*** rest. Paul refers here to those who have unbelieving partners (Barrett). ***ἐγώ*** "I." Paul means that he is not now repeating the teaching of Christ, who is not likely to have said anything on the subj. He is, however, w. inspiration speaking w. apostolic authority (RP). ***εἰ*** w. an ind. "if," introduces a condition which is assumed true. ***ἄπιστος*** unbelieving. ***συνευδοκεῖ*** pres. ind. act. to be pleased together w., to agree together, to approve, to consent. ***οἰκεῖν*** pres. act. inf. to live. Used in the sense of being

13 married. ***μὴ ἀφιέτω*** pres. imp. *ἀφίημι* s.v.11. ■ ***γυνὴ*** woman, wife. The context indicates that it is "a Christian woman" (Bar-

14 rett). ■ ***ἡγίασται*** perf. pass. *ἁγιάζω* to separate, to sanctify, to set apart for God's service, to consecrate. He was set apart to the service of God, as the guardian of one of His chosen ones (Hodge). The perf. tense refers to the lasting condition (Grosheide). ***ἐν*** "in the wife"; that is, through the close tie w. her (Grosheide). ***ἐπεὶ ἄρα*** "since otherwise," "since on the contrary supposition it follows . . ." (Lightfoot, *Notes*). ***ἀκάθαρτος***

15 not clean. (For the neg. pref., s. Rom. 1:20.) ■ ***εἰ δέ*** "but if." The particle introduces a condition which is assumed to be true. ***ἄπιστος*** unbelieving. ***χωρίζεται*** pres. ind. pass. to separate, to separate one's self, to divorce. In the papyri the word was used as a technical expression for divorce (BS, 247). ***χωριζέσθω*** pres. imp. pass. ***δεδούλωται*** perf. ind. pass. *δουλόω* to enslave, to be a slave, to be under bondage. ***ἐν τοῖς τοιούτοις*** "in such cases." ***ἐν εἰρήνῃ*** the prep. may be used in a double sense "God has called you *into* a peace *in* which He wishes you to live" (IBG, 79). ***κέκληκεν*** perf. ind. act. *καλέω* to call. The perf. empha-

16 sizes the continuing results or condition (s. Rom. 3:21). ■ ***σώσεις*** fut. *σῴζω* to save, to rescue.

17 ■ ***εἰ μή*** except, only. This looks back to v.15, which contemplates the possibility in certain circumstances of separation (Barrett). (S. also BD, 191.) ***ἑκάστῳ*** each one. The word is the subject of the main clause but appears in the dat. through inverse attraction to the subordinate clause (s. RG, 717; BD, 151).

ἐμέρισεν perf. ind. act. μερίζω to divide, to distribute. The perf.
looks at the completed action in the past and the continuing
results in the present "has assigned his lot in life once for all."
The word here refers entirely to the external conditions of life
(Lightfoot, *Notes*). **περιπατείτω** pres. act. imp. περιπατέω to
walk about, to conduct one's life. The pres. tense emphasizes the
continual or habitual action. **διατάσσομαι** pres. ind. mid. to
command, to ordain, to order. The word was a military term
(RWP), a technical term used in connection w. wills, as well as
a general word for commanding (MM). ■ **περιτετμημένος** 18
perf. pass. part. περιτέμνω to circumcise. **ἐκλήθη** aor. pass.
καλέω. **ἐπισπάσθω** pres. mid. imp. ἐπισπάω a medical technical term "to pull over the foreskin." A method used to conceal
circumcision (BAG; SB IV, 33f.; Lietzmann; 1 Macc. 115).
ἀκροβυστία uncircumcision. **κέκληται** perf. pass. καλέω. The
perf. emphasizes the continuing result. **περιτεμνέσθω** pres.
pass. imp. περιτέμνω to circumcise. ■ **τήρησις** keeping, watch- 19
ing, guarding. (For nouns ending w. this suf. which expresses
action, s. MH, 373f.) **ἐντολῶν** gen. pl. obj. gen. ■ **κλήσει** call- 20
ing. **ᾗ** rel. pron. dat. sing. fem. locative referring to the state in
which he is when he is called by God to become a Christian
(Barrett). **ἐκλήθη** aor. pass. **μενέτω** pres. imp. μένω to remain.
■ **ἐκλήθης** aor. pass., s.v.18. **μελέτω** pres. imp. μέλει imperson- 21
al verb used w. dat. to be a concern to someone "don't let it be
a concern to you," "don't worry about it," "stop being concerned about it" (FCS, 175; for the force of the imp., s. Rom
6:11, 12; MKG, 272). **ἀλλ'** "but." The word has here its full
adversative force (FCS, 177). **εἰ καί** "if, indeed" (FCS, 178;
Thrall, 81). **ἐλεύθερος** free. **γενέσθαι** aor. mid. inf. γίνομαι.
(For an extensive discussion of slavery in the ancient world w.
the discussion of why and how a slave was set free, s. FCS,
29–125.) **μᾶλλον** comp. adv. πολύ "rather," "by all means."
χρῆσαι aor. mid. imp. χράομαι to use, to live according to. The
object to be supplied would be God's calling "by all means, live
according to (your calling in Christ)." The believer's existence
is no longer determined by his legal status but if he is to be freed
he is to make better use of his vocation (s. FCS, 175–179f.;
Grosheide). ■ **γὰρ** "for." This introduces an explanation and 22
further reason why they are not to worry about being in slavery
(FCS, 177). **ἀπελεύθερος** freedman. The following gen. describes who had freed him and to whom he now belongs. (For
the social standing and the rights of a freedman as well as his
obligations to the one who has freed him, s. FCS, 72–82.) ■ 23
τιμῆς price, gen. sing. gen. of price. **ἠγοράσθητε** aor. pass.

ἀγοράζω to buy at the market place, to purchase (s. APC, 53–59; TDNT; CBB). The pass. indicates another did the pur-
24 chasing and the aor. looks at the completed transaction. ■ **ἐν ᾧ**
"in which." It refers to the state or condition. **ἐκλήθη** aor. pass., s.v.18. **μενέτω** pres. imp. s.v.20. **παρὰ** w. dat. along side of, in the presence of. All secular conditions whether of family life, or caste, or service, are capable of being made the expression of a Christian character (RP).
25 ■ **παρθένος** virgin. It has been suggested that the word here refers to young widows or widowers who have only been married once and the question had been raised whether a second marriage was wrong (s. J.M. Ford, "Levirate Marriage in St. Paul (I Cor. VII)," NTS, 10 [April, 1964], 361–365). Another suggestion is that it refers to engaged couples w. the meaning "fiance" and the entire section (verses 25–38) concerns engagement (J.K. Elliott, "Paul's Teaching on Marriage in I Cor.: Some Problems Considered," 19 [January, 1973], 219–225). **ἐπιταγή** commandment (s.v.17); that is, an expressed command, whether a directly recorded saying of our Lord (as in v. 10) or a direct intimation to the apostle by revelation (Lightfoot, *Notes*). **δίδωμι** pres. ind. act. to give. Though Paul is giving his own opinion, it does not mean that this section is not inspired by the Holy Spirit. **ἠλεημένος** perf. pass. part. ἐλεέω to show mercy, pass. to receive mercy. The word indicates to see someone in need and to have pity and compassion on them and to kindly help him out of his need (s. TDNT; CBB; Trench, *Synonyms*, 166–171). The perf. looks at the completed state or condition and the part. could be used in a causal sense (Barrett). **πιστὸς**
26 true, faithful, trustworthy. ■ **νομίζω** to consider, to think, to be of the opinion. **ὑπάρχειν** pres. act. inf. to be, to exist. Infinitive used in indirect discourse. **διὰ** w. acc. because of. **ἐνεστῶσαν** perf. act. part. ἐνίστημι to stand on, to be present. **ἀνάγκη** necessity, compulsion of any kind, distress, calamity. It refers to the whole state of things between the first and second coming of Christ (Godet). **ὅτι** used after the main verb in a recitative sense equivalent to quotation marks (RWP). **τὸ οὕτως εἶναι**
27 pres. inf. "the being so" (s. BD, 205f.). ■ **δέδεσαι** perf. ind. pass. 2nd per. sing. δέω to bind, Used w. dat. to indicate the pers. w. whom one is bound. The perf. indicates the continuing state resulting from a previous action. (For the lively style of this section, s. BD, 242.) **ζήτει** pres. imp. ζητέω to seek. The pres. imp. w. the neg. could mean "do not immediately . . . ," or "do not always . . . ," or "do not continue . . ." (MKG, 272). **λύσις** loosing, releasing. **λέλυσαι** perf. ind. pass. 2nd per. sing. λύω

to loose, to release. ■ **ἐὰν καί** "and if." It introduces a third-class 28
condition indicating the condition is possible. (For the meaning
"although," s. BD, 190.) **γαμήσῃς** aor. subj. γαμέω to marry,
ingressive aor. to get married. **ἥμαρτες** aor. ind. act. ἁμαρτάνω
to sin, gnomic aor. indicating that which is always true (Lietzmann; s. BD, 171; Funk, 621). **γήμῃ** aor. subj. γαμέω. **θλῖψις**
tribulation, pressure, affliction. **τῇ σαρκί** dat. of reference, possibly instrumental dat. or dat. of disadvantage. **ἕξουσιν** fut. ἔχω.
τοιοῦτοι such ones. **φείδομαι** pres. mid. to spare, conative pres.
"I am trying to spare" (Barrett). ■ **φημί** to say. **καιρὸς** time, 29
time period. **συνεσταλμένος** perf. pass. part. συστέλλω to
draw together, to limit, to shorten. The time has been drawn
together so as to be small in amount (RP). **λοιπός** finally, henceforth. The word can be inferential or progressive (s. Blomqvist,
100–103; Thrall, 25–30). **ἔχοντες** pres. part. ἔχω. The part. is
used w. the particle for an assumed condition (RWP). **ὦσιν** pres.
subj. εἰμί. ■ **κλαίοντες** pres. part. to weep, to cry. **κατέχοντες** 30
pres. act. part. to hold down, to hold firm, to possess, "as not
entering upon full ownership." Earthly goods are a trust, not a
possession (RP). ■ **χρώμενοι** pres. mid. part. χράομαι to use, 31
to make use of. (For the use of the acc. w. this verb, s. RG, 476.)
καταχρώμενοι pres. mid. part. καταχράομαι to make full use
of, to use to the utmost, "using it down to the ground," "using
it completely up" (RP). (For the use of this word in the papyri,
s. MM.) **παράγει** to pass by, to pass alongside of, to pass away.
The pres. tense emphasizes the continual action. **σχῆμα** bearing, manner, outward appearance, form, shape (BAG; TDNT).
κόσμος world. It refers to the world's resources and its opportunities (Bruce). ■ **ἀμερίμνους** without care, free from care, with- 32
out worry or concern. (For the neg. pref., s. Rom. 1:20.)
μεριμνᾷ pres. ind. act. to have care or concern, to worry about
something, gnomic pres. indicating a general truth (s. SMT, 8;
Funk, 615). **ἀρέσῃ** aor. subj. ἀρέσκω to please. ■ **γαμήσας** 33
aor. part. γαμέω. **τὰ τοῦ κόσμου** "things belonging to the
world," gen. of relationship (s. BD, 89). ■ **μεμέρισται** perf. ind. 34
pass. μερίζω to divide. The perf. tense emphasizes the state or
condition. **ᾖ** pres. subj. εἰμί. **ἁγία** holy, dedicated, consecrated.
τῷ σώματι dat. of reference. The passage indicates that the
human spirit is distinct from the body (s. SBT, 140). **γαμήσασα**
aor. act. part. fem., s.v.33. ■ **αὐτῶν** own, refl. use of the pron. 35
or possibly the intensive use (s. RG, 687). **σύμφορον** that which
is carried together, beneficial, advantageous, profitable, here
used as a noun, benefit, advantage. **βρόχος** noose, a noose or
slipknot used for lassoing animals (RWP). **ἐπιβάλω** aor. subj.

ἐπιβάλλω to cast upon, to put upon w. the purpose of catching, "to cast a noose upon one" is a figurative expression, originally borrowed from the chase, for the idea of depriving of freedom (bringing under, binding and limiting relations) (Meyer). **εὔσχημον** well-shaped, proper, good order, decorum, decency. The word denotes perf. fitness (Godet). **εὐπάρεδρον** constant, lit. well sitting beside, "for the good position beside the Lord" (RWP). The verb is used in 1 Cor. 9:13 for "waiting upon the altar" (Barrett). **ἀπερισπάστως** adv. unhindered, lit. without anything drawn around (RWP), without distraction.

36 ■ **ἀσχημονεῖν** pres. act. inf. to act without decorum, to behave in a dishonorable way (for the noun, s.v.35). **ἐπί** w. acc. toward. **παρθένον αὐτοῦ** "his virgin." This refers either to a father and his daughter or to a man and woman who have entered upon a spiritual marriage and now live together without physical relations or a case of levirate marriage and the word means "young widow" or it refers to a man and woman who are an engaged couple (s. Barrett; s. also v. 25). **ᾖ** pres. subj., s.v.34. **ὑπέρακμος** past the bloom of youth, beyond marriageable age. The prep. in compound may be understood to express intensification rather than the temporal sense; that is, w. strong passion, oversexed (BAG; s. also Barrett). **ὀφείλει** pres. ind. act. one is obligated, it is necessary. The word expresses a moral obligation. **ποιείτω** pres. imp. 3rd per. sing. **ποιέω**. **γαμείτωσαν** pres. imp. 3rd per. pl. γαμέω to marry. Present tense of the imp.
37 points to a general truth. ■ **ἕστηκεν** perf. ἵστημι to stand. **ἐν τῇ καρδίᾳ** "in his heart." Here the heart is the center of man from which decisions come (PAT, 328). **ἑδραῖος** firm, steadfast. **ἀνάγκην** necessity, s.v.26. **ἐξουσία** authority. **κέκρικεν** perf. κρίνω to judge, to come to a decision, to decide. **τηρεῖν** pres. act. inf. to keep. The meaning is probably "to keep his virgin as she is" (Barrett). The inf. is used in indirect discourse giving the content of the decision. **καλῶς** adv. well. (For the adj., s.v.1.)
38 ■ **γαμίζων** pres. act. part. to marry. Verbs w. this ending are generally causative, "to give in marriage," but the word may also mean "to marry," "to enter into marriage" (s. MM; Weiss; Lietzmann). **ἑαυτοῦ** his. The reflex. here appears to have lost refl.
39 force (IBG, 120). **κρεῖσσον** comp. ἀγαθός "better." ■ **δέδεται** perf. ind. pass. δέω to bind. The perf. emphasizes the state or condition resulting from the act of marriage. **ὅσον** rel. pron. as much as, as long as. **ζῇ** pres. ind. act. ζάω to live. **κοιμηθῇ** aor. pass. subj. κοιμάομαι to go to sleep. The term for Christian death (EGT). **ᾧ** rel. pron. masc. dat. sing. "to whom." The dat. is used w. the verb "to be married to." **γαμηθῆναι** aor. pass. inf.

γαμέω pass. to be married to, epexegetic inf. used to explain the
freedom of the widow (s. Funk, 663f.). ■ **μακαριωτέρα** comp. 40
μακάριος happy (s. TDNT). **ἐάν** w. subj. introduces a condition
which is probable. **μείνῃ** aor. subj. μένω to remain.

Ch. 8

■ **περί** w. gen. "concerning," "about." Paul begins to treat 1
a second point concerning which the Corinthians had questioned
him (Grosheide). **εἰδωλόθυτον** that which was offered as a sacrifice to an idol. The word is of Jewish origin (s. TDNT). Various
types of choice animals without blemish were offered to the
gods. Part of the meat was burned on the altar and part of it was
used for a sacred banquet w. the deity as the honored guest and
that which was left was sold at the marketplace (s. OCD, 944;
Bruce). The Jews called this meat from sacrifices for the dead;
that is, "idols," and the use of such meat was strictly forbidden
(s. SB III, 377). **οἴδαμεν** defective perf. w. pres. meaning. Paul
uses the 1st per. pl. to include himself w. the readers (Lietzmann). **γνῶσις** knowledge. Paul's use of knowledge is not something purely intellectual. It is knowledge which has results and
leads to action, especially religious action (Grosheide). Here it
is not a reference to gnosticism which developed later (s. PCG,
39f.). **φυσιοῖ** pres. ind. act. to puff up, to blow up like a billows.
The pres. is gnomic emphasizing a general truth. ■ **ἐγνωκέναι** 2
perf. act. inf. γινώσκω. The perf. emphasizes a knowledge
which is acquired and is one's possession. The inf. is used in
indirect discourse. **ἔγνω** aor. ind. act. γινώσκω ingressive aor.
"come to know" (RWP). ■ **ἔγνωσται** perf. ind. pass. he has 3
come to be known and is still known by God (Lenski). ■ **βρῶσις** 4
eating. (For nouns ending w. this suf. indicating action, s. MH,
373.) **εἴδωλον** idol. Paul calls that which the statute represents
an idol (Schlatter). **οὐδείς** no one, nobody, used as an adj. "no."
εἰ μή except. ■ **εἴπερ** if indeed, if after all. Here used in a 5
concessive sense (s. BD, 237). **λεγόμενοι** pres. pass. part. λέγω
to say, pass. to be called, "those who continually are called gods"
or "so called gods" (Grosheide). **εἴτε . . . εἴτε** "just as indeed."
θεοὶ πολλοί many gods (s. Acts 17:16). ■ **εἷς** one god followed 6
by the word in apposition "the father." **κύριος** lord, a title used
to indicate deity of Jesus Christ. (For a collection of the evidence
proving that the Jews at the time of Christ used this term for
God, s. Joseph A. Fitzmyer, "Der semitische Hintergrund des
neutestamentlichen Kyriostitels," *Jesus Christus in Historie und
Theologie*, 267–298). **ἐκ** and **εἰς** indicate the origin and goal of
God's creation. **ἡμεῖς δι᾽αὐτοῦ** "we through Him." Like all men

we are created by Christ but we are also redeemed by Him
(Grosheide).
7 ■ **ἡ γνῶσις** "the knowledge." The article points to the
specific knowledge he is discussing in this context. **συνηθείᾳ**
familiarity, custom, instrumental dat. **συνείδησις** conscience (s.
Rom. 2:15; TDNT; PAT, 402–446; CBB). **μολύνεται** pres. pass.
8 μολύνω to stain, to pollute, to contaminate, to defile. ■
παραστήσει fut. ind. act. παρίστημι to present, to present for
approbation or condemnation (RP). **ἐὰν** w. subj. introduces a
condition which is possible. **φάγωμεν** aor. subj. ἐσθίω to eat.
ὑστερούμεθα pres. ind. mid. ὑστερέω to fall short, to lack (s.
Rom. 3:23). **περισσεύομεν** pres. ind. act. to have an abun-
9 dance. ■ **μή** lest. Used w. aor. subj. to express a neg. imp. (s. BD,
184). **πρόσκομμα** stumbling, hindrance. **γένηται** aor. mid.
10 subj. γίνομαι. **ἀσθενής** weak. ■ **ἴδῃ** aor. subj. ὁράω to see.
εἰδώλειον idol temple, idol shrine. **κατακείμενον** pres. mid.
part. κατάκειμαι to lie down, to recline at the table. It would
not be uncommon to be invited to a meal in the temple as is
evident from some "invitation cards" found among the papyri (s.
Bruce). **οὐχὶ** used to introduce a question which expects the
answer yes. **ἀσθενοῦς ὄντος** weak, used w. part. in apposition
to the personal pron. αὐτοῦ. **ὄντος** pres. part. gen. sing. εἰμί.
Perhaps the causal use of the part. **οἰκοδομηθήσεται** fut. ind.
11 pass. οἰκοδομέω to build up, to strengthen. ■ **ἀπόλλυται** pres.
ind. pass. ἀπόλλυμι to ruin; that is, "to come to sin." It means
not to show one's self as a Christian (Grosheide). **ἀσθενῶν** pres.
part. ἀσθενέω to be weak. **ἀπέθανεν** aor. ind. act.
12 ἀποθνήσκω to die. ■ **ἁμαρτάνοντες** pres. act. part.
ἁμαρτάνω to sin. **τύπτοντες** pres. part. **τύπτω** to wound, to
strike w. the fist, staff, whip (RWP). The part. could be conditional or indicating the means or manner. **ἀσθενοῦσαν** pres.
13 part., s.v.11. ■ **διόπερ** therefore, for this very reason. **εἰ** w. ind.
Used to introduce a condition which is assumed to be true.
σκανδαλίζει to cause one to stumble, to offend (s. TDNT;
NTW, 111–114). **οὐ μή** not in anywise. (For the use of this
strong neg., s. M 188f.) **φάγω** aor. subj., s.v.8. **σκανδαλίσω**
aor. subj.

Ch. 9

1 ■ **ἐλεύθερος** free, the freedom of a Christian (Morris). **οὐχὶ**
used in questions expecting the answer yes. **ἑώρακα** perf. ind.
act. ὁράω to see. The perf. pictures the lasting results of having
seen. Having seen the Lord was one of the prerequisites for
2 apostleship (s. Acts 1:22; s. also 1 Cor. 1:1; TDNT). ■ **εἰ** w. ind.

used to introduce a condition which is assumed to be true.
ἄλλοις "to others," dat. of respect or relation "in the estimation
of others" (s. Funk, 721f.; MT, 238; Barrett). **ἀλλά** "but at
least." A contrast used w. the emphatic article (BD, 226).
σφραγίς seal, a confirming and guaranteeing sign as well as a
sign of authority (s. TDNT; CBB).
■ **ἐμή** "my," emphatic by position. **ἀπολογία** defense. 3
Used elsewhere of defense in a law court (Barrett).
ἀνακρίνουσιν pres. part. ἀνακρίνω to examine, perhaps in the
sense cross-examine, conative pres. those who would like to
examine (Barrett). ■ **μὴ οὐκ** The first neg. is used in the question 4
expecting the answer no and the second neg. negates the verb
"you would not say that we do not have the authority, would
you?" (s. BD, 220f.; RG, 1173). **φαγεῖν** aor. act. part. ἐσθίω to
eat. **πεῖν** aor. act. inf. πίνω to drink. The inf. is used to explain
the content of the authority. ■ **ἀδελφήν** sister; that is, a Chris- 5
tian, one who belongs to the same religious belief (s. CBB;
TDNT). **περιάγειν** pres. act. inf. to lead around. The word does
not emphasize the traveling together on a journey but rather it
means "to have constantly w. one's self"; that is, being married
(Conzelmann). ■ **ἤ** or. The word continues the question. 6
ἐργάζεσθαι pres. mid. inf. to work; that is, to do manual labor.
■ **στρατεύεται** pres. mid. ind. to be a soldier, to do military 7
service, to serve in the army. The pres. tense is gnomic emphasizing a timeless truth (s. SMT, 8). **ὀψωνίοις** provisions, soldiers' wages (s. Rom. 6:28). The dat. could be instrumental. The
soldiers' pay was probably a denarius a day, out of which they
had to equip themselves, secure any simple luxuries, or bribe the
centurions for remissions of duties (BC V, 428). **ποτέ** at any
time, ever. **ἀμπελῶνα** vineyard. (For the exact rules governing
the workers eating of the harvest, s. SB III, 379f.) **ποιμαίνει**
pres. ind. act. to tend a flock. **ποίμνη** flock. **γάλακτος** milk.
■ **οὐ** not. The word negates the verb rather than determining the 8
question (s.v.4.). ■ **γέγραπται** perf. pass. γράφω. The perf. 9
emphasizes the standing legal authority of that which was written (s. MM). **κημώσεις** fut. κημόω to muzzle. The fut. is used
under Semitic influence of the legal language of the OT and
expresses a categorical imp. (BG, 94). The Jewish concern for
animals distinguished them from other nations (SB III, 382).
βοῦς ox. **ἀλοῶντα** pres. act. part. acc. sing. masc. ἀλοάω to
thrash, to tread or trample out. Sledges were drawn by teams of
oxen . . . , and encircled the pile of grain heaped in the center of
the thrashing floor (ZPEB V, 739; IDB IV, 637). **μή** Used to
introduce questions expecting the answer no. **μέλει** pres. ind.

act. to have concern. Used impersonally followed by the dat. of interest and the gen. of thing, "aren't the things of oxen a con-
10 cern to God?" ■ **δι' ἡμᾶς** "because of us, for our sakes." Either a reference to men in general or specifically to teachers. **πάντως** assuredly, entirely; that is, in every case (Grosheide). **γάρ** for. In replies it affirms what was asked, giving the reason for a tacit "yes," "to be sure, just so" (BD, 236). **ἐγράφη** aor. pass. γράφω. **ὀφείλει** pres. ind. act. to be obligated to, ought, should. It generally shows a moral obligation. **ἀροτριῶν** pres. act. part. ἀροτριάω to plow. **ἀροτριᾶν** pres. act. inf. Used to complete the main verb showing what the obligation is. **μετέχειν** pres. act.
11 inf. to share in, to partake of. ■ **εἰ** w. ind. introducing a condition which is assumed to be true. **ἐσπείραμεν** aor. ind. act. σπείρω to sow, to sow seeds. **μέγα** great. **σαρκικά** fleshly, pertaining to the flesh. (For the meaning of this suf., s. MH, 378.) The word here is not identical w. "sinful." The contrast is one between heavenly and earthly, or between spiritual and the material (Grosheide). **θερίσομεν** fut. ind. act. θερίζω to harvest, to reap. (For the use of the fut. w. **εἰ** w. the meaning "if subsequently,
12 as actually happened, we . . . ," s. BD, 189.) ■ **ὑμῶν** "over you" (RG, 500). **ἐξουσίας** authority, gen. after a verb of sharing. **μετέχουσιν** pres. ind. act. μετέχω to partake in, to share.

ἐχρησάμεθα aor. mid. χράομαι to use, to make use of. **στέγομεν** pres. ind. act. to cover, to protect or keep by covering, to bear up against, to endure (T). **ἐγκοπή** a cutting in, hindrance. Used in the papyri in the literal sense of cutting down (a tree) (MM). **δῶμεν** aor. act. subj. δίδωμι to give. The subj. is used to
13 express purpose. ■ **ἐργαζόμενοι** pres. mid. part. ἐργάζομαι to work, here to officiate in religious matters. **τὰ ἐκ τοῦ ἱεροῦ** the things from the temple or holy place; that is, the altar or the sacrifice. Thus the last clause defines the first (Grosheide). **θυσιαστήριον** altar, place of sacrifice (for this suf. indicating the place where an action takes place, s. MH, 342–343) "at the altar." The dat. is pure locative (RG, 521). **παρεδρεύοντες** pres. act. part. to sit constantly beside, to attend constantly (AS). (For the religious connotation of the word in the papyri, s. MM.) **συμμερίζονται** pres. ind. mid. to share a portion together. The customs Paul refers to were widespread in antiquity. Those who held sacred offices on behalf of others might reasonably expect
14 to be provided for. This Jesus Himself recognized (Barrett). ■ **διέταξεν** aor. ind. act. διατάσσω to give an order, to command. The tense of the verb indicates that Paul was consciously alluding to a "past" origin in the teaching of Jesus (JNP, 96). **καταγγέλλουσιν** pres. act. part. masc. dat. pl. καταγγέλλω to

proclaim, to make a solemn proclamation (s. CBB). The dat. is dat. of favor or advantage (Godet). **ἐκ** from. The prep. gives the source of income. **ζῆν** pres. act. inf. ζάω to live. The inf. is used
in indirect speech (s. BD, 200; IBG, 153). ■ **ἐγὼ δὲ** but I (em- 15
phatic). He now applies the principle to himself and the apostle gives a further reason for the renunciation of his undoubted rights (Hering). **κέχρημαι** perf. ind. mid. χράομαι to use followed by the object in the dat. The change of tenses from the aor. to the perf. brings it down to the pres. moment "I have not availed myself" (RP). **γένηται** aor. mid. subj. γίνομαι. Subjunctive used in expressing purpose. **ἐν** in, in my case (Barrett). **ἀποθανεῖν** aor. act. inf. ἀποθνήσκω to die, an epexegetical inf. explaining what is better. **ἤ** or. Paul breaks the construction abruptly (s. MT, 343). **καύχημα** boasting, reason or ground for boasting. **κενώσει** fut. κενόω to make empty, to make void.
■ **εὐαγγελίζωμαι** pres. mid. subj. εὐαγγελίζομαι to proclaim 16
good news, to evangelize (s. TDNT; CBB; MTW, 41f.). **ἀνάγκη** compulsion, necessity. The word in the NT does not have the meaning "fate" (s. TDNT; Gustav Stählin, "Das Schicksal Im Neuen Testament und bei Josephus," *Josephus-Studien*, 321f.). **ἐπίκειται** perf. ind. pass. ἐπιτίθημι to place upon, perf. lies upon. The perf. emphasizes the pres. condition and the meaning is "presses upon me" (RP). **οὐαὶ** woe, alas! An interjection denoting pain or displeasure (BAG), followed by the dat. of
disadvantage. **εὐαγγελίσωμαι** aor. mid. subj. ■ **ἑκὼν** willingly, 17
gladly, of one's own freewill. **πράσσω** to do, to practice. The pres. tense emphasizes habitual action and the word is used in a first-class conditional clause which assumes the reality of the condition. **μισθός** payment, reward. Paul's purpose is to intimate that he does not seek his reward in the receiving of financial compensation (Grosheide). **ἄκων** unwilling, not of one's own freewill (for the neg. pref., s. Rom. 1:20). **οἰκονομία** stewardship, responsibility. The word indicates the task given to responsible and faithful servants who were appointed over the economy or particular area of responsibility in the household. The word stresses obligation, responsibility, and faithfulness of the servant to his master in carrying out the entrusted task (s. TDNT). (For the use of the word in patristic writers, s. PGL.) **πεπίστευμαι** perf. ind. pass. πιστεύω to believe, to entrust. The perf. emphasizes the completed state or condition reaching
to the pres. time. ■ **μού** "my," emphatic by position. **ἵνα** here 18
does not express purpose but gives the content of the reward (s. BD, 202). **εὐαγγελιζόμενος** pres. mid. part., s.v.16. **ἀδάπανος** without expense, free of charge. **θήσω** fut. ind. act. τίθημι to

place, to present. **εἰς τό** w. inf. used to express purpose. **καταχρήσασθαι** aor. mid. inf. καταχράομαι to make full use of, to use completely, to use to the uttermost. The prep. in compound is perfective (RWP; s. 1 Cor. 7:31).

19 ■ **ὢν** pres. act. part. εἰμί to be. The part. here is concessive "although I am free." **ἐδούλωσα** aor. ind. act. δουλόω to enslave, to make a slave of someone. **πλείονας** comp. πολύς more, the majority or it has the meaning "others, even more"
20 (BD, 127). **κερδήσω** fut. ind. act. κερδαίνω to win. ■ **ἐγενόμην** aor. mid. γίνομαι. **τοῖς Ἰουδαίοις** the individual use of the article "the Jews w. whom I had to deal on each occasion" (BD, 137). **ὑπό** w. acc. "under." The "law" here is the Torah, as written in the Pentateuch and expounded by orthodox Jewish
21 rabbis (MS, 135). ■ **ἄνομος** lawless, without the law, however, not in the sense of leading an unregulated and irresponsible life (MS, 135). The addition of the gen. **ἄνομος θεοῦ** indicates that "the law of God" is something wider and more inclusive than the "law, in the sense of Torah" (MS, 137). **ἔννομος** legal, subject to law, obedient to the law, "under legal obligation to Christ" (Barrett). (For the relation of this to the spiritual life and walk according to the precepts of Christ, s. MS, 137–148.) **κερδάνω**
22 aor. act. subj. κερδαίνω s.v.19. ■ **γέγονα** perf. ind. act. γίνομαι to become. The change from aor. to perf. is significant; this is the permanent result of his past action (RP). **πάντως** by all means. **σώσω** fut. σῴζω to rescue, to save. (For the use of the fut. in
23 purpose clauses, s. MT, 100.). ■ **συγκοινωνός** one who shares together, fellow partaker, fellow participant. **γένωμαι** aor. mid. subj. γίνομαι. Subjunctive used in a purpose clause.

24 ■ **οἴδατε** defective perf. w. a pres. meaning to know. **στάδιον** stadium, a running track which was a long parallelogram about 200 yards long and 30 yards wide (s. OCD, 1010f.; Oscar Bronner, "The Apostle Paul and the Isthmian Games," BA, 25 [February, 1962], 1–31; A.H. Harris, *Sport in Greece and Rome*, 27–33; DGRA, 1055f.). **τρέχοντες** pres. act. part. τρέχω to run. **εἷς** one. **βραβεῖον** prize. The prize given to the winner of an athletic contest. The prize was generally a wreath but the winner was also rewarded w. fame and popularity. **καταλάβητε** aor. act. subj. καταλαμβάνω to attain, to grasp and hold, effective aor. w. the perfective use of the prep. in compound (RWP). The example of the runners in the arena sets the stage for the
25 theme of self-control which follows (PAM, 87). ■ **ἀγωνιζόμενος** pres. mid. part. ἀγωνίζομαι to engage in an athletic contest, to strive. (For the attitude of Greeks, Romans, and Jews toward the athletic contest, s. PAM, 16–75; for the

particular neg. attitude of the Jews, s. SB IV, 401–405.) **πάντα**
acc. of general reference "in regards to all things."
ἐγκρατεύεται pres. ind. mid. to exercise self-control. The pres.
is gnomic and emphasizes that which is always true. All the
endeavors of the athlete are in vain if he has not trained his body
and abstained from all that might in any harm his physical condition (PAM, 87). **φθαρτός** perishable. **ἄφθαρτος** inperishable.
λάβωσιν aor. act. subj. λαμβάνω to receive. Paul is not speaking of agonizing for the prize of eternal life but rather for the goal
of faithfully proclaiming the gospel (PAM, 87f.). ■ **τοίνυν** ac- 26
cordingly, therefore. It is used to draw an inference. **ἀδήλως**
uncertainly, "I do not run as one who has no fixed and certain
goal" (PAM, 90; s. also Weiss). **πυκτεύω** to fight w. the fist, to
box (s. A.H. Harris, *Sport in Greece and Rome*, 22–25; DGRA,
974). Paul turns to the picture of the boxer in order to rein-
troduce the principle of self-restriction and self-negation (PAM,
90). **ἀήρ, - έρος** air. **δέρων** pres. act. part. to beat. The word
could signify the failure of the pugilist to make his blows tell or
his actions in carrying on mock contest of a shadow boxer
(PAM, 90). ■ **ὑπωπιάζω** to strike under the eye, to beat black 27
and blue. **δουλαγωγῶ** to lead into slavery, to make a slave or
to treat one as a slave. The two verbs give the picture of the
athlete who does all to discipline himself and to keep his body
under rigorous control, in order that it might serve and not
hinder his progress to the goal (PAM, 91). **πως** "lest by any
means." **κηρύξας** aor. act. part. **κηρύσσω** to preach, to proclaim as a herald (s. TDNT). The part. is temporal expressing
antecedent time, "after I have preached." **ἀδόκιμος** rejected as
unusable. Used of metals and coins which were rejected for not
standing the test (RWP). **γένωμαι** aor. mid. subj. s.v.23. Paul's
fear is that he will be unfaithful in carrying out his commission
of preaching the gospel as expected of him (PAM, 96).

Ch. 10

■ **ἀγνοεῖν** pres. act. inf. ἀγνοέω not to know, to be igno- 1
rant. Used w. acc. and is supplementary to the verb θέλω. (For
the neg. force of the pref., s. Rom. 1:21.) **πάντες** all. The main
emphasis in vv. 1–4 rests on the word "all." Paul had received
the same privileges (s. Bruce; Grosheide). **διῆλθον** aor.
διέρχομαι to go through, to pass completely through. The prep.
in compound is perfective and local (s. MH, 301f.). ■ **εἰς** into. 2
ἐβαπτίσαντο aor. mid. βαπτίζω to baptize. It means to im-
merse in Moses; that is, to bring in close relationship w. Moses
(Grosheide). The mid. is permissive mid. Some accept the pass.

as the true reading here (s. BD, 166), and the pass. is explained
as a permissive pass. "to allow one's self to be . . ." (MT, 57).
3 ■ **τὸ αὐτό** "the same." **πνευματικός** spiritual, that which pertains to the spirit. The word is either spiritual in contrast to
material or spiritual in its relation to the Holy Spirit. **βρῶμα**
4 food. **ἔφαγον** aor. act. ἐσθίω to eat. ■ **ἔπιον** aor. ind. act. πίνω
to drink. **πόμα** that which one drinks, drink. **ἔπινον** impf. The
impf. pictures the manner of action and shows the continual
access to the supernatural source of supply (RWP; BD, 169).
ἀκολουθούσης pres. act. part. fem. ἀκολουθέω to follow. (For
the Jewish tradition that the well which followed the Israelites
in the wilderness, s. SB IV, 406f.; Targum Onkelos and Rashi at
Numbers 21:16–19; for the DSS, s. CD 6:3–9.) **πέτρα** rock (s.
Matt. 16:18). **ἦν** impf. εἰμί. It was not that Christ was the literal
rock but He was the spiritual rock that followed and from which
Israel drank. The benefits enjoyed by the people are spiritual
because they came from Christ who is the source of all blessings
5 (Grosheide; s. also TDNT). ■ **εὐδόκησεν** aor. εὐδοκέω to be
pleased w. Its use w. the prep. **ἐν** denotes a Semitic influence (s.
BD, 111). **κατεστρώθησαν** aor. ind. pass. καταστρώννυμι to
stretch or spread down as of a couch, to lay low, as if by a
6 hurricane (RWP). ■ **τύπος** type, example. The word is used here
in the sense of "an awful, warning example" (Barrett; s. also
CBB; TDNT). **ἐγενήθησαν** aor. pass. γίνομαι. Instead of the
usual sing. of the verb after a neuter pl. subject the verb here is
pl. through the attraction of the pred. (EGT). **εἰς τό** w. inf. used
here to express purpose; that is, neg. purpose "that we should not
be." **ἐπιθυμητάς** one who lusts, one who has a strong desire.
The noun is followed by the obj. gen. indicating the object of the
strong desire. (For nouns w. this ending indicating the agent
performing an action, s. MH, 365f.) **ἐπεθύμησαν** aor. ind. act.
ἐπιθυμέω to have strong desire, to lust after, to lust. Lust is
strong desire of any sort, but in the NT it is more commonly used
7 of evil passions than good desires (Morris). ■ **γίνεσθε** pres. mid.
imp. The pres. imp. w. the neg. is often used to stop an action
in progress, "do not continue" (s. MKG, 272f.). **γέγραπται**
perf. ind. pass. γράφω, "it stands written." The term was used
of authoritative documents (s. MM). **ἐκάθισεν** aor. καθίζω to
take one's seat, to sit. **φαγεῖν** aor. act. inf. ἐσθίω to eat. **πεῖν**
aor. act. inf. πίνω to drink. The inf. is used to express purpose.
ἀνέστησαν aor. ἀνίστημι to rise up, to get up. **παίζειν** to
play, to amuse one's self, to dance. This word as well as the
eating and drinking were considered by the rabbis to mean the
8 committing of idolatry (s. SB III, 410). ■ **πορνεύωμεν** pres.

subj. πορνεύω to engage in unlawful sexual acts, to commit fornication. The subj. is hortatory "let us not." **ἐπόρνευσαν** aor. ind. act. **ἔπεσαν** aor. πίπτω to fall. **εἴκοσι τρεῖς** twenty-three
χιλιάς thousand. ■ **ἐκπειράζωμεν** pres. subj. ἐκπειράζω to 9
try, to put to the test (s. Matt. 4:1). The prep. in compound is perfective and might suggest the daring of the act or an effort to put to a decisive test (MH, 309), hortatory subj. **ὄφις** snake. **ἀπώλλυντο** impf. mid. ἀπόλλυμι to be destroyed, to perish. The impf. pictures the continual action, they continue to perish
day by day (RWP). ■ **γογγύζετε** pres. act. imp. γογγύζω to 10
murmur, to complain, to give audible expression to unwarranted dissatisfaction (Lenski). It contains the idea of a judgment and a condemnation of God by man who instead of giving God thanks and showing obedience sets himself up as a judge over God (s. TDNT; CBB). **καθάπερ** just as. **ἐγόγγυσαν** aor. ind. act. γογγύζω and, w. the result that (Barrett). **ἀπώλοντο** aor. ind. mid. ἀπόλλυμι. **ὀλοθρευτής** one who destroys, the destroyer. Perhaps a reference to the angel of destruction whom the rabbis called Mashhith (s. SB III, 421f.; Jastrow II, 851; s.
Exod. 12:23; TDNT). ■ **τυπικῶς** adv. typically (s.v.6). 11
συνέβαινεν impf. συμβαίνω to happen. Used w. dat. which indicates to whom the events happened. The impf. pictures the enumerated events as in process of happening; the sing. sums them up as one series (RP). **ἐγράφη** aor. pass. γράφω. **νουθεσία** admonition, warning (s. TDNT). **τέλη τῶν αἰώνων** the ends of the ages. In Jewish writing the term means the beginning of redemption or the time of the appearing of the Messiah or the general meaning "the end" (s. SB III, 416). (For the apparently general use of the term in the DSS, s. 1 QS 4:16f.) Paul believes he and his correspondents are living in the last days of world history before the breaking in of the Messianic Age (Barrett). **κατήντηκεν** perf. ind. act. καταντάω to come down to a meeting, to arrive at a goal, to come to. The word appears in the papyri as a technical term for the inheritance that comes to an heir (s. TDNT; BAG; MM). It may be that this refers not
to "us" but to those of Israel (MT IV, 85). ■ **ὥστε** therefore, thus 12
then. It indicates that this exhortation to watchfulness is the inference to be drawn from the foregoing examples (Godet). **δοκῶν** pres. act. part. δοκέω to seem, to be of the opinion, to think. **ἑστάναι** perf. inf. ἵστημι to stand. **βλεπέτω** pres. imp. beware. The pres. tense indicates the necessity of continual watchfulness. **μή** w. subj. lest. It introduces a neg. purpose clause. **πέσῃ** aor. subj. πίπτω to fall, perhaps here to fall into
sin (Weiss). ■ **πειρασμός** testing, trying, temptation. The verb 13

came to signify the trying intentionally, and w. the purpose of discovering what of good and evil, or power or weakness, was in a person or thing (Trench, *Synonyms*, 280). **εἴληφεν** perf. ind. act. λαμβάνω to take. The words imply that there was a certain temptation which had captured the Corinthians and which subdued them (Grosheide). **εἰ μή** except. **ἀνθρώπινος** human, that which is according to human strength, bearable (Weiss; BAG). The suf. signifies material or kind (MH, 359). **ἐάσει** fut. ἐάω to allow. The verb is followed by the inf. w. the subject of the inf. in the acc. **πειρασθῆναι** aor. pass. inf. πειράζω. The pass. indicates that the temptation is from without. **ὑπὲρ** w. acc. above, beyond. **ὃ** rel. pron. which includes the unexpressed demonstrative pron. "beyond that which" (s. BD, 154). **ποιήσει** fut. ποιέω. **σὺν** w., in connection w.; that is, "w. the temptation." **ἔκβασις** a way out, escape. In the papyri it has the meaning "end," "completion" (MM). **δύνασθαι** pres. mid. inf. to be able. The inf. either explains the way of escape or gives purpose or result of God's making a way of escape (s. BD, 206). **ὑπενεγκεῖν** aor. act. inf. ὑποφέρω to carry under, to bear, to endure.

14 ■ **διόπερ** wherefore, for which very reason, "the conclusion
of this" (Barrett; DM, 245; Blomqvist, 136f.). **εἰδωλολατρία**
15 idolatry, the service and worship of idols. ■ **φρόνιμος** wise,
understanding, sensible, the ability to make a decision (s.
TDNT). **κρίνατε** aor. imp. κρίνω to judge. **ὑμεῖς** you yourself.
16 ■ **ποτήριον** cup, the cup of blessing was a technical Jewish term
used for the cup of wine drunk at the end of a meal. The most
honored guest at the table took the cup, lifted it up and said the
benediction (Barrett; SB IV, 627ff.). **εὐλογοῦμεν** pres. ind. act.
to bless, to give thanks. The pres. tense views the general Christian practice without going into details (RP). **οὐχί** introduces a
question expecting the answer yes. **κοινωνία** fellowship, common participation (Barrett; s. also CBB; TDNT). **αἵματος τοῦ
Χριστοῦ** gen. sing. obj. gen. "a participation in the blood of
Christ" (RWP). **τὸν ἄρτον** acc. by inverse attraction to the rel.
pron. (s. BD, 154; RG, 717f.). **κλῶμεν** pres. ind. act. κλάω to
break. **σώματος τοῦ Χρ.** "the body of Christ." A reference to
the church as the body of Christ and the fellowship among
17 believers (Kümmel in Lietzmann). ■ **ὅτι** because. **οἱ πάντες** the
all, "we the whole, the whole number." These words are in
apposition w. the subject (RWP). **μετέχομεν** pres. ind. act. to
18 share w., to be partners in. ■ **κατὰ σάρκα** "according to the
flesh," a reference to historical Israel (Conzelmann). **ἐσθίοντες**
pres. act. part. ἐσθίω. **θυσία** sacrifice. **θυσιαστήριον** altar,

place of sacrifice. ■ **οὖν** then. **εἰδωλόθυτον** that which is sacri- 19
ficed to an idol (s. 1 Cor. 8:1). ■ **ἅ** rel. pron. including the 20
demonstrative pron. which is not expressed (s.v.13). **δαιμονίοις**
"to demons" dat. of advantage. Heathen sacrifices were sacrifices to demons (s. CBB; TDNT; SB III, 51f.; RAC IX, 546–797).
■ **οὐ δύνασθε** pres. ind. mid. "you are not able." The pres. tense 21
emphasizes that which is always true. **ποτήριον** cup, the common meal and the common drinking of the heathen created a
close and meaningful relationship between the human partners
and between the god to whom they ate and drank. This was
expecially true when they drank from a common cup (RAC II,
41). **πίνειν** pres. act. inf. **τράπεζα** table indicating a common
meal, gen. after a verb of sharing. ■ **ἤ** or. **παραζηλοῦμεν** pres. 22
ind. act. to provoke to jealousy, to cause one to be jealous. (For
the prep. compound, s. MH 320.) **μὴ** introduces a question
which expects the answer no. **ἰσχυρότεροι αὐτοῦ** "strong as he
(is)," gen. of comparison.

■ **ἔξεστιν** "it is lawful," "it is allowed." **συμφέρει** pres. 23
ind. act. to bring together, to help, to confer a benefit, to be
advantageous or profitable or useful (BAG). The pres. tense
indicates that which is always true. **οἰκοδομεῖ** pres. ind. act. to
build up, to edify. It means to cause to advance spiritually
(Grosheide). ■ **μηδεὶς** no one. **τὸ ἑαυτοῦ** "the thing of himself," 24
"that which is his own," "his own ends" (Barrett). **ζητείτω** pres.
act. imp. ζητέω to seek. The pres. tense points to a habitual
action. ■ **μάκελλον** stall or shop on the marketplace where 25
meat and other foods were sold. Because of the nearness to the
temple, it was possible that some of the meat in the marketplace
had been sacrificial offerings (s. Lietzmann; TDNT; H.J. Cad-
bury, "The *Macellum* of Corinth," JBL 53 [1934], 134–141;
Barrett NTS, 11 [January, 1965], 144). **πωλούμενον** pres. pass.
part. πωλέω to sell. A middle to lower class household in Corinth buying its supplies in the *Macellum* would often make pur-
chases that had no connection w. idolatry (Barrett NTS, 11
[January, 1965], 146). **ἐσθίετε** pres. act. imp. to eat, the imp. of
permission "you may eat" (s. RG, 948). (For a discussion of
Plutarch's arguments against eating meat, s. PTW, 301–316.)
ἀνακρίνοντες pres. act. part. ἀνακρίνω to examine, to make
inquiry. The word was used in a judicial sense of conducting a
hearing or investigation (BAG). Jews were only allowed to buy
meat from the Gentiles if it could be established that it was not
meat offered to idols (s. SB III, 420f.). **συνείδησις** conscience
(s. Rom. 2:15; PAT, 416–420). ■ **τοῦ κυρίου** "belongs to the 26
Lord." **πλήρωμα** fullness, the total content. ■ **εἰ** "if." It views 27

the possibility as a reality. **καλεῖ** pres. ind. act. to call, to invite. Christians were evidently frequently invited to dinners by the unbelievers and some of these dinners may have been connected w. heathen gods. (For a study of such invitations w. examples, s. Chan-Hie Kim, "The Papyrus Invitation," JBL, 94 [September, 1975], 391–402.) **πορεύεσθαι** pres. mid. inf. πορεύομαι to go. **παρατιθέμενον** pres. pass. part. παρατίθημι to place be-
28 fore. ■ **ἐὰν** used w. subj. to introduce a condition which is possible. **εἴπῃ** aor. subj. λέγω. **ἱερόθυτον** that which is sacrificed in a temple. It is different from a word in chapter 8:1; 10:19 and is more appropriate on pagan lips or, in pagan company (Bruce). **μηνύσαντα** aor. act. part. μηνύω to make known, to
29 give information, to reveal. ■ **τὴν ἑαυτοῦ** his own. **ἱνατί** why. **κρίνεται** pres. ind. pass. κρίνω to judge, pass. to be judged, to
30 be exposed to judgment (Barrett). ■ **χάριτι** "w. thanks," "w. thanksgiving," dat. of manner (BD, 106). The word "grace" not only meant the gift which was given but the thanks which was expressed for the gift (s. TDNT). **βλασφημοῦμαι** pres. ind. pass. βλασφημέω to slander, to defame, to injure the reputation of someone (BAG). **οὗ** "that which," rel. pron. used including
31 the idea of the demonstrative pron. ■ **ποιεῖτε** pres. act. imp. to
32 do. The pres. tense points to a habitual action. ■ **ἀπρόσκοπος** without offense, without causing others to stumble (RP). Used in the papyri in the sense of "free from hurt or harm" (MM) and in the sense of "not causing injury" (Preisigke). **Ἰουδαίοις** Jews (s. Malcolm Love, "Who Were the IOUDAIOI?," Nov T, 18 [April, 1976], 101–130). **γίνεσθε** pres. mid. imp. **ἐκκλησίᾳ**
33 church, dat. of disadvantage. ■ **πάντα** acc. of general reference. **σωθῶσιν** aor. pass. subj. σῴζω to rescue, to save. Used in a purpose clause.

Ch. 11

1 ■ **μιμητής** imitator, one who mimics another, from the verb μιμέομαι to imitate, to mimic. The ending of the noun indicates the agent who performs an action (s. MH, 365). **γίνεσθε** pres. mid. imp. γίνομαι. **Χριστοῦ** Paul's appeal to the character of Jesus of Nazareth shows Paul's interest in the earthly life of Christ (JNP, 109).

2 ■ **ἐπαινῶ** pres. ind. act. to praise. **πάντα** acc. of reference. **μέμνησθε** perf. ind. mid. μιμνῄσκομαι to remember. The perf. indicates that the Corinthians remembered continually (Grosheide). **παρέδωκα** aor. ind. act. παραδίδωμι to deliver over, to pass on. Often used in the sense of a teacher passing on material which he has learned (s. TDNT; CBB). **παράδοσις**

tradition, that which is passed on. **κατέχετε** pres. ind. act. to
hold down, to hold fast, to possess (s. MM). ■ **εἰδέναι** perf. inf. 3
οἶδα. Defective perf. w. pres. meaning to know. **κεφαλή** head,
in its metaphorical sense it may apply to the outstanding and
determining part of a whole, but also to origin. Paul does not say
that the man is the lord of the woman; he says that he is the
origin of her being (Barrett; s. also TDNT). ■ **προσευχόμενος** 4
pres. mid. part. *προσεύχομαι* to pray. **κατὰ κεφαλῆς** down
from the head; that is, the veil hanging down from the head (RG,
606f.; s. also MT, 268). **καταισχύνει** pres. ind. act. to put to
shame, to shame, to disgrace. Since the Christian man reflects
the glory of Christ if he were to wear a veil concealing his head,
he would rob his own head of its chief function of reflecting the
glory of Christ (Barrett). ■ **ἀκατακαλύπτῳ** dat. sing. uncov- 5
ered. For a Jewish woman to appear outside of the house w. an
uncovered head was shameful and her husband could divorce
her (SB III, 427). The Jewish sense of a woman's head covering
indicated the special hairstyle she was to wear which consisted
of plaited hair held together w. bands and coverings (s. SB III,
428f.). The women of Tarsus were to have their face covered
when they appeared on the street. This was an old custom which
was retained in Tarsus (DC 33:48). **τὸ αὐτό** "one and the same
thing w...." (RWP). **ἐξυρημένῃ** perf. pass. part. *ξυράω* to
shave. For the Jews a woman w. a shaved head was particularly
ugly (SB III, 434). In Cyprus a woman guilty of adultery was to
have her hair cut off and was considered a harlot (DC 64:3). A
woman w. a shaved head was also the sign of mourning
(DC 64:16; s. also *De Dea Syria*, 6; s. also Barrett). ■ 6
κατακαλύπετεται pres. ind. mid. to cover one's self, to cover
one's self w. a veil. The pres. tense is used to express a general
principle. **κειράσθω** aor. imp. mid. *κείρω* to shear, to cut w.
scissors (Lietzmann). **αἰσχρός** shame, disgrace, followed by the
dat. of disadvantage. **κείρασθαι** aor. mid. inf. The inf. w. the
article is used as the subject of the clause (s. Funk, 657).
ξυρᾶσθαι pres. mid. inf. *ξυράω* to shave, to cut w. a razor (s.
Lietzmann; s. also v. 5). **κατακαλυπτέσθω** pres. mid. imp.
■ **ὀφείλει** one ought to, one is obligated to. The word indicates 7
moral obligation. **κατακαλύπτεσθαι** pres. mid. inf., s.v.5.
εἰκὼν image. **δόξα** glory. **ὑπάρχων** pres. act. part. to exist, to
be; causal use of the part. ■ **καὶ γὰρ** "for even," "yes, even" 9
(BD, 236). **ἐκτίσθη** aor. ind. pass. *κτίζω* to create. **ἀνήρ** man,
male. ■ **ἐξουσία** authority, the right to perform an act. The 10
covered head is the woman's authority to pray and worship since
it shows her belonging to and obedience to her husband (Schlat-

ter, s. also M.D. Hooker, "Authority on Her Head: An Examination of First Corinthians 11:10," NTS, 10 [April, 1964], 410–416). **ἐπὶ τῆς κεφαλῆς** "upon her head." **δία τοὺς ἀγγέλους** "because of the angels." Angels were considered to be the guardians of the order of creation (Hooker, 412f.), and were considered to be present at a worship service (Schlatter). (For Qumran parallels to angels being present at worship services, and the interpretation that the lack of covering for a woman signified a physical defect which excluded one from worship, s. Fitzmyer,
11 *Essays*, 187–204). ■ **πλήν** however, nevertheless, in any case. It is used in an adversative and modifying sense to conclude a discussion and emphasize what is essential (BD, 234; Blomqvist, 82f.). **χωρίς** without, separated from. **ἐν κυρίῳ** in the Lord or perhaps "in the Lord's intention"; that is, in the original creation
12 and its restoration (Barrett). ■ **διά** w. gen. "through." **ἐκ τοῦ θεοῦ** "from, out of God." The man is the woman's initial cause, she is his instrumental cause, but both owe their origin to God
13 (s. RP). ■ **κρίνατε** aor. imp. act. κρίνω to judge, to decide. **πρέπον** pres. act. part. n. sing. that which is fitting to the circumstances, that which is proper. Followed by the acc. w. the inf.
14 **προσεύχεσθαι** pres. mid. inf. προσεύχομαι to pray. ■ **φύσις** "nature herself." **κομᾷ** pres. subj. act. κομάω to have long hair, to let one's hair grow long. **ἀτιμία** dishonor. Jewish men wore middle length hair which was usually well-groomed (SB III, 440–442). Sometimes long hair was associated w. homosexuality (Weiss; Philo, *The Special Laws*, III, 37), but long hair was not uncommon for philosophers, farmers, barbarians, etc. (DC 35:
15 11). ■ **κομή** long hair, the hairdo which was neatly held in place by means of ribbon or lace. What is required by these verses is an orderly hairdress which distinguishes a woman from a man (Grosheide). **ἀντί** w. gen. instead of. **περιβολαίου** that which is thrown about, a wrap, a covering. **δέδοται** perf. ind. pass.
16 δίδωμι to give. ■ **δοκεῖ** pres. ind. act. to seem to be, to seem, to intend to be. **φιλόνεικος** strife-loving, contentious, quarrelsome. **συνήθεια** custom, habit, usage. He means we have no such custom such as women praying or prophesying w. head uncovered (Morris).
17 ■ **παραγγέλλων** pres. act. part. παραγγέλλω to transmit a message along from one to another, to declare, to order, to charge. Used especially of the order of the military commander which is passed along the line by his subordinates (T 343). The part. indicates contemporaneous time, "in giving this charge." **κρεῖσσον** comp. of ἀγαθός more prominent, preferable, more advantageous, better. **ἧσσων** comp. of κακός inferior, weaker,

lesser, for the worse. (For both of these words, s. BAG.)
συνέρχεσθε pres. ind. mid. to come together. ■ **πρῶτον μέν** 18
"first of all," "in the first place." It is not formally caught up by such a companion phrase as "in the next place," unless we so regard v. 34b (Bruce). **συνερχομένων** pres. mid. part. συνέρχομαι to come together, gen. abs. "when you come together." **σχίσμα** division. **ὑπάρχειν** pres. act. inf. used in direct discourse. **μέρος τι** partly, acc. of extent "to some part"
(RWP). ■ **δεῖ** followed by the inf. it is necessary to. The word 19
generally expresses logical necessity. **αἵρεσις** division, different opinion (s. MM). **δόκιμος** that which is approved after examination, genuine (s. BS, 259–262; TDNT). **φανερός** open to sight, visible, w. reference to outward appearance, manifest as opposed
to conceal (AS, 104). **γέγωνται** aor. subj. mid. γίνομαι. ■ 20
συνερχομένων pres. mid. part. to come together, to assemble. **οὖν** then, now. The word indicates the continuation of the subject from one thought to another or the introduction of a new phase of thought (DM, 253). **τὸ αὐτό** the same, here "assemble together" or "assemble together at the same place." **κυριακός** belonging to the Lord. The word was used in the papyri in the sense of belonging to the Caesar or Imperial (s. Deissmann; BS, 217–219; LAE, 362f.; TDNT) (s. also Rev. 1:10). **δεῖπνον** din-
ner, the main meal, supper. ■ **ἕκαστος** each, each one for him- 21
self. It was not the Lord who was determining the celebration but the individual (Conzelmann). **προλαμβάνει** pres. ind. act. to take before. The prep. here is temporal, "each one takes it before others have theirs" (Barrett). (For the examples in the papyri and the suggested "weakening" of the prep. in compound, s. MM.) **φαγεῖν** aor. act. inf. ἐσθίω to eat. The prep. used w. inf. to indicate the area in which some were going ahead of others. They took what they had brought along and did not permit others, the poor, to eat from their portion (Grosheide). **ὃς μεν . . . ὃς δέ** "the one, the other." **πεινᾷ** pres. ind. act. to be hungry. **μεθύει** pres. ind. act. to be drunk. The pres. tense vividly points out the action that was in progress. It could also point to a habitual action. (For a description of the common meal associated w. the Lord's Supper, s. IDB II, 53–54; for the common meal of the Greeks and the Romans other than the agape, s. Bengel,
Lietzmann.) ■ **μὴ οὐκ** used in a question expecting the answer 22
no; "it is certainly not that you do not have houses, is it?" **ἐσθίειν** pres. act. inf. to eat. Used w. prep. to express purpose "for eating and drinking." **καταφρονεῖτε** pres. ind. act. followed by the gen. to think down upon, to despise. **καταισχύνετε** pres. ind. act. to put to shame. The pres. tense

could be conative "are you trying to put to shame?" (s. Barrett). **ἔχοντας** pres. act. part. ἔχω to have. Adjectival part. used as a noun "those who do not have." **εἴπω** aor. act. subj. λέγω to say. Deliberative subj. "what shall I say?," "what should I say?" **ἐπαινέσω** fut. ind. act. or aor. subj. ἐπαινέω to praise. (For an excellent article regarding the struggle between the rich and poor and the social problems at the Lord's Supper in Corinth, s. G. Theissen, "Soziale Integration und sakramentales Handeln," Nov T, 16 [July, 1974], 179–206.)

23 ■ **ἐγώ** "I." Strongly emphasized and stands in contrast to
those at Corinth. **παρέλαβον** aor. ind. παραλαμβάνω to receive. The word corresponds to the technical term in the rabbinical literature, *quibbel*, meaning to receive tradition which has been passed on (s. PRJ, 248; SB III, 444). **ἀπό** from. The prep. can indicate that Paul did not receive his information directly by revelation (Grosheide). It may be, however, that he received the interpretation of the information from the Lord (Barrett). **παρέδωκα** aor. ind. act. παραδίδωμι to pass on, to hand down. The word corresponds to the rabbinical technical term *masar* indicating the passing down of tradition. The words mean the chain of historical tradition that Paul received goes back unbroken to the words of Jesus Himself (Ladd, 389). (For the use of *masar* in the DSS, s. CD 3:3.) **ὅτι** introduces the content of that which was received. **παρεδίδοτο** impf. pass. παραδίδωμι to deliver over, to betray. The impf. implies that this betrayal was
24 still going on (Grosheide). **ἔλαβεν** aor. λαμβάνω. ■
εὐχαριστήσας aor. act. part. εὐχαριστέω to give thanks, temporal use of the part. "after he had given thanks." **ἔκλασεν** aor. ind. act. κλάω to break. **μου** "my." Strongly emphasized by its position. **τὸ ὑπὲρ ὑμῶν** "which was (given) on behalf of you." The word to be supplied here is "given" (s. Luke 22:19). **ποιεῖτε** pres. imp. ποιέω, The pres. tense emphasizes the repeated action. **ἀνάμνησις** memorial, remembrance. The word indicates to call back again into memory a vivid experience (s. TDNT). The object of recalling to memory is expressed by the obj. use
25 of the poss. adj. (s. BD, 149). ■ **ὡσαύτως** in the same manner.
ποτήριον cup. (For the cup of blessing which the honored guest lifted up and said the benediction, s. SB IV, 630f.; TDNT.) **μετὰ** w. acc. after. **δειπνῆσαι** aor. act. inf. δειπνέω to dine, to eat the main meal. **διαθήκη** covenant, treaty (s. Matt. 26:28). **ἐν τῷ ἐμῷ αἵματι** "in my blood." Blood indicated a life given up in death which was the penalty for breaking the covenant (s. Cleon Rogers, "The Covenant with Moses and its Historical Setting," JETS, 14 [1971], 152). **ὁσάκις** as often as, used w. **ἐάν** w. the

meaning "every time." The usual construction for a general
temporal clause of repetition (RWP). **πίνητε** pres. subj. *πίνω* to
drink. ■ **γάρ** "for." Introduces the apostle's explanation of the 26
Lord's command (RP). **ἐσθίητε** pres. subj. *ἐσθίω*.
καταγγέλλετε pres. ind. act. *καταγγέλλω* to proclaim. It is
used in the sense of making a solemn announcement by word of
mouth (Barrett; CBB). **ἄρχι** until. **οὗ** when. **ἔλθῃ** aor. act. subj.
ἔρχομαι. Subjunctive may have an affinity w. a final clause (BD,
193) w. the idea "until the goal is reached, that is till he comes"
(Otfried Hofius, " 'Bis dass er kommt': I Kor. XI. 26," NTS, 14
[April, 1968], 439–441).

■ **ὥστε** wherefore, it follows. The word is used to draw a 27
conclusion. **ὅς ἄν** whoever. **ἐσθίῃ** pres. subj. **ἀναξίως** adv.
unworthily, not in accordance w. their value (Grosheide). **ἔνοχος**
guilty of, guilty of violating (Hering). When the dat. is used it
indicates a crime of which one is guilty; when the gen. is used
it indicates against which or against whom the crime is committed (Weiss). ■ **δοκιμαζέτω** pres. imp. 3rd per. sing. to examine, 28
to approve after examination (s. TDNT). *δοκιμάζω*. Used in an
indefinite and at the same time general sense "one" (BAG).
■ **κρίμα** judgment. The suf. indicates the result of an action; that 29
is, the result of making a decision (s. MH, 355). **ἑαυτῷ** reflex.
pron. dat. of disadvantage. **διακρίνων** pres. act. part. to judge
between, to determine, to distinguish. The part. could be conditional (RWP) or causal. ■ **ἀσθενής** weak, sickly. **ἄρρωστος** 30
powerless, feeble, ill. **κοιμῶνται** pres. ind. pass. *κοιμάω* to fall
asleep, to die. The pres. tense indicates either an action in
progress or a repeated action. **ἱκανός** a sufficient number, a large
amount, many. ■ **εἰ** w. ind. used to introduce a contrary to fact 31
conditional clause. **διεκρίνομεν** impf. *διακρίνω* s.v.29.
ἐκρινόμεθα impf. pass. to judge, pass. to be judged. ■ 32
κρινόμενοι pres. pass. part. conditional use of the part. "if we
are being judged," "when we are being judged." **παιδευόμεθα**
pres. ind. pass. to discipline, to train a child through discipline.
(For this figure of speech and the training of children in the
ancient world, s. TDNT; RAC VI, 502–559.) **κατακριθῶμεν**
aor. pass. subj. *κατακρίνω* condemn, to reach a verdict or decision against someone. Subjunctive used in a neg. purpose clause.
■ **ὥστε** wherefore, so. The word draws a conclusion from the 33
previous discussion, pres. mid part. to come together, s.v.18.
ἐκδέχεσθε pres. mid. imp. *ἐκδέχομαι* to wait upon, to wait in
turn (RWP). It is implied that a proper distribution of food
should first be made, and that all then should eat together (Barrett). ■ **πεινᾷ** pres. ind. act. to be hungry, s.v.21. **ἐν οἴκῳ** at 34

home. ***συνέρχησθε*** pres. mid. subj. *συνέρχομαι*. ***ὡς ἄν*** whenever. ***ἔχθω*** aor. subj. *ἔρχομαι*. ***διατάξομαι*** pres. fut. mid. *διατάσσω* to put in order.

Ch. 12

1 ■ ***πνευματικός*** spiritual. The suf. indicates "that which pertains to the spirit" (s. MH, 378f.). The word can be either masc. (spiritual people) or n. spirit (spiritual things, gifts) (s. Pearson, 47f.; Grosheide). ***ἀγνοεῖν*** pres. act. inf. *ἀγνοέω* to be
2 ignorant (s. 1 Cor. 10:1). ■ ***ἦτε*** impf. *εἰμί*. ***ἄφωνος*** without speech, dumb. ***ὡς ἄν*** used w. impf. for the notion of repetition (RG, 974). ***ἤγεσθε*** impf. pass. *ἄγω* to lead. ***ἀπαγόμενοι*** pres. pass. part. *ἀπάγω* to lead away, to carry away. It suggests moments of ecstasy experienced in heathen religion, when a human
3 being is possessed by a supernatural (Barrett). ■ ***ἐν*** in, through, in control of. ***λαλῶν*** pres. act. part. *λαλέω* to speak. ***ἀνάθεμα*** that which is set apart for a deity, that which is abandoned by the gods, a curse, cursed (Grosheide; TDNT). The reference is to demonic powers and the control of these powers over the lives of the Corinthians before they became Christians. It was possible that the demons used the gift of ecstatic speech to curse Jesus (s. Pearson, 49–50f.). ***εἰπεῖν*** aor. act. inf. *λέγω*. ***κύριος Ἰησοῦς*** "Jesus is Lord" (s. 1 Cor. 8:6). ***εἰ μή*** except. (For the view that Paul is primarily referring to a ruler of the synagogue who is reported to have tutored a Jewish Christian to say these words in order to save membership in the community, s. J.D.M. Derrett, "Cursing Jesus [1 Cor. 13:3]: The Jews as Religious 'Persecutors'," NTS, 21 [July, 1975], 544–554).
4 ■ ***διαίρεσις*** distribution (RP) difference, variety (Conzel-
6 mann). ■ ***ἐνέργημα*** performance, that which was accomplished through energy. These are the results or effects of the working given by God (RP). ***ἐνεργῶν*** pres. act. part. *ἐνεργέω* to perform, to be at work, to be effective, to produce. ***τὰ πάντα ἐν πᾶσιν*** "all things in all." The second "all" could be n. or masc. but the emphasis in the passage is on the working of God within
7 men (Morris). ■ ***δίδοται*** pres. pass. *δίδωμι* to give. The pres. tense points to the habitual and repeated action. ***φανέρωσις*** manifestation, a making clear. ***συμφέρον*** pres. act. part. n. sing. *συμφέρω* to bring together, to confer a benefit, to be advantageous, profitable or useful (BAG). Used here w. prep. meaning
8 "w. a view to advantage" that is, "the profit of all" (RP). ■ ***κατὰ τὸ αὐτὸ πνεῦμα*** "acording to the same spirit." The prep. gives
9 the norm or standard. ■ ***πίστις*** faith. Faith here is to be connected w. the miracles referred to in the next few lines (Barrett).

ἰαμάτων healing. The plural relates to the different classes of
sicknesses to be healed (Godet). ■ **διάκρισις** a judging between 10
things, distinguish, discerning. **ἑρμηνεία** interpretation. ■ 11
ἐνεργεῖ pres. ind. act. to work in, to energize. The word is often
used of the working of the power of God in a miraculous way
(s. MNTW, 46–54). **διαιροῦν** pres. act. part. διαιρέω to distribute. **ἰδίᾳ** individually, by one's self, privately. **καθώς** just as,
accordingly. **βούλεται** pres. ind. mid. βούλομαι to will, to determine. The pres. tense emphasizes the habitual or repeated
action. He gives not according to the merit or wishes of men, but
according to his own will (Hodge).
■ **καθάπερ** just as. **σῶμα** body. (For this comparison, s. 12
SBT, 235f.) **μέλος** member. **ὄντα** pres. part. εἰμί. The part.
could be concessive, "although they are many." **οὕτως καὶ ὁ
Χριστός** "so also is Christ." Paul draws a comparison and uses
the corporate rather than the solely individual Christ (SBT,
235). ■ **καὶ γάρ** "for even," "yes, even" (BD, 236). **εἰς ἓν σῶμα** 13
"into one body." The prep. describes the result of the process
(Barrett; Weiss). **ἐβαπτίσθημεν** aor. ind. pass. βαπτίζω. Paul
is not referring to water baptism but to the spiritual transformation which puts the believer "in Christ," and which is the effect
of receiving the gift of the Spirit which takes place at conversion
(s. BHS, 130f.). **ἐποτίσθημεν** aor. ind. pass. ποτίζω to cause
to drink, to give to drink, to water, to irrigate (s. MM; BHS, 131).
■ **ἔστιν** is, consists of. The article w. the subject, "the body" is 14
generic, "a body" (Barrett). ■ **ἐὰν** w. subj. "if," "in case." **εἴπῃ** 15
aor. subj. λέγω. **ὅτι** because. **οὐ . . . οὐκ.** The double negatives
cancel each other and are equivalent to a positive statement
(BD, 223; but s. also RWP). **παρά** "because of this" "along side
of this," "on that score," "for that reason" (IBG, 51). The prep.
w. acc. is causal (RG, 616). ■ **οὖς** ear. ■ **ἀκοή** hearing. 16/17
ὄσφρησις smelling. If the whole body were only one member
the condition would be sad (Grosheide). ■ **νῦν δὲ** "but now," 18
"but, as it is" (RP). **ἔθετο** aor. ind. mid. τίθημι to place, to put.
ἓν ἕκαστον each one. **ἠθέλησεν** aor. ind. act. θέλω to wish, to
will. God made unity, but not uniformity. The aor. refers to the
act of creation (RP). ■ **εἰπεῖν** aor. act. inf. λέγω. **χρείαν ἔχω** 21
Used w. object in the gen. ■ **ἀλλά** adversative use "on the 22
contrary" (RWP). **μᾶλλον** much rather, to a greater degree.
δοκοῦντα pres. part. δοκέω to seem to be, to consider to be,
generally followed by the inf. **ἀσθενέστερος** comp. ἀσθενής
weaker. The delicate organs, such as the eye; invisible organs,
such as the heart (Barrett). **ὑπάρχειν** pres. act. inf. to be, to
exist. The inf. is used in connection w. part. even though the two

23 are separated (s. BD, 250). **ἀναγκαῖος** necessary. ■
ἀτιμότερος comp. ἄτιμος without honor, comp. less honorable. **περισσότερος** comp. περισσός greater, more. **περιτίθεμεν** pres. ind. act. περιτίθημι to place around, to clothe. The pres. tense is gnomic pointing to that which is always true. **ἀσχήμων** unpresentable, indecent, the unpresentable, that is, private parts (BAG). (For the ancient world's ideas concerning the genitals, s. RAC X, 1–52.) **εὐσχημοσύνη** decency, propriety, presentability. Here it is used in the sense, "or treated
24 w. greater modesty" (BAG). ■ **εὐσχήμων** n. pl. presentable, decent. **συνεκέρασεν** aor. συγκεράννυμι to mix together, to blend together. God mixed the members of the body (Grosheide) in order that it might function harmoniously. **ὑστερουμένῳ** pres. mid. or pass. part. to come short, ὑστερέω to fail, to be inferior, to lack. **δούς** aor. act. part. δίδωμι to give. The part. expresses manner telling how the mixing was done.
25 ■ **ᾖ** pres. subj. εἰμί. The subj. is used here to express purpose; in this case neg. purpose. **σχίσμα** division, that which results from a splitting (s. 1 Cor. 1:10). **μεριμνῶσιν** pres. subj.
26 μεριμνάω to exercise care for, to exercise concern for. ■
πάσχει pres. ind. to suffer. **συμπάσχει** pres. ind. to suffer together. **δοξάζεται** pres. ind. pass. δοξάζω to honor, pass. to be honored, to be thought well of. **συγχαίρει** pres. ind. to rejoice together. The pres. tenses are gnomic indicating that which is generally true.

27 ■ **ἐκ μέρους** "from a part." The idiom here means "in-
28 dividually" (Barrett). ■ **ἔθετο** aor. mid. τίθημι s.v.18. **δεύτερον** acc. sing. secondly. **τρίτον** acc. sing. thirdly. The acc. is used adverbially. The notion of subordination is to be found in these words (Godet). **ἰαμάτων** gen. pl. healings. **ἀντιλήμψις** nom. pl. helpful deeds, assistance. The basic meaning of the word is an undertaking on behalf of another and is used both in the papyri and the LXX in the sense of help either from God or from men (s. BS, 92; MM). **κυβέρνησις** administration, lit. it refers to the steering of a ship. The pl. indicates proofs of ability to hold a leading position in the church (BAG; TDNT). The verb is applied to the management of a household in an inscription
29 (MM). ■ **μή**. Used to introduce questions in which the answer
30 "no" is expected, "all are not apostles are they?" ■
31 **διερμηνεύουσιν** pres. ind. act. to translate, to interpret. ■
ζηλοῦτε pres. imp. ζηλόω to covet, to be zealous for, to earnestly desire. Believers may desire a gift, the Spirit gives them as He wills (s. Bengel). **μείζων** comp. μέγας large, great.

καθ᾽ ὑπερβολήν lit. "according to the excess." It is best taken to describe the "way" and indicates "a way beyond all comparison" (RWP).

Ch. 13

■ **ἐὰν** w. subj. The word introduces a condition which may 1
be possible, "supposing that." **γλῶσσα** tongue, language. The
dat. form is here instrumental. **ἀγάπη** love. (For a study of this
important word, s. TDNT; CBB; MNTW; James Moffatt, *Love
in the New Testament*, especially 178–187; Trench, *Synonyms*,
41–44; s. also 1 John 2:5.) **γέγονα** perf. act. γίνομαι to become.
The perf. would indicate what a per. has become and continues
to be (s. McKay). **χαλκός** copper, brass, bronze. Used w. the
following word to indicate a "gong" (BAG; Conzelmann). **ἠχῶν**
pres. act. part. ἠχέω to sound, to ring, to echo, to roar. In
connection w. the previous word it indicated a gong which produced a hollow echoing groaning noise (Weiss). **κύμβαλον**
cymbal. Cymbals played a part in the Jewish worship service but
even a greater role in the heathen worship of the goddess Cybele
and Bacchus (s. TDNT; DGRA, 381f.). **ἀλαλάζον** pres. act.
part. ἀλαλάζω loud sounding, clashing. lit. used in the sense of
"raise a war cry, shouting w. triumphant or joy" (AS). ■ **ἔχω** 2
pres. subj. after **ἐὰν. εἰδῶ** subj. οἶδα. **πᾶσαν τὴν γνῶσιν** all
knowledge. Used w. article it means "all that there is in its
entirety" (BD, 144). **πᾶσαν τὴν πίστιν** "all the faith."
μεθιστάναι pres. act. inf. μεθίστημι to remove, to transfer
from one place to another. A proverbial expression meaning "to
make what seems impossible possible" (Barrett; s. also Matt.
17:20). The inf. is used to express results. **οὐθέν** nothing, an
absolute zero (RWP). ■ **ψωμίσω** aor. subj. ψωμίζω. The word 3
means either "to spend everything on food," or "to break into
crumbs" (Grosheide). The word lit. means "I feed w. small morsels," as a child, or invalid. The meaning here is "if, for the
purpose of alms giving, I divide all my property in fragments"
(Barrett). **ὑπάρχοντα** pres. act. part. acc. pl. ὑπάρχω to exist.
The part. in pl. means goods, possessions, property. Although
giving to charity was held in high esteem by the rabbis and
thought to have gained great merit, there were requirements
prohibiting one from giving all of his goods; for example, in a
year he was not to give more than 20% of his entire possessions
(s. SB III, 451; IV, 536–558). **παραδῶ** aor. subj. παραδίδωμι
to give, to hand over. **καυχήσωμαι** aor. mid. subj. καυχάομαι
to boast, to glory. (For a discussion of the variant reading
καυθήσομαι fut. subj. pass. καίω to set fire, to burn, s. TC,
563f.; Barrett; Weiss.) **ὠφελοῦμαι** pres. ind. pass. ὠφελέω to

profit, to be of value. The gifts are not valueless, but he is (RP).
4 ■ **μακροθυμεῖ** pres. ind. act. to be longsuffering, to be
patient. It is a long holding out of the mind before it gives room
to action or passion—generally to passion (Trench; *Synonyms*,
196). It is the steadfast spirit which will never give in (NTW, 83;
s. also TDNT). The idea of the word is that it takes a long time
before fuming and breaking into flames. The pres. tense emphasizes the continual and habitual state or action. **χρηστεύεται**
pres. mid. to be useful, to be kind and gracious, to show kindness,
one who renders gracious, well-disposed service to others (EGT;
TDNT; Trench; *Synonyms*, 323f.). (For verbs w. this ending
conveying the idea of "being or behaving, or acting as," s. MH,
400.) **ζηλοῖ** pres. ind. act. to be fervent, to boil w. envy, to be
jealous (s. TDNT). **περπερεύεται** pres. mid. to brag, to boast,
one who talks a lot and acts presumptuously; ostentation is the
chief idea and ostentatious boasting leads easily to the next point
(RP; s. TDNT). **φυσιοῦται** pres. mid. φυσιόω to puff up, to
5 puff one's self out like a pair of bellows (RWP). ■ **ἀσχημονεῖ**
to behave indecently or in a shameful manner. Love is tactful
and does nothing that would raise a blush (RP). **παροξύνεται**
pres. pass. παροξύνω to irritate, to promote to anger, pass. to
be irritated, to be touchy. Selfishness generates the irritability
(EGT). **λογίζεται** pres. mid. to credit someone's account, "doth
not register the evil." Love stores up no resentment and bears
6 no malice (RP; s. also TDNT). ■ **συγχαίρει** pres. ind. act. to
rejoice together, to join in rejoicing. Here the rejoicing is at the
7 truth rather than w. the truth (Barrett). ■ **στέγει** pres. ind. act.
to cover (as a roof). The meaning is either to cover in the sense
of to protect as a roof or to bear up as to support as a roof
(Barrett) or to endure, forbear (s. RP). **ὑπομένει** to endure, to
bear up patiently (s. TDNT; Trench; *Synonyms*, 195f.).
8 ■ **οὐδέποτε** never. **πίπτει** pres. act. to fall, to fail.
καταργηθήσονται fut. ind. pass. καταργέω to render inoperative, to make ineffective or powerless. **παύσονται** fut. ind. mid.
παύω to cause to rest, to cause to cease, mid. "they shall make
themselves cease or automatically cease of themselves" (RWP).
(For the dying out and the little use of the gift of tongues in the
post-apostolic church, s. Cleon L. Rogers, Jr., "The Gift of
Tongues in the Post-Apostolic Church," Bib Sac, 122 [April,
1965], 134–143; S.D. Currie, "'Speaking in Tongues': Early
Evidence Outside the New Testament Bearing on *GLOSSAIS*
9 *LALEIN*," Interp., 19 [July, 1965], 277–294.) ■ **ἐκ μέρους** in
10 part, partially, Both usages in this v. are emphatic (RWP). ■
ὅταν w. subj. when, whenever. **ἔλθῃ** aor. subj. ἔρχομαι.

καταργηθήσεται fut. ind. pass. s.v.8. ■ **ἤμην** impf. εἰμί. 11
νήπιος infant, child, minor. **ἐλάλουν** impf. ind. act. λαλέω to
speak, customary impf. "I used to speak." **ἐφρόνουν** impf. ind.
act. φρονέω to think. It points to the thoughts, the interest, and
the striving of a child (Lenski), customary impf. **γέγονα** perf.
ind. act. γίνομαι not to be viewed as an aoristic perf. (s. BD,
177) but as a normal perf. emphasizing the resultant condition
or state of the subject (s. M 143f.; RG, 900). **κατήργηκα** perf.
ind. act. s.v.8. Here it has the meaning "to put aside." ■ **ἄρτι** 12
now. A contrast between this dispensation and the fut. (Grosheide). **ἔσοπτρον** mirror. In Gr. literature a mirror symbolized
clarity and self-recognition (Conzelmann). Mirrors of the ancient world were generally made from polished metal and the
Corinthian mirrors were famous (RP; Conzelmann; DGRA,
1052f.). (For the legend of letting a mirror down in a spring
before the temple of Demeter and looking in the mirror to see
if the sick person was to get well or die, s. Pausanias, *Description
of Greece* VII, XXI, XII; VIII, XXXVII, VII.) **αἴνιγμα** riddle,
an indistinct image (BAG). **πρός** before, facing, here "face to
face." **ἐπιγνώσομαι** fut. ind. mid. ἐπιγινώσκω to know, to
have specific knowledge. The prep. in compound is directive (s.
MH, 312). **ἐπεγνώσθην** aor. ind. pass. The words bring out the
inadequacy of man's present knowledge of God in contrast w.
God's knowledge of man now and the knowledge of God that
man will have in the future (Barrett). ■ **νυνί** now, logical not 13
temporal. **μένει** pres. ind. act. to remain. **μείζων** comp. μέγας
large. The comp. is used here to express the superl. "greatest."
(For the contrast of Paul's treatment of love w. the ancient view
of virtue, s. Günther Bornkamm, "Der köstlichere Weg: I Kor.
13," *Gesammelte Aufsätze* I, 93–112.)

Ch. 14

■ **διώκετε** pres. imp. to hunt, to pursue. The pres. imp. calls 1
for a habitual action. **ζηλοῦτε** pres. imp. to be zealous, to earnestly desire, s. 1 Cor. 12:31. **μᾶλλον** adv. The comp. may
retain its comp. meaning or it may be used to express the superl.
(s. Barrett). **προφητεύητε** pres. subj. to prophesy. The subj. is
used to express the aim of the pursuit and desire (s. EGT). ■ 2
γλῶσσα tongue, language (s. TDNT). **οὐδεις ἀκούει** "no one
hears" that is, "no one can understand" (Barrett). However, it
is possible that the verb retains its normal meaning. **πνεύματι**
dat. sing. If it refers to the Holy Spirit it is instrumental (Bruce).
If it is locative it refers to the human spirit (Grosheide). ■ 3
οἰκοδομή edification, building up. **παράκλησις** exhortation,

encouragement, consolation (s. MNTW, 128–135; TDNT; CBB). **παραμυθία** encouragement, consolation. A synonym w. the previous word. This word, however, is not used in the NT to describe God's consolation (Conzelmann; s. also TDNT).
4 ■ **ἑαυτόν** himself. Chrysostom says "What a difference between one person and the church " (RP). **ἐκκλησία** church, assembly. Without the article it refers to the local assembly, the assembly of which he is one member (Barrett). **οἰκοδομεῖ** pres. ind. act. to edify, to build up. The pres. tense emphasizes the continual
5 action that which is habitual or always true. ■ **θέλω** to wish, to desire, to want. It is normally followed by the inf. expressing the object of the desire. In this v. it is also followed by **ἐκτὸς εἰ μή** w. the subj. (s. M 208). **διερμηνεύῃ** pres. subj. διερμηνεύω to translate. The prep. in compound may indicate either "being a go-between" or "thoroughness." One who interprets his own words intervenes between unintelligible utterance and the hearers (RP). **λάβῃ** aor. subj. λαμβάνω. The subj. is used to express purpose. The aor. is ingressive "may get edification" (RWP).
6 ■ **νῦν δέ** "and now." The particle is logical not temporal (s. Weiss). **ἐάν** w. subj. introduces a condition which is supposable (RWP) "in case." **ἔλθω** aor. subj. ἔρχομαι. **ὠφελήσω** fut. ὠφελέω to profit, to benefit. Here followed by the acc. **λαλήσω** fut. λαλέω. **ἐν** through, the instrumental use of the prep. **ἀποκάλυψις** unveiling, revelation. **γνῶσις** knowledge. **προφητείᾳ** prophecy. The proclamation of a prophet. The revelation and knowledge are the internal gifts of which prophecy
7 and teaching are the external manifestation (RP). ■ **ὅμως.** The word could be viewed as displaced and have the meaning "nevertheless," "all the same," or it could be viewed as from the adv. and have the meaning "likewise" (s. BD, 234; MT, 337; BAG). **ἄψυχος** lifeless. (For the neg. force of the perf., s. Moorhouse, 47ff.) **αὐλός** flute. The word could refer to various types of wind instruments and was popular in social, religious, and military life (s. DGRA, 1131; RP). **κιθάρα** lyre, a stringed musical instrument resembling our guitar. It was used in education, lyric poetry, religion, and entertainment (s. OCD, 709; Conzelmann; KP III, 1580). There was a large music hall (odeion) located in Corinth which would seat around 18,000 (s. E.G. Wright, *Biblical Archaeology*, 262). **διαστολή** difference, distinction. **φθόγγος** sound, musical sound, note. It could refer to the notes on a lyre or stops of a flute (s. OCD, 705–713). **δῷ** aor. subj. δίδωμι to give. **γνωσθήσεται** fut. ind. pass. γινώσκω. **αὐλούμενον** pres. pass. part. αὐλέω to play the flute. Here "that which is being played on the flute." **κιθαριζόμενον** pres. pass.

part. κιθαρίζω to play on the harp or lyre. The pres. part.
emphasizes the continuous contemporaneous action, "that
which is being played on the lyre." ■ **ἄδηλος** not clear, uncer- 8
tain, indistinct. **παρασκευάσεται** fut. mid. παρασκευάζω to
prepare, mid. to prepare one's self, to make one's self ready, to
make preparations. **πόλεμος** war, battle (s. Trench; *Synonyms*,
322). ■ **εὔσημος** intelligible, that which is well-marked. The 9
adv. was used in the papyri in the sense of "legible," "clearly"
(s. MM). **δῶτε** aor. subj. δίδωμι. **γνωσθήσεται** fut. ind. pass.
s.v.7. **λαλούμενον** pres. pass. part. λαλέω. **ἔσεσθε** fut. εἰμί.
Used in a periphrastic construction which emphasizes the linear
or continuous action (s. IBG, 18). ■ **τοσοῦτος** so great. Here it 10
indicates a number indefinite but very great (Meyer). **τύχοι** aor.
opt. τυγχάνω to happen, to occur. Used in the construction **εἰ
τύχοι** as a fourth-class conditional clause "if it should happen"
(RWP). Used idiomatically w. the meaning "perhaps." **ἄφωνος**
without sound, voiceless; that is, "meaningless sound" (RP).
■ **εἰδῶ** subj. οἶδα. **βάρβαρος** barbarian. It denotes a man whose 11
language sounds like "bar bar," that is, whose language makes
no sense (Morris). **ἐν ἐμοί** "in my case," "in my judgment" (M,
103). ■ **οὕτως** because, since, in the NT it is regularly causal 12
(BD, 238). **ζηλωτής** zealot, one who is zealous for something,
enthusiast. **πνευμάτων** gen. pl., obj. gen. indicating the object
of the strong desire. The pl. refers to the various manifestations
of the Spirit (Lenski). **ζητεῖτε** pres. imp. ζητέω to seek, to seek
after. The pres. tense indicates the continuing of an action in
progress or the continual action which is to be habitual (s. MKG,
272). **περισσεύητε** pres. subj. περισσεύω to increase, to
abound. The increase could be numerically or spiritually. ■ 13
προσευχέσθω pres. imp. 3rd per. sing. προσεύχομαι to pray.
διερμηνεύῃ pres. subj., s.v.5. The one who spoke in tongues
evidently knew when he was going to use the gift for he is to pray
that he may interpret so that the whole church may be edified.
■ **προσεύχωμαι** pres. subj. **πνεῦμά μου** "my spirit." It could 14
refer to the human spirit of Paul (Barrett) or the Holy Spirit or
the spiritual gift given by the Holy Spirit (s. Weiss; PAT, 190f.).
ἄκαρπος unfruitful. ■ **προσεύξομαι** fut. mid. The fut. is asser- 15
tive or volitive expressing the determined decision of Paul's will
(s. SMT, 34; M, 150; RG, 874). **πνεύματι** instrumental dat.
ψαλῶ fut. ψάλλω to sing a hymn, to sing praises. ■ **εὐλογῇς** 16
pres. subj. 2nd per. sing. εὐλογέω to speak well of, to praise, to
bless, to give thanks. **ἀναπληρῶν** pres. act. part. ἀναπληρόω
to fill, here to fill up the place; that is, "he who fills the role of"
(Barrett). **ἰδιώτης** unskilled, unlearned, a layman in contrast to

an expert (s. BAG; TDNT). (For the use of this word and those related to it in the papyri, s. MM; Preisigke I, 689f.) **ἐρεῖ** fut. λέγω. **τὸ ἀμήν** amen. It was the Jewish and Christian custom to express agreement and concurrence w. the prayer by responding amen (s. SB III, 456; Barrett). (For the use of the term in the DSS, s. 1 QS 1:20; 2:10, 18.) **ἐπί** w. dat. to; that is, in response
17 to. **ἐπειδή** since, because. ■ **καλῶς** adv. well. **εὐχαριστεῖς**
18 pres. ind. act. to give thanks. **οἰκοδομεῖται** pres. pass. ■
μᾶλλον adv. comp. μάλα followed by the gen. of comparison
19 w. the meaning "more than." ■ **θέλω** I wish, I prefer (RP; LAE, 187, 190). **πέντε** five, a round number, as used in Judaism (Barrett; SB III, 461). **λαλῆσαι** aor. act. inf. **κατηχήσω** aor. act. subj. κατηχέω to instruct, to teach, Paul only uses the word in the sense of theological instruction (Conzelmann). **μίριοι** ten thousand.

20 ■ **παιδία** little children. **γίνεσθε** pres. imp. The pres. imp. w. the neg. is a command to stop an action which is in progress, "do not continue" (s. MKG, 72). **φρέσιν** dat. pl. φρήν Only used here and in the pl. w. the meaning thinking, understanding (BAG). Dative of respect or reference, "in reference to understanding." **κακίᾳ** wickedness, maliciousness, and ill-will (RP),
21 dat of reference. **τέλειος** mature. ■ **γέγραπται** perf. ind. pass. γράφω to write. The perf. points to the continuing authority of that which stands written (s. MM). **ἑτερόγλωσσος** other tongues, strange languages. **χεῖλος** lip. **εἰσακούσονται** fut. mid. εἰσακούω to hear into, to attend to. (For the prep. in
22 compound, s. MH, 304.) ■ **ὥστε** therefore. The word draws a conclusion from the previous. **εἰς** after the verb to be it may have a Semitic meaning "to serve as" (s. BD, 80; but also s. Barrett). **σημεῖον** sign. (For a study of this v., s. J.P.M. Sweet, "A Sign for Unbelievers: Paul's Attitude to Glossolalia." NTS, 13 [April,
23 1967], 240–257.) ■ **συνέλθῃ** aor. act. subj. **συνέρχομαι** to come together, to assemble. **ἐπὶ τὸ αὐτό** "to the same place," "together." **λαλῶσιν** pres. subj. **εἰσέλθωσιν** aor. act. subj. εἰσέρχομαι. The subjunctives are used in a third-class conditional clause in which the condition is possible. **ἰδιώτης** s.v.16. **ἐροῦσιν** fut. ind. act. λέγω. **ὅτι.** It introduces either indirect discourse "that" or introduces a direct quotation and is used as quotation marks. **μαίνεσθε** pres. ind. mid. to be mad, to be crazy. The question introduced by the neg. expects the answer
24 yes. ■ **προφητεύωσιν** pres. subj. The pres. tense emphasizes the continual action. **ἐλέγχεται** pres. ind. pass. to convict, to so present the evidence that one is driven to the conclusion that the argument is correct (s. TDNT; T). **ἀνακρίνεται** pres. ind. pass.

ἀνακρίνω to examine, to cross-examine, to put through a course
of questioning as when one is questioned and examined by a
judge in a court (Lenski). ■ **πέσων** aor. part. πίπτω to fall. 25
προσκυνήσει fut. προσκυνέω to worship, to fall down and
worship. Used to designate the custom of prostrating one's self
before a person and kissing his feet, the hem of his garment, the
ground, etc. (BAG; s. also TDNT; CBB). The verb is followed
by the dat. **ἀπαγγέλλων** pres. act. part. to solemnly declare,
part. of manner.

■ **τί οὖν ἐστιν** "what then is the result of this discussion?" 26
(RP) s.v.15. **ὅταν** w. pres. subj. "whenever," "as often as."
συνέρχησθε pres. mid. subj. συνέρχομαι to come together, to
assemble. The pres. is iterat. and points to a reoccurring action.
ψαλμός song, hymn. The word signifies the singing of praises
to God (EGT). Those present may have composed a song or
have sung a Christian hymn (Grosheide). **ἔχει** pres. ind. to have,
each one had these gifts because they were given by the Spirit
(s. Grosheide). **ἑρμηνεία** translation, interpretation. **πρός** w.
acc. for, leading to (s. IBG, 53). **οἰκοδομή** edification, holding
up. **γινέσθω** pres. imp. γίνομαι. The pres. imp. is a command
for habitual action. ■ **εἴτε** if, whether. The construction 27
"whether . . . or" is begun but left unfinished (RP). **κατά** w. acc.
used in a distributive sense "by twos" (s. MT, 268). **πλεῖστον**
adv. superl. πολύς. Used as adverbial acc. "at the most" (RWP).
ἀνὰ μέρος "in turn" (s. IBG, 67; MT, 265). In the Jewish
synagogue service there were at least seven readers of Scripture
who read at least three verses in turn (s. SB III, 465f.; IV, 154–
171; HJP II, ii, 79–83; JPF II, 927–933). **εἷς** one, someone.
διερμηνευέτω pres. imp. s.v.5. ■ **διερμηνευτής** translator, in- 28
terpreter. **σιγάτω** pres. imp. σιγάω to be silent. The pres. tense
indicates that he is not even to speak in a tongue once (RWP).
The command indicates that the per. could control the use of the
gift. **λαλείτω** pres. imp. ■ **λαλείτωσαν** pres. imp. 3rd per. pl. 29
διακρινέτωσαν pres. imp. 3rd per. pl. διακρίνω to separate, to
make a distinction, to pass judgment on (BAG). ■ **ἀποκαλυφθῇ** 30
aor. pass. subj. ἀποκαλύπτω to reveal. **καθημένῳ** pres. mid.
part. κάθημαι to sit, dat. as indirect object. It was the prophet
who stood while the congregation sat (Lietzmann; s. also Luke
4:16). ■ **καθ᾽ἕνα** "one by one," distributive use of prep. (s. MT, 31
268). **μανθάνωσιν** pres. subj. μανθάνω to learn. The conjunc-
tive is used to express purpose. **παρακαλῶνται** pres. pass. subj.
παρακαλέω to exhort, to encourage, to comfort (s. MNTW,
128–135). ■ **καί** also. **πνεύματα** pl. s.v.12. It is the manifesta- 32
tion of the Spirit or the divine influence under which the proph-

ets spoke (Hodge). **ὑποτάσσεται** pres. ind. mid. to be in subjection, to be obedient. The prophet exercised self-control and control over the gift. A preacher without self-control is no true
33 prophet (RP). ■ **ἀκαταστασία** disorder, disturbance, confusion. The disorder could refer to disorder or confusion in the
assembly (Barrett) or it could refer to the disorder if the Spirit
was not in harmony w. Himself (Conzelmann).

ὡς "as." These words should not be taken w. the preceding
34 but w. the words which follow (Grosheide). ■ **ἐκκλησίαι**
churches, assemblies. Here it refers to the local gathering.
ἐπιτρέπω to allow, to permit followed by the inf. In the Jewish
synagogue women were not allowed to speak in public and took
no active part in the conduct of divine service (JPF II, 920f.; SB
35 III, 467f.). ■ **μαθεῖν** aor. act. inf. **μανθάνω**. **θέλω** to wish, to
desire, to will. **ἐν οἴκῳ** "at home." **ἴδιος** own. **ἐπερωτάτωσαν**
pres. imp. **ἐπερωτάω** to ask, to ask about something. The prep.
in compound is directive (s. MH, 314). **αἰσχρός** shameful, disgraceful. Plutarch wrote that not only the arm but the voice of
a modest woman ought to be kept from the public, and she
should feel shame at being heard, as at being stripped (Barrett).
(For a discussion on this passage in the light of other Scriptures
36 dealing w. women in church life, s. PWC, 70–80.) ■ **ἐξῆλθεν** aor.
ind. **ἐξέρχομαι** to go out. **κατήντησεν** aor. ind. **καταντάω** to
reach, to arrive. The question is "were you the starting point of
the gospel? or were you its only destination?" Paul is attacking
the abuses of the Corinthians by pointing out they were not the
source of the gospel (s. RP).

37 ■ **δοκεῖ** pres. ind. act. to suppose. The ind. is used in a
first-class conditional clause which assumes that the condition is
true. **ἐπιγινωσκέτω** pres. imp. **ἐπιγινώσκω** to recognize, to
acknowledge completely. **ἐντολή** commandment. The following
38 gen. "lord" could be poss. gen. or gen. of source. ■ **ἀγνοεῖ** pres.
ind. act. to be ignorant, to disregard. **ἀγνοεῖται** pres. ind. pass.
39 to be ignored, to be disregarded (s. BAG). ■ **ὥστε** therefore. The
word sums up and draws a conclusion of the previous discussion.
ζηλοῦτε pres. act. imp. s.v.1. **κωλύετε** pres. imp. to hinder, to
restrain, to forbid. The pres. imp. w. neg. means either to stop
an action in progress or it forbids an habitual action (s. MKG,
40 272f.). ■ **εὐσχημόνως** adv. decently. **τάξις** "according to order,"
orderly. Josephus uses the neg. of this word to say that the
Roman army did not erect its camp in disorderly parties (Josephus, *Wars* III, 77). Josephus also uses the word indicating that
the Essenes only spoke "in turn" (Josephus, *Wars* II, 132). Paul

uses the word to suggest the idea of members of the church doing things at one time, not all at once (Barrett).

Ch. 15

■ **γνωρίζω** to make known, "I draw your attention" (Bar- 1
rett). The word was used to introduce a solemn statement (Conzelmann). **εὐηγγελισάμην** aor. ind. mid. εὐαγγελίζομαι to proclaim good news. The aor. views the total ministry of Paul emphasizing the one gospel which he preached. **παρελάβετε** aor. ind. act. παραλαμβάνω to receive, to receive as authoritative teaching which was passed on (s. 1 Cor. 11:23). **ἑστήκατε**
perf. ind. act. ἵστημι to stand. ■ **σῴζεσθε** pres. pass. σῴζω to 2
rescue, to save. The pres. pass. indicates a continuous action which was being performed on the believers. **τίνι λόγῳ** "by, in which word." The interrogative pron. is used here as a normal rel. pron. (s. RG, 737f.). **εἰ** "if." The condition is assumed as a reality. **κατέχω** to hold down, to hold fast. **ἐκτὸς εἰ μή** except. (For the construction, s. BD, 191.) **εἰκῇ** adv. without cause, in vain, to no purpose, without due consideration (BAG). **ἐπιστεύσατε** aor. ind. to believe. Not that Paul really entertains this as a serious possibility, but if the denial of the Resurrection is carried to its logical conclusion, then it would be shown that their belief was fruitless, perhaps because it was exercised super-
ficially or "at random" (Bruce). ■ **παρέδωκα** aor. παραδίδωμι 3
to deliver over, to pass on, to pass on authoritative teaching (s. 1 Cor. 11:23; for a detailed study of this passage, s. RH, 76–89). **ἐν πρώτοις** "first of all." The words may indicate priority either in time or importance (Barrett). **παρέλαβον** aor. ind. act. s. 1 Cor. 11:23. **ἀπέθανεν** aor. ind. act. ἀποθνήσκω to die. **κατὰ τὰς γραφὰς** "according to the scriptures." The phrase can be taken to mean "even as the whole tone of the O.T. so foretold concerning Him" (s. Kenneth O. Gangel, "According to the
Scriptures," Bib Sac, 125 [April, 1968], 123–128). ■ **ἐτάφη** aor. 4
ind. pass. θάπτω to bury. **ἐγήγερται** perf. ind. pass. ἐγείρω to raise. The perf. emphasizes that Christ is risen and indicates a continuing condition which has given rise to a new state of affairs. Christ continues in the risen state (McKay, 12; s. also GI, 113). **τῇ ἡμέρᾳ τῇ τρίτῃ** on the day the third, dat. of time.
■ **ὤφθη** aor. pass. ὁράω to see, pass. to be seen, to appear. He 5
could be seen by human eyes, the appearances were not just visions (Grosheide). **εἶτα** then, next, adv. denoting sequence
(AS). ■ **ἔπειτα** there upon, thereafter, then. **ἐπάνω** above, over. 6
(For the use of the adv. w. numbers, s. BD, 99.) **πεντακόσιοι** 500. **ἐφάπαξ** (from ἐπί and ἅπαξ), at once, at one time. **πλείων** comp. πολύς pl. "the majority." **μένω** pres. act. to

remain. **ἄρτι** now. Paul was writing 20 years or so later (Barrett).
7 **ἐκοιμήθησαν** aor. pass. *κοιμάομαι* pass. to fall asleep. ■
πᾶσιν place after the substitutive in order to emphasize the
8 substitutive (BD, 144). ■ **ἔσχατον** last. Used either in the sense that Paul is the last of those to be granted such an appearance or the last of the apostles or he refers to himself as the least of the apostles (s. PAA, 105). **ὡσπερεί** like, as though, as it were. **ἔκτρωμα** untimely birth, miscarriage. The term points to the results of the birth and was used to indicate that which is incapable of sustaining life of its own volition and requires divine intervention if it is to continue. It emphasizes Paul's weakness and his dependence on God's grace (s. PAA, 104–105; Schlat-
9 ter). ■ **ἐλάχιστος** superl. of *μικρός*. The smallest, the least. The true superl. followed by the gen. of comparison. **ἱκανός** worthy, competent, fit. **διότι.** A strengthened form of *ὅτι* "because."
10 **ἐδιώξα** aor. *διώκω* to hunt, to pursue, to persecute. ■ **ἡ εἰς ἐμέ**. The article is used as a rel. pron. "which was extended to me" (RP). **κενός** empty,in vain, without success. **ἐγενήθη** aor. pass. *γίνομαι*. **περισσότερος** comp. *περισσός* more than sufficient, abundantly. Followed by the comp. gen. **ἐκοπίασα** aor. ind. *κοπιάω* to labor, to work to the point of exhaustion, to work hard (s. TDNT). It points to the weariness which follows on this straining of all his powers to the utmost (Trench; *Synonyms*,
11 378). ■ **κηρύσσομεν** pres. ind. act. The pres. denotes a constant fact (Godet). **ἐπιστεύσατε** aor. ind. act. The aor. points to the fact of belief.

12 ■ **εἰ** w. the ind. is used to introduce a condition which is accepted as true. **κηρύσσεται** pres. ind. pass. The pres. points to the continual proclamation. **ἐγήγερται** perf. ind. pass., s.v.4. The perf. means "he lives at the present as the risen Savior" (Grosheide). **ἀνάστασις** resurrection. It is possible that the opponents of Paul who deny a resurrection of the dead were those who were influenced by a Hellenistic, dualistic concept of after-life current among the sacramentally oriented popular cults (J.H. Wilson, "The Corinthians Who Say There Is No Resurrection of the Dead," ZNW, 59 [1968], 103; for the views of resur-
14 rection in the ancient world, s. RAC I, 919–938; TDNT). ■ **κένος** empty, s.v.10. Take out the resurrection, and there is nothing left (Barrett). **ἄρα** "then." The word implies the inevi-
15 table nature of the conclusion (Grosheide). ■ **εὑρισκόμεθα** pres. ind. pass. *εὑρίσκω* to find, pass. to be found. The word is often used of moral judgments respecting character, and conveys the idea of discovering or detecting (RP). **ψευδομάρτυς** false witness. The following gen. is either obj. "a false witness about

God," or subj. gen. "a false witness claiming to be from God." Such a false witness would make his message a myth, a human composition which arises from human wishes, and at the same time he would be claiming that his message was the word of God (Schlatter). **ἐμαρτυρήσαμεν** aor. ind. act. μαρτυρέω to serve as a witness, to give witness. **κατά** w. the gen. "again." **ἤγειρεν**
aor. ἐγείρω to rise. **ἄρα** therefore. ■ **εἰ γάρ** if indeed. A 16
strengthened form of the particle introducing a condition which
is assumed as true "if, as they say, it is true that . . ." (BD, 237).
■ **μάταιος** vain, empty. The word emphasizes the aimlessness 17
and the leading to no object or end (s. Trench; *Synonyms*, 180f.;
s. also CBB). ■ **κοιμηθέντες** aor. pass. part. κοιμάομαι to fall 18
asleep. **ἀπώλοντο** aor. ind. mid. ἀπόλλυμι to ruin, to destroy,
to perish. ■ **εἰ** w. the ind. Assumes the condition is true. 19
ἠλπικότες perf. act. part. ἐλπίζω to hope. The part. could be used as a periphrastic perf. emphasizing the continual condition or state of hoping (RWP), or the part. could be considered to be substitutive "we are hopers" (Barrett). **ἐλεεινότεροι** comp. ἐλεεινός pitiable, one who is to be pitied. The comp. is used w. a superl. followed by the gen. of comparison "more deserving of compassion" (RP; s. also BD, 33f.).

■ **νυνί** "now," not temporal but logical and returns to real- 20
ity (Schlatter). **ἀπαρχή** firstfruit. The word means the first installment of the crop which foreshadows and pledges the ultimate offering of the whole (Barrett). The word was used in various ways in the papyri: a birth certificate, a certificate of authorization, a yearly offering for a god, inheritance tax (s.
Preisigke; MM). **κεκοιμημένων** perf. pass. part., s.v.6. ■ 21
ἐπειδή since, because. **δι'** w. gen. "through." ■ **ὥσπερ** as, just 22
as. **ἀποθνῄσκουσιν** pres. ind. act. to die. The pres. tense is frequentative and describes action which reoccurs from time to time w. different individuals (M, 114). **ζωοποιηθήσονται** fut.
ind. pass. ζωοποιέω to make alive. ■ **ἕκαστος** each. **τάγμα** 23
rank, order, often used in the military sense denoting a body of troops which can be disposed according to the decision of the commanding officer or it could be applied to any sort of group and could also mean place or position (Barrett; s. also 1 Cor. 14:40). **ἔπειτα** then, after, thereafter. **παρουσίᾳ** presence, arrival, coming. The word was used as a technical expression for the arrival or visit of the king or emperor (LAE, 368). It was also
used for the appearance of a god (Conzelmann; s. TDNT). ■ 24
εἶτα then, after this. The word may indicate that there is also to be an interval between his coming and the end (s. RP; Weiss). **τὸ τέλος** completion, end. The word was used as a technical

phrase denoting the final consummation (PRJ, 295). **ὅταν** when, whenever. **παραδιδοῖ** pres. act. subj. παραδίδωμι to give over, to turn over to someone. The pres. tense pictures a fut. proceeding (RWP). **τῷ θεῷ καὶ πατρί.** The definite article has here the force of demonstrative w. the meaning of a rel. pron. that is, "to the one who is God and Father" (Weiss). **καταργήσῃ** aor. subj. καταργέω to make ineffective, to abolish, to bring to an end (s. TDNT). **ἀρχή** rule, ruler. The nouns here represent the evil
25 powers under whose control the world has come (Barrett). ■ **δεῖ**
impersonal verb, it is needful, it is necessary, the necessity arises out of the sovereign plan of God (s. TDNT). **οὗ** until. **θῇ** aor.
26 subj. τίθημι to place, to put. ■ **ἔσχατος ἐχθρός.** Used as a
pred. "as the last enemy." **καταργεῖται** pres. ind. pass. s.v.24.
27 ■ **πάντα γάρ.** The first word is emphatic (RP) and the particle
gives a causal explanation. **ὑπέταξεν** aor. ὑποτάσσω to subject. **εἴπῃ** aor. subj. λέγω. Used to introduce a scriptural quotation "now when it says" (Barrett). **ὑποτέτακται** perf. ind. pass. ὑποτάσσω. **δῆλος** clear, plain. **ἐκτός** outside, except.
28 **ὑποτάξαντος** aor. act. part. ■ **ὑποταγῇ** aor. subj. pass.
ὑποταγήσεται fut. ind. pass. **αὐτός** himself. The word is used as an intensifying pronominal adj. (Funk, 562f.). **ᾖ** pres. subj. εἰμί. The subj. is used in a purpose clause. **πάντα ἐν πᾶσιν.** Paul refers neither to pantheism nor universalism, but speaks of the new heaven and new earth in which all things are in harmony w. God (s. Barrett; Godet).
29 ■ **ἐπεί** since, otherwise. **τί** what. **ποιήσουσιν** fut. ind. act.
to do. Here it means either "what will they have recourse to?" or "what will they gain?" (RP). **βαπτιζόμενοι** pres. pass. part. βαπτίζω to baptize. The substantival use of the part. w. the article suggests a particular group, not all Christians (Barrett). **ὑπέρ** w. gen. for, on behalf of. (For literature regarding "baptism for the dead," s. Conzelmann; ZPEB I, 469f.; TDNT; CBB.) **ὅλως** at all, never. **τί καί β.** . . . "why then," "why at all, still?"
30 (BD, 228). ■ **κινδυνεύομεν** pres. ind. act. to be in danger. The
pres. tense emphasizes the constant or continual state of danger. **πᾶσαν ὥραν** every hour, acc. of time, "hourly." The acc. of
31 time means all through every hour (RWP). ■ **καθ' ἡμέραν** dis-
tributive use of the prep. "day after day," "daily." **ἀποθνῄσκω** pres. ind. act. to die, here "to be in danger of death," or it may mean that Paul abandons life daily and, knowing that he may die, he continually prepares himself for death (Grosheide). **νή.** A particle used in solemn oaths and means "truly," "yes" (RG, 1150) and is followed by the acc. of the person or thing by which one swears or affirms "yes, truly by my pride in you" (BAG).

■ **εἰ** Used w. ind. to introduce a condition accepted as true. **κατά** 32
in accordance w. human standards, "on partly human terms"
(Barrett). **ἐθηριομάχησα** aor. ind. θηριομαχέω to fight w.
wild animals. It is uncertain if Paul is speaking literally or figuratively. If figuratively the "beasts" may have been the legalists or
Judaizers (Robert E. Osborne, "Paul and the Wild Beasts," JBL,
85 [June, 1966], 230). It may have been evil men whose association corrupts. If there were no resurrection of the body, his
struggles at Ephesus had been in vain (Abraham J. Malherbe,
"The Beasts at Ephesus," JBL, 87 [March, 1968], 80). **ὄφελος**
profit, benefit, good. **φάγωμεν** aor. subj. ἐσθίω to eat. **πίωμεν**
aor. subj. πίνω to drink. The two subjs. are cohortative "let us."
αὔριον tomorrow. **ἀποθνήσκομεν** pres. ind. act. s.v.3. The
pres. is used here to express fut. time. (For the quotation from
Isa. 23:13, s. Barrett; for other parallels, s. LAE, 296; Conzelmann.) ■ **πλανᾶσθε** pres. imp. pass. πλανάω to lead astray, to 33
deceive. The pres. imp. w. the neg. is a command to stop an
action in process. The pass. is permissive pass. "don't allow
yourself to be deceived" (s. BD, 165). **φθείρω** pres. ind. act. to
corrupt, to ruin, gnomic pres. indicating that which is always
true. **ἦθος** custom, way, moral. **χρηστός** useful, good. **ὁμιλία**
association, company. A possible quotation from Menander,
Thais (for further possible parallels from Menander, s. F.W.
Danker, "Menander and the New Testament," NTS, 10 [April,
1964], 365–368). ■ **ἐκνήψατε** aor. act. imp. ἐκνήφω become 34
sober, come to one's senses, to wake up. The prep. in compound
points to sobriety attained out of drunkenness (MH, 309). The
aor. imp. calls for immediate action (s. MKG, 272). **δικαίως**
adv. righteously, truly, really, indeed (s. Lietzmann-Kümmel,
194). **ἁμαρτάνετε** pres. imp. to sin. The pres. imp. w. the neg.
is a command not to continue an action in progress or a command not to always do an action (s. MKG, 272f.). **ἀγνωσία**
ignorance followed by the obj. gen. shame.

■ **ἐρεῖ** fut. λέγω. **ποῖος** what sort of, what kind of. **σώματι** 35
dat. sing. instrumental dat. ■ **ἄφρων** fool, one who is ignorant, 36
one who does not have or use understanding (s. TDNT).
σπείρεις pres. ind. act. to sow. **ζῳοποιεῖται** pres. pass. to make
alive, s.v.22. **ἀποθάνῃ** aor. subj. to die, s.v.3. ■ **γενησόμενον** 37
fut. mid. part. γίνομαι "the body that it will become." Perhaps
Paul chose the analogy of the seed precisely because it implies
continuity as well as discontinuity (Ronald J. Sider, "The Pauline Conception of the Resurrection Body in I Corinthians 15:35–
54," NTS, 21 [April, 1975], 432). **γυμνός** naked, bare. **κόκκος**
grain. **εἰ τύχοι** aor. opt. τυγχάνω to happen. The opt. is used

in the idiom meaning "perhaps" (s. BAG). **σῖτος** wheat. **λοιπός** remaining. (For rabbinic parallels which use the analogy of bare grains arising w. many coverings to describe the Resurrection, s.
38 PRJ, 305; SB III, 475.) ■ **ἠθέλησεν** aor. ind. act. θέλω to wish, to will; that is, God gives the seed a body in accordance w. His
39 past decision at creation (Sider, 432). **σπέρμα** seed. ■ **κτῆνος** animal, a domesticated animal. **πτηνός** adj. feathered. Used as a substitutive "bird." **ἰχθύς** fish. The distinction made between different kinds of flesh was common to rabbinical thought but not as familiar to Hellenistic thinking (SB III, 475f.; PRJ, 305f.).
40 ■ **ἐπουράνιος** heavenly, celestial; that is, upon heaven or existing in heaven (RWP), not the heavenly body of human beings or angels (Grosheide). **ἐπίγειος** earthly, terrestrial; that is, the bodies of everything that lives on earth (Grosheide). **δόξα** good opinion, reputation, brightness, splendor, glory (s. AS; TDNT;
41 CBB). ■ **σελήνη** moon. **ἀστήρ** star. The lack of the article points to a characteristic of the class or of the single thing (BD, 132). **γάρ** "yes, and . . ." (Barrett). **διαφέρω** to differ. The stars differed in brilliance or brightness (s. Conzelmann; Barrett).
42 ■ **οὕτως** so, thus. Paul now applies the preceding remarks (Grosheide). **σπείρεται** pres. ind. pass. s.v.36. **φθορά** corruption, that which is subject to decay. Corruption is also viewed as an evil power which affects all of creation as a result of Adam's sin (Sider, 433). **ἀφθαρσία** incorruption, that which is not sub-
43 ject to decay and control by sin. ■ **ἀτιμία** dishonor. The word was sometimes used of loss of the rights of citizenship. A corpse
44 has no rights (Morris). **ἀσθενείᾳ** weakness. ■ **πνευματικός** natural, that which pertains to the soul, a physical body which is suited to earthly life (SBT, 156) and is subject to sin (Sider, 433ff.). **ψυχικός** spiritual, that which pertains to the spirit. It refers to a physical body renovated by the Spirit of God and therefore suited to heavenly immortality (SBT, 166; Sider, 435). (For the suf. which denotes an ethnical or dynamic relation, s.
45 MH, 378.) ■ **γέγραπται** perf. pass. γράφω "it stands written." The perf. denotes the abiding authoritative character of that which was written (s. MM). **ἐγένετο** aor. ind. mid. γίνομαι. Followed by the prep. w. acc. in the place of a pred. nom. "the first Adam became a living soul" (s. MH, 462; BD, 86). **ζῶσαν** aor. act. part. ζάω to live. **ζωοποιοῦν** pres. act. part. ζῳοποιέω to make alive, life giving. It was in His saving work for men that
46 Christ became a life-giving Spirit (Morris). ■ **πρῶτον** used as the pred. **πνευματικόν** "spiritual (body)." **ἔπειτα** then, s.v.23.
47 ■ **ἐκ γῆς** "out of the ground," "earthly." The absence of the article stresses that the essential thing is the earth's specific

quality (BD, 132). ***χοϊκός*** dusty. The word stresses mortality
due to earthly origin (SBT, 166). ■ ***οἷος*** correlative pron. ex- 48
pressing quality, of what sort, such as (s. RG, 291, 731).
ἐπουράνιοι heavenly, celestial. ■ ***ἐφορέσαμεν*** aor. φορέω to 49
wear. Used in the papyri in the sense of wearing clothes, a
breastplate or a badge (MM; Preisigke). ***εἰκών*** image (s. TDNT;
CBB). ***φορέσομεν*** fut. ind. act. The reading of the fut. is accepted instead of the aor. subj. since the context is didactic and
gives a promise instead of hortatory (s. Weiss; TC, 569).
■ ***φημί*** to say. ***σάρξ κακ αἷμα*** "flesh and blood." The 50
phrase means our present mortal nature and refers to those who
are still living (RP; s. also Barrett). ***κληρονομῆσαι*** aor. inf.
κληρονομέω to inherit, to receive as an inheritance. ■ ***πάντες*** 51
οὐ here = οὐ πάντες "not all of us." (For the position of the
neg., s. BD, 224; MT, 287.) ***κοιμηθησόμεθα*** fut. ind. act.
κοιμάομαι s.v.6. ***ἀλλαγήσομεθα*** fut. ind. pass. ἀλλάσσω to
change, to alter. ■ ***ἄτομος*** indivisible, because of smallness, "in 52
a moment" (BAG). ***ῥιπή*** throwing, rapid movement, for example, the "casting" of a glance takes an extremely short time.
Here, "in the twinkling of an eye" (BAG). ***ἐσχάτη σάλπιγξ***
the last trumpet, the last in a series of trumpets. According to
the Jewish view the Resurrection occurred w. the sound of the
trumpet and there were seven trumpets sounded for the various
stages of resurrection. At the seventh trumpet all were made
alive and stood up on their feet (s. TDNT; SB III, 481).
σαλπίσει fut. ind. pass. σαλπίζω to sound a trumpet. Here
used impersonally, "the trumpet will sound," "the trumpet shall
trumpet" (RG, 392). ***ἐγερθήσονται*** fut. ind. pass., s.v.4.
ἄφθαρτος incorruptible, s.v.42. ■ ***φθαρτός*** corruptible, that 53
which is subject to decay, s.v.32. ***ἐνδύσασθαι*** aor. mid. inf.
ἐνδύω to put on, to put on as clothing. ***θνητός*** mortal, that
which is subject to death (s. M, 222). ***ἀθανασία*** immortality,
that which is not subject to death. ■ ***γενήσεται*** fut. γίνομαι. 54
γεγραμμένος perf. pass. part. γράφω s.v.45. ***κατεπόθη*** aor.
ind. pass. καταπίνω to drink down, to swallow down. The prep.
in compound is perfective, "to swallow up." ***εἰς νίκην*** "into
victory." The translation of the Semitic phrase meaning "forever," "permanently," "successfully" (s. SL, 153–156; s. also SB
III, 481f.). ■ ***κέντρον*** sting. The word represents death as a 55
venomous creature, a scorpion, or a hornet which is rendered
harmless (RP). ■ ***διδόντι*** pres. act. part. dat. sing. δίδωμι to 57
give. The pres. tense is used to emphasize the certainty of the
victory (Barrett). ■ ***ἑδραῖος*** firm, steadfast. ***ἀμετακίνητος*** un- 58
moveable, not capable of being moved from its place.

περισσεύοντες pres. act. part. περισσεύω to abound, to be in abundance. **εἰδότες** perf. part. οἶδα to know. **κόπος** effort, labor, s.v.10. **κενός** empty, vain, s.v.14.

Ch. 16

1 ■ **λογεία** collection, contribution. The word appears in the
papyri in the sense of collection, particularly in the sense of
religious collections for a god or temple (s. LAE, 105f.; BS, 142f.,
219f.; MM; TDNT). (For the other words Paul uses in speaking
of this collection, s. RP.) **ὥσπερ** just as. **διέταξα** aor. ind.
διατάσσω to arrange, to order, to command, to give express
2 commands (s. MH, 302). **ποιήσατε** aor. imp. ποιέω to do. ■
κατά w. acc. the distributive use of the prep., "on every first day
of the week" (RP). **μία σαββάτου** a Hebraic expression for
"the first day of the week"; that is, Sunday (s. Hering; Conzelmann). **τιθέτω** pres. imp. 3rd sing. τίθημι to set, to lay, used w.
the prepositional phrase "by himself"; that is, in his home
(RWP). **θησαυρίζων** pres. act. part. θησαυρίζω to store up, to
save up, part. of means or manner explaining how each one is to
lay aside. **ὅτι ἐάν** the generalized rel. pron. "whatever."
εὐοδῶται pres. pass. subj. εὐοδοῦμαι. The form could possibly
be perf. ind. pass. or more unlikely perf. subj. pass. (s. M, 54),
lit. to send well on one's way, to be lead along a good road. It
then has the meaning to get along well, to prosper, to succeed,
and was used of having success in business (BAG; Lietzmann).
ὅταν when, whenever. **ἔλθω** aor. subj. ἔρχομαι. **γίνωνται** pres.
3 mid. subj. γίνομαι subj. used in a purpose clause. ■
παραγένωμαι aor. mid. subj. παραγίνομαι to arrive. The subj.
is used w. the indefinite temporal conj. "whenever I arrive"
(RWP). **δοκιμάσητε** aor. subj. δοκιμάζω to approve after examination, to accept as proven, to approve. In an inscription the
verb is almost a technical term for passing as fit for a public office
(MM). It was also used to indicate a government approved doctor (Preisigke). **δι' ἐπιστολῶν** "through letters," "w. letters."
Commendatory letters were well known in antiquity (Barrett;
Conzelmann; s. also 2 Cor. 3:1). **πέμψω** fut. πέμπω to send.
ἀπενεγκεῖν aor. act. inf. ἀποφέρω to carry away, to take home,
to bring to its destination. It was not the removal of the money
from Corinth, but its being conveyed to Jerusalem, that was the
important point (RP), inf. used to express purpose. **χάρις** grace,
4 generosity, favor (s. TDNT; Trench, *Synonyms*, 167). ■ **ἄξιος**
that which is equal in weight, worthy, right. Paul would make the
journey if circumstances were such that the work demanded him
going (s. Grosheide). **ᾖ** subj. εἰμι. **πορεύεσθαι** pres. mid. inf. to

travel, to make a journey. The inf. is used w. the adj. **πορεύσονται** fut. mid. πορεύομαι.

■ **διέλθω** aor. subj. διέρχομαι to pass through. The follow- 5
ing verb is pres. tense used to express the fut. (s. BD, 168). ■ 6
πρὸς ὑμᾶς "w. you." (For the prep. w. acc. denoting position, s. IBG, 52f.) **τυχόν** aor. act. part. n. sing. τυγχάνω to happen, to occur. The aor. part. is used here as an adv. meaning "possibly," "perhaps" (s. RWP). **παραμενῶ** fut. παραμένω to remain, to stay, to remain w. someone. The contrast is w. "passing through" Macedonia. **παραχειμάσω** fut. παραχειμάζω to spend the winter. Once winter is passed ships can sail again. The winter season would thus compel Paul to sojourn at Corinth (Grosheide). **προπέμψητε** aor. subj. προπέμπω to send forth, to help on one's journey w. food, money by arranging for companions, means of travel, etc. (BAG). **πορεύωμαι** pres. mid.
subj., s.v.4. ■ **πάροδος** a passing visit, here "in passing" (s. RP). 7
ἰδεῖν aor. inf. ὁράω to see. **ἐπιμεῖναι** aor. inf. ἐπιμένω to remain, to stay for a time. **ἐπιτρέψῃ** aor. subj. ἐπιτρέπω to
allow, to permit. ■ **πεντηκοστή** Pentecost. Paul was using the 8
Jewish calendar. (For the Jewish celebration of Pentecost, s.
Acts 2:1.) ■ **μοί** "to me," "for me," dat. of advantage. **ἀνέῳγεν** 9
perf. ind. pass. ἀνοίγω to open, perf. "to stand open." The verb is intransitive and means "stands wide open" (RWP). The term "door" is a metaphor for "opportunity" (Bruce). **ἐνεργής** effective, active, powerful. The opening of the door promises a rich field of labor (BAG). (For the usages of the word in the papyri, such as a mill "in working order" or things or persons which were "active," s. MM; Preisigke.) **ἀντικείμενοι** pres. mid. part. ἀντίκειμαι to lie against someone, to oppose, to be in opposition, to resist.

■ **ἔλθῃ** aor. subj. ἔρχομαι. **ἀφόβως** without fear. Paul is 10
not thinking about the outward dangers but about the opposition that he himself faced (Schlatter). **γένηται** aor. mid. subj. γίνομαι to become, to be. **ἐργάζεται** pres. ind. act. to carry out, to accomplish, to work at. The pres. tense indicates the pres.
continual and habitual action. ■ **ἐξουθενήσῃ** aor. act. subj. 11
ἐξουθενέω to consider as nothing, to despise. The prep. in compound not only has a perfective force but it also makes the trans. idea clear (MH, 310). **προπέμψατε** aor. imp., s.v.6. **ἐκδέχομαι** to expect, to wait for. The idea of the prep. in compound is "to be ready for" (s. MH, 310).

■ **περί** concerning. This may mean that the Corinthians in 12
their letter had inquired about Apollos (Barrett). **πόλλα** n. pl. used here as an adverb, earnestly, often. **παρεκάλεσα** aor. ind.

act. **παρακαλέω** to exhort, to encourage, to ask. **πάντως** adv. at all, "simply" (Barrett). **θέλημα** wish, will. It refers to either God's will or the will or wish of Apollos (RP). **ἐλεύσεται** fut. ind. mid., s.v.5. **εὐκαιρήσῃ** aor. act. subj. **εὐκαιρέω** to find a good time, to have opportunity.
13 ■ **γρηγορεῖτε** pres. imp. γρηγορέω to watch, to stay awake, to be alert. The pres. imp. is a command for habitual action. **στήκετε** pres. imp. στήκω from the verb ἕστηκα perf. from ἵστημι to stand, to stand fast. **ἀνδρίζεσθε** pres. mid. imp. ἀνδρίζομαι to conduct one's self in a manly or courageous way (BAG). The word is common in the LXX in exhortations (s. Josh. 1:6, 7, 9) (RP). Aristotle uses the word indicating the display of courage which he describes as the mean between fear and confidence (*Nichomachean Ethics* III, VI, 1, 12). The word was also used in the papyri in the exhortation "therefore do not
14 be fainthearted but be courageous as a man" (s. MM). ■ **γινέσθω** pres. mid. imp. γίνομαι.
15 ■ **οἴδατε** defective perf. w. a pres. meaning to know. **ἀπαρχή** firstfruit (s. 1 Cor. 15:20). **ἔταξαν** aor. τάσσω to appoint. They had appointed themselves to the service of their
16 fellow Christians. It was a self-imposed duty (RP). ■ **ὑποτάσσησθε** pres. mid. subj. ὑποτάσσω to subject one's self, to be in subjection. **συνεργοῦντι** pres. act. part. συνεργέω to work w., to work together, to cooperate. **κοπιῶντι** pres. act. part. κοπιάω to labor, to work to the point of exhaustion (s. 1
17 Cor. 15:10). ■ **ἐπί** w. the dat. over, on the occasion of. **παρουσία** coming, arrival. **ὑστέρημα** lack, want, that which comes short. Paul could mean that he had missed his Christian friends, and this trio had renewed his acquaintance w. the city (Morris). **ἀνεπλήρωσαν** aor. ind. act. ἀναπληρόω to fill up
18 again, to supply. ■ **ἀνέπαυσαν** aor. ind. ἀναπαύω to give intermission from labor, to refresh (AS). **ἐπιγινώσκετε** pres. act. imp. to recognize, to acknowledge. **τοιοῦτος** such a one, one belonging to this class or having this quality.
19 ■ **ἀσπάζονται** pres. ind. mid. to greet. **πολλά** n. pl. used
20 as an adv. heartily, s.v.12. ■ **ἀσπάσασθε** aor. mid. imp. **φίλημα** kiss. In the ancient world it was customary to give a kiss as a greeting both at the meeting and at the departure. The kiss as symbol of love, fellowship, and thankfulness may have been at this time a liturgical act indicating the forgiveness which had been received and the willingness to partake of the Lord's Supper (s. TDNT; Conzelmann).
21/22 ■ **ἀσπασμός** greeting. ■ **φιλεῖ** pres. ind. act. to love (s. TDNT). **ἤτω** pres. imp. εἰμί. **ἀνάθεμα** anathema, dedicated for

destruction, cursed. **μαράναθά** or to be divided as **μαρὰν ἀθά,** an Aramaic expression. The first possible division would be a pres. imp. "our Lord, come!" and understood as a prayer either in a Eucharistic or eschatological context. The second possible division "our Lord comes!" is fut. ind. or as perf. ind. "our Lord is here!" and is understood as a confession. (For a discussion of this phrase, s. EJC, 121–124; TDNT.)

2 CORINTHIANS

Ch. 1

1 ***οὔσῃ*** pres. part. *εἰμί*. ***ὅλος*** whole, entire, complete. ***τῇ Ἀχαΐᾳ*** Achaia. It refers to the Roman province which included the whole of Greece (s. ZPEB I, 35f.; KP I, 32–38; Strabo XVII. 3. 25), and included Corinth as the capital, Cenchraea (s. Rom. 16:1) and Athens (s. Windisch).

3 ■ ***εὐλογητός*** blessed, a Jewish ascription of praise to God acknowledging Him as the source of all blessing (s. TDNT; TDOT; CBB). ***οἰκτιρμῶν*** gen. pl. compassion, lament, or sorrow which arises from the pitiful state of the object; then the feeling of compassion and understanding (s. TDNT). The gen. may be Semitic and indicates the character or attribute (s. BG, 14f.). ***παράκλησις*** encouragement, consolation, comfort. It is the standing beside a person to encourage him when he is under-
4 going severe testing (Hughes; s. also MNTW). ■ ***παρακαλῶν*** pres. act. part. "the one who encourages or stands beside to comfort." ***ἐπί*** w. dat. "on," "on the occasion of." ***θλίψις*** pressure, affliction, crushing (Plummer; Trench, *Synonyms*, 202f.). ***εἰς τό*** followed by the acc. w. the inf. used to express purpose. ***δύνασθαι*** pres. mid. inf. *δύναμαι*. ***θλίψει*** here without the article "in any kind of affliction." Used previously w. the article it means "all tribulation actually encountered." Here "in any which may be encountered" (BD, 114; MT, 200). ***ἧς*** rel. pron. fem. sing. The gen. instead of the acc. is by attraction to the case of its antecedent (s. BD, 154). ***παρακαλούμεθα*** pres. ind. pass. *παρακαλέω*. The pres. tense points to the continual action or its iterat. and points to the comfort received every time trouble
5 and afflictions arise. ■ ***περισσεύει*** to abound, to overflow. ***πάθημα*** suffering. ***χριστοῦ*** to follow Christ is to follow Him into suffering. In this also the disciple must expect to be identi-
6 fied w. the master (Hughes; s. also John 15:20). ■ ***θλιβόμεθα*** pres. ind. pass. *θλίβω* pass. to be afflicted, to suffer pressure (s.v.4). ***ὑπέρ*** w. the gen. "w. a view to" (IBG, 65). It points to that which one wants to attain (BD, 121). ***τῆς ὑμῶν παρακλήσεως*** "your comfort" obj. gen. ***ἐνεργουμένης*** pres. mid. or pass. part. *ἐνεργέω* to be effective, pass. "is made to

work" by him who bestows it. The mid. appears better "which makes itself felt," "takes effect" (Plummer; Barrett). **ὑπομονή** remaining under, patience, endurance. It was used of the endurance of that which has come upon man against his will. In classical Gr. it is used also of the ability of a plant to live under hard and unfavorable circumstances. It was later used of that quality which enabled men to die for their god (NTW, 59f.; TDNT; RAC IX, 243–294). **ὧν** rel. pron. gen. pl. The gen. instead of the acc. is because of attraction to the antecedent "the same sufferings." **καί** also. **πάσχομεν** pres. ind. act. The pres.
points to the continual suffering or to the repeated suffering.
■ **βέβαιος** firm, certain (s. 1 Cor. 1:6). **εἰδότες** perf. part. from 7
defective verb οἶδα to know. **κοινωνός** partner, one who has a common share w. another, common participant. Used in the papyri for a partner in business or a participant in a sacrifice (s. MM). Followed by the gen. indicating the thing which is shared. **παράκλησις** comfort, encouragement. s.v.3.
■ **ἀγνοεῖν** pres. act. inf. not to know, to be ignorant. **ὑπέρ** 8
w. gen. "concerning" (s. IBG, 65). **γενόμενος** aor. mid. part. γίνομαι to become, to happen. **Ἀσία** Asia; that is, the Roman province, whose capital was Ephesus (Barrett). (For Paul's affliction in Asia, s. Hughes.) **καθ' ὑπερβολή** lit. "a throwing beyond" then "beyond measure," "exceedingly." **ὑπέρ** w. acc. above, beyond (s. IBG, 64), "beyond the normal power of endurance" (Hughes). **ἐβαρήθημεν** aor. ind. pass. βαρέω to weigh down, pass. to be burdened down. Used in the papyri of misfortune or injustice (BAG; MM). **ἐξαπορηθῆναι** aor. pass. inf. ἐξαπορέομαι to be without a way out, to be in utter despair. The prep. in compound is perfective (MH, 310). The inf. is used to express result, "so that we were utterly without way of escape" (Plummer). **ζῆν** pres. act. inf. ζάω to live, to remain alive, to continue to live. The gen. of the inf. is used w. the verb
explaining the despair, "even to live" (s. M, 217f.). ■ **ἀλλά** "yes 9
indeed," "certainly." The word is confirmatory or emphatic (s. DM, 240). **ἑαυτοῖς** "within ourselves." (For the strengthening of the reflex. which was frequent in Attic, s. BD, 148.) **ἀποκρίμα** response, verdict. A technical term used for an official decision in answer to the petition of an embassy (s. J. Hemer, "A Note on II Cor. 1:9," TB, 23 [1972], 104f.; MM; BS, 257). **ἐσχήκαμεν** perf. ind. act. ἔχω. The perf. tense means "having gotten, I continue to have" and indicates that though the sentence was not immediately carried out, it remained in force (K.L. McKay, "Syntax in Exegesis," TB, 23 [1972], 48; Barrett). The action completed in the past is conceived in terms of pres. time

for the sake of vividness. This vivid perf. indicates the experience was a dreadful memory to Paul (RG, 896–897). **ἵνα** used here to express purpose, not result, and expresses God's purpose (Windisch). **πεποιθότες** perf. act. part. πείθω to persuade, perf. to have been persuaded, to trust in. **ὦμεν** pres. subj. εἰμί. Used in a periphrastic construction. The neg. suggests the discontinuance of an existing condition (Barrett). **ἐγείροντι** pres. act. part. ἐγείρω to raise. Perhaps an allusion or quotation from the second prayer of the "Eighteen Petition Prayer" which was quoted three times a day by every Israelite (s. HJP 2 II, 85–89; s. also JPF II, 801; M Berakoth 4, 1–7, s. especially 5, 2; SB IV, 208–
10 249). ■ **τηλικοῦτος** so great, terrible. **ἐρρύσατο** aor. ind. mid. ῥύομαι to rescue. The prep. seems to imply peril rather than death personified but the use of this prep. w. the verb is a common expression (s. Job 33:30; 2 Tim. 4:17, 18) (Plummer). **ῥύσεται** fut. ind. mid. **ἠλπίκαμεν** perf. ind. act. ἐλπίζω to hope. The perf. means "towards whom we have set our hope, and
11 continue to do so" (EGT). ■ **συνυπουργούντων** pres. act. part. συνυπουργέω to work together, to cooperate. The word could mean cooperation w. Paul or cooperation w. one another or cooperation w. God (s. Barrett). The part. is used in a gen. abs. which is either temporal "while" or manner "in that." **δέησις** prayer, request. **προσώπος** face, here it may have the meaning "person," "from many persons" (Plummer) or it may retain the lit. meaning "face" and be a picture of "many upturned faces" (RWP; s. also Hughes). **εἰς** "for," "to," here in the sense of "the gracious gift for us." **διὰ πολλῶν** "through many." The word may be viewed as n. w. the meaning "through many prayers" (Schlatter) but as masc. it may be taken w. the verb "may be thanked for by many" or w. the word "gift" w. the meaning "the gift which reached us by the agency of many" (s. IBG, 108). **εὐχαριστηθῇ** aor. pass. subj. εὐχαριστέω to give thanks. The subject of the pass. verb is "the gracious gift" that is, Paul's deliverance (Bultmann) and the pass. is to be understood as "that you might give thanks for the gift" (s. Lietzmann-Kümmel, 197).
12 ■ **καύχησις** boasting, glorying. The ending of the noun means "the act of glorying" but in v. 14 the word is "the thing boasted of" (RWP). **μαρτύριον** witness, testimony, evidence (s. Plummer). The word is an explanation of the previous pron. "this." **συνείδησις** conscience (s. Rom. 2:15). **ἁπλότητι** simplicity, frankness. (For a defense of the variant reading ἁγιότητι "holiness," s. Hughes; for the adopted reading, s. TC, 575.) **εἰλικρινεία** sincerity, purity (s. 1 Cor. 5:8; for a discussion of the etymology "judged by the sun," "determined by sunlight,"

s. GEW I, 450; s. also Hughes). **θεοῦ**. Probably subj. gen. "God-given simplicity and sincerity" (Plummer). **σαρκικός** fleshly. Fleshly wisdom is the merely human wisdom which is not the work of the Holy Spirit but of the human nature itself enlightened and unimproved guided by the sinful lust of the flesh (Meyer; s. Rom. 7:14). **ἀνεστράφημεν** aor. ind. pass. ἀναστρέπω pass. to turn back and forth, to conduct one's self, to live in the sense of the practice of certain principles. It is always used w. the kind of behavior more exactly described (BAG; s. also MM). **περισσοτέρως** adv. comp. of **περισσός** abundantly, comp. more abundantly, even more. Here in an elative sense "especially" (BAG). ■ **ἄλλα** "other things." **γράφομεν** pres. ind. act. 13
The pres. tense refers to all the letters that Paul writes (Hering). **ἀλλ' ἤ** except (s. BD, 233). **ἀναγινώσκετε** pres. ind. act. to read. **ἐπιγινώσκω** to acknowledge, to know w. certainty. He is referring to the certainty of the Corinthians' knowledge of his character through first-hand experience (Hughes). **τέλος** completion, end. **ἕως τέλους** "to the end," perhaps w. the meaning
"completely" (Barrett). **ἐπιγνώσεσθε** fut. ind. mid. ■ 14
ἐπέγνωτε aor. ind. act. ἐπιγινώσκω s.v.13. **ἀπὸ μέρους** partially. The phrase determines the degree of recognition (Windisch). **ὅτι** "that." Here it is not causal (s. Plummer). **καύχημα** boasting, ground of boasting, s.v.12. The apostle shares the experience of the community because both share something which originates beyond them. For this reason Paul can write "I hope . . . that you can be proud of us as we can be of you, on the day of the Lord Jesus" (PAA, 234). (For this word and the boasting of the apostle, s. PAA, 233–238; CBB; TDNT.)

■ **πεποίθησις** trust, confidence, s.v.9. **ἐβουλόμην** impf. 15
mid. βούλομαι to will, to decide. The word implies an act of will, a decision (Barrett). The impf. pictures his former state of mind (RWP). **πρότερον** adv. formerly, earlier, at first. **ἐλθεῖν** aor. act. inf. ἔρχομαι. **δεύτερος** second. **χάρις** grace, benefit, favor. They would have had two opportunities of receiving spiritual communication from him in person (Hughes). **σχῆτε** aor. act. subj. ἔχω to have, aor. to get, to receive (M, 110, 247).
Subjunctive used in a purpose clause. ■ **δι' ὑμῶν** w. gen. 16
"through you" (s. Plummer). **διελθεῖν** aor. act. inf. διέρχομαι to pass through. **προπεμφθῆναι** aor. pass. inf. προπέμπω to send forth, to outfit for a trip (s. 1 Cor. 16:6). The infinitives are
to be taken w. the main verb of v. 15. ■ **βουλόμενος** pres. mid. 17
part. βούλομαι s.v.15. **μήτι ἄρα.** Used to introduce a question in which an indignant neg. answer is called for (RWP), "do you think then?" (Barrett). **ἐλαφρία** lightness, fickleness, vacilla-

tion. **ἐχρησάμην** aor. ind. mid. χράομαι to use. **βουλεύομαι** to make plans, to consider, to decide (s. Windisch). **ἵνα** w. subj. Normally introduces a purpose clause but in this case the idea of result is possible, "w. the result that" (s. Hughes; BD, 198). **ᾖ** pres. subj. εἰμί. **καί** yes. The duplication of the words "yes" and "no" strengthens the picture of the untrustworthy man who
18 affirms just as fervently as he afterwards denies (Meyer). ■
19 **πιστός** faithful, trustworthy. ■ **γάρ** "for." The position of the word emphasizes the gen. **τοῦ θεοῦ** "God's" (BD, 251) "for it is this faithful God's Son" (Plummer). **κηρυχθείς** aor. pass. part. κηρύσσω to proclaim, to preach, to herald (s. TDNT). **ἐγένετο** aor. mid. γίνομαι here, "to be." **γέγονεν** perf. ind. act. The perf. emphasizes the continuing state or condition "in Him, yes was
20 and continues to be a reality" (Hughes). ■ **ὅσος** rel. pron. indicating quantity "how many." **ἐπαγγελία** promise. **τὸ ἀμήν** amen. A Heb. word meaning "true," "trustworthy" and was used as a strengthening and confirming statement (s. Barrett; CBB; TDNT). The use of the article w. the word means "the custom-
21 ary amen" (Plummer). ■ **βεβαιῶν** pres. act. part. βεβαιόω to make firm, to confirm. The word was used in the papyri of making a legal guarantee and appears often in the guarantee clause of a bill of sale (Preisigke; MM; BS, 104–109). **χρίσας** aor. act. part. χρίω to anoint. The anointing here refers to the anointing of the Holy Spirit at conversion which every believer
22 receives (s. BHS, 131–134). ■ **σφραγισάμενος** aor. mid. part. σφραγίζω to seal. Goods were sealed as a guarantee indicating not only ownership but also guaranteed the correctness of the contents (BS, 239; MM; and especially TDNT). **δούς** aor. act. part. δίδωμι to give. **ἀρραβών** pledge, earnest, down payment. The term means a deposit which is in itself a guarantee that the full amount will be paid (Hughes; s. also SB III, 495). **τοῦ πνεύματος** gen. of apposition "the guarantee consisting of the Spirit" (MT, 214).

23 ■ **ἐπικαλοῦμαι** pres. ind. mid. to call upon someone, to invoke, to call upon someone as a witness. The article used w. the object "God" may be the article of previous reference meaning "I call *this* God, the God whom I have just described" (Plummer). **ἐπί** w. acc. "against." Used w. the verb meaning "he should punish me if I lie" (Lietzmann). **φειδόμενος** pres. mid. part. φείδομαι to spare, to hold back. Followed by the gen. the part. can be causal or express purpose (s. RWP). **ἦλθον** aor. ind.
24 act. ἔρχομαι. ■ **κυριεύω** to be lord, to exercise authority. **συνεργός** fellow-worker. **χαρά** joy. **τῇ πίστει** instrumental dat. (Barrett) or locative indicating the sphere (Plummer).

ἑστήκατε perf. ind. act. ἵστημι perf. to stand. It emphasizes the steadfastness.

Ch. 2

■ **ἔκρινα ἐμαυτῷ** aor. κρίνω to judge, to decide, to make 1
up one's mind. Used w. the dat. of advantage "I decided this for
my own sake" (EGT; RG, 539). **λύπη** sorrow. **ἐλθεῖν** aor. act.
inf. ἔρχομαι. The inf. explains Paul's decision. ■ **λυπῶ** pres. 2
ind. act. to cause sorrow, to make sorry. **καί** then. This word
accepts the previous statement, and the question shows what a
paradox it involves (Plummer). **εὐφραίνων** pres. act. part. to
make happy, to make joyful, to cause one to have good thinking
(s. RWP). **ἐξ** out of. The prep. may suggest "sorrow that arises
from me, on my account, sorrow that is occasioned rather than
caused by my presence" (Barrett). ■ **ἔγραψα** aor. ind. act. "I 3
wrote." The reference may be to a lost letter that Paul wrote
between 1 and 2 Cor. or it may refer to 1 Cor., particularly to
1 Cor. 16:5ff. (s. Hughes for a discussion of the identity of the
epistle). **αὐτό** pron. 3rd per. sing. n. The words here may be
taken in three ways. One an adverbial acc. "precisely this reason," two the direct object of the verb, three a summary of the
content of the letter "I wrote to just this effect" (Barrett). **ἐλθών**
aor. act. part. ἔρχομαι. Temporal use of the part. "when I
come." **σχῶ** aor. subj. ἔχω to have, to receive (s. 2 Cor. 1:15).
ἔδει impf. δεῖ should, must, it is necessary. Imperfect used for
an unrealized pres. obligation (RWP). **πεποιθώς** perf. act. part.
πείθω persuade, perf. to have confidence in, to be confident, to
be persuaded. ■ **θλίψις** pressure, trouble, affliction (s. 2 Cor. 4
1:4). **συνοχῆς** holding together, distress, anguish. The lit. meaning is compression and in the papyri it refers to "imprisonment"
(MM). (For other usages of the word, s. TDNT.) **ἔγραψα** aor.
ind. act. **διά** w. the gen. "through," "with." It expresses attendant circumstances (IBG, 57). **δάκρυον** tear. These words are
expressive of deep emotion and intense distress (Plummer).
λυπηθῆτε aor. subj. pass. s.v.2. Subjunctive used in a neg. purpose clause. **γνῶτε** aor. subj. γινώσκω to know.
περισσοτέρως adv. comp. πολύς here: "especially" (s. 2 Cor.
1:12).
■ **εἰ**. Introduces a condition assumed to be true. **λελύπηκεν** 5
perf. ind. act. λυπέω s.v.2. The perf. indicates that the pain
continues to be felt (Windisch). **ἀπὸ μέρους** in part, to some
extent. The phrase may indicate either that not quite all the
Corinthians had been distressed (Plummer) or it limits the extent
of the effect (Barrett). **ἐπιβαρῶ** pres. subj. ἐπιβαρέω to weigh

down, to burden. Perhaps w. the meaning "in order not to heap
up too great a burden of words," to exaggerate (s. BAG;
6 Hughes). ■ **ἱκανός** sufficient, enough. The use of n. instead of
the fem. may be explained as a latinism w. the meaning *satis*, i.e.
"sufficient" (s. Hughes). **τοιοῦτος** such, such a pers. **ἐπιτιμία**
punishment, rebuke. The word does not have here the classical
meaning of "possession of political rights," but in the legal sense
of "penalty" (s. Plummer; MM). **ὑπὸ τῶν πλειόνων** "by the
7 majority," "by the main body of the church" (Barrett). ■
τοὐναντίον on the contrary. **μᾶλλον** rather. This word may
indicate that there were still some who felt that the punishment
was insufficient (Plummer). **χαρίσασθαι** aor. mid. inf.
χαρίζομαι to be friendly to someone, to be gracious to someone. It occurs in the LXX w. the meaning "to give a gift." Here
it has the meaning "to forgive" (s. TDNT; Windisch).
παρακαλέσαι aor. act. inf. παρακαλέω to encourage, to exhort, to urge on. It is the word used of the speeches of leaders
and of soldiers who urge each other on. It is the word used to
send hesitant soldiers and sailors courageously into battle
(MNTW, 134). The inf. here are used to express results.
περισσότερος comp. περίσσος exceeding the usual number
or size. Comparative used in the sense of superl. greater, even
more, here, "excessive sorrow" (BAG). The dat. is instrumental.
καταποθῇ aor. pass. subj. καταπίνω to swallow. The prep. is
intensive "to swallow down," "to swallow up completely" or "to
8 engulf" (s. Hughes). ■ **κυρῶσαι** aor. act. inf. κυρόω to legally
confirm, to ratify. In the papyri the word was used before the
confirming of a sale or the ratification of an appointment (s.
MM). The call for the confirmation of love may have been a
request for a formal act by the congregation to reinstate the
offender in the communion of the church and to assure him of
9 their love (Hodge). ■ **ἔγραψα** aor. ind. act. s.v.4. **γνῶ** aor. subj.
γινώσκω. The subj. is used in expressing purpose. The aor. is
ingressive "to come to know" (RWP). **δοκιμή** approval, proof.
The word indicates the results of a test. **εἰς πάντα** "in every
respect," "in all things." **ὑπήκοος** obedience. Paul wanted to
know the church's obedience to his apostolic authority (Bruce).
10 ■ **χαρίζομαι** s.v.7. **κεχάρισμαι** perf. ind. mid. The perf.
denotes the continuing state or condition of forgiveness. **εἴ τι
κεχάρισμαι** "if I have had anything to forgive." He is not
suggesting a doubt as to whether he has granted forgiveness, but
he puts the fact of there being something for him to forgive as
a mere hypothesis (Plummer). **δι' ὑμᾶς** prep. w. the acc. "because of you," "on account of you." **ἐν προσώπῳ Χριστοῦ** lit.

"before the face of Christ." It is a Semitic construction w. the meaning "in the presence of" (Hughes). ■ **πλεονεκτηθῶμεν** 11
aor. pass. subj. πλεονεκτέω to take advantage of. The arrogant, greedy, defrauding of someone often through trickery and treacherous means (NTW; TDNT). **νόημα** thought, purpose, design, in the sinister sense "devices," 'wiles," "plots," i.e., "evil schemings." The word signifies the function of the intellective faculty (Hughes). **ἀγνοοῦμεν** pres. ind. act. ἀγνοέω to be ignorant, to be unknowing. (For the neg. pref., s. Moorhouse, 41–66.)

■ **ἐλθών** aor. part. ἔρχομαι, temporal use of the part. **εἰς** 12
τὴν Τρῳάδα. The article indicates "to the Troas where we had agreed to meet" (BD, 137). (For an excellent article dealing w. the history and geography of Troas as well as the NT references to this important city, s. C.J. Hemer, "Alexandria Troas," TB, 26 [1975], 79–112.) **θύρα** door. Used as a symbol of missionary opportunity. **ἀνεῳγμένης** perf. pass. part. ἀνοίγνυμι to open, perf. pass. "to be standing open." Here was a Roman and cosmopolitan population, reinforced by temporary sojourners suffering in forced delays far from their homes in many parts of the Roman world (Hemer, 103). **ἐν κυρίῳ** "in the Lord." The Lord Christ is both the content of the apostle's message and also the
sphere of his opportunity (Hughes). ■ **ἔσχηκα** perf. ind. act. 13
ἔχω. The perf. may have the idea of an aor. (BD, 177) but Paul may have wished to accent the strain of his anxiety up to the time of the arrival of Titus (RG, 901). **ἄνεσις** relief. **τῷ πνεύματι** "in my spirit," locative use of the dat. Paul writes of his inward distress through anxiousness to hear Titus's report concerning the Corinthians (SBT, 144). **τῷ μὴ εὑρεῖν** aor. act. inf. εὑρίσκω to find, instrumental use of the inf. "by the not finding Titus as to me" (RWP; MT, 142). **ἀποταξάμενος** aor. mid. part. ἀποτάσσω mid. to say good-by, to bid farewell to friends (Plummer). **ἐξῆλθον** aor. ind. act. ἐξέρχομαι to depart.

■ **χάρις** thanks, preceded by the dat. indicating to whom 14
thanks is given. **πάντοτε** always. **θριαμβεύοντι** pres. act. part. θριαμβεύω to lead in a triumph. The picture is the triumphal entry of a military hero into the city of Rome (Lamar Williamson, Jr., "Led in Triumph: Paul's Use of Thriambeuo," *Interpretation*, 22 [July, 1968], 322). The victorious Roman general marched into the city in a long procession preceded by the city magistrates. They were followed by trumpeters, then the spoils taken from the enemy followed by white oxen intended for sacrifice, then the captives headed by the king of the conquered country, then officials of the victorious army and musicians dancing and playing, and at last the general himself in whose

honor the whole wonderful pagent was taking place (s. ELR, 115–118; DGRA, 1163–1167; KP V, 973–975; H.S. Versnel, *Triumphus* [Leiden, 1970]); Rory B. Egan, "Lexical Evidence on Two Pauline Passages," Nov Test, 19 [January, 1977], 22–62). Paul represents himself as one of the victorious general's soldiers sharing in the glory of his triumph (Barrett). **ὀσμή** fragrance, sweet smell. It was customary for the triumphal processions to be accompanied by the release of sweet odors from the burning of spices in the streets (Hughes). **φανεροῦντι** pres. act. part. φανερόω to manifest. The manifestation here is not in
15 the eschatological sense but in the missionary sense. ■ **εὐωδία**
aroma, fragrance. **σῳζομένοις** pres. pass. part. σῴζω to save, to rescue. **ἀπολλυμένοις** pres. pass. part. ἀπόλλυμι to destroy,
16 pass. to perish, to be perishing. ■ **ἐκ θανάτου εἰς θάνατον**
"from death unto death." The rabbis used similar words concerning the law. For some it was a medicine unto healing and to others a medicine unto death (s. SB III, 498; Barrett). **ἱκανος** sufficient, adequate, "who is sufficient for these responsibilities?" What kind of a minister ought he to be who preaches a gospel which may prove fatal to those who come in contact w.
17 it? (Plummer). ■ **οἱ πολλοί** the majority. **καπηλεύω** to peddle,
to pawn off a product for gain. The word is used in the LXX in Isa. 1:22 for those who mix wine w. water in order to cheat the buyers (Plummer). It is used by Plato to condemn the pseudo-philosophers (Windisch). It was used in the papyri for a wine dealer and for the running of a junk store (s. MM; Preisigke). The word refers to those who would peddle or merchandise the Word of God for profit. **ἀλλά**. The repetition of this word gives emphasis in an ascending scale (Plummer). **κατέναντι** before, in the presence of. **ἐν Χριστῷ** in union or fellowship w. Christ.

Ch. 3

1 ■ **ἀρχόμεθα** pres. ind. mid. 1st per. pl. ἄρχομαι to begin.
This is sort of an echo of the supposed criticism (Plummer). **συνιστάνειν** pres. act. inf. συνιστάνω (συνίστημι) to place together, to introduce, to commend. (For the form, s. BD, 46.) **χρῄζω** to need. **συστατικός** recommendation. **ἐπιστολή** letter. Letters of recommendation were generally requests for help and hospitality for aid in seeking employment or instruction based on the virtues of the one introduced and the opportunity of the recipient to express his loyalty to the writer (William Baird, "Letters of Recommendation: A Study of II Corinthians 3:1–3," JBL, 80 [June, 1961], 168f.; for examples, s. LAE, 158;
2 1 Cor. 16:3). ■ **ἐγγεγραμμένη** perf. pass. part. ἐγγράφω to

write in, to inscribe. **καρδίαις ἡμῶν.** A reference to Paul's own heart (Baird) or it refers to both Paul and Timothy. **ἀναγινωσκομένη** pres. pass. part. ἀναγινώσκω to read. The pres. tense indicates continual reading, in an iterat. sense. **ὑπὸ πάντων ἀνθρώπων** "by all men." Paul is not referring to the receiving of the letter but the carrying of it. Like a papyrus roll, it is sealed within him to be revealed to all men when w. open
heart he declares to them the Christian's faith (Baird, 170). ■ 3
φανερούμενοι pres. pass. part. φανερόω to make clear, to manifest. **διακονηθεία** aor. pass. part. fem. διακονέω to serve, to minister to. The verb is often used in the sense of "to deliver a message" (BAG). **μελας** black. The n. of the adj. has the meaning "ink." Ink could be blotted out or washed off (Plummer), instrumental dat. (For the making of ink and the use of ink by the rabbis, s. SB III, 499f.) **ζῶντος** pres. act. part. to live, "the spirit of the living God" was the agent of the Corinthians' conversion (Barrett). **πλάξ** flat stone, tablet. Used in reference to the tablets of the law (BAG). **καρδίαις σαρκίναις** "fleshly hearts." Used in apposition to "tablets." The ending of the adj. "fleshly" denotes the material out of which something is made (s. MH 378).

■ **πεποίθησις** confidence. The substitutive is derived from 4
the perf. of πείθω. The word is emphatic by its position (Meyer).
■ **ἱκανός** sufficient, qualified, capable. **λογίσασθαι** aor. mid. 5
inf. λογίζομαι to consider, to reckon. Used here in its widest sense of carrying on any of the ordinary processes of reasoning (EGT). The inf. expresses either results or is a further explanation of "sufficient." **ἱκανότης** sufficiency, capability. The adj. was sometimes used in the LXX to translate *Shaddai* as the name of God (s. TDNT) and the thought may be "our sufficiency
comes from the Sufficient One" (Plummer). ■ **ἱκάνωσεν** aor. 6
ind. act. ἱκανόω to make sufficient. Verbs w. this ending are usually causal. The verb is followed by the double acc. "as ministers" (s. MT, 246f.). The aor. points to the time when Paul was called to be an apostle (Plummer). **διαθήκη** covenant, agreement (s. Jer. 31:31–34; Matt. 26:28). **γράμμα** that which was written, letter of the alphabet, letter. **ἀποκτεννει** pres. ind. act. to kill. (For the form, s. BAG.) The law demands perf. obedience and pronounces the sentence of death on the disobedient (Hodge; s. also Windisch). **ζῳοποιεῖ** pres. ind. act. to make alive. The indwelling Christ has replaced the old Torah written on tablets of stone and has become a Torah written within (PRJ, 226).

■ **εἰ . . . πῶς οὐχὶ μᾶλλον** (v.8). Paul uses here argument 7

from the greater to the lesser (s. Rom. 5:9). **διακονία τοῦ θανάτου** obj. gen. "a ministry leading to death." **ἐντετυπωμένη** perf. pass. part. *ἐντυπόω* to imprint, to engrave. (For the rabbinical view of the tables engraved in stone, s. SB III, 502–513.) **ἐγενήθη** aor. ind. pass. *γίνομαι* to become, to come into existence, to be. **ἀτενίσαι** aor. act. inf. *ἀτενίζω* to gaze, to look intently. The rabbis felt that the shining of Moses' face was either from the glory of the Lord or from the writing of the law or from the tablets of the law or from Moses' position as mediator or even from Moses' humility (s. SB III, 513–516). **καταργουμένην** pres. pass. part. *καταργέω* to render inoperative, to make of no effect, to do away w., to abolish. The pres. part. indicates the continual action which was taking place at that time. The glory was very splendid but it was very transit
8 (Plummer). ■ **μᾶλλον** comp. of the adv. *μάλα* "rather," "even more." It introduces the conclusion of the argument started in v.7. **ἔσται** fut. *εἰμί*. This is a logical, not a chronological fut.
9 (Barrett). ■ **κατάκρισις** condemnation, a judgment against someone. **περισσεύω** to abound, followed by the dat. which
10 indicates the area in which the abundance is found. ■ **καὶ γάρ** "for even." A more precise grounding of the previous statement (Meyer). **δεδόξασται** perf. ind. pass. *δοξάζω* to think well of, to glorify, pass. to be made glorious. **δεδοξασμένον** perf. pass. part. **μέρος** part. **ἐν τούτῳ τῷ μέρει** 'in this part," "in respect to." **ἕνεκεν** = *ἕνεκα* w. the gen. "because of," "on account of." **ὑπερβαλλούσης** pres. act. part. fem. *ὑπερβάλλω* to go above and beyond, to surpass, pres. part. surpassing, extraordinary,
11 outstanding (BAG). ■ **εἰ γάρ** "for if," a continuation of the explanation and support of his argument. **μένον** pres. act. part. n. sing. *μένω* "that which remains." The pres. tense emphasizes the continual existence in contrast to that which is passing away.
12 ■ **ἔχοντες** pres. act. part. *ἔχω*. **παρρησία** lit. "speaking all" then "speaking openly" and then the further developed meaning "boldness," "courage," "great freedom" (s. Barrett; TDNT; Windisch). **χρώμεθα** pres. mid. subj. *χράομαι* to make use of, to use, followed by the dat. hortatory subj. "let us make
13 use of." ■ **καὶ οὐ**. Introduces an abbreviated main clause "we do not do as" (s. BD, 255). **ἐτίθει** impf. ind. act. **τίθημι** to place, customary impf. "used to place" (RWP). **κάλυμμα** that which covers, veil. **πρός** followed by the inf. indicates purpose "w. a view to" (s. MT, 144). **ἀτενίσαι** aor. act. inf. s.v.7. **εἰς τὸ τέλος** "unto the end." They should not see the disappearing of the glory on Moses' face and recognize that his service was coming
14 to an end (Schlatter). ■ **ἐπωρώθη** aor. ind. pass. *πωρόω* to

harden, to make insensitive, to cover w. thick skin, to petrify
(RWP). **νόημα** mind. Here the word means "the thinking faculty" (Plummer). **ἀνάγνωσις** reading. A reference to the public
reading of the law. (For the reading of the Scriptures in the
synagogue, s. JPF II, 927–933; SB IV, 154–165.) **παλαιός** old.
ἀνακαλυπτόμενον pres. pass. part. ἀνακαλύπτω to unveil, to
reveal. The part. refers to the veil which is not lifted. The whole
sentence illustrates the deep tragedy of Judaism. They hold the
law high and read it in their worship services and they do not
see that it is the document which only pronounces their condemnation (Windisch). **ὅτι** because. **καταργεῖται** pres. pass.
καταργέω to render inoperative, to do away w. (s.v.6, 7). ■ 15
ἡνίκα when followed by **ἄν** w. the subj. introducing an indefinite temporal clause "whenever" (RWP; BD, 237).
ἀναγινώσκηται pres. pass. subj. ἀναγινώσκω to read, to read
aloud. **ἐπὶ τὴν καρδίαν** "upon their heart." The heart is viewed
as the center of man's being, the spring of will and activity, the
seat of the affections and the understanding (Hughes). **κεῖται**
pres. ind. mid. to lie. ■ **ἐπιστρέψῃ** aor. pass. subj. ἐπιστρέφω 16
to turn, mid. and pass. to turn one's self. The prep. in compound
is directive "to turn to." The word gives a graphic parallel to the
account in Exod. 34 where Moses turned from the people and
went in before the Lord, thereupon removing the veil from his
face. The word also involves a deeper significance, for it is used
for the act of turning to the Lord and here involves the experience of evangelical conversion (Hughes). **περιαιρεῖται** pres.
pass. περιαιρέω to take away, to take away from around. The
compound verb expresses the removing of something which envelops (Plummer), but the prep. may be intensive, i.e. "to
remove completely" (MH, 321; s. also Hughes). ■ **οὗ** rel. pron. 17
"where." **ἐλευθερία** freedom, liberty, the end of the dominance
of the written law means liberty (Barrett; s. also CBB; TDNT).
■ **πάντες** "all." This stands in contrast to Moses and the old 18
covenant. **ἀνακεκαλυμμένῳ** perf. pass. part., s.v.14. The perf.
indicates the continual state resulting from a previous action.
The veil, once lifted, remains lifted (Hughes).
κατοπτριζόμενοι pres. mid. part. κατοπτρίζω act. "to produce a reflection," mid. "to look at one's self in a mirror." Here
"to look at something as in a mirror, to contemplate something"
(BAG). The pres. part. shows that the beholding is continuous
and free from interruption (Hughes). **μεταμορφούμεθα** pres.
ind. pass. μεταμορφέω to transform, to change the inward reality to something else (Trench, *Synonyms*, 264; TDNT; Plummer). **ἀπὸ δόξης εἰς δόξαν** "from glory unto glory." Christians

seeing in Jesus the image of God, are not deified but are transformed into the same image; the glory they share w. Him ever increasing from one stage of glory to a higher stage (Barrett). **κυρίου πνεύματος** "from the Lord of the Spirit," i.e., from the Lord who sends the Spirit or it may be taken to mean "of the Lord who is Spirit." (For the varying interpretations of this phrase, s. Hughes.)

Ch. 4

1 ■ **διὰ τοῦτο** "because of this." This is either reference to the preceding, i.e., because the gospel is good news of the glory of God or it looks forward, i.e., because of what is said in the next clause (Barrett). **ἔχοντες** pres. act. part. ἔχω to have, to possess. **καθώς** just as, in accordance w. **ἠλεήθημεν** aor. ind. pass. ἐλεέω to show mercy, pass. to be shown mercy, to obtain mercy. Mercy indicates the compassionate removal of misery (s. Trench, *Synonyms*, 169; TDNT; CBB). **ἐγκακοῦμεν** pres. ind. act. 1st per. pl. to give into evil, to lose courage. It is the faint-hearted coward (RWP). The word is also used in the papyri in
2 the sense of treating someone badly (Preisigke). ■ **ἀπειπάμεθα** aor. ind. mid. ἀπειπάμην (ἀπολέγομαι) to speak forth, to speak off or away from, to renounce (RWP). The aor. is timeless and does not mean that he had previously practiced what he says that he has renounced (Plummer). **κρυπτός** hidden. **αἰσχύνη** shame. Τὰ κρυπτὰ τῆς αἰσχύνης "the hidden things of shame," i.e., the things one hides because one is ashamed of them (Lietzmann; for a discussion of the various views of this phrase, s. Bultmann). **περιπατοῦντες** pres. act. part. to walk, to conduct one's life. **πανουργία** (πᾶν ἔργον) readiness to do anything. In an unfavorable sense, it has the meaning "cunning, craftiness, trickery." The man who practices this is ready to do anything, up to every trick (Hughes; TDNT). **δολοῦντες** pres. act. part. δολόω to use deceit, to use bait, to ensnare, to corrupt w. error, to falsify, to corrupt (RWP; T; Trench, *Synonyms*, 228–231). **φανέρωσις** openness, clearness, manifestation. The word is selected in opposition to "the hidden things of shame" (Plummer). **συνιστάνοντες** pres. act. part. (s. 2 Cor. 3:1).
3 **συνείδησις** conscience (s. Rom. 2:15). ■ **εἰ** w. the ind. assumes the reality of the condition. **καί** even, i.e., "even if." With this construction there is sometimes a tone of contempt and the matter is belittled (RG, 1026). **κεκαλυμμένον** perf. pass. part. καλύπτω to veil, to hide. The perf. looks at the state or circumstance and is used w. an adj. (IBG, 18). **ἀπολλυμένοις** pres. pass. part. ἀπόλλυμι to ruin, pass. to perish, to be lost. The

durative verb is perfective and indicates the inevitable doom and the fact that the goal is ideally reached. A complete transformation of its subjects is required to bring them out of the ruin
implicit in their state (M, 114f.). ■ **αἰών** age. It refers to all that 4
floating mass of thoughts, opinions, maxims, speculations, hopes, impulses, aims, aspirations at any time current in the world (Trench; *Synonyms*, 217f.; s. also TDNT). **ἐτύφλωσεν** aor. ind. act. τυφλόω to blind. **νόημα** thought, thinking, the ability to reason (s. 2 Cor. 2:11; 3:14). **ἄπιστος** unbelieving. The fault that leads to their destruction is their own (Barrett). **εἰς τό** w. the inf. can express either purpose or results (s. IBG, 143). **αὐγάσαι** aor. act. inf. αὐγάζω. The verb has two meanings (1) to see distinctly or to gaze upon (2) to illumine or beam upon and is used in Lev. 13 and 14 w. the meaning "to appear bright" (Hughes). **φωτισμός** illumination followed by the gen. of origin "light from the gospel" (MT, 218). **εἰκών** image, the resemblence of something to a prototype from which it is derived and in whose essence it shares. Christ shares in God's real being and is a perfect manifestation of that being (Hughes; s. also TDNT;
CBB). ■ **κύριον** double acc., i.e., "Christ Jesus as Lord." ■ **ὅτι** 5/6
"because." This explains why they must preach Christ and not themselves (Plummer). **ὁ θεός** the Creator of the old creation is also the Creator of the new creation. **λάμψει** fut. ind. act. λάμπω to shine, to shine forth (s. TDNT). The fut. used to express a command is a translation of the Heb. jussive (s. BD, 183; BG, 94). **φωτισμός** illumination, enlightenment followed by the gen. of origin or subj. gen., i.e., "the illumining which the knowledge of the glory produces" (Plummer). **πρόσωπον** face, countenance, per. (BG, 184).

■ **θησαυρός** treasure, that which is valuable and expensive. 7
ὀστράκινος made of clay, earthenware, pottery. Corinthian pottery was well-known in the ancient world (Strabo, *Geography* VIII, 6.23) and Paul may have been referring to the small pottery lamps which were cheap and fragile or he may have referred to earthenware vases or urns. The point seems to be that the valuable treasure is contained in weak, fragile, and valueless containers (s. Hughes; SB III, 516). The ending of the word signifies material out of which something was made (MH, 359). **σκεῦος** vessel. **ὑπερβολή** excess, abundance, extraordinary quality of character (BAG). **ᾖ** pres. subj. εἰμί. The particle w. the subj. generally indicates purpose but here it may have a causal idea
(BG, 140–141). ■ **θλιβόμενοι** pres. pass. part. θλίβω to subject 8
to pressure, to afflict, that which presses upon or burdens the spirit (Trench; *Synonyms*, 202; TDNT). **στενοχωρούμενοι**

pres. pass. part. *στενοχωρέω* to pressure into a narrow place. It speaks of the narrowness of room, confined space, and then painfulness of which this is the occasion (Trench; *Synonyms*, 203; TDNT). **ἀπορούμενοι** pres. mid. part. *ἀπορέω* to be at a loss, to be in doubt, to be perplexed, to be despondent. In the papyri it was used of one who was ruined by creditors and was at his wits end (MM). **ἐξαπορούμενοι** pres. mid. part. *ἐξαπορέομαι* to be completely baffled (Barrett). The prep. in compound is perfective and shows the despondency in its final
9 result of despair (M, 237). ■ **διωκόμενοι** pres. pass. part. *διώκω* to hunt, to hunt down like an animal, to persecute. **ἐγκαταλειπόμενοι** pres. pass. part. *ἐγκαταλείπω* to desert, to abandon one in difficulty. The word occurs in the LXX in God's promises not to forsake His own (Deut. 31:6–8; Joshua 1:5; 1 Chron. 28:20; Ps. 36:25; 28; s. also Plummer, Bultmann). **καταβαλλόμενοι** pres. pass. part. *καταβάλλω* to throw down, to knock down, to strike down w. force. The word was used of throwing an opponent down in wrestling (Windisch) or of striking someone down w. a sword or another weapon (Plummer). **ἀπολλύμενοι** pres. mid. or pass. part. *ἀπόλλυμι* to destroy, to perish. The parts. used in this passage are either to be connected w. the verb "we have" in v.7 or they are to be considered exam-
10 ples of abs. part. standing here for the ind. (s. Hughes). ■ **πάντοτε** always. **νέκρωσις** dying, the process of dying (Hughes), slaying, putting to death. It refers to Paul's constant exposure to death (Hodge). **περιφέροντες** pres. act. part. to carry about, to bear about. The pres. tense emphasizes the continual action. The missionaries were perpetually being delivered to death for Christ's sake. They were never free from peril (Plummer). **φανερωθῇ** aor. pass. subj. *φανερόω* to make clear, to manifest. The subj. is used w. the particle to express purpose.
11 ■ **ἀεί** always. **γάρ** for. The particle gives an explanation of the preceding. **ζῶντες** pres. act. part. *ζάω* to live, "the living," "we are ever a living prey" (Plummer). **παραδιδόμεθα** pres. ind. pass. *παραδίδωμι* to deliver over, to hand over. The pres. tense emphasizes the continual danger that is faced. **διά** w. acc. "because." **θνητός** mortal, subject to death. It emphasizes the
12 material, weakness, and transitoriness of the body (Meyer). ■ **ὥστε** therefore. It is used here as an inferential particle meaning "and so, accordingly" (IBG, 144). **ἐνεργεῖται** pres. ind. mid.
13 *ἐνεργέω* to work, to be at work. ■ **τὸ αὐτὸ πνεῦμα τῆς πίστεως** "the same spirit" followed by the obj. gen. i.e., the spirit who engenders faith (Barrett). **γεγραμμένον** perf. pass. part. *γράφω* to write, perf. "that which stands written." It refers

to an authoritative document (s. MM; BS, 250). **ἐπίστευσα** aor. ind. act. πιστεύω to believe. Paul quotes Ps. 116:10 as rendered in the LXX (s. Hughes). **ἐλάλησα** aor. ind. act. λαλέω to speak.
■ **εἰδότες** perf. part. οἶδα defective perf. w. pres. meaning "to 14
know." The verb expresses knowledge grasped directly or intuitively by the mind (s. Donald W. Burdick, "**οἶδα** and **γινώσκω** in the Pauline Epistles," ND, 344–356). **ἐγείρας** aor. act. part. ἐγείρω to raise up. **ἐγερεῖ** fut. ind. act. ἐγείρω. **παραστήσει** fut. ind. act. παρίστημι to present, to cause to stand in the presence of someone (Hughes), to present as a bride is presented
to the bridegroom (Plummer). ■ **πλεονάσασα** aor. act. part. 15
fem. sing. πλεονάζω to make more through the more, to expand, to become more, to increase. Perhaps the idea is "the increasing numbers" (IBG, 108). **πλείων** comp. πολύς, **οἱ** πλ the majority, the many. **εὐχαριστία** thanksgiving. The acc. is the object of the verb **περισσεύσῃ**. **περισσεύσῃ** aor. act. subj. **περισσεύω** to increase, to cause to abound, to make extremely rich (BAG).

■ **διό** wherefore. **ἐγκακοῦμεν** pres. ind. act. to lose courage 16
(s.v.1). **ἀλλ᾽εἰ** w. ind. introduces a condition assumed to be true. **ἔξω** outward w. the article "the external." **ἡμῶν** poss. gen. (For the position of the pron., s. BD, 148.) **διαφθείρεται** pres. ind. pass. to decay. The pres. tense pictures the process of continual decay. **ἔσω** inward w. the article "the inward." **ἀνκαινοῦνται** pres. ind. pass. ἀνακαινόω to renew again. The pres. tense
emphasizes the continual renewal. ■ **παραυτίκα** momentary. It 17
indicates a short amount of pres. time including the idea temporary i.e., till life ends or the Lord comes (Plummer; Windisch). **ἔλαφρός** light, not heavy (s. Matt. 11:30). Affliction for Jesus' sake however crushing it may seem, is in fact light, a weightless trifle (Hughes). **θλῖψις** pressure, tribulation, affliction. **ὑπερβολή** excess (s.v.7.) **εἰς ὑπερβολήν** for or to excess. The two phrases form a double expression which cannot lit. be translated. The meaning is "out of all proportion" (Barrett). **βάρος** weight. Paul's choice of the expression "the weight of glory" may be influenced from the fact that in Heb. "weight" and "glory" come from the same root (Bruce). **κατεργάζεται** pres. ind. mid. to produce, to accomplish and it implies a prolonged
process, a working out (Plummer). ■ **σκοπούντων** pres. act. 18
part. σκοπέω to fix one's gaze upon, to concentrate one's attention upon. The part. is used as a gen. abs. (Hughes). **βλεπόμενα** pres. pass. part. The part. is used as an adj. "the things being seen," i.e., "visible things." **πρόσκαιρος** for a time, temporary.

Ch. 5

1 ■ ***οἶδα*** defective perf. w. a pres. meaning to know (s. 2 Cor.
4:14). ***ἐπίγειος*** upon the earth, earthly. Death involves the loss,
not only of physical corporeality but also of earthly corporate-
ness (M.J. Harris, ND, 319). ***σκῆνος*** tent, gen. of apposition
"our earthly tent-dwelling," "the tent which forms our earthly
house" (Harris, ND, 318). The figure of a tent picturing the
human body suggests impermanence and insecurity and is a
common picture of earthly life and its setting in the body (Barrett). From a Jewish point of view the tent could be a reference
to the Feast of Tabernacles picturing that the Christian would
have to live in a booth before reaching the promised land (PRJ,
313). (For other references to the figure of the tent, s. Windisch;
Harris, ND, 318.) ***καταλυθῇ*** aor. pass. subj. *καταλύω* to destroy. In reference to the tent metaphor it describes the act of
dismantling a tent (Hughes). ***οἰκοδομή*** house, building. ***ἐκ θεοῦ***
"from God." The phrase indicates the source of the building as
contrasted w. the earthly tent. ***ἔχω*** to have, to possess. (For the
pres. tense w. the meaning "to possess," s. M 110.)
ἀχειροποίητος verbal adj. (*χείρ*, hand, *ποιέω*, to make), not
made w. hands, not handmade, i.e., not of this creation
(Hughes), supernatural, spiritual (Plummer). ***αἰώνιος*** eternal,
everlasting, not in the sense of pre-existent but it indicates in-
2 definite durability (Plummer). ■ ***καὶ γάρ*** "for even," "yes,
even" (s. BD, 326). ***στενάζομεν*** pres. ind. act. to sigh, to groan
because of an undesirable circumstance (BAG). The pres. tense
emphasizes the continual groaning in this life. ***οἰκητήριον*** a
place of living. It denotes a permanent abode or home (s. Jude
6) (Plummer). ***ἐπενδύσασθαι*** aor. mid. inf. *ἐπενδύομαι* to put
3 on over, to put on upon one's self (RWP). ■ ***εἴ γε*** "of course if"
"if, indeed" (Hughes; IBG, 165). ***ἐνδυσάμενοι*** aor. mid. part.
ἐνδύομαι to put on, to be clothed. (For the variant reading "to
be unclothed," s. TC, 579f.) ***γυμνός*** naked, unclothed.
εὑρεθησόμεθα fut. ind. pass. *εὑρίσκω* to find, pass. to be
found, to be discovered. Paul's desire not to be found naked
reveals not only a characteristically Jewish horror of nakedness,
but also that he does not use it in its normal Hellenistic sense
4 (Barrett). ■ ***καὶ γάρ*** s.v.2. ***ὄντες*** pres. part. *εἰμί*. The part. w.
the article indicates the group to which the subject belongs—"we
who are in the tent," i.e., the earthly body (Barrett).
βαρούμενοι pres. pass. part. *βαρέω* to make heavy, to burden,
to weigh down. The part. is used adverbially "we groan as
weighted down," since we are under a constant depressing burden (Lenski). ***ἐφ' ᾧ = ἐπὶ τούτῳ ὅτι*** "in view of the fact that"

(M, 107) "because" (MT, 272). **ἐκδύσασθαι** aor. mid. inf. ἐκδύομαι to take off, to be unclothed. **καταποθῇ** aor. pass. subj. καταπίνω to drink down, to swallow down, pass. to be swallowed up. **θνητός** that which is mortal. It refers to our entire mortal existence (Lenski). The ending of the verbal adj. indicates "libel to death" (RG, 1097; s. also BD, 36). ■ **κατεργασάμενος** 5
aor. mid. part. κατεργάζομαι to produce, to prepare, to produce a condition or atmosphere, to prepare one for a circumstance (Windisch). **εἰς αὐτὸ τοῦτο** "for this very purpose." **θεός** God. The word here is in a position of emphasis (Hughes). **δούς** aor. act. part. δίδωμι to give. **ἀρραβών** earnest, down payment (s. 2 Cor. 1:22; s. also MM).

■ **θαρροῦντες** pres. act. part. θαρρέω to be of good cheer, 6
to be of good courage, to be confident. The part. is in anacolouthon, a break in the sentence structure, and the sentence begins again in v.8 (Barrett). **πάντοτε** always esp. in view of death. **εἰδότες** perf. act. part. οἶδα (s. 2 Cor. 4:14). **ἐνδημοῦντες** pres. act. part. ἐνδημέω to be at home, to be one among his own people, to live in a place (s. RWP). **ἐκδημοῦμεν ἀπὸ** pres. ind. act. to be gone, to be away from home, to be abroad, to immigrate (Hughes). (For the use of the words "be at home" and "to be abroad," "to be away from home," s. MM; Preisigke.) ■ 7
περιπατοῦμεν pres. ind. act. to walk, to conduct one's life. **εἶδος** appearance. The word refers to the thing seen, the form or an appearance of an object (Hughes), "we conduct our lives on the basis of faith, not the appearance of things" (Barrett).
■ **εὐδοκοῦμεν** pres. ind. act. to be well-pleased, to consent, here 8
"we wish rather," "we prefer" (BAG). **ἐκδημῆσαι** aor. act. inf. (s.v.6). ■ **φιλοτιμούμεθα** pres. ind. mid. to love, honor, then to 9
be ambitious, to devote one's self zealously to a cause, to be ambitious (s. Hughes). **εὐάρεστος** pleasing. The word is used in Titus 2:9 of slaves who give satisfaction to their masters (BAG).
■ **πάντας** all. Used w. the article it means here "the sum total 10
of us" (MT, 201; s. also BG, 61). **φανερωθῆναι** aor. pass. inf. φανερόω to make clear, to manifest, pass. to be made manifest. They not only have to appear, but have to have their whole character made manifest (Plummer). **δεῖ** it is necessary. **ἔμπροσθεν** w. the gen. "before." **βῆμα** step, platform, tribunal. This was a tribunal where official decisions were given (RAC II, 129–130; for a good description of the "judgment seat" found at the city of Corinth, s. IB I, 683–684). The word was also used in the papyri in the official sense "tribunal, judgment seat" (MM). **κομίσηται** aor. mid. subj. κομίζω to bring, mid. to carry off, to get for one's self, to receive, to receive as recompense

(BAG). In the NT the mid. has the meaning "to receive back" or "to receive what is one's own" (Hughes; s. also MM). **τὰ διὰ τοῦ σώματος** "the things (done) through the body." The phrase expresses personal agency in which the body acts as the subject of the doing (SBT, 187). This gives the body its positive meaning for eternity (Schlatter). **ἔπραξεν** aor. ind. act. **πράσσω** to do. The aor. pictures the whole life of the individual Christian as seen as a unity. With the prep. the phrase means "w. reference to what he did" (Hughes). **φαῦλος** worthless, bad, of no account, good-for-nothingness. The word indicates the impossibility of any true gain ever coming forth from it, and the notion of worthlessness is the central notion (Trench, *Synonyms*, 317).

11 ■ **εἰδότες** perf. act. part. **οἶδα** defective perf. w. pres. meaning to know (s. 2 Cor. 4:14). **φόβος τοῦ κυρίου** "fear of the Lord." The fear excited by the thought of standing before the judgment seat of Christ and having one's whole life exposed and estimated (Plummer). The gen. is obj. gen. **πείθομεν** pres. ind. act. to persuade. The pres. tense may be conative, "we try to persuade" (Barrett; SMT, 8). **συνείδησις** conscience (s. Rom. 2:15). **πεφανερῶσθαι** perf. pass. inf. (s.v.10). The perf. indicates Paul's true and integral self has been and continues to be
12 manifested in the conscience of the Corinthians (Hughes). ■
συνιστάνομεν pres. ind. act. to commend (s. 2 Cor. 3:1). **ἀφορμή** occasion, basis of operation, a place to start from (Plummer). In the papyri the word was used w. the meanings "incitement" or "prompting," "occasion" or "opportunity" (s. MM). **διδόντες** pres. act. part. **δίδωμι**. A circumstantial part. to be translated as a main verb. Paul is fond of continuing a construction begun w. a finite verb by means of coordinated part. (BD, 245; IBG, 179; MT, Style 89). **καύχημα** a boast, the ground or matter of glorying (AS). **ἔχητε** pres. act. subj. **ἔχω**. The meaning is "in order that you may have a refutation of those who glory in appearance and not in heart" (Hughes). The subj.
13 is used to express purpose. ■ **ἐξέστημεν** aor. ind. act. **ἐξίστημι**
to stand out of one's self, to be beside one's self. The word indicates mental imbalance (s. Windisch). **θεῷ** dat. of advantage. **σωφρονοῦμεν** pres. ind. act. to be sane, to be sensible, to be in control of one's facilities (s. TDNT; Trench, *Synonyms*, 69–72). (For an example of a heathen prophetess who did not utter her prophecies in wild ecstasy but in self-control and moderation, s.
14 DC I, 56.) ■ **ἀγάπη τοῦ Χριστοῦ** either obj. gen., i.e. "Paul's
love for Christ" or subj. gen. "Christ's love for Paul." It is perhaps best taken as subj. gen. indicating the love which originates or ends w. God in Christ, i.e. Christ's love for him which is prior

to and the explanation of his love for Christ (Hughes; s. also
Barrett; RG, 499). **συνέχει** pres. ind. act. to hold together, to
press together, to constrain. The verb implies the pressure which
confines and restricts as well as controls (Plummer; Barrett). The
pres. tense indicates the continual habit of life. **κρίναντας** aor.
act. part. κρίνω to judge, to decide. The aor. may be perfective
aor. indicating the judgment or decision which Paul had come
to. The word points to a judgment formed in the past perhaps at
or soon after his conversion (Hughes). **ἀπέθανεν, ἀπέθανον**
aor. ind. act. ἀποθνήσκω to die. **ἄρα** therefore, "that means
that" (Barrett; s. also BD, 235). **οἱ πάντες** all w. the article the
word denotes the class named is taken as a whole, i.e. "the sum
total of all" (s. BG, 61; MT, 201). ■ **ζῶντες** pres. act. part. ζάω 15
to live. **μηκέτι** = οὔκετι no longer. **ἑαυτοῖς** reflex. pron. 3rd-
per. pl. dat. of advantage "to live for the advantage of one's self."
ζῶσιν pres. act. subj. Subjunctive used to express purpose.
ἀποθανόντι aor. act. part. dat. of advantage or personal interest. **ἐγερθέντι** aor. pass. part. ἐγείρω to raise, pass. to be raised.
■ **ὥστε** wherefore. The word is used to draw a conclusion. 16
κατά w. acc. "according to," "according to the standard of."
Both prep. phrases "according to the flesh" in this v. are to be
taken w. the verbs and not w. the nouns. It is fleshly knowledge
that Paul repudiates (Barrett). **εἰ καί** "even if." The words introduce a condition assumed to be true. It indicates that Paul and
others really did have a fleshly knowledge of Christ (s. John W.
Fraser, "Paul's Knowledge of Jesus: II Cor. 5:16 Once More,"
NTS, 17 [April, 1971], 300). **ἐγνώκαμεν** perf. ind. act.
γινώσκω to know. Personal acquaintance of "others" is not
what is meant here. Paul has a way of looking at, regarding,
understanding Christ; now he has a new way of understanding
others, including Christ (Fraser, 299). (For arguments showing
that Paul was not denying knowledge of the historical Jesus, s.
Barrett; JNP, 89ff.; Hughes.) **νῦν οὐκετι** "now no longer." This
does not mean that Paul had no interest in the historical Jesus,
His example, teaching and the traditions about Him. He knew
about Jesus. The basic meaning is that Paul had a new, fuller
understanding of the "whole Christ" by the Spirit and by faith;
and he sees others in a new way according to their standing w.
Him, in the "new creation" (Fraser, 312). ■ **ὥστε** wherefore. 17
Paul draws a second conclusion. **κτίσις** creation. The one who
is in Christ and has experienced the new birth is a part of the new
creation. The rabbis used the term "new creature" to describe
those whose sins had been forgiven (s. SB II, 415; III, 519; for
further parallels w. rabbinic teaching regarding the new creation,

s. PRJ, 119ff.). **ἀρχαῖος** old, that which comes from an earlier
time. **παρῆλθεν** aor. ind. act. παρέρχομαι to go by, to pass
away. The aor. is perfective and points to the finality. **γέγονεν**
perf. ind. act. γίνομαι. The perf. indicates the continuing state
or condition (s. McKay). (For a discussion of the new life in
18 Christ, s. Ladd, 479f.) ■ **καταλλάξαντος** aor. act. part.
καταλλάσσω to effect a change, to exchange, to reconcile. The
prep. in compound is perfective "to effect a thorough change
back" (s. MH, 298). Reconciliation indicates that Christ's death
removed God's enmity against man (s. APC, 186–223; TDNT;
CBB). **δόντος** aor. act. part. δίδωμι to give. **καταλλαγή** reconciliation, gen. of description. It refers to the office and duty of
19 announcing this reconciliation (Hodge). ■ **ὡς ὅτι** "namely, that
. . ." "how that . . . ." The force of the words is declarative of
what has immediately preceded (Hughes; Alford; s. also RG,
1033). **κόσμος** world, world of human beings. The acc. is the
direct object of the part. It is the world God reconciles.
καταλλάσσων pres. act. part. The part. may be taken as part
of a periphrastic impf. (Barrett; MT, 88). **λογιζόμενος** pres.
mid. part. λογίζομαι to place to one's account, to reckon. A
formula used in rabbinic writing (s. SB III, 121f.) and a common
formula in the papyri in the commercial sense of putting down
to one's account (s. MM; Preisigke). **αὐτοῖς** "against them" dat.
of disadvantage. The pl. pron. takes up the phrase "the world"
(Barrett). **παράπτωμα** transgression, a false step, blunders (s.
Trench; *Synonyms*, 245f.; TDNT). **θέμενος** aor. mid. part.
20 τίθημι to place, to put. ■ **ὑπέρ** on behalf of, representing. Perhaps the prep. also has the idea of "in place of" (Hughes).
πρεσβεύω to be an ambassador, to carry out the office of an
ambassador. (For verbs w. this ending marking the exercise of
a profession, s. MH, 398.) This was the regular word in the Gr.
east for the emperor's legate (s. MM; TDNT; LAE, 378; Windisch). **ὡς.** Followed by the gen. abs. it always gives a subj. view
of that which is stated by the gen. abs. The statement is correct.
It may be translated "seeing that" (Plummer). **παρακαλοῦντος**
pres. act. part. παρακαλέω to urge, to ask, to entreat. **δεόμεθα**
pres. ind. mid. to ask, to request, to ask for a specific thing. The
pres. tense indicates the continual or habitual action.
καταλλάγητε aor. pass. imp. ingressive aor. "become recon-
21 ciled to God" (Plummer). ■ **γνόντα** aor. act. part. γινώσκω to
know. It expresses knowledge gained by experience (s. D.W.
Burdick, ND, 344ff.). The part. could be used in a concessive
sense "although he knew no sin." **ἁμαρτίαν . . . ἐποίησεν** "he
made to be sin." The reference may be an allusion to the scape-

goat at the Day of Atonement (Windisch) or it may refer to the suffering servant of Isa. 53 w. the idea of sacrifice prominent (s. Bruce). God placed our sins on the sinless Jesus and as our substitute in our place God punished Him w. death (Lietzmann). **γενώμεθα** aor. mid. subj. γίνομαι to become. **δικαιοσύνη** "the righteousness of God." This is the righteousness both that God requires and that He provides in justification. Paul relates being "in Christ" to justification (s. GW, 141f.).

Ch. 6

■ **συνεργοῦντες** pres. act. part. συνεργέω to work w. 1
someone, to cooperate, to work together. The complement to be
supplied after "working w." can only be God (Barrett). The part.
can be taken as causal. **παρακαλοῦμεν** pres. ind. act. to encourage, to exhort, followed by the acc. w. the inf. **κενός** empty,
without results, in vain. **δέξασθαι** aor. mid. inf. δέχομαι to
receive. The aor. may point to the time of conversion and Paul
exhorts them not to have accepted the grace of God in vain, i.e.
not to show by their behavior now that they accepted it then to
no profit (Plummer). The fear is not that they would lose their
salvation but that they would not effectively carry out the ministry of reconciliation which had been committed to them (compare 2 Cor. 5:18). ■ **λέγει** pres. ind. act. It is used without a 2
stated subject and it may mean either "He (God) says," or "it
(Scripture) says" (Hughes). **δεκτός** (verbal adj. δέχομαι) acceptable, welcome, favorable (BAG). **ἐπήκουσα** aor. ind. act.
ἐπακούω to listen to, to hear. It is a technical term for hearing
prayer (Barrett). **ἐβοήθησα** aor. ind. act. βοηθέω to help.
εὐπρόσδεκτος easily acceptable, pleasant, welcome. Used of a
time which is favorable for bringing God's grace to fruition
(BAG). **σωτηρία** salvation. The gen. in the phrase "day of
salvation" could be gen. of direction or purpose (BD, 92), i.e. "a
day for salvation," "a day for the proclamation of salvation." It
would then refer again to the fulfilling of the ministry of reconciliation (s. 2 Cor. 5:18). ■ **μηδεμίαν** fem. acc. sing. μηδείς, 3
μία, έν no. A strengthened form used w. another neg. w. the
meaning "no (offense) at all" (BAG). **διδόντες** pres. act. part.
δίδωμι to give. The pres. tense points to the habitual, continual
action. **προσκοπή** a striking against, an occasion of stumbling,
to do something which causes others to stumble (T). It indicates
the causing of the foot to strike and the person to stumble (Lenski). **μωμηθῇ** aor. pass. subj. μωμάομαι to find a defect, to find
fault w., to blame someone (s. Windisch). The word often implies
ridicule as well as blame, w. disgrace as a result (Plummer). The

4 subj. is used to express purpose. ■ **ἐν παντί** "in everything," "in
every way." **συνιστάνοντες** pres. act. part. συνιστάνω
(συνίστημι) to bring together, to recommend, to commend (s.
2 Cor. 3:1). **θεοῦ διάκονοι** "as ministers of God." The nom.
means "as God's servants we commend ourselves" (s. RG, 454).
The word emphasizes the personal service rendered to another
(s. TDNT; CBB). **θλίψις** pressure, affliction (s. 2 Cor. 1:4).
ἀνάγκη necessity, anguish. Here it is used in the sense of suffering, quite possibly it means "tortures" (Barrett). **στενοχωρία**
narrow space, "tight places" (RWP), distress (s. 2 Cor. 4:8).
5 ■ **πληγή** stripe, wound. **ἀκαταστασία** instability, often from
politics (RWP), disorders. These things consist of troubles inflicted by men (Plummer). **κόπος** work, labor. The word implies
toil unto fatigue, the weariness which follows on the straining of
all his powers to the utmost (s. Trench; *Synonyms*, 379).
ἀγρυπνία without sleep, sleeplessness. It refers to the times
when Paul voluntarily went without sleep or shortened his hours
of rest in order to devote more time to his evangelical work, to
his care of all the churches, and to prayer (Hughes). **νηστεία**
fasting, the voluntary foregoing of food in order to get more
work done (Plummer). This triplet consists of those troubles
which Paul took upon himself in the prosecution of his mission
6 (Plummer). ■ **ἁγνότης** purity. The word probably refers to purity of life and motive in the comprehensive sense (Hughes), perhaps in the sense of "innocence" (Barrett). **γνῶσις** knowledge.
μακροθυμία longsuffering, patience. It describes the steadfast
spirit which will never give in, which can endure delay and bear
suffering and is used of God's patience toward sinful men and
of the attitude which Christians are to display (NTW, 83–85;
TDNT). It refers to a long holding out of the mind before it gives
room to action or passion—generally to passion (Trench; *Synonyms*, 196). **χρηστότης** usefulness, kindness. **ἀνυπόκριτος**
without hypocrisy, love that is not entirely geniune, i.e. admixed
w. insincerity or self-seeking (Hughes). (For the prefix used to
7 negate the word, s. Moorhouse, 47ff.) ■ **διά** w. gen. "through,"
"w." **ὅπλα** used only in the pl. "weapons." Followed by the gen.
δικαιοσύνης which refers either to the weapons provided by
righteousness, i.e. subj. gen. or to the weapons used in the defense of righteousness (s. Windisch; s. also MRP, 161). **δεξιός**
right, "for the right hand." **ἀριστερός** left, "for the left hand,"
i.e. "right hand and left hand weapons," offensive and defensive
8 armor, the shield being carried on the left arm (Plummer). ■
ἀτιμία dishonor, disgrace. **δυσφημία** slander, evil report.
9 **εὐφημία** praise, good report. **πλάνος** deceiver. ■ **ἀγνοούμενοι**

pres. pass. part. *ἀγνοέω* to be ignorant, pass. to be unknown. It refers to "being non-entities, not worth knowing," without proper credentials (Plummer). They did not receive recognition in the world of their day because the world, the literature, politics, and scholarship took no notice of them and they were not the source of daily conversation and were not sought out as great orators (Windisch). ***ἐπιγινωσκόμενοι*** pres. pass. part. *ἐπιγινώσκω* to recognize, to acknowledge, pass. to be recognized. They received their recognition from God and hopefully by the Corinthians themselves (Barrett). ***ἀποθνῄσκοντες*** pres. act. part. *ἀποθνῄσκω* to die. ***ἰδού*** "see!" "behold," suddenly and contrary to hope (Bengel). ***ζῶμεν*** pres. ind. act. *ζάω* to live, to be alive. As an apostle, Paul was like a man under sentence of death (Barrett). ***παιδευόμενοι*** pres. pass. part. *παιδεύω* to punish, to discipline. God disciplines His servants for His servants' good (Barrett). ***θανατούμενοι*** pres. pass. part. *θανατόω* to kill, to put to death. See Ps. 118:18, "the Lord hath chastened me sore; but he hath not delivered me over to death." Let believers regard their afflictions not as indications of God's disapprobation, but rejoice in them as opportunities graciously afforded them to glorify His name (Hodge). ■ ***λυπούμενοι*** pres. pass. 10
part. *λυπέω* to cause pain or grief, pass. to be sorry, to be grieved. ***πτωχός*** poor, extremely poor, destitute poverty. It describes the abject poverty which has lit. nothing and which is in imminent danger of real starvation (NTW; TDNT). ***πλουτίζοντες*** pres. act. part. *πλουτίζω* to make rich, to make wealthy. ***ἔχοντες*** pres. act. part. *ἔχω* to hold down, to hold as a possession. (For parallel statements in the ancient world, s. Lietzmann; David L. Mealand, " 'As Having Nothing, and Yet Possessing Everything' II Cor. 6:10c," ZNW, 67 [1976], 277–279.)

■ ***στόμα*** mouth ***ἀνέῳγεν*** perf. ind. act. *ἀνοίγω* to open, 11
perf. to be opened, to stand open. The phrase means "I am speaking to you frankly, w. an open heart, hiding nothing of my life from you" (Hering). ***πεπλάτυνται*** perf. ind. pass. *πλατύνω* to make wide, to open wide, pass. to be wide open, to have the heart wide open means "there are no secrets in it." Paul tells them "there is room for you in it, and I long to have you there"
(Barrett). ■ ***στενοχωρεῖσθε*** pres. ind. pass. *στενοχωρέω* to 12
make narrow, to crowd, to restrict, pass. to be restricted. ***σπλάγχνα*** pl. inward parts. It properly refers to the contents of the breast, i.e. the heart, lungs, liver and is used to describe the seat of the deepest emotions and is the strongest word in Gr. for the feeling of compassion (Hughes; MNTW, 156; TDNT).

13 ■ **ἀντιμισθία** recompense, paying back. The use of the acc.
may be an adverbial acc. (IBG, 160), or it may be acc. in apposition to the sentence (s. IBG, 35; MT, 245). **ὡς τέκνοις λέγω** "I
speak as to children." It is in the nature of things that paternal
love should meet w. the response of filial love (Hughes).
14 ■ **γίνεσθε** pres. mid. imp. *γίνομαι*. The pres. imp. w. the
neg. is used either to stop an action in progress or to prohibit a
habitual action (s. MKG, 272f.). **ἑτεροζυγοῦντες** pres. act. part.
ἑτεροζυγέω to yoke w. a different yoke, to draft animals that
need different kinds of yokes, because they are of different species (BAG), to use a double harnass (Barrett). Paul is probably
referring to the prohibitions found in Deut. 22:10 and Lev. 19:
19. (For the rabbinical development of this prohibition, s. M.
Kilaim VIII, 2f.) The concept of the yoke was used in relation
to marriage and in relation to teachers who agreed in their doctrine. A mixed marriage or cooperation w. one who had a different doctrine was considered to be "unequally yoked" Schlatter).
The use of the part. w. this verb is sometimes used to denote the
beginning of a state or condition "do not lend yourselves to . . ."
(BD, 180). **ἄπιστος** unbelieving, unbeliever. The dat. is used in
connection w. the verb "yoked together" (Windisch). **μετοχή**
having a part in, partaking, partnership. **κοινωνία** fellowship, to
have things common or together (s. TDNT; RAC IX, 1100–
1145; CBB). **πρὸς σκότος** w. darkness. (For the term "dark-
15 ness" particularly in the DSS, s. John 1:5.) ■ **συμφώνησις**
harmony, agreement. The verb related to this noun was used in
the papyri w. the meaning "agree w.," "agree together" (s. MM).
βελιάρ a Heb. word meaning "worthless" and was used in
Jewish writings and the DSS to describe Satan, the prince of
lawlessness and darkness (s. Hughes; Bruce; Barrett; TDNT).
16 ■ **συγκατάθεσις** approval, accent, agreement, union. Used in
the papyri of a decision arrived at by a group, an agreement
(BAG). **νάος** temple. The term was properly used of the innermost sanctuary of a temple where the divine presence was supposed to be located (Hughes). **ζῶντος** pres. act. part. *ζάω* to live.
ὅτι. Used to introduce direct speech and is the equivalent of
quotation marks (s. BD, 205; 246f.). **ἐνοικήσω** fut. ind. act.
ἐνοικέω to live in, to dwell in. **ἐμπεριπατήσω** fut. ind. act.
ἐμπεριπατέω to walk about in, to walk about among. **ἔσομαι**
fut. ind. *εἰμί*. (For Paul's use of the OT in the Pharisaic practice
of putting together various Scriptures to prove a point, s. BE,
17 115ff.) ■ **ἐξέλθατε** aor. act. imp. *ἐξέρχομαι* to go out.
ἀφορίσθητε aor. pass. imp. *ἀφορίζω* to separate, pass. to be
separated. **ἀκαθάρτος** unclean. **ἅπτεσθε** pres. mid. imp.

ἅπτομαι to touch, followed by the gen. **εἰσδέξομαι** fut. ind.
mid. εἰσδέχομαι to receive, to receive w. favor (Plummer).
■ **ἔσομαι, ἔσεσθε** fut. s.v.16. **εἰς**. The prep. is used in a Hebraic 18
way to introduce the pred. nom. (s. BG, 10f.). **παντοκράτωρ**
almighty, all powerful, omnipotent.

Ch. 7

■ **ἔχοντες** pres. act. part. ἔχω. The pres. tense points to the 1
continuous possession. **ἐπαγγελία** promise. **καθαρίσωμεν**
aor. act. subj. καθαρίζω to cleanse, to purify. (For examples of
this verb used w. the prep., s. BS, 216f.) The hortatory use of the
subj. "let us . . . ." The aor. tense indicates that a complete break
should be made (Hughes). **μολυσμός** that which stains, defilement, pollution. **σαρκὸς καὶ πνεύματος** "flesh and spirit." The
terms refer to the outward and inward man both of which would
be contaminated by contact w. heathen forces (s. Schlatter).
ἐπιτελοῦντες pres. act. part. ἐπιτελέω to complete, to perfect,
to bring to the goal. The word can also refer to the discharging
of religious duties (s. Barrett). The prep. in compound is directive indicating the concentration of the verb's action upon some
object (MH, 312). The pres. tense points to a continual advance
in holiness (Hughes). **ἁγιωσύνη** holiness. **φόβος θεοῦ** "the fear
of God." The gen. is objective gen.
■ **χωρήσατε** aor. act. imp. χωρέω to make room for, to 2
provide a place for, "make room for us in your hearts" (RWP).
ἠδικήσαμεν aor. ind. act. ἀδικέω to wrong someone, to treat
someone unjustly, to injure (s. BAG). **ἐφθείραμεν** aor. ind. act.
φθείρω to corrupt, to ruin. It may refer to money, or morals,
or doctrine (Plummer). **ἐπλεονεκτήσαμεν** aor. ind. act.
πλεονεκτέω to take advantage of someone in order to gain
something, to defraud for the purpose of gain. It refers to the
selfish attitude of one who is willing to go to all lengths to satisfy
his selfishness (s. TDNT; NTW). The three aor. tenses point
back to a definite occasion (Hughes). ■ **κατάκρισις** condemna- 3
tion, the rendering of a decision against someone. **προείρηκα**
perf. ind. act. προλέγω to say before. The prep. in compound
is temporal. **εἰς τό** w. the inf. used to express purpose (s. MT,
143). **συναποθανεῖν** aor. act. inf. συναποθνῄσκω to die w.
someone, to die together. **συζῆν** pres. act. inf. συζάω to live
together. ■ **παρρησία** freedom in speaking, openness, boldness 4
(s. 2 Cor. 3:12). **καύχησις** boasting. **πεπλήρωμαι** perf. ind.
pass. πληρόω to fill, pass. to be filled. The perf. indicates "I was
filled then and am still" (Plummer). The dat. occurs here as
instrumental instead of the classical gen. (s. BD, 104).

ὑπερπερισσεύομαι pres. ind. pass. to cause someone to overflow, pass. to overflow, to be overflowing (s. BAG). **ἐπί** w. the dat. "amid all my afflictions" (Plummer).
5 ■ **καὶ γάρ** "for even." **ἐλθόντων** aor. act. part. ἔρχομαι gen. abs. "when we had come." **ἔσχηκεν** perf. ind. act. ἔχω. (For the use of the perf. here, s. 2 Cor. 2:13.) **ἄνεσις** relief. **θλιβόμενοι** pres. act. part. θλίβω to exercise pressure on someone, to afflict. The part. is used independently in the sentence and in this case has the character of the ind. (s. M, 182; RG, 1135). **μάχη** battle, fight. The fights without were presumably against adversaries, whether Christian or non-Christian—Paul had many (Barrett). **φόβος** fear. The fears within were perhaps for the safety of Titus, who might have been carrying a large sum of money, and was seriously overdue, and for the success of the
6 work in Corinth (Barrett; s. also Windisch). ■ **παρακαλῶν** pres. act. part. The pres. tense refers to the habitual character of the comforting God (s. 2 Cor. 1:4). **παρεκάλεσεν** aor. ind. act. παρακαλέω to comfort, to encourage. **ταπεινός** humble, used here in the psychological sense "downcast," "depressed"
7 (Hughes). **παρουσία** arrival. ■ **παράκλησις** comforting, consolation, comfort, encouragement. **παρεκλήθη** aor. ind. pass. s.v.6. **ἐφ᾽ὑμῖν** "over you," "upon you" (RWP). **ἀναγγέλλων** pres. act. part. to report, to announce. The part. is used as a nom. abs. (Lietzmann). **ἐπιπόθησις** longing, yearning. The prep. in compound is directive indicating a "longing towards" (RWP). **ὀδυρμός** lamentation, mourning. Evidently the expression of regret for having saddened Paul by the disorders tolerated in the church (s. Meyer). **ζῆλος** zeal, intense interest. **ὥστε** w. the inf. and the so-called subject of the inf. is used to express result. **μᾶλλον** comp. "rather." It is used either in the sense "I rejoiced rather than mourning," or "I rejoiced the more" (s. Barrett;
8 Windisch). ■ **ὅτι** because. **εἰ καί** "if even," "although." (For this construction, s. 2 Cor. 4:3.) **ἐλύπησα** aor. ind. act. λυπέω to cause pain, to make sorry. **μεταμέλομαι** pres. ind. mid. to be sorry, to regret. The verb indicates to change one's feelings about something (s. TDNT; Trench; *Synonyms*, 255–261; CBB). **μετεμελόμην** impf. ind. mid. The impf. is used in the concessive clause w. the meaning "although I was in a regretful mood at
9 first" (RWP). **πρὸς ὥραν** "for a moment," "for an hour." ■ **ἐλυπήθητε** aor. ind. pass. s.v.8. **μετάνοια** repentence. It indicates the changing of one's thinking regarding a matter (s. TDNT; Windisch; CBB). **κατὰ θεόν** "according to God," "in the way of God's will" (Barrett). **ζημιωθῆτε** aor. pass. subj. ζημιόω to inflict injury or punishment, pass. to suffer damage

or loss, to sustain injury. The pass. is the permissive pass. "to
permit one's self to sustain loss" (BAG). **ἐκ** from. Used here in
the causal sense "because of us" (MT, 260). ■ **λύπη** pain, sor- 10
row. **ἀμεταμέλητος** verbal adj. "not to be regretted." It refers
to either "repentence" or to "salvation" or to both; i.e. "repent-
ence-unto-salvation" (s. Hughes; Barrett). (For the prefix as a
neg., s. Moorhouse, 47ff.) **ἐργάζεται** pres. ind. mid. to work, to
produce. **κατεργάζεται** pres. ind. mid. to work out, to produce
its fulfillment in. The compound is intensive and designed to
emphasize the inevitability of the outworking of death in the
sorrow of the world (Hughes). ■ **λυπηθῆναι** aor. pass. inf. 11
λυπέω. The inf. is used as a noun (s. BD, 205f.). **πόσος** "how
large?" **κατειργάσατο** aor. ind. mid. s.v.10. **σπουδή** eagerness,
earnestness, diligence. (For the use of the word in the papyri and
examples, s. MM.) **ἀλλά** "but," "yea." The word is used to
introduce an additional point in an emphatic way (BD, 233).
ἀπολογία defense; i.e. a defense against an accusation (Barrett). **ἀγανάκτησις** indignation. Here it indicates the indignation at the shame brought upon the church (Plummer).
ἐπιπόθησις longing, yearning, s.v.7. **ζῆλος** zeal, s.v.7.
ἐκδίκησις vengeance, punishment. Perhaps it has the idea of
"requital" i.e. seeing that justice is done by bringing the guilty
person to ecclesiastical discipline (Hughes). **συνεστήσατε** aor.
ind. act. συνίστημι to commend. **ἁγνός** pure, immaculate,
without guilt. **εἶναι** pres. inf. The inf. is used here w. the verb
"you have demonstrated yourselves to be pure." (For the construction, s. BD, 209.) **πρᾶγμα** matter, affair. ■ **ἄρα** then, so, 12
therefore, consequently (s. BD, 235). **ἔγραψα** aor. ind. act.
γράφω to write. **ἕνεκεν** w. the gen. "because of," "on account
of," "for the sake of." **ἀδικήσαντος** aor. act. part. ἀδικέω to
wrong someone, s.v.2. **ἀδικηθέντος** aor. pass. part. ἀδικέω
pass. to be wrong, here "the one who was wronged." The word
has a strong legal flavor w. the active indicating the person who
was guilty and had committed wrong and the pass. indicating the
party against whom the crime was committed (s. Windisch),
followed by the gen. of the inf. "for the sake of," "on account
of." It is used w. the inf. to express purpose (s. IBG, 83; MT,
144). **φανερωθῆναι** aor. pass. inf. φανερόω to make clear,
to manifest. **ἐνώπιον** in the presence of, before. ■ 13
παρακεκλήμεθα perf. ind. pass. παρακαλέω s.v.6. The perf.
tense means "we have been comforted and continue to be so"
(Hughes).

παράκλησις comforting, consolation, s.v.7.
περισσοτέρως comp. of adv. strengthened by **μᾶλλον** = "the

more exceedingly." (For examples of this construction, s.
Hughes; BD, 129; MT, 29.) **ἐχάρημεν** aor. ind. pass. χαίρω to
rejoice, to be glad. **ἀναπέπαυται** perf. ind. pass. ἀναπαύω to
refresh, to give rest. The compound verb expresses a temporary
relief, e.g. a truce as distinct from a peace (Plummer; s. also
MM). The perf. indicates that at the time of writing Titus was
14 still in a state of refreshment (Hughes). ■ **ὅτι** because. **εἰ** w. the
ind. introduces a condition which is assumed to be true. **τι** acc.
"anything." **κεκαύχημαι** perf. ind. mid. καυχάομαι to glory,
to boast. The perf. brings out the fact that Paul kept up this
boasting about the Corinthians when he was speaking to Titus
(Lenski). **κατῃσχύνθην** aor. ind. pass. καταισχύνω to put to
shame. **ἐγενήθη** aor. ind. pass. γίνομαι to become. The perfective use of the aor. "our boasting before Titus proved to be the
15 truth" (Barrett). ■ **σπλάγχνα** the inward parts, the affections (s. 2 Cor. 6:12). **περισσοτέρως** abundantly, s.v.13.
ἀναμιμνησκομένου pres. pass. part. ἀναμιμνήσκω to remind
someone of something, pass. to remember, to recall. The part. is
used as a gen. abs. expressing contemporaneous time. **τρόμος**
trembling. The phrase "w. fear and trembling" indicates "a nervous anxiety to do one's duty" (Plummer). **ἐδέξασθε** aor. ind.
16 mid. δέχομαι to receive. ■ **ἐν παντί** "in everything." **θαρρῶ**
pres. ind. act. θαρρέω to be confident, to be courageous. The
basic meaning of the word is "to dare," "to be bold or daring"
(TDNT) but was used also in the papyri in the sense of "to have
confidence in" (s. MM).

Ch. 8

1 ■ **γνωρίζω** to make known, to cause to know, here "we
draw your attention to" (Barrett). **χάρις** grace. The word here
means the generous giving on the part of Christians which is
considered as a gift of thanksgiving (s. GNT, 174f.; TDNT;
CBB). **δεδομένην** perf. pass. part. δίδωμι to give. The grace of
generosity was given to the churches by God (Lietzmann). The
perf. emphasizes the state or condition. The prep. **ἐν** has almost
the meaning of the dat.; i.e. "in the case of the churches" (s. BD,
118). Although the area of Macedonia which included Philippi,
Thessalonica, and Beroea had at one time been rich, the Romans
had taken possession of the gold and silver mines and the coun-
2 try was like a lacerated and disjointed animal (Plummer). ■
δοκιμῇ proof, test as of metal (RWP). **θλῖψις** pressure, affliction. **περισσεία** abundance, superfluity, surplus (s. LAE, 84).
κατὰ βάθους "down to depth," "rock bottom." Their poverty
had already reached the lowest stage (Plummer; s. also Barrett).

πτωχεία poverty. The word describes abject poverty, which has
lit. nothing and which is in imminent danger of real starvation
(NTW, 110; s. also TDNT). In many parts of the Roman Empire
the bulk of the urban population seems to have been very poor;
probably because of high taxes, high rent, and high prices for
food (s. Jones, 38; A.M.H. Jones, *The Greek City*, 269; RAC I,
698–705). **ἐπερίσσευσεν** aor. ind. act. *περισσεύω* to abound,
to overflow. **ἁπλότης** generosity, liberality. The basic meaning
of the word is "simplicity," "single-mindedness" and indicates
the true open-heartedness and generosity toward others in which
there is no duplicity of motive (Hughes). ■ **παρά** w. acc. 3
"beyond." **αὐθαίρετος** (*αὐτος, αἱρέω* to choose) voluntarily, of
one's own accord; i.e. "spontaneously and voluntarily, out of
one's own initiative, without request and without coercion"
(Windisch; s. also Plummer). ■ **παράκλησις** beseeching, urg- 4
ing. **δεόμενοι** pres. mid. part. to ask, to beg. **κοινωνία** fellowship, sharing (s. TDNT; for the rabbinical practice of sharing
through a collection, s. SB III, 316). **ἅγιοι** holy ones, saints. A
term of honor used for the church in Jerusalem. ■ **ἠλπίσαμεν** 5
aor. ind. act. *ἐλπίζω* to hope, to expect. **ἔδωκαν** aor. ind. act.
δίδωμι to give. Not only have they given grace and a proof of
fellowship, but they have altogether given their own selves (Bengel). **θέλημα θεοῦ.** Everywhere in Paul's writings the impulse
to faithful service is traced up to God's grace (EGT). ■ **εἰς τό** 6
w. the inf., used here to introduce results "in such a manner that
we have urged" (BD, 207; s. also RG, 1003; IBG, 141).
παρακαλέσαι aor. act. inf. *παρακαλέω* to urge, to beseech, to
ask. **ἵνα** "that." It introduces the content of the request (Barrett). **προενηρξάτο** aor. ind. mid. *προενάρχομαι* to begin
previously. **ἐπιτελέσῃ** aor. subj. *ἐπιτελέω* to complete, to bring
to the goal. The prep. in compound is perfective (RWP). ■ 7
περισσεύετε pres. ind. act. to abound, to overflow, followed by
dat. of reference "to abound in reference to." **ἵνα** used w. subj.
to introduce an imp. (s. BD, 195f.; MT, 94f.; BG, 141f.).

■ **ἐπιταγή** command. **διά** w. gen. "through." This gives the 8
motive which justifies the request. **γνήσιος** genuine, sincere.
The primary sense "born in wedlock" is overshadowed by
derived application (MM). **δοκιμάζων** pres. act. part.
δοκιμάζω to approve by testing, to accept as proven, to approve
(s. BAG). ■ **διά** w. acc. "because of." **ἐπτώχευσεν** aor. ind. act. 9
πτωχεύω to be poor, ingressive aor. to become poor, to be
reduced to abject poverty. The aor. tense makes it evident that
the whole event of the Incarnation is referred to, and is viewed
as one act (s. Fred. B. Craddock, "The Poverty of Christ; An

Investigation of II Cor. 8:9," Interp. 22 [April, 1968], 165ff.).
πτωχεία poverty, s.v.2. **πλουτήσητε** aor. subj. πλουτέω to be
rich, ingressive aor. to become rich; i.e. w. the heavenly riches
of union w. God in Christ and the assurance of eternal life
10 (Plummer). ■ **γνώμη** opinion, advice. **συμφέρει** to bring together, to be advantageous, profitable or useable (BAG). **οἵτινες**
"who," "those who." It is used to emphasize persons belonging
to a certain class and emphasizes the characteristic quality (s.
IBG, 124; BAG). **τὸ ποιῆσαι** aor. act. inf. The inf. w. the article
is used as a noun (s. BD, 205). **προενήρξασθε** aor. ind. mid.,
s.v.6. **ἀπὸ πέρυσι** "last year," "from last year" (RWP). If Paul
was writing these words in the autumn of A.D. 57, the Corinthian
collection would have been initiated not less than some nine
months and up to as much as twenty-one months previously
11 (Hughes). ■ **ἐπιτελέσατε** aor. imp. act., s.v.6. **προθυμία** readiness, forwardness, eargerness (s. RWP). **τοῦ θέλειν** pres. act.
inf. The inf. is used as a noun. **ἐπιτελέσαι** aor. act. inf., s.v.6.
ἐκ τοῦ ἔχειν pres. act. inf. used w. prep. "out of the having"; i.e.
"according to one's resources," "according to your means" (MT,
144). The construction is probably meant to accent the ability
12 growing "out of" the possession of property (RG, 1074). ■
πρόκειται pres. ind. mid. to be present, to lie before one. **καθὸ
ἐάν** "according to whatever he may have." The amount that a
man may have is indefinite, therefore the subj. is used, but his
not having is a definite fact therefore the ind. (Plummer; s. also
RG, 967). **εὐπρόσδεκτος** acceptable, well-received. (For the
13 same principle in Judaism, s. SB III, 523.) ■ **ἄνεσις** relief, s. 2
Cor. 2:13. **ἰσότης** equality. Used here w. the prep. "according
14 to equality" (s. Hughes; s. also v. 11). ■ **περίσσευμα** abundance. **εἰς** for. The expression **γίνεσθαι εἰς** means "to be extended to" (Hughes). **γένηται** aor. mid. subj. used w. the parti-
15 cle to express purpose. ■ **τὸ πολύ** one must supply either
"have"; i.e. "the one who has much" (s. RG, 1202), or supply
the word "gathered"; i.e. "he who has gathered much." This
arises from the context of the quotation from Exod. 16:18
(Hughes). **ἐπλεόνασεν** aor. ind. act. πλεονάζω to have an
abundance, to have more than enough. **ἠλαττόνησεν** aor. ind.
act. ἐλαττονέω to have little, to lack, to not have enough.
16 ■ **δόντι** aor. act. part. dat. sing. δίδωμι (variant reading
διδόντι pres. act. part. dat. sing.). **αὐτην** "same"; i.e., the same
zeal that I have myself, and have now described (Barrett).
17 **σπουδή** encouragement, exhortation. ■ **ἐδέξατο** aor. ind. mid.
δέχομαι to receive, to welcome. **σπουδαιότερος** comp.
σπουδαῖος zealous, the elative comp. "very zealous" (BD, 127;

s. also MT, 30). **ὑπάρχων** pres. act. part. ὑπαρχω to exist, to
be. **αὐθαίρετος** of one's own accord, s.v.3. **ἐξῆλθεν** aor. ind.
act. ἐξέρχομαι to go out, to depart, epistolary aor. which views
the action as past at the time the letter is read and refers to Titus'
present trip (s. MT, 72f.). **πρός** to, unto. ■ **συνεπέμψαμεν** aor. 18
ind. act. συμπέμπω to send together, epistolary aor. "we are
now sending" (Barrett). **ἔπαινος** praise. **ἐν** "in," "in the matter
of." The prep. gives the sphere in which the praise occurs and
gives in reality the reason for the praise. ■ **χειροτονηθείς** aor. 19
pass. part. χειροτονέω to stretch out the hand, to vote by holding up the hand, to elect, to appoint (s. MM). The verb may indicate that the churches elected by voting (Lenski) or it may simply point to the selection and appointment but it does not refer to ordination (Hughes). (For the use of the part. as continuing the construction begun w. the finite verb, s. BD, 245.) **συνέκδημος** traveling companion, one who goes out w. another. (For a discussion of the identity of the person and his identification as Tychicus, s. Hughes.) **διακονουμένῃ** pres. pass. part. διακονέω to minister (s. TDNT). **πρός**. The prep. can refer either to "the brother appointed to promote the glory" or to "the fund being ministered to promote the glory" (s. Plummer). **προθυμία** readiness, s.v.11. ■ **στελλόμενοι** pres. mid. 20
part. στέλλομαι to avoid, to take precautions. Perhaps the word is used here as a nautical metaphor w. the meaning "to furl or shorten the sail, when coming to shore or in order to avoid danger in navigation" (s. Hughes). (For the use of the part. as an example of *anacoluthon*, s. RG, 431.) **μωμήσηται** aor. mid. subj. μωμάομαι to blame. The subj. is used to express neg. purpose "lest anyone blame us" (RWP). **ἁδρότης** that which is thick or bulky, abundant, wealth (Hughes). Here it refers to a
large sum of money (Barrett). ■ **προνοοῦμεν** pres. ind. act. to 21
plan beforehand, to think of beforehand, to care for, to take into consideration. **καλός** good, that which suits the occasion, that which is fitted to the purpose (s. TDNT). **ἐνώπιον** in the presence of, before ■ **συνεπέμψαμεν** aor. ind. act., s.v.18. 22
ἐδοκιμάσαμεν aor. ind. act. δοκιμάζω to approve after testing (s. TDNT; CBB). **σπουδαῖος** zealous, s.v.17. **πολύ** n. of the adj. used as an adv. "more." **πεποίθησις** confidence. **εἰς** in, into,
toward. ■ **ὑπέρ** for, concerning, about. (For the prep. w. this 23
meaning, s. BD, 121; M, 105.) **κοινωνός** partner. **συνέργος** fellow-worker. **ἀπόστολος** official messenger, envoy. The word was used in Jewish writings to denote the official messenger who brought or delivered the collection (s. SB III, 316f.; s. also CBB; TDNT). **δόξα Χριστοῦ** "glory of Christ"; i.e., the glory belong-

24 ing to Him or the glory designed for Him. ■ **ἐνδείξις** demonstration, evidence, proof. **καύχησις** boasting. **ἐνδεικνύμενοι** pres.
pass. part. ἐνδείκνυμι to demonstrate, to show proof, to give
visible proof. **εἰς πρόσωπον.** A Semitic expression meaning "in
the presence of" (Hughes).

Ch. 9

1 ■ **περισσός** superfluous. **τὸ γράφειν** pres. act. inf. w. the
article. The inf. explains that which is superfluous and the article
indicates that chapters 8 and 9 belong together. The pres. tense
points to the act of writing, "it is superfluous for me to go on
2 writing to you like this" (Barrett). ■ **προθυμία** readiness (s. 2
Cor. 8:11). **καυχῶμαι** pres. ind. mid. to boast, to glory. The
pres. tense emphasizes Paul's continual boasting on their behalf
(s. Plummer). **παρέσκεύασται** perf. ind. pass. παρασκευάζω
to prepare, to make preparations, to make ready. The perf. emphasizes the past completed action w. the pres. continuing state;
i.e., "stands prepared" (RWP). **ἀπὸ πέρυσι** "last year" (s. 2
Cor. 8:10). **ζῆλος** zeal. **ἠρέθισεν** aor. ind. act. ἐρεθίζω to stir
up, to stimulate, to excite. **πλείονες** comp. "the majority" (s. 2
3 Cor. 2:6). ■ **ἔπεμψα** aor. ind. act. epistolary aor. "I am sending."
ἀδέλφους "the brothers." The article indicates those who were
previously mentioned. **τὸ ὑπὲρ ὑμῶν.** The article is repeated
here in order to avoid misunderstanding (BD, 141). **κενωθῇ** aor.
pass. subj. κενόω to empty, to make void, effective use of the
aor. "to be proven empty" (Barrett; s. also DM, 196f.). **καθὼς
ἔλεγον** impf. ind. act. The impf. emphasizes the repeated action
"just as I repeatedly said" (Plummer). **παρεσκευασμένοι** perf.
pass. part., s.v.2. The part. is used w. the subj. of the verb to be
to express the perf. pass. subj. in a final clause "that you may
4 really be prepared" (RWP). ■ **ἔλθωσιν** aor. subj. ἔρχομαι.
εὕρωσιν aor. subj. εὑρίσκω. **ἀπαρασκευάστους** unprepared.
καταισχυνθῶμεν aor. pass. subj. καταισχύνω to put to
shame, pass. to be put to shame. **ὑπόστάσις** basis, foundation,
support, ground of hope or confidence, assurance (Hughes;
5 s. also Heb. 11:1). ■ **ἀναγκαῖος** necessary, compelling.
ἡγησάμην aor. ind. mid. ἡγέομαι to consider. **παρακαλέσαι**
aor. act. inf. παρακαλέω to ask, to urge, to encourage.
προέλθωσιν aor. act. subj. προέρχομαι to go ahead, to go
before. **προκαταρτίσωσιν** aor. act. subj. προκαταρτίζω
to arrange beforehand, to organize beforehand.
προεπηγγελμένην perf. pass. part. προεπαγγέλλω to promise before. The perf. part. emphasizes the continuing state; i.e.,
"that which was promised before and the promise remains val-

id." **ἕτοιμος** ready. Used w. the inf. to express purpose.
πλεονεξία selfishness, greed. The word indicates the greedy,
grasping for more at the expense of others (s. NTW, 97–99; CBB;
TDNT). The idea here is "ready as a gift and not as something
wrung from you" (Barrett).

■ **σπείρων** pres. act. part. σπείρω to sow, to sow seed. 6
φειδομένως. An adv. developed from a part. from φείδομαι to
spare, to be miserly, adv. sparingly, "in a miserly manner"
(BAG; Hughes). **θερίσει** fut. ind. act. θερίζω to reap, to gather
a harvest. **ἐπὶ εὐλογίας**. The prep. has an adverbial force and
the noun means a gift freely and spontaneously bestowed and
thus constituting a blessing to the recipient. The total phrase is
used as an adv. w. the meaning "generously," "bountifully"
(Hughes). ■ **προῄρηται** aor. mid. subj. προαιρέω mid. to deter- 7
mine beforehand, to decide. The word refers to the deliberate
choosing (Plummer). **ἀνάγκη** necessity, compulsion. **ἱλαρός**
cheerful. **δότης** one who gives, giver. Paul evidently alludes to
Prov. 22:9. ■ **δυνατεῖ** pres. ind. act. δυνατέω to make able, to 8
enable, to be able. The pres. tense emphasizes the continual
ability of God. **περισσεῦσαι** aor. act. inf. περισσεύω to
abound, to have more than enough, to overflow. **αὐτάρκεια**
sufficiency, self-sufficiency. The word indicates being independent of external circumstances, especially of the services of other
people (Plummer). (For the use of the word in the ancient world
both among the Stoic philosophers and also the common people,
s. Windisch; Barrett; TDNT; MM.) **περισσεύητε** pres. subj.
Subjunctive used to express purpose. **πᾶν ἔργον** "every good
work." The meaning here is that the less a man requires for
himself, the greater means he will have for relieving the wants
of others (Plummer). ■ **ἐσκόρπισεν** aor. ind. act. σκορπίζω to 9
scatter, to disperse, to distribute. **ἔδωκεν** aor. ind. act. δίδωμι
to give, gnomic aor. used in a proverb-like expression (Barrett).
πένης poor. The word describes the man for whom life and
living is a struggle, the man who is the reverse of the man who
lives in affluence (NTW, 110). ■ **ἐπιχορηγῶν** pres. act. part. 10
ἐπιχωρέω to supply, to furnish, to provide. **βρῶσις** eating.
χορηγήσει fut. ind. act. χορηγέω "to lead chorus," "to supply
the chorus" for a drama. A service which cost the persons who
undertook it a large outlay; "to supply anything plentifully"
(Plummer). **πληθυνεῖ** fut. πληθύνω increase, to multiply.
αὐξήσει fut. αὐξάνω increase, to cause to grow. **γένημα** produce, the yield of a harvest, particularly the fruit or juice of the
grape vine (Hughes). **δικαιοσύνη** righteousness, perhaps in the
sense of "almsgiving," "benevolence" (SB III, 525; MRT, 161)

or it is used to connote righteousness of life of which charity is
11 an expression (GW, 154). ■ **πλουτιζόμενοι** pres. pass. part.
πλουτίζω to make rich, to enrich. (For the construction w. the
part., s. BD, 245f.) **ἁπλότης** liberality (s. 2 Cor. 8:2).
κατεργάζεται pres. ind. mid. to produce. **εὐχαριστία** thanks-
12 giving. ■ **διακονία** ministry, service. The meaning here is
"ministration," "execution" (Barrett). **λειτουργία** ministry,
service. In classical Gr. the word was used of wealthy citizens
who rendered to the public service in financing choruses for
dramas. In Jewish in koine usage it indicated religious service or
freewill service (s. Plummer; MM; TDNT; Lietzmann).
προσαναπληροῦσα pres. act. part. fem sing.
προσαναπληρόω to fill, to fill up. The prep. in compound
means "to fill up by adding to" (RWP). **ὑστέρημα** that which
lacks, deficiency, shortcoming, need, want. **περισσεύουσα**
pres. act. part. fem. sing., περισσεύω s.v.8. The collection has
a twofold effect: it fills up what is lacking to their poorer brethren
of the necessities of life as well as causing an overflow of praise
13 and gratitude to God (Hughes). ■ **δοκιμή** approval, proven, that
which has been tested and approved (s. 2 Cor. 2:9). **δοξάζοντες**
pres. act. part. δοξάζω to glorify, to cause one to think well of
someone. (For the construction of the part., s.v.13.) **ὑποταγή**
obedience, subordination of one's self. **ὁμολογία** confession.
The word is used specifically to introduce or express a conviction; i.e., the obj. *confession* which especially has reference to
"confessing Christ or the teaching of His church" (ECC, 17).
ἁπλότης liberality. The word indicates singleness of purpose
leading to liberality in giving to others (Hughes). **κοινωνία** fellowship. Here it is used in the sense of "participation in the
14 collection" (Barrett; s. also 2 Cor. 8:4). ■ **δέησις** request, petition. The word implies special petition for the supply of wants
(Plummer; s. also Trench; *Synonyms*, 189). The dat. indicates
accompanying circumstances; i.e., the intercession accompanies
their longing (Plummer). **ἐπιποθούντων** pres. act. part.
ἐπιποθέω to long for someone, to earnestly desire (s. Hering).
The part. is used in a gen. abs. (RWP). **ὑπερβάλλουσα** pres.
act. part. ὑπερβάλλω to throw beyond, to surpass. Here it refers
15 to the surpassing grace or generosity (Barrett). ■ **ἀνεκδιήγητος**
verbal adj. indescribable, not able to recount or to describe or to
set forth in detail (Lenski). God's exquisite working cannot be
fully described w. human words (Windisch). (For the neg. prefix,
s. Moorhouse, 47ff.) **δωρέα** gift, that which is freely given.

Ch. 10
■ **αὐτὸς δὲ ἐγώ** "now I myself." Paul is now calling atten- 1
tion to a specially personal matter (EGT). (For a defense of the
authenticity of chapters 10 through 13, s. Hughes.) **πραΰτης**
meekness. It denotes the humble and gentle attitude which expresses itself in particular in a patient submissiveness to offense,
free from malice and desire for revenge (R. Leivestad, "The
Meekness and Gentleness of Christ, II Cor. 10:1," NTS, 12
[January, 1966], 159; s. also NTW, 103f.; TDNT; Windisch).
ἐπιείκεια fitting, suitable, reasonable, fair. When applied to
authorities it denotes indulgence, equity, lenience. It also
denotes a humble, patient steadfastness, which is able to submit
to injustice, disgrace, and maltreatment without hatred and malice, trusting in God in spite of it all (Leivestad, 157, 158; s. also
TDNT; Trench; *Synonyms*, 153–157; NTW, 38f.). These words
indicate that Paul knew of the historical Jesus and refers to His
character (s. JNP, 108f.). **κατὰ πρόσωπον** "face to face," "present in person" (s. Hughes). **ταπεινός** low, humble. Used here
in the bad sense meaning "downcast" and expresses depression
when it is the effect of the want of courage (Hodge). **θαρρέω**
pres. ind. act. to be confident, to be courageous. ■ **δέομαι** to ask, 2
to beg. **θαρρῆσαι** aor. act. inf. The article is used w. the inf. and
the neg. expressing the direct object of the verb (s. RWP; BD,
105). The aor. inf. is the ingressive aor. "to become courageous."
παρών pres. part. **πάρειμι** to be present, adverbial use of the
inf. "when I am present." **πεποίθησις** having been persuaded,
confidence. **ᾗ** rel. pron. dat. sing. instrumental use "with which,"
"by which." **λογίζομαι** to judge, to reckon, to think. **τολμῆσαι**
aor. act. inf. τολμάω to be bold, to dare. **κατὰ σάρκα** "according to flesh"; i.e., according to fleshly principles.
περιπατοῦντας pres. act. part. **περιπατέω** to walk, to walk
about, to conduct one's life. ■ **ἐν σαρκί** "in the flesh"; i.e., in 3
the element of flesh, living his life, like every other man, subject
to the laws and limitations which are common to human flesh
(Hughes). (For Paul's style of using the same word or word stem
in close proximity, s. BD, 258.) ■ **ὅπλα** (pl.) weapons, instru- 4
ments of warfare. A general word used for both defensive and
offensive weapons (s. TDNT; Windisch). (For a brief description
of the weapons of the Roman army, s. ELR, 106; OCD, 121f.)
σαρκικός fleshly, pertaining to the flesh. The ending of the
word indicates "like the flesh" (s. MH, 378). **δυνατός** powerful.
θεῷ dat. The dat. indicates either personal interest "to or for
God"; i.e., employed on God's behalf (Barrett; BG, 20) or it may
be viewed as an intensive dat. corresponding to the Hebraic

construction indicating a superl. force; i.e., "divinely powerful" (s. Hughes; IBG, 184; MH, 443). **καθαίρεσις** tearing down, pulling down, destroying. **ὀχύρωμα** stronghold, fortress. In the papyri the word also had the meaning "prison" (MM). Paul may have had Prov. 21:22 in mind (Hughes). **λογισμός** calculation, reasoning, reflection, thought (BAG). **καθαιροῦντες** pres. act.
5 part. to tear down, to destroy. ■ **ὕψωμα** that which is lifted up, high, exalted. **ἐπαιρόμενον** pres. mid. part. **ἐπαίρω** to lift up, mid. to exalt one's self. The metaphor here is from walls and towers standing defiantly and the verb may be pass.; i.e., "erected" (Plummer). **αἰχμαλωτίζοντες** pres. act. part. αἰχμαλωτίζω to take one captive w. a spear, to bring into captivity, to bring into subjection. The pres. tense points to the continual struggle and warfare. **νόημα** thought, purpose, design (s. 2 Cor. 3:14). **ὑπακοή** obedience. **τοῦ Χριστοῦ** obj. gen.
6 "obedience to Christ." ■ **ἕτοιμος** ready. Used w. **ἔχοντες** pres. act. part. w. the meaning "to be ready," "to be prepared." **ἐκδικῆσαι** aor. act. inf. **ἐκδικέω** to punish, to avenge (s. BAG; TDNT). **παρακοή** disobedience. **ὅταν** used w. subj. "when," "whenever." **πληρωθῇ** aor. pass. subj. **πληρόω** to fill, pass. to be filled, the effective aor. "to reach completion" (Barrett).
7 ■ **κατὰ πρόσωπον** "according to the face"; i.e., "before your face." **βλέπετε** pres. ind. act. or better pres. act. imp. βλέπω "look at what is before your eyes," "face the obvious facts" (Hughes). **εἴ τις** used w. ind. to introduce a condition which is assumed to be true "if anyone." **πέποιθα** perf. ind. act. w. a pres. meaning to have confidence; i.e., to have been persuaded, to trust. **ἑαυτῷ** dat. of reflex. pron.; i.e., 'to have confidence or trust in one's self." **Χριστοῦ εἶναι** pred. gen. used w. the inf. in indirect discourse "confidence that he belongs to Christ" (s. RWP). **λογιζέσθω** pres. mid. imp. λογίζομαι to think, to consider, to reckon. **ἑαυτοῦ** "for himself," let him then consider once more for himself (Meyer). (For a study of Paul's opponents at Corinth, s. Hughes; C.K. Barrett, "Paul's Opponents in Sec-
8 ond Corinthians," NTS, 17 [April, 1971], 233–254.) ■ **ἐάν τε γάρ** "for if." (For the use of the particles here, s. Thrall, 96; BD, 229f.; Barrett.) **περισσότερον** comp. **περισσόν** abundant, comp. "somewhat more abundantly." **καυχήσωμαι** aor. mid. subj. καυχάομαι to boast, to glory. **ἐξουσία** authority. **ἧς** rel. pron. gen. sing. gen. by attraction. **ἔδωκεν** aor. ind. act. **δίδωμι**. **οἰκοδομή** building up, edification. **καθαίρεσις** tearing down, s.v.4. (cf. Jer. 1:10). **αἰσχυνθήσομαι** fut. ind. pass. αἰσχύνω
9 to put to shame, pass. to be put to shame. ■ **δόξω** aor. act. subj. δοκέω to appear, to seem to be. **ὡσάν** = **ὡς ἄν** "as it were" (M,

167). ***ἐκφοβεῖν*** pres. act. inf. *ἐκφοβέω* to terrify, to frighten, to
distraction. The prep. in compound is intensive (Hughes). ■ ***ὅτι*** 10
equivalent to quotation marks introducing a direct quotation. ***φησίν*** pres. ind. act. 3rd sing. *φημί* to say; i.e., "one says." It may be however that Paul is quoting a particular person (Barrett). ***βαρύς*** heavy, weighty. ***παρουσία*** presence. Followed by the gen. ***τοῦ σώματος*** it emphasizes the external presence; i.e., the visible and tangible presence in the physical body (s. SBT, 48). ***ἀσθενής*** weak. ***ἐξουθενημένος*** perf. pass. part. *ἐξουθενέω* to despise, to consider one of no account. The perf. emphasizes the state or condition; i.e., "despised," "counted as nothing."
■ ***λογιζέσθω*** pres. mid. imp. 3rd sing., s.v.7. ***οἷος*** such a one. 11
τοιοῦτος "what sort of." The pron. is qualitive (RWP). ***παρόντες*** pres. act. part. s.v.2.

■ ***τολμῶμεν*** pres. ind. act. *τολμάω* to be bold, to dare, 12
s.v.2. ***ἐγκρῖναι*** aor. act. inf. *ἐγκρίνω* to judge among, to class or categorize. ***συγκρῖναι*** aor. act. inf. *συνκρίνω* to judge together, to compare. ***συνιστανόντων*** pres. act. part. *συνίστημι* to commend, to recommend (s. 2 Cor. 3:1). ***αὐτοί*** "they themselves." ***μετροῦντες*** pres. act. part. *μετρέω* to measure. The part. is used in the role of a pred. "they do not realize that they are measuring themselves by their own standards" (MT, 160). ***συνιᾶσιν*** pres. ind. act. *συνίημι* to understand, to
comprehend, to realize. ■ ***ἄμετρος*** unmeasured, immeasurable. 13
The phrase here means "we shall not boast excessively" (Barrett; s. also IBG, 71). ***καυχησόμεθα*** aor. mid. subj., s.v.8. ***μέτρον*** measure. ***κανών, όνος*** rule, measuring rod, the fixed bounds of a territory (s. TDNT; Plummer). It may be that Paul has in mind the marked out lanes as used by runners in athletic contests (Hughes). ***οὗ*** rel. pron. gen. sing. gen. by attraction (s. RG, 719). The repetition of ***μέτρον*** in the gen. may be due to attraction and the word may be considered as in apposition to the rel. pron. (Hughes). ***ἐμέρισεν*** aor. ind. act. *μερίζω* to measure out, to distribute, to deal out, to assign. ***ἐφικέσθαι*** aor. mid. inf. *ἐφικνέομαι* to reach, to come to. The inf. is used to express
result (Windisch). ***ἄχρι*** w. the gen. unto, as far as. ■ 14
ἐφικνούμενοι pres. mid. part. ***ὑπερεκτείνομεν*** pres. ind. act. to stretch out beyond, to overstretch, "we are not overextending ourselves beyond the limits set by God" (BAG). ***ἐφθάσαμεν*** aor. ind. act. *φθάνω* to arrive first, to come before others, to precede (s. Hughes). ***ἐν τῷ εὐαγγελίῳ*** "in the gospel"; i.e., in
preaching the gospel as its ministers and envoys (Barrett). ■ 15
ἄμετρον without measure, s.v.13. ***καυχώμενοι*** pres. mid. part., s.v.8. ***ἀλλότριος*** another, belonging to another (RWP). ***κόπος***

work. **αὐξανομένης** pres. pass. part. αὐξάνω to cause to grow, pass. to grow, to increase gen. abs. "as your faith increases" (Barrett). **μεγαλυνθῆναι** aor. pass. inf. μεγαλύνω to make large, to magnify, to enlarge. The inf. is used in indirect discourse, explaining what the "hope" is (RWP). **κανών** s.v.13. **εἰς περισσείαν** "unto abundance"; i.e., "in the highest degree possible" (Lietzmann). Paul expected a brilliant and glorious tri-
16 umph in Corinth (Windisch). ■ **ὑπερέκεινα** beyond; i.e., "the lands that lie beyond you" (BAG; s. also RG, 297). **εὐαγγελίσασθαι** aor. mid. inf. εὐαγγελίζομαι to proclaim the good news, to preach the gospel, to evangelize. **ἕτοιμος** ready, prepared, s.v.6. **καυχήσασθαι** aor. mid. inf., s.v.8. The idea is "without boasting of work already done in another's field" (s.
17/18 Hughes). ■ **καυχάσθω** aor. mid. imp., s.v.8. ■ **συνιστάνων** pres. act. part., s.v.12. **δόκιμος** approved, approved after a test.

Ch. 11

1 ■ **ὄφελον** "oh that," "would that" (BAG; for the form, s. RG, 1003; BD, 37). The word has become a particle w. the impf. or aor. ind. used to express an unattainable wish (BD, 181). **ἀνείχεσθε** impf. ind. mid. ἀνέχω to endure, to put up w. **μου** "w. me" gen. following the verb. **μικρόν τι** a little, adv. acc.; i.e., acc. of general reference "in reference to a little foolishness" (RG, 486). **ἀφροσύνη** lack of sense, foolishness. **ἀλλὰ καί** "but indeed." **ἀνέχεσθε** pres. ind. act. or pres. act. imp. The ind. appears to be better "but indeed you do already bear w. me"
2 (Hughes). ■ **ζηλόω** pres. ind. act. to be jealous. **ζῆλος** jealously. The word is taken up in a metaphor drawn from marriage (Barrett). **ἡρμοσάμην** aor. ind. mid. ἁρμόζω to fit together, to join, to harmonize, to give in marriage, to betroth (BAG). The mid. is probably used purposely to bring out the apostle's personal interest (MM). **ἑνὶ ἀνδρί** "to one man." The emphasis is on the fact that there is one person, and only one, to whom the Corinthians owe their allegiance (Barrett). **παρθένος** virgin. **ἁγνός** pure, chaste, undefiled. **παραστῆσαι** aor. act. inf. παρίστημι
3 to present, inf. used to express purpose. ■ **φοβέομαι** to fear, to be afraid. **μή** followed by the subj. "lest by any means" (RWP). **ὄφις** snake. **ἐξηπάτησεν** aor. ind. act. ἐξαπατάω to deceive. The prep. in compound is perfective "to completely deceive" (s. 1 Tim. 2:14). **πανουργία** craftiness (s. 2 Cor. 4:2). **φθαρῇ** aor. pass. subj. φθείρω to corrupt. **νόημα** thought, purpose, design.
4 **ἁπλότης** simplicity, sincerity. **ἁγνότης** purity. ■ **εἰ** w. the ind. introduces a condition which is assumed to be true. **ἐρχόμενος** pres. mid. part. **ἐκηρύξαμεν** aor. ind. act. κηρύσσω to pro-

claim, to proclaim as a herald (s. TDNT; CBB). **ἐλάβετε** aor.
ind. act. λαμβάνω. **ἐδέξασθε** aor. ind. mid. δέχομαι to receive,
to welcome. **ἀνέχεσθε** pres. ind. mid., s.v.1. ■ **λογίζομαι** to 5
consider, to judge, to reckon. **μηδέν** = **οὐδέν** acc., acc. of
reference; i.e., "in reference to nothing," "in no way at all"
(Barrett). **ὑστερηκέναι** perf. act. inf. ὑστερέω to come behind,
to lack. **ὑπερλίαν** exceedingly, beyond measure, super. Paul's
description is vibrant w. sarcasm "extra-super-apostles"
(Hughes). ■ **εἰ δὲ καί** "but even if." **ἰδιώτης** a private person, 6
distinction to one who holds an office or to one who has special
ability or knowledge, a layman, one who is unskilled (s. TDNT;
Barrett; RWP). The word is followed by the dat. of reference.
ἀλλ᾽οὐ τῇ γνώσει "but not really in knowledge." **ἐν παντί** "in
every respect." **φανερώσαντες** aor. act. part. φανερόω to make
clear, to manifest.

■ **ἤ** "or." **ταπεινῶν** pres. act. part. ταπεινόω to make low, 7
to bring low, to make humble. **ὑψωθῆτε** aor. pass. subj. ὑψόω to
lift up, to exalt. The subj. is used to express purpose. **ὅτι** because.
δωρέαν adv. "freely," "without charge," emphatic juxtaposi-
tion; "*God's gospel*," that most precious thing—*for nothing*!"
(Plummer). **εὐηγγελισάμην** aor. ind. mid. εὐαγγελίζω to proclaim good news, to preach the gospel, to evangelize (s. TDNT;
CBB). ■ **ἄλλος** "other"; i.e., in distinction to the churches in 8
Corinth. **ἐσύλησα** aor. ind. act. συλάω to plunder. The word
was used either for the robbing of temples or for the plundering
of soldiers (s. Hughes; Barrett). **λαβών** aor. act. part. λαμβάνω.
ὀψώνιον wages, pay. **ὑμῶν διακονίαν** (s. Rom. 6:23). ■ **παρών** 9
pres. part. πάρειμι to be present. **ὑστερηθείς** aor. pass. part.,
s.v.5. **κατενάρκησα** aor. ind. act. καταναρκάω to make or
become numb, to be a burden. A noun based on the simplex of
the verb was used for an electric eel which numbed its victims
by an electric shock (s. Lenski; LS). The prep. in compound
is perfective (s. MH, 316). **ὑστέρημα** need, lack, want.
προσανεπλήρωσαν aor. ind. act. προσαναπληρόω to fill up,
to fill up in addition. The prep. in compound signifies the adding
of something and may indicate that the gift from Macedonia
supplemented the amount which Paul earned (Hughes). **ἀβαρής**
free from weight, not burdensome. **ἐτήρησα** aor. ind. act.
τηρέω to guard, to keep. The aor. summarizes the past ministry
of Paul. **τηρήσω** fut. ind. act. ■ **ἔστιν.** The verb is emphatic by 10
its position in the sentence. **ἀλήθεια Χριστοῦ** "the truth of
Christ." The expression here reveals the intensity of Paul's feelings and is to be taken as a solemn assertion (Bruce). (See also
IBG, 112.) **καύχησις** boasting. **φραγήσεται** fut. ind. pass.

φράσσω to fence in, to stop, to block in. The figure may be that
of blocking or barricading a road or damming a river but in each
case the central idea is that of blockage (Hughes; RWP). **κλίμα**
11 province, district, region (s. BAG). ■ **διὰ τί** "why?" **οἶδα** defective perf. w. the pres. meaning "to know." (For this word, s. ND,
344–356.)
12 ■ **ποιήσω** fut. ind. act. **ἐκκόψω** aor. act. subj. ἐκκόπτω to
cut off, subj. used to express purpose. **ἀφορμή** opportunity, base
of operation (s. 2 Cor. 5:12). **θελόντων** pres. act. part. θέλω to
wish, to desire, to want to. **καυχῶνται** pres. ind. mid. to boast,
to glory. **εὑρεθῶσιν** aor. pass. subj. εὑρίσκω to find, pass. to be
13 found. ■ **τοιοῦτοι** such ones. **ψευδαπόστολοι** false apostles,
pseudo-apostles. **ἐργάτης** one who works. **δόλιος** deceitful,
tricky, cunning, treacherous. The basic meaning of the word is
"bait for fish" then "any cunning contrivance for deceiving or
catching" (s. LS). **μετασχηματίζεται** pres. ind. mid. to transform one's outward appearance, to disguise (s. Barrett; TDNT;
s. also 1 Cor. 4:6). The pres. tense points to that which Satan
14 habitually does (Plummer). ■ **θαῦμα** wonder, marvel. **ἄγγελος**
φωτός angel of light. The term may have been used to indicate
15 "a messenger of God" (s. Lietzmann; Schlatter). ■ **διάκονοι**
αὐτοῦ "his ministers" obj. gen. i.e. "those who serve Satan."
ἔσται fut. εἰμί.
16 ■ **μή** used w. aor. subj. in a neg. prohibition (s. RG, 933).
δόξῃ aor. act. subj. δοκέω to suppose, to think. The prohibitive
aor. subj. could be used to prevent an action from arising without
involving the notion "immediately" (MKG, 273). The aor. tense
implies that no one did (s. RG, 853). **ἄφρων** fool, one who does
not think. **εἶναι** inf. used in indirect discourse. **εἰ δὲ μή γε** "and
even if," "otherwise" (s. Barrett; BD, 191, 226). **δέξασθε** aor.
mid. imp. δέχομαι to accept, to receive, to welcome. **κἀγώ** =
καὶ ἐγω "I also," "I too." **μικρόν τι** s. 2 Cor. 11:1.
καυχήσωμαι aor. mid. subj., s.v.12, subj. used to express pur-
17 pose. ■ **κατά** w. the acc. "according to," "according to the
standard." Paul is not claiming to be uninspired but the expression means "in accordance w. the character or example of
Christ" (Hughes). **ὑπόστασις** basis, confidence, followed by
the descriptive or adjectival gen. "boastful confidence" (Barrett;
18 for this word, s. also Heb. 11:1). ■ **καυχήσομαι** fut. ind. mid.,
19 s.v.12. ■ **ἡδέως** adv. ἡδύς glad, adv. gladly, joyously. Paul is
using irony of the sharpest kind (BD, 262). **ἀνέχεσθε** pres. ind.
mid. to endure, to bear w. someone, followed by the gen. (s.v.1.).
φρόνιμος wise, understanding. **ὄντες** pres. part. εἰμί. The part.
could be concessive "although" or causal "because you are sensi-

ble." ■ **καταδουλοῖ** pres. ind. act. to enslave. Used in a condi- 20
tional clause which assumes the reality of the condition.
κατεσθίω to eat up, to devour. The prep. in compound is perfective. The reference may be to one who takes advantage of the
privilege of receiving maintenance, "if anyone eats you out of
house and home" (Barrett). **λαμβάνει** pres. ind. act. to take, to
receive, i.e. "catch you" as birds in a snare, or fish w. bait
(Plummer). **ἐπαίρεται** pres. ind. mid. to lift one's self up, to
exalt one's self. The exaltation is essentially self-exaltation, carnal, and worldly in character (Hughes). **δέρει** pres. ind. act. to
skin, to strike. The reference may be to physical violence or it
may be used to express verbal affronts (s. Windisch; Hughes).
The pres. tenses of the verb here may be explained as conative
or tendential and picture an action which is an attempt and
represents the idea of that which is intended, that which tends
toward realization (s. DM, 186; BD, 167; RG, 880). The prep.
used w. the verb "strike" often directs to a part of the body to,
or on, which an act is done (MT, 256). ■ **κατὰ ἀτιμίαν** "ac- 21
cording to dishonor." Here Paul used intense irony (RWP). **ὡς**
ὅτι "as that," i.e. "as people have been saying, that" (Hughes).
ἠσθενήκαμεν perf. ind. act. ἀσθενέω to be weak, to be powerless. The charge here may be of weakness caused by fear or
caution (BAG). **ἐν ᾧ** "in whatever." In whatever matter any
person exhibits real courage, the apostle does not fear comparison (Plummer). **κἀγώ** = **καὶ ἐγώ** "I also," "I too." The personal
pron. is strongly emphasized. ■ **Ἑβραῖοι** "Hebrews." The term 22
emphasizes the pure-blooded Jew and sometimes it can emphasize a Hebrew-speaking Jew or a Jew of Palestine (s. TDNT;
Lietzmann; Windisch; Barrett). **Ἰσραηλίτης** "Israelite." The
term emphasizes the social and religious character as well as the
national promises and blessings from God (s. Windisch; TDNT).
σπέρμα seed, descendant. The emphasis here may be from a
theological point of view (Barrett), particularly emphasizing the
promises made by God (Windisch). ■ **διάκονοι Χριστοῦ** "min- 23
isters of Christ." The gen. is obj. gen.; i.e., those who minister
or serve Christ. **παραφρονῶν** pres. act. part. to be beside one's
self, to be mentally deranged, "I am talking like a mad man" (s.
MM). **ὑπέρ** over, beyond. Here used as an adv. "more," "to a
higher degree, better" (BD, 121; s. also MT, 250). **κόπος** work,
toil. The word emphasizes the weariness which follows on the
straining of all of his powers to the utmost (Trench; *Synonyms*,
378). **περισσοτέρως** adv. comp. of **περισσός** abundant. Used
here in the superl. sense as elative "very abundantly." It may
mean "more abundantly than most men" or "than you would

believe" (Plummer). **φυλακή** prison, guarding. Places of confinement both public and private were used during the investigation as the accused awaited his trial. Most of the prisons were dark w. very little room, no sanitary facilities and inadequate food. (For prisons in the ancient world, s. RAC IX, 318–345; DGRA, 240f.; KP I, 1053, 1496; OCD, 879, 1099; TDNT.) **πληγή** strike, blow, wound, or bruise as the result of a blow (s. BAG). **ὑπερβαλλόντως** adv. built from the part. beyond measure, very exceedingly. **θάνατοι** pl. "deaths," i.e. "situations in which I was in danger of death" (Barrett). **πολλάκις** often.
24 ■ **πεντάκις** five times. **τεσσεράκοντα** forty. **παρὰ μίαν** "except one." This was the Jewish method of punishment based on Deut. 25:2f. The person had his two hands bound to a pillow on either side and his garments were removed so that his chest was bare. With a whip made of a strap of calf hide and two other straps of donkey hide connected to a long hand piece, the person received one-third of the thirty-nine stripes in front and two-thirds behind while he was bending low. During this time the reader reads over and again Deut. 28:58 (s. M Makkoth; SB III,
25 527–530). ■ **τρίς** three times. **ἐρραβδίσθην** aor. ind. pass. ῥαβδίζω to beat w. rods. This refers to the Roman method of beating or punishment which was often used as police coercion (s. Acts 16:22; TDNT; RAC IX, 469–490). In Paul's case it was probably a punishment prescribed by city magistrates (BAG). **ἅπαξ** once, one time. **ἐλιθάσθην** aor. ind. pass. λιθάζω to stone (s. Acts 14:19). **ἐναυάγησα** aor. ind. act. ναυαγέω to suffer shipwreck. (For the possible voyages during which Paul may have been involved in shipwrecks, s. Hughes.) **νυχθήμερον** "night-day." This refers to the Heb. custom of reckoning the day of 24 hours from evening to evening. The word may be viewed as adverbial or as the direct object of the verb (Hughes). **βυθός** deep. **πεποίηκα** perf. ind. act. The perf. shows that the dreadful experience is vividly before the apostle's mind, and possibly indicates that the occurence was recent (Plummer; s. also M,
26 144). ■ **ὁδοιπορία** walking journey, journey. **κίνδυνος** danger. The following gens. tell where the danger comes from. **ποταμός** river. The rivers were sometimes difficult to cross, some changed in a moment from half-dry riverbeds to rushing torrents (Barrett). **λῃστής** robber, bandit, one who uses weapons and violence in robbing others. (For a good description of bandits and robbers in the ancient world, s. Martin Hengel, *Die Zeloten* [Leiden: E.J. Brill, 1976] 25–47; TDNT.) **γένος** generation, contemporary, those descendant from a common ancestor (BAG). Here it refers to the Jews. **ἐρημία** desert, an isolated place.

ψευδάδελφος false brother. ■ **κόπος** work, s.v.23. **μόχθος** toil, 27
labor. The word is active indicating struggle and toil (Plummer).
ἀγρυπνία wakefulness. It refers evidently to the sleepless nights
Paul spent in work and ministry (Windisch). **λιμός** hunger.
δίψος thirst. **νηστεία** fasting. The word refers to the foregoing
of meals in order that Paul's work as a minister of Christ might
not be interrupted (Hughes). **ψῦχος** cold. **γυμνότης** nakedness.
Perhaps the last two descriptions recall when Paul was thrown
into prison, or drenched by rain, or stripped by brigands (Plummer). ■ **χωρίς** apart, besides. **παρεκτοś** external, i.e. the out- 28
ward suffering or it may imply an exception, i.e., "apart from the
things that I have not mentioned" (s. Hughes). **ἐπίστασις** pressure, stress. The word here probably refers to the "daily pressure
of responsibility" (Hughes). **μέριμνα** concern, care. ■ **ἀσθενέω** 29
to be weak, s.v.21. **σκανδαλίζεται** pres. ind. pass. to cause to
stumble. The word means rather "to catch in a death trap," pass.
"to be caught." It refers to the moral offense that kills spiritually
(s. Lenski). **πυροῦμαι** pres. ind. pass. to set on fire, to enflame.
When a brother stumbles, Paul is set on fire w. grief (RWP).

■ **καυχᾶσθαι** pres. mid. inf. καυχάομαι to boast, to glory. 30
τὰ τῆς ἀσθενείας "things belonging to my weakness."
καυχήσομαι fut. ind. mid. ■ **εὐλογητός** blessed (s. 2 Cor. 1:3). 31
ψεύδομαι to lie. ■ **ἐθνάρχης** ethnarch. (For a discussion of 32
aretas in this passage, s. Hughes.) **ἐφρούρει** impf. ind. act.
φρουρέω to watch, to guard, to guard by posting sentries. The
impf. pictures the continual action in the past **πιάσαι** aor. act.
inf. πιάζω to seize, to arrest. The inf. is used to express purpose
(Barrett). Perhaps Paul escaped from Damascus in A.D. 37 which
would make his conversion around A.D. 34 (s. Hughes; Windisch). ■ **θυρίς** window. A small opening in the wall is still 33
shown as the "little door" through which St. Paul was let down
(Plummer). **σαργάνη** basket, rope basket. **ἐχαλάσθην** aor. ind.
pass. χαλάω to let down. **διά** through. **τεῖχος** wall. **ἐξέφυγον**
aor. ind. act. ἐκφεύγω to escape. The prep. in compound is
perfective indicating that the escape was successful.

Ch. 12

■ **καυχᾶσθαι** pres. mid. inf. **δεῖ** it is necessary. **συμφέρον** 1
pres. act. part. συμφέρω expedient. In Paul's usage the word
points to the welfare not of the individual but of the Christian
society (Barrett). The part. is used as an acc. abs. (s. RG, 1130).
ἐλεύσομαι fut. ind. mid. ἔρχομαι to come. **ὀπτασία** vision.
ἀποκάλυψις unveiling, revelation. **κυρίου.** The gen. could be
subj. gen., i.e. "visions and revelations from the Lord" (Barrett)

or it could be the obj. gen., i.e. visions and revelations which
2 have the Lord as their object (Hughes). ■ **ἄνθρωπος** man. It was
part of rabbinic style to substitute an impersonal word, e.g.,
"man" for the 1st and 2nd person when one talked of himself (SB
III, 530f.). **ἔτος** year. **δεκατέσσαρες** fourteen. **ἐκτός** w. gen.
"out of." The possibility of separability of the inner man from the
body is presented in this verse (s. SBT, 146f.). **ἁρπαγέντα** aor.
pass. part. ἁρπάζω to seize, to snatch, to take by force, to catch
up. (For various parallels to Paul's experience, s. Barrett; Windisch.)
τρίτου οὐρανοῦ "the third heaven." Perhaps the expression
means into the highest heaven where the presence of
God is. Paul was granted the sight of the glory that lies ahead
and was thereby fortified to enter patiently all the suffering
4 which awaited him (s. Hughes; SB V, 531f.). ■ **ἡρπάγη** aor. ind.
pass., s.v.2. **παράδεισος** paradise. The word refers to a blissful
abode within the very courts of heaven itself (s. Hughes; Luke
23:43). **ἤκουσεν** aor. ind. act. ἀκούω. **ἄρρητος** verbal adj. "unspeakable,"
"unutterable." The word was often used of divine
secrets which were not intended for human beings (s. Windisch;
Barrett). **ῥῆμα** word. **ἐξόν** pres. part. n. sing. **ἔξεστιν** "it is
allowed." The word is to be taken in connection w. **ἀνθρώπῳ,**
5 i.e., "which it is not lawful for a man to speak" (Plummer). ■
ὑπέρ on behalf of, for the benefit of. **καυχήσομαι** fut. ind. mid.
6 καυχάομαι to glory. **εἰ μή** except. **ἀσθένεια** weakness. ■ **ἐάν.**
Used to introduce a conditional clause in which the condition is
considered to be probable. **θελήσω** aor. act. subj. θέλω to wish,
to will, to choose. The verb properly carries w. it an element of
deliberate preference (Barrett). **ἔσομαι** fut. εἰμί. **ἄφρων** foolish,
senseless, without reason. It expresses a want of mental
sanity and sobriety, a reckless and inconsiderate habit of mind
(AS). **ἐρῶ** fut. ind. act. λέγω. **φείδομαι** pres. ind. mid. to spare,
to refrain from doing something. The inf. as object is to be
supplied, i.e. "refrain from boasting" (BAG). The pres. tense
could be taken as conative "but I am trying to spare you" (Barrett).
εἰς ἐμέ "unto me." Used w. the verb in the sense "to
reckon to my account." The expression occurs often in commercial
language (s. Lietzmann). **λογίσηται** aor. mid. subj.
λογίζομαι to reckon, to put to one's account. **ὑπέρ** beyond,
7 more than. **ἐξ ἐμοῦ** "from me." ■ **ὑπερβολή** excess, extraordinary
quality or character, instrumental dat. **ὑπεραίρωμαι** pres.
mid. subj. ὑπεραίρω to lift up beyond, mid. to lift one's self up
beyond, to exalt one's self. The prep. in compound has the sense
of "excess" (MH, 326). The subj. is used to express purpose and
the clause is placed first for emphasis (s. MT, *Style*, 94). **ἐδόθη**

aor. ind. pass. δίδωμι to give. **σκόλοψ** stake, a stake used for
impaling or torturing someone, a sharpened wooden staff, thorn,
or splinter (s. Windisch, Barrett, Hughes). (For a discussion as
to what the thorn was, s. Hughes; Windisch; T.Y. Mullens, "The
Thorn in the Flesh," JBL, 76 [1957], 299f.) **τῇ σαρκί** The dat.
is either dat. of advantage "for my flesh" or locative "in my
flesh" (s. RG, 538). **κολαφίζῃ** pres. act. subj. to strike w. the fist,
to beat (s. Mark 14:65). (For a listing of the various interpretations given to this phrase, s. BAG.) The pres. tense refers to
either a constant buffeting or a reoccurring (Hughes). ■ **τρίς** 8
three times. **παρακάλεσα** aor. ind. act. παρακαλέω to ask, to
entreat. **ἀποστῇ** aor. act. subj. ἀφίστημι to depart, to go away.
The verb is generally used of persons not things (Hughes). ■ 9
εἴρηκεν perf. ind. act. λέγω. The perf. implies that the words
remain w. Paul as an abiding source of assurance and comfort
(Bruce; s. also IBG, 15). **ἀρκεῖ** pres. ind. act. to be sufficient, to
be enough. **τελεῖται** pres. ind. pass. to bring to completion, to
bring to perfection. The pres. tense emphasizes the continuous
action "my power is being perfected in weakness" (M, 130).
ἥδιστα superl. of the adv. ἡδύς gladly, elative use of the superl.
"very gladly." **μᾶλλον** rather. The comp. is not to be connected
w. the previous adv. (s. BD, 129). **καυχήσομαι** fut. ind. mid.,
s.v.1. **ἐπισκηνώσῃ** aor. subj. ἐπισκηνόω to take up one's residence, to abide, to dwell. There may be a reference to the she-
china glory of God dwelling in a tent or tabernacle. Paul may
mean that the power of God descends upon him and makes its
abode in the frail tabernacle of his earthly body (Hughes). **ἐπ' ἐμέ**
"upon me," "by me." ■ **διό** therefore. **εὐδοκῶ** pres. ind. act. to 10
take pleasure in. **ὕβρις** insulting injury. It refers to treatment
which is calculated publicly to insult and openly to humiliate the
person who suffers from it (MNTW, 83; s. also TDNT; Plummer). **διωγμός** persecution. **στενοχωρία** distress (s. 2 Cor. 6:4;
4:8). **ὑπὲρ Χριστοῦ** "on behalf of Christ." **ὅταν** whenever.
δυνατός strong, powerful.

■ **γέγονα** perf. ind. act. γίνομαι to become. The verb is 11
emphatic and means that which was expected or predicted has
come to pass (Plummer). **ἄφρων** fool, s.v.6. **ἠναγκάσατε** aor.
ind. act. ἀναγκάζω to compel. **ὤφειλον** impf. ind. act. ὀφείλω
to be obligated, to be under moral obligation, to ought. The impf.
expresses an unfulfilled obligation (RWP; BD, 181).
συνίστασθαι pres. pass. inf. to commend (s. 2 Cor. 3:1).
ὑστέρησα aor. ind. act. ὑστερέω to lack, to come behind.
ὑπερλίαν exceedingly, beyond measure, super (s. 2 Cor. 11:5).
εἰ καί "if also," "although." The condition is treated as a matter

of indifference and something which makes no real difficulty
12 (RG, 1026). ■ **σημεῖον** sign. **κατειργάσθη** aor. ind. pass.
κατεργάζω to produce, to bring about. **σημείοις** instrumental
13 dat. **τέρας** to wonder. ■ **ὅ** acc. of reference "in regard to what?"
"wherein?" **ἡσσώθητε** aor. ind. pass. ἑσσόομαι to make less,
to make inferior, pass. to be defeated, to be weaker than or
inferior to, here "in what respect, then, are you worse off than
the other churches?" (BAG). **ὑπέρ** w. acc. "than." The prep. is
used to express the comp. **κατενάρκησα** aor. ind. act.
καταναρκάω to burden, to be a burden (s. 2 Cor. 11:9).
χαρίσασθε aor. mid. imp. χαρίζομαι to show grace, to forgive.
14 **ἀδικία** wrong, a wrong act. ■ **ἰδού** behold, look. **τρίτον τοῦτο**
"This is the third time." **ἑτοίμως** adv. ἕτοιμος ready. Used w.
the verb ἔχειν "to have readiness"; i.e., "to be ready to do
something." **ἐλθεῖν** aor. act. inf. ἔρχομαι. (For a discussion of
Paul's third visit to Corinth, s. Hughes.) **καταναρκήσω** fut. ind.
act., s. 2 Cor. 11:9. **ζηῶ** pres. ind. act. to seek followed by the
pl. article w. the gen. "to seek after your possessions." The pres.
tense indicates the continual and habitual action. **ὀφείλει** pres.
ind. act. s.v.11. The pres. tense is gnomic and is used to express
customary actions and general truths (SMT, 8). **γονεῖς** parents.
θησαυρίζειν pres. act. inf. to store up treasures, to accumulate
15 money. ■ **ἥδιστα** superl. adv. ἡδύς gladly, elative use of the
superl. "most gladly." **δαπανήσω** fut. ind. act. δαπανάω to
spend money, to spend money freely. (For the use of the word
in the papyri, s. MM; Preisigke.) **ἐκδαπανηθήσομαι** fut. ind.
pass. ἐκδαπανάω pass. "to be spent out," "to be utterly spent."
The prep. in compound is perfective (RG, 596). **περισσοτέρως**
adv. comp. περισσός abundantly, comp. "more abundantly."
ἧσσον adv. comp. ὀλίγον little, comp. "less." **ἀγαπῶμαι** pres.
16 ind. pass. ἀγαπάω to love. ■ **ἔστω** imp. εἰμί "let it be." The
previous sentence is to be considered as the subject of the imp.
(RG, 596). **κατεβάρησα** aor. ind. act. καταβαρέω to put
weight on someone, to be burdensome, to put a burden on someone. **ὑπάρχων** pres. act. part. ὑπάρχω to be, to exist, to be by
constitution (Hughes). **πανοῦργος** (πᾶν, ἔργον) "every work,"
"up to every trick," "crafty and unscrupulous" (Hughes). **δόλος**
guile, craftiness, trickery (s. 2 Cor. 4:2). **ἔλαβον** aor. ind. act.
λαμβάνω to take, to catch. The metaphor is from hunting or
fishing; he entrapped or caught them in his wiliness (Plummer).
17 ■ **μή** introduces a question expecting the answer no. **τίνα** any,
anyone. The anacolouthon is resumed by the personal pron. in
the prep. phrase "through him," i.e. "any one of whom I sent—I
did not defraud you through him, did I?" (For the construction,

s. RG, 436; IBG, 176; BG, 10; BD, 234.) **ἀπέσταλκα** perf. ind.
act. ἀποστέλλω to send, to send as an authoritative representative. The perf. indicates that Paul had sent someone "from time
to time" (M, 144) and is a perf. of repeated action or of broken
continuity (RG, 893, 896). **ἐπλεονέκτησα** aor. ind. act.
πλεονεκτέω to take advantage of someone often out of selfish,
greedy arrogance (s. NTW, 97–99). ■ **παρεκάλεσα** aor. ind. 18
act. παρακαλέω to ask, to beseech, to exhort. **συναπέστειλα**
aor. ind. act. συναποστέλλω to send someone w. another. to
send together. **μήτι** interrogative particle used in questions expecting the answer no or "certainly not" (s. BD, 220). **οὐ** used
in questions which expect the answer yes. **περιεπατήσαμεν**
aor. ind. act. περιπατέω to walk, to conduct one's life. **ἴχνος**
step, footstep. Used here in the pl. "in the same footsteps."
■ **πάλαι** long ago, in the past time. Used w. the pres. tense 19
which gathers up past and pres. into one phrase "you have been
thinking this all the time" or as a question "have you been
thinking all this time?" (M, 119; s. also RG, 879). **δοκεῖτε** pres.
ind. act. to suppose, to think. (For the pres. tense, s. the previous
word.) **ἀπολογούμεθα** pres. ind. mid. to defend one's self. This
was a term used in law courts (Hughes). **κατέναντι** over against,
before. **ἀγαπητός** verbal adj. beloved. **οἰκοδομή** building up,
edification. ■ **φοβέομαι** pres. mid. ind. to fear, to be afraid. **μή** 20
πως lest, lest by any means. (For the use of these words w. verbs
of fearing, s. RG, 995; SMT, 95.) When followed by the subj. it
indicates fear of an uncertain thing in the fut. (MT, 99). **ἐλθών**
aor. act. part. ἔρχομαι temporal or conditional use of the part.
οὐχ οἵους = οὐ τοιούτους, οἵους = "not such ones as." **εὕρω**
aor. subj. εὑρίσκω to find. **ἔρις** strife, quarreling. **ζῆλος** jealous,
envying. **θύμος** anger, sudden flare up of burning anger (s.
Trench; *Synonyms*, 130). **ἐριθεία** selfishness, intrigue (s. Phil.
2:3). **καταλαλιά** speaking against someone, backbiting.
ψιθυρισμός whispering (s. Rom. 1:29). **φυσίωσις** inflated
opinion (Barrett). **ἀκαταστασία** disorder. ■ **πάλιν** again. The 21
word could refer either to the part. or to the main verb (s.
Barrett; Hughes). **ἐλθόντος** aor. act. part. ἔρχομαι to come.
The part. is used as a gen. abs. "when I come" (s. BD, 218).
ταπεινώσῃ aor. act. subj. ταπεινόω to make low, to humiliate.
The subj. is used in a neg. purpose clause which goes back to the
verb in v. 20 "I fear" (RWP). **πενθήσω** aor. act. subj. πενθέω
to express sorrow for one who has died, to mourn.
προημαρτηκότων perf. act. part. προαμαρτάνω to sin previously. The perf. tense of the part. indicates that the sinning began
early and continued and refers to persistence in sexual sin by the

members of the Corinthian church during a previous period (Barrett; Hughes). **μετανοησάντων** aor. act. part. μετανοέω to change one's thinking, to repent. The aor. tense in contrast to the previous perf. indicates that the repentence which might have ended the sinning did not take place (Barrett). **ἀκαθαρσία** uncleanness. The word refers to sexual sins of impurity. **πορνεία** fornication, illicit sexual activity (s. TDNT). **ἀσέλγεια** not bridled, unrestrained, lawless insolence, sheer animal lust. It is the vice of a man who has no more shame than an animal in the gratification of his physical desires (NTW, 27; s. also Trench; *Synonyms*, 53f.).

Ch. 13

1 ■ **τρίτον τοῦτο** "this third time" (s. Hughes; Hodge). **ἐπί** w. the gen. "upon," "on the basis of"; i.e. "on the basis of the testimony." **δύο καὶ τρεῖς** "two or three." **σταθήσεται** fut. ind. pass. ἵστημι to stand, pass. to be established. **ῥῆμα** word, matter. The matter between Paul and the Corinthians is to be brought in order by the third visit which would be in line w. this
2 statement from Deut. 19:15 (s. Windisch). ■ **προείρηκα** perf. ind. act. **προλογέω** to say previously, to say beforehand, to tell in advance. It is possible that the idea of the word is "to warn" (Barrett). **παρών** pres. part. πάρειμι to be present, temporal use of the part. **δεύτερον** second, the second time. **ἀπών** pres. part. ἄπειμι to be absent. **προημαρτηκόσιν** perf. act. part. προαμαρτάνω to sin beforehand (s. 2 Cor. 12:21). **ἔλθω** aor. act. subj. ἔρχομαι. **εἰς τὸ πάλιν** "again," "for another visit" (IBG, 69). **φείσομαι** fut. ind. mid. φείδομαι to spare. It primarily means "to spare in battle—not to kill when the opportunity to do so exists." It then comes to mean "to have mercy
3 upon" (Barrett). ■ **ἐπεί** "since." Used in a causal sense "because." **δοκιμή** proof, that which passes an examination (s. 2 Cor. 2:9). **ζητεῖτε** pres. ind. act. to seek. **τοῦ ἐν ἐμοὶ λαλοῦντος Χριστοῦ.** The gen. indicates that which was to be proven: "proof that Christ is speaking in me." **ἀσθενεῖ** pres. ind. act. ἀσθενέω to be weak. **δυνατεῖ** pres. ind. act. δυνατέω to be strong, to be
4 mighty. ■ **καὶ γάρ** "for even" (Hughes). **ἐσταυρώθη** aor. ind. pass. σταυρόω to crucify. **ἐκ** "out of." The prep. here is used in the causal sense (MT, 259f.). **καὶ γάρ** "for also" (Hughes), "for indeed" (Barrett). **εἰς ὑμᾶς** "toward you." It is probably to be taken w. the verb "we shall live" (Hughes).
5 ■ **ἑαυτούς** "yourselves." **πειράζετε** pres. act. imp. to try, to examine (s. Trench; *Synonyms*, 280). **δοκιμάζω** pres. act. imp. to test, to prove, to approve after examination. In the NT

the word almost always implies that the proof is victorously
surmounted, the proven is also approved (Trench; *Synonyms*,
278; s. also Hughes). **ἐπιγινώσκετε** pres. ind. act. to recognize,
to know. The prep. in compound is directive and directs the
knowledge to the specific object (s. MH, 312). **εἰ μήτι** "if perhaps," "unless indeed." **ἀδόκιμος** disapproved, rejected after
examination, not usable. ■ **γνώσεσθε** fut. ind. mid. *γινώσκω* 6
to recognize. ■ **εὔχομεθα** pres. ind. mid. to pray, followed by 7
the gen. indicating the contents of the prayer. **μὴ ποιῆσαι** aor.
act. inf. used w. the neg. The subject of the inf. is not clear either
"that you may do no evil thing" or "that God may do no harm"
(s. Barrett). **δόκιμος** approved, approved after testing.
φανῶμεν aor. act. subj. *φαίνομαι* to appear. **ὦμεν** pres. subj.
εἰμί. ■ **ἀλήθεια** truth. The word may be used here in a general 8
sense (Barrett). ■ **ὅταν** when, whenever. **ἀσθενῶμεν** pres. act. 9
subj. *ἀσθενέω* s.v.3. **ἦτε** pres. subj. **εἰμί**. **κατάρτισις** perfect-
ing, fitting together. It is used in the sense of setting bones or
reconciling parties and refers here to the growth in holiness
(Plummer). ■ **ἀποτόμως** adv. cut off, curt, sharply, severely (s. 10
RWP; BAG). **χρήσωμαι** aor. mid. subj. *χράομαι* to use.
οἰκοδομη building up, edification. **καθαίρεσις** tearing down,
destroying.

■ **λοίπον** acc. of the adj. used as an adv. "finally." **χαίρετε** 11
pres. act. imp. rejoice. **καταρτίζεσθε** pres. pass. imp.
καταρτίζω to restore, pass. to be restored. **παρακαλεῖσθε**
pres. imp. pass. *παρακαλέω* to exhort, to encourage (s. TDNT;
MNTW, 134). **φρονεῖτε** pres. act imp. *φρονέω* to think, here
"be of the same mind," "be harmonious in thought and aim"
(Plummer). **εἰρηνεύετε** pres. act. imp. to be peaceable, to live in
peace. **ἔσται** fut. *εἰμί*. ■ **ἀσπάσασθε** aor. mid. imp. 12
ἀσπάζομαι to greet. **φίλημα** kiss (s. 1 Cor. 16:10).

■ **κοινωνία τοῦ ἁγίου πνεύματος** "the fellowship of the 13
Holy Spirit." The gen. could be obj. gen., i.e., the fellowship or
participation which has the Holy Spirit as its object or it could
be subj. gen., i.e. the fellowship or participation which comes
from the Holy Spirit (s. TDNT; Barrett).

GALATIANS

Ch. 1

1 **ἀπό** "from." The prep. indicates source and Paul states that his apostleship did not have a group of men (pl.) as its source. (For the term "apostle," s. 1 Cor. 1:1.) **διά** "through." The prep. denotes the means or agency. It points to the medium through which one would have conveyed the office of his apostleship. **ἐγείραντος** aor. act. part. ἐγείρω to raise up. The context indicates that the resurrection of Christ has a special bearing on Paul's apostleship: "I was commissioned by the risen and glorified Lord: I am in all respects an apostle, a qualified witness of His resurrection, and a signal instance of His power" (Lightfoot).
4 ■ **δόντος** aor. act. part. δίδωμι to give, to bestow (s. Gal. 2:20). The idea involved is a delivering up of one's self for a specific purpose (Guthrie). **ἐξέληται** aor. mid. subj. ἐξαιρέω to take out, to remove, to deliver. It denotes a rescue from the power of (Burton). The subj. is used to express purpose. **ἐνεστῶτος** perf. act. part. ἐνίσταμι to have come, to be present. The word points
5 to the pres. transitory age (Lightfoot; s. also Eadie). ■ **ἀμήν** truly. Used to emphasize and substantiate a statement (s. TDNT; CBB; Matt. 5:18).

6 ■ **θαυμάζω** pres. act. ind. to marvel, to wonder, to be astonished. The pres. tense points to the pres. continual attitude of Paul. **οὕτως ταχέως** "so quickly." Paul was astonished at the ταχέως w. which the Galatians were responding to a counterfeit gospel (Guthrie; Mussner). **μετατίθεσθε** pres. mid. ind. to transfer, to remove, to desert, to change one's opinion. The word was used of desertion or revolt in a military or political defection and it frequently had the idea of a change in religion, philosophy, or morals (Lightfoot; TDNT). **καλέσαντος** aor. act. part. The aor. points to the time when the Galatians received the gospel (Mussner). **ἕτερον** another. It expresses a difference in kind (Guthrie; TDNT; Lightfoot; Burton). The rabbis used a similar term for those who had rejected to receive traditions (Mussner).
7 ■ **εἰ μή** "except." The words limit that which went before (Ridderbos). **ταράσσοντες** pres. act. part. ταράσσω to shake back and forth, to trouble, to disturb. **θέλοντες** pres. act. part. to wish,

to desire. **μεταστρέψαι** aor. act. inf. μεταστρέφω to turn
about, to change from one thing to another, to change to the
opposite, to pervert (Burton; Lightfoot). The aor. tense would
indicate a complete and thorough change. ■ **εὐαγγελιζηται** 8
aor. mid. subj. εὐαγγελίζω to proclaim good news, to preach the
gospel. The aor. points to the act of one time preaching the
gospel. **εὐηγγελισάμεθα** aor. mid. ind. **ἀνάθεμα** accursed,
dedicated for destruction (s. TDNT). **ἔστω** pres. imp. εἰμί. ■ 9
προειρήκαμεν perf. ind. act. προλέγω to say beforehand, to
say previously. The perf. points to the abiding authority of that
which was said. **παρελάβετε** aor. ind. act. παραλαμβάνω to
receive from someone. The verb expresses the communication
of authorized Christian teaching (Guthrie).
■ **πείθω** pres. ind. act. to persuade, to win the favor of 10
someone (Burton). The pres. tense is conative indicating the
trying or attempting (BD, 167; RG, 880). **ζητέω** pres. ind. act.
to seek. **ἀρέσκω** pres. act. inf. to please, to cause pleasure. The
inf. gives the content of the verb "seek." **ἤρεσκον** impf. ind. act.
ἀρέσκω. The verb is used in a contrary to fact conditional
clause and the impf. indicates an incompleted action. **ἤμην** impf.
εἰμί.
■ **γνωρίζω** to make known, to make clear, to certify. It has 11
the effect of suggesting a somewhat formal statement to follow
(EBC, Vol. 10). **εὐαγγελισθέν** aor. pass. part., s.v.8. ■ **οὐδέ** not, 12
not even. The word indicates either "even I who so naturally
might have been taught of men did not . . ." or it might mean "I
as little as the other apostles," i.e., "I (distinctly emphatic)—as
little as any others did not . . ." (Ellicott; s. also Burton).
παρέλαβον aor. ind. act., s.v.9. **ἐδιδάχθην** aor. pass. ind.
ἀποκάλυψις unveiling, revelation. The word indicates that it
was an opening up of what was previously secret. The following
gen. is best taken as obj. gen. indicating that Christ was the
object of the revelation (Guthrie).
■ **ἠκούσατε** aor. ind. act. ἀκούω. **ἀναστροφή** manner of 13
life. It refers to Paul's ethical conduct (Ridderbos). **ὑπερβολή**
throwing beyond, beyond measure, in excess. **ἐδίωκον** impf. ind.
act. διώκω to pursue, to hunt, to persecute. The impf. pictures
the persistent and continual action in the past. **ἐπόρθουν** impf.
ind. act. πορθέω to ravage, to destroy. It was used of soldiers
ravaging a city (Burton). The impf. is conative "I was trying to
devastate it." ■ **προέκοπτον** impf. ind. act. προκόπτω to cut 14
forward (as in a forest), to blaze a way, to go ahead, to advance
(RWP). Saul of Tarsus was so intent in his ambition to further
the cause of Judaism that he did not hesitate to cut down all

opposition and in this respect he outstripped his contemporaries (Guthrie). **ὑπέρ** beyond, over, above. The prep. used w. the acc. designates that which excels or surpasses and is a type of comp. (BD, 121). **συνηλικιώτης** one of the same age, contemporary. **γένος**. Here it has the connotation "of my people" (Ridderbos). **περισσοτέρως** adv. comp. περισσός abundantly, extremely. **ζηλωτής** enthusiast, one who is zealous for a cause, followed by the gen. indicating that which one is zealous of. (For a study of the word, s. TDNT; Hengel, *Zeloten*, 67–78.) **ὑπάρχων** pres. act. part. ὑπάρχω to be, to exist, to be by constitution (s. 2 Cor. 12:16). **πατρικός** pertaining to a father, fatherly. (For the meaning of the suf., s. MH, 378.) **παράδοσις** passing on from one to another, tradition. In connection w. Judaism it refers to that body of oral teaching which was complementary to the written law and in fact possessed equal authority to the law (Guthrie).
15 ■ **εὐδόκησεν** aor. ind. act. εὐδοκέω to please, to be well-pleased, followed by the inf. **ἀφορίσας** aor. act. part. ἀφορίζω to divide w. a boundary, to mark off from others w. a boundary, to set apart. The idea here is "to set aside for special purpose" (Ridderbos). **κοιλία** body cavity, womb, i.e., "from before my birth," "before I had any impluses, any principles of my own"
16 (Lightfoot). **καλέσας** aor. act. part. ■ **ἀποκαλύψαι** aor. act. inf. ἀποκαλύπτω to unveil, to reveal. Infinitive used to express purpose. **ἐν ἐμοὶ** "in me" or simply "to me," "me." With verbs of knowing and making known, the prep. designates not only the person through whom the communication comes, but also the one who receives it (Ridderbos; BD, 118). **εὐαγγελίζωμαι** pres. mid. subj. Subjunctive used in a purpose clause. **ἔθνος** nation, pl. Gentiles. **εὐθέως** adv. immediately. **προσανεθέμην** aor. mid. ind. προσανατίθεμι lit. "to lay on one's self in addition." When used w. the gen. it suggests the gaining of information by communicating w. others (Guthrie; Lightfoot; s. also Mussner).
17 ■ **ἀνῆλθον** aor. ind. act. ἀνέρχομαι to go up. **ἀπῆλθον** aor. ind. act. ἀπέρχομαι to go away. **ὑπέστρεψα** aor. ind. act. ὑποστρέφω to return. The prep. in compound has the sense of "back" (s. MH, 327).
18 ■ **ἔπειτα** "then." The word draws particular attention to the next event in order of sequence (Guthrie). **ἔτος** year. **ἱστορῆσαι** aor. act. inf. ἱστορέω to inquire, to visit places or persons (Burton; s. also MM; Preisigke). **ἐπέμεινα** aor. ind. act. ἐπιμένω to remain. (For the prep. in compound, s. MH, 312.)
19 ■ **εἰ μή** "except." (For the possible ways of understanding these words, s. L. Paul Trudinger, "A Note on Galatians 1:19," Nov T, 17 [July, 1975], 200–202.) (For a discussion of the various

interpretations related to James, the brother of the Lord, s. Eadie; Lightfoot, 252–291.) ■ **ψεύδομαι** pres. mid. ind. to lie. (For 20
a comparison of Paul's statement to the oaths offered during Roman court procedures, s. J.P. Sampley, " 'Before God, I Do Not Lie' [Gal. 1:20]," NTS, 23 [July, 1977], 477–482.) ■ **κλῖμα** 21
region, area. ■ **ἀγνοούμενος** pres. pass. part. ἀγνοέω to be 22
ignorant, not to know, pass. to be unknown. The pres. tense stresses the continuity of the state of not knowing (Guthrie).
■ **ἀκούοντες** pres. act. part. **διώκων** pres. act. part., s.v.13. ■ 23/24
ἐδόξαζον impf. ind. act. δοξάζω to glorify, to cause one to think highly of another. The impf. indicates "they began to glorify." **ἐν ἐμοί** "in me." The prep. constitutes the ground or basis of the action "they found in me occasion and reason for praising God" (Burton).

Ch. 2

■ **ἔπειτα** then (s. Gal. 1:18). **ἔτος** year. **ἀνέβην** aor. ind. 1
act. ἀναβαίνω to go up. **μετά** w. the gen. "with," "accompanied by." It suggests that Paul was the leader (Guthrie). **συμπαραλαβών** aor. act. part. συμπαραλαμβάνω to take along w., to take someone along as a traveling companion, to take someone along as a helper. The word is applied to a private companion or minister, who is not sent forth on the mission of an envoy, but is taken by the envoy on their authority (Ramsey;
s. also MM). ■ **ἀποκάλυψις** unveiling, revelation, used w. the 2
prep. "in obedience to such a revelation" (Burton). **ἀνέθεμην** aor. mid. inf. ἀνατίθημι to lay something before someone for consideration, to relate w. a view to consulting (BAG; Lightfoot). **ἴδιος** one's own, used in the idomatic construction κατ' ἰδίαν "privately." **δοκοῦσιν** pres. act. part. δοκέω to seem to be, to appear. Used in this construction "οἱ δοκοῦντες εἰναί τι" "those who seem to be something." It is used in the sense of "the authorities" and the word itself implies position of honor (Meyer; Guthrie). **μή** "lest." Used w. the subj. to express a neg. purpose or to prohibit that which is feared (s. 2 Cor. 12:20). **τρέχω** pres. act. subj. to run. The preaching of the gospel is pictured as a runner of a race and his concern about his eventual success or failure in the race. The pres. subj. expresses the fear of continuous fruitless effort into the fut. (s. PAM, 100f.). **ἔδραμον** aor. ind. act. τρέχω. The ind. is used of that which has already taken place or is entirely independent of the will. The fact of having run in the past is no longer dependent of the will
of him who fears (BD, 188; PAM, 101; Schlier). ■ **ὤν** pres. act. 3
part. εἰμί. The part. is concessive "although . . ." **ἠναγκάσθη**

aor. pass. ind. ἀναγκάζω to exert pressure on someone, to
compel, to coerce. The aor. is effective or resultative affirming
that an action attempted in the past was accomplished (SMT,
42). **περιτμηθῆναι** aor. pass. inf. περιτέμνω to circumcise (s.
Rom. 2:25; Neil J. McEleney, "Conversion, Circumcision and
4 the Law," NTS, 20 [April, 1974], 319–341). ■ **δέ** "but." The
structure and grammatical connection of this verse is not clear.
(For a discussion of the various possibilities, s. Lightfoot; Burton;
Mussner.) **παρείσακτος** secretly brought in, smuggled in along
side of, sneaked in (BAG). The word could also simply mean
"alien," "foreign" (s. Eadie; MM). **ψευδάδελφος** false brother.
ὅστις "who," "one who." The word specifies the class to which
one belongs (Ellicott; RG, 727). **παρεισῆλθον** aor. ind. act.
παρεισέρχομαι to come in along side of, to slip into. The word
usually implies "stealth" (Burton). The metaphor is that of spies
or traitors introducing themselves by stealth into the enemy's
camp (Lightfoot). **κατασκοπῆσαι** aor. act. inf. κατασκοπέω
to spy out, to examine carefully. The form is used most frequently
where the notion of treachery is prominent (Lightfoot). (See
Josh. 2:2, 3.) The aor. may refer to the act as done before they
were detected (Eadie). The inf. is used to express purpose.
ἐλευθερία freedom. **καταδουλώσουσιν** fut. ind. act.
καταδουλόω to enslave, to bring down to bondage, to completely
enslave. The prep. in compound is perfective (MH, 316).
5 ■ **εἴξαμεν** aor. ind. act. εἴκω to yield, to give into, to give way,
to allow. **ὑποταγῇ** submission, dat. of reference or respect, i.e.,
"we did not yield w. respect to the submission." The definite
article refers to the matter under discussion; i.e., circumcision
(Guthrie). **διαμείνῃ** aor. act. subj. διαμένω to remain permanently,
to continue throughout. The idea of "firm possession" is
enforced by the compound verb, by the past tense, and by the
6 prep. (Lightfoot). ■ **ὁποιός ποτε** "what kind of people they
were." The general rel. pron. refers to quality (s. BD, 159;
Schlier). **διαφέρει** "it makes a difference," "it matters." Used
here w. the neg. "it makes no difference to me." **προσανέθεντο**
aor. mid. ind. προσανατίθημι to add something in addition,
here it has the sense "to teach in addition to what I have already
learned" (s. Burton). Paul means that no restrictions were set to,
no further and extraneous requirements were laid upon, the
fundamental proclamation of the gospel (PAA, 146). (For Paul's
view of his apostleship and authoritative message in relation to
the other apostles, s. David M. Hay, "Paul's Indifference to
7 Authority," JBL, 88 [March, 1969], 36–44.) ■ **τοὐναντίον** "on
the contrary." **πεπίστευμαι** perf. pass. ind. πιστεύομαι pass.

to be entrusted w. something. **ἀκροβυστία** foreskin, uncircum-
cised. **περιτομή** circumcised. ■ **ἐνεργήσας** aor. act. part. 8
ἐνεργέω to be at work, to be active, to effect, to produce results
(Burton; Mussner). The verb is followed by the dat. of advantage. **εἰς**. The prep. points to the goal of the active working of
God (Mussner). **ἀποστολή** apostleship. The word is the act of
fulfilling the commission, i.e., the establishment of Christian
communities (PAA, 148; Robert Duncan Culver, "Apostles and
the Apostolate in the New Testament," Bib Sac, 134 [April,
1977], 131–143). **ἐνήργησεν** aor. act. ind. ἐνεργέω. **γνόντες**
aor. act. part. γινώσκω to know, to recognize. **δοθεῖσαν** aor.
pass. part. δίδωμι. **στῦλος** pillar. The metaphor was used by the
Jews in speaking of the great teachers of the law (Lightfoot; s.
also SB III, 537). **δεξία** right. **ἔδωκαν** aor. act. ind. δίδωμι.
κοινωνία fellowship. In modern parlance this means that they
all shook hands to signify agreement (Guthrie). (For the term
"fellowship," s. CBB; TDNT; RAC IX, 1100–1145.) ■ 10
μνημονεύωμεν pres. act. subj. μνημονεύω to remember.
ἐσπούδασα aor. ind. act. σπουδάζω to be diligent, to be eager.
αὐτὸ τοῦτο "this very thing." **ποιῆσαι** aor. act. inf. to do.

■ **ἀντέστην** aor. act. ind. ἀνίστημι to stand against, to 11
oppose. **κατεγνωσμένος** perf. pass. part. καταγινώσκω to
condemn, pass. to be condemned. Peter was condemned either
by his own contradictory actions (Lightfoot) or by his own conscience. (For this view as well as examples from the papyri, s.
MM; Schlier.) ■ **ἐλθεῖν** aor. act. inf. ἔρχομαι. The inf. is used 12
w. the prep. to express previous or antecedent time "before . . ."
(MT, 144). **συνήσθιεν** impf. ind. act. συνεσθίω to eat together. The impf. expresses the habitual action of the past "he
used to eat regularly w. Gentiles." **ὑπέστελλεν** impf. ind. act.
ὑποστέλλω to withdraw. The impf. is inceptive "he began to
withdraw." **ἀφώριζεν** impf. act. ind. ἀφορίζω to separate (s.
Gal. 1:14). The impf. is inceptive. **φοβούμενος** pres. mid. part.
φοβέομαι to fear, to be afraid. The part. is causal. ■ 13
συνυπεκρίθησαν aor. pass. ind. συνυποκρίνομαι to act as a
hypocrite w. another. The basic meaning of the word is "to
answer from under" and refers to actors who spoke under a mask
in playing a part. The actors hid their true selves behind the role
they were playing. The word indicates the concealing of wrong
feelings, character, etc. under the pretense of better ones (Burton; Guthrie; TDNT). **συναπήχθη** aor. pass. ind. συναπάγω
to lead away together. The pass. of the word suggests that Barnabas did not play an active part in the hypocrisy and the meaning of the verb implies that Barnabas was swept off his balance

14 (Guthrie). ■ **ὀρθοποδοῦσιν** pres. act. ind. to walk correctly, to
walk straight or upright. Followed by the prep. the verb means
"they were not walking on the straight path towards the truth of
the gospel" (Mussner). **ὑπάρχων** pres. act. part. ὑπάρχω to
exist, to be. **ἐθνικῶς** adv. "in the manner of a heathen." **ζῇς**
pres. ind. act. ζάω to live. The ind. is used in a conditional clause
which assumes the reality of the condition. **Ἰουδαΐζειν** pres. act.
inf. to live as a Jew, to adopt Jewish customs (Lightfoot).
15 ■ **φύσις** nature, here in the dat. "by nature," "by birth."
The verb to be supplied is to be taken as concessive "though we
are Jews by nature and not sinners of Gentile origin" (Burton;
16 Mussner). **ἁμαρτωλός** sinner. ■ **εἰδότες** perf. act. part. οἶδα
defective perf. w. the pres. meaning "to know." (For a study of
this verb, s. ND, 344ff.) **δικαιοῦται** pres. pass. ind. δικαιόω to
declare righteous. (For the meaning of this term, s. Rom. 2:13.)
The pres. tense indicates that which is always true. The pass.
points to the fact that one does not justify himself but is declared
righteous by another. The neg. w. the pres. tense indicates that
justification can never at any time be achieved by works of the
law. **ἐάν μή** "if not," "except." The expression is properly ex-
ceptive and introduces an exception related to the main verb.
Here it can be translated "but only" (Burton). **ἐπιστεύσαμεν**
aor. ind. act. The aor. could be ingressive aor. "we have come
to believe" (Ridderbos). **δικαιωθῶμεν** aor. pass. subj.
17 **δικαιωθήσεται** fut. pass. ind. ■ **δικαιωθῆναι** aor. pass. inf.
εὑρέθημεν aor. pass. ind. **ἆρα** here to be taken as the interrogative particle rather than an inferential particle. It expresses
bewilderment as to a possible conclusion "is Christ then a minister of sin?" (s. Lightfoot; Mussner). **γένοιτο** aor. mid. opt.
γίνομαι "let it not be," "certainly not!" This represents a characteristic Pauline reputation of an unthinkable suggestion
18 (Guthrie). ■ **κατέλυσα** aor. ind. act. καταλύω to tear down, to
destroy, to annul, to abrogate. **οἰκοδομέω** pres. ind. act. to build
up. The pres. tense suggests a maxim which would always be true
(s. Eadie). **παραβάτης** one who goes beyond the boundary,
transgressor. **συνιστάνω** pres. ind. act. to constitute, to prove.
Used w. the double acc. Used w. the reflex. pron. as one of the
accs. it means "to prove one's self something or someone," "to
19 recommend or present one's self as such" (Ridderbos). ■ **ἐγώ.**
The idea here is "I Paul, the natural man, the slave of the old
covenant" (Lightfoot). **γάρ** for. This explicative shows how this
rehabilitation of the law actually amounts to a transgression of
its true principles (Ellicott). **ἀπέθανον** aor. ind. act.
ἀποθνῄσκω to die, followed by the dat. of reference. **ζήσω** aor.

act. subj. ζάω followed by the dat. of advantage "to live for God." **συνεσταύρωμαι** perf. pass. ind. συνσταυρόω to crucify together. The perf. tense suggests that Paul is thinking of that specific completed event which marked his identification w. Christ and which has had an enduring effect upon his life (Guthrie). ■ **οὐκέτι** no longer. **ἀγαπήσαντος** aor. act. part. ἀγαπάω 20
to love. **παραδόντος** aor. act. part. παραδίδωμι to give over,
to give. Christ's self-giving upon the cross was a definite act of
love. ■ **ἀθετέω** pres. ind. act. to set aside, to reject. In the papyri 21
it was used of loans which were repaid and cancelled and for the rejection of certain officials who were described as inefficient and incapable of doing their duty. It was also used of grain which was rejected by the inspector as unfit for food (MM). **δωρέαν** gratuitously, i.e. "without (giving or receiving) pay" (Burton).

Ch. 3

■ **ἀνόητος** foolish, without thinking. It describes the acting 1
in a spirit which manifests the absence of wisdom (Eadie). **ἐβάσκανεν** aor. ind. act. βασκαίνω to bewitch, to cast a magic spell, to seek to bring damage to a person through an evil eye or through a spoken word (s. Lightfoot; TDNT; MM). One ancient writer felt that one could ward off the evil spell by spitting three times (BAG). **προεγράφη** aor. pass. ind. προγράφω to write before, to write up in public. The word was used to describe all public notices or proclamations and indicates a public announcement in which the validity of a particular fact or a particular condition is proclaimed (Lightfoot; Ridderbos; TDNT). **ἐσταυρωμένος** perf. pass. part. σταυρόω to crucify. The perf. tense indicates a state or condition and stresses the abiding significance of the event (Guthrie; s. also McKay). The lack of the article stresses the character; i.e. "a crucified one." (For a description of crucifixion in the ancient world, s. Martin Hengel, *Crucifixion in the Ancient World and the Folly of the Message
of the Cross* [Philadelphia: Fortress Press, 1977].) ■ **μαθεῖν** aor. 2
act. inf. μανθάνω to learn. **ἐλάβετε** aor. act. ind. λαμβάνω to
receive. **ἀκόη** hearing. ■ **ἐναρξάμενοι** aor. mid. part. ἐνάρχω 3
to begin. **πνεύματι** and **σαρκί** are dats. of instrument. **ἐπιτελεῖσθε** pres. mid. ind. ἐπιτελέω to accomplish, to complete, to finish, to come to the intended goal. ■ **τοσοῦτος** so 4
great, pl. "so great things." **ἐπάθετε** aor. ind. act. πάσχω to experience. The word may mean "to experience evil," i.e. "to suffer" or it may be used in a neutral sense "to experience" (s. Burton; Mussner). **εἰκῇ** in vain. **εἴ γε καί** "if it be really." The phrase leaves a loophole for doubt implying an unwillingness to

5 believe on the part of the speaker (Lightfoot). ■ **ἐπιχορηγῶν**
pres. act. part. ἐπιχορηγέω to supply. The simple verb means
"to defray the expense of providing a 'chorus' at the public feast"
and the prep. expresses strongly the idea "to supply abundantly"
(Burton; s. also 2 Cor. 9:10). The pres. tense implies the permanency of the action (Ellicott). **ἐνεργῶν** pres. act. part. ἐνεργέω
6 to be energetic, to work. ■ **καθώς** "just as." The word indicates
that Paul is drawing a parallel between Abraham's justification
and present-day justification (Mussner). **ἐπίστευσεν** aor. ind.
act. **ἐλογίσθη** aor. ind. pass. λογίζομαι to place to one's account, to account, to reckon.
7 ■ **γινώσκετε** pres. ind. or imp. **ἄρα** so, therefore. It is used
8 as a particle of inference. ■ **προϊδοῦσα** aor. act. part. προοράω
to see beforehand, to foresee. The word indicates that the faith
element in God's method of justification is timeless (Guthrie).
δικαιοῖ pres. ind. act. to justify, to declare righteous. **ἔθνος**
nation, Gentile. **προευηγγελίσατο** aor. mid. ind.
προευαγγελίζομαι to proclaim the good news beforehand. **ὅτι**
recitative use introducing a direct quotation and is equivalent to
quotation marks. **ἐνευλογηθήσονται** fut. ind. pass. ἐνευλογέω
to bless. (For the term "blessing," "to bless," s. Cleon Rogers,
"The Covenant with Abraham and Its Historical Setting," Bib
9 Sac, 127 [April, 1970], 241–256.) ■ **ὥστε** therefore. The word
draws a conclusion from the previous material. **εὐλογοῦνται**
10 pres. ind. pass. εὐλογέω to bless. ■ **ὅσοι** as many as. **κατάρα**
curse. This was the covenant curse for disobedience to the conditions of the Mosaic covenant (s. CBB; TDNT). **γέγραπται** pres. pass. ind. "it stands written." The perf. indicates that the authority of the document is binding (s. MM). **ἐπικατάρατος** curst, cursed. (For a discussion of the Heb. word "curst" as used here in the quotation from Deut. 27:26, s. TDOT, H.C. Brichto, *The Problem of "Curse" in the Hebrew Bible* [Philadelphia: Society of Biblical Literature, 1968].) **ἐμμένει** pres. ind. act. to remain in, to continue in. The pres. tense indicates the need for unbroken and continual observance of the whole law. **γεγραμμένοις**
perf. pass. part. **ποιῆσαι** aor. act. inf. The inf. is used to express
11 purpose. ■ **δικαιοῦται** pres. pass. ind. **δῆλος** clear, evident.
12 **ζήσεται** fut. ind. mid. ζάω to live. ■ **ποιήσας** aor. act. part.
13 ■ **ἐξηγόρασεν** aor. ind. act. ἐξαγοράζω to buy out of the
market place, to redeem, to randsom from slavery (s. APC; TDNT). **γενόμενος** aor. mid. part. γίνομαι. The part. gives the means or way in which the action of the main verb was accomplished. **κρεμάμενος** pres. mid. part. κρέμαμαι to hang. **ξύλον** wood, tree (s. Acts 10:39). (For the view that Paul combines

Deut. 21:22–23 w. a reference to Isaac in Gen. 22, s. Max Wilcox, " 'Upon the Tree'—Deut. 21:22–23 in the New Testament," JBL, 96 [March, 1977], 85–99.) ■ **γένηται** aor. mid. subj. 14
γίνομαι. The subj. is used to express purpose. **ἐπαγγελία** promise. The gen. **ἐπαγγελίαν τοῦ πνεύματος** is obj. gen., i.e. the promise which has the Spirit for its object (Eadie). **λάβωμεν** aor. act. subj. λαμβάνω to receive.

■ **ὅμως** even though, nevertheless, w. the possible transla- 15
tion "even though it is only a man's will, nevertheless." However it may be used to introduce a comparison and have the translation "also," "likewise" (s. BD, 234). **κεκυρωμένην** perf. pass. part. κυρόω to validate, to ratify. **διαθήκη** agreement, treaty, covenant. However it may have the meaning "will," "testament" (s. Guthrie; APC; TDNT). **ἀθετεῖ** pres. ind. act. to annul (s. Gal. 2:21). **ἐπιδιατάσσεται** pres. mid. ind. to add on to. The prep. in compound indicates "to make additional prescriptions" (Burton). The pres. tenses here are gnomic indicating that which is
always true. ■ **ἐρρέθησαν** aor. pass. ind. λέγω. ■ **τοῦτο δὲ** 16/17
λέγω "now this I say." Paul comes to his real purpose and proceeds to apply the figure of v. 15 arguing from the lesser to the greater; i.e., if this is true among human beings and their agreements, it is even more true in respect to God and His promises (s. Ridderbos). **προκεκυρωμένην** perf. pass. part. προκυρόω to ratify beforehand, to confirm previously. The perf. tense points to the lasting authority of the legal ratification. **ἔτος** year. **γεγονώς** perf. act. part. γίνομαι. **ἀκυρόω** pres. act. ind. to make invalid, to annul either by rescinding or overriding or otherwise (Burton; s. also MM; BS, 228). **καταργῆσαι** aor. act. inf. καταργέω to render inoperative, to make of no effect. The inf. is used w. the prep. to express either purpose or result (s. MT,
143). ■ **κληρονομία** inheritance. **οὐκέτι** no longer. 18
κεχάρισται perf. mid. ind. χαρίζομαι to give graciously (s.
TDNT). ■ **παράβασις** stepping over the boundary, transgres- 19
sion. **χάριν** used w. gen. "on account of," "because of." **προσετέθη** aor. pass. ind. προστίθημι to add to. **ἄχρις** until. **ἔλθῃ** aor. act. subj. ἔρχομαι. **τὸ σπέρμα** "the seed," "the offspring" has already been identified as Christ in v. 16 (Guthrie). **ἐπήγγελται** perf. pass. ind. ἐπαγγέλλω to promise. **διαταγείς** aor. pass. part. διατάσσω to enact "a law." It is a technical term for the carrying out of laws and ordinances (Ridderbos). (For the Jewish view concerning the activity of angels in the giving of the
law, s. SB III, 554–556.) ■ **μεσίτης** mediator, one who stands 20
between two parties. **ἑνός** one. (For a discussion of the meaning of this passage, s. EBC, Vol. 10; Burton; Guthrie; Mussner; U.

Mauser, "Galater III 20: Die Universalität des Heils," NTS, 18
[April, 1967], 258–270.)
21 ■ **γένοιτο** aor. mid. opt. γίνομαι (s. Gal. 2:17). **ἐδόθη** aor.
pass. ind. δίδωμι. The ind. is used in a contrary to fact conditional clause. **δυνάμενος** pres. mid. part. to be able.
ζωοποιῆσαι aor. act. inf. ζωοποιέω to make alive. The purpose
of the law was not to make alive but to give Israel a rule of life
22 in the promised land. ■ **συνέκλεισεν** aor. ind. act. συγκλείω
to lock up together, to shut in on all sides. The verb indicates
there is no possibility of escape (Guthrie). **δοθῇ** aor. pass. subj.
δίδωμι. The subj. is used in a purpose clause. **πιστεύουσιν**
pres. act. part. The dat. is the indirect object.
23 ■ **ἐλθεῖν** aor. act. inf. ἔρχομαι. The inf. is used w. the prep.
to express antecedent time "before" (s. MT, 144). **πίστις** "the
faith," i.e. before the salvation given in Christ was revealed as
the object of faith (Ridderbos). **ἐφρουρούμεθα** impf. pass. ind.
φρουρέω to guard. The verb carries the idea of setting a guard
to protect (Guthrie). It has the idea of a garrison keeping ward
over a town (MM; s. also Preisigke). **συγκλειόμενοι** pres. pass.
part. **μέλλουσαν** pres. act. part. μέλλω to be, about to be. It is
used w. the inf. to express the fut. **ἀποκαλυφθῆναι** aor. pass.
24 inf. ἀποκαλύπτω to unveil, to reveal. ■ **παιδαγωγός** custodi-
an, male nursemaid. He was a slave employed in Gr. and Roman
families to have general charge of a boy in the years from about
6 to 16, watching over his outward behavior and attending him
whenever he went home, as for example to school (Burton; s.
also Mussner; TDNT; CC, 144f.; DGRA, 847). **γέγονεν** perf.
ind. act. γίνομαι. **δικαιωθῶμεν** aor. pass. subj. The subj. is used
25 in a purpose clause. ■ **ἐλθούσης** aor. act. part. ἔρχομαι.
27 ■ **ἐβαπτίσθητε** aor. pass. ind. βαπτίζω to baptize. Baptism was the sign of an entry into a new kind of life (Guthrie).
ἐνεδύσασθε aor. mid. ind. ἐνδύομαι to put on, to put on a
garment. Just as a garment which one puts on envelops the
person wearing it and identifies his appearance in his life, so the
person baptized in Christ is entirely taken up in Christ and in the
28 salvation brought by Him (Ridderbos). ■ **ἔνι.** Used w. the neg.
it means "there is not" and is a statement of a fact rather than
a possibility (RWP). **ἐλεύθερος** free. **ἄρσην** male. **θῆλυς**
29 female. ■ **κατ᾽ ἐπαγγελίαν** "according to promise."
κληρονόμος heir. It does not mean that the believer receives
the land promises of Abraham but rather that he partakes of the
spiritual blessing of justification which is through faith.

Ch. 4

■ λέγω δέ "I mean that." Paul begins w. an explanation of 1
his reference to the heirs (Guthrie). **ἐθ' ὅσον χρόνον** "for as
long a time as," "as long as." **κληρονόμος** heir. The term was
used in the inscriptions of Asia Minor to indicate "a son after
he has succeeded to the inheritance" as the representative of his
father, undertaking all the duties and obligations of his father
(Ramsey). **νήπιός** infant, properly "one without understanding"
(Burton). Here it describes "a minor" in any stage of his minority
(Lightfoot). **διαφέρει** pres. ind. act. to differ. **ὤν** pres. part. act.
εἰμί. The part. is concessive "although he is lord over all." ■ 2
ἐπίτροπος guardian, a general term referring to someone to
whom the whole care of the underaged boy is entrusted (Ridderbos). **οἰκονόμος** steward, trustee. The word usually denotes a
slave acting as a house steward for his master, or an employed
steward acting as an agent for his principal, or a treasurer (Burton). **προθεσμία** appointed day, fixed time. It was customary
in the ancient world for the father to set a fixed time or day on
which the son entered manhood (s. Lightfoot; Burton; Ramsey;
DGRA, 462, 630f.). ■ **οὕτως** "so," "thus." Paul now applies the 3
illustration. **ἤμεν** impf. εἰμί. **στοχεῖα τοῦ κόσμου** rudimentary
elements. It may mean the elementary teaching referring to the
elementary truths of natural religion or the elementary rules and
regulations or it may refer to elementary spirits; i.e., the spiritual
forces behind the world (Guthrie; s. also TDNT; Burton; Col.
2:8). **ἤμεθα** impf. εἰμί. **δεδουλωμένοι** perf. pass. part. The perf.
indicates the state of slavery. The part. is used in a past perf.
periphrastic construction (s. RWP). ■ **πλήρωμα** that which is 4
filled up, fullness. It refers here to the appointed time of the
father (s.v.2.). God had prepared the whole world for the coming
of His Son at this particular time in history (s. Guthrie).
ἐξαπέστειλεν aor. ind. act. ἐξαποστέλλω to send out from, to
send forth. The word indicates to send someone as an authoritative representative w. a specific task (s. TDNT; CBB).
γενόμενον aor. mid. part. γίνομαι. The part. is used to define
the principle clause (Ellicott). ■ **ἐξαγοράσῃ** aor. act. subj. 5
ἐξαγοράζω to buy out of the marketplace, to redeem (s. Gal.
3:13). **υἱοθεσία** adoption (s. Rom. 8:15). **ἀπολάβωμεν** aor. act.
subj. ἀπολαμβάνω to receive from someone, to receive. ■ 6
κρᾶζον pres. act. part. κράζω to cry out. **ἀββά** (Aramaic)
father. This was the language of the children and a daily but
polite form of address to the father (Mussner; TDNT; CBB).
■ **ὥστε** therefore. It is used to draw a conclusion from the 7
previous "it becomes apparent" (Ridderbos). **οὐκέτι** no longer.

8 ■ **εἰδότες** perf. act. part. οἶδα (s. Gal. 2:16). **ἐδουλεύσατε**
aor. ind. act. to be enslaved. **οὖσιν** pres. part. εἰμί. The dat.
9 indicates the one to whom they were enslaved. ■ **γνωσθέντες**
aor. act. part. γινώσκω. The part. could be temporal "after you
have come to know" or it could be causal "because you have
come to know." **ἐπιστρέφετε** pres. ind. act. to turn to someone
or something. The prep. in compound is directive. The pres.
tense points to an action which is in progress. **ἀσθενής** weak,
without strength. **πτωχός** poor, beggarly. The heathen religions
were feeble and poor as beggars for they bring no rich endowment of spiritual treasures (Lightfoot). **ἄνωθεν** anew, again.
Used in the expression "once more" which strongly expresses
the completeness of their reversion (Guthrie). **δουλεύσαι** aor.
10 act. inf. ■ **παρατηρεῖσθε** pres. mid. ind. παρατηρέω to observe, to observe closely, to watch carefully (s. Eadie; for the
prep. in compound, s. MH, 319). **μήν** month. The pl. "months"
may be used for monthly reoccurring events (Burton). **ἐνιαυτός**
year. (For a detailed discussion of these religious elements, s.
11 Mussner.) ■ **φοβέομαι** pres. mid. ind. to be afraid, to fear. **μή**
lest, used here w. the ind. following a verb of fearing. The ind.
indicates that the anxiety is directed toward something which
has already taken place (BD, 188). **εἰκῇ** in vain. **κεκοπίακα**
perf. ind. act. κοπιάω to labor, to toil, to work to exhaustion.
The pres. tense draws attention to what Paul fears may be the
permanent result of his past effort (Guthrie).
12 ■ **γίνεσθε** pres. mid. imp. Paul appeals to the Galatians to
become as he is in reference to freedom from the law and to the
freedom which they have as sons of God (Schlier). **δέομαι** pres.
mid. ind. to beseech, to beg. **ἠδικήσατε** aor. ind. act. ἀδικέω
13 to wrong someone, to injure someone. ■ **ἀσθένεια** weakness,
disease, sickness, ailment. (For the various views regarding
Paul's sickness, s. 2 Cor. 12:7; Lightfoot; Ramsey, 422f.)
εὐηγγελισάμην aor. mid. ind. εὐαγγελίζομαι to preach the
good news, to preach the gospel. **τὸ πρότερον** "the first time."
14 The word can mean "at first" or "formerly" (Guthrie). ■
πειρασμός temptation, trial (s. Trench; *Synonyms*, 280).
ἐξουθενήσατε aor. act. ind. ἐξουθενέω to consider as nothing,
to despise. **ἐξεπτύσατε** aor. act. ind. ἐκπτύω to spit out. The
spitting out may refer to contempt and scorn or it may have
referred to an attempt to ward off evil spirits (BAG) or it may
refer to the fact that they did not spit out the message which Paul
preached (Mussner; s. also MM). **ἐδέξασθε** aor. mid. ind.
15 δέχομαι to receive, to welcome. ■ **ποῦ** where. Used to state a
question. **μακαρισμός** happiness, blessedness (s. Matt. 5:3).

μαρτυρέω pres. ind. act. to testify, to bear witness.
ἐξορύξαντες aor. act. part. ἐξορύσσω to dig out, to tear out.
ἐδώκατε aor. ind. act. δίδωμι. Used in a contrary to fact conditional clause (RWP). ■ **ὥστε** "therefore," "so then." Used here 16
w. a question "can it be that I have become your enemy?"
(Lightfoot). **γέγονα** perf. ind. act. γίνομαι. **ἀληθεύων** pres.
act. part. ἀληθεύω to speak the truth. The part. indicates the
means "by speaking the truth." ■ **ζηλοῦσιν** pres. ind. act. to be 17
zealous, to busy one's self about someone, to take interest in,
"they pay court to" (Lightfoot; s. also Gal. 1:14). **καλῶς** well,
"in no honorable way" (Eadie). **ἐκκλεῖσαι** aor. act. inf.
ἐκκλείω to shut out, to exclude. **ζηλοῦτε** pres. act. subj. (For the
subj. form of this verb, s. BD, 46.) ■ **ζηλοῦσθαι** pres. pass. inf. 18
πάντοτε always, "but it is good to be courted fairly at all times"
(Eadie). **παρεῖναί** pres. inf. πάρειμι to be present. The inf. is
used w. the prep. to express contemporaneous time "when I am
present w. you" (s. MT, 144f.). ■ **πάλιν** again. **ὠδίνω** to have 19
birth pains. (For childbearing and the figure of childbearing in
the ancient world, s. RAC IX, 37–217.) **μέχρις οὗ** until.
μορφωθῇ aor. pass. subj. μορφόω to form, pass. to take on
form, to be formed. The form means the essential form rather
than outward shape. The idea is therefore of real Christlike
character (Guthrie; s. also TDNT). ■ **ἤθελον** impf. ind. act. 20
θέλω. The impf. is used to express an unfulfilled desire "I could
wish" (RG, 886). **ἀλλάξαι** aor. act. inf. ἀλλάσσω to change.
ἀπορέομαι pres. mid. ind. to be at a loss, to be at one's wits end,
to be perplexed (s. Guthrie). **ἐν** "in respect to you" (Burton).
■ **λέγετε** pres. act. imp. **θέλοντες** pres. act. part. ■ 21/22
γέγραπται perf. pass. ind. The form was used to express an
authoritative document (s. MM). **ἔσχεν** aor. act. ind. ἔχω to
have. **παιδίσκη** maidservant. **ἐλεύθερος** free. ■ **γεγέννηται** 23
perf. pass. ind. γεννάω to bear, to bear a child. **ἐπαγγελία**
promise. ■ **ἀλληγορούμενα** pres. pass. part. ἀλληγορέω to 24
allegorize, to use an allegory. Paul is using a historical event as
an example. (For the allegorical interpretation in Paul's time, s.
BE, 126ff.; Eadie; TDNT.) **δουλεία** bondage. slavery. **γεννῶσα**
pres. act. part. The part. is adj. in force and timeless (Burton).
ἥτις. The indefinite rel. pron. denotes an attribute which essentially belongs to the nature of the antecedent (Ellicott). ■ **τό**. 25
The article is n. and refers to the word Hagar as applied to the
mountain (RWP). **συστοιχεῖ** pres. act. ind. to line up in the
same rank (in a military sense), here, to correspond to (Guthrie).
δουλεύει pres. act. ind. to be in bondage, to be in slavery, i.e.
in spiritual bondage w. her children just as Hagar was in social

26 bondage w. her child Ishmael (Lightfoot). ■ **ἥτις** which (s.v.24).
27 ■ **εὐφράνθητι** aor. pass. imp. εὐφραίνομαι to rejoice. **στεῖρα**
sterile, barren. **τικτοῦσα** pres. act. part. τίκτω to bear a child.
ῥῆξον aor. act. imp. ῥηγνυμι to break, to burst, to break loose,
here "to break forth and shout." **βόησον** aor. act. imp. βοάω to
cry aloud. **ὠδίνουσα** pres. act. part. to have labor pains, s.v.19.
ἔρημος desolate. **μᾶλλον** more, more than. **ἐχούσης** pres. act.
part. (For Isa. 54:1 in the rabbinical literature, s. SB III, 574.)
29 ■ **γεννηθείς** aor. pass. part. **ἐδίωκεν** impf. act. ind. διώκω to
hunt, to persecute. The impf. pictures the continual action in the
30 past. ■ **κληρονομήσει** fut. ind. act. κληρονομέω to inherit.
31 ■ **διό** therefore. It draws a conclusion from the previous discussion and summarizes the section. (For a discussion of this allegory in relation to the argument of Galatians, s. C.K. Barrett, "The
Allegory of Abraham, Sarah, and Hagar in the Argument of
1 Galatians," R, 1–16.) ■ **ἐλευθερία** freedom. (For the meaning
of this word, s. CBB; TDNT; RAC VIII, 269–306.) The dat.
could be instrumental or it may be a dat. of purpose or designation (Ridderbos). **ἠλευθέρωσεν** aor. act. ind. ἐλευθερόω to
free, to free from slavery. A slave was free under Gr. law for he
had freedom to act as his own legal person, freedom from seizure
of property, freedom to earn his own living as he might choose,
and freedom to dwell where he wished (FCS, 115; for a discussion of the ways in which a slave could be freed, s. FCS, 88–120).
στήκετε pres. act. imp. στήκω to stand fast. The pres. tense
indicates a continual and habitual action. **ζυγός** yoke. **δουλεία**
slavery, bondage. **ἐνέχεσθε** pres. mid. imp. ἐνέχομαι to be had
in, to be ensnared. The pres. tense calls for the stopping of an
action in progress "cease to be entangled" (Burton). The mid.
voice could be permissive "stop allowing yourselves to be entangled."

Ch. 5

2 ■ **ἴδε** aor. act. imp. ὁράω "look!" "see." **ἐγὼ παῦλος** "I
Paul," very emphatic emphasizing Paul's authority (Schlier).
περιτέμνησθε pres. mid. subj. περιτέμνω to circumcise, here
the mid. is permissive to allow one's self to be circumcised.
ὠφελήσει fut. ind. act. ὠφελέω to be of value, to profit, to be
an advantage, followed by the acc. of respect, i.e. "Christ will be
3 an advantage to you in respect to nothing." ■ **περιτεμνομένῳ**
pres. mid. part. permissive mid. **ὀφειλέτης** one who is morally
4 obligated to fulfill a debt, debtor. **ποιῆσαι** aor. act. inf. ■
κατηργήθητε aor. pass. ind. καταργέω to make idle or inactive, to render invalid, followed by the prep. "to be separated

from," "to be loosed from" (AS). **δικαιοῦσθε** pres. pass. ind.
δικαιόω to declare righteous, to justify. The pres. tense is connative indicating an attempt "you are trying to be justified" (s.
DM, 186). **ἐξεπέσατε** aor. act. ind. ἐκπίπτω to fall out of.
Originally used for the falling out of a flower, then "to be loos-
ened from something," "to loose one's grasp of" (Ridderbos). To
attempt to be justified by the law is to reject the way of grace—
justification by faith. ■ **ἀπεκδεχόμεθα** pres. mid. ind. to wait 5
expectingly, earnestly but patiently for someone or something.
The first prep. in compound intensifies the verb and the second
prep. in compound indicates "to be receiving from a distance"
i.e. "to be intently awaiting" (Burton; s. also MM). ■ **ἰσχύει** 6
pres. ind. act. to be strong, to have power. When used of things
it means "to be serviceable" (Guthrie). **ἀκροβυστία** foreskin,
uncircumcision. **ἐνεργουμένη** pres. mid. part. ἐνεργέω to be
act., mid. to demonstrate activity, to work, to work effectually.
■ **ἐτρέχετε** impf. ind. act. τρέχω to run, to run a race (s. 7
Gal. 2:2). **καλῶς** well. **ἐνέκοψεν** aor. ind. act. ἐγκοπτω to cut
in, to hinder. The word suggests a breaking into or obstruction
of the Galatian Christians in their course of following the truth.
The picture is that of the runner who has allowed his progress
to be blocked or who is still running, but is on the wrong course
(PAM, 136f.). **πείθεσθαι** pres. mid. inf. to obey. The prep. is
used to express results. ■ **πεισμονή** persuasion. The word can 8
have an act. or pass. sense (Mussner). **καλοῦντος** pres. act. part.
"the one who does the calling" is obviously God (EBC, Vol 10).
■ **ζύμη** yeast, leaven (s. Matt. 13:33). **φύραμα** that which is 9
mixed, a lump or batch of dough (BAG). **ζυμοῖ** pres. ind. act.
to leaven, to ferment (s. 1 Cor. 5:6f.). The pres. tense is gnomic
to express the continuing truth of a proverb or saying. ■ 10
πέποιθα perf. ind. act. to be persuaded, to have confidence.
(For the instructions employed by Paul after this verb, s. Burton.) **φρονήσετε** fut. ind. act. φρονέω to think, to hold an
opinion, to set one's mind on something, to have an attitude or
thought. **ταράσσων** pres. act. part. ταράσσω to shake back
and forth, to disturb, to trouble. **βαστάσει** fut. ind. act.
βαστάζω to carry, to bear. Paul thinks of the heavy weight
which will press down upon those seeking to impose a load of
Judaism on these Christians (Guthrie). **κρίμα** judgment. ᾖ pres.
subj. εἰμί. ■ **διώκομαι** pres. pass. ind. διώκω to hunt, to hunt 11
down, to persecute. **ἄρα** then, "so it appears!" The word introduces a false statement or inference which is here used ironically (Lightfoot). **διώκομαι** perf. pass. ind. διώκω s.v.4.
σκάνδαλον. The arm or stick on which bait was fixed in a trap,

that which trips one up, offense, cause of stumbling (s. NTW,
111–114; TDNT). **σταυρός** cross. The gen. can be either gen.
of explanation, i.e., the "cause of offense which is the cross," or
it could be causal "the offense which the cross causes" (Muss-
12 ner). ■ **ὄφελον** "I would," "oh, that," "would that," a fixed form
functioning as a particle to introduce unobtainable wishes (BAG;
BD, 181f.). Here it is used w. the fut. ind. for an obtainable wish
even though strictly speaking fulfillment is inconceivable and
this impossibility is forgotten only for the moment (BD, 181,
194). **ἀποκόψονται** fut. mid. ind. ἀποκόπτω to cut off. Here
to castrate. Paul expresses the wish that his opponents would not
stop w. circumcision, but would go on to emasculation (Burton).
Perhaps there is also a reference to the practices of the ancient
cult of cybele (s. TDNT; BAG *De Dea Syria—The Syrian Goddess*, 51 [Edited by Harold W. Attridge and Robert A. Oden,
Missoula, Mont.: Scholars Press, 1976]; Strabo XIII, 4, 14).
ἀναστατοῦντες pres. act. part. ἀναστατόω to upset, to trouble, to disturb. It was used in the papyri in the sense of upsetting
or disturbing one's mind (RWP; MM).
13 ■ **ἐκλήθητε** aor. pass. ind. καλέω. **τὴν ἐλευθερίαν** object
of a verb to be supplied ἔχετε. **ἀφορμή** properly it refers to the
place from which an attack is made, i.e. "a base of operation,"
"opportunity," "occasion" (Burton; Guthrie). **δουλεύετε** pres.
act. imp. to perform the duties of a slave. **ἀλλήλοις** (dat.) one
14 another, dat. of advantage. ■ **πεπλήρωται** perf. ind. pass.
πληρόω to fulfill. **ἀγαπήσεις** fut. ind. act. ἀγαπάω to love. **ὁ**
15 **πλησίον** neighbor. ■ **δάκνω** pres. ind. to bite. **κατεσθίω** pres.
ind. to eat up. The two presents are connative indicating the
attempt (Burton) and the indicatives are used in a conditional
clause which assumes the condition as true. **βλέπετε** pres. act.
imp. **μή** used w. the subj. to express a neg. purpose. **ἀναλωθῆτε**
aor. pass. subj. ἀναλίσκω to consume, to devour. These verbs
suggest wild animals engaged in deadly struggle (Burton).
Strength of soul, health of body, character and resources are
consumed by broils and struggles (Bengel).
16 ■ **περιπατεῖτε** pres. act. imp. περιπατέω to walk, to walk
about, to conduct one's life. The pres. tense indicates a continual
habitual action. **ἐπιθυμία** desire, lust. The prep. in compound
is directive. **οὐ μή** used w. the subj. as a strong neg. "not at all"
(s. M, 188ff.). **τελέσητε** aor. act. subj. τελέω to fulfill, to bring
17 to the goal, to perform. ■ **ἐπιθυμεῖ** pres. act. ind. to desire, to
yearn, to long for. The use of the verb brings the more act. side
of the lust of the flesh (Guthrie). **ἀντίκειται** pres. mid. ind. to
lie opposite, to oppose. The pres. tense indicates continual oppo-

sition. **θέλητε** pres. act. subj. **ποιῆτε** pres. act. subj. The subj.
is used to express purpose or result. (For a discussion, s. Mussner.) ■ **ἄγεσθε** pres. pass. ind. ἄγω to lead, pass. to be lead. Here 18
the Spirit is regarded as a guide, to whom the believer is expected
to submit himself (Guthrie). ■ **φανερός** clear, manifest. 19
πορνεία illicit sexual activity (s. TDNT). **ἀκαθαρσία** uncleanness, impurity. **ἀσέλγεια** unrestrained living, unbridled acts of
indecency which shock the public (Lightfoot; TDNT; s. also 2
Cor. 12:21). ■ **εἰδωλολατρία** worship of idols, idolatry. 20
φαρμακεία the use of medicine or drugs, the use of drugs for
magical purposes, magic, sorcery (Burton; Guthrie; Rev. 9:21).
ἔχθρα hostility. **ἔρις** strife. **ζῆλος** jealousy. **θύμος** anger, a terrible flair up of temper (s. Trench; *Synonyms*, 130; TDNT; CBB).
ἐριθεία selfishness, self-seeking ambition (s. 2 Cor. 12:20; Phil.
2:3). **διχοστασία** dissension. **αἵρεσις** faction. It is the result of
the former—divisions organized into factions (Eadie), cliques.
■ **φθόνος** envy, the desire to appropriate what another pos- 21
sesses. The word "jealousy" in v. 20 refers to the desire of being
as well off as another and the word "envy" refers to the desire
to deprive another of what he has (s. Lightfoot; Eadie; CBB).
μέθη drunkenness (s. Rom. 13:13). **κῶμος** carousing, drinking
party (s. Rom. 13:13). **ὅμοιος** that which is like another.
προλέγω to say beforehand, to tell forth, to tell publicly, to
warn. The meaning here may be "to predict" (Burton).
προεῖπον aor. act. ind. προλέγω. **τοιοῦτος** of such a kind, such
as this. **πράσσοντες** pres. act. part. πράσσω to do, to practice.
κληρονομήσουσιν fut. ind. act. κληρονομέω to inherit.

■ **καρπός** fruit, that which is produced by growth (s. CBB; 22
TDNT). The gen. "of the Spirit" indicates the source or cause
of the fruit. **ἀγάπη** love. The word includes both love for God
and love for fellowman. **χαρά** joy. It is joy grounded in conscience relationship to God (Burton). **εἰρηνη** peace.
μακροθυμία longsuffering, patient endurance under injuries
inflicted by others (Lightfoot; CBB; TDNT; s. Rom. 2:4).
χρηστότης kindness, gentleness. It refers to a kindly disposition toward one's neighbors (Lightfoot). **ἀγαθωσύνη** goodness.
It refers to active goodness as an energetic principle (Lightfoot;
s. also Trench; *Synonyms*, 231f.; TDNT; CBB). **πίστις** faith,
faithfulness. ■ **πραΰτης** meekness, gentle submissiveness (s. 23
Burton; 2 Cor. 10:1). **ἐγκράτεια** self-control, the holding in of
passions and appetites (Eadie; Burton). ■ **ἐσταύρωσαν** aor. act. 24
ind. σταυρόω to crucify. The aor. points to a completed action
in the past and might most naturally refer to conversion (Guthrie). **πάθημα** passion, affections (s. Trench; *Synonyms*, 323).

25 ■ **ζῶμεν** pres. act. ind. ζάω to live. The ind. is used in a conditional sentence which views the condition as real. **στοιχῶμεν** pres. act. subj. στοιχέω to stand in a row, to walk in a straight line, to behave properly. The word was used for movement in a definite line, as in military formation or in dancing (Ridderbos). Here it means "to walk (in a straight line)," "to conduct one's self (rightly)" (Burton). The pres. tense points to the continual
26 and habitual action. The subj. is cohortatory "let us walk." ■ **γινώμεθα** pres. mid. subj. to become, hortatory subj. used w. the neg. **κενόδοξος** empty glorying, vain glory, vain-minded. It refers to one who knows how or who attempts to achieve unfounded respect and by his actions demonstrates big talk, boasting, and ambition (Mussner; Burton). **προκαλούμενοι** pres. mid. part. προκαλέω to invite or challenge to combat, to provoke (Eadie). **φθονοῦντες** pres. act. part. φθονέω to be envious (s.v.21). The two parts. describe the means or manner of the action in the main verb.

Ch. 6

1 ■ **προλημφθῇ** aor. pass. subj. προλαμβάνω to overtake by surprise, to overpower before one can escape (Lightfoot; Eadie). **παράπτωμα** the results of stepping aside, trespass. The aspect of stepping aside may have been chosen because of its appropriateness to the Christian life as a walk by the Spirit (Guthrie). **καταρτίζετε** pres. act. imp. καταρτίζω to restore, to correct. It is used especially as a surgicial term, of setting a bone or joint (Lightfoot). **πραΰτης** meekness, gentleness, submissiveness (s.v.23; s. also 2 Cor. 10:1). **σκόπων** pres. act. part. σκοπέω to look at, to observe, to consider, to give heed to. The verb indicates being sharply attentive, very diligent and the pres. tense indicates continually doing so (Ridderbos). **πειρασθῇς** aor. pass. subj. πειράζω to try, to attempt. The subj. may be used to express purpose or it may be used after a verb of fearing, i.e.
2 "consider or give heed lest you be tempted" (Burton). ■ **ἀλλήλων** (gen.) one another. **βάρος** burden, that which is heavy. **βαστάζετε** pres. act. imp. βαστάζω to carry, to bear, to carry away, to endure (s. MM). **ἀναπληρώσετε** fut. act. ind. ἀναπληρόω to fill, to fill up, to fulfill. The prep. in compound
3 gives the idea of a complete filling, of a filling up (Eadie). ■ **δοκεῖ** pres. act. ind. to think, to suppose. **ὤν** pres. part. εἰμί. The part. is temporal or "temporal—concessive," i.e., "when, although he is nothing" (s. Ellicott). **φρεναπατᾷ** pres. act. inf. to lead one's mind astray, to deceive. The word brings out the idea
4 of "subjective fantasies" which deceive (Lightfoot; RWP). ■

δοκιμαζέτω pres. act. imp. δοκιμάζω to examine, to approve after testing or examination. The word was used for testing of metals to see whether they were pure (Guthrie). **καύχημα** the
ground or reason for boasting. ■ **φορτίον** burden, a load which 5
one is expected to bear. It was used as a military term for a man's
pack or a soldier's kit (Lightfoot). **βαστάσει** fut. act. ind. ■ 6
κοινωνείτω pres. act. imp. κοινωνέω to share w. someone, to exercise fellowship. The apostle is thinking here especially of material things (Ridderbos). **κατηχούμενος** pres. pass. part. κατηχέω to instruct, pass. to be instructed, to be taught. **κατηχοῦντι** pres. act. part. The dat. is dat. of advantage and is
used w. the main verb "to share w. someone." ■ **πλανᾶσθε** pres. 7
pass. imp. πλανάομαι to deceive, to lead astray. **μυκτηρίζεται** pres. pass. ind. μυκτηρίζω to turn up the nose at, to treat w. contempt, to ridicule. The idea is to make God ridiculous by outwitting Him and evading His laws (Burton). **ἐάν** used to make the rel. pron. general "whatever." **σπείρῃ** pres. act. subj. σπείρω to sow, to sow seeds. The pres. tenses are gnomic indicating that which is always true. **θερίσει** fut. ind. act. θερίζω
to harvest, to gather. ■ **σπείρων** pres. act. part. **φθόρα** corrup- 8
tion, rottenness, no one would bother to harvest a field of decaying matter. The "corruption" stands for that which results in
death (Guthrie). **αἰώνιος** eternal. ■ **ποιοῦντες** pres. act. part. 9
The "doing the good" describes what the action of the main verb is. **ἐγκακῶμεν** pres. act. subj. ἐγκακέω to grow weary, to give into evil, to lose heart and become a coward (Lightfoot; s. also Luke 18:1). **καιρός** season, time, dat. of time "in its own season," "at the time of harvest." It indicates there is an appointed time for the spiritual reaping (Guthrie). **ἐκλυόμενοι** pres. pass. part. ἐκλύω to loosen out, to relax, to faint, to be exhausted as
a result of giving in to evil (RWP). ■ **ἄρα** so, then. It is used to 10
draw a conclusion from the previous. **εργαζώμεθα** pres. mid. subj. ἐργάζομαι to be active, to work effectively. The subj. is hortatory "let us work." **οἰκεῖος** household, members of a household.

■ **ἴδετε** aor. act. imp. ὁράω. **πηλίκος** how large. **ἔγραψα** 11
aor. act. ind. At this point Paul may have taken the pen from the amanuensis and have added his concluding remarks in his own handwriting which consisted of larger letters than the smaller and neater script of the amanuensis (Guthrie; s. also Richard N.
Longenecker, "Ancient Amanuenses," ND, 281–297). ■ **ὅσοι** 12
"as many as." **εὐπροσωπῆσαι** aor. act. inf. εὐπροσωπέω to play a good role, to please, to make a fair appearance (s. Burton). **ἐν σαρκί** "in the flesh." **ἀναγκάζω** pres. act. ind. to compel, to

coerce (s. Gal. 2:3). The pres. tense is conative "they are trying to coerce." **περιτέμνεσθαι** pres. pass. inf. περιτέμνω to circumcise. **σταυρός** cross. The dat. is causal "because of the cross" (s. BD, 105). **διώκωνται** pres. pass. subj. διώκω to hunt, to persecute, pass. to suffer persecution. The subj. is used in
13 a purpose clause. ■ **περιτεμνόμενοι** pres. pass. part.
φυλάσσουσιν pres. act. ind. to guard, to observe.
καυχήσωνται aor. mid. subj. καυχάομαι to glory. The subj. is
14 used in a purpose clause. ■ **γένοιτο** aor. mid. opt. γίνομαι,
followed by the inf. **εἰ μή** "except." **δι' οὗ** "through which."
ἐσταύρωται perf. ind. pass. σταυρόω to crucify, to put to
death by crucifixion. The perf. tense indicates the continuing
15 and lasting state or condition. ■ **περιτομή** circumcision.
16 **ἀκροβυστία** foreskin, uncircumcision. **κτίσις** creation. ■
κάνων rod, measuring rule, standard. (For this word, s. 2 Cor. 10:13.) **στοιχήσουσιν** fut. act. ind. to walk the line, to walk according to a standard (s. Gal. 5:25). **ἔλεος** mercy. **καὶ ἐπὶ τὸν Ἰσραήλ** "and upon the Israel of God." The phrase is not to be taken as an explanation of the preceding but as a separate entity or group. His thoughts turn to his own brethren after the flesh and he pauses to specify those who were once Israelites according to the flesh but now are the Israel of God (Ellicott).
17 ■ **τοῦ λοιποῦ.** The gen. means "in respect of remaining
time" (RWP). **κόπος** trouble. **παρεχέτω** pres. act. imp. παρέχω to furnish, to provide, to cause. **στίγμα** mark, brand. It was the custom to mark slaves by scars (Ramsey) and religious tattooing also played a great role in antiquity (BAG; The Assyrian Goddess, 59). Paul is speaking of the permanent marks which he bore of persecution undergone in the service of Christ (Lightfoot; s. also TDNT). **βαστάζω** to carry, to bear. The pres. tense
18 indicates the continual bearing. ■ **ἀμήν** "so let it be." A Hebraic
word used to emphasize and confirm a statement. Paul means to add weight to his conclusion (Guthrie).

EPHESIANS

Ch. 1

οὖσιν pres. part. εἰμί. **τοῖς ἁγίοις τοῖς οὖσιν** "to the 1
saints who are . . ." The dat. indicates to whom this letter was
written. The term "saints" are those who are cleansed by the
blood of Christ, and by the renewing of the Holy Ghost, and thus
separated from the world and consecrated to God (Hodge; s. also
TDNT). ■ **χάρις** grace, the undeserved and unmerited favor of 2
God (s. TDNT; CBB). **εἰρήνη** peace. Probably to be understood
in the term of the Heb. concept of "shalom" indicating "spiritual
prosperity" (Barth; TDNT; CBB).

■ **εὐλογητός** blessed. Verbal adjs. w. this ending indicate 3
one who is worthy, i.e. "worthy of blessing" (Abbott; s. also 2
Cor. 1:3). **εὐλογήσας** aor. act. part. εὐλογέω to bless, to endow
one w. the ability to succeed (s. TDOT; TDNT). **ἐπουράνιος**
"in the heavenlies." The term is to be understood in a local sense
indicating the sphere of the blessings which are related to the
Spirit. The term refers to heaven as seen in perspective of the
new age brought about in Christ and for this reason it is so
closely linked w. the Spirit of that age (A.T. Lincoln, "A Re-
examination of 'The Heavenlies' in Ephesians," NTS, 19 [July,
1973], 471; s. also Barth). ■ **καθώς** just as, because. Here the 4
word combines the comp. and causal idea (Schlier; BD, 236).
ἐξελέξατο aor. mid. ind. ἐκλέγω to choose out, to select. The
word involves three ideas: the stem of the word indicates "the
telling over"; the prep. in compound indicates the rejection of
some and acceptance of others; and the mid. voice indicates "the
talking to (for) Himself" (Lightfoot, *Notes*). **καταβολή** throwing down, foundation. (For the various usages of the word, s.
Barth; TDNT.) The meaning of the phrase "before the foundation of the world" means "from all eternity" (Abbott). **εἶναι**
pres. inf. Infinitive used to express purpose. **ἄμωμος** without
blame, unblemished, used of the absence of defects in sacrificial
animals (BAG). **κατενώπιον** prep. used w. a gen. "in the presence of" (s. RG, 644). **ἀγάπῃ** "in love." The phrase is best
understood as being joined w. the part. in v. 5 (s. Eadie). ■ 5
προορίσας aor. act. part. προορίζω to mark out w. a boundary

beforehand, to foreordain, to predestinate (s. TDNT; L.C. Allen, "The Old Testament Background of (προ) ὁρίζειν in the New Testament," NTS, 17 [October, 1970], 104–108). The part. is causal giving the reason for the election (Abbott). **υἱοθεσία** adoption (s. Rom. 8:15). **εὐδοκία** good pleasure, satisfaction. The election and predestination is God's absolute act of free love which is grounded totally in Himself and there was nothing apart
6 from Him which gave His will direction (Gaugler). ■ **ἔπαινος** praise. **δόξα** glory (s. TDNT). **ἧς** rel. pron. The gen. is by attraction to its antecedent. **ἐχαρίτωσεν** aor. act. ind. χαριτόω to bestow grace, to give grace. The word means "begracing w. grace" and indicates exclusive and abundant demonstration of grace (Barth; s. also TDNT; Robinson; Luke 1:28). **ἠγαπημένῳ** perf. pass. part. ἀγαπάω to love. The pass. part. indicates the one who is in the state or condition of being loved, "the be-
7 loved." ■ **ἀπολύτρωσις** purchasing w. a price, redemption (s. Rom. 3:24; Abbott; Lightfoot; *Notes*). **ἄφεσις** releasing, forgiveness. **παράπτωμα** falling aside, transgression. The word signifies the actual and numerous results and manifestations of our
8 sinful nature (Eadie). ■ **ἧς** rel. pron. gen. by attraction rather than acc. **ἐπερίσσευσεν** aor. act. ind. περισσεύω to cause to overflow, to cause to abound. **φρόνησις** understanding. It refers to the display of wisdom in operation (Simpson). It is the ability to discern modes of action w. a view to their results (Lightfoot;
9 *Notes*). ■ **γνωρίσας** aor. act. part. γνωρίζω to make known. **προέθετο** aor. mid. ind. προτίθημι to place before. The prep. in compound can be local, i.e. "to set before one's self," i.e. "to
10 purpose" (Abbott). ■ **οἰκονομία** household management, administration (s. TDNT; BAG). **πλήρωμα** fullness. **ἀνακεφαλαιώσασθαι** aor. mid. inf. ἀνακεφαλαιόω to gather again under one head, to sum up, to gather up into one. (For this word, s. Barth; Robinson; Abbott.) The prep. in compound refers to the prior dispersion of the elements and the substitutive of the verb describes the ultimate aggregation in one; thus the whole compound involves the idea of "unity" effected out of diversity (Lightfoot; *Notes*). The inf. is used to explain the preceding.
11 ■ **ἐκληρώθημεν** aor. pass. ind. κληρόω to appoint by lot, pass. to be appointed by lot, to be destined, to be chosen (BAG). **προορισθέντες** aor. pass. part. s.v.5. **πρόθεσις** purpose, s.v.9. **ἐνεργοῦντος** pres. act. part. ἐνεργέω to be effective, to be energetic, to work, to accomplish (s. Robinson). **βουλή** counsel, will. It expresses counsel w. reference to action (Westcott). The word solemnly represents the almighty Will as displaying itself in action (Ellicott). **θέλημα** will. It denotes the will in general

(Westcott). ■ **προηλπικότας** perf. act. part. προελπίζω to 12
hope before, to hope beforehand. The prep. in compound is
temporal but its significance is not clear. It could indicate the
hope before the event (EGT) or the hope of the Jewish Christians prior to the conversion of the heathen (Abbott; Barth) or
it could refer to the hope or belief "before Christ actually came"
(Westcott). The perf. tense indicates that the hope continues.
The part. is in apposition to the subject of the inf. "we." ■ 13
ἀκούσαντες and **πιστεύσαντες** aor. act. part. The parts. are
temporal and express contemporaneous time "when you believed," "at the time you believed" (Simpson). **ἐσφραγίσθητε**
aor. pass. ind. σφραγίζω to seal. Seals were used as a guarantee
indicating not only ownership but also to guarantee the correctness of the contents (s. 2 Cor. 1:22). **ἐπαγγελία** promise. ■ 14
ἀρραβών down payment, pledge. It indicates a deposit which
is in itself a guarantee that the full amount will be paid. The down payment is of the same kind as the full payment (s. 2 Cor. 1:22; Abbott; Lightfoot; *Notes*). **κληρονομία** inheritance. **περιποίησις** possessing, possession, that which is one's own (CBB).

■ **ἀκούσας** aor. act. part., temporal use of the part. ■ 15/16
εὐχαριστῶν pres. act. part. εὐχαριστέω to give thanks. The
part. is used supplementary to complete the main verb. **μνεία**
remembrance. **ποιούμενος** pres. mid. part. used w. the previous
noun w. the sense to make mention of, esp. in the sense of
mentioning someone in prayer (BAG). ■ **δῴη** aor. opt. δίδωμι. 17
The volitive opt. is used to express a wish or desire in prayer (s.
RG, 939f.). (For the view that the form is subj. rather than opt.,
s. BD, 187.) **ἀποκάλυψις** unveiling, revelation. **ἐπίγνωσις** recognition, knowledge. The word means knowledge directed
toward a particular object "perceiving, discerning, recognizing."
The gen. following the word denotes the object of the knowledge
(s. Robinson, 254). ■ **πεφωτισμένους** perf. pass. part. φωτίζω 18
to enlighten, to illuminate, to give light. It refers to the ministry
of the Holy Spirit who continually illuminates spiritual truths (s.
1QS 2, 3; s. also Gnilka). The perf. tense points to the continuous
process (Barth). The grammatical structure of the part. could be
an anacoluthon or a third predicate of the main verb or an acc.
abs. (s. RWP). **εἰδέναι** perf. act. inf. **οἶδα** (s. ND, 344ff.).
κλῆσις calling. ■ **ὑπερβάλλον** pres. act. part. ὑπερβάλλω to 19
throw beyond, to exceed, to surpass. **μέγεθος** greatness. **πιστεύοντας** pres. act. part. **ἐνεργία** working, the effectual working of ability (Schlier; Robinson; TDNT). **κράτος** might, power. The word refers to strength regarded as abundantly effec-

tive in relation to an end to be gained or dominion to be exercised (Westcott; TDNT). **ἰσχύς** strength, strength which one
has, power in possession, ability, or latent power (Eadie;
20 Schlier). ■ **ἐνηργηκεν** perf. ind. act. ἐνεργέω to be at work, to
work effectually. **ἐγείρας** aor. act. part. ἐγείρω to raise.
καθίσας aor. act. part. καθίζω to cause to sit, to seat. **δεξία**
right, right hand. Christ seated at the right hand pictures His
place of honor and authority (s. David M. Hay, *Glory at the
Right Hand: Psalm 110 in Early Christianity* [Nashville: Abing-
don Press, 1973]; for a critical approach of this theme, s. W.R.G.
Loader, "Christ at the Right Hand—Ps. CX. 1 in the New Testament," NTS, 24 [January, 1978], 199–217). **ἐπουράνιος** heav-
21 en, heavenly place. s.v.3. ■ **ὑπεράνω** high above, far above.
ἀρχή rule, ruler. **κυριότης** lordship, dominions. In Jewish writings the terms were used to designate angelic powers and their
ranks (s. SB III, 581; Abbott; Barth). **ὀνομαζομένου** pres. pass.
part. ὀνομάζω to name. **μέλλοντι** pres. act. part. dat. sing.
22 masc. μέλλω to be about to, coming. ■ **ὑπέταξεν** aor. act. ind.
ὑποτάσσω to subject. **ἔδωκεν** aor. act. ind. δίδωμι to give. The
verb is followed by the indirect object, i.e., "he gave Him as head
over all things to the church." Rather than speaking only of
Christ as being "the Head of the church," Paul refers to the
cosmic rule of Christ and implies that Christ is the sovereign
head of all things (George Howard, "The Head-Body Metaphors
23 of Ephesians," NTS, 20 [April, 1974], 353f.). ■ **πληρουμένου**
pres. mid.-pass. part. πληρόω to fill. The part. could be pass.
(Robinson) or it could also be mid., i.e., "the one who fills for
himself" (Howard, 351; s. also Abbott).

Ch. 2

1 ■ **ὄντας** pres. part. εἰμί. **παράπτωμα** transgression (s.
2 Eph. 1:7). ■ **ἐν αἷς** strictly speaking the antecedent of the rel.
pron. is **ταῖς ἁμαρτίαις** but logically it refers to both "sins" and
"transgressions." **ποτέ** at that time, formerly. **περιεπατήσατε**
aor. act. ind. περιπατέω to walk about, to conduct one's life.
The aor. views the total past life in summary fashion as a point.
ἀήρ air, atmosphere, the realm in which the evil powers operate
(s. Abbott; Barth; Hodge). **τοῦ πνεύματος.** The gen. is best
understood as being in apposition to the words **τῆς ἐξουσίας
τοῦ ἀέρος** (s. Ellicott). **ἀπείθεια** disobedience. The phrase
"sons of disobedience" is a Hebraic expression indicating that
their chief characteristic is that of "disobedience" (s. BG, 16).
3 ■ **ἀνεστράφημεν** aor. pass. ind. ἀναστρέφομαι to conduct
one's life. The word refers to the social action whereas the verb

"walk" in v. 2 is used more of personal action (Westcott).
ἐπιθυμία desires, strong lust. **σαρκός** gen., subjective gen. indicating the source of the desires. **ποιοῦντες** pres. act. part.
διάνοια understanding, intelligence, mind, disposition, thought
(BAG). **ἤμεθα** impf. εἰμί. **φύσις** nature. **ὀργή** wrath, anger (s.
Rom. 1:18). ■ **πλούσιος** rich. **ἔλεος** mercy, compassion, pity. 4
The word indicates the emotion aroused by someone in need and
the attempt to relieve the person and remove his trouble (CBB;
TDNT; Trench; *Synonyms*, 166f.). **ἠγάπησεν** aor. act. ind.
ἀγαπάω to love. ■ **συνεζωοποίησεν** aor. act. ind. 5
συζωοποιέω to make alive together w. The word is a synonym
for the verb "to raise" but it can also have the meaning "to keep
alive" or "to preserve life" (Barth). **σεσῳσμενοι** perf. pass.
part. σῴζω to rescue, to save. The perf. tense points to the
completed action w. a continuing result thus emphasizing the
continual state or condition. ■ **συνήγειρεν** aor. act. ind. 6
συνεγείρω to raise together w. Believers not only receive life,
but they experience a resurrection (Eadie). **συνεκάθισεν** aor.
act. ind. συνκαθίζω to cause to sit down together w. another.
ἐπουράνιος heavenly (s. Eph. 1:3). ■ **ἐνδείξηται** aor. pass. 7
subj. ἐκδείκνυμι to demonstrate, to display, to show, to prove.
ἐπερχομένοις pres. mid. part. ἐπέρχομαι to come upon, approaching. The times after the coming of the Lord are viewed as
being already "on the approach" (Meyer). **ὑπερβάλλον** pres.
act. part. ὑπερβάλλω to throw beyond, to exceed, to surpass.
The part. is used in the sense "surpassing, extraordinary, outstanding" (BAG). **χρηστότης** usefulness, goodness, kindness.
The word involves the idea of the exercise of kindness toward
another (Abbott; s. also Trench; *Synonyms*, 232f.; TDNT). ■ **τῇ** 8
χάριτι instrumental dat. "by grace." The definite article appears
w. the word because it is the grace already mentioned (Abbott).
διὰ πίστεως "through faith." The prep. indicates the channel
through which salvation comes (s. Ellicott). Faith is not viewed
as a positive work or accomplishment of the individual (s. Gaugler). **θεοῦ** the gen. is emphasized by its position before the
substitutive and stands in emphatic contrast w. the personal
pron. "from you" (Abbott). ■ **καυχήσηται** aor. mid. subj. 9
καυχάομαι to boast, to glory. The subj. is used in a neg. purpose
clause. ■ **ποίημα** that which is made, work. The word can also 10
have connation of a "work of art," esp. a poetic product, including fiction (Barth). **κτισθέντες** aor. pass. part. κτίζω to create.
The word points to God's new creation in Christ. (For this aspect
of Paul's teaching against its Jewish background, s. PRJ, 119ff.)
ἐπί w. the dat. "for." The prep. indicates the goal or purpose. It

primarily designates movement ending in a definite spot (IBG, 50). **προητοίμασεν** aor. act. ind. προετοιμάζω to prepare beforehand. The prep. refers to a period before the action described in the part. "created" and describes the means by which the end is secured according to divine arrangement (s. Eadie). **περιπατήσωμεν** aor. subj. The subj. is used in a purpose clause.
11 ■ **διό** therefore. **μνημονεύετε** pres. act. imp. μνημονεύω to remember. The word calls for repentence, decision, and gratitude (Barth). **ποτέ** formerly. **ἔθνος** nation, pl. Gentile, the non-Jewish world. **ἐν σαρκί** "in the flesh." The words suggest the external and temporary nature of the distinction (Robinson). **λεγόμενοι** pres. pass. part. **ἀκροβυστία** foreskin, uncircumcision. **περιτομή** circumcision (s. TDNT; Barth; CBB).
12 **χειροποίητος** verbal adj. handmade. ■ **ἦτε** impf., s.v.3. **καιρός** time, season, dat. of time. **ἀπηλλοτριωμένοι** perf. pass. part. ἀπαλλοτριόω to estrange, to alienate. The perf. tense indicates the state or condition. **πολιτεία** citizenship, state, commonwealth. It indicates the government of Israel framed by God in which religion and polity were co-joined (Eadie). **ξένος** stranger followed by the gen. of separation "strange to something" (BD, 98). **διαθήκη** covenant, treaty. **ἐπαγγελία** promise. **ἔχοντες** pres. act. part. **ἄθεος** without God, godless, atheist. The perf.
13 negates the stem of the word (s. Moorhouse, 47ff.). ■ **ὄντες** pres. act. part., s.v.1. **μακράν** adv. far, far off. **ἐγενήθητε** aor. pass. ind. **ἐγγύς** near. The terms "far" and "near" were used in rabbinical writings and indicated among other things non-Jews (far) and Jews (near) or those who were righteous and near God or those who were godless and far away (s. SB III, 585–587).
14 ■ **ἡ εἰρήνη**. The article used w. the pred. noun presents the pred. as something well known or as that which alone merits the designation, i.e., the only thing to be considered (BD, 143). **ποιήσας** aor. act. part. **ἀμφότερος** both, i.e., both Jews and Gentiles (Abbott). The n. is used if it is not the individual but a general quality that is to be emphasized (BD, 76). **μεσότοιχον** middle wall, dividing wall. (For a discussion of the various views concerning the "middle wall," s. Barth.) The context identifies the "wall" in four ways: it is the fact of separation between Israel and the nations; it has to do w. the law and its statutes and interpretations; it is experienced in the enmity between Jews and Gentiles; it also consists of the enmity of both Jews and Gentiles against God (Barth). **φραγμός** fence, partition. It signified originally a fence or railing erected for protection rather than separation (Barth). **λύσας** aor. act. part. λύω to loose, to destroy, to break down. The aor. tense points to the completed action.

ἔχθρα enmity, hostility. ■ **ἐντόλη** command. **δόγμα** decree. 15
The law consisted of, i.e. was "in decrees." **καταργήσας** aor.
act. part. καταργέω to invalidate, to nullify, to annul, to make
of no effect (Simpson). **κτίσῃ** aor. act. subj. κτίζω to create. The
subj. is used to express purpose. **ποιῶν** pres. act. part. ■ 16
ἀποκαταλλάξῃ aor. act. subj. ἀποκαταλλάσσω to change,
to exchange, to turn from hostility to friendship, to reconcile.
The double prep. in compound may be intensive (Abbott; s. also
Barth) or there may be a hint at a restoration to a primal unity
(Ellicott; s. also Col. 1:20). **σταύρος** cross. The term reveals two
things: Christ's death is shameful among men, not honorable; it
corresponds to death on the gallows. Also, it is an execution in
which God's curse was borne (Barth). **ἀποκτείνας** aor. act. part.
ἀποκτείνω to put to death, to kill. The part. is used to express
means. ■ **ἐλθών** aor. act. part. ἔρχομαι. **εὐηγγελίσατο** aor. 17
mid. ind. εὐαγγελίζομαι to proclaim good news. ■ 18
προσαγωγή entrance, access. The word was used of a solemn
approach to a deity and of access to a king's presence (Simpson).
■ **ἄρα** therefore. The word marks the progress in the argument 19
and has a connective sense implying a consequence. The double
particles (**ἄρα οὖν**) in combination are intended to imply logical
connection, the one simply reinforcing the other and both are
used to sum up the argument of the whole section (Thrall, 11;
Eadie). **οὐκέτι** no longer. **πάροικος** one living along side, alien.
A resident alien was subject to only a part of the law of the land
and enjoyed only corresponding legal protection according to
the OT meaning (Barth; s. also TDOT under "ger").
συμπολίτης fellow citizen. **οἰκεῖος** one's own household,
family. When used of persons it means "of one's family," strictly
of kinsmen, sometimes loosely of familiar friends (Robinson).
■ **ἐποικοδομηθέντες** aor. pass. part. ἐποικοδομέω to build 20
upon. **θεμέλιος** foundation. **ἀκρογωνιαῖς** foundation stone,
cornerstone, keystone. The word could refer either to the cornerstone or to the keystone in an archway (s. TDNT; 1 Peter
2:6). ■ **οἰκοδομή** building. **συναρμολογουμένη** pres. pass. 21
part. συναρμολογέω to fit together. In construction terms it
represents the whole of the elaborate process by which stones are
fitted together: the preparation of the surfaces, including the
cutting, rubbing, and testing; the preparation of the dowels and
the dowel holes, and finally the fitting of the dowels w. molten
lead (Robinson, 262). **αὔξω** pres. ind. act. to increase, to grow.
The pres. tense indicates the continual development. **νάος** temple. ■ **συνοικοδομεῖσθε** pres. pass. ind. συνοικοδομέω to 22
build together, pass. to be built together, i.e., together w. the

others. The pres. tense is used because the building is still going on (Abbott). ***κατοικητήριον*** place of dwelling, a place of settling down. (For the suf. indicating place or locality, s. MH, 343.) The prep. indicates the goal or intention.

Ch. 3

1 ■ ***τούτου χάριν*** "because of this," "on account of this,"
"for this reason." The illusion is not only to building God's house
on a firm foundation, but also to the unification of Jews and
Gentiles (Barth). ***δέσμιος*** prisoner. ***ἔθνος*** people, nation, pl.
2 "Gentile." ■ ***εἴ γε*** "if indeed," "surely." The particles here are
used to express assurance (s. Thrall, 87f.). ***ἠκούσατε*** aor. act.
ind. ἀκούω. ***οἰκονομία*** administration, responsibility. The term
was used of the administrative responsibility given to a servant
over a household (s. Eph. 1:10; TDNT). ***δοθείσης*** aor. pass.
3 part. δίδωμι. ***εἰς ὑμᾶς*** "for you"; i.e. for your benefit. ■ ***κατὰ***
w. the acc. according to. Used here in an adverbial sense "by way
of revelation" and expresses the mode of the making known
(Meyer). ***ἀποκάλυψις*** unveiling, revealing, revelation.
ἐγνωρίσθη aor. ind. pass. γνωρίζω to make known.
μυστήριον mystery, that which a human being cannot know but
which is revealed by God (s. TDNT; ZPEB IV, 327–330).
προέγραψα aor. act. ind. προγράφω to write beforehand. It
refers to the previous part of this letter (Schlier). ***ἐν ὀλίγῳ*** "in
4 a few words," "in brief." ■ ***πρὸς ὅ*** "to that which," "w. reference
to," i.e., "w. reference to what I have said" (s. Abbott; Barth).
ἀναγινώσκοντες pres. act. part. ἀναγινώσκω to read, temporal use of the part. "when you read." ***νοῆσαι*** aor. act. inf. νοέω
to perceive, to come to the knowledge of, to apprehend, to
understand, to gain an insight into (BAG). ***σύνεσις*** understand-
5 ing, insight. ■ ***γενεά*** generation. The dat. could be dat. of time
"in other generations" (Robinson) or it could be dat. of indirect
object "to other generations" (Barth). ***ἀπεκαλύφθη*** aor. pass
6 ind. ἀποκαλύπτω to unveil, to reveal. ■ ***εἶναι*** pres. inf. εἰμί.
The inf. is used to explain the content of the divine revelation.
συγκληρονόμος fellow-heir. ***σύσσωμος*** fellow members of a
body, belonging to the same body. ***συμμέτοχος*** fellow partaker,
co-sharer. The word was used in the papyri of those who were
7 "joint possessors" of a house (MM). ***ἐπαγγελία*** promise. ■
ἐγενήθη aor. pass. ind. γίνομαι. ***κατά*** w. the acc., s.v.3. ***δωρέα***
gift, followed by the gen. of apposition (Eadie) or the gen. of
8 source. ***ἐνέργεια*** working, effectual working (s. Robinson). ■
ἐλαχιστότερος (comp. of the superl. ἐλάχιστος), less than the
least, "the smallester," "leaster" (Barth). The form was used to

designate the deepest self-abasement (Eadie). Paul may be making an allusion to his own name (Simpson). (For the form, s. BD, 34.) **ἐδόθη** aor. pass. ind. δίδωμι. **εὐαγγελίσασθαι** aor. mid. inf. εὐαγγελίζω to proclaim the good news, to preach the gospel. **ἀνεξιχνίαστος** not able to track out, untraceable (s. Rom 11:33). ■ **φωτίσαι** aor. act. inf. φωτίζω to illuminate, to bring 9
into light, to shed light upon. **ἀποκεκρυμμένου** perf. pass. part. ἀποκρύπτω to hide. The perf. part. indicates the state or condition "that which was hidden." **κτίσαντι** aor. act. part. κτίζω to
create. ■ **γνωρισθῇ** aor. pass. subj., s.v.3. **ἐπουράνιος** heavenly 10
(s. Eph. 1:3). **πολυποίκιλος** many sided, variegated, very-varied. The word was used to describe robes or hems (Robinson).
■ **πρόθεσις** purpose, design (s. Eph. 1:11). The gen. following 11
the word could be descriptive gen. "eternal purpose" or poss. gen. "the purpose that runs through the ages" (Abbott) or it could be obj. gen. "purpose about the ages," "the design concerning the ages." (For this view and a discussion of other views,
s. Barth.) **ἐποίησεν** aor. ind. act. ■ **παρρησία** speaking freely, 12
confidence, boldness. **προσαγωγή** entrance, access (s. Eph.
2:18). **πεποίθησις** having been persuaded, confidence. ■ **διό** 13
therefore. **αἰτέομαι** pres. mid. ind. to ask, to request. **ἐγκακεῖν** pres. act. inf. to give in to evil, to be a coward, to be discouraged, to grow weary (s. Gal. 6:9; Luke 18:1). **θλῖψις** pressure, tribulation, trouble.

■ **κάμπτω** to bow. **γόνυ** knee. (For a discussion of the 14
position of kneeling in prayer, s. Barth.) ■ **πατρία** family, de- 15
scendant from a common father. It always refers to a concrete group of people. (For a discussion of the meaning of the term in this passage, s. Barth; SB III, 594.) **ὀνομάζεται** pres. pass. ind.
ὀνομάζω to name, to give a name to a thing. ■ **δῷ** aor. act. subj. 16
δίδωμι. The subj. is used w. the particle to give the content of Paul's prayer. **δυνάμει** "w. power," "w. infused strength," dat. of instrument (Ellicott; Abbott). **κραταιωθῆναι** aor. pass. inf. κραταιόομαι to strengthen, to fortify, to brace, to invigorate
(Simpson; s. also Eph. 1:19). **ἔσω** inner. ■ **κατοικῆσαι** aor. act. 17
inf. κατοικέω to dwell, to live in, to settle down. The verb denotes permanent habitation as opposed to sojourning or an occasional visit (Barth). The inf. could be used as a type of apposition explaining the previous inf. (Schlier). **ἐρριζωμένοι** perf. pass. part. ῥιζόω to cause to take root, pass. to be or to become firmly rooted or fixed (BAG). The perf. looks at the continuing state or condition. **τεθεμελιωμένοι** perf. pass. part. θεμελιόω to lay a foundation, to establish, to strengthen. The illusion is to the solid basement of the spiritual temple described

18 in chapter 2 (Eadie). ■ **ἐξισχύσητε** aor. act. subj. ἐξισχύω to be able, to be fully able, to be strong enough. The prep. in compound is perfective and indicates a strength exerted till its object is attained (MH, 310). **καταλαβέσθαι** aor. mid. inf. καταλαμβάνω to grasp mentally, to comprehend (s. Abbott).
19 **πλάτος** breath. **μῆκος** length. **ὕψος** height. **βάθος** depth. ■ **γνῶναι** aor. act. inf. γινώσκω. **ὑπερβάλλουσαν** pres. act. part. ὑπερβάλλω to throw beyond, to excel, to surpass (s. Eph. 1:19). **πληρωθῆτε** aor. pass. subj. πληρόω to fill (s. Eph. 1:23).
20 ■ **δυναμένῳ** pres. mid. part. dat. of advantage. **ποιῆσαι** aor. act. inf. **ὑπερεκπερισσοῦ** superabundantly, quite beyond all measure. The form is used as the highest form of comparison imaginable (BAG). **αἰτουμεθα** pres. mid. ind. to ask, s.v.13. **νοέω** pres. act. ind. to understand, s.v.4. **ἐνεργουμένη** pres. mid. part. ἐνεργέομαι to be active, to be effective (s. Robinson).
21 ■ **γενέα** s.v.5. **ἀμήν** truly. Used after a statement to add confirmation (s. TDNT).

Ch. 4

1 ■ **παρακαλέω** pres. act. ind. to beseech, to exhort, to encourage. The word signifies a will of the writer that is at the same time warm, personal, and urgent (Barth; TDNT; NTW). **δέσμιος** prisoner. **ἀξίως** adv. worthily. The adj. has the basic meaning "that which balances the scales," "equivalent" (TDNT). **περιπατῆσαι** aor. act. inf. περιπατέω to walk about, to conduct one's life. The inf. is used to express the content of Paul's urging. **ἧς** rel. pron. gen. sing. gen. by attraction to its
2 antecedent (RWP). **ἐκλήθητε** aor. pass. ind. καλέω to call. ■ **ταπεινοφροσύνη** lowly thinking, humility. The word refers to the quality of esteeming ourselves as small but at the same time recognizing the power and ability of God (s. TDNT; Trench; *Synonyms*, 148; CBB; RAC III, 735ff.). **πραΰτης** meek, gentle. The humble and gentle attitude which expresses itself in a patient submissiveness to offense, free from malice and desire for revenge (s. Matt. 5:5; TDNT; CBB). **μακροθυμία** longsuffering (s. Gal. 5:22). **ἀνεχόμενοι** pres. mid. part. ἀνέχομαι to bear, to bear up, to hold one's self up. The word indicates to have patience w. someone till the provocation is past (Eadie). **ἀλλήλων**
3 (gen. pl.) one another. ■ **σπουδάζοντες** pres. act. part. σπουδάζω to give diligence, to be eager, to make every effort. **τηρεῖν** pres. act. inf. to guard, to keep, to maintain (Schlier). **ἑνότης** unity. **σύνδεσμος** that which binds together, a bond. The word denotes that which keeps something together (Barth).
4/5 ■ **καθώς** just as. **ἐλπίς** hope. ■ **βάπτισμα** baptism.

■ ***ἕκαστος*** each, dat. of the indirect object. ***ἐδόθη*** aor. pass. 7
ind. *δίδωμι*. ***μέτρον*** measure. ***δωρέα*** gift. Unity is not uniformity, for it is quite consistent w. variety of gifts and offices in the
church (Eadie). ■ ***διὸ λέγει*** "therefore he says." This formula 8
introduces a citation from the OT and is characterized by the
absence of a legalistic and polemic undertone. It is an urgent
invitation to listen attentively (Barth; s. also BE, 107ff.).
ἀναβάς aor. act. part. *ἀναβαίνω* to ascend, to go up. ***ὕψος***
height. ***ᾐχμαλώτευσεν*** aor. act. ind. *αἰχμαλωτεύω* to lead
captive. The allusion is to a triumphal possession in which
marched the persons taken in war (Eadie; s. also 2 Cor. 2:14).
■ ***ἀνέβη*** aor. act. ind. *ἀναβαίνω* to go up, to ascend. ***κατέβη*** 9
aor. act. ind. *καταβαίνω* to go down, to descend. ***τὰ κατώτερα
μέρη*** the lower parts, the lower regions. The following gen. "of
the earth" could be gen. of apposition and the reference could
be to the Incarnation and Christ's coming to earth (RWP; s. also
Barth; Hodge). ■ ***καταβάς*** aor. act. part. *καταβαίνω*. 10
ὑπεράνω w. the gen. "high above." ***πληρώσῃ*** aor. act. subj.
πληρόω to fill (s. Eph. 1:23). ■ ***ὁ μέν . . . ὁ δέ*** "the one . . . the 11
other." ***εὐαγγελιστής*** one who proclaims the good news, evangelist. An evangelist was one who proclaimed the gospel which
he had received from the apostle. He was particularly a missionary who brought the gospel into new regions (s. Schlier; Barth;
TDNT; CBB). ***ποιμήν*** shepherd, pastor. The image of a shepherd w. his flock pictures the relation of a spiritual leader to
those committed to his charge (Eadie). ***καί*** "and." Often the
word has the meaning "that is" or "in particular" and indicates
that the "shepherds" and "teachers" are viewed as one common
group, i.e., "teaching shepherds" (Barth). ■ ***καταρτισμός*** 12
equipping. The word was a medical technical term for "the setting of a bone" (BAG). The noun describes the dynamic act by
which persons or things are properly conditioned (Barth).
οἰκοδομή building, building up, edify. The word is an expression
of development (Meyer). ■ ***μέχρι*** until. ***καταντήσωμεν*** aor. 13
act. subj. *καταντάω* to come to, to arrive at, to reach, to attain
to, to come down to the goal. The subj. is used in a temporal
clause w. a purpose idea (RWP). ***ἐπίγνωσις*** knowledge, knowledge directed toward a particular object (s. Robinson). ***τέλειος***
that which has reached the set goal, perfect, mature. (For a
discussion of the various views regarding the "perfect man," s.
Barth.) ***ἡλικία*** age, full age, ripeness of full age. The word can
also mean development in stature but is best understood as "mature age" (s. Eadie; Abbott). ■ ***μηκέτι*** no longer. ***ὦμεν*** pres. 14
subj. *εἰμί*. ***νήπιος*** baby, immature. It refers to the immaturity

of children in opposition to the perfection of the perfect man (Barth). **κλυδωνιζόμενοι** pres. pass. part. κλυδωνίζομαι driven by waves, to be agitated by waves (RWP). **περιφερόμενοι** pres. pass. part. περιφέρω to carry about, to carry around, to be borne to and fro. (For this figure of speech, s. Abbott.) **ἄνεμος** wind. **διδασκαλία** teaching. **κυβεία** dice playing. It means "wicked dice playing" and refers to intentional fraud (BAG; Barth; Ellicott). **πανουργία** cleverness, trickery. **μεθοδεία** following after, deceit, scheming (RWP; Barth). **πλάνη** wandering, roaming. Used figuratively of wandering from the path of truth: "error," "delusion," "deceit" (BAG).

15 ■ **ἀληθεύοντες** pres. act. part. ἀληθεύω to be truthful, to tell
the truth, to deal truly. Verbs ending in the suf. express the doing
of an action which is signified by the corresponding noun (Abbott). With this verb the relationship of quality passes to that of
action (MH, 399). **αὐξήσωμεν** aor. act. subj. αὐξάνω to grow,
to increase (s. Eph. 2:21). **τὰ πάντα** acc. of general reference
"in respect to all things." It may, however, be viewed adverbially
16 "in every way," "totally" (Barth). ■ **συναρμολογούμενον** pres.
pass. part. συναρμολογέω to join together, to fit together (s.
Eph. 2:21). **συμβιβαζόμενον** pres. pass. part. συμβιβάζω to
bring together, to unite, pass. to be held together. It refers to a
body which is held together by sinews, ligaments, joints (BAG).
It refers to a correlation as of a functioning organism (Simpson).
ἀφή joint, contact, touching, i.e., "contact w., the supply" (s.
Abbott). **ἐπιχορηγία** supply. The simple noun originally indicated a payment for the cost of bringing out a chorus at a public
festival. Then it signified provisions for an army or expedition.
The word w. the prep. in compound was a technical term describing the provision of food, clothing, etc., which a husband is
obligated to make for his wife. Here it indicates that the body
receives from the head what nourishment, life, and direction it
needs (Barth; s. also Robinson). **ἐνέργειαν** function. It refers to
the working process (Robinson). **αὔξησιν** part. αὐξάνω growing, pres. mid. ind. The mid. is used of the body promoting its
own growth (Abbott).

17 ■ **μαρτύρομαι** pres. mid. ind. to testify, to bear witness.
περιπατεῖν pres. act. inf. to walk about, to conduct one's life.
The inf. is used either to express a command or as obj. of the
verb. The pres. tense points to a habitual action. **καθώς** just as.
ἔθνος people, nation, pl. Gentiles, heathen, those who were not
Jews. **ματαιότης** vanity, emptiness, vain. The word contains the
idea of aimlessness, the leading to no object or end, vanity (s.
Trench; *Synonyms*, 180–184; s. also TDNT). (For the Jewish

indictment of the Gentiles, s. Barth; SB III, 600; JPFC II,
1065ff.) **νοῦς** mind, thinking facility, reasoning capacity. ■ 18
ἐσκοτωμένοι perf. pass. part. σκοτόω to darken. The perf.
part. is used in a periphrastic construction indicating the continuing darkened condition. **διάνοια** thinking through, understanding, intelligence, the mind as the organ of thinking (BAG). **ὄντες** pres. part. εἰμί. **ἀπηλλοτριωμένοι** perf. pass. part. ἀπαλλοτριόω to estrange, to alienate. The perf. tense emphasizes the continuing state or existence "being alienated from the life of God." It does not imply that they had at one time enjoyed that life: it means simply "being aliens" from it (Robinson). **ἄγνοια** ignorance, lack of knowledge. It refers to the inability to comprehend and see the light (Barth). **πώρωσις** hardening. The word could be used in a medical sense for callous hardening
(RWP; CBB; Barth). ■ **ἀπηλγηκότες** perf. act. part. ἀπαλγέω 19
to cease to feel pain or grief, to become callous, insensible to pain (T). The translation "past feeling" expresses the sense accurately (Abbott). **παρέδωκαν** aor. act. ind. παραδίδωμι to deliver over to, to hand over to. **ἀσέλγεια** unrestrained living (s. Gal. 5:19). **ἐργασία** working, producing, performance, practice (Robinson). **ἀκαθαρσία** uncleanness, filthiness, impurity (Barth; s. also Gal. 5:19). **πλεονεξία** insatiable craving, greed, giving rein to appetites and desires which are against the laws of
God and man (NTW, 99; Barth; s. also Rom. 1:29). ■ **ἐμάθετε** 20
aor. act. ind. μανθάνω to learn. ■ **ἠκούσατε** aor. act. ind. 21
ἀκούω. **ἐδιδάχθητε** aor. pass. ind. διδάσκω to teach, pass. to
be taught. ■ **ἀποθέσθαι** aor. mid. inf. ἀποτίθημι to put off, to 22
remove as one puts off clothes. The inf. is used to denote the substance of what they had been taught (Eadie). The aor. tense denotes a once and for all, definite, concluding action: the stripping off is to be done at once, and for good (Barth). **ἀναστροφή** manner of life (s. Eph. 2:3). **παλαιός** old. **φθειρόμενον** pres. pass. part. φθείρω to corrupt. The whole character representing the former self was not only corrupt but ever growing more and more corrupt. This is indicated by the pres. tense (s. Westcott). Every trait of the Old Man's behavior is putrid, crumbling, or inflated like rottening waste or cadavers, stinking, ripe for being disposed of and forgotten (Barth). **ἐπιθυμία** strong desire, lust.
ἀπάτη deceit. ■ **ἀνανεοῦσθαι** pres. pass. inf. ἀνανεόω to 23
make new again, to renew. The pres. tense emphasizes the continuing renewing. ■ **ἐνδύσασθαι** aor. mid. inf. ἐνδύομαι to put 24
on. Often used in the sense of putting on a garment. The inf. gives the positive side of v. 22. **κτισθέντα** aor. pass. part. κτίζω to create. **ὁσιότης** piety, holiness. It indicates fulfilling the di-

vine demands which God places upon men (CBB; TDNT; Ellicott).
25 ■ **ἀποθέμενος** aor. mid. part., s.v.22. **ψεῦδος** lie. **λαλεῖτε**
pres. act. imp. The pres. imp. points to a habitual action which
is to characterize the life. **πλησίον** one who is close by, neigh-
26 bor. **ἀλλήλων** one another, s.v.2. **μέλος** member. ■ **ὀργίζεσθε**
pres. mid. imp. ὀργίζω to be angry. A quotation from Ps. 4:5
(LXX). **ἁρμαρτάνετε** pres. act. imp. to sin. **ἐπιδυέτω** pres. act.
imp. ἐπιδύω to go down, to set. The day of the anger should be
the day of reconciliation (Barth). **παροργισμός** anger, angry
mood, a violent irritation is meant, expressed by either hiding
one's self from others or by flaming looks, harmful words, incon-
27 siderate actions (Barth). ■ **δίδοτε** pres. act. imp. **τόπος** place.
28 **διάβολος** slanderer, devil. ■ **κλέπτων** pres. act. part. **κλέπτω**
to steal. The pres. part. indicates the continuous action, i.e., "the
one stealing." **μηκέτι** no longer. **κλεπτέτω** pres. act. imp. The
pres. imp. w. the neg. calls for the stopping of an action in
progress. **κοπιάτω** pres. act. imp. **κοπιάω** to grow weary, to
work w. effort, to labor (AS). **ἐργαζόμενος** pres. mid. part. to
work. **ἔχῃ** pres. act. subj. Subjunctive used in a purpose clause.
μεταδίδωμι pres. act. inf. to give w., to share. The inf. could
express purpose or result. **χρεία** need, necessity. **ἔχοντι** pres.
act. part. (For the sharing among the Dead Sea community, s.
29 CD, 14:12f.) ■ **σαπρός** rank, foul, putrid, rotten, worthless,
disgusting (Simpson; Abbott). **ἐκπορευέσθω** pres. mid. imp.
ἐκπορεύομαι to go out, to come out. **οἰκοδομή** building, edify.
δῷ aor. act. subj. δίδωμι. The subj. is used in a purpose clause.
χάρις grace. Used w. this verb it means "to confer a favor," i.e.,
to give pleasure or profit. The meaning is, "that it may benefit
30 the hearers" (Hodge). **ἀκούουσιν** pres. act. part. dat. pl. ■
λυπεῖτε pres. act. imp. λυπέω to cause sorrow, to grieve. The
pres. imp. w. the neg. is used to forbid a continual and habitual
action. The Spirit who makes men attest to the truth is put to
shame when the saints "lie" to one another and utter "foul talk"
(Barth). **ἐσφραγίσθητε** aor. pass. ind. σφραγίζω to seal (s.
Eph. 1:13; 2 Cor. 1:22). **ἀπολύτρωσις** release through the pay-
31 ment of a price, redemption (s. Rom. 3:24). ■ **πικρία** bitterness.
It is a figurative term denoting that fretted and irritable state of mind that keeps a man in perpetual animosity—that inclines him to harsh and uncharitable opinions of men and things—that makes him sour, crabby and repulsive in his general demeanor—that brings a scowl over his face and infuses venom into the words of his tongue (Eadie). **θυμός** anger. It expresses the temporary excitement or passion (Abbott; Trench; *Synonyms*,

130f.). **ὀργή** wrath. It refers to the more subtle and deep-flowing
anger (Abbott; s. also Trench; *Synonyms*, 130f.; TDNT).
κραυγή clamor, outcry, shouting. It is the cry of strife (Ellicott).
βλασφημία slander, speaking evil of someone. It is a more
enduring manifestation of inward anger, that shows itself in
reviling. These two words are the outward manifestation of the
foregoing vices (Ellicott). **ἀρθήτω** aor. pass. imp. αἴρω to pick
up and carry away, to take away, to make a clean sweep (RWP).
κακία malice, badness. It is a generic term and seems to signify
"badhardiness," the root of all those vices (Eadie). ■ **γίνεσθε** 32
pres. mid. imp. **χρηστός** useful, worthy, good, kind, benevolent
(BAG; TDNT; CBB; Gal. 5:22). **εὔσπλαγχνος** in the lit. and
physical sense "having healthy bowels." The inward organs were
considered the seat of emotion and intention. The word then
means "compassionate," "tender-hearted" (Barth; TDNT; s.
also 1 Peter 3:8). **χαριζόμενοι** pres. mid. part. χαρίζομαι to
forgive, to exercise grace in freely forgiving. **καθώς** just as.
ἐχαρίσατο aor. mid. ind.

Ch. 5

■ **γίνεσθε** pres. mid. imp. **μιμητής** imitator. **ἀγαπητός** 1
beloved. ■ **περιπατεῖτε** pres. act. imp. περιπατέω to walk 2
about, to conduct one's life. **καθώς** just as. **ἠγάπησεν** aor. act.
ind. ἀγαπάω to love (s. John 3:16). **παρέδωκεν** aor. act. ind.
παραδίδωμι to deliver over. The verb expresses wherein his
love was shown (Abbott). **προσφορά** offering. The word generally denotes offerings which consist of products from the field
and trees (Barth). **θυσία** sacrifice. The word describes the offering of animals from the flock or stable which were killed at the
holy place and portions of which were burned upon the altar
(Barth). **ὀσμή** smell. **εὐωδία** sweet odor, fragrance. The phrase
"odor of fragrance" is a fig. designation for the acceptableness
of the offering (Meyer). ■ **πορνεία** illicit sex activity (s. TDNT). 3
ἀκαθαρσία uncleanness, impurity, filthiness (s. Eph. 4:19; Gal.
5:19). **πλεονεξία** greediness (s. Rom. 1:29; Eph. 4:19). **μήδε**
emphatic neg. "not even." **ὀνομαζέσθω** pres. pass. imp.
ὀνομάζω to name, pass. to be named. Here "let it not be even
mentioned by name" (Ellicott). **πρέπει** pres. act. ind. to be
fitting, to be suitable, to be proper. ■ **αἰσχρότης** shameful, filthy 4
or obscene speech, perhaps also w. the idea of "shameful conduct" (Abbott; Barth). **μωρολογία** foolish talk, silly talk. It is
that "talk of fools," which is foolishness and sin together
(Trench; *Synonyms*, 121). It is where a mere laugh is aimed at
even without wit (Bengel). **εὐτραπελία** coarse jesting. It implies

the dexterity of turning a discourse to wit or humor; and lastly deceptive speech, so formed that the speaker easily contrives to wriggle out of its meaning or engagements (Eadie). Ephesus was especially known for producing facetious orators (Barth). **ἀνῆκεν** impf. act. ind. ἀνήκει impersonal, it is proper, it is fitting. The impf. is used of necessity, obligation, duty and is used here in the sense "what is (really) not proper" (but yet happens) (BD, 181). **μᾶλλον** rather. **εὐχαριστία** thanksgiving. Gratitude is here singled out as the basic structural feature of the
5 Christian's ethic (Barth). ■ **ἴστε** pres. act. ind. or imp. οἶδα. The form is probably best understood as imp. and perhaps a Hebraism used w. the following part. w. the meaning "know of a surity" (s. M, 245; MH, 222; ND, 352; Barth). **γινώσκοντες** pres. act. part. **πόρνος** one who practices sexual immorality, fornicator. **πλεονέκτης** one who is greedy (s. Rom. 1:29). **ὅ ἐστίν** "that is to say." A formulaic phrase used without reference to the gender of the word explained or to that of the word which explains (BD, 73). **εἰδωλολάτρης** one who serves an idol, idolator. **κληρονομία** inheritance.
6 ■ **ἀπατάτω** pres. act. imp. ἀπατάω to lead astray, to mislead, to deceive. **κενός** empty, without content, "empty words" or words which have not inner substance and kernel of truth, hollow sophistries and apologies for sin (Trench; *Synonyms*, 180). **διὰ ταῦτα γάρ** refers not only to v. 6, but also to the previous verses. **ὀργή** wrath. **ἀπείθεια** disobedience, "sons of disobedience" is a Semitic expression indicating that the chief
7 characteristic of the per. is disobedience (s. BG, 15f.). ■ **συμμέτοχος** fellow partaker, partner, one who shares together
8/9 w. another. ■ **ἦτε** impf. εἰμί. **ποτέ** formerly. ■ **ἀγαθωσύνη**
10 goodness (s. Gal. 5:22). ■ **δοκιμάζοντες** pres. act. part. δοκιμάζω to approve after examination, to arrange and execute a test, to accept and heed the results of a test, to carry out a careful examination, to find out by experience (s. Barth). **εὐάρεστος** well-pleasing, acceptable, followed by the dat. of
11 advantage. ■ **συγκοινωνεῖτε** pres. act. imp. συγκοινωνέω to join in fellowship w. someone, to have part in a thing (Abbott). The pres. imp. w. the neg. forbids a continual and habitual act (MKG, 272f.). **ἄκαρπος** unfruitful. **ἐλέγχετε** pres. act. imp. ἐλέγχω to bring to light, to expose, to reveal hidden things, to convict or convince, to reprove, to correct, to punish, to discipline. (For the variant meanings, s. Barth; TDNT; Robinson.)
12/13 ■ **κρυφῇ** hidden, secret. **γινόμενα** pres. mid. part. ■ **ἐλεγχόμενα** pres. pass. part., s.v.11. **φῶς** light. **φανεροῦται** pres. pass. ind. φανερόω to make clear, to make known, pass.

to become visible or known, to be revealed (BAG). ■ 14
φανερούμενον pres. pass. part. **διὸ λέγει** (s. Eph. 4:8). Paul evidently uses a free adaptation of Isa. 26:19 and 61:1 (RWP; s. also Eadie). **ἔγειρε** pres. act. imp. ἐγείρω to rise, to wake up. **καθεύδων** pres. act. part. καθεύδω to sleep, to be asleep. **ἀνάστα** aor. act. imp. ἀνίσταμαι to stand up, to get up. **ἐπιφαύσει** fut. act. ind. ἐπιφαύσκω to shine upon. The means employed by the Messiah are compared to the rays of the rising sun. God's glory or light appearing over Israel exerted the life-giving power (Barth).

■ **βλέπετε** pres. act. inf. to watch, to give heed. **ἀκριβῶς** 15
accurately, carefully. **περιπατέω** pres. act. ind. to walk about, to conduct one's life. The pres. tense points to the continual action. **ἄσοφος** unwise. **σοφός** wise. The applying of acquired
knowledge (s. TDNT). ■ **ἐξαγοραζόμενοι** pres. mid. part. 16
ἐξαγοράζομαι to buy up at the market place. Either w. the meaning "seizing the opportunity," "making your market to the full from the opportunity of this life" (Abbott) or w. the meaning "buying back (at the expense of personal watchfulness and self-denial) the pres. time, which is now being used for evil and godless purposes" (MM). **καιρός** time, opportunity. **πονηρός**
evil, active evil. ■ **γίνεσθε** pres. mid. imp. **ἄφρων** without 17
understanding, senseless. The word refers to imprudence or folly in action (Abbott). **συνίετε** pres. act. imp. συνίημι to understand, the ability to bring things together and see them in relation to one another. The saints are encouraged to make use of
their reasoning power (Barth). ■ **μεθύσκεσθε** pres. mid. imp. 18
μεθύσκομαι to get drunk, to be drunk. In Philo's treatise entitled "On Drunkenness" he characterizes drunkenness generally as a mark of the blind and foolish man who is a slave to the material world (CBB). Others describe drunkenness as producing inability to preserve one's self-control and forcing one to commit many distasteful acts (DC XXXVII, 55). The religious aspects of drunkenness were seen in the Bacchus festivals in the worship of Dionysus (s. Barth; KP II, 77–85; OCD 352f.; DGRA, 410–414; Cleon Rogers, "The Dionysian Background of Ephesians 5:18," Bib Sac 136 [July, 1979], 249–257). The neg. w. the pres. imp. calls for a discontinuation of an action in progress or is used to prohibit a habitual action. **ἀσωτία** excess. The word indicated one who himself cannot save or spare thus one who extravagantly squanders his means, and then it chiefly denoted a dissolute, debauched, profligate manner of living (Trench; *Synonyms*, 54f.; s. also Josephus; *Jewish War*, IV, 651f.; MM; TDNT). The excesses and the flagrant and senseless activi-

ties connected w. the religious celebrations to Dionysus were well-known to the ancient world. The worshipers felt that they were united, indwelled, and controlled by Dionysus who gave them special powers and abilities (s. the references by the previous word; s. also H.J. Rose, *Religion in Greece and Rome,* 60f. [New York: Harper and Brothers, 1959]; Rogers, Bib Sac 136 [July, 1979], 249–257). **πληροῦσθε** pres. pass. imp. πληρόω to fill, pass. to be filled. The idea of the word is "control." The indwelling Spirit of God is the One who should continually control and dominate the life of the believer. This stands in marked contrast to the worshipers of Dionysus. The pres. tense calls for a habitual and continuing action. The pass. could be
19 permissive pass. "allow yourselves to be . . ." (s. BD, 165). ■
λαλοῦντες pres. act. part. The following parts. indicate the outworking or practice of being filled w. the Spirit (s. Schlier). **ψαλμός** song of praise, psalm. The verb meant primarily the plucking of the strings and the noun was used of sacred songs chanted to the accompaniment of instrumental music (Abbott; Eadie; Barth). **ὕμνος** hymn. It refers to sacred poetical compositions whose primary purpose is to praise (Eadie). **ᾠδή** song. This was the general word which originally meant any kind of song but was specially used of lyric poetry (Abbott). **ᾄδοντες** pres. act. part. ᾄδω to sing. **ψάλλοντες** pres. act. part. ψάλλω to play on strings, to sing to the accompaniment of a harp, to sing praise
20 (BAG). ■ **εὐχαριστοῦντες** pres. act. part. εὐχαριστέω to be
21 thankful, to give thanks. **πάντοτε** always. ■ **ὑποτασσάμενοι**
pres. mid. part. ὑποτάσσομαι to line one's self up under, to submit. Used in a military sense of soldiers submitting to their superior or slaves submitting to their masters. The word has primarily the idea of giving up one's own right or will, i.e., "to subordinate one's self" (s. RWP; TDNT; Barth). **ἀλλήλοις** dat. pl. "to one another." **φόβος** fear, reverence.
22/23 ■ **ἴδιος** one's own. ■ **κεφαλή** head. The word speaks of
24 authority and direction (s. Eadie). **σωτήρ** savior, protector. ■
ὑποτάσσεται pres. mid. ind., s.v.21. The pres. tense points to
25 the continual action or state. **οὕτως** so. ■ **οἱ ἄνδρες** voc. "you
men." The Attic Gr. used the nom. w. the article only in addressing inferiors in a rather harsh manner. However, the NT does not follow this practice and uses the nom. w. the article as the voc. sometimes under Semitic influence (s. BD, 81f.; MT, 31f.). **ἀγαπᾶτε** pres. act. imp. ἀγαπάω to love. The pres. imp. calls for a continual habitual action. **καθώς** just as. **ἠγάπησεν** aor. act. ind. **παρέδωκεν** aor. act. ind., s.v.2. In a time when marriages were arranged and morals were so loose, to fulfill the

commands of subordination and love was not an easy task. (For marriage and the home in the ancient world, including both Jewish and Gentile, s. SB III, 610–613; JPFC II, 748–769; Barth 655–662, 700–720; W.K. Lacey, *The Family in Classical Greek* [London: Thames & Hudson, 1972]; Heinrich Greeven, "Ehe nach dem Neuen Testament," NTS, 15 [July, 1969], 365–388.)
■ **ἁγιάσῃ** aor. act. subj. ἁγιάζω to sanctify, to make holy, to 26
set apart. (For the relation of this word to the marriage ceremony, s. Barth.) **καθαρίσας** aor. act. part. καθαρίζω to cleanse. **λουτρόν** bath. Since a bridal bath was the practice both among Jews and Gentiles, Paul may be making allusions to this custom (s. SB I, 506; DGRA, 737). Barth's objection that such an allusion would mean that the bridegroom would be said to have given the bride a bath is to press the allusion too far (s. Barth, 694). The case is either locative or instrumental. **ῥῆμα** word, spoken word. Perhaps the reference is to the gospel which is
proclaimed. ■ **παραστήσῃ** aor. act. subj. παρίστημι to 27
present. **ἔνδοξος** glorious. **ἔχουσαν** pres. act. part. acc. fem. sing. **σπίλος** spot, speck, fleck, stain. **ῥυτίς** wrinkle, fold. The word referred to a wrinkle or fold on the face. The terms used here are taken from physical beauty, health, and symmetry, to denote spiritual perfection (Eadie). **τοιοῦτος** such a thing. **ᾖ** pres. subj. εἰμί. Subjunctive used in a purpose clause. **ἄμωμος**
blameless. ■ **ὀφείλω** pres. act. ind. to owe someone a debt, to 28
be obligated, to ought to. The word indicates moral obligation (s. TDNT). The pres. tense indicates the continual existence of the
obligation. **ἀγαπῶν** pres. act. part. ■ **ἐμίσησεν** aor. act. ind. 29
μισέω to hate. The aor. is gnomic and expresses something which is always true. **ἐκτρέφει** pres. act. ind. to nourish, to nourish children to maturity (T). The prep. in compound is perfective. The pres. tense of a linear verb denotes the whole process leading up to an attained goal (M, 114). **θάλπει** pres.
act. ind. to cherish, to show affection and tender love. ■ **μέλος** 30
member. ■ **ἀντὶ τούτου** because of this, for this reason. 31
καταλείψει fut act. ind. καταλείπω to leave behind. **προσκοληθήσεται** fut. pass. ind. προσκολλάομαι to be glued to, to be joined to. The previous word suggests the complete separation from all former ties and this word gives the
forming of a new relation. **ἔσονται** fut. mid. ind. εἰμί. ■ 32
μυστήριον (s. Eph. 3:3). The word refers to that which is incapable of being discovered by human being but also that which is revealed by God. Here it has to do w. the mystical union of
Christ and His church. ■ **πλήν** in any case, however. The word 33
is used for breaking off discussion and emphasizing what is im-

portant (BAG). **ἀγαπάτω** pres. act. imp. **φοβῆται** pres. mid. subj. φοβέομαι to reverence, to show respect.

Ch. 6

1 ■ **ὑπακούετε** pres. act. imp. ὑπακούω to listen to, to obey.
2 **γονεῖς** parent. ■ **τίμα** pres. act. imp. τιμάω to count as valuable, to value, to honor, to revere (BAG; TDNT). **ἐντολή** commandment. **ἐπαγγελία** promise. (For the Jewish teaching regarding this commandment and the position of children in the
3 family, s. SB I, 705–717, III, 614; JPFC II, 769f.) ■ **εὖ** adv. well.
γένηται aor. mid. subj. γίνομαι. **ἔσῃ** fut. mid. ind. 2nd per.
sing. εἰμί. It is possible that the fut. is used here because there
was no aor. subj. of the verb (Abbott). **μακροχρόνιος** long-
4 lived, long-timed (s. Eadie). ■ **παροργίζετε** pres. act. imp.
παροργίζομαι to anger, to make angry, to bring one along to
a deep-seated anger. The prep. in compound indicates an "onward motion" (MH, 320; s. also Schlier; TDNT; Eph. 4:26). The
neg. w. the pres. imp. is used to prevent a habitual action.
ἐκτρέφετε pres. act. imp. ἐκτρέφω to nourish, to provide for w.
tender care (s. Eph. 5:29). (For the responsibility of the father
for the children in a Jewish family, s. JPFC II, 769f.) **παιδείᾳ**
education, child training, discipline. The word indicates the discipline used to correct the transgression of the laws and ordinances of the Christian household (Trench; *Synonyms*, 112; s.
also TDNT). **νουθεσίᾳ** admonition. It refers to the training by
word—by the word of encouragement, when this is sufficient,
but also that of remonstrance, of reproof, of blame, where these
may be required (Trench; *Synonyms*, 112; s. also TDNT).
5 ■ **φόβος** fear, reverence. **τρόμος** tremble. The words only
express anxious solicitude about the performance of duty, so that
there is no allusion to the hardness of the service (Abbott).
6 **ἁπλότης** simplicity, sincerity, uprightness (BAG). ■
ὀφθαλμοδουλία eyeservice. It is labor when the master is
present, but relaxation and laziness as soon as he is gone (Eadie).
ἀνθρωπάρεσκος men pleaser, one who tries to please men at
7 the sacrifice of principle (BAG). **ποιοῦντες** pres. act. part. ■
εὔνοια good will. It suggests the ready good will, which does not
wait to be compelled (Robinson). **δουλεύοντες** pres. act. part.
8 ■ **εἰδότες** perf. act. part. οἶδα. **ἕκαστος** each. **ποιήσῃ** aor. act.
subj. **κομίσεται** fut. mid. ind. κομίζομαι to receive, to receive
back, i.e., to receive as a deposit; hence here it implies an adequate return (Abbott). **εἴτε . . . εἴτε** whether . . . or. **ἐλεύθερος**
9 free. ■ **ποιεῖτε** pres. act. ind. **ἀνιέντες** pres. act. part. ἀνίημι to
loosen up, to relax, "to let up on" (RWP). **ἀπειλή** threatening.

προσωπολημψία the accepting of one's person, partiality.
■ **τοῦ λοιποῦ** finally, for the remaining. **ἐνδυναμοῦσθε** 10
pres. pass. imp. ἐνδυναμόω to empower, pass. to be
strengthened. **κράτος** strength. **ἰσχύς** might. (For these two
words, s. Eph. 1:19.) ■ **ἐνδύσασθε** aor. mid. imp. ἐνδύομαι to 11
put on, to clothe one's self. **πανοπλία** full armor, complete armor. This included such things as a shield, sword, lance, helmet, greaves, and breastplate (T; for a description of a Roman soldier and his armor, s. CC, 207f.; Josephus; *Jewish Wars*, III, 93ff.). Since armor of a soldier was often a display of splendor, Barth prefers the translation "the splendid armor" (s. Barth, 793–795). **τοῦ θεοῦ** gen. of source or origin indicating that God provides the armor (Eadie). **στῆναι** aor. act. inf. ἵσταμι to stand. The word could be used in a military sense indicating either "to take over," "to hold a watch post," or it could also mean "to stand and hold out in a critical position on a battlefield" (Barth). **μεθοδεία** scheming, craftiness. **διάβολος** slanderer, devil. ■ **πάλη** struggle, wrestling. The word refers partic- 12
ularly to a "hand-to-hand fight" (Barth). Wrestling was a fight characterized by trickery, cunningness, and strategy (DGRA, 817; KP IV, 1436; CC, 143f.). **κοσμοκράτωρ** world ruler. (For
a discussion of the spiritual warfare in the DSS, s. 1QM.) ■ 13
ἀναλάβετε aor. act. imp. ἀναλαμβάνω to take up. The word was used as a military technical term describing the last preparation and final step necessary before the actual battle begins (Barth). The aor. imp. demands an immediate action. **δυνηθῆτε** aor. pass. subj. Subjunctive used in a purpose clause. **ἀντιστῆναι** aor. act. inf. ἀνθίσταμι to spend against, to resist. **κατεργασάμενοι** aor. mid. part. κατεργάζομαι to accomplish, to carry out. Although the word may mean "to carry to victory," it here means not only "having made all necessary preparations," but indicates having done everything which the crisis demands, in order to quail the foe and maintain the position (Eadie; s. also Barth). ■ **στῆτε** aor. act. imp. ἵσταμι ingres- 14
sive aor. "take your stand" (RWP). **περιζωσάμενοι** aor. mid. part. περιζώννυμι to bind around one's self, to gird one's self. The Roman soldiers wore one of at least three wide belts or girdles. The breech-like leather apron worn to protect the lower abdomen or the sword-belt which was buckled on together w. the sword as the decisive step in the process of preparing one's self for battle and the special belt or sash designating an officer or high official (Barth; TDNT). **ὀσφῦς** hips. **ἐνδυσάμενοι** aor. mid. part. **θώραξ** breastplate. The word denotes a piece of armor that can mean everything that was worn at different periods to

protect the body between the shoulders and the loins. The average Roman soldier wore a piece of metal, but those who could afford it used the very best available: a scale or chain mail
15 that covered chest and hips (Barth; DGRA, 711f.). ■
ὑποδησάμενοι aor. mid. part. ὑποδέομαι to bind under, to strap on. It may refer to the *caliga*, the strong and heavy shoe worn by the Roman soldiers. This shoe was thickly studded w. hobnails or it may refer to the more elegant shoe, the *calceus*, which was worn by men of higher rank (s. DGRA, 233f.). **τοὺς πόδας** acc. of general reference. **ἑτοιμασίᾳ** preparation, readiness. The word may however in this context have the meaning "firmly" and express solidity, firmness, solid foundation (Barth).
16 ■ **ἀναλαβόντες** aor. act. part. ἀναλαμβάνω to take up, s.v.13.
θυρεός shield. It refers to the large door-shaped shield in contrast to the small round convex shield. The reference is to the Roman soldiers *scutum* which had an iron frame and sometimes a metal boss in the center at the front. Often the several layers of leather were soaked in water before the battle in order to put out the incendiary missiles of the enemy (Barth). **δυνήσεσθε** fut. mid. ind. **βέλος** dart, arrow. The term could be used of any type of missile (Barth). **πεπυρωμένα** perf. pass. part. πυρόω to set on fire. The perf. pass. part. indicates that the arrows were set on fire and are burning. These were arrows or spears tipped w. tow and dipped in pitch (Barth; s. also Josephus; *Jewish Wars*, III, 173). **σβέσαι** aor. act. inf. σβέννυμι to put out, to quench.
17 ■ **περικεφαλαία** a protection around the head, helmet. The
Roman soldier wore a bronze helmet equipped w. cheek pieces. The helmet was a heavy decorative and expensive item which had an inside lining of felt or sponge which made the weight bearable. Nothing short of an axe or hammer could pierce a heavy helmet (Barth; TDNT). **σωτήριον** salvation, gen. of apposition. **δέξασθε** aor. mid. imp. δέχομαι to take, to receive. **μάχαιρα** sword. It signifies the short, straight sword used by the
18 Roman soldier (Barth; DGRA, 577; TDNT). ■ **δέησις** request,
prayer, petition. It is generally a petition for particular benefits or a petition arising from a particular need (s. Trench; *Synonyms*, 189; CBB; TDNT). **προσευχόμενοι** pres. mid. part. προσεύχομαι to pray. This is the general word which was used for making a petition to a divine being, i.e., to pray (s. CBB; TDNT; Trench; *Synonyms*, 188f.). **καιρός** time, occasion, opportunity. **εἰς αὐτό** "for this." **ἀγρυπνοῦντες** pres. act. part. ἀγρυπνέω to stay awake, to lie sleepless, to pass a sleepless night, to suffer from insomnia, to be watchful, to be vigilant (Barth). **προσκαρτέρησις** perseverance, constancy (s. LAE,

102). The verb was used in the papyri in the sense of holding out
or waiting, e.g., waiting until one's trial came before the court or
diligently remaining at one's work (s. Preisigke). ■ **δοθῇ** aor. 19
pass. subj. *δίδωμι*. **ἄνοιξις** opening. **στόμα** mouth. **παρρησία**
speaking everything, speaking openly, boldness (s. TDNT).
γνωρίσαι aor. act. inf. *γνωρίζω* to make known. **μυστήριον**
mystery (s. Eph. 3:3). ■ **πρεσβεύω** to be an ambassador or 20
envoy, to travel or work as an ambassador (BAG; s. also 2 Cor.
5:20). **ἅλυσις** chain. The description of an ambassador in chains
could be a paradox in three aspects. The term "chain" could
indicate a necklace worn by ambassadors to reveal the riches,
power, and dignity of the government they represent, but Paul's
chain is one of an iron prison chain. The word could also refer
to imprisonment, and because an ambassador normally would
not be arrested, Paul indicates the wrong he is suffering. Finally,
a delegate who is in prison knows that the end of his mission is near (Barth). **παρρησιάσωμαι** aor. mid. subj.
παρρησιάζομαι to speak everything, to speak openly and
frankly, to speak boldly, to be bold. **δεῖ** it is necessary. **λαλῆσαι**
aor. act. inf.

■ **εἰδῆτε** perf. act. subj. *οἶδα*. **γνωρίσει** fut. act. ind. s.v.19. 21
ἀγαπητός beloved. ■ **ἔπεμψα** aor. act. ind. *πέμπω* to send. **εἰς** 22
αὐτὸ τοῦτο for this very reason. **γνῶτε** aor. act. subj. *γινώσκω*.
Subjunctive used in a purpose clause. **παρακαλέσῃ** aor. act.
subj. *παρακαλέω* to comfort, to encourage (TDNT; MNTW,
134).

■ **ἀγαπώντων** pres. act. part. *ἀγαπάω* to love. **ἀφθαρσία** 24
not corruptible, incorruption. The word does not point merely
to time but to character (Abbott; s. also Rom. 2:7; 1 Cor. 15:52).

PHILIPPIANS

Ch. 1

1 ***οὖσιν*** pres. part. masc. dat. pl. *εἰμί.* ***σύν*** w. dat. The prep.
implies close fellowship or cooperation (DM, 111). ***ἐπίσκοπος***
overseer, superintendent, bishop. The word was used for one
who had the responsibility of oversight. It is important to note
that Paul here uses the pl. and that elsewhere the term is used
interchangeably w. "elder" (s. CBB; TDNT; Lightfoot, 95–99;
Gnilka; ZPEB I, 617–620; Vincent).
3 ■ ***εὐχαριστέω*** pres. act. ind. to give thanks. ***μνεία*** remembrance, mention. Used w. the prep. to express the thought "as
4 often as I make mention of you (in prayer)" (BAG). ■ ***πάντοτε***
every time, always. ***δέησις*** request, petition, generally a specific
petition arising from a need (s. Eph. 6:18). ***ποιούμενος*** pres.
mid. part. The mid. voice of this verb is used where it has for
object a noun denoting action, w. which it forms a periphrasis
5 equivalent to a simple verb, i.e., "to pray" (BG, 72f.). ■
κοινωνία fellowship, sharing. The word signifies "your cooperation toward, in aid of the gospel." The word refers not only to
financial contributions but also denotes cooperation in the widest sense, their participation w. the apostle whether in sympathy
or in suffering or in active labor (Lightfoot; s. also TDNT; CBB;
6 RAC IX, 1100–1145). ■ ***πεποιθώς*** perf. act. part. *πέποιθα* to
persuade, perf. to be convinced, to be sure, to be certain. (For
the construction of the verb followed by a noun clause, s. BD,
204.) The part. may have a faint causal force (Ellicott). ***αὐτὸ
τοῦτο*** "this very thing," "just this (and nothing else)" (BD, 151).
ἐναρξάμενος aor. mid. part. *ἐναρχομαι* to begin. The prep. in
compound represents the action of the verb as more directly
concentrated on the object (Ellicott). ***ἐπιτελέσει*** fut. act. ind.
ἐπιτελέω to complete, to bring to the goal. The prep. in compound is directive and the verb indicates "will carry it on
7 towards completion, and finally complete" (Vincent). ■ ***κάθως***
just as. The word has a slight causal sense and is often used to
introduce new ideas (Gnilka). ***ἐστὶν δίκαιον ἐμοί*** "it is right for
me." Although the expression may have been a daily figure of
speech (Lohmeyer) the word does contain an ethical and general

moral sense which has its foundation in the moral relation of
man to God (Vincent; MRP, 148). **φρονεῖν** pres. act. inf. to be
minded. The word denotes a general disposition of mind (Vincent). **ἔχειν** pres. act. inf. used w. the prep. in a causal sense. The
words form an expression of heartfelt love on the part of the
apostle toward his readers (Meyer). **δέσμος** bond. **ἀπολογία**
defense, defense against a judicial accusation. The word may be
more general including all of Paul's efforts, whatever put forth,
to defend the gospel (Vincent). **βεβαίωσις** confirmation, a legal
technical term for guaranteeing or furnishing security (BAG; s.
also BS, 104–109; MM). **συγκοινωνός** sharers together w.
someone, fellow partakers. **ὄντας** pres. part. εἰμί. Causal use of
the part. ■ **ἐπιποθέω** pres. act. ind. to long for, to yearn after. 8
The prep. in compound signifies direction; but the idea of straining after the object being thereby suggested, the idea implied is
"eagerness" (Lightfoot). **σπλάγχνον** the inward parts, i.e., the
heart, liver, lungs which were collectively regarded as the seat
of feeling and is the strongest word in Gr. for the feeling of
compassion (s. Vincent; MNTW, 156f.; TDNT; CBB). ■ 9
προσεύχομαι to pray. (For the prayer words and syntactical
constructions, s. PIP, 173f.) **ἔτι** yet. **μᾶλλον** more. The phrase
"more and more" accentuates their need for unremitting
progress (PIP, 209). **περισσεύῃ** pres. act. subj. περισσεύω to
overflow, to abound. The pres. tense is progressive and expresses
the desire "may continue to abound" (Vincent). **ἐπίγνωσις**
knowledge, recognition. The prep. in compound indicates a
knowledge directed toward an object. Here the word indicates
a firm conception of those spiritual principles which would guide
them in their relations w. one another and the world (EGT).
αἴσθησις insight, perception, discernment. The word was originally used of sense perception but is applicable to the inner
world of sensibility and refers to moral and spiritual perception
related to practical applications (EGT; Lightfoot). ■ 10
δοκιμάζειν pres. act. inf. to approve after testing (s. TDNT).
The inf. w. the prep. could express either purpose or result (MT,
143). **διαφέροντα** pres. act. part. διαφέρω to differ. Here it
refers to what is worthwhile, excellent, vital (PIP, 209).
εἰλικρινής pure, genuine, sincere. The etymology "tested by
sunlight" is possible but uncertain (s. GEW I, 459; Vincent;
Lohmeyer; TDNT). **ἀπρόσκοπος** without stumbling, without
offense. The word means either "not stumbling" or "not causing
others to stumble" (Vincent). ■ **πεπληρωμένοι** perf. pass. part. 11
πληρόω to fill. The perf. views the completed state or condition.
ἔπαινος praise.

12 ■ **γινώσκειν** pres. act. inf. to know, to realize. **μᾶλλον**
rather, i.e., rather than the reverse, as might have been anticipated (Lightfoot). **προκοπή** cutting forward, advance, progress, furtherance. (For the verb, s. Gal. 1:14.) **ἐλήλυθεν** perf. ind.
13 ἔρχομαι. ■ **φανερός** clear, manifest. **γενέσθαι** aor. mid. inf. γίνομαι. Infinitive used w. a particle to express actual result (s. BD, 197f.). **πραιτώριον** praetorian guard, praetorium. The word refers either to the elite troops or to the headquarters used by such troops (s. Vincent; Lightfoot; Gnilka; ZPEB IV, 832–
14 834; CC, 198f.; KP IV, 1116–1117). ■ **πλείονες** "the majority" (s. BD, 127). **πεποιθότας** perf. act. part., s.v.6. **περισσοτέρως** adv. comp. περισσός abundantly. Here it denotes the "increased zeal" of the brethren, when stimulated by St. Paul's endurance (Lightfoot). **τολμᾶν** pres. act. inf. to dare. Infinitive used to express actual results (s.v.13). **ἀφόβως** adv. fearless.
15 ■ **καί.** Used here in a contrasting force and introduces another and a different class (Vincent). **φθόνος** envy. **εὐδοκία** goodwill. The word refers to the good motives and well wishes
16 from which an action comes (s. TDNT; Gnilka). ■ **οἱ μέν . . . οἱ δέ** "the ones . . . the others." **εἰδότες** perf. act. part. οἶδα. **ἀπολογία** defense (s.v.7). **κεῖμαι** to lie, to recline. Figuratively
17 to be appointed, to be destined (BAG). ■ **ἐριθεία** selfishness. Originally, the character of a worker for pay. A hired worker was looked down upon because his laboring was wholly for his own interest (EGT; s. also Phil. 2:3). **καταγγέλλουσιν** pres. act. ind. to proclaim, to proclaim w. authority. The prep. in compound is perhaps intensive "making fully known" (Ellicott; Vincent; CBB). **ἁγνῶς** adv. purely w. the neg. "w. mixed" impure motives (Lightfoot). **οἰόμενοι** pres. mid. part. οἴομαι to suppose, to imagine. It denotes a belief or judgment based principally upon one's own feelings, or the peculiar relations of outward circumstances to one's self (Vincent). **θλῖψις** pressure, tribulation. **ἐγειρεῖν** pres. act. inf. to raise up. Used in the context "to make
18 my chains gaul me" (Lightfoot). ■ **γάρ** then, assuredly (s. Thrall, 44). **πλήν** except, but, nevertheless. The particle is used in an adversitive sense (s. Blomqvist, 75–100; Thrall, 20f.). **τρόπος** manner, fashion. **εἴτε** whether. **πρόφασις** pretense, pretext, excuse. The word indicates the "ostensible reason" for which a thing is done, and generally points to a false reason as opposed to the truth (MM; BAG). Here it is using the name of Christ as a cover or mask for personal and selfish ends (Vincent). The dat. expresses the manner (Ellicott). **καταγγέλλεται** pres. pass. ind. **ἀλλὰ καί.** The two particles are combined in a progressive sense "further," "what is more," "moreover" (s. Thrall, 14ff.).

χαρήσομαι fut. mid. (BD, 42) ind. χαίρω to be glad, to rejoice.
The fut. is volitive indicating a decision of the will (s. RG, 889)
and is a progressive fut. which affirms that an action will be in
progress in fut. time (SMT, 32). ■ **οἶδα** defective perf. w. a pres. 19
meaning to know. The word speaks of the possession of knowledge which is grasped directly or intuitively by the mind (s. ND,
344f.). **τοῦτο** this, i.e., "this state of things," these perplexities
and annoyances (Lightfoot). **ἀποβήσεται** fut. mid. ind.
ἀποβαίνω to come from, to come back, to turn out (RWP).
ἐπιχορηγία supply (s. Eph. 4:16; Gal. 3:5). ■ **ἀποκαραδοκία** 20
intense expectation, earnest watching. The word is composed of
the prep. "away," the noun "head" and the verb "to watch" and
indicates watching something w. the head turned away from
other objects (Vincent). It indicates the concentrated intense
hope which ignores other interests and strains forward as w.
outstretched head (EGT; s. also Rom. 8:19; Gnilka).
αἰσχυνθήσομαι fut. pass. ind. αἰσχύνομαι to be ashamed, to
be put to shame. **παρρησία** speaking all things, forthrightness
of speech then more broadly "boldness," esp. the courage appropriate to the free man, which acts openly even in a hostile atmosphere (Beare). **μεγαλυνθήσεται** fut. pass. ind. μεγαλύνω to
make large, to magnify. ■ **ζῆν** pres. act. inf. ζάω to live. The 21
articular inf. is used as the subject of the sentence "the act of
living." The pres. tense is continuous (Vincent). **ἀποθανεῖν** aor.
act. inf. ἀποθνήσκω to die. The articular inf. is used as the
subject. **κέρδος** gain, profit. The word was used of something
advantageous and in the pl. sometimes refers to money (BAG;
MM; for other examples, s. Lohmeyer). (For a discussion of this
verse, s. D.W. Palmer, " 'To Die Is Gain.' Philippians 1:21," Nov
T, 18 [July, 1975], 203–218.) ■ **αἱρήσομαι** fut. mid. ind. 22
αἱρέομαι to take, to pick, mid. to choose. **γνωρίζω** to understand, to know, to declare, to make known. The latter meaning
is better in this context (s. Lightfoot; Vincent). ■ **συνέχομαι** 23
pres. pass. ind. συνέχω to hold together, to hem in on both
sides. The idea is that of a strong pressure bearing upon him from
two sides and keeping him motionless (EGT; Lightfoot). **δέ** and,
now. It introduces an explanation and at the same time separates
it from that which is to be explained (Vincent). **ἐπιθυμία** desire.
ἔχων pres. act. part. **ἀναλῦσαι** aor. act. inf. ἀναλύω to break
up, to unloose, to undo. It is used of loosening a ship from its
moorings, of breaking camp, and of death (Vincent; cf. 2 Cor.
5:1). The inf. w. the prep. is used to supply the limits of the noun
"desire" (MT, 143). **κρεῖσσων** comp. stronger, better. ■ 24
ἐπιμένειν pres. act. inf. to remain, to stay. The prep. in com-

pound implies rest in a place and hence at a more protracted stay
(Ellicott). **ἀναγκαιότερος** comp. ἀναγκαῖος necessary, comp.
25 more necessary. ■ **μενῶ** fut. act. ind. μένω to remain.
παραμενῶ fut. act. ind. παραμένω to remain w. someone, to
stand by. In the koine the word often had the idea of "service"
26 (MM; Preisigke; Lohmeyer). ■ **καύχημα** ground or reason for
boasting. Here it is their knowledge and possession of the gospel
(EGT). **περισσεύῃ** pres. act. subj. to overflow, to abound. The
subj. is used to express purpose. **παρουσία** arrival, presence.
27 ■ **ἀξίως** adv. worthily (s. Eph. 4:1). **πολιτεύεσθε** pres.
mid. imp. πολιτεύομαι to be a citizen, to conduct one's self as
a citizen. Paul may be alluding to the fact that the city of Philippi
had the Roman status of "colonia," which meant that the city
was a "mini-Rome" (s. DGRA, 315–320; IDB I, 657; s. also
A.N. Sherwin White, *The Roman Citizenship* [Oxford: At the
Clarendon Press, 1973]). (For verbs w. this suf. meaning "to play
the part of," "to act as," s. MH, 398–400.) The pres. imp. calls
for a continual and habitual action. **ἐλθών** aor. act. part.
ἔρχομαι. **ἰδών** aor. act. part. ὁράω. The parts. could be conditional or translated as a main verb (s. Vincent). **ἀπών** pres. part.
ἄπειμι to be away from, to be absent. **στήκετε** pres. ind. act.
στήκω to stand, to stand firm, to hold one's ground. The word
indicates the determination of a soldier who does not budge one
inch from his post (Lohmeyer). **ψυχή** soul. It indicates the mind
as the seat of sensation and desire (Vincent; TDNT; PAT).
συναθλοῦντες pres. act. part. συναθλέω to contend or strug-
28 gle along w. someone (BAG). ■ **πτυρόμενοι** pres. pass. part.
πτύρω to frighten, to startle, to terrify. The metaphor is from a
timid horse (Lightfoot). Perhaps an allusion to Cassius who at
the battle of Philippi committed suicide at the fear of defeat
(CAH X, 24). **ἀντικειμένων** pres. mid. part. ἀντίκειμαι to line
up against, to oppose, to be an adversary. **ἥτις** which, "seeing
it is." The rel. has an explanatory force and takes its gender from
the predicate but agrees logically w. the part. in the nom. (Vincent). **ἔνδειξις** evidence, proof. The word was used as an Attic
law term (EGT). **ἀπώλεια** destruction. Here it is the destruction which consists in the loss of eternal life (Vincent; s. also
29 TDNT). ■ **ἐχαρίσθη** aor. pass. ind. χαρίζω to give graciously,
"God has granted you the high privilege of suffering for Christ;
this is the surest sign, that He looks upon you w. favor" (Lightfoot). **πάσχειν** pres. act. inf. to suffer. The articular inf. is used
30 as the subject of the verb. ■ **ἀγών** conflict, struggle. The word
pictures Paul's apostolic life of service (PAM, 183). **ἔχοντες**
pres. act. part. **οἷος** which kind of. **εἴδετε** aor. act. ind. ὁράω.

Ch. 2

■ **παράκλησις** comfort, consolation, exhortation, encour- 1
agement (s. TDNT; MNTW, 128ff.). **παραμύθιον** encouragement, esp. as consolation or alleviation (BAG). The prep. in
compound may have the force of "aside," i.e., "the converse
which draws the mind aside from care" (MM). **κοινωνία** fellowship. **σπλάγχνα** tender affection, mercy (s. Phil. 1:8).
οἰκτιρμός compassion. It signifies the manifestation of tender
feelings in compassionate yearnings and actions (Lightfoot). ■ 2
πληρώσατε aor. act. imp. πληρόω to fill. The particle **ἵνα**
"that" is used to introduce the object of the request and blends
in the purpose of making it (Ellicott; s. also BD, 199f.). **φρονῆτε**
pres. act. subj. φρονέω to think, to hold an opinion, to have
thoughts or an attitude, to be minded or disposed (BAG). The
pres. tense implies a continual habitual attitude. **ἔχοντες** pres.
act. part. **σύμψυχος** harmonious, united in spirit (BAG). The
following words appear on the grave stone of a man and his wife:
"we spoke the same things, we thought the same things and we
go the inseparable way in Hades" (s. Lohmeyer; BS, 256).
φρονοῦντες pres. act. part. ■ **ἐριθεία** selfishness, selfish ambi- 3
tion. The word is related to a noun which originally meant "a day
laborer" and was used esp. of those cutting and binding wheat
or of those who were spinners or weavers. The word later
denotes the attitude of those who worked for wages and particularly it denoted a self-seeking pursuit of political office by unfair
means. It then came to be used of "party squabbles," of the
jockeying for position and the intriguing for place and power.
Finally, it meant "selfish ambition," the ambition which has no
conception of service and whose only aims are profit and power
(s. BAG; TDNT; GEW I, 558; NTW, 39ff.). **κενοδοξία** empty
praise, vainglory. It refers to personal vanity (Lightfoot; s. also
Gal. 5:26). **ταπεινοφροσύνη** lowly thinking, humility. The
word indicates the recognition of personal insufficiency of one's
self but the powerful sufficiency of God (TDNT; CBB; Gnilka).
ἀλλήλους one another. **ἡγούμενοι** pres. mid. part. ἡγέομαι to
consider, to count as. The word implies a conscious sure judgment resting on a careful weighing of the facts (Vincent).
ὑπερέχοντας pres. act. part. ὑπερέχω w. the gen. to have over
and beyond, to excel or surpass, to be superior (RWP; Ellicott).
■ **τὰ ἑαυτῶν** "the things of others," i.e., "others, different from 4
those named." (For the contrast, s. BD, 161.) **ἕκαστος** each,
each one. **σκοποῦντες** pres. act. part. σκοπέω to look at, to
consider, to regard as one's aim. Used w. the article and the
reflex. pron. it means "to consult one's own interest" (Light-

5 foot). ■ **φρονεῖτε** pres. act. imp., s.v.2. **ἐν ὑμῖν** "in you," i.e.,
"in your community (of faith and love)," "in your common life"
6 (Beare). ■ **μορφή** form. The outward display of the inner reality
or substance. Here it refers to the outward display of the divine
substance, i.e., divinity of the preexistent Christ in the display
of His glory as being in the image of the Father. (For a study of
this word, s. Martin, 99–133; Lightfoot, esp. 127–133; TDNT;
CBB; T.F. Glasson, "Two Notes on the Philippians' Hymn: II.6–
11," NTS, 21 [October, 1974], 133–139; Vincent, 78ff.)
ὑπάρχων pres. act. part. ὑπάρχω to be, to exist. The word
expresses continuance of an antecedent state or condition (AS;
s. also 2 Cor. 12:16). **ἁρπαγμός.** The word has either an active
sense "robbing" or a pass. sense "prize gained through robbery."
Perhaps the meaning is that Christ did not use His equality w.
God in order to snatch or gain power and dominion, riches,
pleasure, worldly glory. He did not reach out of His favored
place and grasp at authority (s. Meyer; Martin, 152). (For detailed studies on this difficult word, s. Martin, 134–164; Lightfoot, 133–138; Glasson, 133–137; TDNT; Lampe.) **ἡγήσατο**
aor. mid. ind. ἡγέομαι to consider. (For the view that the verb
in connection w. the previous noun means "to treat as a piece
of good fortune," "to regard as a lucky find," "to prize highly,"
"to welcome eagerly," s. Martin, 143f.; Lightfoot, 138.) **ἴσος**
equal, exactly equal, equal in number, size, quality. The n. pl. can
be used of an adv. which in turn is used here as an adj. w. the
verb "to be" (s. BAG; BD, 224; s. also TDNT). The acc. is used
w. the articular inf., "to be equal w. God," to form the acc. of
object in a double acc. construction; "He did not regard the
being equal w. God (acc. of object) as a robbing (pred. acc.)."
7 (For this construction, s. BD, 86; RG, 479ff.) ■ **ἑαυτόν** Himself.
The word is emphasized by its position in the sentence.
ἐκένωσεν aor. act. ind. κενόω to empty, to make empty, to
make of no effect. The word does not mean He emptied Himself
of His deity, but rather He emptied Himself of the display of His
deity for personal gain. The word is a graphic expression of the
completeness of His self-renunciation and His refusal to use
what He had to His own advantage (Vincent; Martin, 195; for
a study of the word, s. TDNT; Martin, 165–196; CBB). **δοῦλος**
slave. **λάβων** aor. act. part. λαμβάνω. **ὁμοίωμα** likeness. The
phrase expresses the fact that His mode of manifestation resembled what men are. The apostle views Him solely as He could
appear to men (Vincent). This, however, does not deny His true
humanity. **γενόμενος** aor. mid. part. γίνομαι. **σχῆμα** outward
appearance. The word was used of a king who exchanges his

kingly robe for sackcloth (BAG; s. also Lightfoot, 127–133; CBB; TDNT; Martin, 207f.). **εὑρεθείς** aor. pass. part. The parts.
are manner and indicate how Christ emptied Himself. ■ 8
ἐτάπείνωσεν aor. act. ind. **ταπεινόω** to make low, to humble. **ὑπήκοος** obedient. **μέχρι** until, unto, "even unto death," i.e., to the extent of death (Vincent). **δέ** and, even, yea. It introduces another and more striking detail of the humiliation, and leads on to a climax not only death but a death of suffering shameful and accursed, the most ignominious of deaths (Vincent; Ellicott). (For the horrors and the attitude of the ancient world toward the despicable death by crucifixion which was a form of punishment reserved for slaves, rebels and the lowest criminals, s. Blinzler; Martin Hengel, *Crucifixion in the Ancient World and the Folly of the Message of the Cross* [Philadelphia: Fortress Press, 1978].)
■ **διό** wherefore, in consequence of this voluntary humiliation, 9
in fulfillment of divine law which He Himself enuniciated (Lightfoot; s. also Martin, 231ff.). **ὑπερύψωσεν** aor. act. ind. ὑπερυψόω to exalt, to exalt above and beyond, to highly exalt. The force of the prep. in compound is not to describe a different stage in Christ's existence in a comp. sense, but to contrast His exaltation w. the claim of other high powers, and thereby to proclaim His uniqueness and absoluteness (Martin, 241; s. also Beare). **ἐχαρίσατο** aor. mid. ind. χαρίζομαι to give out of grace, to grant graciously. Now after a career of self-humbling and obedience there comes to Him in the Father's good pleasure the very thing He might have grasped (Martin, 236; s. also Phil.
1:29). ■ **γόνυ** knee. **κάμψῃ** aor. act. subj. **κάπτπω** to bend, to 10
bow. The subj. is used to express purpose. **ἐπουράνιος** heavenly, heaven (s. Eph. 1:3). **ἐπίγειος** earthly, on the earth. **καταχθόνιος** under the earth. Christ is acknowledged as Lord of all angelic forces, esp. malevolent demons and they are compelled to admit that He is victor; and they show their submission by their prostration before Him (Martin, 261; for a discussion of this threefold division of the universe, s. Martin 257–265).
■ **γλῶσσα** tongue. **ἐξομολογήσεται** aor. mid. subj. 11
ἐξομολογέομαι to admit openly, to acknowledge, to recognize, to acclaim (s. Martin, 263; TDNT; Beare). The subj. is used to express purpose. **εἰς δόξαν θεοῦ πατρός** "for the glory of God the Father." The Lord Jesus was neither selfish nor did He seek vainglory but even in His exaltation all praise, honor, and power finally belonged to God the Father (s. Martin, 273).

■ **ὥστε** wherefore, so then, consequently. The particle 12
draws a conclusion from the preceding as Christ was perfectly obedient, therefore, w. like subjection to Him the readers are to

carry out their own salvation (Vincent). **ἀγαπητός** beloved. **καθώς** just as. **πάντοτε** always. **ὑπηκούσατε** aor. act. ind. ὑπακούω to answer the door, to obey as a result of listening, to obey, to be obedient. The prep. in compound contains the idea of "submission" (MH, 327; Vincent). **παρουσία** presence. **πολλῷ μᾶλλον** much more. **ἀπουσία** absence. **τρόμος** trembling. The expression "w. fear and trembling" indicates a nervous and trembling anixety to do right (Lightfoot). **κατεργάζεσθε** pres. mid. imp. κατεργάζομαι to work out, to work on to the finish. The prep. in compound is perfective and views the linear progress down to the goal "work on to the
13 finish" (RWP; M 114ff.). ■ **θεός.** The word is placed first as the subject not as the pred.: God is the agent (Meyer). **γάρ** for. It gives the reason for the entire previous verse and supplies at once the stimulus to and the corrective of the precept in the preceding (Vincent; Lightfoot). **ἐνεργῶν** pres. act. part. ἐνεργέω to work effectually and productively, to put forth power. The word describes the energy and the effective power of God Himself in action (Vincent; MNTW, 46–54). **εὐδοκία** good pleasure, satisfaction, "in fulfillment of His benevolent
14 purpose" (Lightfoot; s. also Phil. 1:15). ■ **ποιεῖτε** pres. act. imp. **γογγυσμός** murmuring, an expression of dissatisfaction, grumbling, muttering in a low voice. The word was used in the LXX for the murmuring of Israel against God (T; TDNT). **διαλογισμός** inward questionings, dispute, discussion, skeptical questioning or criticism (Vincent). It refers to the intellectual
15 rebellion against God (Lightfoot). ■ **γένησθε** aor. mid. subj. γίνομαι. **ἄμεμπτος** unblamed, without blame (s. Eph. 1:4; 5:27; Trench; *Synonyms*, 379). **ἀκέραιος** unmixed, unadulterated, pure, sincere. The word was used of pure wine and of unalloyed metal (Lightfoot). **ἄμωμος** without spot, without blemish (Trench; *Synonyms*, 380). **μέσον** in the midst of, in the middle of. The n. as an adv. was used as a prep. w. the gen. (RG, 644). **γενέα** generation. **σκολιός** curved, crooked. **διεστραμμένης** perf. pass. part. διαστρέφω twisted, distorted, to twist in two. It denotes an abnormal moral condition. The perf. expresses a state or condition consequent to an action (s. Vincent; Matt. 17:17). **φαίνομαι** pres. mid. ind. φαίνω act. to shine, to give light, to be bright, mid. to appear, to be visible, to make one's appearance, to show one's self (s. BAG). The pres. tense points to the continual action. **φωστήρ** luminary, the light given off by heavenly bodies, mainly the sun and moon, the "lights," or "great lights" (Trench; *Synonyms*, 164; TDNT; s. also Gen. 1:14, 16; s. also 1QS 10:3; 1QM 10:11; 1QH 1:11; 7:25; 9:26).

(For the Jewish teaching regarding those who shine as luminiar-
ies, s. SB I, 236; III, 621.) ■ **λόγον ζωῆς** word of life, i.e., the 16
word which brings life and which is life. **ἐπέχοντες** pres. act.
part. ἐπέχω to hold fast, to hold forth. The latter sense would be "to hold out" and the metaphor may be that of offering food or wine (Lightfoot; s. also MM). The part. would express means. **καύχημα** reason for boasting, ground of glorying. It is not a boasting in meritorious effort but the sign of the completion of a divinely assigned commission (PAM, 104; Lohmeyer). **κένος** empty, in vain. The word fits well into the picture of the runner and his eventual success or failure in the race (PAM, 100). **ἔδραμον** aor. act. ind. τρέχω to run. The word pictures Paul's work as an apostle spreading the gospel under the figure of a runner. The word indicates the strenuous effort and exertion involved. Paul's fear is that his own interest might impede the gospel or the threat of the introduction of the law as a condition for salvation or the possibility of unfaithfulness on the part of the Philippians might make his efforts fruitless or in vain (PAM, 107). **ἐκοπίασα** aor. act. ind. καπιάω to work hard, to labor. This verb is qualified by the first and both verbs designate the intense labor and efforts of Paul toward the one goal (PAM,
109f.). ■ **καί** even. The word refers to the whole clause (Vin- 17
cent). **σπένδομαι** pres. pass. ind. σπένδω to pour out as a drink offering. A drink offering, usually a cup of wine, was poured out on the ground to honor deity. Paul is again referring to the prospect of martyrdom which he faces, and thinks of himself, his life's blood, as a libation poured forth to God (Beare). **θυσία** sacrifice. The prep. can mean "upon the sacrifice" or "in addition to the sacrifice" (s. Vincent). **λειτουργία** service, religious or sacred service. (For the development of this word, s. Lightfoot; s. also BS, 140f.; TDNT.) **συγχαίρω** pres. act. ind. to
rejoice together, to rejoice w. someone. ■ **χαίρετε** and 18
συγχαίρετε pres. act. imp.

■ **ταχέως** quickly, soon. **πέμψαι** aor. act. inf. πέμπω to 19
send. The inf. explains the content of Paul's hope. **εὐψυχέω** pres. act. subj. to be glad, to have courage. The word is found in the papyri in the salutation of a letter of condolence (MM). **γνούς** aor. act. part. γινώσκω. The part. is used temporally "when I
know," "after I know." ■ **ἰσόψυχος** likeminded, having the 20
same mind, having equal power, confident (s. Gnilka). The word may have the meaning "precious as life" (s. GELS, 75). **γνησίως** adv. genuinely, legitimate birth, not spurious (RWP). **μεριμνήσει** fut. act. ind. μεριμνάω to give one's thoughts to a matter, to be concerned (EGT). The fut. points to the time

21 when Timothy would come to them (Ellicott). ■ **οἱ πάντες** all.
The article w. the adj. excludes every exception (Lohmeyer; s.
22 also RG, 773f.). **ζητοῦσιν** pres. act. ind. to seek. ■ **δοκιμή**
approval, acceptance after being tested (s. TDNT). **ἐδούλευσεν**
23 aor. act. ind. to serve as a slave, to serve. ■ **ὡς** w. ἄν = ὅταν
"whenever," "as soon as." The construction is temporal and indicates the uncertainty which surrounds the whole prospect (EGT; s. also BD, 237f.). **ἀφίδω** aor. act. subj. ἀφοράω to look away, to see. The prep. in compound implies looking away from the pres. circumstances to what is going to happen, which will decide the question of his sending Timothy (Vincent). **ἐξαυτῆς**
24 at once, immediately, soon thereafter. ■ **πέποιθα** perf. ind. act.
πείθω to persuade, perf. w. the pres. meaning to be convinced, to be sure, to be certain (BAG). The perf. expresses a state or condition "I am convinced" (s. BD, 176). **ἐλεύσομαι** fut. mid. ind. ἔρχομαι.
25 ■ **ἀναγκαῖος** compelling, necessary. **ἡγησάμην** aor. mid.
ind., s.v.6. **συνεργός** fellow worker. **συστρατιώτης** fellow soldier. **ἀπόστολος** missionary, not apostle in the official sense, but a messenger sent on a special commission (Vincent). **λειτουργός** minister. The word was used of a public official in civil service, then it was also used for one ministering in religious
26 ceremonies (s.v.17; s. also TDNT; CBB). **χρεία** need. ■ **ἐπειδή**
since, since then, because. It presents the reason for Paul feeling compelled to send Epaphroditus (s. Ellicott). **ἐπιποθῶν** pres. act. part. ἐπιποθέω to yearn after, to long for (s. Phil. 1:8). The part. is used in a periphrastic impf. construction "he was yearning after" (RWP). **ἀδημονῶν** pres. act. part. ἀδημονέω to be distressed. Although the root meaning of the word is not clear (s. GEW I, 20), the word describes the confused, restless, half-distracted state which is produced by physical derangement, or by mental distress, as grief, shame, disappointment, etc. (Lightfoot). **ἠκούσατε** aor. act. ind. ἀκούω. **ἠσθένησεν** aor. act. ind.
27 ἀσθενέω to be without strength, to be weak, to be sick. ■ **καὶ**
γάρ "for even," "—yes, even" (BD, 236). **παραπλήσιον** w. the dat. near to. **ἠλέησεν** aor. act. ind. ἐλεέω to have mercy, to show mercy. **λύπη** sorrow. **σχῶ** aor. act. subj. ἔχω to have, aor. to get, to receive (s. M, 110). The subj. is used in a neg. purpose
28 clause. ■ **σπουδαιοτέρως** adv. comp. of σπουδαῖος w. haste,
comp. w. special urgency (BAG), "w. increased eagerness," on account of this circumstance (Lightfoot). **ἔπεμψα** aor. act. ind. epistolary aor. (EGT). **πάλιν** again. The word is to be taken w. the main verb "rejoice" rather than w. the part. (Vincent). **ἀλυπότερος** comp. ἄλυπος without grief, free from sorrow.

(For the neg. character of the alpha privative, s. Moorhouse, 47ff.) Comparative "less sorrowful." The joy felt by the Philippians will mitigate the sorrow (in his confinement) of the sympathizing apostle (Ellicott). ὦ pres. subj. εἰμί. Subjunctive used
in a purpose clause. ■ **προσδέχεσθε** pres. mid. imp. 29
προσδέχομαι to receive, to receive favorably, to welcome. **τοιοῦτος** such a one, one w. such characteristics. **ἔντιμος** in honor, prized, precious, pred. acc. in a double acc. construction
"hold such ones in honor" (s. RWP). ■ **ἤγγισεν** aor. act. 30
ind. ἐγγίζω to come near, to draw near, to be near. **παραβολευσάμενος** aor. mid. part. παραβολεύομαι to gamble, to play the gambler, to expose one's self to danger. The word has connotations of gambling or playing dice by which high sums were often at stake (s. OCD, 338f.). The word was used in the papyri of one who in the interest of friendship had exposed himself to dangers as an advocate in legal strife by taking his clients' causes even up to emperors (MM; LAE, 88). The word was later used of merchants who for the sake of gain exposed themselves to death (PGL, 1008). The word was used of a fighter in the arena who exposed himself to the dangers of the arena (PGL, 1009). In the post-apostolic church a group called the "paraboloni" risked their lives by nursing the sick and burying the dead (Lightfoot; Vincent). (For the use of the dat. w. this verb, s. M, 64.) **ἀναπληρώσῃ** aor. act. subj. ἀναπληρόω to fill up, to make complete, to fill a gap, to replace. Used w. the gen. of a per. it means "to make up for someone's absence or lack," "to represent one who is absent" (BAG). **ὑστέρημα** that which is lacking, deficiency. There is no rebuke in the word for the only "deficiency" is that they could not be w. him themselves, to do him service (Beare). **λειτουργίας** service, ministry (s.v.17).

Ch. 3

■ **τὸ λοιπόν** finally. With this Paul probably intends to 1
draw to a close the general admonitions and then takes up specific matters in the latter part of the letter (s. Victor Paul Furnish, "The Place and Purpose of Philippians 3," NTS, 10 [October, 1963], 80–88). **τὰ αὐτά** "the same things." Paul perhaps means the same warnings and directives Epaphroditus and Timothy would orally communicate when they visit the Philippians in per. (Furnish, 86). **ὀκνηρός** causing fear or reluctance, troublesome (BAG). **ἀσφαλής.** The word is taken from a verb meaning "to trip up," "to overthrow," "to cause to fall or stumble." With the neg. prefix the adj. is used to describe anything which has stability and firmness enough *not* to be overthrown. It carries then the

idea of "certain, dependable knowledge" (s. Furnish, 83ff.; s. also Luke 1:4).

2 ■ **βλέπετε** pres. act. inf. "continually be on the lookout for" (s. Vincent). **κύων** dog. The Jews considered dogs to be the most despised and miserable of all creatures and used this to describe Gentiles. Perhaps it was because of the herds of dogs which prowled about eastern cities, without a home and without an owner, feeding on the refuge and filth of the streets, quarreling among themselves and attacking the passerby, that the Jews used this designation (Lightfoot; s. also SB III, 621; I, 722–726; TDNT; OCD, 358; KP II, 1245–1249). Paul uses the term here of those who prowl around the Christian congregations, seeking to win converts (s. Beare). **ἐργάτης** worker. **κατατομή** inci-
3 sion, mutilation. Used in contrast to circumcision (RWP). ■ **περιτομή** circumcision (s. Gal. 2:3). **λατρεύοντες** pres. act. part. λατρεύω to minister, to serve (s. TDNT; Phil. 2:17). **καυχώμενοι** pres. mid. part. καυχάομαι to boast, to glory. **πεποιθότες** perf. act. part. πείθω to persuade, perf. to be per-
4 suaded, to be confident, to have confidence (s. Phil. 2:24). ■ **καίπερ** "even though," "although." It is used to clarify the concessive sense of the part. (BD, 219; s. also Blomqvist, 47). **ἔχων** pres. act. part. concessive use of the part. **πεποίθησις** trusting, confidence. **δοκέω** pres. act. ind. to suppose, to seem, to think. Here "if anyone is disposed to think" (Vincent). **πεποιθέναι** perf. act. inf., s.v.3. **μᾶλλον** more, to a higher
5 degree. ■ **περιτομῇ** dat. of respect, "w. respect to circumcision an eighth-day one" (BD, 105; often called "dat. of reference," e.g. DM, 85; MT, 238). **ὀκταήμερος** eighth day, on the eighth day. The normal procedure was circumcision on the eighth day after birth, but under certain circumstances the circumcision could be on the ninth, tenth, eleventh or twelfth day (s. SB IV, 23ff.; M Shabbath, 19.5). **φύλη** tribe. **Ἑβραῖος** Hebrew. The term emphasized not only the rights and privileges belonging to the Jewish nation, but also emphasized that those who lived in the Diaspora, i.e., outside of Palestine, had remained true to the religious practices and especially regarding the language. Paul was trained in the use of the Heb. tongue by Heb.-speaking parents (Vincent; s. also Lightfoot; JPFC I, 184–225; s. also MM). **νόμος** law. Used here without the article. It emphasizes
6 law in the abstract, as a principle of action (Lightfoot). ■ **ζῆλος** zeal (s. Gal. 1:14). **διώκων** pres. act. part. διώκω to pursue, to persecute. **γενόμενος** aor. mid. part. γίνομαι. **ἄμεμπτος** with-
7 out blame (s. Phil. 2:15). ■ **κέρδος** profit, gain (s. Phil. 1:21). **ἥγημαι** perf. mid. ind. ἡγέομαι to consider, to reckon, to count

as (s. Phil. 2:6). The perf. indicates a completed action w. continuing results "I have counted (and they are now to me)" (Ellicott). **ζημία** loss. Used for a loss at sea (Acts 27:10) and used
in the papyri of a commercial or business loss (MM). ■ **μενοῦν** 8
γε. The presence of so many particles is clearly for the purpose
of emphasis (DM, 255) and could be translated "yes the previous
is true but more than that I also. . . ." **ὑπερέχον** pres. act. part.
n. sing. ὑπερέχω. The n. sing. is used as an abstract noun followed by the gen. "the surpassing greatness" (BAG; BD, 138; s.
also Phil. 2:3). **γνῶσις** knowledge. It is the personal knowledge
and acquaintance w. Christ. It is the knowledge of one who loves
and knows himself beloved (s. Beare). **ἐζημιώθην** aor. pass. ind.
ζημιόω pass. to suffer loss. The aor. points to the definite period
of his conversion. In that great crisis all his legal possessions
were lost (Vincent). **σκύβαλον** refuse. It refers either to human
excrement, the portion of food rejected by the body as not being
nutritive or it refers to the refuse or leavings of a feast, the food
thrown away from the table (Lightfoot; s. also TDNT; MM).
κερδήσω aor. act. subj. κερδαίνω to gain, to win. The subj. is
used in a purpose clause. ■ **εὑρεθῶ** aor. pass. subj. εὑρίσκω to 9
find, pass. to be found. The idea involved is a revelation of true
character (EGT). The subj. is used in a purpose clause. **διὰ
πίστεως Χριστοῦ** "through faith in Christ," obj. gen. **ἐπὶ τῇ
πίστει** "on the basis of faith," "resting upon faith" (Vincent).
■ **γνῶναι** aor. act. inf. γινώσκω to know, to recognize, to know 10
personally through experience, to appropriate. The word often
implies a personal relation between the knower and the known,
involving the influence of the object of knowledge upon the
knower (Vincent; s. also TDNT; ND, 344ff.; CBB). The inf. is
used to express purpose or perhaps intended results (s.
Funk, 706). **κοινωνία** fellowship. **πάθημα** suffering.
συμμορφιζόμενος pres. pass. part. συμμορφίζω to grant or
invest w. the same form, pass. to be conformed to, to take on the
same form as. This seems to be a reference to the kind of death
Paul was to die (BAG; Meyer). ■ **εἴ πως** if perhaps. The word 11
introduces a clause expressing a possibility which is the object
of hope or desire (SMT, 111; s. also BD, 191). **καταντήσω** aor.
act. subj. καταντάω to reach, to arrive at a destination.
ἐξανάστασις resurrection, rising up.

■ **οὐχ ὅτι** "not that." The words serve to correct a false 12
impression that might have arisen from his preceding words.
ἔλαβον aor. act. ind. λαμβάνω (s. RWP), to receive, to obtain.
The aor. points to the time of Paul's conversion "not as though
by my conversion I did once attain" (Lightfoot). **τετελείωμαι**

perf. pass. ind. τελειόω to reach the goal, to perfect, pass. to be
perfect. The perfection referred to is moral and spiritual perfection (Vincent). The perf. tense describes his pres. state "not as
though I were now already perfected" (Lightfoot). **καταλάβω**
aor. act. subj. καταλαμβάνω to seize, to grasp, to lay hold of.
The subj. is used w. the particle in a 3rd-class conditional clause
which is a sort of purpose clause or aim (RWP; s. also RG, 1017).
ἐφ' ᾧ "for which," "for the reason that, because" (BD, 123). The
phrase can also express purpose "whereunto" (Lightfoot).
13 **κατελήμφθην** aor. pass. ind. καταλαμβάνω. ■ **οὔπω** not yet.
λογίζομαι pres. mid. ind. to reckon, to consider.
κατειληφέναι perf. act. inf. καταλαμβάνω. The prep. in compound is perfective "to grant completely" (RWP). **ἕν δέ** "but one
thing." The verb "I say" could be supplied (Lohmeyer) or the
verb "I do" is to be understood (Vincent). **ὀπίσω** behind.
ἐπιλανθανόμενος pres. mid. part. ἐπιλανθάνομαι to forget.
The prep. in compound is directive (s. MH, 312).
ἐπεκτεινόμενος pres. mid. part. ἐπεκτείνομαι to stretch one's
self out for, to stretch one's self out toward. The metaphor is
from the foot race and the word pictures the body of the racer
bent forward, his hand outstretched toward the goal, and his eye
fastened upon it (Vincent). The word is followed by the dat.
14 ■ **σκοπός** a mark on which to fix the eye, goal. Paul is evidently
referring to the goal of a foot race. (For a description of the
stadium and the foot race, s. DGRA, 1055f.; Oscar Broneer,
"The Apostle Paul and the Isthmian Games," BA, 25 [February,
1962], 1–31.) The prep. has the sense of "down," i.e., "bearing
down upon" (Vincent). Paul's picture is of a runner who has just
turned the curve or gone around the post and is now in the home
stretch where he can see the goal (s. Lohmeyer; PAM, 141).
βραβεῖον prize, a prize awarded the winner at the games. **ἄνω**
above, upward. The word could be an adv. telling where the
calling comes from or it could point to the direction in which the
calling leads "upward," "heavenward" (s. PAM, 149). **κλῆσις**
15 calling. ■ **ὅσοι** "as many as," "those who." **τέλειος** perfect,
mature. The word refers to "grown men" as opposed to children
(Lightfoot). **φρονῶμεν** pres. act. subj. φρονέω to think, to have
an attitude (s. Phil. 2:2, 5), co-hortative subj. **ἑτέρως** adv. "otherwise." **ἀποκαλύψει** fut. act. ind. ἀποκαλύπτω to unveil, to
16 reveal. ■ **πλήν** nevertheless. The word is used at the conclusion
of a section in order to bring out the main point of discussion
"just one thing more" (s. RG, 1187; Blomqvist, 75ff.).
ἐφθάσαμεν aor. act. ind. φθάνω to come to, to arrive at, to
attain, dramatic aor. used to express what has just taken place

(RG, 842). **στοιχεῖν** pres. act. inf. to walk in line, to march in battle order. The word refers to walking according to principles of a system (s. Vincent; TDNT). The inf. is used in the sense of an imp. This construction generally follows an imp. and the command is carried on by the inf. (RG, 943; s. also BD, 196f.; IBG, 126).

■ **συμμιμηταί** fellow imitator. **γίνεσθε** pres. mid. imp. 17
σκοπεῖτε pres. act. imp. **σκοπέω** to look at, to fix one's attention upon, to mark. Here "to mark and follow" (Lightfoot; s. also
Rom. 16:17). **περιπατοῦντας** pres. act. part. **περιπατέω** to
walk, to conduct one's life. **κάθως** just as. **τύπος** that which is
formed by a blow or impression, pattern, type, example (T; s.
also TDNT). ■ **κλαίων** pres. act. part. **κλαίω** to cry, to weep, 18
to weep audibly. The stress of St. Paul's grief would lie in the fact
that they degraded the true doctrine of liberty (Lightfoot).
σταυρός cross. ■ **ἀπώλεια** ruin, destruction. **κοιλία** stomach. 19
(For a description of the luxury of Roman eating, s. DGRA,
303–309; s. also LAE, 164f.) The word may be used as a general
term to include all that belongs most essentially to the bodily,
fleshly life of man and therefore inevitably perishes (EGT).
αἰσχύνη shame. **ἐπίγειος** earthly, upon the earth. **φρονοῦντες**
pres. act. part., s. Phil. 2:5. ■ **πολίτευμα** citizenship. The word 20
means either "the state, the constitution, to which as citizens we
belong" or "the functions which as citizens we perform" (Lightfoot; s. also Vincent; TDNT; Phil. 1:27). **ὑπάρχει** pres. act. ind.
to exist, to be (s. 2 Cor. 12:16). **ἀπεκδέχομεθα** pres. mid. ind.
to expect anxiously, to await eagerly. The preps. in compound
indicate the eager but patient waiting (s. Gal. 5:5). ■ 21
μετασχηματίσει fut. act. ind. **μετασχηματίζω** to refashion,
to change, to change the outward form or appearance. The
meaning of the word would be illustrated not merely by changing
a Dutch garden into an Italian garden, but by transforming a
garden into something wholly different, as into a city (Trench;
Synonyms, 263; s. also Lightfoot, 130f.; Phil. 2:6). **ταπείνωσις**
lowliness, humble, insignificant. **σύμμορφος** conformed, the
changing of the inward and outward substance, conforming to or
w. something (s. Phil. 2:6). **ἐνέργεια** working. The act. and
productive power of God at work (s. Phil. 2:13; MNTW, 46–54).
ὑποτάξαι aor. act. inf. **ὑποτάσσω** to place under, to subdue,
to subject, to place under one's authority. **αὐτός** himself. The
pron. is used here in a reflex. sense (BD, 148).

Ch. 4

1 ■ **ὥστε** wherefore, therefore. It draws a conclusion from chapter
3 verses 17–21 (EGT). **ἀγαπητός** beloved. **ἐπιπόθητος** longed
for, desired (s. Phil. 1:8). The word is a verbal adj. (RWP; M,
221; MH, 370). **στήκετε** pres. act. imp. στήκω to stand, to
stand firm (s. Phil. 1:27).
2 ■ **παρακαλέω** to beseech, to urge, to encourage (s. TDNT;
MNTW, 128ff.). **φρονεῖν** pres. act. inf. to be minded, to have
3 an attitude or disposition, to think (s. Phil. 2:2). ■ **ναί** yes, yea.
The particle is a confirmation of an assertion (s. Ellicott; RG,
1150). **ἐρωτάω** pres. act. ind. to ask, to request, to ask something
of someone. (For examples in the papyri, s. BS, 276ff.; MM.)
γνήσιος legitimately born, genuine, true, sincere (s. Phil. 2:20).
σύζυγος yoked together, yokefellow, voc. masc. sing. Some
view this as a proper name, i.e., "Synzygus" (s. Vincent).
συλλαμβάνου pres. mid. imp. συλλαμβάνομαι to take and
bring together, to lay hold of, to help, to assist (s. MM).
συνήθλησαν aor. act. ind. συναθλέω to fight alongside, to
contend w. someone against a common enemy, to labor together
(s. Phil. 1:27). **καί** also. The word may be retrospective referring
to the "true yokefellow" (Lightfoot) or it may be pleonastic, i.e.,
superfluous (BD, 228). **λοιπός** rest. **συνεργός** fellow worker.
4 ■ **χαίρετε** pres. act. imp. rejoice. The pres. imp. calls for a
continual and habitual action. **πάντοτε** always. **ἐρῶ** fut. act. ind.
5 λέγω. ■ **τὸ ἐπιεικές** reasonableness in judging. The word signifies a humble, patient stedfastness, which is able to submit to
injustice, disgrace, and maltreatment without hatred and malice,
trusting in God in spite of all of it (Leivestad, 158; s. 2 Cor. 10:1;
Trench; *Synonyms*, 154). **γνωσθήτω** aor. pass. imp. γινώσκω.
ἐγγύς near. The word could imply "near in space" or "near in
time." Here the phrase probably expresses general expectation
6 of the speedy second coming of Christ (Vincent). ■ **μεριμνᾶτε**
pres. act. imp. μεριμνάω to be anxious, to be troubled, to care
for something, to be fretful (Beare). **δέησις** request, generally a
request arising from a specific need (s. Eph. 6:18). **εὐχαριστία**
thanksgiving. It expresses that which ought never to be absent
from any of our devotions; namely, the grateful acknowledgment
of past mercies, as distinguished from the earnest seeking of fut.
(Trench; *Synonyms*, 191). **αἴτημα** request, a thing asked for.
The word in the pl. indicates the several objects of the request
(Lightfoot; s. also Trench; *Synonyms*, 191). **γνωριζέσθω** pres.
7 pass. imp. γνωρίζω to make known. ■ **ὑπερέχουσα** pres. act.
part. ὑπερέχω to rise above, to be superior, to surpass (Vincent;
s. also Phil. 2:3; 3:8). **φρουρήσει** fut. act. ind. φρουρέω to

guard. The word is a military term picturing soldiers standing on
guard duty and refers to the guarding of the city gate from
within, as a control on all who went out (BAG; EGT). The fut.
preceded by an imp. and joined by "and" has the character of
a result clause in a Semitic type of conditional sentence, i.e.,
"make your request known, then the peace of God will guard
your hearts" (s. Beyer, 238–255; BD, 227). **καρδία** heart. The
heart is the center of each per. from which thoughts and affections flow (PAT, 326). **νόημα** thought, act of the will which
issues from the heart (Vincent; PAT, 327).

■ **τὸ λοιπόν** "finally" (s. Phil. 3:1). **ὅσος** whatever. 8
ἀληθής truth. **σεμνός** worthy of respect or honor, noble, dignified, reverent. The word implies that which is majestic and awe-
inspiring (BAG; Trench; *Synonyms*, 347; Lohmeyer). **ἁγνός**
pure, morally pure, undefiled. In the LXX it signifies ceremonial
purification (s. Vincent; Lohmeyer; Trench; *Synonyms*, 333).
προσφιλής acceptable, pleasing, lovely. It refers to "those
things whose grace attracts" (EGT). **εὔφημος** well-sounding,
praiseworthy, attractive, appealing (BAG). **ἀρετή** virtue, the
most comprehensive Gr. term for moral excellence and the central theme of Gr. ethics (Beare; s. also TDNT; CBB; Cremer; PS,
152ff.). (For a comparison of Paul and Stoicism, and esp. w.
Seneca, s. Lightfoot, 270–333; PS; Beare, 42f.) **ἔπαινος** praise.
λογίζεσθε pres. mid. imp. λογίζομαι to consider, to reckon, to
take into account, to think on, "use your facilities upon them"
(Ellicott; s. also Vincent). The pres. tense calls for a continual or
habitual action. ■ **καί** "also." The word here is ascensive but its 9
other occurences in this v. are copulative, i.e., "and" (Ellicott).
ἐμάθετε aor. act. ind. μανθάνω to learn. **παρελάβετε** aor. act.
ind. παραλαμβάνω to receive, to receive tradition or that
which is passed on (s. TDNT). **ἠκούσατε** aor. act. ind. ἀκούω.
εἴδετε aor. act. ind. ὁράω. The last two verbs "heard and saw"
refer to Paul's personal contact w. the Philippians (Vincent).
πράσσετε pres. act. imp. πράσσω to do, to practice. The verb
contains the idea of continuity and repetition of action (Trench;
Synonyms, 361). The pres. tense calls for a continual practicing.
ἔσται fut. εἰμί. (For the construction of the imp. plus "and" plus
the fut. forming a type of conditional sentence w. the fut. used
in a result clause, s.v.7.)

■ **ἐχάρην** aor. pass. ind. χαίρω to rejoice, to be glad (s. 10
Phil. 1:18). The aor. is epistolary aor. (Vincent). **μεγάλως** adv.
"greatly." **ἤδη ποτέ** "now at last." The word indicates that there
was an indefinite interval of delay but has more the notion of
culmination rather than time (RG, 1147). **ἀνεθάλετε** aor. act.

ind. ἀναθάλλω to sprout again, to shoot up, to blossom again, to put forth new shoots (RWP; Lightfoot). The prep. in compound probably contains a causative idea (MH, 295). **φρονεῖν** pres. act. inf. (s. Phil. 2:2). The inf. is used as the obj. of the verb "you caused your thought for me to sprout and bloom afresh, like a tree putting out fresh shoots after the winter" (Vincent). **ἐφ' ᾧ** "upon which," "upon whom." The phrase could indicate the object of their thinking (Ellicott) or it could be taken as causal (BD, 123). **ἐφρονεῖτε** impf. act. ind. The impf. emphasizes the continual action in the past "you were all along taking thought" (Vincent). **ἠκαιρεῖσθε** impf. mid. ind. ἀναιρέομαι to have no opportunity, to lack opportunity, to lack a convenient
11 time. ■ **οὐχ ὅτι** "not that." It is used to avoid a misunderstanding "my meaning is not . . ." (Meyer). **ὑστέρησις** coming short, lack. **ἐγώ** "I" strongly emphatic. **ἔμαθον** aor. act. ind., s.v.9. The aor. is effective aor. pointing to the completion of the process. **αὐτάρκης** content, being self-sufficient, having enough. The word indicates independence of external circumstances and often means the state of one who supports himself without aid from others (Lightfoot; BAG). The word indicates an inward self-sufficiency, as opposed to the lack or the desire of outward
12 things (Vincent). ■ **ταπεινοῦσθαι** pres. pass. inf. ταπεινόω to make low, pass. to be brought low. Here it has to do w. the physical rather than the moral or spiritual and is used in respect to the needs of daily life (EGT). The inf. is used as the object of the verb. **περισσεύειν** pres. act. inf. to overflow, to abound. **μεμύημαι** perf. pass. ind. μυέω to initiate, pass. to be initiated, to be instructed, a t.t. of the mystery religions (BAG). The perf. emphasizes the completed action w. a continuing state or result. **χορτάζεσθαι** pass. inf. χορτάζω to fill, pass. to be full. The word was used primarily of feeding and fattening animals in a stall (Vincent). **πεινᾶν** pres. act. inf. πεινάω to be hungry. **ὑστερεῖσθαι** pres. mid. inf. ὑστερέομαι to come short, to fall
13 behind, to lack, to suffer need. ■ **ἰσχύω** pres. act. ind. to be strong, to have strength, to be able (s. Eph. 1:19). **ἐνδυναμοῦντι** pres. act. part. ἐνδυναμόω to empower, to give strength, to
14 infuse strength into someone (Vincent). ■ **πλήν** "nevertheless," "however" (s. Phil. 3:16). **καλῶς** well. **ἐποιήσατε** aor. act. ind. **συγκοινωνήσαντές** aor. act. part. συγκοινωνέω to participate in something w. someone, to share together w. someone (s. Phil. 1:7). **θλῖψις** pressure, trouble, tribulation.
15 ■ **δέ** "and." It marks the transition to his first experience of their generosity (EGT). **ἀρχή** beginning. **ἐξῆλθον** aor. act. ind. ἐξέρχομαι to go out. **ἐκοινώνησεν** aor. act. ind. κοινωνέω to

have fellowship, to share, to be a partner. ***εἰς λόγον*** "as to an account." He used a metaphor from the business world. The Philippians by their contributions had "opened an account" w. him (Vincent; for the commercial t.t., s. also BAG; LAE, 117; MM). ***δόσις*** giving. The word is very common in financial transactions and is used for a payment or an installment (s. MM; Preisigke). ***λῆμψις*** receiving. This was also a t.t. in the business world meaning the receiving of a payment and was used in connection w. the word "giving" in the sense of "credit and
debit" (s. Vincent; MM; Lohmeyer). ■ ***ἅπαξ*** once. ***δίς*** twice. 16
Used together in the sense of "not merely once but twice" (Vincent). ***χρεία*** need. ***ἐπέμψατε*** aor. act. ind. *πέμπω* to send.
■ ***ἐπιζητῶ*** pres. act. ind. to seek after. The prep. in compound 17
is directive indicating the concentration of the action upon some object (MH, 312). ***δόμα*** that which is given, gift. ***πλεονάζοντα*** pres. act. part. *πλεονάζω* to increase, to become more, to multiply. The commercial or business metaphor is continued and their
earthly investment accrues heavenly dividends. ■ ***ἀπέχω*** pres. 18
act. ind. to have in full, to receive in full. The word was also a commercial t.t. meaning "to receive a sum in full and give a receipt for it." (For examples, s. BAG; MM; BS, 229; LAE, 111.) ***πεπλήρωμαι*** perf. pass. ind. *πληρόω* to fill, pass. to be filled. The perf. emphasizes the continuing state. ***δεξάμενος*** aor. mid. part. *δέχομαι* to receive. The part. expresses contemporaneous action "when I receive." ***ὀσμή*** smell. ***εὐωδία*** aroma, fragrance, "a scent of sweet savor" was a t.t. indicating the acceptance and pleasantness of a sacrifice (s. Gnilka). ***δεκτός*** acceptable.
εὐάρεστος pleasing. ■ ***πληρώσει*** fut. act. ind. ***ἐν δόξῃ*** "in 19
glory." Used here as an adv. indicating the mode or manner of the fulfillment "gloriously," i.e. in such wise that His glory will be manifested (Vincent).

■ ***ἀσπάσασθε*** aor. mid. imp. *ἀσπάζομαι* to greet, to give 21
greetings. ■ ***μάλιστα*** especially. ***οἱ ἐκ τῆς Καίσαρος*** "the 22
members of Caesar's household." Probably slave and freedmen attached to the palace (Lightfoot, esp. 171–178).

COLOSSIANS

Ch. 1

2 ***οἱ ἅγιοι***. The adjs. can be taken w. the substitutive "the
holy brothers" or it can be taken as a substitutive indicating a
definite class of people "the holy ones" (s. Moule; Martin,
NCB). **πίστος**. The adjs. can mean "believing" or "faithful."
The latter sense is perhaps preferable and has the idea "trustworthy, stedfast, unswerving" (Lightfoot).
3 ■ **εὐχαριστοῦμεν** pres. act. ind. to give thanks. The pl.
could be epistolary pl., i.e. "I thank" or a real pl., i.e. "Timothy
and I thank" (s. Moule). **πάντοτε** always. It could be taken
either w. the part. or w. the main verb. The latter is probably
more accurate (s. Lohse). **προσευχόμενοι** pres. mid. part.
προσεύχομαι to pray. The pres. tense points to a repeated
4 action. ■ **ἀκούσαντες** aor. act. part. The part. could be temporal
"after we heard" or causal "because we heard" (Martin, NCB).
He heard from Epaphras for the apostle had no direct personal
5 knowledge of the Colossian church (Lightfoot). ■ **διά** w. acc.
because. **ἐλπίς** hope. The prep. phrase can be taken either w. the
main verb as the ground of thanksgiving or w. the words faith
and love indicating the reason for these (s. Abbott; Eadie;
Moule). (For the psychological necessity of hope in one's life, s.
Basil Jackson, "Psychology, Psychiatry and the Pastor: Relationships Between Psychiatry, Psychology, and Religion," Bib
Sac, 132 [January, 1975], 3–15.) **ἀποκειμένην** pres. mid. part.
ἀπόκειμαι to put up, to store up, to put away for one's use. As
an extension of a royal Persian custom Hellenistic rulers would
lay up in store goods for faithful servants (Lohse; s. also TDNT).
προηκούσατε aor. act. ind. προακούω to hear beforehand, to
hear previously, i.e. they had heard the gospel before they had
heard the false teaching (Moule). **ἀληθείας** gen. of quality belonging to logos followed by the gen. **λόγος** which explains the
6 words "the word of truth" (Abbott). ■ **παρόντος** pres. act. part.
πάρειμι to arrive and be present (Lohmeyer). The prep. combines the idea of the gospel being present w. the idea of the
gospel coming to them (s. Abbott; Lightfoot). **κάθως** just as.
καρποφορούμενον pres. mid. part. καρποφορέω to bear fruit.

The mid. emphasizes that the gospel bears fruit of itself. The
part. is used in a periphrastic construction emphasizing the continuity of the process (RWP). **αὐξανόμενον** pres. mid. part.
αὐξάνομαι to grow, to increase, to develop. The word refers to
the outward expansion as the previous part. refers to the personal inner working (Abbott). **ἀφ' ἧς ἡμέρας** "from which
day." The fruitfulness and growing started on the day they received the grace of God (s. Lohse). **ἠκούσατε** aor. act. ind.
ἀκούω. **ἐπέγνωτε** aor. act. ind. ἐπιγινώσκω to know, to
recognize. It implies not so much developed knowledge as active
conscience recognition, of taking knowledge of (Abbott). The
aor. is ingressive "you came to know." **χάρις** grace. It refers to
God's unmerited and undeserved help to someone in need and
here indicates the message of salvation in the gospel (s. TDNT;
CBB). **ἐν ἀληθείᾳ** "in truth," i.e., the grace of God "as it truly
is" (Moule). ■ **ἐμάθετε** aor. act. ind. μανθάνω to learn. 7
ἀγαπητός one who is loved, beloved. **σύνδουλος** fellow slave.
πιστός faithful. **διάκονος** minister, one who ministers to the
needs of another (s. TDNT) ■ **δηλώσας** aor. act. part. δηλόω 8
to make plain, to make clear. **ἐν πνεύματι** "in the Spirit." It is
to be connected w. agape and expresses the ground of their love,
which was not individual sympathy, personal acquaintance, or
the like, but belonged to the sphere of the Holy Spirit's influence
(Abbott).

■ **καί** "also." The word is to be taken w. the main verb 9
(Lohse). **ἠκούσαμεν** aor. act. ind., s.v.6. **παυόμεθα** pres. mid.
ind. to cease. (For the 1st per. pl., s.v.3.) **προσευχόμενοι** pres.
mid. part., s.v.3. **αἰτούμενοι** pres. mid. part. αἰτέω to ask, to
request. The mid. indicates that one is asking something for
himself. The mid. was often used in a commercial sense and was
also used of requests addressed to God (s. BD, 165f.; M, 160f.).
ἵνα "that." The particle is used to introduce the content of the
prayer (s. Lohse). **πληρωθῆτε** aor. pass. subj. πληρόω to fill.
The pass. is used as a substitute for God's name "may God fill
you" (Lohse). The pass. is followed here by the acc. (s. BD, 87).
ἐπίγνωσις knowledge. The knowledge here is not of other
worlds but of the will of God (Lohse). The concept of knowledge
in Colossians is related more to the concept of knowledge found
in the DSS rather than that in the gnostic philosophy (s. Edwin
Yamauchi, "Qumran and Colosse," Bib Sac, 121 [April, 1964],
141–152; for specific references in the DSS and other literature,
s. Lohse; s. also CBC; Eph. 1:17). **σοφία** wisdom. The word
indicated for the Gr. the mental excellency in its highest and
fullest sense (Lightfoot; Abbott). The OT concept was that of

applying the knowledge of God's will to life's situations (s. TDNT; Lohse). **σύνεσις** understanding, insight. The word refers to the putting together the facts and information and drawing conclusions and seeing relationships. **πνευματικῇ** spiritual. The prevailing meaning of the word in the NT is "of, or belonging to the Holy Spirit" (Eadie; for the suf. of the adj., s. MH,
10 378). ■ **περιπατῆσαι** aor. act. inf. περιπατέω to walk about, to conduct one's life. The inf. is used to express intended or potential results (s. IBG, 141; BD, 197f.; S. Lewis Johnson, Jr., "Spiritual Knowledge and Walking Worthily of the Lord," Bib Sac, 118 [October, 1961], 342). According to the teaching of the Dead Sea community, those who walked according to the spirit of truth will walk pleasing before God. (For this teaching and the references in the DSS, s. Lohse.) **ἀρεσκεία** pleasing. The word was often used in a neg. sense of trying to gain favor from someone and describes that cringing subservient attitude which one has who would do anything to please a benefactor (Abbott; Johnson, 342; s. also MM; TDNT). **καρποφοροῦντες** pres. act. part., s.v.6. The pres. tense indicates that fruit-bearing for believers is to be a continuous thing and the act. voice may point to external diffusion or it may simply direct attention away from the inherent energy of the fruit-bearing instrument, the Christian (Johnson, 342). **αὐξανόμενοι** pres. mid. part., s.v.6. **τῇ ἐπιγνώσει.** The dat. could be either locative, i.e. "growing in knowledge," or it could be instrumental, i.e. "growing by knowledge." The simple instrumental dat. represents the knowledge of God as the dew or the rain which nurtures the growth of the
11 plant (Lightfoot). ■ **δύναμις** power, might. **δυναμόυμενοι** pres. pass. part. δυναμόω to make powerful, to strengthen. **κράτος** strength, might. It refers to the inherent strength which displays itself in the rule over others (s. TDNT; GEW II, 8; s. also Eph. 1:19). Here it refers to the might which is characteristic of His glory (Eadie; s. also Moule). **μακροθυμία** patience, longsuffering. It refers to the self-restraint which does not hastily retaliate a wrong (Lightfoot; s. also TDNT; NTW, 83–85; s. also Gal.
12 5:22; Rom 2:4). ■ **εὐχαριστοῦντες** pres. act. part., s.v.3. **ἱκανώσαντι** aor. act. part. ἱκανόω to make sufficient, to qualify, to authorize. This is a qualification for inheritance due solely to the grace of God (Johnson, 344). **μερίς** part, portion. **κλῆρος** lot. The phrase is not exactly equivalent to the word "inheritance" since it designates only the allotted part. The gen. is either apposition "the portion which consists in the lot" or it is partitive "to have a share in the lot" (Abbott). (For the teaching of inheritance in the DSS, s. Lohse.) **φῶς** light. The inheri-

tance is "in the light" because He who is the Light dwells there
and fills heaven w. His marvelous light (Johnson, 344). ■ 13
ἐρρύσατο aor. mid. act. *ῥύομαι* to rescue, to deliver. (For the
relation of rescuing or deliverance w. the OT and the Dead Sea
community, s. Lohse.) ***ἐξουσία***. The word properly means "liberty of action," i.e., freedom to do something without any hindrance. In relation to others it means "authority" and here refers
to the characteristic and ruling principle of the region in which
they dwelled before conversion to Christ (Abbott; TDNT).
μετέστησεν aor. act. ind. *μεθίστημι* to remove from one place
to another, to transfer. The word was often used to signify deportation of a body of men or the removal of them to form a colony
(Eadie). ***βασιλεία*** kingdom. ***τῆς ἀγάπης*** objective gen. "the
Son who is the object of His love" (Abbott). ■ ***ἐν ᾧ*** "in whom." 14
The reference is to Christ and the rel. sentence speaks of the new
life which we have received in Christ (Lohse). ***ἀπολύτρωσις***
redemption, complete release based on the payment of a price
(s. Rom. 3:24; LAE, 327; s. also the references to the DSS listed
by Lohse). ■ ***εἰκών*** image, copy. In Gr. thought an image shares 15
in reality what it represents. Christ is the perfect likeness of God.
The word contains the idea of representation and manifestation
(s. CBB; Moule; Lightfoot; TDNT; Lohse). ***ἀόρατος*** not capable of being seen, invisible. ***πρωτότοκος*** firstborn. The word
emphasizes the preexistence and uniqueness of Christ as well as
His superiority over creation. The term does not indicate that
Christ was a creation or a created being. (For this important
word, s. Lohse; Lightfoot; Abbott; Moule; Martin; PJR, 150f.;
SB III, 626; TDNT; CBB; GI, 122–126; CEJC, 53f.) ***κτίσις***
creation. ■ ***ἐν αὐτῷ*** "in Him." The prep. denotes Christ as the 16
"sphere" within which the work of creation takes place (Bruce).
All the laws and purposes which guide the creation and government of the universe reside in Him (Lightfoot). The prep. is
possibly both instrumental and local (Moule). He is not in all
things but all things are in Him and this difference is not insignificant (s. Fred B. Craddock, " 'All Things in Him': A Critical
Note on Col. I.15–20," NTS, 12 [October, 1965], 78–80).
ἐκτίσθη aor. pass. ind. *κτίζω* to create. ***ὁρατός*** visible. ***εἴτε***
whether. ***κυριότης*** lordship. ***ἀρχή*** beginning, ruler. ***δι᾽αὐτοῦ***
"through Him." The prep. w. the gen. describes Christ as the
immediate instrument of creation (Abbott; s. also Lightfoot). ***εἰς
αὐτόν*** "for Him, unto Him." The prep. indicates that Christ is
the goal of creation (Lohse). The rabbis taught that the world
was created for the Messiah (SB III, 626). ***ἔκτισται*** perf. pass.
ind. The perf. tense emphasizes the duration and persistence of

17 the act of creation (Ellicott). ■ **αὐτός.** The pron. is used emphatically "He Himself" in contrast to the created things (Abbott). Here it means "*He* and no other" (MT, 40). **πρό** before.
The prep. could refer to priority in time or in rank but the idea
of time is here more suitable. Used w. the pres. tense of the verb,
the idea expresses immutability of existence, i.e., "His existence
is before all things" (Abbott; s. also Moule, Lightfoot).
συνέστηκεν perf. act. ind. συνίσταμι to place together, to
stand together, to hold together, to cohere. He is the principal
of cohesion in the universe (Lightfoot). God Himself is the uni-
fying band which encompasses everything and holds it together.
This applies not only to the largest things of the universe, but
18 also to the smallest things of the universe (Lohse). ■ **ἀρχή**
beginning, origin. The word refers to priority in time and to
originating power (Lightfoot; s. also Moule). **γένηται** aor. mid.
subj. γίνομαι. The purpose clause indicates "that He Himself in
all things (material and spiritual) may come to hold the first
place" (RWP). **πρωτεύων** pres. act. part. **πρωτεύω** to be first,
to have first place, to hold the chief place. (For the quotation
from Meander—"Never does a house fail to come to grief, where
19 woman takes the lead in everything"—, s. MM.) ■ **εὐδόκησεν**
aor. act. ind. εὐδοκέω to be pleased. The subject here is "God."
πλήρωμα fullness. It could refer either to the totality of the
divine powers and attributes (Lightfoot) or perhaps better it
refers to the fullness of saving grace and power which belongs
to one constituted as "savior" (Eadie; s. also S. Lewis Johnson,
"From Emnity to Amity," Bib Sac, 119 [April, 1962], 141–142).
κατοικῆσαι aor. act. inf. κατοικέω to live, to dwell, to settle
down. The word indicates "permanent abode" (Lightfoot). The
aor. could be ingressive aor. "to take up one's permanent
20 abode" (Johnson, 142). ■ **ἀποκαταλλάξαι** aor. act. inf.
ἀποκαταλλάσσω to exchange hostility for friendship, to reconcile. (For this word, s. Johnson, 143; TDNT; CBB; APC,
186–223; MNTW, 101ff.) The prep. in compound has the meaning "back" and implies a restitution to a state from which one
has fallen. The meaning is "to effect a thorough change back"
(MH, 298; Lightfoot). **εἰρηνοποιήσας** aor. act. part.
εἰρηνοποιέω to make peace. The part. describes the means of
the reconciliation. The insertion of the part. indicates that reconciliation is not to be thought of as a cosmic miracle which merely
changed the state of the universe outside of man but shows that
reconciliation is primarily concerned w. the restoration of relationships (R.P. Martin, "Reconciliation and Forgiveness in
Colossians," RH, 113). Peace is more than an end to hostilities.

It has a positive content and points to the presence of positive blessings and is concerned w. spiritual blessings and prosperity of the whole man (CNT, 251). **σταυρός** cross.
■ **καί** and, also. The word indicates that this message of 21
reconciliation is also applicable to those at the church of Colossae (Lohse). **ποτέ** once, formerly. **ὄντας** pres. act. part. εἰμί. **ἀπηλλοτριωμένους** pres. pass. part. ἀπαλλοτριόω to estrange, to alienate. The part. is used in a periphrastic construction and w. the perf. tense it expresses more forcibly the settleness of the alienation (Abbott; s. also Eph. 2:12). **ἐχθρός** hostility. The adj. is act. rather than pass. (Lightfoot). **διάνοια** mind. The hostile minds of the Colossian Christians have turned into a willing and glad subservience; and the ultimate result of this interchange of attitude toward God will be perfection in sanctification (Ladd, 455). ■ **νυνί** now. **ἀποκατήλλαξεν** aor. act. ind. 22
ἀποκαταλλάσσω s.v.20. The verb has a soteriological meaning, which embraces both the "overcoming of the cosmic hostility through the lordship of Christ" and the restoration of sinful men to God's favor and family (Martin, RH, 114). (For a discussion of the pass. as a variant reading, s. TC, 621f.; Lohse.) **παραστῆσαι** aor. act. inf. παρίστημι to present. The inf. can be used to express either purpose or result. The picture here may be a sacrificial metaphor (Moule) or it may be a legal word indicating that one is placed before a court of justice (s. Lohse). **ἄμωμος** without spot, without blemish. In the LXX the word was used as a t.t. to designate the absence of anything amiss in a sacrifice, of anything which would render it unworthy to be offered (Trench; *Synonyms*, 379). **ἀνέγκλητος** without accusation, unaccused, free from any charge at all. It is a legal word indicating that there is no legal or judicial accusation which can be brought against a person (Trench; *Synonyms*, 381; TDNT; s. also Abbott; Lohse). **κατενώπιον** before, "right down in the eye
of" (RWP). ■ **εἴ γε** "if," "assuming that" (Abbott). The particle 23
introduces a conditional clause which the author assumes to be true. **ἐπιμένετε** pres. act. ind. to remain, to continue. The prep. in compound adds to the force of the linear action of the pres. tense "to continue and then some" (RWP). **τεθεμελιωμένοι** perf. pass. part. θεμελιόω to lay the foundation of something, pass. to be founded. The word refers to the sure foundation (Abbott; s. also TDNT). The perf. emphasizes the completed state or condition. **ἑδραῖος** firm. This word refers to the firmness of the structure (Abbott). (For DSS parallels to the figure of a building used to describe the people of God, s. Lohse.) **μετακινούμενοι** pres. mid. or pass. part. μετακινέω to move

from one place to another, to shift from one place to another.
The pres. tense stresses the "not constantly shifting" (Abbott).
κηρυχθέντος aor. pass. part. **κηρύσσω** to preach, to proclaim,
to herald, to proclaim as a herald (TDNT; CBB). **ἐγενόμην** aor.
mid. ind. *γίνομαι*.
24 ■ **πάθημα** that which is suffered, suffering. (The suf. in the
word indicates a pass. idea or the result of an action; MH, 355.)
ὑπὲρ ὑμῶν "on behalf of you," "for you." The prepositional
phrase is to be connected w. the word "suffering" (Eadie).
ἀνταναπληρόω pres. act. ind. to fill up. The idea of the prep.
in compound may be reciprocal or it may signify that the supply
comes "from an opposite quarter" or it may contain the idea of
substituting for that which is lacking (s. MH, 297; Lightfoot;
Lohse; S. Lewis Johnson, "The Minister of the Mystery," Bib
Sac, 119 [July, 1962], 228ff.). **ὑστέρημα** lacking, that which is
lacking. **θλῖψίς** pressure, tribulation, affliction. The sufferings of
Paul were the afflictions of Christ because He suffered in and w.
Paul because of his identification w. Christ in mystical union
(Johnson, 231; for a discussion of the various interpretations, s.
25 Moule). **σάρξ** flesh. ■ **οἰκονομία** stewardship. The word indicated the responsibility, authority, and obligation given to a
household slave (s. Eph. 1:10; Lohse; J. Reumann, "OIKO-
NOMIA—Terms in Paul in Comparison with Lukian Heilsges-
chichte," NTS, 13 [January, 1967], 147–167). **δοθεῖσαν** aor.
pass. part. *δίδωμι*. **πληρῶσαι** aor. act. inf. *πληρόω* to fill, to
fulfill. The word has the sense of "doing fully," "carrying to
26 completion" (Moule). ■ **μυστήριον** mystery, that which is hidden and undiscoverable by human means, but that which has
been revealed by God (s. Eph. 3:3; Johnson, 231f.; Lohse;
Moule). **ἀποκεκρυμμένον** perf. pass. part. *ἀποκρύπτω* to
hide, to veil, to conceal. The perf. part. emphasizes the state or
condition. **ἀπό** from. The prep. is doubtless temporal (Lightfoot). **αἰῶνες** age. The pl. indicates successive periods of time
(s. TDNT). **γενεά** generation, an age includes many generations
(Abbott). **ἐφανερώθη** aor. pass. ind. *φανερόω* to make clear, to
27 manifest. ■ **ἠθέλησεν** aor. act. ind. *θέλω*. **γνωρίσαι** aor. act.
inf. *γνωρίζω* to make known. **δόξης** glory. The word became a
comprehensive word for God's glorious presence (Moule; s. also
CBB; TDNT). **ἔθνος** folk, Gentile. **ἐν ὑμῖν** "in you," "among
you." For Christ to be "among" the Gentiles involved being "in"
28 those who believed (Johnson, 232). ■ **καταγγέλλω** pres. act.
ind. to proclaim. The word indicates an official proclamation
(Lohmeyer; CBB). The pres. tense emphasizes the continual and
habitual action. **νουθετοῦντες** pres. act. part. **νουθετέω** to ad-

monish, to correct through instruction and warning (s. TDNT).
The part. is a part. of manner defining more nearly the manner
or accompaniments of the proclamation (Ellicott).
διδάσκοντες pres. act. part. **παραστήσωμεν** aor. act. subj.,
s.v.22. The subj. is used in a purpose clause. **τέλειος** perfect,
mature (s. Lohse). ■ **κοπιάω** pres. act. ind. to work, to labor, to 29
labor w. wearisome effort, to work to exhaustion (T; TDNT).
ἀγωνιζόμενος pres. mid. part. *ἀγωνίζομαι* to strive, to exert
effort. The athletic picture behind this word emphasizes Paul's
missionary work, w. all its attendant toil, its tireless exertion, and
its struggles against all manner of setbacks and opposition
(PAM, 175). **ἐνέργεια** working, effectual working. The word is
used of the effective working of God's power (MNTW, 46–54).
ἐνεργουμένην pres. mid. part. *ἐνεργέω* to work effectively, to
be effectual (TDNT).

Ch. 2

■ **εἰδέναι** perf. act. inf. *οἶδα* defective perf. w. a pres. 1
meaning to know. **ἡλίκος** how great. **ἀγών** struggle. The picture
is that of an athletic contest which is strenuous and demanding.
The struggle here is not the struggle against God but pictures the
intense effort of the one praying as he struggles within himself
and against those who oppose the gospel (s. PAM, 113f.; 123f.).
ἑόρακαν perf. act. ind. *ὁράω* to see. (For the form of this verb,
s. BD, 44.) **ἐν σαρκί** "in the flesh." This is to be taken w. the
noun "my face" and implies that they had a knowledge of Him,
though not personal (Abbott). ■ **ἵνα** "that." The word in- 2
troduces the purpose of the struggle. **παρακληθῶσιν** aor. pass.
subj. *παρακαλέω* to comfort, to encourage (s. Phil. 2:1).
συμβιβασθέντες aor. pass. part. *συμβιβάζω* to bring together, to unite, to knit together. The meaning here could be "to
instruct," "to teach" (s. Dibelius; Lohse; TDNT). The part. is a
part. of manner. **πληροφορία** full assurance, firm conviction,
confidence. The gen. is descriptive, i.e. "the wealth consists" of
conviction (Moule). **σύνεσις** understanding, insight.
ἐπιγνωσις knowledge (s. Col. 1:9). **μυστήριον** mystery (s. Col.
2:26). The gen. **τοῦ θεοῦ** is possessive and the next gen.
Χριστοῦ "Christ" is in apposition to the word "mystery"
(Moule; Lightfoot). ■ **θησαυρός** storehouse, treasure. **γνῶσις** 3
knowledge. **ἀπόκρυφος** hidden. It is in Christ that all the treasures of divine wisdom and knowledge have been stored up—
stored up in hiding formerly, but now displayed to those who
have come to know Christ (Bruce). ■ **ἵνα** "that," "in order that." 4
The particle may be used to express purpose "I say this in order

that . . ." or it is equally possible that it has an imperatival sense: "Let no one . . ." (MT, 102). **παραλογίζηται** pres. mid. subj. *παραλογίζομαι* to reckon wrong, to cheat by false reckoning, to deceive by false reasoning (T). The word was used in the papyri of a keeper of a state library who had shown a willingness to "make a wrong use of" certain documents. Paul uses the word here to point to drawing an erroneous conclusion from the reasoning submitted (MM). The prep. in compound has the idea of counting "beside" or counting "aside" w. the idea of "miscalculating" (s. MH, 319; RWP). **πιθανολογία** "persuasive speech." The word was used by classical writers for probable reasoning and opposed to demonstration (Abbott). The word is used in the papyri in a court case of those who sought persuasive words to keep the things obtained by robbery (Lohse; MM). The terminology used here is practically equivalent to our English expression, "to talk someone into something" (S. Lewis Johnson, "Beware of Philosophy," Bib Sac, 119 [October, 1962],
5 304). ■ **γάρ** "for." The particle gives the reason how Paul who was unknown to the Colossians and not present w. them can give such a warning. Through the Holy Spirit he is so bound to them as though he were w. them (Dibelius). **ἄπειμι** to be away from someone, to be absent. **χαίρων** and **βλέπων** pres. act. parts. **τάξις** an orderly arrangement used in the military sense of a rank or orderly array (Lightfoot; s. also Lohse). **στερέωμα** that which is firm, hard, solid. (For the root meaning, s. GEW II, 790f.) Firmness, solidity. Here it is probably a continuation of the military metaphor and means "a solid front," "a closed phalanx" (Lightfoot).

6 ■ **παρελάβετε** aor. act. ind. *παραλαμβάνω* to receive, to receive through transmission, to receive through teaching and is equivalent to the rabbinical terms for receiving and passing on tradition (Johnson, 305f.; Lohse; TDNT). **περιπατεῖτε** pres. act. imp. *περιπατέω* to walk about, to walk, to conduct one's life. The command is for the Colossians to conduct their life in accord w. the truth of Paul's preaching and not in accord w. enticing words of the heretics (Johnson, 306). The pres. tense
7 calls for a continual and habitual action. ■ **ἐρριζωμένοι** perf. pass. part. *ῥιζόω* to cause to take root, pass. to be or to become firmly rooted or fixed. The word was also used in the metaphor of the building and pictured the firm and solid foundation (s. BAG; Lohse; TDNT; Eph. 3:17). The perf. tense points to the past completed action w. the continuing results or condition. The tense pictures the settled state brought about by conversion. The following parts. in the pres. tense emphasize the continuing

development which is always advancing (Abbott). **ἐποικοδομούμενοι** pres. pass. part. ἐποικοδομέω to build up, to build up upon. **βεβαιούμενοι** pres. pass. part. βεβαιόω to make firm, to establish, to strengthen (BAG; TDNT). The pres. tense gives the idea "being more and more established" (Abbott). **πίστις** faith. The word could be used in the subjective sense and the dat. would be instrumental "by your faith." Faith would be as it were the cement of the building (Lightfoot). It is, however, more probable that faith is to be taken in its objective sense referring to the doctrines of the Christian faith (Eadie; Johnson, 303). **ἐδιδάχθητε** aor. pass. ind. **περισσεύοντες** pres. act. part. περισσεύω to overflow, to abound. **εὐχαριστία**
thanksgiving. ■ **βλέπετε** pres. act. imp. beware. The word is 8
normally followed by the subj. but the ind. in this case shows that the danger is real (Lightfoot). **ἔσται** fut. ind. **συλαγωγῶν** pres. act. part. συλαγωγέω to carry off as booty or as a captive. The word was used in the sense of "to kidnap" (Dibelius; Johnson, 306) and here is the figure of carrying someone away from the truth into the slavery of error (BAG). **κενός** empty. **ἀπάτη** deceit. **παράδοσις** tradition, that which is given over from one to another. **ἄνθρωπος** man, i.e., "man-made tradition which is to be contrasted w. the true, living, divine 'tradition' just alluded to" (Moule). **στοιχεῖον** component parts of a series, elementary things. The word could refer to elemental powers, i.e., "cosmic spirits" or more probably to "elementary teaching" (Johnson, 308; Moule; Dibelius; Lohse; TDNT). (For studies regarding the heresy at Colossae, s. Martin, 12ff.; Martin, NCB, 9–19; Andrew J. Bandstra, "Did the Colossian Errorists Need a Mediator?"
ND, 329–343; s. also the various articles in CC.) ■ **κατοικέω** 9
pres. act. ind. to settle down, to be at home (s. Col. 1:19). The pres. tense indicates the continual state and points to the pres. reality (Lohse). **πλήρωμα** fullness (s. Col. 1:19). **θεότης** divine nature, deity. The word differs from the expression "Godhead" in Rom. 1:21 in that it emphasizes not so much divine attributes but divine nature or essence. They were no mere ways of divine glory which gilded Him lighting up His person for a season and w. a splendor not His own; but He was and is absolute and perfect God (Trench; *Synonyms*, 8; TDNT; Lightfoot). **σωματικῶς** adv. bodily. The word refers to the human body of Christ (Johnson, 310) indicating also the full humanity of Jesus which was not a humanity which was simply a covering for His
deity (s. Lohse; TDNT; Moule; Lohmeyer). ■ **πεπληρωμένοι** 10
perf. pass. part. πληρόω to fill, to make full. The perf. is used in a periphrastic construction and accentuates the abiding results

of believers' completeness through union w. the exalted Lord. In Him they find their needs fully met (Johnson, 310). **κεφαλή** head. The word here probably notes primarily supremacy but it also emphasizes that the head is the center of vital force, the source of all energy and life (Lightfoot). **ἀρχή** beginning, princi-
11 pality. ■ **περιετμήθητε** aor. pass. ind. περιτέμνω to circumcise (s. Gal. 2:3). **περιτομή** circumcision. **ἀχειροποίητος** not made w. hands. **ἀπέκδυσις** putting off. The prep. in compound express a complete putting off and laying aside (Abbott). **σάρξ** flesh. The reference here could be to the putting off of the fleshly nature of man, i.e., the crucifixion of the old man (S. Lewis Johnson, "The Sufficiency of Union with Christ," Bib Sac, 120 [January, 1963], 15) or it could be a reference to the physical
12 death of Christ, i.e., His crucifixion (s. Moule; SBT, 41f.). ■ **συνταφέντες** aor. pass. part. συνθάπτω to bury together. **συνηγέρθητε** aor. pass. ind. συγεγείρω to raise up together w. someone, to be co-resurrected. **ἐνέργεια** effective working, divine working (s. Col. 1:29). **ἐγείραντος** aor. act. part. ἐγείρω to raise up, to resurrect. The rite of baptism typified the reality of death and resurrection. Death is the neg. side and the resur-
13 rection is the positive (Johnson, 16). ■ **ὄντας** pres. part. εἰμί. **παράπτωμα** transgression (s. Eph. 2:1). The dat. could be locative or instrumental describing either the circumstances (Moule) or the reason for them being dead (Lightfoot). **ἀκροβυστία** foreskin, uncircumcision. **συνεζωοποίησεν** aor. act. ind. συζωοποιέω to make alive together (s. Eph. 2:5). **χαρισάμενος** aor. mid. part. χαρίζομαι to grant as a favor, to give graciously, to forgive out of grace (Abbott; s. also TDNT;
14 CBB). ■ **ἐξαλείψας** aor. act. part. ἐξαλείφω to wash over, to wipe out. The word was used for wiping out a memory of an experience or for cancelling a vote or annulling a law or cancelling a charge or debt. It was also used for "the washing out" the writing on a papyrus (s. NTW, 46–48; MM; Preisigke I, 507; Moule). **κατά** w. the gen. "against." **χειρόγραπον** handwriting. It was used as a t.t. for a written acknowledgment of debt. It is an "I.O.U.," a statement of indebtedness, personally signed by the debtor (Abbott; Moule; LAE, 334). (For a description of the Jewish certificate of indebtedness, s. SB III, 628; Lohse.) **δόγμα** decree. The word referred to a legal obligation which was a binding law or edict which was placed on a public place for all to see (s. TDNT; Lohmeyer; Lohse; Martin, NCB). The dat. is a dat. of description, i.e., a document containing or consisting of "decrees" (IBG, 45; s. also MT, 219). **ὑπεναντίος** opposed, against, hostile, directly opposed. It described the act. hostility

(Lightfoot). **ἦρκεν** perf. act. ind. *αἴρω* to take away. The perf. tense stands in contrast to the aor. in this section and fixes attention on the pres. state of freedom resulting from the action which was esp. before the apostle's mind (Abbott). **μέσον** middle, combined w. the verb is a strong expression meaning "and put out of sight" (Lightfoot). **προσηλώσας** aor. act. part. *προσηλόω* to nail to. The part. is modal and describes the manner in which Christ removed the handwriting. He nailed the Mosaic law with all its decrees to His cross and it died w. Him
(Ellicott). **σταυρός** cross. ■ **ἀπεκδυσάμενος** aor. mid. part. 15
ἀπεκδύομαι to strip off, to put off as one puts off a garment. Christ divested Himself at the cross of the evil powers which had struggled w. Him so strongly during His ministry in attempts to force Him to abandon the pathway of the cross (Johnson, 20). **ἐδειγμάτισεν** aor. act. ind. *δειγματίζω* to display, to expose, to display as a victor displays his captives or trophies in a triumphal procession (Lightfoot). **παρρησία** openness, boldness, confidence (s. Abbott; Lightfoot). **θριαμβεύσας** aor. act. part. *θριαμβεύω* to lead in a triumph. It pictures a victorious general leading his prisoners in a triumphal procession (Moule; s. also 2 Cor. 2:14). See also Rory B. Egan, "Lexical Evidence of Two Pauline Passages," Nov T, 19 [January, 1977], 34–62). (For a study of these verses, s. Ralph P. Martin, "Reconciliation and Forgiveness in Colossians," RH, 116–124.)

■ **κρίνετω** pres. act. imp. *κρίνω* to judge, to take one to 16
task (Abbott). The pres. imp. w. the neg. calls for the stopping of an action in progress or indicates that an action should not be a habitual one (s. MKG, 272f.). **βρῶσις** eating. **πόσις** drinking. Here it refers to indulgence in wine (Dibelius). The idea that man could serve deity or draw near to deity or prepare one's self for the reception of a revelation through ascetic living and fasting was widespread in the ancient world (Lohse). **μέρος** part. Used in the construction in **ἐνμέρει** w. the meaning "in respect to," "in the matter of" (Abbott). **ἑορτή** festival. Here it refers chiefly to the annual festival like the Passover, Pentecost, etc. (Lightfoot). **νεομηνία** new moon. This describes the monthly festival and the following word "sabbath" refers to the weekly
holy day (Lightfoot). ■ **σκία** shadow. The word indicates either 17
a "shadow" which in itself has no substance but indicates the existence of a body which casts the shadow (Abbott), or it indicates a dim outline, a sketch of an object in contrast w. the object itself. This would mean that the OT ritual observances were dim outlines of the NT redemptive truths (S. Lewis Johnson, "The Paralysis of Legalism," Bib Sac, 120 [April, 1963], 112). (For the

use of the figure of a shadow in Josephus and rabbinical writings, s. SB III, 628.) **μελλόντων** pres. act. part. μέλλω to be about
18 to. Here it has the meaning "things coming." ■ **καταβραβευέτω** pres. act. imp. καταβραβεύω to decide against someone, to give judgment against someone (Abbott; Lohse; s. also Preisigke I, 744; Lohmeyer). **θέλων** pres. act. part. The verb here followed by the prep. could be taken as a septuagintism and translated "being bent upon" (Fred O. Francis, "Humility and Angelic Worship in Colossians 2:18," CAC, 167). **ταπεινοφροσύνη** lowliness, humility. The word was often used in connection w. the fasting and several Jewish Christian writings specify that the consequence of this ascetic practice is entrance into the heavenly realm (Francis; CAC, 168ff.). **θρησκεία** worship. The word can be used in a variety of ways but stands for the act of worship (Francis, CAC, 180). **τῶν ἀγγέλων** gen. pl. The word is normally taken as obj. gen., i.e., "the worship given to angels," but it is also possible and more probable that the gen. is subj. gen. and refers to the worship the angels performed (Francis; CAC, 177–180). **ἑόρακεν** perf. act. ind., s.v.1. **ἐμβατεύων** pres. act. part. ἐμβατεύω to enter into, to penetrate. Perhaps the meaning here is the entering into heavenly spheres as a sort of superspiritual experience. (For various contexts in which this word appears and a discussion of this interpretation, s. CAC, 171–176; cf. also PGL, 453; for other views s. also Abbott; Lohse; Johnson, 111.) **φυσιούμενος** pres. pass. part. φυσιόω to puff up, to blow up, pass. to be puffed up. Their profession of humility was a cloak for excessive pride
19 (Lightfoot). **νοῦς** mind, thinking facility. ■ **κρατῶν** pres. act. part. κρατέω to hold fast to someone, to remain closely united w. someone (BAG; s. also Lohse). **κεφαλή** head, "the Head" regarded as a title, so that a person is at once suggested, and the rel. which follows is masc. (Lightfoot). **σῶμα** body. Here it refers to the church as the "body of Christ" consisting of the saints and deriving its unity and growth from Christ (s. SBT, 224). **ἁφή** ligament. The word could refer to the "nerves" (Meyer) or to the "joints" of the body as contacts between the members (Lightfoot). (For a study of the words, s. Robinson, Eph. 4:16; Lightfoot.) **σύνδεσμος** band, that which binds together. In relation to the figure of the church being the body of Christ, these words refer to believers in the body of Christ, who are to exercise their spiritual gift in the church for the edification of the whole body (Johnson, 115). **ἐπιχορηγούμενοι** pres. pass. part. ἐπιχορηγέω to furnish or provide, to support, pass. to be supported, to receive help (BAG). **συμβιβαζόμενον** pres. pass.

part., s.v.2. **αὔξει** pres. act. ind. to grow. The pres. tense emphasizes the continual growth. **αὔξησις** growth. The acc. is cognate acc. here being the acc. of the inner content and is used for emphasis (s. BD, 84f.; RG, 478; DM, 94). Growth does not come through a denial of certain foods but rather growth comes from God.

■ **ἀπεθάνετε** aor. act. ind. ἀποθνήσκω to die. The ind. is 20
used in a conditional clause which assumes the reality of the
condition. **στοιχεῖον** elementary teachings, s.v.8. **ζῶντες** pres.
act. part. The part. used w. the particle is concessive. The particle
here gives the subj. motivation of the subject or action, i.e., "w.
the assertion that, on the pretext that, w. the thought that" (BD,
219). **δογματίζεσθε** pres. mid. ind. to issue a decree, mid. to
subject one's self to decrees. The mid. is permissive mid. "why
are you allowing yourselves to be subjected to authoritative decrees?" (s. RG, 808; MT, 57) ■ **ἅψῃ** aor. mid. subj. ἅπτομαι to 21
touch, to take hold of, to grasp. **γεύσῃ** aor. mid. subj. γεύομαι
to taste, to partake of, to enjoy. **θίγῃς** aor. act. subj. θιγγάνω
to touch. (For a comparison of the words for "touch" and that
the first word may be used in a sexual sense, s. Lightfoot; Abbott;
Schweizer.) ■ **ἀπόχρησις** consuming, consumption, using up. 22
The prep. in compound is perfective, completely using up (MH,
299; Ellicott). **ἔνταλμα** commandment. **διδασκαλία** teaching,
doctrine. ■ **ἔχοντα** pres. act. part. The part. is used w. ἐστίν to 23
form a periphrastic pres. ind. (RWP) and this points out that the
character of the precepts is such that a word of wisdom belongs
to them (Abbott). **ἐθελοθρησκία**. The word could mean "self-
chosen worship" (Hendriksen; Martin; Lohse) or it could mean
"would-be worship" (Francis; CAC, 181f.; MH, 290; s. also BD,
64). **ταπεινοφροσύνη** s.v.18. **ἀφειδία** unsparing, severity,
hard treatment (S. Lewis Johnson, "Human Taboos and Divine
Redemption," Bib Sac, 120 [September, 1963], 210).
πλησμονή filling up, satisfaction, gratification, but it may be
used in the bad sense "indulgence of the flesh" (s. BAG; Lightfoot; Abbott).

Ch. 3

■ **συνηγέρθητε** aor. pass. ind. συνεγείρω to raise up to- 1
gether, pass. to be coresurrected. The ind. is used in a conditional clause which assumes the reality "if then (as is the case) you were raised together w. Christ" (EGT). The aor. looks at the completed action. **ἄνω** above, "the things above." The words are used to mean "the heavenly world" (Lohse; s. also TDNT). (For a contrast of "things above and things below" in Jewish writings,

s. SB I, 395, 977; II, 116, 133, 430; III, 630.) **ζητεῖτε** pres. act. imp. ζητέω to seek. The pres. tense calls for a continual and habitual action. **δεξία** right, right hand (s. Eph. 1:20). **καθήμενος** pres. mid. part. κάθημαι to sit. The sitting at the right hand was considered to be a place of honor (s. Schweizer).
2 ■ **φρονεῖτε** pres. act. imp. φρονέω to think, to be minded. The verb in this v. differs so far from that employed in the preceding, that it refers more to an inner disposition, while the former is
3 rather practical pursuit (Eadie; s. also Phil. 2:2, 5). ■ **ἀπεθάνετε** aor. act. ind. ἀποθνήσκω to die. **κέκρυπται** perf. pass. ind. κρύπτω to hide. The idea of life being hidden in God suggests three thoughts, i.e., secrecy where the believer's life is nurtured by secret springs; safety, "w. Christ in God" marks a double protection; identity, the believer is identified w. the risen Lord (Johnson, 212). The perf. tense views the completed state arising
4 from a past action. ■ **ὅταν** w. the subj. "whenever." **φανερωθῇ** aor. pass. subj. φανερόω to make plain, clear, to manifest. Here it refers to the coming of the Lord at which time the veil will be removed so that the things which are now hidden from our eyes will be illuminated in a bright light (Lohse). **φανερωθήσεσθε** fut. pass. ind.

5 ■ **νεκρώσατε** aor. act. imp. νεκρόω to put to death. The meaning here is to be compared to Rom. 6:11 and contains the idea "reckon as dead" (Bruce). **μέλος** member. The members of the body were used to carry out the desires. According to the rabbis there are as many commandments and restraints in the law as the body has members and the "Evil Impulse" is said to be king over 248 members (s. Schweizer) and the two great passions which the "Evil Inclination" plays the most upon are the passions of idolatry and adultery (s. S. Schechter, *Some Aspects of Rabbinic Theology*, 250). **πορνεία** illicit sex, sexual activity apart from marriage. Sexual activity was often connected w. the idolatrous worship of false gods (s. TDNT; Gal. 5:19). **ἀκαθαρσία** uncleanness, filthiness (s. Gal. 5:19). **πάθος** passion. The word indicates a drive or force which does not rest until it is satisfied (s. Trench; *Synonyms*, 324). **ἐπιθυμία** desire, lust. The word is wider than the previous word and reaches to all evil longing (Lightfoot). **πλεονεξία** insatiable selfishness, greed (s. NTW, 97; TDNT). **εἰδωλολατρία** idolatry. The accs. in this v. are accs. of general reference, i.e. "put to death the
6 members in reference to . . ." (s. DM, 93; RG, 486). ■ **ὀργή** wrath, anger. It refers to the deep-seated anger of God which displays itself in eternal punishment which will come upon those who practice sexual sins, uncontrolled greed and service to idols

(s. TDNT; CBB; Lohse). ■ **περιπατήσατε** aor. act. ind. 7
περιπατέω to walk about, to conduct one's life. The verb used
w. the prep. indicates "to take part in" (BAG). The aor. is
constative summing up their whole life of the past (RWP; DM,
196; Funk, 620f.). **ἐζῆτε** impf. ind. act. ζάω to live. The impf.
is customary impf. indicating the continual action of the past
time "you used to live." ■ **ἀπόθεσθε** aor. mid. imp. ἀποτίθημι 8
to take off from one's self, to change one's clothes, to remove
one's clothes from one's self, to put off. **θυμός** anger. It refers
to a burning anger which flares up and burns w. the intensity of
a fire (s. Trench; *Synonyms*, 130f.; TDNT). **κακία** malice. It
refers to the vicious nature which is bent on "doing harm to
others" (Lightfoot; s. also Trench; *Synonyms*, 37ff.; TDNT).
βλασφημία slander. It indicates the attempt to belittle and
cause someone to fall into disrepute or to receive a bad reputation (s. TDNT; for examples from the DSS, s. Lohse).
αἰσχρολογία filthy talk, dirty speech, abusive language (s.
Lightfoot; MM). ■ **ψεύδεσθε** pres. mid. imp. to lie. The pres. 9
imp. w. the neg. forbids a manner of life. **ἀπεκδυσάμενοι** aor.
mid. part. ἀπεκδύομαι to take off completely, to strip off of
one's self. The part. is causal and contains the motive for the
preceding exhortation (Abbott). Paul means: if the old man really has been put off, one must not at a critical moment revert to
the way one acted before his conversion. (For this and a discussion of the origin of Paul's metaphor along w. various parallel
usages, s. P.W. van der Horst, "Observations on a Pauline Expression," NTS, 19 [January, 1973], 185; 181–187.) **παλαιός**
old. **πρᾶξις** deed. The pl. describes the individual deeds which
characterized the former life. ■ **ἐνδυσάμενοι** aor. mid. part. 10
ἐνδύομαι to put on one's self, to cloth one's self. The part. is
causal (Hendriksen). **νέος** new. The word only expresses newness in point of time (Abbott; Lightfoot; Trench; *Synonyms*,
219f.). **ἀνακαινούμενον** pres. pass. part. ἀνακαιόω to make
new again, to renew. The idea of "new" is that of newness in
quality (s. Rom. 12:2; TDNT). The prep. in compound does not
suggest the restoration of the original state, but the contrast to
that which has lately existed (Abbott). The pres. tense points to
the continual action "which is ever being renewed" (Lightfoot).
The pass. indicates that the action is performed by another.
ἐπίγνωσις knowledge, "thorough knowledge" (Abbott; s. also
Col. 1:9). **εἰκών** image (s. TDNT; CBB). **κτίσαντος** aor. act.
part. κτίζω to create. **αὐτόν** "him." The reference is to the "new
man" rather than "man" in general (Ellicott). ■ **ὅπου** where. 11
περιτομή circumcision. **ἀκροβυστία** foreskin, uncircumci-

sion. **βάρβαρος** barbarian. The word properly denoted one who spoke an inarticulate, stammering, unintelligible language and was adopted by Gr. exclusiveness and pride to stigmatize the rest of mankind and denoted one who was not a Gr. (s. Lightfoot; Lohse; TDNT). **ἐλεύθερος** free, one who had been freed from slavery.

12 ■ **ἐνδύσασθε** aor. mid. imp., s.v.10. **ἐκλεκτός** chosen, elect. If God chose them as members of His new creation, they must fulfill the command to conduct themselves accordingly. **ἠγαπημένοι** perf. pass. part. ἀγαπάω to love. The perf. tense points to a past completed action w. a continuing state or results. **σπλάγχνα** heart. It denotes esp. the nobler inward parts, heart, liver, and lungs and figuratively it refers to the seat of the emotion (Abbott; s. also MNTW, 156; TDNT; Phil. 2:1). **οἰκτιρμός** compassion (s. Phil. 2:1). **χρηστότης** kindness. It is kindness expressed in attitude and deed. It is the friendly and helpful spirit which seeks to meet the needs of others through kind deeds (s. TDNT; Gal. 5:22). **ταπεινοφροσύνη** lowliness in thinking, humility. It is the recognizing of one's own weakness but also the recognition of the power of God (TDNT; CBB). **πραΰτης** meekness. The word indicates an obedient submissiveness to God and His will w. unwavering faith and enduring patience which displays itself in a gentle attitude and in kind acts toward others, and this often in the face of opposition. It is the restrained and obedient powers of the personality brought into subjection and submission to God's will by the Holy Spirit (s. Gal. 5:23). **μακροθυμία** longsuffering. It is a long holding out of the mind before it gives room to action or passion. It indicates the patient longsuffering in bearing injustices or unpleasant circumstances without revenge or retaliation but w. a view or hope for a final goal or betterment (s. Trench; *Synonyms*, 196; TDNT; Gal.
13 5:23). ■ **ἀνεχόμενοι** pres. mid. part. ἀνέχομαι to endure, to bear w., to put up w. someone (BAG). The part. describes the manner or means. The pres. tense emphasizes the continual action. **χαριζόμενοι** pres. mid. part. χαρίζομαι to be gracious, to forgive. **ἑαυτοῖς** = ἀλλήλοις. (For the reflex. pron. used instead of the reciprocal pron., s. BD, 150; MT, 37f.) The reflex. pron. here may suggest the performance of an act faintly resembling that of Christ, namely, of each one toward all, —yea even to themselves included, Christians being members one of another (Ellicott). **ἔχῃ** pres. act. subj. The pres. tense has the idea of "having" rather than the idea of "getting" as expressed by the aor. (s. M, 110). The subj. is used in a conditional clause where the condition is viewed as possible. **μόμφη** blame, cause for

complaint. The verb from which this noun is taken means "to
find fault w. someone," "to be dissatisfied w. someone," and
refers most commonly to errors of omission so the noun here is
regarded as a debt which needs to be remitted (Lightfoot; s. also
TDNT). **ἐχαρίσατο** aor. mid. ind. The aor. points to the completed action. ■ **ἐπί** w. the dat. the prep. could mean "in addition 14
to" or "on the top of all the others" or it may have an elative
force and mean "above all," i.e., love is the most important moral
quality in the believer's life (s. Moule; S. Lewis Johnson, "Christian Apparel," Bib Sac, 121 [January, 1964], 30). **σύνδεσμος**
that which binds or holds something together, bond. **τελειότης**
perfection, complete maturity. The gen. could be an obj. gen., i.e.
"the bond producing perfection" (s. MT, 212; Lohse), or it could
be a type of descriptive gen. indicating the bond which signifies
or indicates perfection. The word here is the full expression of
the divine life in the community, devoid of bitter words and
angry feelings, and freed from the ugly defects of immorality and
dishonesty (Bruce). ■ **βραβευέτω** pres. act. imp. 3rd per. sing. 15
βραβεύω to referee, to be an umpire, to call a decision, to decide
between (s. TDNT; Lohse; Lightfoot). **ἐκλήθητε** aor. pass. ind.
καλέω to call. **εὐχάριστος** thankful. The word indicates the
obligation of being thankful to someone for a favor done. The
thankfulness arises out of the grace of God and that which He
has done (s. TDNT). **γίνεσθε** pres. mid. imp. The pres. tense
indicates a continual action pointing to a habit of life. ■ 16
ἐνοικείτω pres. act. imp. 3rd per. sing. ἐνοικέω to live in, to
dwell in, to take up one's residence in, to make one's home
among (Moule; s. also Preisigke I, 493). **πλουσίως** adv.
πλούσιος extravagantly rich, richly. **διδάσκοντες** pres. act.
part. **νουθετοῦντες** pres. act. part. νουθετέω to admonish, to
correct one who is at fault through admonition (s. Col. 1:28).
ψαλμός psalm. It was often used of the psalms in the OT and
has the idea of a song w. musical accompaniment (s. Trench;
Synonyms, 296; Lightfoot; Lohse). **ὕμνος** hymn. The word is
used of a song which is a praise to God (s. Trench; *Synonyms*,
297f.; Lightfoot). **ᾠδή** song. This is the general word for any kind
of a song (Trench; *Synonyms*, 300f.; Lightfoot). **ᾄδοντες** pres.
act. part. ᾄδω to sing. ■ **ἐάν** used w. the subj. and generalizes 17
the object "whatever," "everything whatever" (s. RWP). **ποιῆτε**
pres. act. subj. **εὐχαριστοῦντες** pres. act. part. εὐχαριστέω to
give thanks.

■ **ὑποτάσσεσθε** pres. mid. imp. ὑποτάσσω mid. to be in 18
subjection, to subject one's self. Submission for Paul is a voluntary submission based on one's own recognition of God's order

(Crouch, 110; s. also Eph. 5:21). (For references to the position
of women in the ancient world, s. Crouch, 107.) **ἀνῆκεν** impf.
ind. act. ἀνήκει it is fitting, it is proper. The impf. is used w. a
pres. meaning in an expression of necessity, obligation, or duty
19 (BD, 181; s. also RG, 919f.; MT, 90f.). ■ **ἀγαπᾶτε** pres. act.
imp. The pres. imp. calls for a continual attitude and positive
expression. **πικραίνεσθε** pres. mid.-pass. imp. πικραίνω to
make bitter, to embitter, to become bitter. The verb has the idea
of being sharp, harsh, and bitter. It speaks of friction caused by
impatience and thoughtless "nagging." If love is absent, such
obedience will not be secured by perpetual irritation and fault-
finding (s. TDNT; Moule; Eadie). The pres. imp. w. the neg.
forbids a habitual action.
20 ■ **ὑπακούετε** pres. act. imp. ὑπακούω to listen to, to obey.
γονεῖς (pl.) parents. **εὐάρεστος** well-pleasing, commendable.
The word is generally used in the Bible to mean "pleasing to
21 God" (Moule). ■ **ἐρεθίζετε** pres. act. imp. ἐρεθίζω to excite, to
provoke, to irritate (Abbott). **ἀθυμῶσιν** pres. act. subj. ἀθυμέω
to be without courage or spirit, to lose heart, to become spiritless,
i.e., "to go about their task in a listless, moody, sullen frame of
mind" (Lightfoot). A child frequently irritated by overseverity
or injustice, to which, nevertheless, it must submit, acquires a
spirit of sullen resignation, leading to despair (Abbott).
22 ■ **ὀφθαλμοδουλία** eye service. It might mean "merely
such service as can be seen," i.e., superficial work—not dusting
behind the ornaments, not sweeping under the wardrobe but the
context suggests rather going through the outward movements
of the work "without a corresponding keenness of will behind
them" (Moule). The word could also have the idea of "when the
master's eye is upon you" (S. Lewis Johnson, "The New Man
in the Old," Bib Sac, 121 [April, 1964], 113). **ἀνθρωπάρεσκος**
men-pleaser, one who tries to please men at the sacrifice of
principle (BAG). **ἁπλότης** singleness. The phrase used here
means "w. undivided service" (Lightfoot). **φοβούμενοι** pres.
mid. part. φοβέομαι to be afraid, to fear, to fear the Lord
(Christ) is the leading principle of Christian conduct (Lohse).
23 ■ **ἐάν**. Used w. the subj. and the rel. pron. w. the meaning
"whatever" (s.v.17). **ποιῆτε** pres. act. subj., s.v.17. **ἐργάζεσθε**
pres. mid. imp. ἐργάζομαι to work, to work energetically, to
24 work diligently (Lightfoot). ■ **εἰδότες** perf. act. part. οἶδα.
ἀπολήμψεσθε fut. mid. ind. ἀπολαμβάνω to receive from
someone. The prep. denotes that the recompense comes immediately from Christ, its possessor (Eadie). **ἀνταπόδοσις** receiving
from another in return, recompensing, requittal. The prep. in

compound expresses the idea of full, complete return (Hendriksen). **κληρονομία** inheritance, gen. of apposition, the reward which consists in the inheritance. There is a special point in the word, inasmuch as slaves could not be inheritors of an earthly possession (Abbott). **δουλεύετε** pres. act. imp. or ind. to serve as a slave. The form could be either imp. (Lohse; Moule) or ind.
(Lightfoot). ■ **ἀδικῶν** pres. act. part. ἀδικέω to commit an 25
unrighteous act, to wrong (s. TDNT). The sentence is an explanation and gives a general law applicable to all. **κομίσεται** fut. mid. ind. κομίζω to carry off safe, mid. to bear for one's self, to receive (AS). **ἠδίκησεν** aor. act. ind. ἀδικέω. **προσωπολημψία** the accepting of one's face or person, partiality (s. Moule; TDNT).

Ch. 4

■ **ἰσότης** equality, fairness. **παρέχεσθε** pres. mid. imp. 1
παρέχω to give, to grant, mid. to show one's self to be something, here "exhibit on your part fairness to the slaves." The idea is "reciprocation." The master's duty as corresponding to the slaves (Lightfoot; s. also BAG; BD, 166).

■ **προσκαρτερεῖτε** pres. act. imp. προσκαρτερέω to ad- 2
here to, to persist in, to busy one's self w., to busily engage in, to be devoted to (BAG; s. also TDNT). **γρηγοροῦντες** pres. act. part. γρηγορέω to be awake, to stay awake, to be watchful, to be vigilant. Perhaps Paul was reminded of the literal sleep which he had heard about in the story of the passion or of the Transfiguration (Moule). **εὐχαριστία** thanksgiving (s. Col. 3:17). ■ 3
προσευχόμενοι pres. mid. part. προσεύχομαι to pray. **ἅμα** to gather at the same time, "praying at the same time also for us" (BD, 220). **ἀνοίξῃ** aor. act. subj. ἀνοίγω to open. The picture of an open door stood for "opportunity." (For rabbinical examples, s. SB III, 631; TDNT.) **λόγου** "the word," obj. gen. "a door for preaching" (RWP). **λαλῆσαι** aor. act. inf. **μυστήριον** mystery (s. Col. 1:26; Eph. 3:3). **δέδεμαι** perf. pass. ind. δέω to bind.
The perf. emphasizes the continuing state or condition. ■ 4
φανερώσω aor. act. subj. φανερόω to make clear, to manifest. **δεῖ**. Used w. the acc. and the inf. "it is necessary." The word denotes the logical necessity (s. AS; for the root meaning of the
word, s. GEW I, 375). ■ **περιπατεῖτε** pres. act. imp. 5
περιπατέω to walk about, to walk, to conduct one's life. **ἔξω** outside. The expression "those outside" is equivalent to the rabbinical term denoting those who belong to another religious group and is used here to denote those who are "non Christians" (s. SB III, 362; TDNT; Lohse). **καιρός** time, opportunity. The

word does not emphasize a point of time but rather a time space
filled w. all kinds of possibilities (s. TDNT; Lohse).
ἐξαγοραζόμενοι pres. mid. part. ἐξαγοράζω to buy at the
market place. The prep. in compound is probably intensive and
the object of the verb is viewed as a commodity to be eagerly
6 bought (s. Eph. 5:16; Moule; Lightfoot). ■ **πάντοτε** always.
ἅλας salt. **ἠρτυμένος** perf. pass. part. ἀρτύω to season. The
figure of speech as salt was used in the ancient world of sparkling
conversation, speech dotted w. witty or clever remarks (Hendriksen; Moule; Lohse; SB III, 631). Here it indicates speech
which gives a flavor to the discourse and recommends it to the
pallet as well as speech which preserves from corruption and
renders wholesome (Lightfoot). **εἰδέναι** perf. act. inf. οἶδα. The
inf. is used to express results. **πῶς** how. The conversation must
not only be opportune in regards to time; it must also be appropriate as regards the person (Lightfoot). **ἀποκρίνεσθαι** pres.
mid. inf. to answer.
7 ■ **τὰ κατ᾽ ἐμέ** "the things related to me," "my affairs."
γνωρίσει fut. act. ind. γνωρίζω to make known. **ἀγαπητός**
beloved. **πίστος** true, faithful. **διάκονος** minister (s. Col. 1:23).
8 **σύνδουλος** fellow servant. ■ **ἔπεμψα** aor. act. ind. πέμπω to
send. **γνῶτε** aor. act. subj. γινώσκω. The subj. is used in a
purpose clause. **παρακαλέσῃ** aor. act. subj. παρακαλέω to
exhort, to encourage, to comfort (s. TDNT; MNTW, 128ff.).
9 ■ **ὧδε** here.
10 ■ **ἀσπάζεται** pres. mid. ind. to greet. **συναιχμάλωτος**
fellow prisoner. The term denotes properly "a prisoner of war"
but it also occurs in the general sense (s. TDNT; Moule).
ἀνεψιός cousin (s. Lightfoot). **ἐλάβετε** aor. act. ind. λαμβάνω
to receive. **ἐντολή** command. **ἔλθῃ** aor. act. subj. ἔρχομαι.
11 **δέξασθε** aor. mid. imp. δέχομαι to receive, to welcome. ■
λεγόμενος pres. pass. part. **ὄντες** pres. part. εἰμί. **περιτομή**
circumcision. **συνεργός** fellow worker. **ἐγενήθησαν** aor. pass.
ind. γίνομαι. **παρηγορία** encouragement, comfort. The word
appears on gravestones and in a letter of condolence w. the
12 meaning "comfort" (s. MM; Lohse; Lightfoot). ■ **ἐξ ὑμῶν** "one
who belongs to you," "who is one of you," i.e., a native or at least
an inhabitant of Colossae (Lightfoot). **ἀγωνιζόμενος** pres. mid.
part. ἀγωνίζομαι to struggle, to agonize. It is the zeal and
intensity of prayer which is emphasized (PAM, 123). **σταθῆτε**
aor. pass. subj. ἵστημι to place, pass. to stand. The word conveys the idea of standing firm (Abbott). **τέλειος** perf., mature.
πεπληροφορήμενοι perf. pass. part. πληροφορέω to fill completely, pass. to be fully convinced, to be assured through, rich,

gratifying insight into all spiritual matters is meant; understanding which not only penetrates the mind but also fills the heart
w. satisfying conviction (Hendriksen; BAG). ■ ***μαρτυρέω*** pres. 13
act. ind. to witness, to testify. ***πόνος*** labor, strenuous work. It is labor such as does not stop short of demanding the soul strength of a man; and this exerted to the uttermost, if he is to accomplish the task which is set before him. It is the standing word by which the laborers of Hercules are expressed (Trench;
Synonyms, 378). ■ ***ιατρος*** doctor, physician. (For information 14
concerning physicians and medicine in the ancient world, s. RAC I, 720–724; OCB, 660–664; DGRA, 747–748; Preisigke
III, 123; ZPEB IV, 788f.) ***ἀγαπητός*** beloved. ■ ***ἀσπάσασθε*** 15
aor. mid. imp. **Νύμφαν**. The manuscript evidence is divided as to whether the name refers to a woman or a man (s. TC, 627; Lightfoot). ***κατ᾽οἶκον*** at home, at one's house. The use of the home for Christian assembly is well attested in the NT period (s.
Martin; Lightfoot). ■ ***ὅταν*** w. the subj. "when," "whenever." 16
ἀναγνωσθῇ aor. pass. subj. *ἀναγιγνώσκω* to read. ***ποιήσατε*** aor. act. imp. ***τὴν ἐκ Λαοδικείας*** "the letter that is at Laodicea" (s. BD, 225). (For the suggestion that the Laodicean letter was written by Epaphras, s. C.P. Anderson, "Who Wrote the 'Epistle From Laodicea'?" JBL, 85 [December, 1966], 436–440.)
ἀναγνῶτε aor. act. subj. *ἀναγιγνώσκω*. ■ ***εἴπατε*** aor. act. 17
imp. *λέγω*. ***βλέπε*** pres. act. imp. to see, to take heed, to keep an eye on (RWP). ***διακονία*** ministry, service (s. Col. 1:23; TDNT). ***παρέλαβες*** aor. act. ind. *παραλαμβάνω* to receive, to receive from someone. The word suggests a mediate rather than a direct reception; Archippus received the charge immediately from St. Paul, though ultimately from Christ (Lightfoot). ***πληροῖς*** pres. act. subj. The pres. tense points to a continual action. It refers to a lifetime job (RWP).

■ ***ἀσπασμός*** greeting. ***μνημονεύετε*** pres. act. imp. 18
μνημονεύω to remember. The verb is followed by the gen. ***δέσμος*** bond. The chain clanked afresh as Paul took the pen to sign the salutation (RWP).

1 THESSALONIANS

Ch. 1

1 ***ἐν***. The prep. could be local and emphasizes that the church is in the atmosphere of the divine (Frame). They live "in" Him day by day. All their deeds are done in Him (Morris). The prep. could also be taken in an instrumental sense which means that for the believer salvation lies "in" what God accomplished by Christ's life, death, and resurrection (Best).

2 ■ ***εὐχαριστοῦμεν*** pres. act. ind. to give thanks, to thank. The pres. tense stresses the continual action. ***πάντοτε*** always. ***μνεία*** remembrance, mention. The word indicates "remembrance" in a special case, i.e., "the direction of the memory to some particular object" (Lightfoot, *Notes*). ***ποιούμενοι*** pres. mid. part. used in connection w. the previous noun w. the meaning "making mention," "remembering." (For examples in the papyri and inscriptions, s. Milligan.) This is the first of three modal parts. describing the nature of the perpetual thanksgiving (Milligan). ***ἀδιαλείπτως*** constantly, without interruption, un-
3 ceasingly (s. Rom. 1:9; 1 Thess. 5:17). ■ ***μνημονεύοντες*** pres. act. part. μνημονεύω to remember. The verb regularly means "to call something to mind," or "to make mention of it" (Moore). ***ὑμῶν*** your. The word is placed emphatically at the head of three phrases and should be taken w. each (Best). ***ἔργον*** work. The word refers to active work (Lightfoot). The word could also involve the results of the activity, i.e., "achievement" (Best). The word comprehends the whole Christian life work, as it is ruled and energized by faith (Milligan). ***κόπος*** labor. The word denotes arduous, wearying toil involving sweat and fatigue (Moore). The word emphasizes the weariness which follows on this straining of all of one's powers to the utmost (Trench; *Synonyms*, 378). ***ὑπομονή*** endurance. It is the spirit which bears things, not simply w. resignation, but w. blazing hope. It is the spirit which bears things because it knows that these things are leading to a goal of glory (NTW, 60; s. also TDNT; CBB). The gens. "faith, love and hope" are subj. gens. (MT, 211).
4 ***ἔμπροσθεν*** in the presence of. ■ ***εἰδότες*** perf. act. part. οἶδα. (For the meaning of this word, s. ND, 344–356.) ***ἠγαπημένοι***

perf. pass. part. ἀγαπάω. The perf. pass. part. stresses continuing love which God shows to men (Morris). **ἐκλογή** choosing,
election. ■ **ἐγενήθη** aor. pass. ind. γίνομαι to become, to come. 5
The word is significant as pointing to a result reached through the working of an outside force (Milligan). **εἰς ὑμᾶς** "unto you," "to you." The prep. w. the acc. is used here as an equivalent to the dat. (s. RG, 594). **οὐκ . . . ἐν λόγῳ μόνον** "not in word alone," i.e., "our preaching was not merely declamation, a hollow and heartless rhetoric" (Lightfoot; *Notes*). **δύναμις** power. The word is generally used by Paul of divine energy (Moore). **πληροφορία** full assurance, conviction, confidence (Lightfoot; *Notes*; s. also Col. 4:12). **οἷος** what sort of, what kind of, what manner of. The qualitative pron. brings out the interest and advantage of those for whom that power was exercised (Milligan). **ἐγενήθημεν** aor. pass. ind. γίνομαι to become. The sense here is "came to be," "proven to be" (Ellicott). **ἐν ὑμῖν** "in your
midst." **δι' ὑμᾶς** "because of you," "for your sake." ■ **μιμητής** 6
imitator, one who imitates another particularly by following one's example or one's teaching (s. TDNT; von Dobschütz). **ἐγενήθητε** aor. pass. ind., s.v.5. **δεξάμενοι** aor. mid. part. δέχομαι to receive, to welcome. The part. expresses contemporaneous or identical action "in that you welcomed" (Frame). **θλῖψις** pressure, tribulation (s. TDNT). **χαρά** joy. The gen. following this word is a gen. of originating cause "joy inspired
by, preceding from the Holy Spirit" (Milligan). ■ **ὥστε** w. the 7
inf. used here to introduce a result clause which expresses actual results rather than merely contemplated results (Milligan; s. also Funk, 707). **τύπος** example, type. Originally the word denoted the mark left by a blow. Then it was used in the ethical sense of a pattern of conduct but more usually, as here, of an example to
be followed (Morris). ■ **ἐξήχηται** perf. pass. ind. ἐξηχέομαι to 8
sound forth, to sound out. The word suggests an echoing like thunder or sounding out as a trumpet (Moore; s. also Lightfoot; Milligan). Although the metaphor is not clear, the word indicates that a sound is made and it is heard spreading out from a center over an area (Best). The perf. denotes the continuing activity (Morris). **τόπος** place. The definite article w. **θεόν** indicates their faith in the true God and contrasts their present attitude to God w. their past pagan attitude to idols (Frame). **ἐξελήλυθεν** perf. act. ind. ἐξέρχομαι to go out. The perf. indicates the continuing result. **χρεία** need, necessity. **λαλεῖν** pres.
act. inf. to speak. The inf. is used to explain the need. ■ **αὐτοί** 9
"they themselves," i.e. people generally (Moore). **ἀπαγγέλλω** pres. act. ind. to report. The pres. tense indicates a continuous

and repeated action. **ὁποῖος** what sort of. **εἴσοδος** entrance. The word indicates here the "act of entering" rather than the "means of entering" and points to the nature of the entrance, how happy and successful it was (Milligan). **ἔσχομεν** aor. act. ind. ἔχω. **ἐπεστρέψατε** aor. act. ind. ἐπιστρέφω to turn one's self to or toward. The prep. in compound is directive. **εἴδωλον** idol (cf. Acts. 17:16). **ζῶντι** pres. act. part. ζάω to live. The living God is not merely one who is alive but one who gives life, both the life of creation and the new life of redemption (Best). **ἀληθινός** genuine, true, real. The adj. w. this ending express the material out of which anything is made, therefore the word signifies "genuine" made up of that which is true and is used to distinguish the true God from idols and all other false gods (Trench;
10 *Synonyms*, 27). ■ **ἀναμένειν** pres. act. inf. to wait, to wait for. The leading thought here seems to be to wait for one whose coming is expected, perhaps w. the added idea of patience and confidence (Milligan). The pres. tense points to the continual waiting. The inf. is used to express purpose. **ἤγειρεν** aor. act. ind. ἐγείρω to raise. **ῥυόμενον** pres. mid. part. ῥύομαι to rescue, to deliver. The word indicates a deliverance and the avoidance of great danger (Moore). **ὀργή** wrath, deep-seated anger (s. TDNT; Morris). **ἐρχομένης** pres. mid. part. The part. is emphatic by position and emphasizes the approaching anger (Best).

Ch. 2

1 ■ **οἴδατε** perf. ind. act. defective perf. w. a pres. meaning "you yourselves know." **εἴσοδος** entrance (s. 1 Thess. 1:9). **κενός** empty, vain. The reference is to the essential content of the apostle's preaching rather than to its results (Milligan). The word refers to "hollow, empty, wanting in purpose and earnestness" (Lightfoot; *Notes;* s. also Trench; *Synonyms*, 180). **γέγονεν** perf. act. ind. γίνομαι. The perf. tense indicates the lasting effects of Paul's preaching (Lightfoot; *Notes;* s. also Best).
2 ■ **προπαθόντες** aor. act. part. προπάσχω to suffer beforehand, to suffer previously. **ὑβρισθέντες** aor. pass. part. ὑβρίζω to abuse, to treat shamefully. The word expresses insulting and outrageous treatment and esp. treatment which is calculated publicly to insult and openly to humiliate the person who suffers from it (MNTW, 83; s. also TDNT). Both parts. are to be taken w. the main verb and are either temporal, i.e. "after having suffered previously and having been shamefully treated" or they could be concessive "although . . ." (Frame). **ἐπαρρησιασάμεθα** aor. mid. ind. παρρησιάζομαι to speak freely, to speak all things, to be bold and courageous. The word

was used in classical Gr. to signify freedom of speech or expression, often w. a political connotation (Moore). **λαλῆσαι** aor. act. inf. λαλέω. **ἀγών** conflict, effort. The word implies the intense effort and strenuous exertion in Paul's preaching the gospel esp. in the fact of hostility and conflict which he had w. the
Jews at Thessalonia (PAM, 112–114). ■ **παράκλησις** exhorta- 3
tion, encouragement, appeal. The word implies an appeal, having for its object the direct benefit of those addressed, and which may be either hortatory or conciliatory according to circumstances. The word was used to encourage soldiers before going into battle and it was said that "encouragement" was necessary for hired soldiers but for those who fight for life and country no exhortation is required (Milligan; s. also MNTW, 128f.; TDNT). **ἐκ πλάνης** "out of error." The word is used either in the active sense of "deceit," "the leading astray," or in a pass. sense "error" (Lightfoot; *Notes;* s. also Best). **ἐξ ἀκαθαρσίας** "out of impurity." The word could refer to sexual or moral impurity but here it is more general and means that Paul does not preach from any impure motives, e.g. ambition, pride, greed, popularity (Best). **ἐν δόλῳ** "in guile." The word meant a bait or trap and then any
form of trick or strategy (s. Moore; Milligan). ■ The word is to 4
be taken in connection w. **οὕτως** w. the meaning "just as . . . so . . ." **δεδοκιμάσμεθα** perf. pass. ind. δοκιμάζω to prove, to approve after examination or testing. The word was used in classical Gr. w. the technical sense to describe the passing as fit for election to a public office (Milligan; s. also TDNT). The perf. tense indicates a lasting approval and not something over and done w. (Moore). **πιστευθῆναι** aor. pass. inf. πιστεύομαι to entrust. The inf. is explanatory serving to define more nearly that to which the approval was directed (Ellicott). **ἀρέσκοντες** pres. act. part. ἀρέσκω to please someone. The word is found in inscriptions of people who have served their fellow citizens and it conveys the sense of service and obedience (Moore). **δοκιμάζοντι** pres. act. part. δοκιμάζω to approve after testing. Here is is Paul's inner life in its totality of thought and intention
which God scrutinizes (Best). ■ **ποτέ** ever, used w. the neg. 5
"never." **κολακεία** flattery. The word contains the idea of deception for selfish ends. It is flattery not merely for the sake of giving pleasure to others but for the sake of self-interest. It is deception by slick eloquence, the idea being to win over the hearts in order to exploit them (Lightfoot; *Notes;* Moore; s. also Frame; Milligan). (For the use of the word in Dio Chrysostom, s. DCNT, 200f.) **ἐγενήθημεν** aor. pass. ind. γίνομαι to demonstrate one's self as (s. 1 Thess. 1:5). **πρόφασις** cloak, pretense.

The word denotes that which one puts on for appearance and w. the definite design to color or to cloak something else. It therefore denotes pretext, the outward show (Lünemann). **πλεονεξία** greed, selfishness. It is the disregard for the rights of others in order to meet one's own selfish desires to have more and more
6 (s. TDNT; NTW, 97f.). ■ **ζητοῦντες** pres. act. part. ζητέω to seek. The pres. tense points to a continual and habitual action.
7 ■ **δυνάμενοι** pres. mid. part. concessive use of the part. which qualifies the fact, "we never came requiring honor," by asserting the principle that the authority demand for honor inheres in their place of preponderance of Christ's apostles (Frame). **βάρος** weight, burden. Here the word is used in the sense of honor, authority, dignity, importance. The aspect of the word is closely related to the Heb. root *kbd* (Milligan; Best). **ἤπιος** gentle. (For the variant reading νήπιος "infants" and the textual problem, s. TC, 629f.) ὡς used w. the comparative particle and the subj. implying "a standing contingency," i.e. "as it may be at any time" (Milligan). **τρόφος** one who nourishes or feeds, nurse, wet nurse, nursing mother (s. Best; for a parallel in the DSS, s. 1QH 7.20f.; 9.29–32). A wet nurse in the ancient world not only had strict contractual stipulations, but often came to be a very trusted person whose influence lasted a lifetime (s. RAC I, 381–385; "Engagement of a Wet Nurse" No. 146, CPJ II, 15–19). **θάλπῃ** pres. act. subj. θάλπω to warm, to foster, to nourish, to cherish. In Deut. 22:6 it is used of a bird warming her
8 eggs (Moore; s. also Milligan; GEW I, 651). ■ **ὁμειρόμενοι** pres. mid. part. ὁμείρομαι to have a kindly feeling, to long for someone. The derivation of the word is uncertain (s. Lightfoot; *Notes;* Morris; MH, 251). It is used on a grave inscription describing the parents' sad yearning for their dead child and seems to indicate deep affection and great attraction (Moore; s. also MM). **εὐδοκοῦμεν** pres. act. ind. εὐδοκέω to be well-pleased, to be gladly determined. The word draws attention to the hearty good will attending the writer's attitude (Milligan). Although the form is pres. ind. it is probably a case where the impf. is used without the augment (s. Best; BD, 37). **μεταδοῦναι** aor. act. inf. μεταδίδωμι to share. It is the giving of something by which the giver retains a part and the receiver has a part so that they both share in the matter (von Dobschütz). **ψύχη** soul, life. The word signifies here the life of the individual person which is shared w. another. It is the life of the individual as it is manifested in behavior and refers to the observable totality of Paul's earthly existence (PAT, 346f.). **διότι** therefore, because. The word apparently always has a causal force in the NT (Milligan).

ἀγαπητός beloved. ■ **μνημονεύετε** pres. act. ind. or imp. 9
μνημονεύω to remember. **κόπος** exhausting labor (s. 1 Thess.
1:3). **μόχθος** toil. The word refers to the trouble and pain of
arduous work and the leading notion is that of struggling to
overcome difficulties (Moore; Lightfoot; *Notes*). **ἐργαζόμενοι**
pres. mid. part. ἐργάζομαι to work. There were no paid teachers
in Palestine. It was necessary therefore for a rabbi to have some
other means of income than the gifts that might now and then
be made to him (Morris; s. also the rabbinical examples quoted
by Morris; Best). **πρός**. The prep. is used w. the inf. to indicate
purpose (s. MT, 144; BG, 135). **ἐπιβαρῆσαι** aor. act. inf.
ἐπιβαρέω to place a weight on someone, to be burdensome, to
make demands (Moore; s. also Milligan). **ἐκηρύξαμεν** aor. act.
ind. ■ **ὁσίως** adv. piously, holy. The word describes one's duty 10
toward God (Lightfoot; *Notes;* Trench; *Synonyms*, 328f.; TDNT;
CBB). **δικαίως** adv. righteously. The word indicates one's duties
toward men but it also stresses a righteous life before God
(Lightfoot; *Notes;* Best). **ἀμέμπτως** adv. blamelessly.
πιστεύουσιν pres. act. part. The dat. could be dat. of reference
"in reference to you believers" or it could be dat. of advantage
"to the benefit of you believers" or it could be locative "among
you believers." (For the various views, s. Best.) ■ **καθάπερ** just 11
as, in accordance w. The first part of the word marks comparison
and the last part the latitude of the application. It introduces a
confirmatory appeal to the individual experience of the hearers
(Ellicott; s. also Milligan). ■ **παρακαλοῦντες** pres. act. part. 12
παρακαλέω to exhort, to encourage, to console. The word indicates "to exhort to a particular line of conduct" (Lightfoot;
Notes; TDNT; s. also v. 3). **παραμυθούμενοι** pres. mid. part.
παραμυθέομαι to encourage. The word indicates "to encourage to continue in a course" (Lightfoot; *Notes*). The word is
addressed to the feelings rather than to the will (Milligan).
μαρτυρόμενοι pres. mid. part. μαρτύρομαι to summon to witness, to solemnly charge (Milligan). **περιπατεῖν** pres. act. inf.
to walk, to conduct one's life. The inf. is used w. the prep. to
express either purpose (Morris) or to express the content of the
command or entreaty (M, 219). **ἀξίως** adv. worthily (s. Eph.
4:1). **καλοῦντος** pres. act. part. (For the variant reading of the
aor. part., s. TC, 630; Best.)

■ The second **καί** in the expression "we also" indicates a 13
reciprocal relation between writers and readers (Frame) and
does not necessarily indicate that Paul was answering a letter
from the Thessalonians (s. Morris; Moore). **εὐχαριστοῦμεν**
pres. act. ind. to give thanks. **ἀδιαλείπτως** without interrup-

tion, continually, regularly (s. Rom. 1:9; 1 Thess. 1:2). **παραλάβοντες** pres. act. part. παραλαμβάνω to receive, to receive from another, a t.t. used for the reception of tradition which was conveyed (s. Col. 2:6). **ἀκοή** hearing, report, message (Best). **παρ' ἡμῶν** "from us." The phrase is to be connected w. the part. and indicates the immediate source of the message delivered and received, while the emphatic **τοῦ θεοῦ** "from God" is added to point to its real source (Milligan). The gen. "from God" is therefore a subj. gen. "preceding from God, having God as its author," as its empathic position requires (Lightfoot; *Notes*). **ἐδέξασθε** aor. mid. ind. δέχομαι to receive, to welcome. **καθὼς** just as. **ἀληθῶς** adv. truly. **ἐνεργεῖται** pres. mid. ind. to work effectually, to work efficiently and productively. The word is used to describe the energy and effective power of God Himself (s. MNTW, 46–54; TDNT). **πιστεύουσιν** pres.
14 act. part. ■ **μιμητής** imitator (s. 1 Thess. 1:6). **ἐγενήθητε** aor. pass. ind., s.v.5. **οὐσῶν** pres. part. εἰμί. **ἐπάθετε** aor. act. ind. πάσχω to suffer. The word is used regularly to indicate good fortune (Moore). **ἴδιος** one's own. **συμφυλέτης** countryman. This expression may be in part geographical and include Thessalonian Jews, but it points to a large Gentile element in the
15 opposition (Morris). ■ **ἀποκτεινάντων** aor. act. part. ἀποκτείνω to kill. **ἐκδιωξάντων** aor. act. part. ἐκδιώκω to hunt down, to hunt out, to persecute. The prep. in compound may indicate "to drive out w. the intention of persecuting" (Moore). **ἀρεσκόντων** pres. act. part., s.v.4. **ἐναντίος** oppos-
16 ing, contrary to, hostile toward. ■ **κωλυόντων** pres. act. part. κωλύω to hinder, to prevent, to forbid. The pres. tense would be conative as well as indicating a continual action "they are continually trying to hinder." **ἔθνος** nation, Gentile. **λαλῆσαι** aor. act. inf. **σωθῶσιν** aor. pass. subj. σῴζω to rescue, to save. The subj. is used in a purpose clause. **εἰς**. The prep. is used w. the articular inf. to express purpose (Ellicott; Morris; MT, 143). **ἀναπληρῶσαι** aor. act. inf. ἀναπληρόω to fill up, to fill up to the full. The word indicates "to fill up the measure" of their sins, implying that the process of filling had already begun, drop after drop being poured into the cup of their guilt (Lightfoot; *Notes*). **πάντοτε** always. **ἔφθασεν** aor. ind. act. φθάνω to arrive, to reach. The word could have two meanings here. It could mean "anger hangs over them and is just about to fall on them" or it could mean "anger has fallen on them and they now experience it." (For a discussion of these two meanings as well as the meaning of the aor., s. Best.) **ὀργή** wrath, anger (s. TDNT; CBB). **εἰς**

τέλος. The phrase means either "at last" or "to the end" (Morris).
■ **ἀπορφανισθέντες** aor. pass. part. ἀπορφανίζομαι to 17
make one an orphan by separation. The word could be used of
a parentless child, or of childless parents, and even in a general
sense of any severe deprivation or desolation (Moore), i.e. "we
are like children who have lost their parents" (Lightfoot; *Notes;*
s. also TDNT). The pass. voice points out that the situation was
forced (von Dobschütz) and the aor. tense implies a single action
and not a continued state (Best). **καιρός** time, period of time,
space of time. **προσώπῳ οὐ καρδίᾳ** dat. of reference marking
the true limiting power of the case, the metaphorical place to
which the action is restricted (Ellicott). **πρόσωπον** "face,"
"person" indicates that which the outward connection or relationship is. **καρδία** "heart" indicates the place of the affections
and of the inner connection in love (von Dobschütz).
περισσοτέρως comp. adv. περισσός "more abundantly." The
adv. could have the true comp. force "the more fervently" or it
could be elative "excessively" (s. Frame). **ἐσπουδάσαμεν** aor.
act. ind. σπουδάζω to make haste, to endeavor. **ἰδεῖν** aor. act.
inf. ὁράω to see. **ἐπιθυμία** desire, longing. ■ **διότι** "because" 18
(s.v.8.). **ἠθελήσαμεν** aor. act. ind. θέλω to wish, to desire. The
word probably points to the will which precedes from inclination
(T; Morris). **ἐγώ** "I." This is the first of a number of instances
where Paul speaks for himself alone in these letters (Moore).
Paul's name is used to guarantee the correctness of the "we
desired" (von Dobschütz; for a discussion of the "we" sections
in the Thessalonian letters, s. von Dobschütz, 67f.; Milligan,
131f.). **ἅπαξ** once. **δίς** twice. The two words used together form
an idiomatic expression meaning "and that more than once,"
"several times" (Morris; Best). **ἐνέκοψεν** aor. act. ind. ἐγκόπτω
to cut in. The word was originally used of breaking up a road to
render it impassable and later it was used in a military sense of
making a break through the enemy's line. It was also used in the
athletic sense of cutting in on someone during a race. The general meaning of the word is "to hinder" (s. Milligan; Moore;
TDNT; Gal. 5:7). ■ **καύχησις** boasting. **οὐχί** strengthened 19
form of οὐ used in questions expecting the answer "yes" (s. BD,
220f.). The words "it is certainly you, isn't it?" form a rhetorical
parenthesis interjected into the main sentence to draw special
attention to the position of the Thessalonians (Milligan).
παρουσία coming, presence. ■ **γάρ** "yes, indeed." The particle 20
is used to introduce the answer to a rhetorical question and in
such cases it affirms what was asked, i.e. giving the reason for
a tacit "yes" (BD, 236).

Ch. 3

1 ■ ***διό*** therefore, on which account, i.e. "on account of this very fervent desire, which I was unable to gratify" (Lightfoot; *Notes*). ***μηκέτι*** no longer. ***στέγοντες*** pres. act. part. *στέγω* to cover, to ward off by covering (e.g., a roof covering a house both conceals and wards off), to endure, to bear up under (s. Milligan; Morris; Best). The part. is either temporal or causal. ***εὐδοκήσαμεν*** aor. act. ind. *εὐδοκέω* to be well pleased, to willingly determine, to consider it good (s. 1 Thess. 2:8). ***καταλειφθῆναι*** aor. pass. inf. *καταλείπω* to leave behind, to
2 forsake. The idea here is "willing to be forsaken" (Moore). ■
ἐπέμψαμεν aor. act. ind. *πέμπω* to send. The verb is used w. the prep. ***εἰς*** and the articular inf. to express purpose (Frame). ***τοῦ Χριστοῦ***. The gen. is either subjective or obj. gen. or could indicate both, i.e. Christ is the author and the content of the gospel (Best). ***στηρίξαι*** aor. act. inf. *στηρίζω* to support, to strengthen, to establish. The word has the idea of putting in a buttress as a support (Morris). The inf. is used to express purpose. ***παρακαλέσαι*** aor. act. inf. *παρακαλέω* to exhort, to encourage (s. 1 Thess. 2:11). ***ὑπέρ*** on behalf of, for the advan-
3 tage of (Morris). ■ ***σαίνεσθαι*** pres. pass. inf. *σαίνω* to shake
or wag, used esp. of a dog wagging the tail to allure, to fascinate, to flatter, to beguile, to draw aside from the right path (Lightfoot; *Notes;* Best; Milligan). ***θλῖψις*** pressure, tribulation (s. TDNT). ***κείμεθα*** pres. mid. ind. *κεῖμαι* to lie, to place, used as a perf. pass. of *τίθημι* w. the meaning "to be appointed," "to be des-
4 tined" (s. Best; Milligan; Moore). ■ ***ἦμεν*** impf. *εἰμί*.
προελέγομεν impf. ind. act. *προλέγω* to say beforehand, to foretell. The prep. in compound is predictive and the impf. denotes repeated action (Frame). ***μέλλομεν*** pres. act. ind. to be about to. The word is used w. the pres. inf. to denote a durative fut. ind. "we are going to . . ." (s. MKG, 307f.). ***θλίβεσθαι*** pres. pass. inf. *θλίβω* to put under pressure, pass. to suffer tribulation. ***καθώς*** just as. ***ἐγένετο*** aor. mid. ind. *γίνομαι* to happen, to
5 come to pass. ■ ***κἀγω*** "I also" (Morris). It could also mean "I
actually sent . . . ," or "that is in fact why I sent . . ." (IBG, 167). ***εἰς*** used w. the articular inf. to express purpose. ***γνῶναι*** aor. act. inf. *γινώσκω* ingressive aor. "to come to know" (RWP; s. also ND, 344f.). ***μή πως*** "lest." Used to express neg. purpose particularly in an expression of apprehension. It is used w. the subj. if the anxiety is directed toward warding off something still dependent on the will and w. the ind. if directed toward something which is entirely independent of the will. With the subj. it expresses feared results (s. BD, 188; RG, 988; s. also Gal. 2:2).

ἐπείρασεν aor. ind. act. *πειράζω* to test, to try, to tempt (s.
Trench; *Synonyms*, 278–281). The ind. is used to express fear
regarding a pres. inevitable reality (MT, 99). **πειράζων** pres. act.
part. **κένος** empty (s. 1 Thess. 2:1). **γένηται** aor. act. subj.
γίνομαι. The subj. expresses a fear of an uncertain thing in the
fut. (MT, 99). **κόπος** labor, wearying work (s. 1 Thess. 4:3).
■ **ἄρτι** now, just now. **ἐλθόντος** aor. act. part. *ἔρχομαι* 6
gen. abs. **εὐαγγελισαμένου** aor. mid. part. *εὐαγγελίζομαι* to
bring good news. This is the only place in the NT where the verb
is used without a full and direct reference to the gospel which
is Jesus Christ (Best; s. also Milligan, 141–144; TDNT). **μνεία**
mention, remembrance. Used w. the main verb in the sense of
"to hold, to maintain a recollection." Here it indicates a "kindly
remembrance" toward their former teachers (Milligan).
ἐπιποθοῦντες pres. act. part. *ἐπιποθέω* to long for, to yearn
after. The prep. in compound is directive (s. Lightfoot; *Notes;*
Phil. 1:8; 2:26). The part. further expands the preceding words
and gives an example of their kindly remembrance (Ellicott; von
Dobschütz). **ἰδεῖν** aor. act. inf. *ὁράω*. **καθάπερ** just as (s. 1
Thess. 2:11). ■ **διὰ τοῦτο** "because of this," "for that reason." 7
This is a transitional phrase taking up what precedes, i.e., the
whole of v. 6 (Best). **ἐφ'**= *ἐπί* w. the dat. "because," "because
of." The prep. frequently denotes the basis for a state of being,
action, or result, esp. w. verbs of emotion (BD, 123). **ἀνάγκη**
necessity, distress, affliction. The word is used of outward
calamities or distresses (Milligan). ■ **ζῶμεν** pres. act. ind. to live, 8
"we live once more," i.e., in spite of this distress and affliction
(Lightfoot; *Notes*). **στήκετε** pres. act. ind. to stand, to stand
firm, to stand fast. ■ **εὐχαριστία** thanksgiving, thanks. 9
ἀνταποδοῦναι aor. act. inf. *ἀνταποδίδωμι* to render, to give
back as an equivalent. The prep. in compound implies the
adequacy of the return (Lightfoot; *Notes;* s. also Moore).
ἔμπροσθεν before, in the presence of. ■ **ὑπερεκπερισσοῦ** adv. 10
more than out of bounds, overflowing all bounds, exceedingly,
super abundantly (RWP; Best; s. also Eph. 3:20). **δεόμενοι** pres.
mid. part. *δέομαι* to make a request, to pray. The word embo-
dies a sense of personal need and is very common in petitions
addressed to ruling sovereigns as distinguished form those addressed to magistrates (Milligan; s. also PIP, 19f.). **καταρτίσαι**
aor. act. inf. *καταρτίζω* to fit together, to join together, to
restore, to repair, to equip. The word had a variety of usages
depending upon the context. It was used to reconcile political
factions. It was a surgical term for "setting bones." It was used
for repairing nets (Mark 1:19). It was used of making military

and naval preparations (s. Best; Lightfoot; *Notes;* TDNT). **ὑστέρημα** that which is lacking, deficiency.

11 ■ (For a discussion of the background and form of intercessory wish prayers, s. PIP, 22–44.) **αὐτὸς δέ** . . . "now God Himself." Although this was a conventional liturgical form of address, Paul adds a new depth of meaning and invokes the august majesty and unique power of almighty God, the original Creator and direct Controller of events (PIP, 54). **κατευθύναι** aor. act. opt. κατευθύνω to make straight. The word refers to the leveling or removal of those obstacles which Satan has used to obscure the path (Lightfoot; *Notes;* s. also Milligan). The opt. was often used to express a wish in prayers (PIP, 32f.; s. also M,
12 165f.; RG, 939f.; BD, 194). ■ **πλεονάσαι** aor. act. opt. πλεονάζω to make more, to increase. **περισσεύσαι** aor. act. opt. περισσεύω to cause to overflow. **τῇ ἀγάπῃ**. The dat. could be dat. of reference or locative or perhaps instrumental
13 (Ellicott). ■ **εἰς τό στηρίξαι.** The prep. and the aor. inf. w. the article expresses purpose. (For the meaning of the word "establish," s.v.2.) **ἄμεμπτος** blameless. The prayer gains sublimity in that they must be prepared to stand unblamable in holiness before God as judge, the searcher of the inward motives of men, who tests and tries the hearts of men (PIP, 62; s. also Frame). **ἁγιωσύνῃ** holiness. The word indicates the state or condition of holiness (Lightfoot; *Notes*). **παρουσία** coming, arrival. The word was used as a semi-t.t. for the visit of a king or emperor or for the appearance of a god (MM; LAE, 370ff.; s. also TDNT).

Ch. 4

1 ■ **λοίπον** finally, "as our last matter" (Best; s. also Phil. 3:1). **ἐρωτῶμεν** pres. act. ind. to ask, to request. The word lays stress on the person asked rather than on the thing asked for and it conceives the request in a question form (Milligan; Morris). **παρακαλοῦμεν** pres. act. ind. to beseech, to exhort. **ἵνα** "that." The word introduces the content of the request. **καθώς** just as. **παρελάβετε** aor. act. ind. παραλαμβάνω to receive, to receive from another, to receive tradition or teaching (s. Col. 2:6). **δεῖ** it is necessary. **περιπατεῖν** pres. act. inf. to walk, to walk about, to conduct one's life. **ἀρέσκειν** pres. act. inf. to please. The pres. inf. emphasizes the continual or habitual action (s. 1 Thess. 2:4). **περισσεύητε** pres. act. subj. περισσεύω to overflow, to abound. **μᾶλλον** more, still more. It is the intensive use of the
2 word (Milligan; s. also Moore). ■ **παραγγελία** order, command, instruction. The word often denotes a "word of command" received from a superior officer that it may be passed on

to others. Here the pl. points to special precepts or rules of living,
which the writers had laid down when in Thessalonica, and in
which they had referred to the Lord Jesus as the medium
through whom alone they could be carried into effect (Milligan).
ἐδώκαμεν aor. act. ind. δίδωμι to give. ■ **ἁγιασμός** sanctifica- 3
tion. The process of becoming holy (Moore). **ἀπέχεσθαι** pres.
mid. inf. to hold one's self from, to abstain. The inf. is explanatory defining the neg. side of sanctification (Ellicott). **πορνεία**
sexual sin, illicit sexual activity. Sex was often linked to pagan
religious practice (Best; s. also TDNT; Lightfoot; *Notes*). ■ 4
εἰδέναι perf. act. inf. οἶδα to know. The verb was often used to
describe "know how," the possession of knowledge or skill
necessary to accomplish a desired goal (ND, 347). The word
might mean in this context "to respect" (Frame). **σκεῦος** vessel.
In this context the word could mean either "body" or more
likely "life" (s. Best; Morris; TDNT; T). **κτᾶσθαι** pres. mid. inf.
to acquire. Although the perf. generally means "to possess"
some examples from the papyri indicate the word could also
mean "possess" in the pres. (MM; Milligan; TDNT; Morris). It
is possible that the word reflects a Heb. idiom and has the sense
"to possess a woman sexually" (Best; TDNT). ■ **πάθος** passion. 5
ἐπιθυμία lust, desire. Paul does not forbid desire as a natural
impulse but a "passion of lust," "lustful passion," i.e., a condition
where sense has been converted into the ruling principle or into
passion (Lünemann). **καθάπερ** just as (s. 1 Thess. 2:11). **ἔθνος**
Gentile. **εἰδότα** perf. act. part. οἶδα. ■ **ὑπερβαίνειν** to go 6
beyond, to exceed the proper limits, to transgress. With the acc.
of a person the verb has the sense of "to get the better of, to
override" (Lightfoot; *Notes*). The inf. may be used to express
results or purpose or it may be used parallel to the other inf. in
the section (s. Frame; Best). **πλεονεκτεῖν** pres. act. inf. to claim
more, to have more than one's due, to defraud, to selfishly attempt to gain more at all costs and w. all means disregarding
others and their rights (Moore; TDNT; NTW, 97ff.; CBB).
πρᾶγμα matter. In this case it could mean "in matters of sex"
(TDNT; Best). **ἔκδικος** one who carries out that which is right,
avenger. The word was used in the papyri for the office of an
official legal representative (MM; Preisigke I, 443; III, 110; Milligan). The word may be a compound developed from a prep.
phrase which had the meaning "just as *after* a legal decision" and
the word would thus be one who carries out a sentence (MH,
311). **προείπαμεν** aor. act. ind. προλέγω to say previously, to
say beforehand. The word is not used here in the sense of
"prophesy, predict" (Best). **διεμαρτυράμεθα** aor. mid. ind.

διαμαρτύρομαι to solemnly declare. The prep. in compound
7 has the idea of "thoroughly" (MH, 302). ■ **ἐκάλεσεν** aor. act.
ind. καλέω to call. **ἀκαθαρσία** uncleanness, filthiness, impurity. The prep. used. w. the noun has the meaning "for the purpose
of" (Moore). **ἐν**. The prep. indicates the state of holiness result-
8 ing from the calling (Frame). ■ **τοιγαροῦν** for that very reason
then, therefore (BAG; for its position in usage, s. Blomqvist,
130). **ἀθετῶν** pres. act. part. ἀθετέω lit. "to do away w. what
has been laid down," to reject, to set aside, to spurn, to despise
(Milligan; Frame). **διδόντα** pres. act. part. The pres. tense describes the continual or the continually repeated action.
9 ■ **χρεία** need. **θεοδίδακτος** taught of God. The word
points not so much to "one divine communication" as to "a
divine relationship" established between believers and God:
hence, it is as those who have been born of God, and whose
hearts are in consequence filled by God's Spirit that the Thessalonians on their part can no longer help loving (Milligan). (For
the verbal adj. w. this ending, s. M 221; MH, 370; and for the
compound having an instrumental sense "God-taught," s. MH,
10 271.) **ἀλλήλους** reciprocal pron. "one another." ■ **καὶ γάρ** "for
also, for indeed." The phrase marks this statement as an advance
upon the preceding one. "You are not only taught the lesson, but
you also practice it" (Lightfoot; *Notes*). **μᾶλλον** more (s.v.1).
11 ■ **φιλοτιμεῖσθαι** pres. mid. inf. to make it one's ambition, to be
zealous, to strive eagerly (Milligan). **ἡσυχάζειν** pres. act. inf. to
be at rest, to be quiet, to remain silent, i.e., "to live quietly." The
context suggests that Paul is speaking to those whose brotherly
love expressed itself in busybodying and he directs that these
people should learn to behave and quietly get on w. their own
work (Moore). **πράσσειν** pres. act. inf. to do, to practice. **ἴδιος**
private, one's own. **ἐργάζεσθαι** pres. mid. inf. to work. Although the Gr. generally looked down on manual labor as the
work of slaves and others, the Jews did not have this attitude.
The emphasis here, however, is not on manual labor as opposed
to some other form but upon working as opposed to idling
(Moore; s. also RAC I, 585–590; KP I, 490–494).
παρηγγείλαμεν aor. act. ind. παραγγέλλω to charge, to order, to instruct. In classical writers the word was used of the
orders of military commanders and here brings out the authority
12 w. which the apostle spoke (Milligan). ■ **περιπατῆτε** pres. act.
subj. The subj. is used in a purpose clause. **εὐσχημόνως** decently, becomingly. **πρός** "toward," "w. an eye to" (Frame). **ἔξω**
outside, "those outside" reflects a rabbinic expression and means
anyone and everyone not within the Christian community

(Moore). **ἔχητε** pres. act. subj.
■ **ἀγνοεῖν** pres. act. inf. not to know, to be ignorant. 13
κοιμωμένων pres. mid. part. κοιμάομαι to sleep, to fall asleep.
The pres. tense is probably timeless and denotes a class, "the
sleepers" (Frame; Morris). **λυπῆσθε** pres. pass. subj. λυπέω to
grieve, to pain, pass. to become sad, to be sorrowful, to be distressed. The pres. tense signifies a continuing sorrow (Morris).
λοιπός remaining, here "the others." **ἔχοντες** pres. act. part.
The general hopelessness of the pagan world in the presence of
death is almost too well-known to require illustration (Milligan;
s. also Lightfoot; *Notes;* Morris; LAE, 176–178; s. also Gerhard
Pfohl, *Römische Grabinschriften* [Munich: Ernst Heimeran,
1969]; G. Pfohl, *Griechische Inschriften*, 11–42). ■ **εἰ** "if." The 14
word introduces a condition of the first class, assuming the death
and resurrection of Jesus to be true (RWP). **ἀπέθανεν** aor. act.
ind. ἀποθνῄσκω to die. **ἀνέστη** aor. act. ind. ἀνίστημι to
rise. **κοιμηθέντας** aor. pass. part., s.v.13. **ἄξει** fut. act. ind. ἄγω
to lead, to bring. The prep. phrase is to be taken w. this verb,
"God will bring through Jesus those who have fallen asleep"
(Moore).
■ **ζῶντες** pres. act. part. ζάω to live. **περιλειπόμενοι** pres. 15
pass. part. περιλείπω to leave, to leave behind. The pres. tense
indicates that the action is viewed as going on to the limit of time
designated by the prep. "until" (Frame). **παρουσία** arrival,
coming (s. 1 Thess. 3:13). **οὐ μή** "not in anywise." **φθάσωμεν**
aor. act. subj. φθάνω to precede, to go before. The aor. subj. used
w. the emphatic neg. has the sense of an emphatic fut. ind. (SMT,
78; RG, 929f.). ■ **κέλευμα** command, shout. The word was used 16
in a variety of ways, e.g., it is the cry made by the ship's master
to its rowers, or by a military officer to his soldiers, or by a hunter
to his hounds, or by a charioteer to his horses. When used to
military or naval personnel, it was a battle cry. In most places
it denotes a loud, authoritative cry, often one uttered in a thick
of a great excitement (Morris; s. also Lightfoot; *Notes*).
ἀρχάγγελος archangel. It was a term for those of the uppermost
rank (Best). **σάλπιγξ** trumpet. The trumpet was used by the
Jews in their festival and was also associated w. theophanies and
w. the End and is again linked w. the resurrection of the dead
(Best; s. also TDNT). **καταβήσεται** fut. mid. ind. καταβαίνω
to come down. **ἀναστήσονται** fut. mid. ind. ἀνίστημι to rise.
■ **ἔπειτα** then, following. The word denotes the speedy follow- 17
ing of the event specified upon what has gone before (Milligan;
Ellicott). **ἁρπαγησόμεθα** fut. pass. ind. ἁρπάζω to snatch up,
to seize, to carry off by force, to rapture. The word often denotes

the emotion of a sudden swoop, and usually that of a force which cannot be resisted (Morris). **ἀνάντησις** meeting. The word had a technical meaning in the Hellenistic world in relation to the visits of dignitaries to cities where the visitor would be formally met by the citizens, or a deputation of them, who had gone out from the city for this purpose and would then be ceremonially escorted back into the city (Best). **ἀήρ** air. **πάντοτε** always.
18 **ἐσόμεθα** fut. εἰμί. ■ **ὥστε** therefore. **παρακαλεῖτε** pres. act. imp. s.v.1.

Ch. 5

1 ■ **χρόνος** time. The word expresses simply duration, time viewed in its extension (Milligan; s. also Best; Morris; TDNT). **καιρός** originally, "the fit measure," time. It refers to "the right moment," "the opportunity for doing, or avoiding to do, anything." It is time w. reference to both its extent and character and refers to the kind of events that are taking place (s. Lightfoot; *Notes;* Milligan; Morris; TDNT). **γράφεσθαι** pres. pass.
2 inf. ■ **ἀκριβῶς** accurately, precisely, well (Moore; s. also Luke
3 1:3). ■ **ὅταν** used. w. the subj. "when," "whenever." **λέγωσιν** pres. act. subj. **ἀσφάλεια** safety. The word occurs in the papyri as a law term "bond," "security" (Milligan; MM). **αἰφνίδιος** sudden, suddenly. The word could be an adj., i.e. "sudden destruction comes upon them" or it could be used as an adv. "all of a sudden" (Frame). **ἐφίσταται** pres. mid. ind. ἐφίστημι to approach, to appear, to come upon. It is used of misfortunes which suddenly come upon someone (BAG). **ὄλεθρος** destruction, disaster, ruin. The word is used in the LXX particularly in the prophets w. the meaning "an eschatological destruction" (TDNT; CBB). **ὠδίν** birth pain. **γαστήρ** stomach. **ἐχούσῃ** pres. act. part. used in the expression "to have something in the stomach" w. the meaning "to be pregnant." **οὐ μή** "certainly not." **ἐκφύγωσιν** aor. act. subj. ἐκφεύγω to escape, to escape completely. (For the subj. w. the emphatic neg., s. 1 Thess. 4:15; s.
4 also Luke 21:34–36.) ■ **ἵνα**. Used w. the subj. to express result (s. IBG, 142; BD, 198; RG, 998; MT, 103f.; BG, 122). **καταλάβῃ** aor. act. subj. καταλαμβάνω to seize, to seize w. hostile intent, to overtake, to come upon. Used of the coming of the "day," unexpected by the "sons of darkness" and fraught w.
5 danger for them (BAG). ■ **υἱοί φωτός** "sons of light." The expression "son" followed by the gen. is a Semitic construction meaning "to be characterized by that thing" (Morris; s. also BG, 15ff.; BS, 161–166). (For the use of the term "sons of light" in the DSS, s. 1QM; 1QS I, 9; II, 16; III, 13, 24, 25; John 1:5.)

νυκτός and **σκότους** "of night," "of darkness." The gen. points
to the sphere to which the subjects belong (Milligan). (For the
term "sons of darkness" in the DSS, s. 1QM; 1QS I, 10; John
1:5.) ■ **ἄρα** "therefore," "then." Paul uses this to introduce a 6
new stage in the argument (Best). **καθεύδωμεν** pres. act. subj.
καθεύδω to sleep, cohortative subj. used w. the neg. indicating
a prohibition. **γρηγορῶμεν** pres. act. subj. γρηγορέω to stay
away, to watch, to be vigilant. The word signifies the proper
attitude of the Christian (Moore). The subj. is cohortative and
the pres. tense indicates a continuing attitude. **νήφωμεν** pres.
act. subj. νήφω to be sober, not to be under the influence of
drink. The word points to a condition or moral alertness, the
sense of being so exercised and disciplined that all fear of sleep-
ing again is removed (Milligan; s. also TDNT; Best). ■ 7
καθεύδοντες pres. act. part. **νυκτός** gen. of time "during the
night." The gen. specifies the time within which something occurs, "nighttime action" (MT, 235; DM, 77; BD, 99f.; RG,
494f.). **μεθυσκόμενοι** pres. mid. part. μεθύσκομαι to get
drunk, to make drunk (s. Gal. 5:21; Eph. 5:18). **μεθύω** pres. act.
ind. to be drunk. The pres. tense points to that which generally
happens. ■ **ὄντες** pres. part. εἰμί. **ἐνδυσάμενοι** aor. mid. part. 8
ἐνδύομαι to clothe one's self, to put on. The aor. part. expresses
identical or contemporaneous action in relation to the main verb
(Ellicott; Frame). **θώραξ** breastplate (s. Eph. 6:14). **πίστεως**
and **ἀγάπης** are epexegetical gens. explaining the breastplate
(von Dobschütz; Best). **περικεφαλαία** that which goes around
the head, helmet (s. Eph. 6:17). **ἐλπίδα** hope, appositional to
"helmet" (von Dobschütz). ■ **ἔθετο** aor. mid. ind. τίθημι to 9
place, to destine (s. Best; MT, 55; BD, 165). **ὀργή** wrath, anger.
περιποίησις obtaining, acquiring (Morris; Moore). **διά** w. the
gen. "through." The phrase is to be taken w. "the obtaining of
salvation" (von Dobschütz). ■ **ἀποθανόντος** aor. act. part. 10
ἀποθνήσκω to die. **περί** for. (For the prep. in relation to the
death of Christ as compared to other prep., s. IBG, 63; M, 105;
BG, 96.) **εἴτε** whether. It is used as an alternative condition of
a 3rd-class conditional clause w. the pres. subj. (s. RWP; RG,
1017; BD, 187). **ζήσωμεν** aor. act. subj. ζάω to live. The aor.
points to this "life" as a definite fact secured to us by the equally
definite death of our Lord (Milligan). ■ **διό** therefore. 11
παρακαλεῖτε pres. act. imp. παρακαλέω to encourage, to
comfort (s. 1 Thess. 2:12). **ἀλλήλους** one another. **οἰκοδομεῖτε**
pres. act. imp. οἰκοδομέω to build up, to edify. **καθώς** just as.

■ **ἐρωτυμεν** pres. act. ind. to ask, to request (s. 1 Thess. 12
4:1). **εἰδέναι** perf. act. inf. οἶδα (s. ND, 344ff.). **κοπιῶντας**

pres. act. part. κοπιάω to grow weary, to work w. effort. The word refers to both bodily and mental labor (Milligan; s. also 1 Thess. 1:3). **προϊσταμένους** pres. mid. part. προΐστημι to stand before someone. The word has two possible meanings either "to preside, to lead, to direct"; or "to protect, to care for" (s. Best; TDNT; MM). **νουθετοῦντας** pres. act. part. νουθετέω to put one in mind, to advise, to warn, to admonish. The word is used for the admonition and correction of those who are in
13 error (Moore; TDNT; s. also Col. 1:28). ■ **ἡγεῖσθαι** pres. mid. inf. to consider, to esteem (Morris; for examples in the papyri, s. MM). **ὑπερεκπερισσῶς** adv. exceedingly, very highly (Moore; s. also 1 Thess. 3:10). **εἰρηνεύετε** pres. act. imp. εἰρηνεύω to exercise peace, to be at peace. Verbs w. this suf. are often causative or connote the possession of a quality and this
14 quality sometimes passes to that of action (s. MH, 399f.). ■ **παρακαλέω** pres. act. ind. (s. 1 Thess. 2:12). **νουθετεῖτε** pres. act. imp. s.v.12. **ἄτακτος** without rank, out of rank, disorderly. The word was primarily a military term used of the soldier who is out of step or out of rank or the army moving in disarray. It then was used more generally of whatever is out of order. In the pres. passage the special reference would seem to be the idleness and neglect of duty which characterized certain members of the Thessalonian church in view of the shortly expected *parousia* (Milligan, esp. 152–154; Morris; Best). **παραμυθεῖσθε** pres. mid. imp. παραμυθέομαι to encourage (s. 1 Thess. 2:12). **ὀλιγόψυχος** fainthearted, worried, discouraged, fearful (Best). **ἀντέχεσθε** pres. mid. imp. ἀντέχομαι to lay hold of, to hold firmly to. (For this as well as examples from the papyri, s. Milligan; MM.) **ἀσθενής** without strength, weak. The word probably refers to those who are morally or spiritually weak (Best). **μακροθυμεῖτε** pres. act. imp. μακροθυμέω to be longsuffering. It indicates not giving way to a short or quick temper toward those who fail, but being patient and considerate of them (Milli-
15 gan; s. also TDNT; NTW, 83ff.; Trench; *Synonyms*, 195). ■ **ὁρᾶτε** pres. act. imp. to see, to see to it. The combination of 2nd and 3rd per. in this construction conveys the idea that the whole group is being held responsible for the conduct of each individual. They are not only to abstain from retaliation, but to see that none of their number retaliates (Morris; s. also Frame). **μή** "that," "lest." The neg. is used in an expression of apprehension and the subj. indicates that anxiety is directed toward warding off something still dependent on the will (BD, 188; s. also MT, 98). **ἀντί** w. the gen. "instead of," "in return for." **ἀποδῷ** aor. act. subj. ἀποδίδωμι to give back, to pay back. **πάντοτε** always.

διώκετε pres. act. imp. διώκω to hunt, to pursue, to seek eagerly
(Best).
■ **χαίρετε** pres. act. imp. χαίρω to rejoice. The pres. tense 16
calls for a continual attitude of rejoicing. ■ **ἀδιαλείπτως** adv. 17
without interruption, unceasingly, constantly. The word was
used of that which was continually and repeatedly done; e.g., the
uninterrupted necessary payment of hard taxes; the continual
service or ministry of an official; a continual uninterrupted
cough (Preisigke; MM); repeated military attacks (Josephus,
Jewish Wars I, 252); the continual failing of a military effort
(Josephus, *Jewish Wars* III, 241); the regular and consistent
production of fruit (Josephus, *Jewish Wars* III, 519).
προσεύχεσθε pres. mid. imp. προσεύχομαι to pray. This is
the more comprehensive term for prayer and can include the
other words for prayer (Morris; s. also TDNT). ■ **ἐν παντί** "in 18
every circumstance." This includes even in persecutions and
trials (Milligan). **εὐχαριστεῖτε** pres. act. imp. εὐχαριστέω to
give thanks (s. Col. 3:17). **τοῦτο** "this." Grammatically it could
refer to the last injunction only but it is more likely that Paul
means all three commands to be regarded as a unity (Moore).
■ **σβέννυτε** pres. act. imp. σβέννυμι to put out (a fire), to 19
quench. ■ **προφητεία** prophecy. The gift of speaking for God. 20
ἐξουθενεῖτε pres. act. imp. ἐξουθενέω to consider as nothing,
to make absolutely nothing of, to downgrade, to despise (s. Morris). ■ **πάντα** "all things." Here it is unlimited and refers to "all 21
things whatsoever" (Lightfoot; *Notes*). **δοκιμάζετε** pres. act.
imp. δοκιμάζω to approve after testing (s. 1 Thess. 2:4).
κατέχετε pres. act. imp. κατέχω to hold fast, to lay hold of, to
take possession of (s. MM; Milligan, 155–157). ■ **εἶδος** visible 22
form, outward show. The word could also be used in the sense
of "kind," "species," "class" (Milligan). **πονηροῦ** evil. The
word could be taken either as an adj. or as a noun (s. Ellicott;
Morris). **ἀπέχεσθε** pres. mid. imp. ἀπέχομαι to hold one's self
from, to abstain (s. 1 Thess. 4:3).
■ **ἁγιάσαι** aor. act. opt. ἁγιάζω to sanctify. (For the use 23
of the opt. in prayers to express a wish, s. PIP, 32f.) **ὁλοτελής**
wholly, entirely, "quite completely." The word not only implies
entirety, but involves the further idea of completion (Lightfoot;
Notes; s. also Moore). **ὁλόκληρος** whole, complete, undamaged,
intact (BAG). The point is that no part of the Christian personality should be lacking in consecration (Frame). (For the possible
construction of the entire v., s. PIP, 39ff.; Best.) **ἀμέμπτως** adv.
blamelessly. **παρουσία** arrival, coming (s. 1 Thess. 3:13).
τηρηθείη aor. pass. opt. τηρέω to keep. The word has a sense

24 of protecting, watching over, and guarding (Moore). ■ **καλῶν**
pres. act. part. **ποιήσει** fut. act. ind.
25 ■ **προσεύχεσθε** pres. mid. imp., s.v.17.
26 ■ **ἀσπάσασθε** aor. mid. imp. ἀσπάζομαι to greet.
φίλημα kiss. The kiss was used in the ancient world as a form
27 of greeting (s. Best; Moore; TDNT; 1 Cor. 16:20). ■ **ἐνορκίζω**
to adjure, to cause someone to swear by something, to put someone on their oath (BAG; Morris). The verb is followed by the inf. (s. BD, 199f.) and the one by whom the oath is sworn is in the acc. (BD, 83; RG, 483f.). **ἀναγνωσθῆναι** aor. pass. inf. ἀναγινώσκω to read. From the context it is clear that it is a "public" reading or a reading "aloud" (Milligan). **ἐπιστολή** letter.

2 THESSALONIANS

Ch. 1

εὐχαριστεῖν pres. act. inf. to give thanks (s. Col. 3:17; s. 3
also P.T. O'Brien, "Thanksgiving and the Gospel in Paul," NTS, 21 [October, 1974], 144–155). *ὀφείλομεν* pres. act. ind. to be obligated, ought. The word implies a special, personal obligation rather than one arising out of the nature of things (Best); "we owe it to God" (Moore). (For parallels to the necessity and propriety of giving thanks esp. in the midst of persecution, s. Roger D. Aus, "The Liturgical Background of the Necessity and Propriety of Giving Thanks According to II Thess. 1:3," JBL, 92 [September, 1973], 432–438.) *πάντοτε* always. *καθώς* just as. The word is slightly causal and resumes and explains the obligation to give thanks (Frame). *ἄξιον* fitting. The word indicates that this thanksgiving is also appropriate in the circumstances (Moore). *ὑπεραυξάνει* pres. act. ind. to grow abundantly, to grow over and beyond. It is a figure of the tree of faith growing above measure (RWP). The prep. in compound intensifies and magnifies the normal meaning of the word (Best; MH, 326). *πλεονάζει* pres. act. ind. to increase (s. 1 Thess. 3:12). *ἑκάστου*
each one. ■ *ὥστε* used w. the inf. to express results. *αὐτοὺς* 4
ἡμᾶς "we ourselves." The words are emphatic and may form a contrast. (For the various interpretations, s. Best.) *ἐγκαυχᾶσθαι* pres. mid. inf. to boast. The inf. is used to express results. *ἐν ταῖς ἐκκλησίαις*. The prep. may be used for the normal dat.; i.e., "to the churches" but it is also possible that it has its normal local meaning "within the churches," "among the churches" (s. MT, 264). *ὑπέρ* concerning. *ὑπομονή* patience, endurance. The word indicates a "remaining under"; i.e., "bearing up under" difficult circumstances. It is the Spirit which can bear things, not simply w. resignation, but w. blazing hope. It is not the patience which grimly waits for the end, but the patience which radiantly hopes for the dawn (NTW, 60; s. also TDNT; CBB). *διωγμός* persecution. *θλῖψις* pressure, tribulation. The former is a special term for external persecutions inflicted by the enemies of the gospel; the latter is more general, and denotes tribulation of any kind (Lightfoot; *Notes*). *ἀνέχεσθε* pres. mid.

ind. to hold one's self up, to endure (MH, 295). The pres. tense indicates that trouble did not end for the converts w. the expul-
5 sion of the missionaries (Moore). ■ **ἔνδειγμα** evidence, proof. The ending of the word denotes strictly a result which has been reached, "a thing proved," but frequently in similar cases where the abstract gives place to the concrete the word can hardly be distinguished from "evidence," the actual proof by an appeal to facts (Milligan; but s. Lightfoot; *Notes*). **κρίσις** judging, judgment. **καταξιωθῆναι** aor. pass. inf. καταξιόω to consider or declare worthy. The strengthened form of the verb means "to declare to be worthy," "to deem worthy" (Morris). **ὑπέρ** for, "for the sake of which," "in the name of which," "in the interest of which" (Moore; Morris). **πάσχειν** pres. act. ind. to suffer. The pres. tense denotes the sufferings are still going on (Frame).
6 ■ **εἴπερ** "if on the whole, provided that." The word introduces a conditional clause which assumes the reality of the condition (RWP; s. also von Dobschütz). **παρά** w. dat. The reference is to the righteous judgment of God. **ἀνταποδοῦναι** aor. act. inf. ἀνταποδίδωμι to pay back again, to recompense. The prep. in compound conveys the thought of a full and due requittal (Morris). **θλίβουσιν** pres. act. part. θλίβω to put one under pressure, to cause tribulation, to persecute. The pres. tense indicates that
7 the affliction was in process. ■ **θλιβομένοις** pres. pass. part. **ἄνεσις** loosening, relaxing. In classical Gr. it could refer to the release of a bow string and so comes to mean relaxation and recreation generally. It is the relaxing of the cords of endurance now tightly drawn (Moore; Milligan). **ἀποκάλυψις** unveiling,
8 revelation (s. Milligan, 149f.; TDNT). ■ **πῦρ** fire. **φλόξ** flame. The flaming fire emphasizes the glory of the appearance of the Lord and it may be a reference to judgment (Best; Lightfoot; *Notes;* von Dobschütz). **διδόντος** pres. act. part. **ἐκδίκησις** vengeance. The word indicates full, complete punishment (Milligan). **εἰδόσιν** perf. act. part. dat. pl. οἶδα (s. ND, 344f.). **ὑπακούουσιν** pres. act. part. dat. pl. ὑπακούω to listen to, to obey. The prep. in compound has the idea of "submission" (MH,
9 327). ■ **οἵτινες** who. The rel. pron. is generic indicating ones who belong to such a class, "such people" (Best; s. also MT, 47f.; IBG, 123f.; MKG, 174f.). **δίκη** the standard to which a thing is to conform, right, law, judicial hearing. It then came to express the results of the law suit, "execution of a sentence," "punishment" (s. Milligan; TDNT; GW, 99; CBB; Preisigke). **τίσουσιν** fut. act. ind. τίνω to suffer, to pay a penalty. The word means "to pay a price by way of recompense" (Moore). **ὄλεθρος** destruction, ruination. The word does not mean annihilation, but

implies the loss of all things that give worth to existence (s. MM;
Best; TDNT; 1 Thess. 5:3). The acc. case is in apposition to the
word "penalty" (RWP). **αἰώνιος** eternal. The adj. lit. means
"age long" and everything depends on the length of the age. In
the NT there is never a hint that the coming age has an end
(Morris; GW, 186–189; CBB; TDNT). **ἰσχύς** strength, might,
power (s. Eph. 1:19). ■ **ὅταν** w. the subj. "when," "whenever." 10
ἔλθῃ aor. act. subj. ἔρχομαι. **ἐνδοξασθῆναι** aor. pass. inf.
ἐνδοξάζω to glorify. The prep. in compound is repeated after
the verb and could have either a local meaning "in" or an instrumental meaning "by means of" or a causal meaning "because of"
(Best). The prep. is used to express purpose. **θαυμασθῆναι** aor.
pass. inf. θαυμάζω to marvel, to wonder, pass. to be marveled
at. The inf. is used to express purpose. **πιστεύσασιν** aor. act.
part. 3rd per. pl. The aor. part. focuses attention on the past act
of belief (Best). **ἐπιστεύθη** aor. pass. ind. **μαρτύριον** witness.
■ **εἰς ὅ** "to this end," "w. this in mind." The expression conveys 11
the idea of purpose (Morris; s. also Moore). **προσευχόμεθα**
pres. mid. ind. to pray (s. 1 Thess. 5:17). **ἵνα** "that." The particle
introduces the content of the prayer. **ἀξιώσῃ** aor. act. subj.
ἀξιόω to consider worthy, to reckon as worthy. **κλῆσις** calling.
The gen. is used after the verb "to consider worthy of."
πληρώσῃ aor. act. subj. πληρόω to fill. Here it has the sense
of "accomplishing" (Moore). **εὐδοκία** good pleasure, resolve,
consent, desire (BAG; TDNT). **ἀγαθωσύνη** goodness, obj. gen.
"delight in well doing" (Lightfoot; *Notes;* s. also Gal. 5:22). ■ 12
ἐνδοξασθῇ aor. pass. subj., s.v.10. The subj. is used to express
purpose.

Ch. 2

■ **ἐρωτῶμεν** pres. act. ind. to ask, to request (s. 1 Thess. 1
4:1). **παρουσία** arrival, coming (s. 1 Thess. 3:13).
ἐπισυναγωγή meeting, assembling, gathering together, collection, collecting together (s. LAE, 103f.). The prep. in compound
is directive (MH, 312). The word is used in 2 Maccabees 2:7
indicating a fut. time when God shall gather His people together.
■ **εἰς τό** w. the inf. is used either to express purpose (RWP) or 2
to introduce the object of the verb (Best; s. also MT, 143).
ταχέως quickly, hastily (Lightfoot; *Notes*). **σαλευθῆναι** aor.
pass. inf. σαλεύω to shake, to cause to move to and fro, to cause
to waiver, pass. to be shaken, to be made to waiver or totter
(BAG). By the aor. tense, the suddenness of the shock is emphasized (Moore). **νοῦς** mind, understanding, the reasoning faculty,
man's power of judgment (Best; s. also TDNT). **θροεῖσθαι** pres.

pass. inf. θροέω pass. to be inwardly aroused, to be disturbed, to be frightened (BAG). The pres. tense points to a continued state of agitation following upon a definite shock received and describes a state of "jumpiness" (Milligan; Morris). **πνεῦμα** spirit. It could refer here to some type of spiritual revelation (Lightfoot; *Notes*). **λόγος** word. A general expression which could refer to prophecy or sermon or any verbal communication (Moore). **ὡς** (before ὅτι) "to the effect that" (MT, 137). **ἐνέστηκεν** perf. act. ind. ἐνίστημι to place in, to stand in, perf. to be at hand, to be pres. The word could be translated "is now pres." and the verb is sometimes contrasted w. verbs expressing
3 the fut. idea (Morris; s. also RWP). ■ **ἐξαπατήσῃ** aor. act. subj. ἐξαπατάω to deceive, to deceive completely, to deceive successfully (MH, 311). The subj. is used w. the neg. to express a prohibition. The subj. of prohibition occurs in the 3rd per., esp. in clauses of fear or warning (DM, 171; s. also SMT, 76). **τρόπος** manner. Used in the expression "in no way" (Milligan). **ἔλθῃ** aor. act. subj. ἔρχομαι. **ἀποστασία** falling away, rebellion, revolt, apostasy (s. Best; Moore; TDNT). **ἀποκαλυφθῇ** aor. pass. subj. ἀποκαλύπτω to unveil, to reveal. The word is very significant, not only as marking the "superhuman" character of the one spoken of, but as placing it in mocking counterpart to the revelation of the Lord Jesus Himself (Milligan). **ἀνομία** lawlessness. The word describes the condition not of one living without law, but of one who acts contrary to law (Milligan; s. also Best; for a discussion of the antichrist, s. ZPEB I, 179–181; for the Jewish teaching regarding the antichrist named Armilos who was identified w. the Christ of Christianity, s. SB III, 637–640). The gen. is of Semitic influence and is used as an adj. describing the main quality or character (s. BG, 14f.; MT, 208; Best). **υἱός** son. Used in a Semitic construction followed by the gen. describing the character or quality (BG, 15f.; MH, 441). **ἀπωλεία** ruin, doom, destruction. The Semitic construction means "he who is
4 destined to be destroyed" (Moore; Best). ■ **ἀντικείμενος** pres. mid. part. ἀντίκειμαι to lie against, to oppose. The pres. part. indicates a constant opposing as habitual or as a life style. **ὑπεραιρόμενος** pres. mid. part. ὑπεραίρω to lift up, mid. to lift one's self up, to exalt one's self, to exalt one's self exceedingly, to exalt one's self above measure (Lightfoot; *Notes*). **λεγόμενον** pres. pass. part. **σέβασμα** an object of worship. The ending of the noun indicates a pass. idea; i.e., "something which is reverenced," "something which is worshiped" and the word includes anything at all that could be worshiped (s. MH, 355; Morris; TDNT). **ὥστε.** Used w. the inf. to express results. **αὐτόν** him-

self. **ναός** temple, sanctuary, the innermost part of the temple
(Best). **καθίσαι** aor. act. inf. καθίζω to sit, to take one's seat.
The inf. is used to express result. **ἀποδεικνύντα** pres. act. part.
ἀποδείκνυμι to show off, to exhibit, to display, to prove, to
nominate or proclaim to an office. Here "proclaiming himself
that he is God" (Milligan; s. also Best). **ἑαυτόν** himself. ■ 5
μνημονεύετε pres. act. ind. to remember, to call to remembrance
(s. 1 Thess. 1:3). The verb is used in a question introduced by
the neg. particle which expects the answer yes, "you remember
don't you?" **ὤν** pres. part. εἰμί. ■ **νῦν** now. The word can be 6
logical introducing a new point, but it is almost certainly temporal in the pres. context (Best). **κατέχον** pres. act. part. κατέχω
to hold down, to restrain. Though many explanations for "the
restrainer" have been offered (s. Morris; Best; Milligan, 155–
157) in light of the supernatural character of "the one holding
back," the use of the masc. article in v. 7 (the n. article here is
because the Gr. word for "spirit" is n.), it is best to understand
"the restrainer" as the Holy Spirit (s. TDNT; and for ancient
interpretations in this regard, s. PGL, 731; Milligan).
ἀποκαλυφθῆναι aor. pass. inf. to reveal, s.v.3. The inf. is used
to express purpose. **καίρος** time, opportunity, the moment appointed by God (Moore; s. also 1 Thess. 2:17). ■ **μύστηριον** 7
mystery, that which was unknown and incapable of being known
by man except through a revelation of God (s. TDNT; ZPED IV,
327–330; Best; s. also Eph. 3:3). **ἐνεργεῖται** pres. mid. ind. to
work, to work effectively. The word is often used of supernatural
working (s. Best). **μόνον** only. **ὁ κατέχων ἄρτι** pres. act. part.
The masc. article refers to the pers. of the Holy Spirit (s.v.6.).
ἕως until. **μέσον** mid. midst. **γένηται** aor. mid. subj. γίνομαι.
The phrase means "to be removed," "to be taken away." (For
this meaning as well as a discussion of the passage relating the
"restrainer" to God, s. Roger D. Aus, "God's Plan and God's
Power: Isaiah 66 and the Restraining Factors of 2 Thess. 2:6–7,"
JBL, 96 [December, 1977], 537–553.) ■ **καὶ τότε** "and then." 8
ἀποκαλυφθῆναι fut. pass. ind. to unveil, to reveal, s.v.3.
ἄνομος lawless, s.v.3. **ἀνελεῖ** fut. act. ind. ἀναιρέω to take
away, to do away w., to destroy (s. BAG). **στόμα** mouth.
καταργήσει fut. act. ind. καταργέω to render inactive, to
abolish, to bring to naught, to put out of commission. **ἐπιφάνεια**
manifestation, glorious appearance. The word usually has some
idea of striking splendor and was often used by the Greeks of a
glorious manifestation of the gods (Morris; T; s. also LAE, 373;
Milligan, 148f.). ■ **κατά** according to. The prep. not only refers 9
to the norm, but indicates the source or cause of the miracle (von

Dobschütz). **ἐνέργεια** work, effective work. The word was often
10 used of supernatural work (s. TDNT). **τέρας** wonder. ■ **ἀπάτη**
deception, deceitfulness. **ἀδικία** unrighteousness, wrongdoing.
The combination of the words "deceit" and "unrighteousness"
is evidently thought of here as an active, aggressive power (Milligan). **ἀπολλυμένοις** pres. mid. part. ἀπόλλυμι to destroy, to
ruin. The pres. tense of the verb perfectized by the prep. has the
sense of inevitable doom and indicates the fact that the goal is
ideally reached and a complete transformation of its subjects is
required to bring them out of the ruin implicit in their state (M,
114f.). **ἀνθ' ὧν** "because" (s. Lightfoot; *Notes*). **ἐδέξαντο** aor.
mid. ind. δέχομαι to receive, to receive gladly, to welcome.
11 **σωθῆναι** aor. pass. inf. σῴζω to rescue, to save. ■ **πέμπει** pres.
act. ind. to send. **πλάνη** delusion, error. **εἰς τό** used w. the inf.
to express purpose (von Dobschütz; Milligan). **πιστεῦσαι** aor.
12 act. inf. The inf. is used to express purpose. ■ **κριθῶσιν** aor.
pass. subj. κρίνω to judge. Here "to be judged," "to be condemned" (Best). **πιστεύσαντες** aor. act. part. **εὐδοκήσαντες**
aor. act. part. εὐδοκέω to have pleasure in, to delight in.
13 ■ **ὀφείλομεν** pres. act. ind. to be obligated, to owe a debt,
ought to (s. 2 Thess. 1:3). **εὐχαριστεῖν** pres. act. inf. to give
thanks (s. 2 Thess. 1:3). **ἠγαπημένοι** perf. pass. part. ἀγαπάω.
The perf. tense emphasizes the continual state. **εἵλατο** aor. mid.
ind. αἱρέομαι to choose, to elect, mid. to choose for one's self.
14 **ἀπαρχή** firstfruits. **ἁγιασμός** sanctification. ■ **εἰς ὅ** "unto
which," "whereunto." The phrase is to be taken w. the whole of
the previous expression "salvation ... truth" (Morris).
ἐκάλεσεν aor. act. ind. **περιποίησις** possessing, obtaining (s.
15 1 Thess. 5:9). **τοῦ κυρίου** possessive gen. ■ **ἄρα** "therefore."
The practical conclusion is drawn from what has just been said
(Milligan). **στήκετε** pres. act. imp. στήκω to stand, to stand
fast. **κρατεῖτε** pres. act. inf. κρατέω to hold, to hold fast.
παράδοσις tradition, that which is passed on. Here it refers to
the teaching of the apostle (s. TDNT; Moore; Best). **ἐδιδάχθητε**
16 aor. pass. ind. ■ **ἀγαπήσας** aor. act. part. **δούς** aor. act. part.
δίδωμι to give. **παράκλησις** encouragement, comfort. Here it
refers to consolation and encouragement in the present (Light-
17 foot; *Notes*). ■ **παρακαλέσαι** aor. act. opt. παρακαλέω to
encourage, to comfort (s. TDNT; MNTW; 128). **στηρίξαι** aor.
act. opt. στηρίζω to strengthen, to support (s. 1 Thess. 3:2).

Ch. 3

1 ■ **τὸ λοιπόν** "finally," "as our last matter" (Best; s. also
Phil. 3:1). **προσεύχεσθε** pres. mid. imp. προσεύχομαι to pray.

The pres. tense means "pray continually" (Morris). **ὁ λόγος** the
word. Here "the word of the Lord." **τρέχῃ** pres. act. subj. τρέχω
to run. The word was used in the LXX of the running of a warrior
in battle and the picture of the word as the authorized messenger
of the Lord is then further applied to the prophets as His "runners" (PAM, 49). Paul uses the word here to express his dominating concern for the free course of the gospel. The important
thing here is the swift progress of the Word—if any image is
intended it is that of the herald in his urgency (PAM, 108).
δοξάζηται pres. pass. subj. δοξάζω to think well of, to have a
good opinion of, to glorify, pass. to be glorified. The triumphant
onrush of the gospel brings glory to God, and in its success His
glory is seen because it is God who spreads the gospel and brings
it to success or glory (Best). **καθώς** just as. **πρὸς ὑμᾶς** "w. you,"
"as in your case" (Frame). ■ **ῥυσθῶμεν** aor. pass. subj. ῥύομαι 2
to rescue, to deliver. Paul uses this term to express his second
request and the word often has the idea of deliverance w. power;
however, the use of the prep. here lays stress perhaps on the
deliverance rather than on the power from which it is granted
(Milligan; s. also Morris). **ἄτοπος** out of place, odd, unbecom-
ing, outrageous. The word was used in the papyri in one instance
to describe those who had pulled to pieces a farmer's sheaves of
wheat and thrown them to the pigs, and in another incidence it
was used of parents who publicly announced their prodigal son's
misdeeds "lest he should insult us, or do anything else amiss"
(that is outrageous) (MM; s. also Preisigke). **ἡ πίστις** "the
faith." The word w. the article may signify "the body of Christian teaching" or it may be used in the sense of "trust" (Morris).
■ **στηρίξει** fut. act. ind. στηρίζω to establish, to support, to 3
make firm (s. 1 Thess. 3:2). **φυλάξει** fut. act. ind. φυλάσσω to
guard, to protect. The Lord will also protect them from external
assaults (Milligan). ■ **πέποιθα** perf. ind. act. πείθω to persuade, 4
to have been persuaded, to trust. The perf. tense emphasizes a
state of trust (RWP; s. also Phil. 1:6). **παραγγέλλω** pres. act.
ind. to command, to charge, to instruct. (For the noun, s. 1
Thess. 4:2.) **ποιήσετε** fut. ind. act. ■ **κατευθύναι** pres. act. opt. 5
κατευθύνω to make straight, to guide (s. 1 Thess. 3:11).

■ **στέλλέσθαι** pres. mid. inf. The word originally meant 6
"to get ready," "to equip," esp. referring to equipping an army
for an expedition or for sailing. Then it came to mean "to bring
together" or "to gather up"—as for instance one gathers or tucks
up clothes and from this comes the sense of an inner gathering
up or withdrawl, and so of "flinching" and "avoiding." Here it
is withdrawl from brethren who are out of step (Moore; s. also

Milligan). **περιπατοῦντος** pres. act. part. περιπατέω to walk
about, to conduct one's life. **παράδοσις** tradition, teachings
that were passed down. It refers to the authoritative teaching of
the apostle (s. 2 Thess. 2:15). **παρελάβετε** aor. act. ind.
παραλαμβάνω to receive, to receive that which is passed on (s.
7 Col. 2:6; 1 Cor. 11:23; 15:1). ■ **δεῖ** "it is necessary." The word
indicates a logical necessity arising from the circumstances (s.
AS). **μιμεῖσθαι** pres. mid. inf. to imitate, to mimic (s. 1 Thess.
1:6). **ἠτακτήσαμεν** aor. act. ind. ἀτακτέω to be out of rank, to
be out of order, to be disorderly, to be idle, to be a loafer (s. 1
8 Thess. 5:14; Best). ■ **δωρέαν** freely, "without paying," "gratis."
One example in the papyri speaks of labor or work as "gratis or
at reduced wages" (s. Milligan; MM; Moore). **ἐφάγομεν** aor.
act. ind. ἐσθίω to eat. The phrase "to eat bread" is evidently a
semitism and means "to get a living" (Morris). **κόπος** toil, working until one is weary. **μόχθος** labor, toil, hardship in working.
(For these two words, s. 1 Thess. 2:9; AS.) **ἐργαζόμενοι** pres.
mid. part. ἐργάζομαι to work, to work energetically.
ἐπιβαρῆσαι aor. act. inf. ἐπιβαρέω to be heavy, to be burden-
9 some (s. 1 Thess. 2:9). ■ **τύπος** type, example (s. 1 Thess. 1:7;
TDNT). **δῶμεν** aor. act. subj. δίδωμι. Subjunctive used to ex-
10 press purpose. ■ **καί** "also"; i.e., "not only did we set before you
our own example, but we gave you a positive precept to this
effect, when at Thessalonica" (Lightfoot; *Notes*). **ἦμεν** impf. act.
ind. εἰμί. The impf. indicates continuing action in the past time
for Paul had repeatedly used this injunction in his preaching
(Morris). **ὅτι** recitative use and equivalent to quotation marks in
a direct quote (RWP). **ἐσθιέτω** pres. act. imp. 3rd-per. sing. (s.
11 Best; Moore). ■ **περιεργαζομένους** pres. mid. part.
περιεργάζομαι to work around, to waste one's energy, to be a
busybody. Paul uses here a play on words "busybodies instead
of busy." These people were not simply idle, they were meddling
12 in the affairs of others (Morris; Best; Moore). ■ **τοιοῦτος** "such
ones." **παρακαλέω** pres. act. ind. to urge, to exhort. **ἡσυχία**
quietness, calmness. The expression suggests a manner of life
which is to characterize an activity and signifies the calm and
contentment which are the opposite of busybodying (Moore).
13 **ἐσθίωσιν** pres. act. subj. ■ **ἐγκακήσητε** aor. act. subj.
ἐγκακέω to behave badly in, to be cowardly, to lose courage, to
faint (RWP; s. also Luke 18:1; Gal. 6:9). The aor. subj. is used
w. the neg. in a prohibition in which the aor. is ingressive and
the prohibition is used to forbid a thing not yet done (RG, 852).
καλοποιοῦντες pres. act. part. καλαποιέω to do good, to do
the noble thing. The word "good" carries w. it the thought not

only of what is right in itself, but of what is perceived to be right
and consequently exercises an attractive power (Milligan). ■ 14
ὑπακούω pres. act. ind. to listen to, to obey. **σημειοῦσθε** pres.
mid. imp. σημειόω to mark, to signify, to mark out, to take
note of, "put a tag on that man" (RWP; s. also Lightfoot;
Notes; Moore; MM). **συναναμίγνυσθαι** pres. mid. inf.
συναναμίγνυμι to mix up together, to associate w. someone.
The first prep. in compound denotes "combination," and the
second prep. denotes "interchange" (Lightfoot; *Notes*). The inf.
is used as an indirect command (RWP). **ἐντραπῇ** aor. pass. subj.
ἐντρέπω to turn about, to make one turn about, pass. to put
someone to shame (Moore). ■ **ἡγεῖσθε** pres. mid. imp. ἡγέομαι 15
to consider, to reckon. **νουθετεῖτε** pres. act. imp. νουθετέω to
admonish, to correct (s. 1 Thess. 5:12).

■ **δῴη** aor. act. opt. δίδωμι. The opt. is used to express a 16
wish or desire. **τρόπος** manner, way.

■ **ἀσπασμός** greeting. Paul's greeting in his own hand 17
suggests that the autographs of these letters exhibited two hands, one in the body and the other in the subscription. Paul may have used an amanuensis (Richard N. Longenecker, "Ancient Amanuensis," ND, 290f.). **σημεῖον** sign, mark, token, signification; i.e., the means of authentication. This is the way he indicates that his letters are genuine (Morris).

1 TIMOTHY

Ch. 1

1 **ἐπιταγή** command, commission. The word connotes an order and is used of royal commands which must be obeyed
2 (Kelly; s. also CBB). ■ **γνήσιος** genuine, legitimate, born in lawful wedlock, true. Since Timothy's father was a Gentile and his mother a Jewess, his birth according to Jewish teaching would be illegitimate but his child-relation to Paul was genuine (Schlatter; s. also Kelly). **ἐν πίστει** "in faith," "in the sphere of Christian faith." The stress is on spiritual character, faith in and loyalty to Christ (Lock; Ellicott). **ἔλεος** mercy, compassion, pity. It is the emotion roused by contact w. an affliction which comes undeservedly on someone else. It has special and immediate regard to the misery which is the consequence of sin and is the tender sense of this misery displaying itself in the effort, which only the continued perverseness of man can hinder or defeat, to assuage and entirely remove it (TDNT; CBB; Trench, *Synonyms*, 169).
3 ■ **καθως** "just as." Used in an elliptical construction in which the act of writing is understood as the last part of the construction; i.e., "as I urged, so now I write" (Lock; s. also MM). **παρεκάλεσα** aor. act. ind. παρακαλέω to urge, to exhort. **προσμεῖναι** aor. act. inf. προσμένω to remain, to stay on. The prep. in compound could have a locative sense; i.e., "to remain w. someone" (MH, 324). The inf. is used as the object of the verb "to exhort." **πορευόμενος** pres. mid. part. πορεύομαι to journey, to travel. The part. is temporal "when I was going" and may indicate that he left Timothy enroute for Ephesus and charged him to abide there (Guthrie). **παραγγείλῃς** aor. act. subj. παραγγέλλω to command, to charge, to instruct, to pass on commands from one to another. It is a military term meaning "to give strict orders" and emphasizes that the commanding was to be done authoritatively (Guthrie; Kelly; Ellicott). **ἑτεροδιδασκαλεῖν** pres. act. inf. to teach another doctrine, to teach something totally different (Ellicott). The opponents in the pastoral epistles were not gnostic but rather Jews or Jewish Christians who were teachers of the law,

who taught Jewish myths and genealogies, who forbade marriage and enjoined abstinence from food, who taught that the Resurrection had already occurred and who may have had significant success among the women, esp. because of their teaching about emancipation (s. Robert J. Karris, "The Background and Significance of the Polemic of the Pastoral Epistles," JBL 92 [December, 1973], 549–564; Guthrie, 32–38; PCG, 49ff.; s. also J. M. Ford, "A Note on Proto-Montanism in the Pastoral Epistles,"
NTS 17 [April, 1971], 338–346.) ■ **προσέχειν** pres. act. inf. to 4
turn one's mind to, to pay attention to, to give heed to, to be concerned about, to occupy one's self w. (BAG). **μῦθος** myth, fable, legendary stories, fiction (s. particularly the article by F.F. Bruce in the English edition of CBB; s. also TDNT; Dibelius). **γενεαλογία** genealogy, the tracing of one's ancestors, family tree. In postexilic Judaism there was a keen interest in family trees, and this played a part in controversies between Jews and Jewish Christians (Kelly; s. also Jastrow I, 575; for a lengthy discussion of genealogies in the ancient world, s. RAC IX, 1145–1268). **ἀπέραντος** endless, unrestrained (Guthrie). **ἐκζήτησις** seeking out, speculation, "out-of-the-way researches" (Lock). **παρέχουσιν** pres. act. ind. to cause, to bring about, to give rise to (BAG). **μᾶλλον** rather. **οἰκονομία** administration, office of stewardship; i.e., they do not help them carry out the stewardship entrusted to them by God (Lock; s. also Kelly; TDNT; Eph.
1:10). ■ **παραγγελία** instruction, command, s.v.3. **συνείδησις** 5
conscience. The word indicates "self-judgment" (Guthrie; s. also Rom. 2:15; PAT, 458f.). **ἀνυπόκριτος** without hypocrisy (s. 2
Cor. 6:6). ■ **ἀστοχήσαντες** aor. act. part. ἀστοχέω to miss the 6
mark, to swerve, to fail to aim at. The word indicates "taking no pains to aim at the right path" (Lock; Kelly). **ἐξετράπησαν** aor. pass. ind. ἐκτρέπομαι to turn or twist aside, to turn away. The word was used as a medical t.t. "to be dislocated" (BAG; s. also MM). **ματαιολογία** vain or useless talk, idle chatter, empty
argument (Kelly; MM). ■ **θέλοντες** pres. act. part. The part. 7
could be concessive "although they desire." **νομοδιδάσκαλος** law teachers, a term from Judaism (s. Luke 5:17; Acts 5:34). They sought popularity not only in their subtle and detailed exegesis, but also in a strict legalism and ascetic demands (Jeremias). **νοοῦντες** pres. act. part. νοέω to understand, to comprehend. The pres. tense w. the neg. stresses their continuing inability to understand. The part. has a slight antithetical or perhaps even concessive force (Ellicott). **διαβεβαιοῦνται** pres. mid. ind. to confidently affirm, to strongly affirm, to speak confidently, to insist. The verb means "to make asseveration, or to

give one's opinion in a firm, dogmatic tone" (BAG; Fairbairn). The prep. in compound has the meaning "thoroughly" (MH, 302).

8 ■ **καλός** good, suitable, useful (s. CBB; TDNT). **νομίμως** lawfully; i.e., agreeably to the design of the law (Ellicott). **χρῆται** pres. mid. subj. *χράομαι* to use, to make use of, fol-
9 lowed by the dat. as the object. ■ **εἰδώς** perf. act. part. *οἶδα* to know. Used to express knowledge grasped directly by the mind (ND, 344). **κεῖται** perf. pass. ind. *τίθημι* to place. Here used for the introduction or enactment of a law "to establish" (Fairbairn). **ἀνυπότακτος** not made subject, independent, undisciplined, disobedient, rebellious (BAG). **ἀσεβής** ungodly, irreverent, irreligious. **ἁμαρτωλός** sinful. **ἀνόσιος** unholy. It speaks of one's lack of inner purity (Ellicott; CBB; TDNT). **βέβηλος** profane. It speaks of irreverent and contemptuous behavior toward the things more particularly associated w. the name of God (Fairbairn). **πατρολῴας** one who kills one's father, one who smites his father. **μητρολῴας** one who smites or strikes his mother. The words speak of a most unnatural and shameful violation of the honor due to the parents whether or not it might issue in fatal consequences and was considered a transgression of the fifth
10 commandment (Fairbairn). **ἀνδροφόνος** murderer. ■ **πόρνος** one who practices sexual immorality, an immoral person (BAG; s. also TDNT; CBB). **ἀρσενοκοίτης** homosexual (s. 1 Cor. 6:9). **ἀνδραποδιστής** one who catches the man by the foot, man stealer, kidnapper. It includes all who exploit other men and women for their own selfish ends (RWP; EGT). **ψεύστης** liar. **ἐπίορκος** one who commits perjury, perjurer. The force of the prep. in compound may be "against"; i.e., one goes against his oath (s. MH, 314f.). **ὑγιαινούσῃ** pres. act. part. *ὑγιαίνω* to be healthy, to be sound. The word denotes the wholesomeness or healthiness of true Christian teaching (Guthrie; s. also Kelly). **διδασκαλία** teaching. **ἀντίκειται** pres. mid. ind. to sit against,
11 to be contrary, to be opposite. ■ **μακάριος** blessed. It describes God as containing all happiness in Himself and bestowing it on men (Lock). **ἐπιστεύθην** aor. pass. ind. *πιστεύω* to believe, pass. to be entrusted w.

12 ■ **ἐνδυναμώσαντι** aor. act. part. *ἐνδυναμόω* to empower, to give strength, to enable (s. Phil. 4:13). The aor. is used because the writer's thoughts pass back to the particular time when he received inward strength increasingly (EGT). **ἡγήσατο** aor. mid. ind. *ἡγέομαι* to consider, to reckon, to count. **θέμενος** aor. mid. part. *τίθημι* to place, to appoint. **διακονία** ministry, ser-
13 vice (s. TDNT; CBB). ■ **τὸ πρότερον** formerly, previously, acc.

of general reference of the articular comp., "as to the former time" (RWP). **ὄντα** pres. part. εἰμί. The part. could be temporal or concessive "though I was" (Ellicott). **βλάσφημος** blasphemer, one who slanders God. **διώκτης** one who pursues as a hunter, persecutor. **ὑβριστής** sadist, a violent person. The word indicates one who in pride and insolence deliberately and contemptuously mistreats and wrongs and hurts another person just for hurting sake and to deliberately humiliate the person. It speaks of treatment which is calculated publicly to insult and openly to humiliate the person who suffers it. The word is used in Romans 1:30 to describe a man of arrogant insolence, and pictures one of the characteristic sins of the pagan world (MNTW, 77–85; s. also TDNT; CBB). **ἠλεήθην** aor. pass. ind. ἐλεέω to show mercy, to show compassion and pity, pass. to obtain mercy, to be shown pity (s. 1 Tim. 1:3). **ἀγνοῶν** pres. act. part. ἀγνοέω to be ignorant. Paul is availing himself of the distinction, conventional in Judaism (Lev. 22:14; Num. 15:22–31) and also in the Qumran sect, between "unwitting" and "presumptuous" sins, linking unbelief w. his ignorance. He does not claim that as a result he was without guilt, but mentions the fact as explaining how his career prior to his conversion became the object of God's compassion rather than His wrath (Kelly). **ἐποίησα** aor.
act. ind. ■ **ὑπερεπλεόνασεν** aor. act. ind. ὑπερπλεονάζω to 14
abound over and beyond, to be present in great abundance, to
abound exceedingly. The prep. in compound means "above its
usual measure" and is an attempt to express the superabundance
of divine grace (Lock; Guthrie). ■ **ἀποδοχή** reception, accep- 15
tance, approval. In the koine the word indicates the acceptance
and recognition which someone or something has found (Dibelius; s. also MM). **σῶσαι** aor. act. inf. σῴζω to rescue, to save.
The inf. is used to express purpose. **πρῶτος** first, foremost, chief.
Here the word is used in the sense of "greatest" (Fairbairn). The
verb used in pres. "I am," not "I was." The sinner remains a
sinner even if forgiven; the past is always there as a stimulus to
deeper penitence and service (Lock; s. also Kelly). (Cf. 1 Cor.
15:9; Eph. 3:8.) ■ **ἐνδείξηται** aor. mid. subj. ἐνδείκνυμι to 16
point out, to demonstrate. The prep. in compound suggest a more complete demonstration than the simple verb. It is the laying of the "index" finger, as it were, "on" the object (MH, 305). The subj. is used to express purpose. **μακροθυμία** longsuffering, patience (s. Gal. 5:22). **μελλόντων** pres. act. part. μέλλω to be about to. Use w. the inf. to express the durative fut. (s. MKG, 307). **πιστεύειν** pres. act. inf. Used w. the prep. w. the dat. to mean "to repose one's trust upon" and suggests more of

the state whereas the acc. emphasizes more the initial act of faith (M, 68; s. also Lock). ***αἰώνιος*** eternal, everlasting. The term "everlasting life" emphasizes "life of the age to come" and contains a temporal reference, but stresses the qualitative character. Although Paul regards eternal life as predominately eschatological, he also sees it as a pres. possession of the believer. It is the
17 result of the indwelling Spirit (s. GW, 188ff.). ■ ***ἄφθαρτος*** incorruptible; i.e., immune from decay, immortal (Kelly). ***ἀόρατος*** not able to be seen, invisible.
18 ■ ***παρατίθεμαι*** pres. mid. ind. to place beside, mid. to entrust, to pledge, to deposit w. another. The term here is a banking figure (RWP; MM). ***προαγούσας*** pres. act. part. *προάγω* to go before, to lead before. The phrase may be translated "relying on the prophecies once made about you," or it could mean "the prophecies which pointed me to you" (s. Kelly; Lock). ***στρατεύῃ*** pres. act. subj. *στρατεύω* to fight as a soldier, to war as a soldier. ***στρατεία*** military expedition or campaign, warfare. The cognate acc. or acc. of content; i.e., "to fight a
19 fight" (s. MT, 245; BD, 84f.; RG, 477f.). ■ ***ἔχων*** pres. act. part. to have, to possess (s. M, 110). ***ἀπωσάμενοι*** aor. mid. part. *ἀπωθέομαι* to push away from one's self, to push aside, to reject, to repudiate. The word implies a violent and deliberate rejection (Guthrie). ***ἐναυάγησαν*** aor. act. ind. *ναυαγέω* to make shipwreck, to suffer shipwreck. Paul himself had suffered shipwreck at least four times when he wrote this epistle. He had
20 on each occasion lost everything except himself (EGT). ■ ***παρέδωκα*** aor. act. ind. *παραδίδωμι* to deliver over to (s. 1 Cor. 5:5). ***παιδευθῶσιν*** aor. pass. subj. *παιδεύω* to train through discipline. The word conveys the idea of stern punishment rather then instruction (Kelly). The subj. is used to express purpose. ***βλασφημεῖν*** pres. act. inf. to ridicule, to slander, to slander God, to blaspheme.

Ch. 2

1 ■ ***παρακαλῶ*** pres. act. ind. to urge, to exhort (s. Rom. 12:1). ***πρῶτον πάντων*** "first of all." The words relate not to primacy of time but to primacy of importance (Guthrie). ***ποιεῖσθαι*** pres. mid. inf. to make, to do. The word is used in a causative sense (s. 1 Thess. 1:2). ***δέησις*** intercession, petition. The verb from which the noun is derived had the meaning "to chance upon," then "to have an audience w. a king," to have the good fortune to be admitted to an audience, so to present a petition. The word was a regular term for a petition to a superior and in the papyri it was constantly used of any writing addressed

to the king (Lock; Guthrie; MM; BS, 121f.; Preisigke; TDNT).
ἔντευξις thanksgiving (s. Col. 3:17). ■ **ὑπεροχή** prominence, a 2
place of prominence or authority, used of prominent officials. The word was used in Hellenistic Gr. to indicate the prominent position of a person (BAG; MM; Dibelius). **ὄντων** pres. part. εἰμί. **ἵνα** introduces the result or purpose of the prayer (Lock). (For references to Jewish prayers for those in authority, s. Dibelius.) **ἤρεμος** quiet, tranquil. **ἡσύχιος** still, quiet. **διάγωμεν** pres. act. subj. διάγω to lead, to conduct. **εὐσέβεια** godliness, religious devotion. It refers to the true reverence toward God which comes from knowledge. It is the right attitude to God and to the holiness, the majesty, and the love of God (Lock; MNTW, 66–77; Trench, *Synonyms*, 172ff.; TDNT; CBB; RAC VI, 985–1052). **σεμνότης** gravity. The word denotes moral earnestness, affecting outward demeanor as well as interior
intention (Kelly; Trench, *Synonyms*, 347f.). ■ **τοῦτο** "this." The 3
word refers to the idea of universal prayer for all men (Guthrie; EGT). **καλόν** good (s. 1 Tim. 1:8; Lock, 22f.). **ἀπόδεκτος** acceptable. ■ **σωθῆναι** aor. pass. inf. σῴζω to rescue, to save. 4
Used w. the verb meaning "to wish, to desire" (s. Guthrie). **ἐπίγνωσις** recognition, knowledge, knowledge directed to a
particular object. **ἐλθεῖν** aor. act. inf. ἔρχομαι. ■ **μεσίτης** 5
mediator, go between (s. Gal. 3:19). **ἄνθρωπος** human being, man. The lack of the article emphasizes the character; i.e., "one possessing the nature, and in his work manifesting the attributes,
of humanity" (Fairbairn). ■ **δούς** aor. act. part. δίδωμι. 6
ἀντίλυτρον ransom, the price paid for the release of a slave. The prep. in compound implies an exchange (EGT; s. also Matt. 20:28; Mark 10:45; TDNT; I. Howard Marshall, "The Development of the Concept of Redemption in the New Testament," RH, 153–169; Dibelius). **μαρτύριον** witness, testimony. **καιρός** time, opportunity, season. The dat. is locative "in its due
seasons" (RWP). ■ **ἐτέθην** aor. pass. ind. τίθημι to place, to 7
appoint, to commission. **κῆρυξ** herald, preacher. The herald was someone who had important news to bring. He often announced an athletic event or religious festival, or functioned as a political messenger, the bringer of some news or command from the king's court. He was to have a strong voice and proclaim his message w. vigor without lingering to discuss it. The herald's most important qualification was that he faithfully represent or report the word of the one by whom he had been sent. He was not to be "original" but his message was to be that of another (Victor Paul Furnish, "Prophets, Apostles, and Preachers: A Study of the Biblical Concept of Preaching," *Interpretation* 17

[Jan., 1963], 55; s. also TDNT; CBB). (For the use of the nom. in this construction "to appoint as . . . ," s. RG, 401.) **ψεύδομαι** pres. mid. ind. to lie. (For the import of Paul's statement, s. Gal. 1:20.) **ἐθνῶν** pl. Gentiles, non-Jews. The gen. is obj. gen. **ἐν.** The prep. indicates the sphere in which the apostle performs his mission (Ellicott).

8 ■ **βούλομαι** pres. mid. ind. to purpose, to determine, to will. The apostolic authority is represented in this expression (Bengel). **προσεύχεσθαι** pres. mid. inf. to pray. **τοὺς ἄνδρας** acc. pl. *ἀνήρ* man, male. The word is used here to emphasize the responsibilities of the male members of the congregation. **τόπος** place. The expression is used for public worship (RWP). **ἐπαίροντας** pres. act. part. *ἐπαίρω* to lift toward, to raise up. The most general attitude for prayer in antiquity, for pagans, Jews, and Christians alike, was to stand w. hands outstretched and lifted up, the palms turned upward (Kelly; s. also SB II, 261; IV, 645; DGRA, 16; MM). **ὅσιος** holy. The word stood for that which was in accordance w. divine direction and providence. The word describes the pious, pure, and clean action which is in accordance w. God's command. The hands are holy which have not been given over to deeds of wicked lust (Huther; CBB; Trench, *Synonyms*, 328; TDNT). **ὀργή** anger, wrath. **διαλογισμός** a thinking back and forth, deliberation. The word then took on the meaning doubting or disputing. In relation to prayer in this section the meaning "doubting" is possible (Guthrie) or in relation to the idea of "holy hands" it could have the
9 meaning "disputing," "quarrelsomeness" (Kelly). ■ **ὡσαύτως** just as, likewise. **καταστολή** clothing, apparel. The word could be understood in a wider sense; i.e., "demeanour," "deportment" (MM; Ellicott). **κόσμιος** well-arranged, well-ordered, moderate, modest. **αἰδως** modesty. The word connotes fem. reserve in matters of sex. In the word is involved an innate moral repugnance to the doing of the dishonorable. It is "shamefastness" which shrinks from overpassing the limits of womanly reserve and modesty, as well as from dishonor which would justly attach thereto (Kelly; Trench, *Synonyms*, 68, 71f.). **σωφροσύνη** sobriety, self-control. It stands basically for perfect self-mastery in the physical appetites and as applied to women it too had a definitely sexually nuance. It is that habitual inner self government, w. its constant reign on all the passions and desires (Kelly; Trench, *Synonyms*, 72; s. also TDNT). **κοσμεῖν** pres. act. inf. to put in order, to arrange, to adorn. **πλέγμα** that which is woven or plaited. Here it refers to "hair styles"; i.e., "plaited hair." Both Jewish and Gentile women were noted for

their elaborate hair styles (s. SB III, 428ff.; DGRA, 328–330). In Philo's description of pleasure coming in the guise of a prostitute, he describes such a woman as having her hair dressed in curious and elaborate plaits, her eyes w. pencil lines, her eyebrows smothered w. paint and her costly raiment broided lavishly w. flowers, and w. bracelets, necklaces of gold and jewels hanging around her (Philo, "The Sacrifices of Abel and Cain," 21). **μαργαρίτης** pearl. Pearls were considered to have had the topmost rank among valuables and were considered to be three times more valuable than gold. Pearls were esp. prized by women who used them to adorn their hair, to hang them on their fingers, to use them as earrings, or to use them to decorate their garments and even their sandals (s. Pliny, *Natural History*, IX, 106–123; KP III, 1020–1021; TDNT). **ἱματισμός** garment, clothing. **πολυτελής** very costly, very expensive. The best garments could cost as much as seven thousand denarii and those of inferior quality for commoners and slaves the cost would be between eight hundred and five hundred denarii (the average wage of the working man was one denarius a day). Tarsus was an important weaving center and its garments were classified as some of the best in the ancient world. (For information regarding clothes and the cloth industry under the Roman Empire, s. Jones, 350–364.)
■ **πρέπει** pres. act. ind. to be clearly seen, to resemble, to be 10
fitting or becoming, to suit (AS). **ἐπαγγελλομέναις** pres. mid. part. ἐπαγγέλλω to announce, to proclaim, to profess, to lay claim to, to give one's self out as an expert in something (BAG). The pres. tense emphasizes continual action. **θεοσέβεια** religious, godliness, reverence toward God. The emphasis in this section does not lie on the use of jewelry or clothing, but rather on the fact that true beauty and beautification is not in the
outward appearance (Dibelius). ■ **ἡσυχία** quietness, silence. 11
The word expresses quietness in general (T). (For the relation of this command to the commands of Paul in 1 Cor., s. PWC, 74ff.) **μανθανέτω** pres. act. imp. 3rd per. sing. **ὑποταγή** submission
(s. PWC, 72f.). ■ **ἐπιτρέπω** pres. act. ind. to allow, to permit. 12
The pres. tense emphasizes the continual action and points to an abiding attitude. **αὐθεντεῖν** pres. act. inf. to act on one's own authority, to exercise authority, to have mastery, to be an autocrat, to be dominating (s. AS; MM; Preisigke; Dibelius; LAE,
88f.). **εἶναι** pres. inf. "to be." ■ **ἐπλάσθη** aor. pass. ind. 13
πλάσσω to form, to fashion, to mold, to create. ■ **ἠπατήθη** 14
aor. pass. ind. ἀπατάω to deceive, to trick, to mislead. **ἐξαπατηθεῖσα** aor. pass. part. ἐξαπατάω to deceive completely, to deceive successfully (s. MH, 311). **παράβασις** stepping

over the boundary, transgression (s. Eph. 2:1). **γέγονεν** perf. act. ind. *γίνομαι*. The perf. tense expresses an abiding state (Guth-
15 rie). ■ **σωθήσεται** fut. pass. ind. *σῴζω* to save, to rescue. **τεκνογονία** childbearing. The use of the definite article, "the childbearing," may be a reference to the birth of the Savior (Ellicott; but also s. Guthrie). **ἁγιασμός** sanctification. The word is used here in the act. sense and would refer to the living of a godly life.

Ch. 3

1 ■ **ἐπισκοπή** the office of one who oversees a work, the office of bishop (s. CBB; TDNT; ZPEB I, 617–620). **ὀρέγεται** pres. mid. ind. to stretch one's self out, to aspire to (Guthrie). The verb takes its object in the dat. **ἐπιθυμεῖ** to set one's heart
2 upon, to desire (Guthrie). ■ **δεῖ** "it is necessary." The word speaks of logical necessity according to the binding needs of the circumstances (s. TDNT; AS). Plutarch used the word to describe the character of one who teaches children (*Moralia, The Education of Children*, 7). **ἐπίσκοπος** overseer, bishop, pastor. **ἀνεπίλημπτος** not able to be taken hold of, irreproachable, beyond reproach. The word implies not only that the man is of good report, but that he is deservedly so (AS; MM; Preisigke). **ἄνδρα** acc. sing. "a husband of one wife," "one woman man." The difficult phrase probably means that he is to have only one wife at a time (s. Robert L. Saucy, "The Husband of One Wife," Bib Sac, 131 [July, 1974], 229–240; s. also SB III, 647–650). **νηφάλιος** sober, sober-minded, clearheaded. The word originally connotes abstinence from alcohol, but here it has a wider, metaphorical sense (Kelly). **σώφρων** self-controlled, thoughtful (s. MM; TDNT). **κόσμιος** orderly. It implies well-ordered demeanor, but also the orderly fulfillment of all duties and the ordering of the inner life from which these spring (Lock). **φιλόξενος** hospitable. In his official capacity he has the duty of keeping open house both for delegates traveling from church to church and for ordinary needy members of the congregation (Kelly). **διδακτικός** able to teach, skillful in teaching (BAG; s.
3 also MH, 379). ■ **πάροινος** one who sits long at his wine, one who is a slave of drink (RWP; Kelly). **πλήκτης** not a giver of blows, not given to violence (Kelly). **ἐπιεικής** equity, lenient, kindly, forbearing (s. 2 Cor. 10:1). **ἄμαχος** without fighting, not a fighter, not contentious (RWP; Guthrie). **ἀφιλάργυρος** not a
4 lover of money. ■ **ἴδιος** one's own. **καλῶς** well. **προϊστάμενον** pres. mid. part. *προΐστημι* to stand before, to rule over, to manage. **ἔχοντα** pres. act. part. **ὑποταγή** submission.

σεμνότης dignity, stateliness. It describes the characteristic of the man who carries himself w. the perfect blend of dignity and courtesy, independence and humility to his fellowmen (MNTW, 144; s. also Trench, *Synonyms*, 344f.). The word avoids the suggestion of sternness yet retains the idea of natural respect
(Guthrie). ■ **προστῆναι** aor. act. inf. προΐστημι to rule, to 5
manage, to govern. **ἐπιμελήσεται** fut. mid. ind. ἐπιμελέομαι to care for, to exercise concern for. The prep. in compound is
directive (RWP). ■ **νεόφυτος** newly planted, recent convert. 6
The word was used in a literal sense of newly planted trees (BS, 220f.). **τυφωθείς** aor. pass. part. τυφόω to wrap in smoke, to puff up, pass. to be beclouded w. pride (AS). The part. could be causal or temporal. **κρίμα** judgment. **ἐμπέσῃ** aor. act. subj. ἐμπίπτω to fall into. **διάβολος** slanderer, devil. The gen. could be obj. gen.; i.e., condemnation reserved for the devil; the judgment meeted out for the sin of pride or the gen. could be subj. gen.; i.e., condemnation wrought by the devil; the condemnation brought about by the further intrigues of the devil when a man is once lured into his grasp through pride (Guthrie; s. also Kelly).
■ **ἔξωθεν** outside, "those outside," is a term used for unbelievers 7
(s. 1 Thess. 4:12; Col. 4:5). **ὀνειδισμός** reproach, disgrace, insult. **παγίς** trap, snare. Here the gen. is subj. gen. "the snare made by the devil" (Ellicott).

■ **ὡσαύτως** likewise. **σεμνός** serious, dignified, stately 8
(s.v.4.). **δίλογος** double-tongued. The word could mean "talebearer," suggesting the idea of gossipers (Guthrie; Lock), or it could be "consistent in what one says," i.e., "not saying one thing while thinking another," or "not saying one thing to one man and a different thing to the next" (Kelly). **προσέχοντας** pres. act. part. προσέχω. Used w. the dat. to turn one's mind to, to occupy one's self w. Here "to be addicted to much wine" (BAG). The pres. tense points to an habitual action. **αἰσχροκερδής** greedy of gain. The gain may become shameful when a man makes the acquisition of it, rather than the glory of God, his prime object (EGT; s. also Plutarch, *Moralia, On Love
of Wealth*). ■ **τῆς πίστεως.** The gen. gives the content or sub- 9
stance of "the mystery"; i.e., "the mystery, the substance of which is Christian faith" (Guthrie; Schlatter). **συνείδησις** conscience (s. Rom. 2:15; TDNT; PAT, 402ff.; 458f.). ■ 10
δοκιμαζέσθωσιν pres. pass. imp. 3rd per. pl. δοκιμάζω to approve after testing or examining (s. TDNT; MM). **εἶτα** then. **διακονείτωσαν** pres. act. imp. 3rd per. pl. to serve as a deacon, to minister. **ἀνέγκλητος** without charge, blameless, without accusation, irreproachable. (For examples of this word in the

papyri, s. MM; Preisigke.) **ὄντες** pres. part. *εἰμί*. The part. could
12/13 be conditional. ■ **ἔστωσαν** pres. imp. 3rd per. pl. *εἰμί*. ■
διακονήσαντες aor. act. part. to serve, to minister. **βαθμός** step, base, foundation (for example of a pedestal). The word is used in a fig. sense and may refer to "standing in the sight of God" or it may refer to the repute and influence of the deacons which they would have w. the congregation (s. Guthrie; Kelly). **περιποιοῦνται** pres. mid. ind. *περιποιέω* to make besides, mid. to achieve, to gain for one's self, to acquire for one's self (s. RWP). **παρρησία** speaking all, confidence, assurance, boldness (s. TDNT).
14 ■ **ἐλπίζων** pres. act. part. The part. may be concessive "although I hoped" (Ellicott). **ἐλθεῖν** aor. act. inf. *ἔρχομαι*.
τάχιον adv. comp. *ταχύς* fast, quickly, comp. "more quickly,"
15 "sooner," i.e., "than I at one time thought" (Fairbairn). ■
βραδύνω pres. act. subj. to hesitate, to delay. The subj. is used in a third-class conditional clause expressing that which may be possible (s. RWP). **εἰδῇς** perf. act. subj. *οἶδα*. The word was used to describe "know how"; i.e., the possession of knowledge or skill necessary to accomplish a desired goal (ND, 347f.). **ἀναστρέφεσθαι** pres. mid. inf. to conduct one's self, to behave. The word could well apply to the discharge of official duties and aptly covers conduct expected from, and the mutual relations of, all the groups discussed (Guthrie; Kelly; s. also Lock; MM). **ἥτις** "which indeed," the explanatory use of the indef. rel. (Ellicott; s. also RG, 960). **ζῶντος** pres. act. part. gen. sing. *ζάω* to live. **στῦλος** pillar. **ἑδραίωμα** foundation, buttress, bulwark. (For
16 various views related to this v., s. Guthrie; Kelly; Lock.) ■
ὁμολογουμένως adv. confessedly, by common consent. The word expresses the unanimous conviction of Christians (Kelly; s. also ECC, 129f.). **εὐσέβεια** godliness, piety, religion. The word may perhaps include the thought of doctrine as well as of life (Lock; s. also Kelly). **ἐφανερώθη** aor. pass. ind. *φανερόω* to make visible, to manifest. **σάρξ** flesh; i.e., He appeared on earth as a real man (Kelly). The word does not indicate the nature of natural man which is opposed to God, but in connection w. the OT use of the word it indicates the earthly existence of Jesus (Jeremias). **ἐδικαιώθη** aor. pass. ind. *δικαιόω* to justify, to declare righteous, to vindicate. If the word "spirit" is taken to be parallel to "flesh" the meaning is "declared righteous and shown to be in fact Son of God, in respect to his spiritual nature" and a reference to the Resurrection is implied. If the word "spirit" denotes the Holy Spirit, it means "he was declared righteous through, or by means of, the Holy Spirit" (Kelly; s. also MRP,

154f.). **ὤφθη** aor. pass. ind. ὁράω to see, pass. to be seen, to appear. **ἐκηρύχθη** aor. pass. ind. κηρύσσω to preach, to proclaim as a herald. **ἐπιστεύθη** aor. pass. ind. **ἀνελήμφθη** aor. pass. ind. ἀναλαμβάνω to receive up. The verb is used of the Ascension (s. Acts 1:2, 11, 22).

Ch. 4

■ **ῥητῶς** adv. expressly, clearly, unmistakably, "in express 1
terms." The word indicates that these elements of fut. events
have been distinctly made known (Guthrie; Lock). **ὕστερος**
later, latter, last. **καιρός** period of time, season (s. TDNT;
Trench, *Synonyms*, 209; CBB). **ἀποστήσονται** fut. mid. ind.
ἀφίστημι to go away, to withdraw, to fall away, to become
apostate. The gen. "from the faith" indicates that which they
leave and is used in the obj. sense; i.e., "Christian doctrine,
sound teaching" (s. Kelly). **προσέχοντες** pres. act. part.
προσέχω. Used w. the dat. to give one's attention to, to devote
one's self to, to give heed to (s. 1 Tim. 1:4). **πνεύμασιν** dat. pl.
"spirits." These are evidently supernatural evil spirits who work
through individuals and they stand in contrast to "the Spirit"
mentioned immediately before (Guthrie; EGT; Fairbairn).
πλάνος leading astray, deceptive, deceiving, seducing.
διδασκαλία teaching. **δαιμόνια** demons, s. 1 Corinthians 10:-
20. ■ **ὑπόκρισις** hypocrisy (s. Gal. 2:13). **ψευδολόγος** false 2
speakers, a speaker of that which is not true. This word expresses
perhaps more than "liar," the notion of definite false statements
(EGT). **κεκαυστηριασμένων** perf. pass. part. καυστηριάζω
to brand w. a red hot iron, to sear. The idea of the word may be
that these are people who are in the service of Satan and in
consequence have their conscience stamped w. the brand mark
which indicates his ownership. Another possible alternative interpretation is that their conscience has been "cauterized"; i.e.,
made insensible to the distinction between right and wrong (Kelly). The perf. tense looks at the completed and continuing state
or condition. **συνείδησις** conscience. ■ **κωλυόντων** pres. act. 3
part. κωλύω to hinder, to forbid. **γαμεῖν** pres. act. inf. to marry.
ἀπέχεσθαι pres. mid. inf. to hold one's self apart from, to
abstain. These people may have been those who insisted that the
new age had already been introduced by Christ and they failed
to distinguish the pres. times of refreshing, which the resurrection of Jesus had initiated, from the consummation to be inaugu-
rated by the yet fut. resurrection (s. William L. Lane, "First
Timothy IV.1–3. An Early Instance of Over-Realized Es-
chatology," NTS 11 [Jan., 1965], 164–169). **βρῶμα** that which

is eaten, food. **ἔκτισεν** aor. act. ind. κτίζω to create.
μετάλημψις receiving, reception, sharing. The prep. in compound has the idea of "sharing" (s. MH, 318). **εὐχαριστία**
thanksgiving. **ἐπεγνωκόσι** perf. act. part. dat. pl. ἐπιγινώσκω
to recognize, to know, to know thoroughly. The prep. in com-
4 pound is directive (s. Col. 1:9). ■ **κτίσμα** that which is created,
creation, creature. **ἀπόβλητος** to be thrown away, rejected,
refused. The verbal adj. here has a pass. sense (RWP).
5 **λαμβανόμενον** pres. pass. part. ■ **ἁγιάζεται** pres. pass. ind.
ἁγιάζω to cause to be set apart, to remove from profane or
common use, to sanctify (s. TDNT; CBB). **ἔντευξις** prayer,
request (s. 1 Tim. 2:1).
6 ■ **ὑποτιθέμενος** pres. mid. part. ὑποτίθημι to place under,
to subject (Guthrie). The part. could have a conditional force "if
you suggest" (s. Ellicott), or the part. could be modal. **ἔσῃ** fut.
εἰμί. **ἐντρεφόμενος** pres. pass. part. ἐντρέφω to nourish in. The
metaphor is that of feeding w. the idea of reading and inwardly
digesting and the pres. part. suggests a continual process (Lock;
Guthrie). **διδασκαλία** teaching. **παρηκολούθηκας** perf. act.
ind. παρακολουθέω to follow, to follow beside. The word combines the ideas of "understanding" w. that of "practicing persev-
7 eringly" (Lock). ■ **βέβηλος** permitted to be trodden, accessible,
profane, unhallowed (AS; s. also 1 Tim. 1:9). **γραώδης** characteristic of old women. It is the sarcastic epithet which was
frequent in philosophical polemic and conveys the idea of limit-
less credulity (Kelly). **μῦθος** myth, fable, tale (s. 1 Tim. 1:4). The
"tale" here are such as old women tell to children quite unfit for
strong young men who have been trained to discipline themselves (Lock). **παραιτοῦ** pres. mid. imp. παραιτέομαι to
refuse, to turn away from, to decline, to have nothing to do w.
The word suggests a strong refusal (s. Ellicott; Guthrie).
γύμναζε pres. act. imp. γυμνάζω to exercise. It is not the
self-centered ascetic struggle of the individual for his own moral
and religious perfection, but the training necessary for the unhindered pursuit of God's purposes. Enemies may have accused
Paul of moral laxity since he refused to follow their demands of
abstention, but his exercise was a vigorous development and
application of all his strength and ability that he may serve the
glory of God w. every thought and action (PAM, 174f.).
εὐσέβεια godliness, piety (s. TDNT; CBB; MNTW, 66–77; 1
8 Tim. 2:2). ■ **σωματικός** bodily, that which pertains to the body.
γυμνασία exercise. The "bodily exercise" is a metaphor which
refers back to the errors of the heretics against which the author
has been warning. It is best to see in this phrase not the Hellenis-

tic culture of the body, but an external dualistic asceticism as
propounded by the heretics and reflected in the warnings contained in v. 3 (PAM, 173; s. also TDNT; Jeremias). **ὀλίγος** little,
that which is numerically small and lasts only a short time
(Schlatter). **ὠφέλιμος** useful, profitable. **ἐπαγγελία** promise.
The struggle of Paul and Timothy is not to gain eternal life, but
has as its goal the honor and glory of God, the proclamation and
demonstration of His faithfulness to this promise of life. The
promise of life to all men is the basis and motive for their life's
task (s. PAM, 175ff.). **ἔχουσα** pres. act. part. **μελλούσης** pres.
act. part. μέλλω to be about to, "the coming age" (s. Lane, NTS,
11 [Jan., 1965], 166). ■ **ἀποδοχή** reception, acceptance. ■ 9/10
κοπιῶμεν pres. act. ind. to work hard, to work until one is
weary. **ἀγωνιζόμεθα** pres. mid. ind. to struggle, to exert one's
self. The two words speak of Paul's tremendous efforts and exer-
tions in the proclamation of the gospel (s. PAM, 171–177). The
pres. tense describes the continual action. **ἠλπίκαμεν** perf. act.
ind. ἐλπίζω to hope. The perf. tense implies a continuous state
of hope, i.e., "because we have fixed our hope" (Guthrie). **ζῶντι**
pres. act. part. dat. sing. ζάω to live. The pres. tense indicates
that God is living, and therefore able to give life now and hereaf-
ter (Lock). **μάλιστα** especially.

■ **παράγγελλε** pres. act. imp. παραγγέλλω to transmit a 11
message, to order, to command (s. 1 Tim. 1:3). **δίδασκε** pres.
act. imp. The pres. tense indicates the continuation of an action
and the continual habitual carrying out of the command (s.
Bakker; MKG, 271ff.). ■ **νεότης** youth. **καταφρονείτω** pres. 12
act. imp. 3rd per. sing. καταφρονέω to think down, to despise,
to underrate. In the ancient world a person between 30 and 40
years old could be considered young (Kelly). One rabbi said that
a person at 30 was fit for authority and at 40 he was fit for
discernment (M, Aboth V, 21). **τύπος** type, example. **γίνου**
pres. mid. imp. **ἀναστροφή** behavior. **ἁγνεία** purity. The word
covers not only chastity in matters of sex, but also the innocence
and integrity of heart which are denoted by the related noun in
2 Cor. 6:6 (Kelly). The word refers to purity of act and thought
(Lock). ■ **πρόσεχε** pres. act. imp. s.v.1. The pres. tense calls for 13
a continual action. The verb "to give attendance" implies previous preparation in private (Guthrie). **ἀνάγνωσις** reading. Used
w. the verb it implies a wise choice of the passages to be read;
audible reading; a power of correct exposition (Lock).
παράκλησις exhortation, encouragement (s. TDNT; CBB).
διδασκαλία teaching, doctrine. ■ **ἀμέλει** pres. act. imp. 14
ἀμελέω to be unconcerned about something, to neglect. (For the

pref. as a neg., s. Moorhouse, 47ff.) The pres. imp. w. the neg. could mean "do not immediately . . . ," "do not always . . . ," and "do not continue . . ." (s. MKG, 272). **χάρισμα** that which is a result of grace, free gift, grace gift. It denotes a special endowment of the Spirit enabling the recipient to carry out some function in the community (Kelly; s. also TDNT; CBB). **ἐδόθη** aor. pass. ind. δίδωμι. **προφητεία** speaking for someone, prophecy. **μετά** "with." The prep. does not express instrument or means but merely accompaniment (RWP; EGT). **ἐπίθεσις** placing upon, laying on. **πρεσβυτέριον** assembly of the elders, presbytery. This may be the rendering of a Heb. t.t. which meant "the leaning, or pressing on of elders," which in effect meant, "the leaning or pressing of hands upon someone w. the object of making him an elder or rabbi." In a Christian context it would mean "elder ordination" or "formal ordination to office" (Kel-
15 ly). ■ **μελέτα** pres. act. imp. μελετάω to take care, to practice, to cultivate, to take pains w. something, to think about, to meditate upon (BAG). **ἴσθι** pres. imp. εἰμί "be in them." It is a construction expressing absorption in anything. The mind is to be as immersed in these pursuits as the body in the air it breathes (Guthrie). **προκοπή** advance, progress (s. Phil. 1:12; Gal. 1:14). The expression is a favorite word in Stoic writers of a pupil's progress in philosophy (Lock). **φανερός** clear, obvious, manifest. **ᾖ** pres. subj. εἰμί. The subj. is used to express purpose.
16 ■ **ἔπεχε** pres. act. imp. ἐπέχω to hold upon, to give heed to, to give attention to, to fix attention upon. (For examples from the papyri, s. MM; Preisigke.) **ἐπίμενε** pres. act. imp. ἐπιμένω to remain upon, to continue. The prep. in compound is directive indicating the concentration of the verb's action upon some object (MH, 312). **ποιῶν** pres. act. part. ποιέω. **σώσεις** fut. act. ind. σῴζω to rescue, to save. **ἀκούοντας** pres. act. part.

Ch. 5

1 ■ **ἐπιπλήξῃς** aor. act. subj. ἐπιπλήσσω to strike upon, to strike at, to rebuke sharply. The word contains a note of severity, "to censure severely" (s. MM; Guthrie). The aor. subj. is used w. the neg. in a prohibition and implies that an action is not yet existent and should not arise (MKG, 273). **παρακάλει** pres. act. imp. παρακαλέω to encourage, to exhort. **νεώτερος** comp.
2 νέος young, comp. younger; i.e., "the younger men." ■ **ἀδελφή** sister. **ἁγνεία** purity, chastity (s. 1 Tim. 4:12).
3 ■ **χήρα** widow. **τίμα** pres. act. imp. τιμάω to honor, to show respect. The word would also carry the idea of support in this context (EGT; Schlatter). **ὄντως** adv. from the part. of **εἰμί**

actually, really. Paul means widows who have no other means of
support, who have no opportunity for marriage and who have
given themselves to the service of the Lord (Jeremias; Guthrie).
■ **ἔκγονος** descendant, grandchild (Guthrie). **μανθανέτωσαν** 4
pres. act. imp. 3rd per. pl. The subject of the pl. verb is "such
children and grandchildren" (Lock). **ἴδιος** one's own. **εὐσεβεῖν**
pres. act. inf. to show piety, to show reverence, to fulfill one's
religious obligation (s. 1 Tim. 2:2; MM). **ἀμοιβή** return, recompense (s. MM). **ἀποδιδόναι** pres. act. inf. to give back, to return, to render. Used w. the noun it means "to make a worthy
requittal" (Guthrie). **πρόγονος** one born early or before, parents, forefather, ancestor (s. BAG). **ἀπόδεκτος** acceptable (s. 1
Tim. 2:3). ■ **μεμονωμένη** perf. pass. part. μονόω to leave alone, 5
pass. to be left alone. The perf. tense looks at the continual
condition or state. **ἤλπικεν** perf. act. ind. ἐλπίζω to hope. The
perf. tense and the prep. convey the meaning "has fixed her hope
and keeps it in the direction of God" (RWP; Guthrie).
προσμένει to remain w. something, to continue, to remain w.,
to abide in. The pres. tense emphasizes the continual action.
δέησις request. ■ **σπαταλῶσα** pres. act. part. σπαταλάω to 6
live a luxurious life, to give one's self to pleasure. The word
connotes abandonment to pleasure and comfort (Kelly; s. also
James 5:5). **ζῶσα** pres. act. part. ζάω to live. The part. expresses
contemporaneous action. **τέθνηκεν** perf. act. ind. ἀποθνήσκω
to die, perf. to be dead. ■ **παράγγελλε** pres. act. imp. 7
παραγγέλλω to command, to instruct (s. 1 Tim. 1:3).
ἀνεπίλημπτος without reproach, irreproachable (s. 1 Tim. 3:2).
ὦσιν pres. subj. εἰμί. ■ **ἰδίων** one's own; i.e., the near relatives 8
(EGT). **μάλιστα** especially. **οἰκεῖος** household. It refers to the
members of one's household and refers to one's immediate
family circle (Guthrie; EGT). **προνοεῖ** pres. act. ind. προνοέω
to think of beforehand, to provide for. The object of the verb is
in the gen. (For examples in the papyri, s. MM; Preisigke.)
ἤρνηται perf. mid. ind. ἀρνέομαι to deny. **ἄπιστος** unbeliever, gen. of comparison. **χείρων** comp. κακός bad, comp. worse.
He is worse than an unbeliever because unbelievers perform the
duty (both Jew and Gentile) and because he not only has the law
of nature but the law of Christ to guide him (Lock; s. also JPFC
II, 761; M, Ketuboth V, 8–9; Epictetus III, 18f.). ■ 9
καταλεγέσθω pres. pass imp. καταλέγω to write down in a
list, to enroll. It is a t.t. for being placed on a recognized list or
"catalogue" (Kelly). **ἔλαττον** adv. comp. "less than." **ἔτος** year.
The gen. is gen. of comparison or gen. of quality (s. RG, 516;
BD, 99). **γεγονυῖα** perf. act. part. fem. γίνομαι. The Jews con-

sider that becoming old began w. the 60th year and Orientals regarded it as the time for retiring from the world for quiet
10 contemplation (SB, III, 653; Lock). ■ **μαρτυρουμένη** pres. pass. part. μαρτυρέω to witness, to testify. **ἐτεκνοτρόφησεν** aor. act. ind. τεκνοτροφέω to rear children. **ἐξενοδόχησεν** aor. act. ind. ξενοδοχέω to welcome strangers, to show hospitality. **ἔνιψεν** aor. act. ind. νίπτω to wash. The washing of the feet was a service to visitors which occupied a great place in eastern hospitality. The mistress of the house would act as a servant to the servants of God (Kelly; EGT). **θλιβομένοις** pres. pass. part. θλίβω to put under pressure, to bring about distress, pass. to be under pressure, to be in distress. **ἐπήρκεσεν** aor. act. ind. ἐπαρκέω to help, to aid, to assist, to relieve. **ἐπηκολούθησεν** aor. act. ind. ἐπακολουθέω to follow after. The prep. in compound is directive (MH, 312). The verbs in this v. are used in first-class conditional clauses which assume the reality of the
11 condition. ■ **παραιτοῦ** pres. mid. imp. παραιτέομαι to decline, to refuse; i.e., to refuse to put on the list of widows entitled to special guardianship and sustenance on the part of the church (Fairbairn). **ὅταν** w. the subj. "when," "whenever." **καταστρηνιάσωσιν** aor. act. subj. καταστρηνιάω to feel the impulse of sexual desire, here "to feel sensuous impulses that alienate from Christ" (RWP; BAG). **γαμεῖν** pres. act. inf. to
12 marry. ■ **ἔχουσαι** pres. act. part. **κρίμα** judgment. The meaning is that the widows who forsook their sacred obligation in order to marry would be deserving of censure, for such action would amount to casting aside their first faith, i.e., their pledge of service (Guthrie). **ἠθέτησαν** aor. act. ind. ἀθετέω to set aside,
13 to regard as void, to annul (s. Gal. 2:21). ■ **ἅμα** at the same time. Used here in the phrase "but at the same time also" (BAG). **ἀργός** not working, idle. **μανθάνουσιν** pres. act. ind. to learn. The verb w. a substitutive denoting a profession or occupation was an idiomatic construction signifying "to qualify as such and such" (for example a doctor, wrestler, etc.) (Kelly). **περιερχόμεναι** pres. mid. part. περιέρχομαι to go about, to go around. The word may mean that the younger widows were misusing their opportunities in visitation (Guthrie; s. also EGT). **φλύαρος** gossipy, loose talkers; i.e., babbling out whatever might come into their mind (Fairbairn). **περίεργος** over careful, taking needless trouble, busybodies (Kelly). The word marks a meddling habit, a perverted activity that will not content itself w. minding its own concerns, but must busy itself about those of others (Ellicott; s. also 2 Thess. 3:11). **λαλοῦσαι** pres. act. part. **δέοντα** pres. act. part. τὰ δέοντα "things which are necessary"

w. the neg. "things which are not proper" (s. EGT). ■ **βούλομαι** 14
pres. mid. ind. to will, to desire. Jewish formal law and accepted Jewish custom beyond any doubt agree that a widow's remarriage was both permissible and desirable and she was only required to wait long enough for it to be ascertained that she was not already pregnant at the time of the second marriage. There were, however, in Judaism some groups which considered a widow's abstinence from remarriage to be a pious and proper act (JPFC II, 787–788f.). **τεκνογονεῖν** pres. act. inf. to bear children. **οἰκοδεσποτεῖν** pres. act. inf. to rule over the house, to manage the household, to be master of a house. **ἀφορμή** a starting point, a base of operations, an occasion, opportunity (AS; s. 2 Cor. 5:12). **ἀντικειμένῳ** pres. mid. part. ἀντίκειμαι to lie against, to oppose, to be an adversary. **λοιδορία** abuse, reproach, railing. **χάριν** prep. w. the gen. "on account of,"
"because of." ■ **ἐξετράπησαν** aor. pass. ind. ἐκτρέπομαι to 15
turn from, to go astray, to turn out of the true path (Lock). **ὀπίσω** w. the gen. "after," "behind"; i.e., they follow behind or
after Satan (EGT). ■ **ἐπαρκείτω** pres. act. imp. 3rd per. sing. 16
to help, to assist, s.v.10. **βαρείσθω** pres. pass. imp. βαρέω to burden, pass. to be burdened. The word is used of financial burdens and refers here to financial support (Kelly). **ἐπαρκέσῃ** aor. act. subj. to help, to assist, s.v.10.

■ **καλῶς** adv. "well." **προεστῶτες** perf. act. part. 17
προΐστημι to stand first, to rule. The word means general superintendence, and describes the duties allotted to all presbyters (Guthrie). **διπλοῦς** double. **τιμή** honor (Schlatter), remuneration (Kelly; EGT). **ἀξιούσθωσαν** pres. pass. imp. ἀξιόω to consider worthy, to hold as worthy. **κοπιῶντες** pres. act. part. κοπιάω to work, to labor, to work until one is exhausted. **λόγος** word; i.e., those who preach and teach (Guthrie). **διδασκαλία**
teaching, doctrine. ■ **γραφή** writing, Scripture (s. TDNT). **βοῦς** 18
ox, cow. **ἀλοῶντα** pres. act. part. ἀλοάω to thrash. **φιμώσεις** fut. act. ind. φιμόω to muzzle (s. 1 Cor. 9:9). The fut. is used to express a prohibition and is used in the legal language of the OT almost always as a categorical imp. (BG, 94; s. also RWP).
ἐργάτης worker. **μισθός** wage, salary. ■ **κατηγορία** that 19
which is brought against someone, charge, legal accusation (s. MM; Preisigke). **παραδέχου** pres. mid. imp. παραδέχομαι to
entertain. **ἐκτὸς εἰ μή** "except when" (s. BS, 118). ■ 20
ἁμαρτάνοντας pres. act. part. ἁμαρτάνω to miss the mark, to sin. **ἔλεγχε** pres. act. imp. ἐλέγχω to bring to light, to expose, to demonstrate or prove, to convince or convict someone, to reprove, to correct. Here it may have connotation of refuting

(BAG). **λοιπός** remaining, rest. **ἔχωσιν** pres. act. subj. The subj.
21 is used in a purpose clause. ■ **διαμαρτύρομαι** to charge, to
charge solemnly, to declare solemnly. The prep. in compound
has the idea of "thoroughly" (MH, 302; s. also 1 Thess. 4:6).
ἐκλεκτός chosen, elect. **ἵνα** "that." It introduces the content of
Paul's charge to Timothy. **φυλάξῃς** aor. act. subj. φυλάσσω to
guard, to observe, to keep. **πρόκριμα** a judgment beforehand,
prejudice. **ποιῶν** pres. act. part. **πρόσκλισις** inclining toward,
22 partiality (RWP). ■ **ταχέως** quickly. **ἐπιτίθει** pres. act. imp.
ἐπιτίθημι to place upon, to lay "hands" upon. **κοινώνει** pres.
act. imp. κοινωνέω to have fellowship w., to participate.
ἀλλότριος belonging to another, not one's own. **ἁγνός** pure (s.
23 1 Tim. 4:12). **τήρει** pres. act. imp. τηρέω to keep. ■ **μηκέτι** no
longer. **ὑδροπότει** pres. act. imp. ὑδροποτέω to drink water.
The command to abstain from drinking water exclusively may
have been that contaminated water contributed to Timothy's
indigestion (Guthrie). Epictetus used the word in a positive command "drink only water" to show one's ability in restraint (Epictetus III, 13, 21). **χρῶ** pres. mid. imp. χράομαι to use.
στόμαχος stomach. **πυκνός** often, frequent, numerous.
ἀσθένεια sickness, weakness. (For the text of a memorandum
requesting the purchase of a jar of wine according to doctor's
orders, s. SP I, 396–397.)

24 ■ **πρόδηλος** clear, evident, openly plain, plain before all
(RWP). **προάγουσαι** pres. act. part. fem. προάγω to go before,
25 to go ahead. **κρίσις** judgment. ■ **ὡσαύτως** likewise. **ἄλλως**
otherwise. **ἔχοντα** pres. act. part.; i.e., "those having it otherwise" (RWP). **κρυβῆναι** aor. pass. inf. κρύπτω to hide.

Ch. 6

1 ■ **ὅσοι** as many as. The pron. indicates those who belong
to a particular class or group. **ζυγός** yoke. (For ancient dis-
courses on slavery, s. DC X, XIV, XV; Seneca, *Epistle* 47; s. also
1 Cor. 7:21; Philemon 21.) **δεσπότης** master. **ἡγείσθωσαν**
pres. mid. imp. ἥγεομαι to consider, to reckon, to deem.
διδασκαλία teaching, doctrine. **βλασφημῆται** pres. pass.
2 subj. βλασφημέω to slander, to blaspheme. ■ **ἔχοντες** pres. act.
part. **καταφρονείτωσαν** pres. act. imp. καταφρονέω to think
down upon, to despise. The word means "to treat without the full
consideration due to the other man's station" (Kelly). The pres.
imp. w. the neg. is to prohibit a continual or habitual action (s.
MKG, 272f.). **μᾶλλον** comp. "rather," "more." The word is
intensive and indicates that the Christian master should be
served more; i.e., better (Ellicott; RWP). **δουλευέτωσαν** pres.

act. imp. **ἀγαπητός** beloved. **εὐεργεσία** working well, good
service, good deed, benefit. The word refers to the human kindness not of the masters but of the slaves as shown by their better
service (Lock). **ἀντιλαμβανόμενοι** pres. mid. part.
ἀντιλαμβάνομαι to take part in, to devote one's self to, to
practice. Here "those who devote themselves to kindness"
(BAG).

δίδασκε pres. act. imp. **παρακάλει** pres. act. imp.
παρακαλέω to encourage, to exhort. ■ **ἑτεροδιδασκαλεῖ** pres. 3
act. ind. to teach another doctrine, to teach a completely different doctrine, to teach a false or heretical doctrine (s. Fairbairn).
προσέρχεται pres. mid. ind. to come to, to approach, to attach
one's self to, to consent (Guthrie). The verbs in the ind. are used
in a first-class conditional clause which assumes the reality of the
condition. **ὑγιαίνουσιν** pres. act. part. ὑγιαίνω to be in good
health, to be healthy, to be sound (s. 3 John 2). **εὐσέβεια** godliness (s. 1 Tim. 2:2; 4:7). ■ **τετύφωται** perf. pass. ind. τυφόω to 4
be puffed up, to be proud (s. 1 Tim. 3:6). **ἐπιστάμενος** pres.
mid. part. ἐπίσταμαι to know, to understand. **νοσῶν** pres. act.
part. νοσέω to be sick, to be ailing w., to have a morbid craving
for something (BAG). The disease is intellectual curiosity about
trifles (EGT). **ζήτησις** seeking, speculation. It denotes the
preoccupation w. pseudo-intellectual theorizing (Kelly; s. also 1
Tim. 1:4). **λογομαχία** word war, strife of words. **φθόνος** envy.
ἔρις strife. **βλασφημία** slander, blasphemy. **ὑπόνοια** suspicion, conjecture. The prep. in compound suggests the idea of
thoughts making their way up into the mind (MH, 327). ■ 5
διαπαρατριβή a mutual rubbing or irritation alongside, protracted quarreling, persistent wrangling (RWP; EGT; Kelly;
MH, 303). **διεφθαρμένων** perf. pass. part. διαφθείρω to corrupt. The perf. tense emphasizes the completed state or condition. **νοῦς** mind, understanding. **ἀπεστερημένων** perf. pass.
part. ἀποστερέω to steal, to rob, to deprive. **νομιζόντων** pres.
act. part. νομίζω to suppose. **πορισμός** means of gain. ■ 6
αὐτάρκεια contentment, self-sufficiency. The word was a t.t. in
Gr. philosophy used to denote the wise man's independence of
circumstances (Kelly; Dibelius; s. also Phil. 4:11). ■ 7
εἰσηνέγκαμεν aor. act. ind. εἰσφέρω to bring into. **ἐξενεγκεῖν**
aor. act. inf. ἐκφέρω to carry out of. (For Jewish and Gentile
parallels, s. Kelly; SB III, 655.) ■ **ἔχοντες** pres. act. part. 8
διατροφή food, nourishment. **σκέπασμα** that which covers,
clothing. **ἀρκεσθησόμεθα** fut. pass. ind. ἀρκέω pass. = to be
content, to be satisfied. The fut. probably has an imp. sense as
used in the legal language of the OT (s. BG, 94; EGT). ■ 9

βουλόμενοι pres. mid. part. *βούλομαι* to will, to purpose. **πλουτεῖν** pres. act. inf. to be rich, to be wealthy, **ἐμπίπτουσιν** pres. act. ind. to fall into. The pres. tense indicates that which always or normally happens. **πειρασμός** temptation. **παγίς** snare, trap. **ἐπιθυμία** strong desire. **ἀνόητος** irrational (s. Gal. 3:1). **βλαβερός** harmful, injuring. **βυθίζουσιν** pres. act. ind. to drag to the bottom, to submerge, to drown. The verb is the image of drowning someone in the sea (Kelly; RWP). **ὄλεθρος** destruction. **ἀπώλεια** ruin. The two words are used in the sense of ruin
10 and suggest irretrievable loss (Guthrie). ■ **ῥίζα** root. The pred. nom. without the article emphasizes the character or quality (s. John 1:1). **κακά** evil. The pl. emphasizes evils of all kinds (Kelly). **φιλαργυρία** love of money. (For parallels to this proverbial saying, s. Lock; Kelly; Dibelius; 1 Tim. 3:8). **ὀρεγόμενοι** pres. mid. part. *ὀρέγομαι* to reach out after something, to desire something. The object is in the gen. (s. 1 Tim. 3:1). **ἀπεπλανήθησαν** aor. act. ind. *ἀποπλανάω* to lead astray. **περιέπειραν** aor. act. ind. *περιπείρω* to pierce completely (RWP).
11 ■ **φεῦγε** pres. act. imp. *φεύγω* to flee. **δίωκε** pres. act. imp. *διώκω* to hunt, to pursue. **ὑπομονή** patience, endurance (s. 2 Thess. 1:4). **πραϋπαθία** gentleness, meekness (s. 2 Cor. 10:1;
12 Gal. 5:22). ■ **ἀγωνίζου** pres. mid. imp. *ἀγωνίζομαι* to carry on a contest, to strive, to struggle, to fight. The word includes the effort put forth in the proclamation of the gospel (s. PAM, 178f.). **ἀγών** struggle, contest. In opposition to those who crave material riches, Timothy is to strive after righteousness, godliness, faith, love, patience, and meekness (PAM, 178). **ἐπιλαβοῦ** aor. mid. imp. *ἐπιλαμβάνομαι* to lay hold on, to get a good grip on (RWP). This does not appear as a fut. prize lying at the end of the Agon, but as that which is to be grasped and retained in the pres. Agon of faith (PAM, 179f.). **ἐκλήθης** aor. pass. ind. *καλέω*. **ὡμολόγησας** aor. act. ind. *ὁμολογέω* to agree to, to confess. **ὁμολογία** agreement, confession. It is the acknowledg-
13 ing of Jesus as the Messiah (ECC, 133). ■ **παραγγέλλω** to instruct, to command, to charge (s. 1 Tim. 1:3). **ζῳογονοῦντος** pres. act. part. *ζῳογονέω* to give life to, to make alive. **μαρτυρήσαντος** aor. act. part. *μαρτυρέω* to give witness to, to
14 testify. ■ **τηρῆσαι** aor. act. inf. *τηρέω* to keep. The inf. is used to express the object of the verb "charge" and is used in an indirect command (RWP). **ἄσπιλος** without spot. **ἀνεπίλημπτος** irreproachable (s. 1 Tim. 3:2). **ἐπιφάνεια** manifestation, appearance. The word was a t.t. in the language of contemporary Hellenistic religion for the self-disclosure of a god

or king (Kelly; s. also 2 Thess. 2:8). ■ **καιρός** time, season, 15
opportune time. **δείξει** fut. act. ind. δείκνυμι to show. **μακάριος** happy, blessed. **δυνάστης** potentate. The word was used of one who exercised sovereignty in his own power (Guthrie). **βασιλευόντων** pres. act. part. βασιλεύω to be a king, to rule as king. **κυριευόντων** pres. act. part. κυριεύω to be a lord,
to rule as a lord. ■ **ἀθανασία** not able to die, immortality (s. BS, 16
293). **οἰκῶν** pres. act. part. οἰκέω to dwell. **ἀπρόσιτος** unapproachable (s. SB, III, 656). **εἶδεν** aor. act. ind. ὁράω. **ἰδεῖν** aor. act. inf. ὁράω. **κράτος** power (s. Eph. 1:19).

■ **πλούσιος** rich, wealthy. **παράγγελλε** pres. act. imp. (s. 17
1 Tim. 1:3). **ὑψηλοφρονεῖν** pres. act. inf. to think exalted, to think highly, to be proud and haughty. **ἠλπικέναι** perf. act. inf. ἐλπίζω to hope, perf. to place one's hope upon something or someone and rest there; i.e., "to have hope and continue to hope" (Ellicott). **ἀδηλότης** uncertainty. From the adj. meaning "unseen, unobserved, not manifest," "indistinct" (AS). **παρέχοντι** pres. act. part. παρέχω to give, to grant, to cause, to bring about something for someone (BAG). **πλουσίως** adv.
richly. **ἀπόλαυσις** enjoying, enjoyment, pleasure. ■ 18
ἀγαθοεργεῖν pres. act. inf. to do that which is good, to do good works, to do deeds inherently noble and praiseworthy (Fairbairn). **εὐμετάδοτος** sharing well, generous, ready to impart (MM). **κοινωνικός** ready to share, giving or sharing generously
(BAG; s. also MH, 378). ■ **ἀποθησαυρίζοντας** pres. act. part. 19
ἀποθησαυρίζω to store up, to amass a treasure. The prep. in compound indicates that the rich are exhorted to take "from" their own plenty, and by devoting it to the service of God and the relief of the poor actually to "treasure" it up as a good foundation for the future (Ellicott; s. also Kelly). **θεμέλιος** foundation. **μέλλον** pres. act. part. μέλλω to be about to. Here "for that which is coming," "for the future." **ἐπιλάβωνται** aor. mid. subj. **ὄντως** adv. (from the part. of εἰμί) truly (s. 1 Tim. 5:4).

■ **παραθήκη** that which is placed beside, deposit, trust. It 20
is a legal term connoting something which is placed on trust in another man's keeping (Kelly; s. also MM). **φύλαξον** aor. act. imp. φυλάσσω to guard. **ἐκτρεπόμενος** pres. mid. part. ἐκτρέπομαι to go out of the way, to turn away from. The part. describes the manner or means. **βέβηλος** that which is accessible to all, profane (s. 1 Tim. 4:7). **κενοφωνία** empty talking, uttering emptiness (RWP). **ἀντίθεσις** opposition, objection, contradiction. **ψευδώνυμος** falsely named. **γνῶσις** knowing,
knowledge. ■ **ἐπαγγελλόμενοι** pres. mid. part. 21
ἐπαγγέλλομαι to announce, to proclaim, to profess (s. 1 Tim.

2:10). ***ἠστόχησαν*** aor. act. ind. ἀστοχέω to miss the mark, to fail, to deviate (s. 1 Tim. 1:6).

2 TIMOTHY

Ch. 1

κατά "according to." It gives the standard by which God 1
chose him and to which his apostleship must be true (Lock). The
prep. also denotes the object and intention of the appointment,
"to further, to make known, the promise of eternal life" (Ellicott). ***ἐπαγγελία*** promise. ***ζωή*** life. The gen. gives the content
of the promise. (For a study of the concept of eternal life, s. GW,
163–201; TDNT; CBB.) ***ἐν*** "in." The prep. indicates that the
source and sphere of life is "in Christ Jesus." ■ ***ἀγαπητός*** 2
beloved. ***τέκνον*** child. ***ἔλεος*** mercy (s. 1 Tim. 1:2).
■ ***λατρεύω*** to serve. The word was used esp. of carrying out 3
religious duties particularly of a cultic nature and was used in the
sense of worship (BAG; TDNT). The pres. tense emphasizes the
continual unbroken habit of life "I have been serving" (RWP).
πρόγονος forebearer. The statement must be understood to
mean that Paul thought of Judaism in such close connection w.
Christianity that his present worship of God is in a sense a
continuation of his own Jewish worship (Guthrie). ***ἐν*** "in." The
prep. is local and gives the spiritual sphere in which the worship
was offered (Ellicott). ***συνείδησις*** conscience (s. Rom. 2:15; 1
Tim. 3:9). ***ἀδιάλειπτος*** without interruption, unceasing (s. 1
Thess. 1:2; 5:17; Josephus, *Wars*, V, 71; 279; 298). ***μνεία***
remembrance, mention (s. 1 Thess. 1:2). ***δέησις*** request, prayer.
■ ***ἐπιποθῶν*** pres. act. part. ἐπιποθέω to have a strong desire 4
for, to yearn after. The prep. in compound is directive (s. Phil.
1:8; 1 Thess. 3:6). ***ἰδεῖν*** aor. act. inf. ὁράω. ***μεμνημένος*** perf.
mid. part. μιμνῄσκομαι to remind one's self, to recall to mind,
to remember. The perf. tense emphasizes the continuing state.
δάκρυον tear. ***ἵνα*** "that." Introduces the purpose of Paul wanting to see Timothy (s. Kelly). ***πληρωθῶ*** aor. pass. subj. πληρόω
to fill, pass. to be filled. ■ ***ὑπόμνησις*** remembering, reminder. 5
The word is used properly of an external reminder (Lock).
λαβών aor. act. part. λαμβάνω. The phrase "having received
a reminder" may suggest that Paul had just had news of Timothy
(s. Guthrie). ***ἀνυπόκριτος*** without hypocrisy, genuine. It was a
genuine principle, the opposite of a hypocritical or wavering

profession (Fairbairn). **ἐνῴκησεν** aor. act. ind. ἐνοικέω to live in, to dwell in (s. Col. 3:16). **μάμμη** grandmother. **πέπεισμαι** perf. pass. ind. πείθω to persuade, to be persuaded, perf. "I stand
6 persuaded" (RWP). ■ **αἰτία** cause, reason. **ἀναμιμνῄσκω** pres. act. ind. to remind, to cause to remember. The prep. in compound is causative (MH, 295). **ἀναζωπυρεῖν** pres. act. inf. to stir up smoldering embers into a living flame, to keep at white heat (Lock). The word means either "to kindle afresh" or "to keep a full flame" (AS; s. also MH, 296; RWP). Paul's statement does not necessarily contain a censure since fire in the ancient world was never kept at a continual blaze but rather kept alive through glowing coals which were then rekindled to a flame by a bellows whenever the situation demanded flame (s. Schlatter; TDNT; OCD, 439; Lev. 6:9). **χάρισμα** gift, grace gift.
7 **ἐπίθεσις** laying on. ■ **ἔδωκεν** aor. act. ind. δίδωμι to give. **δειλία** cowardice, timidity. **σωφρονισμός** self-discipline, the power to keep one's self in hand, free from all excitement or
8 hesitation (Lock; s. also TDNT). ■ **ἐπαισχυνθῇς** aor. pass. subj. ἐπαισχύνομαι to be ashamed of. The aor. subj. is used w. a neg. to form a prohibition which is designed to prevent an action from arising (MKG, 273). **μαρτύριον** witness. **δέσμιος** prisoner. **συγκακοπάθησον** aor. act. imp. συγκακοπαθέω to suffer evil together, to take one's share of evil treatment (AS). The aor. imp. indicates that the action is to be done immediately (s.
9 MKG, 272). ■ **σώσαντος** aor. act. part. σῴζω to rescue, to save. **καλέσαντος** aor. act. part. καλέω. **κλῆσις** calling. **ἴδιος** one's own. **πρόθεσις** facing before, purpose (s. Eph. 1:11). **δοθεῖσαν** aor. pass. part. δίδωμι. **αἰώνιος** eternal. This may be a reference to the earliest promise of triumph to the woman's seed (Gen. 3:15), or to the grace of the preexistent Christ (Guth-
10 rie). ■ **φανερωθεῖσαν** aor. pass. part. φανερόω to make visible, to make clear, to manifest. **ἐπιφάνεια** manifestation, appearing (s. 1 Tim. 6:14; 2 Thess. 2:8; TDNT; Dibelius). Here are two thoughts of the divine intervention of a Savior in an hour of need and of the drawing of a new light (Lock). **καταργήσαντος** aor. act. part. καταργέω to render inoperative, to make inactive, to annul (s. Rom. 3:3; 1 Cor. 1:28; Gal. 3:17). **μέν . . . δέ** "on the one hand . . . on the other hand." The particles are ind. at one of connection and contrast (Fairbairn). **φωτίσαντος** aor. act. part. φωτίζω to illuminate, to flood w. light, to bring to light (Kelly). The two part. indicate the meaning or manner in which the manifestation was accomplished. **ἀφθαρσία** incorruptibili-
11 ty, immortality. ■ **ἐτέθην** aor. pass. ind. τίθημι to place, to appoint, to commission (s. 1 Tim. 2:7). **κῆρυξ** proclaimer, her-

ald, preacher (s. 1 Tim. 2:7). ■ **καί** "also." **πάσχω** pres. act. ind. 12
to suffer. The pres. tense indicates a continual action which was
going on at the pres. time. **ᾧ** "whom," dat. case of the rel. pron.
used as object of the verb but the antecedent is not expressed.
Paul knows Jesus Christ whom he has trusted (RWP).
πεπίστευκα perf. act. ind. to believe, to trust in. The word
literally means "to whom I have given my trust" and the perf.
tense indicates "in whom I have put my trust, and still do put
it" (Ellicott). **παραθήκη** that which is committed to another,
deposit. It is a legal term connoting something which one person
places on trust in another's keeping (Kelly; Lock, 90f.; s. also 1
Tim. 6:20). The word is best understood as that which God
entrusted to Paul and the present v. focuses attention on God's
ability to guard (Guthrie; Kelly). **φυλάξαι** aor. act. inf.
φυλάσσω to guard, to protect, to keep watch over, to keep
guard. (For references, s. LS; TDNT.) ■ **ὑποτύπωσις** model, 13
example. The word denotes an outline sketch or ground plan
used by an artist or in literature the rough draft forming the basis
of a fuller exposition (Kelly). **ἔχε** pres. act. imp. to have, to hold.
ὑγιαινόντων pres. act. part. ὑγιαίνω to be healthy, to be sound.
ἤκουσας aor. act. ind. ἀκούω to hear. **ἐν** "in." The prep. specifies the principles in which the example is to be held (Ellicott).
■ **φύλαξον** aor. act. imp. (s.v.12). **ἐνοικοῦντος** pres. act. part. 14
to dwell in.

■ **ἀπεστράφησαν** aor. pass. ind. ἀποστρέφομαι to turn 15
away from, to desert. The verb is a pass. deponent and has its
object in the acc. (s. RG, 484f.). ■ **δῴη** aor. act. opt. δίδωμι to 16
give, to grant. **ἔλεος** mercy (s.v.2). **ἀνέψυξεν** aor. act. ind.
ἀναψύχω to cool again, to refresh. The idea is that the presence
of his friend provided a special tonic (Guthrie; s. also RWP).
ἅλυσις chain. (For prisons and prison conditions in the ancient
world, s. RAC IX, 318–345.) **ἐπαισχύνθη** aor. pass. ind. (s.v.8).
■ **γενόμενος** aor. mid. part. γίνομαι to become, to be, to arrive. 17
The part. is temporal and means "when he arrived and was
there" (Ellicott). **σπουδαίως** adv. diligently, eagerly. **ἐζήτησέν**
aor. act. ind. ζητέω to seek, effective aor. (RWP). **εὗρεν** aor. act.
ind. ■ **εὑρεῖν** aor. act. inf. **ὅσος** as many as, which one, those 18
belonging to this class or group. **διηκόνησεν** aor. act. ind.
διακονέω to minister, to serve. **βέλτιον** adv. comp. ἀγαθός.
The word could be taken as a true comp. "better than I" (RG,
665) or it could have the meaning "very well" (s. BAG; BD,
127).

Ch. 2

1 ■ **ἐνδυναμοῦ** pres. pass. imp. ἐνδυναμόω to enpower,
pass. to be strong (s. Eph. 6:10). **ἐν** "in." The prep. is probably
2 instrumental "by means of" or "in the power of" (Kelly). ■
ἤκουσας aor. act. ind. ἀκούω. **παράθου** aor. mid. imp.
παρατίθημι to place to another's trust, to entrust, to deposit,
to commit for safe keeping (s. MM; for the noun, s. 1 Tim. 1:12).
ἱκανός that which reaches or arrives at a certain standard, sufficient, capable (s. GEW I, 719f.; TDNT; LS). **ἔσονται** fut. εἰμί.
3 **διδάξαι** aor. act. inf. to teach. ■ **συγκακοπάθησον** aor. act.
imp. συγκακοπαθέω to suffer evil together, to endure affliction
together, to take one's share of rough treatment (Kelly; s. also
4 2 Tim. 1:8). ■ **στρατευόμενος** pres. mid. part. στρατεύομαι
to be a soldier. (For a description of the life, training, and discipline of Roman soldiers, s. Josephus, *Jewish Wars*, III, 70–109.)
ἐμπλέκεται pres. mid. ind. ἐμπλέκω to entangle, mid. to entangle one's self. The word pictures a soldier's weapon entram-
melled in his cloak (Guthrie). **πραγματεία** affairs, pursuits. The
soldier does not let himself get involved in the preoccupation
of civil life (Kelly). As applied to ministers this command
requires wholehearted devotion to their work (Lock).
στρατολογήσαντι aor. act. part. to enlist soldiers. It was the
general's duty to see that his soldiers were well equipped and
provided w. food and shelter (s. DC III, 67f.). **ἀρέσῃ** aor. act.
subj. ἀρέσκω to please. The Christian "soldier" has only one
goal and purpose—wholehearted devotion to the given task in
the effort to please his Lord (PAM, 169). The subj. is used in a
5 purpose clause. ■ **ἀθλῇ** pres. act. subj. ἀθλέω to compete in a
contest. **στεφανοῦται** pres. pass. ind. στεφανόω to crown one
w. a victor's crown. **νομίμως** adv. lawfully. There was need for
the athlete's adherence to the laws of the contest and he was not
allowed to lighten his struggle by bypassing the rules. When
applied to Timothy this meant that he as an athlete of Christ
must also be prepared to suffer. The word also contains rejection
of the heretics who do not "contend lawfully" (PAM, 170f.).
6 **ἀθλήσῃ** aor. act. subj. ■ **κοπιῶντα** pres. act. part. κοπιάω to
work, to work until one is exhausted. **γεωργός** farmer (s. 1 Cor.
9:7). **δεῖ** (w. the acc. and the inf.) it is necessary.
7 **μεταλαμβάνειν** pres. act. inf. to partake, to share. ■ **νόει** pres.
act. imp. νοέω to understand, to think over, to consider; i.e.,
"work out what I am getting at" (Kelly). **δώσει** fut. act. ind.
δίδωμι. **σύνεσις** insight, understanding.
8 ■ **μνημόνευε** pres. act. imp. μνημονεύω to remember, to
call to memory. **ἐγηγερμένον** perf. pass. part. ἐγείρω to rise,

pass. to be raised. The perf. tense points to the continual state;
i.e., he was raised and continues to live. Timothy was to remember not just the mere fact of the Resurrection, but was to keep
Him in mind as a living, risen Lord who is able to give His life
to the believer (s. Lock). ■ **κακοπαθῶ** pres. act. ind. to suffer 9
trouble. The pres. tense emphasizes that which is continually
taking place. **δεσμῶν** bond. **κακοῦργος** evil worker, criminal.
The word is used for the criminals who were crucified alongside
Jesus (Luke 23:32f.), and in technical legal parlance it was reserved for burglars, murderers, traitors, and the like (Kelly).
δέδεται perf. pass. ind. δέω to bind. The perf. emphasizes that
the Word of God is not bound; i.e., "has not been and is not now
bound" (Ellicott). ■ **ὑπομένω** pres. act. ind. to remain under, to 10
endure, to endure patiently (s. 1 Thess. 1:3). **ἐκλεκτός** elected,
chosen. **τύχωσιν** aor. act. subj. τυγχάνω followed by the gen.
to reach, to obtain. The subj. is used in a purpose clause. ■ 11
πιστός faithful, trustworthy. **συναπεθάνομεν** aor. act. ind.
συναποθνῄσκω to die together. The ind. is used in a first-class
conditional clause which accepts the condition as a reality.
συζήσομεν fut. act. ind. συζάω to live together, to live w.
someone. ■ **συμβασιλεύσομεν** fut. act. ind. συμβασιλεύω to 12
be king together, to rule w. someone. **ἀρνησόμεθα** fut. mid. ind.
ἀρνέομαι to deny. ■ **ἀπιστοῦμεν** pres. act. ind. ἀπιστέω to 13
be unfaithful, to be untrustworthy. (For the alpha pref., s. Moorhouse, 47ff.) **μένει** pres. act. ind. to remain. **ἀρνήσασθαι** aor.
act. inf.

■ **ὑπομίμνῃσκε** pres. act. imp. ὑπομιμνῄσκω to call to 14
remembrance, to remind someone of something.
διαμαρτυρόμενος pres. mid. part. διαμαρτύρομαι to solemnly charge someone (s. 1 Tim. 5:21). **λογομαχεῖν** pres. act.
inf. to wage a word war. The inf. is used to give the content of
the charge and the pres. tense w. the neg. could indicate the
stopping of an action in progress or it could prohibit the carrying
on of such an action. **χρήσιμος** useful. **καταστροφή** turning
against, overturning, subverting, demoralizing (Kelly).
ἀκουόντων pres. act. part. The gen. is objective gen. ■ 15
σπούδασον aor. act. imp. σπουδάζω to give diligence. The
word contains the notion of persistent "zeal" (Guthrie).
δόκιμος approved after examination or testing (s. TDNT; BS,
259–262; MM; Preisigke). **παραστῆσαι** aor. act. inf.
παρίστημι to stand alongside of, to present. **ἐργάτης** worker.
ἀνεπαίσχυντος not being ashamed, having no occasion to be
ashamed of (Fairbairn). **ὀρθοτομοῦντα** pres. act. part.
ὀρθοτομέω to cut along a straight line, to cut a straight road.

The metaphor could be that of plowing a straight furrow or of a road maker driving his road straight or of a mason squaring and cutting a stone to fit in its proper place or the cutting of a sacrifice or food for household use (s. Lock; EGT; Kelly; MM).
16 ■ **βέβηλος** available for everyone, profane (s. 1 Tim. 4:7). **κενοφωνία** empty or vain talking. In the ancient world useless talking was considered to be caused from a sickness of the soul and demonstrated itself either in the quantity or quality of the speech (s. RAC X, 829–837). **περιΐστασο** pres. act. imp. περιΐστημι to shift around, to avoid, to shun (s. MH, 231). **ἐπὶ πλεῖον** "fair the more"; i.e., "they will arrive at an ever greater measure of godlessness"; i.e., become more and more deeply involved in godlessness (BAG). **προκόψουσιν** fut. act. ind. προκόπτω to set before, to advance, to make progress (s. Gal.
17 1:14). **ἀσέβεια** godlessness (s. TDNT). ■ **γάγγραινα** gangrene, cancer, spreading ulcer. It is a disease by which any part of the body suffering from inflammation becomes so corrupted that unless a remedy be seasonably applied, the evil continually spreads, attacks other parts, and at last eats away at the bones (T). The metaphor illustrates insidiousness and nothing could more suitably describe the manner of advancement of most false teachings, whether ancient or modern (Guthrie). **νομή** pasture, grazing, feeding. It is used of a spreading sore (AS). **ἕξει** fut. act. ind. ἔχω. The true thought is "will spread further into the church
18 and corrupt others" (Lock). ■ **ἠστόχησαν** aor. act. ind. ἀστοχέω to miss the mark, to go astray (s. 1 Tim. 1:6; 6:21). **γεγονέναι** perf. act. inf. γίνομαι. The inf. is used in indirect discourse. **ἀνατρέπουσιν** pres. act. ind. to over turn, to upset,
19 to break down, to ruin (s. MM). ■ **μέντοι** however. The particle gives a strong adversitive sense (RWP; Blomqvist, 27). **στερεός** solid, hard, firm, steadfast, strong (s. BAG). **θεμέλιος** foundation. **ἕστηκεν** perf. act. ind. ἵστημι to stand, perf. to remain standing. **ἔχων** pres. act. part. **σφραγίς** seal. The illusion is to the practice of placing on a building, or its foundation stone, an inscription or other sign to indicate its owner's purpose (Kelly). **ἔγνω** aor. act. ind. γινώσκω (s. ND, 344ff.). **ὄντας** pres. part. εἰμί. **ἀποστήτω** aor. act. imp. 3rd per. sing. ἀφίστημι to depart, to leave, "let everyone stand off from" (RWP). The aor. tense calls for a definite break. **ἀδικία** unrighteousness.
20 **ὀνομάζων** pres. act. part. ὀνομάζω to name. ■ **σκεῦος** vessel. **χρυσοῦς** golden. **ἀργυροῦς** silver. **ξύλινος** wooden. The suf. of the adj. signifies material (MH, 359; s. also MH, 378). **ὀστράκινος** made out of clay, earthenware, pottery. **ἀτιμία**
21 dishonor. ■ **ἐκκαθάρῃ** aor. act. subj. ἐκκαθαίρω to clean out,

to cleanse completely. The purging out relates either to the false
teachers or it denotes inward purification (Guthrie). **ἔσται** fut.
εἰμί. **ἡγιασμένον** perf. pass. part. ἁγιάζω to separate, to sanctify, to set apart for holy use (s. TDNT; CBB). The perf. tense
looks at the completed state or condition. **εὔχρηστος** for good
use, useful. **δεσπότης** master, ruler, lord. The term denotes
absolute ownership and uncontrolled power (T).
ἡτοιμασμένον perf. pass. part. ἑτοιμάζω to prepare. ■ 22
νεωτερικός youthful, that which pertains to youth. (For the suf.,
s. MH, 378.) **ἐπιθυμία** strong desire, passion. **φεῦγε** pres. act.
imp. φεύγω to flee. The pres. imp. calls for a continuous action
which indicates a habit of life and could have an interat. force.
δίωκε pres. act. imp. διώκω to pursue. **εἰρήνη** peace.
ἐπικαλουμένων pres. mid. part. ἐπικαλέω to call upon. ■ 23
μωρός foolish, stupid. **ἀπαίδευτος** without discipline, without
training, uninstructed, uneducated (s. BAG). **ζήτησις** questioning, speculation. **παραιτοῦ** pres. mid. imp. παραιτέομαι to
refuse, to reject. **εἰδώς** perf. act. part. οἶδα. **γεννῶσιν** pres. act.
ind. to give birth to, to produce. The pres. tense points to that
which happens continually. **μάχη** fight, strife. ■ **μάχεσθαι** 24
pres. mid. inf. to fight. The word was generally used of armed
combatants, or those who engage in hand-to-hand struggle. It
was then used of those who engage in a war of words, i.e., "to
quarrel, to wrangle, to dispute" (T). **ἤπιος** gentle. **διδακτικός**
skillful in teaching (s. 1 Tim. 3:2). **ἀνεξίκακος** bearing up w.
evil, ready to put up w. evil, patient of wrong. The word denotes
an attitude of patient forbearance toward those who are in opposition (Guthrie; Kelly; Ellicott; RWP). ■ **πραΰτης** meekness, 25
gentle, submissiveness. It denotes the humble and gentle attitude
which expresses itself in particular in a patient submissiveness to
offense, free from malice and desire for revenge (s. 2 Cor. 10:1).
παιδεύοντα pres. act. part. παιδεύω to train, to train by discipline, to instruct. **ἀντιδιατιθεμένους** pres. mid. part.
ἀντιδιατίθημι to place one's self in opposition, to oppose (s.
MH, 297). **μήποτε** "if perhaps," "in the hope that" (Ellicott; s.
also BD, 188). **δώῃ** aor. act. opt. δίδωμι. The problematic construction may mean "it may be that he will give" (IBG, 157; s.
also MT, 129; BD, 118; RWP). **μετάνοια** change of mind,
change of attitude, repentance (Kelly; s. also TDNT; CBB).
ἐπίγνωσις recognition, acknowledgment, knowledge. ■ 26
ἀνανήψωσιν aor. act. subj. ἀνανήφω to sober up, to return to
sobriety, to return to one's senses. The metaphor implies some
previous duping by evil influences as in the case of intoxication;
the devil's method is "to numb the conscience, confuse the

senses and paralyze the will" (Guthrie; s. also Kelly). **παγίς** snare, trap. **ἐζωγρημένοι** perf. pass. part. **ζωγρέω** to capture alive, to make captive.

Ch. 3

1 ■ **γίνωσκε** pres. act. imp. i.e., "recognize," "realize" (Lock). **ἔσχατος** last. **ἐνστήσονται** fut. mid. ind. **ἐνίστημι** to stand on, to be at hand, to set in (RWP; Ellicott). **καιρός** period of time, season, a particular time. **χαλεπός** difficult, dangerous. It is not merely the outward dangers that might be involved, but the evils that mark them (Ellicott; for the Jewish teaching and description of the difficulties of the last times, s. SB IV, 977–
2 1015.) ■ **ἔσονται** fut. **εἰμί**. **φίλαυτος** lover of one's self, self-loving. **φιλάργυρος** money loving. **ἀλαζών** bragger, boaster. It is one who brags and boasts about his accomplishments and in his boasting he overpasses the limits of truth and stresses the fact to magnify himself in his attempt to impress men (s. MNTW, 38–42; Trench, *Synonyms*, 98–102; TDNT). **ὑπερήφανος** haughty, arrogant, one who shows himself above his fellow (Trench, *Synonyms*, 101f.; TDNT). **βλάσφημος** abusive speech, slanderer. **γονεῖς** parents. **ἀπειθής** disobedient. **ἀχάριστος** not thankful, ungrateful. **ἀνόσιος** unholy, wicked
3 (s. 1 Tim. 1:9). ■ **ἄστοργος** unloving, without family affection, without love of kindred, destitute of love toward those for whom nature herself claims it. The verb without the neg. pref. denotes primarily and properly the love between parents and children (Ellicott; s. also AS). **ἄσπονδος** without a truth, irreconcilable. It denotes a hostility that admits of no truce (Guthrie). The word denotes a man who cannot bring himself to come to terms w. other people (Kelly; s. also Trench, *Synonyms*, 193f.). **διάβολος** slanderer, "setters at variant." These are those who promote quarrels in hope that they may gain from them (Lock). **ἀκρατής** without power, without self-control; i.e., w. respect to both their tongue and to their appetite and everything else (EGT). **ἀνήμερος** not tamed, uncivilized, fear, savage. **ἀφιλάγαθος**
4 without laws for good, haters of good. ■ **προδότης** traitor, betrayer. The word was used of one who betrays his country or one who is a traitor to his oath or one who abandons another in danger (LS; s. also MH, 323). **προπετής** one who falls before or ahead, hasty, reckless, one who is ready to precipitate matters by hasty speech or action (Fairbairn; s. also Lock). **τετυφωμένοι** perf. pass. part. **τυφόω** to fill w. smoke, to be conceited (s. 1 Tim. 3:6; 6:4). **φιλήδονος** pleasure lover.
5 **μᾶλλον** rather. **φιλόθεος** God lover. ■ **ἔχοντες** pres. act. part.

μόρφωσις shaping, bringing into shape, embodiment, outline, outward form, resemblance (LS; BAG). **εὐσέβεια** reverence of God, godliness (s. 1 Tim. 2:2). **ἠρνημένοι** perf. mid. part. ἀρνέομαι to deny. The word involves always more than an act of the mind; it means carrying the ligation into practice (EGT). **καί.** The word seems here to retain its proper force by specifying those particularly who were to be avoided (Ellicott). **ἀποτρέπου** pres. mid. imp. ἀποτρέπομαι to turn from, to turn one's self away from. The verb is a strong one, implying that
Timothy is to avoid them w. horror (Kelly). ■ **ἐνδύνοντες** pres. 6
act. part. ἐνδύνω to enter in, to creep in, to run one's way in. The word implies insidious method (Guthrie). **αἰχμαλωτίζοντες** pres. act. part. αἰχμαλωτίζω to take captive at spear point, to make a prisoner of war, to capture. The word denotes here "getting complete possession of" (Huther). **γυναικάριον** little woman, silly or idle woman. The word is a diminutive and expresses contempt (Fairbairn). **σεσωρευμένα** perf. pass. part. σωρεύω to heap or pile up, to overwhelm. The perf. tense emphasizes the continual state or condition. **ἀγόμενα** pres. pass. part. ἄγω to lead, to drive. **ἐπιθυμία** strong desire, lust. The dat. is instrumental used w. the pass. **ποικίλος** many-colored,
variegated, various, diversified. ■ **πάντοτε** always. 7
μανθάνοντα pres. act. part. The part. refers to the women who apparently desired to listen to other people's advice, but their mind had become so fickle and warped that they had become incapable of obtaining the knowledge of the truth (Guthrie). **μηδέποτε** never. **ἐπίγνωσις** recognition, knowledge (s. Col. 1:9; Eph. 1:17). **ἐλθεῖν** aor. act. inf. ἔρχομαι. **δυνάμενα** pres.
mid. part. ■ **τρόπος** manner, adverbial acc. "in which manner" 8
(RWP). **ἀντέστησαν** aor. act. ind. ἀνθίστημι to stand against, to withstand, to oppose (s. Acts 13:8). **οὕτως** so. It refers rather to the degree of their hostility than to the manner in which it was expressed (EGT). **κατεφθαρμένοι** perf. pass. part. καταφθείρω to corrupt, to corrupt completely, to ruin, pass. to be perverted, to be depraved (BAG; for examples in the papyri, s. also MM). **νοῦς** mind, understanding. **ἀδόκιμος** rejected after trial, disqualified (s. 1 Cor. 9:27). **πίστις** faith. (For Jewish references concerning Jannes and Jambres, s. SB III, 660–664;
s. also CD 5:18; ZPEB III, 403–405.) ■ **προκόψουσιν** fut act. 9
ind. προκόπτω to cut before, to make progress, to advance (s. 2 Tim. 2:16). **ἐπὶ πλεῖον** "farther, very far" (Lock; s. also 2 Tim. 2:16). **ἄνοια** without understanding, foolishness, faithlessness. **ἔκδηλος** clear, evident, very clear. The prep. in compound is

defective (s. MH, 311). **ἔσται** fut. *εἰμί*. **ἐγένετο** aor. mid. ind.
γίνομαι.
10 ■ **παρηκολούθησας** aor. act. ind. *παρακολουθέω* to follow along, to follow closely, to accompany. The word is also a
t.t. defining the relation of a disciple to his master; i.e., "study
at close quarter," "follow in spirit," "carefully note w. a view to
reproducing," and so "take as an example" (Kelly).
διδασκαλία teaching, doctrine. **ἀγωγή** the way one leads his
life, manner of life, the word denotes general behavior, which a
man's closest associate can never fail to know in all its aspects
(Guthrie). **πρόθεσις** purpose; i.e., the guiding motive of his life
and work (Kelly). **μακροθυμία** longsuffering, patient endurance (s. Gal. 5:22; Rom. 2:4). **ὑπομονή** bearing under, patience,
patient and hopeful endurance (s. 2 Thess. 1:4; RAC IX, 243–
11 294). ■ **διωγμός** persecution. **πάθημα** that which is suffered,
suffering. **οἷος** which kind, which sort of. **ὑπήνεγκα** aor. act.
ind. *ὑποφέρω* to bear by being under, to carry or be under a
heavy load, to hold out, to endure. (For examples, s. LS; 1 Cor.
12 10:13.) **ἐρρύσατο** aor. mid. ind. *ῥύομαι* to rescue. ■ **καί . . . δέ**
"but even," "yea and" (Ellicott). **θέλοντες** pres. act. part. to
desire, to want to, to wish. **ζῆν** pres. act. inf. to live. **εὐσεβῶς**
adv. godly, Godfearingly. It denotes living in the right attitude
to God and to things divine. It can sometimes have the meaning
of loyalty or true religion (s. MNTW, 66–76; 1 Tim. 2:2).
διωχθήσονται fut. pass. ind. *διώκω* to hunt, to follow after, to
13 persecute. ■ **γόης** one who gives incantations by howling, one
who practices magic art, sorcerer, swindler, cheat (Ellicott;
BAG). **χείρων** comp. worse. **πλανῶντες** pres. act. part.
πλανάω to lead astray, to deceive. **πλανώμενοι** pres. pass.
14 part. ■ **μένε** pres. act. imp. *μένω* to remain. The pres. imp. calls
for a constant and continual habit of life. **ἔμαθες** aor. act. ind.
μανθάνω to learn. **ἐπιστώθης** aor. pass. ind. **πιστόω** to make
reliable, pass. to be assured of, to be convinced of (s. RWP).
15 **εἰδώς** perf. act. part. **οἶδα** (s. ND, 344ff.). ■ **ὅτι** "that." It
introduces the object of the verb "to know" and presents a
second fact which Timothy was to take into consideration (Ellicott). **βρέφος** child. The Jewish parents' duty was to teach
their children the law when in their fifth year (Lock; s. also M,
Aboth 5:21; SB III, 664–666). **ἱερός** sacred. The term **τὰ ἱερὰ
γράμματα** is the name for the Holy Scriptures of the OT which
was used among Gr.-speaking Jews (Dibelius; but s. also Guthrie; Lock). **τὰ δυνάμενα** pres. mid. part. to be able "which are
able." **σοφίσαι** aor. act. inf. *σοφίζω* to impart wisdom, to make
16 wise. ■ **γραφή** writing, Scripture (s. TDNT; Schlatter; Guthrie).

θεόπνευστος God-breathed, breathed into by God, inspired. The rabbinical teaching was that the Spirit of God rested on and in the prophets and spoke through them so that their words did not come from themselves, but from the mouth of God and they spoke and wrote in the Holy Spirit. The early church was in entire agreement with this view (s. Kelly; SB IV, 435–451; ZPEB III, 286–293; TDNT; Schlatter; Gerhard Delling, "Die biblische Prophetie bei Josephus," JS 109–121). **ὠφέλιμος** profitable. **ἐλεγμός** proving, convicting, reproof; i.e., for refuting error and rebuking sin (Kelly; Lock). **ἐπανόρθωσις** setting up straight in addition, setting right, correction. It is the setting upright on their feet (Lock; for example in the papyri, s. MM; Preisigke).
παιδεία training, instruction, discipline. ■ **ἄρτιος** fit, complete, 17
capable, sufficient; i.e., able to meet all demands (BAG). **ᾖ** subj. εἰμί. The subj. is used in a purpose clause. **ἐξηρτισμένος** perf. pass. part. ἐξαρτίζω completely outfitted, fully furnished, fully equipped, fully supplied. The word was used of documents which were completely outfitted or of a wagon which was completely outfitted or of a completely outfitted rescue boat. (For these and other examples, s. MM; Preisigke; LS.) The prep. in compound is effective (s. MH, 308ff.).

Ch. 4

■ **διαμαρτύρομαι** pres. mid. ind. to solemnly charge (s. 1 1
Tim. 5:21). **μέλλοντος** pres. act. part. μέλλω to be about to. The word was used w. the inf. to express a durative fut. (s. MKG, 307). **κρίνειν** pres. act. inf. **ζῶντας** pres. act. part. ζάω to live. **ἐπιφάνεια** appearance, manifestation. The word was used in reference to the appearance of a god (s. 1 Tim. 6:14; 2 Thess.
2:8). ■ **κήρυξον** aor. act. imp. to proclaim as a herald, to preach 2
(s. 1 Tim. 2:7). **ἐπίστηθι** aor. pass. imp. ἐφίστημι to take one's stand, to stand by, to be at hand. The word was also used in a military sense; i.e., "to stay at one's post," but here it means "to be at one's task" and indicates that the Christian minister must always be on duty (Kelly; Guthrie). **εὐκαίρως** adv. well-timed, suitably, conveniently; i.e., when it is convenient (BAG). **ἀκαίρως** not well-timed, inconveniently; i.e., when it is inconvenient (BAG). **ἔλεγξον** aor. act. imp. ἐλέγχω to prove w. demonstrative evidence, to convict, to reprove. It is so to rebuke another, w. such effectual feeling of the victorious arms of the truth, as to bring one, if not always to a confession, yet at least to a conviction, of sin (Trench, *Synonyms*, 13; s. also TDNT). **ἐπιτίμησον** aor. act. imp. ἐπιτιμάω to rebuke. The word denotes in the NT usage the idea of censure and sharp rebuke (Guthrie; Trench, *Synonyms*, 13; TDNT; s. also Matt. 17:18).

παρακάλεσον aor. act. imp. παρακαλέω to urge, to encourage, to exhort, to admonish (s. 1 Thess. 4:1; Rom. 12:1). **μακροθυμία** longsuffering, patient endurance (s. Gal. 5:22).
3 ■ **ἔσται** fut. εἰμί. **καιρός** season, period of time. **ὑγιαινούσης** pres. act. part. ὑγιαίνω to be well, to be in good health, to be sound. **διδασκαλία** teaching, doctrine. **ἀνέξονται** fut. mid. ind. ἀνέχομαι to bear up, to endure, to put up w. **ἐπιθυμία** strong desire, lust. **ἐπισωρεύσουσιν** fut. act. ind. ἐπισωρεύω to pile upon, to heap upon (s. 2 Tim. 3:7). **κνηθόμενοι** pres. mid. part. κνήθομαι to tickle, to scratch, to itch, pass. to feel an itching. It is used fig. of curiosity that looks for interesting and spicy bits of information. This itching is relieved by the messages of the new teachers (BAG; s. also MM). **ἀκοή** hearing, ear, acc. of general reference; i.e., "being tickled in reference to their
4 hearing" (Kelly). ■ **ἀποστρέψουσιν** fut. act. ind. ἀποστρέφω to turn away from. **μῦθος** myth (s. 1 Tim. 1:4). **ἐκτραπήσονται** fut. pass. ind. ἐκτρέπομαι to turn away from, to turn aside from
5 (s. 1 Tim. 1:6). ■ **νῆφε** pres. act. imp. νήφω to be sober; i.e., to be in a vigilant, wakeful considerate frame of mind taking good heed to what is proceeding around and pursuing its course w. calm and steady aim (Fairbairn). **κακοπάθησον** aor. act. imp. κακοπαθέω to suffer evil, to suffer hardship (s. 2 Tim. 1:8; 2:3). **ἔργον** work, activity. **ποίησον** aor. act. imp. **εὐαγγελιστής** one who proclaims the good news, evangelist. The word was found on a non-Christian inscription w. the meaning "a proclaimer of oracle" (TDNT). The word, however, occurs primarily of those who preach the gospel (TDNT; s. also PGL). **διακονία** ministry, service. **πληροφόρησον** aor. act. imp. πληροφορέω to carry full, to make full, to fulfill, to accomplish (s. LAE, 86f.).
6 ■ **σπένδομαι** pres. pass. ind. to offer, to pour out as a drink offering (s. Phil. 2:17; Kelly). **ἀνάλυσις** lifting up, departure. The word is used as a euphemism for death and evokes the picture of a ship weighing anchor or of a soldier or traveler striking camp (Kelly). **ἐφέστηκεν** perf. act. ind. ἐφίστημι to be
7 present, to be at hand (s.v.2). ■ **ἀγών** struggle, fight. **ἠγώνισμαι** perf. mid. ind. ἀγωνίζομαι to struggle, to exert effort (s. PAM, 182ff.). The perf. tense conveys a sense of finality (Guthrie). **δρόμος** foot race, race (s. PAM, 183f.). **τετέλεκα** perf. act. ind. τελέω to finish, to complete, to arrive at the goal. **τετήρηκα** pres. act. ind. τηρέω to keep. The expression indi-
8 cates "to remain faithful or true" (PAM, 183.). ■ **λοιπόν** finally. **ἀπόκειται** pres. pass. ind. to be laid away (RWP). The word appeared not only in an athletic context, but was also used of the

award made to loyal subjects by oriental sovereigns for services rendered (Guthrie; s. also Dibelius; Kelly). This, however, is not the certainty of the man who now looks forward to the reward which he has merited. It is rather the certainty of faith and hope (PAM, 184). **ἀπόδωσει** fut. act. ind. ἀποδίδωμι to give, to give back, to recompense. The prep. in compound does not necessarily convey any sense of due. Here the prep. only seems to allude to the reward as having been laid up and being taken, so to say, out of some reserve treasure (Ellicott). **ἠγαπηκόσι** perf. act. part. ἀγαπάω to love.

■ **σπούδασον** aor. act. imp. σπουδάζω to make haste, to 9
be zealous or eager, to give diligence, to do one's best (AS; Kelly;
s. also 2 Tim. 2:15). **ἐλθεῖν** aor. act. inf. ἔρχομαι. **ταχέως** adv.
quickly. ■ **ἐγκατέλιπεν** aor. act. ind. ἐγκαταλείπω to aban- 10
don, to desert, to leave one in lurch, to forsake. **ἀγαπήσας** aor.
act. part. **ἐπορεύθη** aor. pass. ind. πορεύομαι to travel. ■ 11
ἀναλαβών aor. act. part. ἀναλαμβάνω to take up, to pick up
(RWP). **ἄγε** pres. act. imp. ἄγω to lead, to take, to bring.
εὔχρηστος useful, serviceable (Guthrie). ■ **ἀπέστειλα** aor. act. 12
ind. ἀποστέλλω to send. ■ **φαιλόνης** cloak. It was a large, 13
sleeveless outer garment made of a single piece of heavy material
w. a hole in the middle through which the head was passed. It
was used for protection against cold and rain, particularly in
traveling. It may have been that Paul felt the need of it because
winter was at hand and his dungeon was cold (Kelly; s. also
DGRA, 848). **ἀπέλιπον** aor. act. ind. ἀπολείπω to leave behind. **φέρε** pres. act. imp. φέρω to carry, to bring. **βιβλίον** book.
μάλιστα especially. **μεμβράνα** parchment, pergamena. The
word denotes a piece of skin or vellum prepared for writing
purposes and was a t.t. for a codex or leaf book made of parchment (Kelly). Paul mave have been referring to OT Scriptures (s.
Charles C. Ryrie, "Especially the Parchments," Bib Sac 117
[July, 1960], 246f.). ■ **χαλκεύς** one who works w. copper, cop- 14
persmith, smith. The word does not mean that he only worked
in copper. The term came also to be used of workers in any kind
of metal (EGT). **ἐνεδείξατο** aor. mid. ind. ἐνδείκνυμι to show,
to demonstrate, to do something to someone. **ἀποδώσει** fut. act.
ind. ἀποδίδωμι to give back. ■ **φυλάσσου** pres. mid. imp. 15
φυλάσσω to guard, mid. to guard one's self, to be on one's
guard. **λίαν** greatly, violently. **ἀντέστη** aor. act. ind.
ἀνθίστημι to stand against, to oppose.

■ **ἀπολογία** legal defense. **παρεγένετο** aor. mid. ind. 16
παραγίνομαι to be alongside of, to stand by, to support. The
verb is technical for a witness or advocate standing forward in

court on a prisoner's behalf (Kelly). **λογισθείη** aor. pass. opt. λογίζομαι to reckon, to place to one's account. The opt. is used
17 to express a wish. ■ **παρέστη** aor. act. ind. παρίστημι to stand by one's side. **ἐνεδυνάμωσεν** aor. act. ind. ἐνδυναμόω to empower, to strengthen. **κήρυγμα** proclamation, that which is proclaimed or preached. **πληροφορηθῇ** aor. pass. subj. (s.v.5). **ἀκούσωσιν** aor. act. subj. **ἐρρύσθην** aor. pass. ind. ῥύομαι to rescue. **στόμα** mouth. **λέων** lion. (For a discussion of the prob-
18 lems involved in the words of Paul, s. Guthrie.) ■ **ῥύσεται** fut. mid. **πονηρός** evil, active evil. **σώσει** fut. act. ind. σῴζω to save, to rescue. **ἐπουράνιος** heavenly (s. Eph. 1:3).
19/20 ■ **ἄσπασαι** aor. mid. imp. ἀσπάζομαι to greet. ■ **ἔμεινεν** aor. act. ind. μένω to remain. **ἀπέλιπον** aor. act. ind. (s.v.13). **ἀσθενοῦντα** pres. act. part. ἀσθενέω to be weak, to be sick.
21 ■ **σπούδασον** aor. act. imp. (s.v.9). **χειμών** winter. **ἐλθεῖν** aor. act. inf.

TITUS

Ch. 1

κατά "according to," i.e., "for (the furtherance of) the faith 1
of God's elect" (Ellicott). ***ἐκλεκτός*** chosen, elect. ***ἐπίγνωσις***
recognition, knowledge (s. Col. 1:9; Eph. 1:17). ***εὐσέβεια*** godliness, reverence for God (s. 1 Tim. 2:2). ■ ***ἐπί*** for, based upon. 2
The prep. suggests that such hope is the basis on which the
superstructure of Christian service is built (Guthrie).
ἐπηγγείλατο aor. mid. ind. ἐπαγγέλλω mid. to promise.
ἀψευδής not a liar, one who does not lie. (For the negating pref.,
s. Moorhouse, 47ff.) ■ ***ἐφανέρωσεν*** aor. act. ind. φανερόω to 3
make clear, to manifest. ***καιρός*** time, season of time, opportune
time. ***ἴδιος*** one's own. ***κήρυγμα*** that which is proclaimed, proclamation. ***ἐπιστεύθην*** aor. pass. ind., pass. to entrust. ***ἐπιταγή***
command (s. 1 Tim. 1:1). ■ ***γνήσιος*** legitimate, true (s. 1 Tim. 4
1:2). ***κοινός*** common, that which all share in.

■ ***χάριν*** prep. w. the gen. "because of," "on account of." 5
ἀπέλιπόν aor. act. ind. ἀπολείπω to leave behind. ***λείποντα***
pres. act. part. λείπω to leave; i.e., "the things remaining," "the
things that are lacking." ***ἐπιδιορθώσῃ*** aor. mid. subj.
ἐπιδιορθόω to set straight thoroughly in addition to, to set in
order. (For the prep. in compound, s. RWP; MH, 313.)
καταστήσῃς aor. act. subj. καθίστημι to appoint (s. Acts 6:3).
πρεσβυτέρους elder. ***διεταξάμην*** aor. mid. ind.
διατάσσομαι to give orders to, to appoint, to arrange, to ordain (s. 1 Cor. 11:34). ■ ***ἀνέγκλητος*** without indictment, un- 6
chargeable, above reproach (s. 1 Tim. 3:10). ***ἔχων*** pres. act. part.
κατηγορίᾳ accusation. ***ἀσωτία*** inability to save, one who
wastes his money often w. the implication of wasting it on pleasures, and so ruining himself; luxurious living, extravagant
squandering of means (Lock; Trench, *Synonyms*, 53f.; TDNT; s.
also Eph. 5:18). ***ἀνυπότακτος*** independent, unruly, insubordinate. ■ ***δεῖ*** "it is necessary," it is a logical necessity. ***ἐπίσκοπος*** 7
overseer, bishop (s. 1 Tim. 3:1, 2). ***οἰκονόμος*** manager of a
household or family, steward. The word emphasizes the commitment of a task to someone and the responsibility involved. It is
a metaphor drawn from contemporary life and pictures the man-

ager of a household or estate (Guthrie; TDNT; s. also 1 Cor. 4:1; Gal. 4:2). **αὐθάδης** self-willed, obstinate in one's own opinion, arrogant, refusing to listen to others. It is the man who obstinately maintains his own opinion or asserts his own rights and is reckless of the rights, feelings and interests of others (Lock; Trench, *Synonyms*, 349f.; MM; TDNT). **ὀργίλος** inclined to anger, quick-tempered (BAG). Words w. this ending often denote "habit," "custom" (Ellicott). **πάροινος** given to drink, heavy drinker (Kelly; s. also 1 Tim. 3:3). **πλήκτης** one who strikes, fighter. The word could be quite literal "not hasty to strike an opponent" (Lock; s. also 1 Tim. 3:3). **αἰσχροκερδής** greedy of shameful gain; i.e., making money discreditably, adopting one's teaching to the hearers in hope of getting money
from them, or perhaps it refers to engaging in discreditable trade
8 (Lock; s. also 1 Tim. 3:8). ■ **φιλόξενος** lover of strangers, hospitable. **φιλάγαθος** lover of that which is good. It denotes devotion to all that is best (Kelly). **ὅσιος** devout, holy (s. 1 Tim. 2:8).
ἐγκρατής control over one's self. It means complete self-mastery, which controls all passionate impulses and keeps the will
loyal to the will of God (Lock; s. also Lock, 148; Gal. 5:23).
9 ■ **ἀντεχόμενον** pres. mid. part. ἀντέχομαι to hold on to, to
hold fast. The prep. in compound appears to involve a faint idea
of holding out against something hostile or opposing. This, however, passes into that of "steadfast application" (Ellicott).
πίστος reliable, trustworthy (Guthrie). **δυνατός** able. **ᾖ** pres.
subj. **εἰμί**. The subj. is used in a purpose clause. **παρακαλεῖν**
pres. act. inf. to exhort, to urge (s. Rom. 12:1; 1 Thess. 4:1).
διδασκαλία teaching, doctrine. The dat. is instrumental.
ὑγιαινούσῃ pres. act. part. **ὑγιαίνω** to be well, to be healthy,
to be sound. **ἀντιλέγοντας** pres. act. part. ἀντιλέγω to speak
against, to oppose, to object. **ἐλέγχειν** pres. act. inf. to convict,
to reprove (s. 2 Tim. 4:2).
10 ■ **ματαιολόγος** worthless words, evil talkers; i.e., using
impressive language w. little or no solid content of truth (Kelly;
s. also 2 Tim. 2:16). **φρεναπάτης** deceivers of the mind, deceivers of thinking, deceiver, subducer. **μάλιστα** especially.
11 **περιτομή** circumcision. ■ **ἐπιστομίζειν** pres. act. inf. to put
something on the mouth, to muzzle, to silence. **ἀνατρέπουσιν**
pres. act. ind. to turn upside down, to upset (s. 2 Tim. 2:18).
διδάσκοντες pres. act. part. The part. gives the means or manner. **αἰσχρός** shameful, ugly, dishonest (BAG). **κέρδος** gain,
12 profit. ■ **ἐξ αὐτῶν** "from them." Paul quotes from Epimenides
of Cnossus, in Crete, a religious teacher and worker of wonders
of the sixth century B.C. (Kelly; s. also Lock; Dibelius; OCD,

399; KP II, 319). **ἴδιος αὐτῶν προφήτης** "one of their own prophets." Epimenides was a famous figure of Crete and was considered to be a prophet. Because a well-known Cretian condemns his own people, the apostle cannot be charged w. censoriousness for his exposures (Guthrie).

ψεύστης liar. **θηρίον** wild animal, beast. **γαστήρ** stomach. **ἀργός** inactive, lazy. The expression "lazy belly" describes their uncontrolled greed (Guthrie; for gluttony in the ancient world,
s. RAC IX, 345–390). ■ **αἰτία** reason, cause. **ἔλεγχε** pres. act. 13
imp. (s. 2 Tim. 4:2). **ἀπότόμως** adv. severely, sharply. **ὑγιαίνωσιν** pres. act. subj. to be well, to be healthy, to be sound.
The subj. is used in a purpose clause. ■ **προσέχοντες** pres. act. 14
part. προσέχω to give heed to, to devote one's self to (s. 1 Tim. 1:4). **μῦθος** myth (s. 1 Tim. 1:4). **ἐντολή** command, rule. **ἀποστρεφομένων** pres. mid. part. ἀποστρέφομαι to turn
one's self from something, to reject. ■ **μεμιαμμένοις** perf. pass. 15
part. μιαίνω to stain, to defile, to pollute. The perf. points to a past completed action w. a continuing result or state or condition. **νοῦς** mind, understanding. **συνείδησις** conscience. ■ 16
ὁμολογοῦσιν pres. act. ind. to confess, to profess. **εἰδέναι** perf. act. inf. οἶδα to know. **ἀρνοῦται** pres. mid. ind. to deny. **βδελυκτός** detestable, abominable. It is an expression of disgust at their hypocrisy (Guthrie). **ὄντες** pres. part. εἰμί. **ἀπειθής** disobedient. **ἀδόκιμος** rejected after trial, disqualified (s. 2 Tim. 3:8).

Ch. 2

■ **λάλει** pres. act. imp. **ἅ** "the things," "the things which." 1
πρέπει pres. act. ind. "it is fitting." The word indicates that which is fitting or suitable to a particular context. **ὑγιαινούσῃ** pres. act. part. ὑγιαίνω to be well, to be healthy, to be sound.
διδασκαλία teaching, doctrine, dat. of respect. ■ **πρεσβύτης** 2
one who is older, an older man. **νηφαλίος** sober. It refers here to general restraint in indulging desires (Kelly; s. also 1 Tim.
3:2). **σεμνός** dignified (s. 1 Tim. 2:2; 3:8). ■ **πρεσβῦτης** older 3
woman. **ὡσαύτως** likewise. **κατάστημα** demeanor, deportment, behavior. The word describes a state of mind (Guthrie). **ἱεροπρεπής** that which is suitable to holiness, reverence, temple-like, like people engaged in sacred duties, "like those employed in sacred service." They are to carry into daily life the demeanor of priestesses in a temple (Lock; MM; Dibelius). **διάβολος** slanderer (s. 2 Tim. 3:3). **δεδουλωμένας** perf. pass. part. to be enslaved. The perf. tense emphasizes the completed state or condition. **καλοδιδάσκαλος** teacher in good. The word

does not refer to formal instruction, but rather the advice and
encouragement they can give privately, by word and example
4 (Kelly). ■ **σωφρονίζωσιν** pres. act. subj. σωφρονίζω to teach
someone self-control, to train someone in self-control (s. Lock,
148f.; TDNT). **νέος** young. **φίλανδρος** husband-loving.
5 **φιλότεκνος** children-loving. ■ **ἁγνός** chaste (s. 1 Tim. 5:22).
οἰκουργός working at home, housekeeping. In a Jewish
household the married woman had to grind flour, bake, launder,
cook, nurse children, make the beds, spin wool, keep the house,
and was also responsible for hospitality and the care of guests
(s. M, Ketuboth, 5:5; JPFC II, 761ff.; SB III, 667).
ὑποτασσομένας pres. mid. part. ὑποτάσσομαι to be in subjection (s. Eph. 5:22). **βλασφημῆται** pres. pass. subj.
βλασφημέω to slander, to speak lightly of sacred things, to
6 blaspheme (s. AS; TDNT). ■ **νεώτερος** comp. νέος younger.
παρακάλει pres. act. imp. παρακαλέω to urge, to exhort (s.
Rom. 12:1; 1 Thess. 4:1). **σωφρονεῖν** pres. act. inf. to be of a
sound mind, to exercise self-control, to have one's total life
7 under control of the mind (s. Lock, 148ff.; TDNT). ■
παρεχόμενος pres. mid. part. παρέχομαι to show one's self to
be something (BAG). **τύπος** example, type, model.
διδασκαλία teaching, doctrine. **ἀφθορία** uncorruptness, sincerity, untaintedness. It is purity of motive, without desire of
gain or respect of persons and purity of doctrine (Lock; Guthrie;
8 MM). **σεμνότης** dignity (s. 1 Tim. 2:2; 3:8, 11). ■ **λόγος** word,
speech. The word denotes the content of what is said (Guthrie).
ὑγιής healthy, sound. **ἀκατάγνωστος** without accusation, unable to be accused, that which cannot be condemned. **ὁ** "he that
is on the contrary part" (Lock). **ἐντραπῇ** aor. pass. subj.
ἐντρέπομαι mid. to turn one on himself and so be ashamed (i.e.,
to blush) (RWP; s. also 2 Thess. 3:14). **ἔχων** pres. act. part.
9 **φαῦλος** bad, worthless. ■ **δεσπότης** master. **εὐάρεστος** well-
pleasing. **ἀντιλέγοντας** pres. act. part. ἀντιλέγω to speak
10 against, to answer back, to talk back. ■ **νοσφιζομένους** pres.
mid. part. νοσφίζομαι to set apart for one's self, to separate or
lay on one's side, to embezzle (RWP; Kelly). **ἐνδεικνυμένους**
pres. mid. part. ἐνδείκνυμι to show one's self, to demonstrate,
to show forth. **κοσμῶσιν** pres. act. subj. κοσμέω to put in
order, to adorn. The word is used of the arrangement of jewels
in a manner to set off their full beauty (Guthrie).
11 ■ **ἐπεφάνη** aor. pass. ind. ἐπιφαίνομαι to appear, pass. to
be made clear, to be made manifest. The essential meaning of the
word is to appear suddenly upon a scene and it is used particularly of divine interposition, especially to aid, and of the dawning

of light upon darkness (Lock; s. also MM). **σωτήριος** saving,
delivering, bringing salvation. Followed by the dat. the word
means "bringing deliverance to" and the phrase "to all men"
belongs to the noun showing the universal scope of Christian
salvation (Guthrie; s. also BAG). ■ **παιδεύουσα** pres. act. part. 12
παιδεύω to train by discipline, to train a child, to instruct. **ἵνα**
that. The particle introduces the purpose of the training.
ἀρνησάμενοι aor. mid. part. ἀρνέομαι to deny, to say no to.
ἀσέβεια godlessness, the rejection of all that is reverent and of
all that has to do with God (s. TDNT). **ἐπιθυμία** strong desire,
lust. **σωφρόνως** adv. w. self-control (s.v.6). **δικαίως** adv. righteously. **εὐσεβῶς** adv. godly, reverently (s. 1 Tim. 2:2). **ζήσωμεν**
aor. act. subj. ζάω to live. The subj. is cohortative "let us live."
■ **προσδεχόμενοι** pres. mid. part. προσδέχομαι to expect, to 13
wait for, to eagerly wait for. **μακάριος** blessed, happy.
ἐπιφανεία appearance (s. 2 Thess. 2:8). ■ **ἔδωκεν** aor. act. ind. 14
δίδωμι to give. **λυτρώσηται** aor. mid. subj. λυτρόομαι to obtain release by the payment of a price, to redeem, to ransom (s.
Matt. 20:28; RAC VI, 54–219). **ἀνομία** lawlessness. **καθαρίσῃ**
aor. act. subj. καθαρίζω to cleanse. The subj. are used in purpose
clauses. **περιούσιος** chosen, special; i.e., something that belongs
in a special sense to one's self (Guthrie). **ζηλωτής** zealous (s.
Gal. 1:14). ■ **ἔλεγχε** pres. act. imp. ἐλέγχω to convince, to 15
convict, to reprove (s. 2 Tim. 4:2). **ἐπιταγή** command, order,
here "w. all impressiveness" (BAG). **περιφρονείτω** pres. act.
imp. περιφρονέω to think around someone, to despise someone, to overlook, to disregard (s. MH, 321).

Ch. 3

■ **ὑπομίμνησκε** pres. act. imp. ὑπομιμνήσκω to call to 1
remembrance, to remind someone of something. **ἀρχή** ruler.
ἐξουσία authority. **ὑποτάσσεσθαι** pres. mid. inf. to be in subjection. **πειθαρχεῖν** pres. act. inf. to be obedient. The inf. are
used in indirect discourse after the verb "to remind." **ἕτοιμος**
prepared, ready. ■ **βλασφημεῖν** pres. act. inf. to slander, to 2
treat w. contempt, to blaspheme. **ἄμαχος** without fighting.
ἐπιεικής forbearing, reasonable, fair (s. 2 Cor. 10:1).
ἐνδεικνυμένους pres. mid. part. ἐνδείκνυμι to demonstrate, to
display. **πραΰτης** meekness, mildness, patient trust in the midst
of difficult circumstances (s. 2 Cor. 10:1). ■ **ἦμεν** impf. εἰμί. 3
ποτέ formerly. **ἀνόητος** without understanding, foolish.
ἀπειθής disobedient. **πλανώμενοι** pres. pass. part.
πλανάομαι to deceive, to lead astray. The word suggests a false
guide leading astray (Guthrie). **δουλεύοντες** pres. act. part. to

be in slavery to. **ἐπιθυμία** strong desire, lust. **ἡδονή** pleasure. **ποικίλος** many-colored, variegated, various (s. 2 Tim. 3:6). **κακία** evil (s. TDNT; CBB). **φθόνος** envy. **διάγοντες** pres. act. part. διάγω to live, to spend time. **στυγητός** hated, hateful, detestable. **μισοῦντες** pres. act. part. μισέω to hate. **ἀλλήλους**
4 kindness, goodness (s. Gal. 5:22). ■ **χρηστότης** love of mankind, love toward men, generosity. While generosity was sometimes attributed to God, inscriptions show that in the Hellenistic age it was the most prized of the stock virtues acclaimed in rulers
5 (Kelly). ■ **τῶν**. The definite article is used here as a rel.; i.e., "not as a result of works, *those* in righteousness which we did" (RWP). **ἐποιήσαμεν** aor. act. ind. **ἔλεος** mercy (s. 1 Tim. 1:2). **ἔσωσεν** aor. act. ind. σῴζω to rescue, to save. **λουτρόν** bath, washing (s. Eph. 5:26; Fairbairn). **παλιγγενεσία** a birth again, regeneration, new birth. The term was current in Stoicism for periodic restorations of the natural world. It was also used in an eschatalogical sense especially by the Jews of the renewing of the world in the time of the Messiah, but here the word takes on a new meaning in view of the Christian new birth which is applied not cosmically but personally (Guthrie; BAG; Lock; Dibelius; s. also TDNT; CBB; RAC IX, 43–171; s. also Matt. 19:28). **ἀνακαίνωσις** renewing, making new (s. Rom. 12:2; Col. 3:10).
6 ■ **ἐξέχεεν** aor. act. ind. ἐκχέω to pour out. **πλουσίως** adv.
7 richly. ■ **δικαιωθέντες** aor. pass. part. δικαιόω to declare righteous, to justify (s. Rom. 2:13; 5:1). The part. is either temporal "after having been justified" or it could be causal "because we have been justified." **κληρονόμος** heir. **γενηθῶμεν** aor. pass. subj. (For an attempt to explain the teaching in light of Philo, s. Stephen Charles Mott, "Greek Ethics and Christian Conversion: The Philonic Background of Titus II 10–14 and III 3–7," Nov T 20 [Jan., 1978], 22–48.)

8 ■ **τούτων** "these things," refers to all that has been included in the previous part of the letter (Guthrie). **βούλομαι** to determine, to will. **διαβεβαιοῦσθαι** pres. mid. inf. to speak confidently, to insist, to confirm, to make a point of (Lock; s. also 1 Tim. 1:7). The pres. tense calls for a continual action. **φροντίζωσιν** pres. act. subj. φροντίζω to take thought of, to give heed to. **προΐστασθαι** pres. mid. inf. προΐσταμι to stand before, to take the lead in, to be careful to busy one's self w. The word has a technical meaning "to practice a profession" (s. RWP; Kelly). **πεπιστευκότες** perf. act. part. **ὠφέλιμος** useful,
9 profitable, serviceable. ■ **μωρός** dull, stupid, foolish (AS). **ζήτησις** questioning, speculation (s. 1 Tim. 1:4). **γενεαλογία** genealogy (s. 1 Tim. 1:4). **ἔρις** strife. **μάχη** fight, controversy.

νομικός pertaining to law, legal. The word here refers to the
Mosaic law (Guthrie). **περΐστασο** pres. mid. imp. περιΐσταμι
to step around, to stand aside, to turn one's self about, to avoid,
to shun (RWP; MM; s. also 2 Tim. 2:16). **ἀνωφελής** useless,
unprofitable. **μάταιος** futile. ■ **αἱρετικός** having the power of 10
choice, a self-chosen party or sect or it could mean "a self-
chosen teaching," i.e., "heresy," "heretical" (s. Lock). **δεύτερος**
second. **νουθεσία** admonition, warning. It is the attempt to
cause a person to correct his wrong by warning or counseling w.
him (s. TDNT; 1 Cor. 10:11; Eph. 6:4). **παραιτοῦ** pres. mid.
imp. παραιτέομαι to ask from, to beg off, to avoid (RWP; s. also
1 Tim. 4:7; 5:11). ■ **εἰδώς** perf. act. part. οἶδα. **ἐξέστραπται** 11
perf. mid. or pass. ἐκστρέφω to turn from, to turn inside out,
to twist, to divert (s. RWP). **τοιοῦτος** such a one. **ἁμαρτάνει**
pres. act. ind. to sin. **ὤν** pres. part. εἰμί. **αὐτοκατάκριτος** condemnation of one's self, self-condemned; i.e., he is condemned
"by his own action" (Lock).

■ **ὅταν** used w. the subj. "when," "whenever." **πέμψω** aor. 12
act. subj. πέμπω to send. **σπούδασον** aor. act. imp. σπουδάζω
to hurry, to endeavor, to do one's best (Kelly). **ἐλθεῖν** aor. act.
inf. ἔρχομαι. **κέκρικα** perf. act. ind. κρίνω to judge, to determine, to decide. The perf. tense looks at the settled decision
which had been reached. **παραχειμάσαι** aor. mid. inf.
παραχειμάζω to spend the winter. ■ **νομικός** pertaining to 13
law, lawyer. The word may be used of an expert in either Heb.
or Roman law. Here it probably refers to a Roman lawyer. If one
did not know the laws of a city, he consulted w. a lawyer (s.
Guthrie; TDNT; MM; Preisigke). **σπουδαίως** speedily, hur-
riedly, earnestly, diligently. **πρόπεμψον** aor. act. imp.
προπέμπω to send forth, to send on. The word often had the
idea of supplying one w. money for material needs for a trip (s.
Rom. 15:24; 1 Cor. 16:6). **λείπῃ** pres. act. subj. λείπω to leave
behind, to lack. The word suggests that Titus was in a position
to provide material assistance (Guthrie). ■ **μανθανέτωσαν** 14
pres. act. imp. **προΐστασθαι** pres. mid. inf. (s.v.8). **ἀναγκαῖος**
necessary. **ὦσιν** pres. subj. εἰμί. **ἄκαρπος** fruitless.

■ **ἀσπάζονται** pres. mid. ind. to greet. **ἄσπασαι** aor. mid. 15
imp. **φιλοῦντας** pres. act. part. φιλέω to love.

PHILEMON

Ch. 1

1 **Δέσμιος** prisoner (s. 2 Tim. 1:8, 16). **Χριστοῦ Ἰησοῦ.** The
gen. expresses to whom Paul belonged and indicates that the
writing is not simply to be looked at as a private letter but
contains a message which those who receive it are obligated to
obey (Lohse). **ἀγαπητός** beloved. **συνεργός** fellow worker.
The term is a frequent name given to Paul's colleagues in the
"work" of the gospel. Just how Philemon had labored w. Paul in
2 missionary service is not clear (Martin; NCB). ■ **ἀδελφή** sister.
Since the women at that time had to do w. the business of the
house, it was important for her what Paul had to say about the
slave Onesimus (Stuhlmacher; Lohse; s. also Titus 2:5).
συστρατιώτης fellow soldier. This was one who engaged in the
same conflicts, faced the same dangers, and fought for the same
goals (s. TDNT).
4 ■ **εὐχαριστῶ** pres. act. ind. to give thanks. It was a common feature of Hellenistic letters that the sender praised the
gods for the health and well-being of his addressees, and assured
them of his prayers on their behalf. Paul gives a distinctly Christian content to the formula by the way in which he goes on to
describe the reason for his thankfulness (Martin, NCB; Lohse;
s. also LAE, 184f.; P.T. O'Brien, *Introductory Thanksgivings in
the Letters of Paul* [Leiden: E.J. Brill, 1977]). **πάντοτε** always.
μνεία mention, remembrance. **ποιούμενος** pres. mid. part. The
construction means "to make mention in prayer" (Moule; s. also
5 1 Thess. 1:2). ■ **ἀκούων** pres. act. part. The part. could be causal
"because I hear" and indicates the cause of Paul's giving thanks
(Vincent). **πρός.** The prep. signifies direction "forward to," "toward." Here it is used of faith which aspires toward Christ
(Lightfoot; s. also Vincent; Ellicott). **εἰς πάντας τοὺς ἁγίους**
"unto all saints." The prep. denotes "arrival" and so "contact,"
i.e., "into," "unto" and is used of love which is exerted upon men
6 (Lightfoot; but s. also MT, 256). ■ **ὅπως** "that," "in order that."
The particle introduces either the aim and purport of Paul's
prayer (Lightfoot) or it simply gives the content of Paul's prayer
(Lohse). **κοινωνία** fellowship, sharing. The word could mean

generosity or participation and the main idea is that Philemon's
faith is to show itself in loving service (Martin, NCB; s. also
TDNT; CBB; RAC IX, 1100–1145). **πίστεώς**. The gen. can be
the obj. gen. (For a discussion of the various problems and interpretations, s. Moule; Stuhlmacher.) **ἐνεργής** active, effective,
productive (s. TDNT; MNTW, 46–54). **γένηται** aor. mid. subj.
γίνομαι. **ἐπίγνωσις** recognition, acknowledgment, knowledge
(s. Col. 1:9). **παντὸς ἀγαθοῦ** "of every good." The words may
refer to that which is God's will and generally refers to something which is done or performed (s. Moule; s. also Stuhlmacher). ■ **ἔσχον** aor. act. ind. ἔχω to have, aor. to get, to receive 7
(s. M, 110). The aor. tense expresses forcibly the moment of joy
which Paul experienced when he heard this good news about
Philemon (EGT). **παράκλησις** encouragement, comfort.
σπλάγχον the inner organs, heart. The term is used here to
denote the total person and his personality at the deepest level
(Martin, NCB; Lohse; TDNT). **ἀναπέπαυται** perf. mid. ind.
ἀναπαύω to cause to rest, to refresh. The word implies "relaxation, refreshment," as a preparation for the renewal of labor or
suffering (Lightfoot). **ἀδελφέ** vocative. The place of the word
here makes it emphatic (EGT).

■ **διό** therefore. **παρρήσία** speaking all things, openness, 8
boldness (s. TDNT). **ἔχων** pres. act. part. The part. is concessive
(IBG, 102). **ἐπιτάσσειν** pres. act. inf. to command. When a
slave ran away, he could be searched for through a wanted list
and if anyone recognized him and caught him, he was to bring
him back to his owner who could punish the slave as he wished.
In such a case it was also possible for one to intercede w. the
master for the slave. (For examples and references, s. Lohse; for
the text of the description of two runaway slaves, s. Moule, 34ff.)
ἀνῆκον that which is required, that which is fitting; i.e. one's
duty (Martin, NCB). ■ **μᾶλλον** rather. **παρακαλέω** pres. act. 9
ind. to urge, to beseech. The verb contains the idea of a request
(s. TDNT; Lohse). **τοιοῦτος** such a one. (For the construction
of this section, s. Lightfoot.) **ὤν** pres. part. εἰμί. **πρεσβύτης** old
man, ambassador. The sense requires Paul's invoking his authority as an ambassador (Martin, NCB). **νυνί** now. **δέσμιος** prisoner (s.v.1). ■ **παρακαλῶ** pres. act. ind. Used w. the prep. here 10
in the sense of "making a request on behalf of someone" (s.
Lohse; Stuhlmacher). **ἐγέννησα** aor. act. ind. γεννάω to bear,
to give birth. Here it is the metaphor of fatherhood "of whose
conversion I was the instrument" (Vincent; Moule). (For references to the DSS and rabbinical literature concerning the metaphor of spiritual parenthood, s. Stuhlmacher; SB, III, 340f.;

11 TDNT.) **δεσμός** bond. ■ **ποτέ** formerly. **ἄχρηστος** useless,
12 unserviceable. **εὔχρηστος** useful, serviceable, profitable. ■
ἀνέπεμψα aor. act. ind. ἀναπέμπω to send again, to send back (s. BAG; Moule). The aor. is an epistolary aor. which is translated by the pres. tense in English. It indicates that Onesimus carried the letter (Lightfoot; Stuhlmacher; s. also BD, 172). **σπλάγχνα** inward organs, heart, "my very heart" (Lightfoot; s.
13 also v. 7; Phil. 1:8; 2:1). ■ **ἐβουλόμην** impf. mid. ind. βούλομαι
to desire, to wish. The word involves the idea of "purpose, deliberation, desire, mind" (Lightfoot; s. also TDNT). The impf. is either an epistolary tense which is rendered in English "I wish" or "I would like" (Moule) or it could be used of a wish which was either impossible to fulfill; i.e., "I could have desired" (s. BD, 181f.; Lightfoot). **κατέχειν** pres. act. inf. to retain, to keep. Although the word is capable of several meanings, the idea here in this construction is "to keep w. me" (Lohse). **ὑπὲρ σοῦ** "instead of you." The idea of substitution is in the word and the prep. was used of one who wrote "for" another who could not write (s. Lohse; LAE, 331; TDNT; Stuhlmacher). **διακονῇ** pres. act. subj. to wait on, to minister to, to minister (s. TDNT). **εὐαγγέλιον** good news, gospel. The gen. may be subjective indicating that his bonds arise from the gospel (Lohmeyer) or it
14 may mean "my imprisonment for the gospel" (Moule). ■ **χωρίς**
w. the gen. without. **γνώμη** opinion, consent. The word was used often in the papyri in this sense (s. Stuhlmacher; Dibelius; Preisigke; MM). **ἠθέλησα** aor. act. ind. θέλω to wish, to desire. The aor. tense describes a definite completed action (s. Lightfoot; EGT). **ποιῆσαι** aor. act. inf. **ἀνάγκη** pressure, necessity, complusion. **τὸ ἀγαθόν σου** "the benefit arising from you," i.e., "the good which I should get from the continued presence of Onesimus and which would be oweing to you" (Lightfoot). **ἑκουσίος** voluntary. Used here w. the prep. "of one's own free
15 will" (BAG). ■ **τάχα** perhaps. **ἐχωρίσθη** aor. pass. ind. χωρίζω
to separate, to depart; i.e. by escaping. The pass. may contain a conviction of the divine overruling and would be parallel to the "divine pass." in Heb. which was a mode of expression to denote the hidden action of God as an agent responsible for what is done (Martin, NCB). **αἰώνιος** eternal. In this context it appears to mean "for good," "permanently" (Moule). **ἀπέχῃς** pres. act. subj. ἀπέχω to have. The word was a commercial t.t. meaning "to receive a sum in full and give a receipt for it." Here the idea
16 is to keep, to keep for one's self (s. BAG; Ellicott). ■ **οὐκέτι** no
longer. **ὑπὲρ δοῦλον** "beyond a slave," "more than a slave" (RWP). **ἀγαπητός** beloved (s.v.1). **μάλιστα** especially. **πόσῳ**

μᾶλλον "how much rather," having first said "most of all to
me," he goes a step further, "more than most of all to thee"
(Lightfoot). **ἐν σαρκί** "in the flesh," i.e., "as a man" (Martin,
NCB).

■ **ἔχεις** pres. act. ind. The ind. is used in a first-class condi- 17
tional clause which accepts the condition as a reality. **κοινωνιός**
sharer, partner. The word denotes those who have common
interest, common feelings, and common work (Lightfoot; s. also
v. 6). **προσλαβοῦ** aor. mid. imp. προσλαμβάνω mid. to take
to one's self, to receive or accept in one's society or into one's
home or circle of acquaintances (BAG). ■ **ἠδίκησεν** aor. ind. 18
act. ἀδικέω to act unjustly, to wrong someone, to injure.
ὀφείλει pres. act. ind. to owe someone a debt. **ἐλλόγα** pres. act.
imp. ἐλλογάω to place on someone's account. The word was a
commercial t.t. meaning "to charge to someone's account" (s.
MM; Preisigke; BAG; Dibelius; Lohse). ■ **ἔγραψα** aor. act. ind. 19
epistolary aor. (s.v.12). **ἀποτίσω** fut. act. ind. ἀποτίνω to
repay, to pay back. The word is a legal t.t. and appears in promissory notes (s. Lohse; LAE, 331f.). **λέγω** pres. act. subj.
προσοφείλω pres. act. ind. to owe a debt besides, to owe in
addition to (s. Ellicott). ■ **ναί** yes. **ὀναίμην** aor. mid. opt. to 20
benefit, to profit. The opt. is used to express a wish and was used
in the formula "may I have joy, profit or benefit" and was used
w. the gen. of the person or thing that is the source of the joy
or profit (s. BAG). **ἀνάπαυσον** pres. act. imp. (s.v.7).

■ **πεποιθώς** perf. act. part. πέποιθα to persuade, perf. to 21
be persuaded, to have confidence (s. Phil. 1:6). **ὑπακοή** listening
to, obedient. **ἔγραψα** aor. act. ind. **εἰδώς** perf. act. part. οἶδα.
ποιήσεις fut. act. ind. (For general discussions of slavery in the
ancient world and esp. of slaves obtaining their freedom, s. FCS;
Lohse; Stuhlmacher, 42–48; DC XIV-XV; Seneca, *Letters to
Lucilus*, 47: DGRA, 1034–1042; KP V, 230–234; CC, 109–112;
1 Cor. 7:21; Rom. 1:1). ■ **ἅμα** at the same time, besides. 22
ἑτοίμαζε pres. act. imp. ἑτοιμάζω to prepare, to prepare a guest
room (s. Stuhlmacher). **ξενία** lodging, a place of entertainment.
It may denote quarters in an inn or a room in a private house
(Lightfoot). **χαρισθήσομαι** fut. pass. ind. χαρίζομαι to give
graciously, to grant somebody to someone (s. Lightfoot; Moule).
The pass. voice suggests that it is God who alone can secure
Paul's release, though Paul relies on the prayers of the community to entreat God for this favor (Martin, NCB).

■ **ἀσπάζομαι** pres. mid. ind. to greet. **συναιχμάλωτος** 23
fellow captive. ■ **συνεργός** fellow worker (s.v.1). (For a discus- 24

sion of churches in homes in the ancient Christian world, s. Stuhlmacher, 70–75.)

HEBREWS

Ch. 1

πολυμερῶς adv. in many ways, in many parts. The word 1
points to the fragmentary character of former revelations. The
revelation of God was essentially progressive (EGT).
πολυτρόπως adv. in many ways, in various manners. It could
refer both to the various geographical locations of the revelation
as well as to the various methods of disclosure; i.e., direct revelation, dreams, visions, etc. (Buchanan; s. also Westcott; Michel).
πάλαι formerly, of old time. The word describes something
completed in the past. Here the thought is of the ancient teachings now long since sealed (Westcott). **λαλήσας** aor. act. part.
λαλέω to speak, w. the dat. to speak to. The aor. tense points
to the completed action. The part. is used temporarily indicating
antecedent time; i.e., "after he had spoken." **πατράσιν** dat. pl.
"to the fathers." **ἐν** "in," "through." The prep. could refer to the
teaching of inspiration which viewed the prophets as being indwelled by the Holy Spirit (Michel; s. also Westcott). ■ **ἐπ᾽** 2
ἐσχάτου at the end. **ἐπ᾽ ἐσχάτου τῶν ἡμερῶν** "the last of these
days." The rabbinic term indicated the time of the Messiah (SB
III, 617; s. also Buchanan; Hughes). **ἐλάλησεν** aor. act. ind.
λαλέω to speak. The aor. tense used both of God speaking by
the prophets and also His speaking by Christ indicates that God
has finished speaking in both cases (Hughes). **ἐν υἱῷ** "in one who
is a son." The absence of the article fixes attention upon the
nature and not upon the personality of the mediator of a new
revelation. God spake to us in one who has this character that
He is Son (Westcott). **ἔθηκεν** aor. act. ind. **τίθημι** to place, to
appoint. **κληρονόμος** heir. The word is derived from the term
"lot" and referred to a situation in which lots were drawn to
divide property or select a winner; the one who drew the lot was
the heir. The word came to be used for dividing the property that
a father left to his children when he died. When there was only
one son, there would only be one heir. Christ is the heir of all
things precisely because God has only one Son and only one heir
(Buchanan; Hughes; s. also TDNT). **ἐποίησεν** aor. act. ind.
ποιέω to make, to create. **τοὺς αἰῶνας** acc. pl. the ages. Ac-

cording to rabbinical use, the word refers not only to the periods
of time, but also to the content of the world (Michel; s. also SB
3 III, 671f.; Bruce). ■ **ὤν** pres. part. εἰμί. The word refers to the
absolute and timeless existence (RWP). **ἀπαύγασμα** radiance.
The active meaning has the idea of emitting brightness and the meaning is that the shekinah glory of God radiated from Him. The pass. idea is not so much that of reflection, but rather the radiation through the source of the light. It is as the sun radiates its rays of light (s. RWP; Hughes; Michel; Westcott; TDNT). **δόξα** glory. It refers to the brilliant radiancy from the person of God (s. TDNT; s. also CBB). **χαρακτήρ** impression, stamp. It refers to an engraved character or impress made by a die or a seal. It also indicates the characteristic trait or distinctive mark. It was used w. special reference to any distinguishing pecularity and hence indicated "an exact reproduction" (Hughes; BAG; MM; TDNT). **ὑπόστασις** essence, substance, nature (s. Heb. 11:1). **φέρων** pres. act. part. φέρω to carry. The concept is dynamic and not static. The Son's work of upholding involves not only support, but also movement. He is the One who carries all things forward on their appointed course (Hughes; Bruce; s. also Michel). **τὰ πάντα** "all things." **τῷ ῥήματι** dat. of instrument. **καθαρισμός** cleansing, purification. **ποιησάμενος** aor. mid. part. ποιέω to make. The use of the mid. suggests the thought that Christ Himself, in His own person made the purification (Westcott). The aor. tense points to the completed action and the temporal part. expresses action which occurred before the main verb. **ἐκάθισεν** aor. act. ind. καθίζω to sit down, to take one's seat. **ἐν δεξιᾷ** (on the right hand). (For the concept of Christ sitting at the right hand, s. Eph. 1:20.) **μεγαλωσύνη** majesty. **ὑψηλός** high, pl. equivalent to the term "in heaven" (s.
4 Michel). ■ **τοσούτῳ** dat. of instrument used w. the comp. "by
how much more" (RWP). **κρείττων** comp. κρατός strong comp. better, superior. The word is characteristic of the epistle (thirteen times) and the idea is that of superiority in dignity or worth or advantage, the fundamental idea being power and not goodness (Westcott). **τοσούτῳ** as great, how great, as much, how much. Used as a correlative w. the comp. in the sense "by as much ... as" (s. BAG; RWP). **διαφορώτερος** comp. διάφορος different, comp. excellent, more excellent. **παρά** "than." The prep. is used w. the acc. after a comp. (s. MT, 251; IBG, 51). **κεκληρονόμηκεν** perf. act. ind. κληρονομέω to inherit, perf. to have inherited, to be an heir (s. Buchanan; Michel; TDNT).

5 ■ **ποτέ** ever. **εἶ** 2nd per. sing. εἰμί. **σήμερον** today. The

day spoken of here is the day of His glorious victory and vindication. The Resurrection, Ascension and glorification should be
viewed as forming a unity, each one contributing to the exaltation of the Son to transendental heights of power and dignity
(Hughes). **γεγέννηκα** perf. act. ind. γεννάω to give birth to, to
bear. This begetting is the begetting of the incarnate Son and it
marks the completion and the acceptance of His redeeming
mission to our world (Hughes). **ἔσομαι** fut. εἰμί. **ἔσται** fut.
■ **ὅταν** when, whenever. **εἰσαγάγῃ** aor. act. subj. εἰσάγω to 6
lead into. The word is probably a Hebraism w. the meaning "to
bring something into the world" and referred either to a birth or
to the entrance into the fut. world. Here it refers either to the
Incarnation or to the enthronement (Michel; s. also Riggenbach). **πρωτότοκος** firstborn (s. Col. 1:18; Michel; TDNT;
Hughes). **οἰκουμένη** world, inhabited world. **προσκυνησάτω**
aor. act. imp. προσκυνέω w. the dat. to fall on the knees before
someone, to worship (s. TDNT; CBB). ■ **πρός** used w. the acc. 7
"to." **ποιῶν** pres. act. part. **πνεῦμα** wind. **λειτουργός** minister.
The description here may be understood in two ways, either as
a personification as when the wind storm and fire do His word,
or as referring to real persons; i.e., the angels can take the form
of wind or fire (Delitzsch; s. also Hughes). **φλόξ** flame. ■ **ὁ θεός** 8
voc. "O God." The article used w. the voc. is due to Semitic
influence (BG, 11; s. also MT, 34). **αἰών** age. Used here in the
expression to mean "eternal" (s. TDNT). **ῥάβδος** scepter.
εὐθύτης strictness, uprightness. ■ **ἠγάπησας** aor. act. ind. 2nd 9
per. sing. ἀγαπάω. **ἐμίσησας** aor. act. ind. 2nd per. sing.
μισέω to hate. The aor. tense could apply to the life and ministry of the incarnate Son on earth (Westcott; s. also Hughes;
Riggenbach). **ἀνομία** lawlessness. **διὰ τοῦτο** because of this.
ἔχρισέν aor. act. ind. χρίω to anoint. The idea is the crowning
of the sovereign w. joy as at the royal banquet (Westcott; s. also
TDNT). **ἔλαιον** oil. **ἀγαλλίασις** joy, gladness. The gen. would
be gen. of description indicating the oil which was used on
occasions of gladness. **παρά.** Used in a comp. "more than,"
"above." **μέτοχος** partner, comrade, colleague. The reference
here is not to angels but to believers who will share His reign in
the age to come (Kent). ■ **κατ' ἀρχάς** "at the beginning," "in 10
the beginning." **ἐθεμελίωσας** aor. act. ind. 2nd per. sing.
θεμελιόω to lay a foundation. ■ **ἀπολοῦνται** fut. mid. ind. 11
ἀπόλλυμι to perish. **διαμένει** pres. act. ind. to remain, to continue throughout. The pres. tense plus the prep. in compound
emphasize the permanent continual existence (s. MH, 301f.).
ἱμάτιον garment. **παλαιωθήσονται** fut. pass. ind. παλαιόω

12 pass. to grow old, to become old, ingressive aor. ■ **ὡσεί** as. **περιβόλαιον** that which one wraps around himself, cloak. The word suggests a costly robe (Westcott). **ἑλίξεις** fut. act. ind. ἑλίσσω to roll up, to fold together. **ἀλλαγήσονται** fut. pass. ind. ἀλλάσσω to change, to change clothes. **εἶ** 2nd per. sing. εἰμί. Used in the sense of "remain," i.e., "but you remain (are) the same." **ἔτη** nom. pl. ἔτος year. **ἐκλείψουσιν** fut. act. ind. ἐκλείπω to leave off, to fail. (For the prep. in compound, s. MH,
13 309.) ■ **εἴρηκεν** perf. act. ind. λέγω. **κάθου** pres. mid. imp., s.v.3. **ἐκ δεξιῶν** "on the right (hand)." **θῶ** aor. act. subj. **τίθημι** to set, to place. **ἐχθρός** one who actively hates, enemy. **ὑποπόδιον** footstool, double acc. used w. the verb (Michel). **ποδῶν** gen. pl. πούς foot. The figure arose from the oriental custom of the victor putting his foot on the neck of the defeated
14 enemy (N. Lightfoot). ■ **λειτουργικός** ministering. The suf. of the word has the idea of "belonging to," "pertaining to," "w. the characteristic of" (s. MH, 378). **διακονία** service (s. TDNT). The rabbinical term "angel of service or ministry" was used of angels who protected or accompanied a person (s. SB III, 680f.). **ἀποστελλόμενα** pres. pass. part. ἀποστέλλω to send out, to commission, to send as an authoritative representative (s. TDNT; CBB). **διά** w. the acc. "because of." **μέλλοντας** pres. act. part. μέλλω to be about to. The word is used w. the inf. to express the fut. (s. MKG, 307f.). **κληρονομεῖν** pres. act. inf. to inherit. **σωτηρία** salvation. Here it is salvation in its ultimate and broadest term (s. Michel; TDNT; CBB; NTW, 114f.). (For the use of the OT by the author of Hebrews, s. N. Lightfoot, 63f.; BE.)

Ch. 2

1 ■ **δεῖ** impersonal used w. the acc. and the inf. "it is binding," "it is necessary." The word marks the logical necessity "we must" (Westcott). **περισσοτέρως** comp. adv. "more abundantly," "more earnestly" (s. BD, 33). The word here could have almost an elative sense "w. extreme care" (Moffatt). **προσέχειν** pres. act. inf. to give heed to, to give attention to. The word is commonly used of bringing a ship to land (EGT). The verb is followed by the dat. **ἀκουσθεῖσιν** aor. pass. part. ἀκούω to hear. **παραρυῶμεν** aor. pass. subj. παραρρέω to flow by. The word was used to describe a river that flows by a place or flows aside from its normal channel in the sense of flooding or escaping its channel. It was used of something slipping from one's memory or of a ring slipping from one's finger or of a crumb going down the wrong way. It also indicated a ship drifting away (s.

Hughes; Buchanan; Moffatt; Michel; Westcott). The pass. signifies to get or to find one's self in a state of flowing or passing by; i.e., in reference to an object which requires close attention
(Delitzsch). ■ **λαληθείς** aor. pass. part. λαλέω. **ἐγένετο** aor. 2
mid. ind. γίνομαι. **βέβαιος** firm, dependable, reliable, guaranteed. The word was used in the papyri in a technical sense for a legal guarantee (BS, 107; s. also BAG; TDNT; s. also 1 Cor. 1:6). **παράβασις** stepping beside, transgression. **παρακοή** hearing beside, disobedience. Both expressions here involve an expressed rejection of the divine will (Riggenbach). **ἔλαβεν** aor. act. ind. λαμβάνω to receive. **ἔνδικος** just, that which conforms to right. The prep. in compound indicates that the word stands in antithesis to the term "unrighteous" (s. MH, 307). **μισθαποδοσία** giving back w. payment, a paying back, recompense, retribution. The word indicates a full recompense as punishment (s. Riggenbach). ■ **ἐκφευξόμεθα** fut. mid. ind. 3
ἐκφεύγω to flee from, to escape. **τηλικοῦτος** so great, so large, so important. **ἀμελήσαντες** aor. act. part. ἀμελέω w. the gen. to be unconcerned about, to neglect. The part. is used conditionally "if we neglect." **λαβοῦσα** aor. act. part. fem. sing. λαμβάνω. **ἀρχὴν λαβοῦσα** lit. "having received a beginning to be spoken," "having begun to be spoken" (RWP). **λαλεῖσθαι** pres. pass. inf. epexegetical describing the "beginning." The pass. used here is the "divine pass." implying that it is God who spoke (Hughes). **ἀκουσάντων** aor. act. part. ἀκούω. This came to the author and his contemporaries from "those who heard" and probably means that they received it from the ear and eyewitnesses—those who saw and heard the very words of Jesus (Buchanan). This information plainly rules out the admissibility of any "first-hand" apostle or disciple as the writer of our epistle (Hughes). **ἐβεβαιώθη** aor. pass. ind. βεβαιόω to make firm, to confirm, to guarantee. A t.t. indicating legal security and validity
(s.v.2; s. also MM). ■ **συνεπιμαρτυροῦντος** pres. act. part. 4
συνεπιμαρτυρέω to witness together w. someone, to join in giving additional testimony. The part. is used in a gen. abs. construction (s. RWP). **τέρας** wonder. **σημεῖον** sign. The word indicates that the event is not an empty ostentation of power, but it is significant in that it points beyond itself to the reality of the mighty hand of God in operation (Hughes). **ποικίλος** various, variegated, manifold. **δύναμις** power, miracle. The word emphasizes the dynamic character of the event w. particular regard to its outcome or effect (Hughes). **μερισμός** dividing, distribution. The following gen. could be subjective gen.; i.e., "distribution which the Holy Spirit gives" or perhaps better obj. gen.

"distribution of the Holy Spirit," i.e., the reference is God's distribution of spiritual gifts to His people (Bruce). **κατά** w. the acc. "according to," "in accordance w." **θέλησις** will, willing. The word describes the active exercise of will (Westcott).
5 ■ **ὑπέταξεν** aor. act. ind. ὑποτάσσω to subordinate, to subject to one's authority. **μέλλουσαν** pres. act. part. μέλλω to be about to, fut. The phrase "the world to come" was considered by the rabbis to be the age of Messiah, the time when the Messiah would rule as king from His throne at Jerusalem (Buchanan; s. also SB IV, Michel). The term refers to the coming age when Christ at His return shall establish His rule as the promised
6 Davidic king (Kent). ■ **διεμαρτύρατο** aor. mid. ind. διαμαρτύρομαι to testify, to solemnly testify, to solemnly declare (s. MH, 302). **πού** where, somewhere. It is characteristic of the author that he is not concerned to provide a precise identification of the sources from which he quotes. It is sufficient for him that he is quoting from Holy Scripture, whose inspiration and authority he accepts without question (Hughes). **τις** someone. **μιμνήσκῃ** pres. mid. ind. 2nd per. sing. to remember. **ἐπισκέπτῃ** pres. mid. ind. 2nd per. sing. to look upon, to visit. The word is used almost exclusively in the LXX, as in the NT,
7 of a visitation for good (Westcott). ■ **ἠλάττωσας** aor. act. ind. ἐλαττόω to make less, to make lower, to reduce in rank (Buchanan). **βραχύ** a little. The word could have a temporal force "for a little while" (Bruce). **παρά** w. the acc. "than." (For the prep. used in a comp. construction, s. Heb. 1:4, 9.) **δόξα** glory.
8 **ἐστεφάνωσας** aor. act. ind. στεφανόω to crown. ■ **ὑπέταξας** aor. act. ind., s.v.5. **ὑποκάτω** under. **ὑποτάξαι** aor. act. inf., s.v.5. The articular inf. is used w. a prep. to express time "when." Although the aor. inf. w. the prep. generally expresses antecedent time while the pres. inf. expresses contemporaneous time, the context must decide and here it could be translated "putting everything in subjection" (MT, 145). **ἀφῆκεν** aor. act. ind. ἀφίημι to leave out, to omit. **ἀνυπότακτος** unsubjected. The verbal adj. here has a pass. sense (RWP). **οὔπω** not yet. **ὁρῶμεν** pres. act. ind. ὁράω to see. **ὑποτεταγμένα** perf. pass. part. ὑποτάσσω s.v.5. The perf. tense indicates the completed state
9 or condition. ■ **βραχύ** temporal "a little while." **παρά** than, s.v.7. **ἠλαττωμένον** perf. pass. part., s.v.7. The perf. emphasizes the completed state or condition and indicates that the human nature which Christ assumed He still retains (Westcott). **πάθημα** suffering. **δόξα** glory (s. Heb. 1:3). **ἐστεφανωμένον** perf. pass. part., s.v.7. **ὅπως** in order that. The particle introduces a purpose clause which is to be taken w. the idea of

"suffering" (s. Moffatt; Bruce). **χάριτι θεοῦ** instrumental "by the grace of God." (For a discussion of the textual variant "without God," s. Michel; TC.) **ὑπέρ** w. the gen. "for," "for the benefit of." **γεύσηται** aor. mid. subj. γεύομαι (w. the gen.) to taste, to taste of. The verb is used in this common idiomatic sense and means "to experience something to the full" (Hughes).

■ **ἔπρεπεν** impf. ind. act. πρέπει used impersonally "it is 10
fitting," "it is appropriate." It was appropriate that action taken to help man should include suffering, since suffering is mankind's common lot (Montefiore; s. also Westcott). **διά** w. the acc. "because of." **διά** w. the gen. "through." The phrases indicate that the sufferings and death of Jesus are not accidental; they form part of the eternal world purpose of God (Moffatt). **ἀγαγόντα** aor. act. part. ἄγω to lead. The part. could refer to Christ who leads sons into glory or it could refer to the subject of the inf.; i.e., God the Father who leads sons into glory (s. Hughes, 101f.; Michel). The aor. part. could express coincident action "by bringing in" (MT, 80) or it could be explained as a proleptic aor. which envisages the work of Christ and its consequences for mankind as a unit (Hughes, 102). **ἀρχηγός** leader, pioneer. In Gr. writings it was used of a "hero" who founded a city, gave it its name, and became its guardian. It also denoted one who was "head" of a family or "founder" of a philosophic school. The term also had a distinct military connotation referring to a commander of an army who went ahead of his men and blazed the trail for them. The idea here is of a leader who opens up a new way (N. Lightfoot; s. also TDNT; MM; Preisigke; Michel). The acc. is to be taken as the object of the inf. **τελειῶσαι** aor. act. inf. τελειόω to complete, to initiate, to perfect, to qualify. To make Jesus fully qualified as "the pioneer of their salvation," the training required involved passing
"through suffering" (Buchanan; s. also Michel; TDNT). ■ 11
ἁγιάζων pres. act. part. ἁγιάζω to sanctify, to consecrate (s. TDNT; CBB). **ἁγιαζόμενοι** pres. pass. part. **ἑνός** gen. of εἷς, **ἐξ ἑνός** "from one," "from one source." The "one" could refer to God indicating that He is the source (s. Bruce) or it could refer to Abraham or Adam indicating the humanity of Christ (s. Hughes). **αἰτία** cause, reason. **δι' ἣν αἰτίαν** "for this reason,"
"because." **ἐπαισχύνεται** pres. mid. ind. to be ashamed. ■ 12
ἀπαγγελῶ fut. act. ind. ἀπαγγέλλω to proclaim, to announce (s. CBB). **μέσον** middle. **ὑμνήσω** fut. act. ind. ὑμνέω to praise,
to sing the praise of someone (AS). ■ **ἔσομαι** fut. εἰμί. 13
πεποιθώς perf. act. part. πέποιθα to persuade, perf. to be persuaded, to be convinced (s. Phil. 1:6). The perf. part. is used in

a periphrastic fut. perf. construction (RWP). **παιδίον** child, lit-
14 tle child. **ἔδωκεν** aor. act. ind. δίδωμι. ■ **ἐπεί** since. **τὰ παιδία**
children. It refers to men and women, creatures of flesh and
blood (Bruce). **κεκοινώνηκεν** perf. act. ind. κοινωνέω followed
by the gen. to share in. The perf. tense describes the constant
human situation (Hughes; s. also Westcott). **αἷμα** blood. **σάρξ**
flesh. The expression "flesh and blood" was the postbiblical Heb.
designation for "men" or "human beings" (Delitzsch).
παραπλησίως adv. coming near, nearly, resembling, in like
manner. **μετέσχεν** aor. act. ind. μετέχω to have a part in, to
share. The aor. tense points to the historical event of the Incarnation when the Son of God assumed this same human nature and
thus Himself became truly man and accordingly truly one w.
mankind (Hughes). **αὐτῶν** gen. used as object of the verb and
refers to "flesh and blood"; i.e., "the human beings."
καταργήσῃ aor. act. subj. καταργέω to render inoperative, to
nullify, to make idle or ineffective, to render impotent as though
no longer existing (Hewitt). **κράτος** power, control (s. TDNT;
Eph. 1:19). **ἔχοντα** pres. act. part. (For rabbinical teaching regarding Satan and his angels and their power over death, s.
Michel; SB I, 144f.; Buchanan.) Here is a paradox. Jesus suffered
and overcame death; the devil, willing death, succumbed (Ben-
15 gel). ■ **ἀπαλλάξῃ** aor. act. subj. ἀπαλλάσσω to change from,
to set free from. The word was used in the papyri for the release
from a place of responsibility; e.g., a marriage contract; the superintendence of land under lease or the release from a munici-
pal office. (For these and other examples, s. MM; Preisigke.) **ζῆν**
pres. act. inf. ζάω to live. **διὰ παντὸς τοῦ ζῆν** "through the
whole of life," "all through the living." (For the use of the prep.
and the inf. here, s. IBG, 56; RWP; MT, 144.) **ἔνοχος** held in,
16 subject to. **δουλεία** slavery, bondage. ■ **δήπου** certainly, surely.
ἐπιλαμβάνεται pres. mid. ind. to take hold of, to seize, to take
to one's self. The word may have in this context the sense of "to
help," "to assist," "to draw someone to one's self to help." (For
this interpretation, s. Bruce; Moffatt; TDNT; for a discussion of
the various meanings and implications of the word, s. Hughes.)
17 ■ **ὅθεν** "from there," "therefore," "wherefore." This seems to be
a favorite word of the writer of this epistle (Riggenbach).
ὤφειλεν impf. act. ind. ὀφείλω to be obligated; i.e., "one must."
The word often implies moral necessity (s. AS; TDNT). **κατὰ
πάντα** "in every respect." **ὁμοιωθῆναι** aor. pass. inf. ὁμοιόω
to make like, pass. to become like. This likeness is nothing less
than complete identification: assimilation, not simulation
(Hughes). **ἐλεήμων** merciful, sympathetic (s. TDNT; CBB).

γένηται aor. mid. subj. γίνομαι. The verb suggests the notion of a result reached through the action of that which we regard as a law (Westcott). **ἀρχιερεύς** high priest. (For the term high priest in Judaism, s. Michel, 165f.; Westcott, 137–141; SB III, 696–700; TDNT; CBB.) **τὰ πρὸς τὸν θεόν** acc. of reference; i.e., "w. reference to the things that pertain to God." The expression points to "all man's relations towards God" (Westcott; s. also Riggenbach). **εἰς** used w. the prep. to express purpose. **ἱλάσκεσθαι** pres. mid. inf. to satisfy, to render well disposed, to conciliate, to propitiate (s. Hughes; APC, 125–185; TDNT;
CBB; Riggenbach). ■ **πέπονθεν** perf. act. ind. πάσχω to suffer. 18
The perf. tense serves to emphasize that, though the temptation Christ suffered in the flesh is a thing of the past, yet its effect is permanent, the effect of compassion and understanding as He aids us in the hour of our temptation (Hughes). **πειρασθείς** aor. pass. part. πειράζω to test, to tempt. The part. describes the manner in which the suffering took place (s. Moffatt). The aor. tense points to the completion of the action. **πειραζομένοις** pres. pass. part. The pres. tense of the part. points to the continuous action that was at that time taking place. **βονθῆσαι** aor. act. inf. βοηθέω to help, to help someone in need (s. Michel).

Ch. 3

■ **ὅθεν** wherefore, therefore, lit. "from which," meaning 1
that the following arguments could be deduced from the conclusion reached above (Buchanan). **κλῆσις** calling. **ἐπουράνιος** heavenly (s. Eph. 1:3). **μέτοχος** one who shares, partner. **κατανοήσατε** aor. act. imp. κατανοέω to put the mind down on a thing, to fix the mind on something, to consider. The word expresses attention and continuous observation and regard (s. RWP; Westcott). **ἀπόστολος** one who is commissioned as an authoritative representative, apostle (s. 1 Cor. 1:1; TDNT; Hughes; Michel; CBB). **ὁμολογία** agreement, confession (s.
ECC; TDNT). ■ **ὄντα** pres. part. masc. acc. sing. εἰμί. 2
ποιήσαντι aor. act. part. Here the word has the idea "to appoint." The word could be used of actions that one undertakes or states of being that one brings about (BAG; Hughes; Moffatt).
■ **πλείων** comp. "greater" followed by the gen. of comparison. 3
δόξα glory. **παρά** "than." (For the prep. used in a comp. construction, s. Heb. 1:4.) **ἠξίωται** perf. pass. ind. ἀξιόω to consider worthy. The perf. tense looks at the state or condition. **ὅσος** how much, as much as. Used in a comp. expression denoting measure and degree (s. AS). **κατά** according to. Used in the comp. construction w. the meaning "as much more . . . as" (s.

BAG). **τιμή** honor. **τοῦ οἴκου** gen. of comparison "than the house." **κατασκευάσας** aor. act. part. κατασκευάζω to equip, to make ready, to construct, to furnish. The word expresses more than the mere construction of the house. It includes the supply of all necessary furniture and equipment (Westcott; s. also Mich-
4 el; MM). ■ **κατασκευάζεται** pres. pass. ind. The pres. is a gnomic pres. indicating that which always occurs as a general rule (s. SMT, 8). **θεός** pres. nom. "is God." The lack of the article w. the pred. nom. emphasizes character or quality (s. John
5 1:1). ■ **θεράπων** server, minister. The word suggests a personal service freely rendered. It denotes both the willing service rendered as well as the relationship between the one serving and the one he serves. It also emphasizes an office which was honorable and dignified. In this case it may have been taken over from the LXX as a translation of the Heb. word (TDNT; EGT; Hughes; Riggenbach). **λαληθησομένων** fut. pass. part. λαλέω. The word indicates that the position of Moses was one which pointed beyond itself to a fut. and higher revelation (Moffatt; s. also
6 Michel). ■ **χρίστος** subject of the unexpressed pred. "is faithful" (Westcott). **ἐσμέν** 1st per. pl. εἰμί. **παρρησία** boldness, confident (s. Michel; TDNT). **καύχημα** boasting, ground of boasting. The following gen. "hope" may be described as a gen. of content or definition: the Christian's hope is the theme of our boasting or glorying (Hughes). **μέχρι** until. **βέβαιος** firm, adverbial acc. "firmly." (For the variant readings and textual problem here, s. TC.) **κατάσχωμεν** aor. act. subj. κατέχω to hold down, to hold fast to.
7 ■ **διό** wherefore, therefore. The particle introducing the quotation looks backward as well as forward (Michel). **ἀκούσητε** aor. act. subj. The subj. is used in a conditional clause.
8 ■ **σκληρύνητε** pres. act. subj. σκληρύνω to dry out, to dry up, to make hard, to harden (Michel). **παραπικρασμός** embittering, exasperation, rebellion. The word is a translation of the Heb. proper name Meribah which means in Heb. "conflict" or "rebellion" (s. Montefiore; Buchanan; Hughes). **κατά** w. the acc. used in a temporal sense "at" (s. IBG, 58). **πειρασμός** tempting, temptation. It is a translation of the Heb. name Massah meaning
9 "tempting" or testing" (s. Buchanan; Montefiore; Hughes). ■ **οὗ** adv. of place "where." **ἐπείρασαν** aor. act. ind. πειράζω to try, to test, to tempt. instrumental use of the prep. "by." **δοκιμασία** proof, testing. The word implies a testing which is intended to
10 bring out the good (s. TDNT). **εἶδον** aor. act. ind. ὁράω. ■ **τεσσεράκοντα** forty. **ἔτα** acc. pl. ἔτος year, acc. of time. The words "forty years" could be taken either w. that which pre-

cedes; i.e., "your fathers put me to the test and saw my works
for forty years," or it could be taken w. what follows; i.e., "for
forty years I was provoked" (Hughes). **προσώχθισα** aor. act.
ind. προσοχθίζω to loath, to be burdened down, to be laden w.
grief, to be exhausted, to be indignant (s. Buchanan). The verb
is followed by the dat. **πλανῶνται** pres. pass. ind. πλανάω to
lead astray, pass. to go astray, to wander astray. **ἔγνωσαν** aor.
act. ind. γινώσκω τὰς ὁδοὺς τοῦ θεοῦ. The word here is not
so much the understanding of the revelatory acts of God and His
leading as it is obedience to God's command (s. Riggenbach).
■ **ὡς** as, according as. **ὤμοσα** aor. act. ind. ὄμνυμι to swear. 11
ὀργή wrath, anger. **εἰ** "if." The word is the translation of the
Heb. particle and is the equivalent of a strong neg. (s. MT, 333;
MH, 468). This construction is in accord w. the Semitic idiom
used in the taking of an oath (s. Buchanan; Michel).
εἰσελεύσονται fut. mid. ind. εἰσέρχομαι to go into.
κατάπαυσις rest (s. TDNT; Michel, 183f.; O. Hofius, *Katapausis. Die Vorstellung vom endzeitlichen Ruheort im Hebräerbrief*
[Tübingen, 1970]).

■ **βλέπετε** pres. act. imp. βλέπω to see, to see to it, to 12
beware. When the word is followed by the neg. and the ind., it
expresses a warning and fear regarding a pres. inevitable reality
and indicates the warning should be taken very seriously (MT,
99; Riggenbach). **ἔσται** fut. εἰμί. **ἀπιστίας** unbelief, gen. of
quality indicating that unbelief characterizes the "evil heart"
(Westcott). **ἀποστῆναι** aor. act. inf. ἀφίσταμι to fall away, to
depart, to leave, to step aside from. The inf. w. the prep. is used
here epexegetically indicating the content of an evil heart (s.
MT, 146; RG, 1073). **ζῶντος** pres. act. part. ζάω to live. The
construction without the article fixes attention upon the character (Westcott). ■ **παρακαλεῖτε** pres. act. imp. παρακαλέω 13
to encourage, to beseech. **ἑαυτούς** yourselves. The reflex. pron.
is deliberately used here instead of the reciprocal pron. "each
other," w. the purpose of emphasizing the close unity of the
Christian body (Westcott), but it may be that the two pron. are
used interchangeably (Hughes). **κατά** w. the acc. used distributively "at each day," i.e., "every day," "daily" (s. IBG, 59;
Westcott; Hughes). **ἄχρις οὗ** "as long as," "while" (RWP).
καλεῖται pres. pass. ind. **σκληρυνθῇ** aor. pass. subj., s.v.8. The
subj. is used in a neg. purpose clause. The pass. could perhaps
be understood as a pass. of permission; i.e., "allow or permit
one's self to be hardened." **ἀπάτη** deceitfulness, dat. of means
used w. a pass. verb. ■ **μέτοχος** partner, sharer, partaker. (For 14
a discussion of this phrase, s. Hughes; Michel.) **γεγόναμεν** perf.

act. ind. *γίνομαι*. The perf. tense signifies that the readers have become and consequently now are partakers of Christ (Hughes). **ἐάνπερ** "if at least" (s. Westcott). **ὑπόστασις** that which underlies, ground, basis. The word then means "confidence," "assurance," "conviction" and refers to the reality, essence, or nature of something, or the ground work or basis of hope (Bruce; Buchanan). **κατάσχωμεν** aor. act. subj. *κατέχω* to hold down,
15 to hold fast. ■ **λέγεσθαι** pres. pass. inf. The inf. used w. the prep.
16 could be temporal or it could also be causal (s. MT, 146). ■ **ἀκούσαντες** aor. act. part. The part. could be concessive "although they had heard." **παρεπίκραναν** aor. act. ind. *παραπικραίνω* to provoke, to exasperate. **ἐξελθόντες** aor. act.
17 part. *ἐξέρχομαι*. ■ **προσώχθισεν** aor. act. ind., s.v.10. **ἁμαρτήσασιν** aor. act. part. masc. pl. dat. **κῶλον** body, corpse.
18 **ἔπεσεν** aor. act. ind. *πίπτω* to fall. ■ **ὤμοσεν** aor. act. ind., s.v.11. **ἀπειθήσασιν** aor. act. part. *ἀπειθέω* to be disobedient,
19 unbelief passed into action (Westcott). ■ **ἠδυνήθησαν** aor. pass. ind. *δύναμαι*. Their exclusion from Canaan was not only a fact, but a moral necessity (Westcott). **εἰσελθεῖν** aor. act. inf. *εἰσέρχομαι*. **ἀπιστία** unbelief. Used w. the prep. and the acc. "because of disbelief."

Ch. 4

1 ■ **φοβηθῶμεν** aor. pass. subj. *φοβέομαι* to be afraid, to fear. The cohortative subj. is used to express a command or excitation in the 1st per.; i.e., "let us fear." **μήποτε** lest. Used after a verb of fear expressing anxiety. Its use w. the subj. indicates that it is a fear of an uncertain thing (MT, 99). **καταλειπομένης** pres. pass. part. *καταλείπομαι* to leave behind, pass. to be left behind. Here the sense is of being "left open" (Bruce). The part. is used in a gen. abs. and could express cause or it could be concessive (s. Riggenbach). **ἐπαγγελία** promise (s. TDNT; CBB; Michel). **εἰσελθεῖν** aor. act. inf. *εἰσέρχομαι*. The inf. is epexegetical and explains what the promise is. **κατάπαυσις** rest (s. Heb. 3:11). **δοκῇ** pres. act. subj. *δοκέω* to appear, to seem, to suppose. The word could also have a forensic idea "to be found" (Michel; Riggenbach). **ὑστερηκέναι** perf. act. inf. *ὑστερέω* to fall short, to be late, to come behind, to fall behind. The verb pictures someone in a company marching together w. others who march faster than he can. He cannot keep up, so he falls behind. Falling behind in religious matters means not being able to fulfill all the demands or commandments; being negligent failing to qualify or measure up (Buchanan). The perf. tense marks not only a present or past

defeat, but an abiding failure (Westcott). ■ **εὐηγγελισμένοι** 2
perf. pass. part. εὐαγγελίζομαι to proclaim good news, pass. to
have good news proclaimed to someone. The part. is used to
build the periphrastic perf. pass. ind. and the perf. emphasizes
the completeness of the evangelization that has taken place, and
thus leaves no room for any excuse to the effect that evangelization had been inadequate or deficient (Hughes). **καθάπερ** just
as. **κακεῖνοι** = καί ἐκεῖνοι "those also." **ἀκοή** hearing. The
gen. is descriptive gen. and emphasizes that the word or message
is associated w. hearing, the implication being that the message
is intended for people to hear and so must be proclaimed
(Hughes). **ὠφέλησεν** aor. act. ind. ὠφελέω to profit, to be profitable. **συγκεκερασμένος** perf. pass. part. συγκεράννυμι to
mix together, to blend, to unite. (For the textual problem here,
s. PC; Hughes.) ■ **εἰσερχόμεθα** pres. mid. ind. Although the 3
pres. tense could be used as a futuristic pres., it is better to take
it as an expression of a pres. fact (Westcott). The pres. tense
could express the idea "we are already in process of entering"
(Montefiore). **πιστεύσαντες** aor. act. part. **εἴρηκεν** perf. act.
ind. λέγω. **ὤμοσα** aor. act. ind. ὄμνυμι to swear, to take an
oath. **ὀργή** anger, wrath. **εἰσελεύσονται** fut. mid. ind.
εἰσέρχομαι. (For the Semitic expression of the oath implying
a strong negative, s. Heb. 3:11.) **καίτοι** used w. the part. expressing a concessive idea "although." **καταβολή** laying down, foundation. **γενηθέντων** aor. pass. part. γίνομαι to become, here
the pass. sense in the perf. "to be completed," "to be finished."
■ **εἴρηκεν** perf. act. ind., s.v.3. **πού** where, somewhere. 4
ἑβδόμης seventh. **κατέπαυσεν** aor. act. ind. καταπαύω to
rest. ■ **ἐν τούτῳ** "in this," "here." ■ **ἐπεί** since, because. 5/6
ἀπολείπεται pres. pass. ind. ἀπολείπω to remain over, to
leave behind, pass. to be left over. **εἰσελθεῖν** aor. act. inf. The
inf. explains what remains to be done. **πρότερον** formerly.
εὐαγγελισθέντες aor. pass. part., s.v.2. **εἰσῆλθον** aor. act. ind.
διά w. the acc. "because," "because of." **ἀπείθεια** unpersuaded,
disobedient. The act. expression of unbelief is manifested in
disobedience (Westcott). ■ **ὁρίζει** to mark out w. a boundary, to 7
appoint, to designate. **σήμερον** today. **τοσοῦτος** so long. Used
in the temporal expression "after so long a time." **προείρηται**
perf. pass. ind. προλέγω to say before, to say previously.
ἀκούσητε aor. act. subj. **σκληρύνετε** aor. act. subj. σκληρύνω
to harden. The aor. subj. is used w. the neg. to express a prohibition. ■ **Ἰησοῦς** Joshua. **κατέπαυσεν** aor. act. ind. καταπαύω 8
to give rest. The ind. is used here in a second-class conditional
clause expressing that which is contrary to fact. **ἐλάλει** impf.

act. ind. λαλέω "he would not speak," "he would not be speak-
9 ing" (RWP). ■ **ἄρα** "so then." The word draws a conclusion
from the preceding argument. **ἀπολείπεται** pres. pass. ind.,
10 s.v.6. **σαββατισμός** sabbath rest. ■ **εἰσελθών** aor. act. part.
εἰσέρχομαι. **κατέπαυσεν** aor. act. ind. to rest, to cease. **ἴδιος**
11 one's own. ■ **σπουδάσωμεν** aor. act. subj. σπουδάζω to be in
a hurry, to make haste, to be in earnest, to concentrate one's energies on the achievement of a goal, to endeavor (Hughes). The subj. is hortatory expressing a command "let us . . . ." **εἰσελθεῖν** aor. act. inf. **ἵνα** "that." **ὑπόδειγμα** example. The word is used here in the sense of a warning sign (Michel). The word refers not to an example of disobedience, but to an example of falling into destruction as a result of disobedience (BAG). **ἀπείθεια** disobedience, s.v.6.

12 ■ **ζῶν** pres. act. part. ζάω to be alive, living. **ἐνεργής** energetic, active, productive. The word is used of activity which produces results and is used often for divine activity which produces effective results (s. MNTW, 46ff.; TDNT). **τομώτερος** comp. τομός sharp, comp. sharper. **ὑπέρ** than. The word is used in a comp. construction; i.e., "sharper beyond," "sharper than." **μάχαιρα** sword (s. Eph. 6:17). **δίστομος** double-edged, two edged. **διϊκνούμενος** pres. mid. part. διϊκνέομαι to pass through, to pierce, to penetrate (cf. Exod. 26:28, LXX). **μερισμός** dividing. **ἁρμός** joint. **μυελός** marrow. The expressions serve to convey effectively the notion of the extreme power of penetration of the word of God, to the very core of man's being (Hughes). **ἐνθύμησις** capable of making a decision, discerning, able to judge, followed by the objective gen. **ἐννοιῶν** thought, reflection, feelings. The word refers to the action of the affections and is related to the will (Westcott; Michel). **ἔννοια** thought, intent. The word refers to the action of reason (West-
13 cott). ■ **κτίσις** creature. **ἀφανής** hidden, not manifest. **γυμνός**
naked, open. **τετραχηλισμένα** perf. pass. part. τραχηλίζω to lay bear, to expose. The figure of speech behind the word is not clear. It has been suggested that it refers to the bending back the neck of a sacrificial victim making ready for the final stroke or it may refer to the wrestler's art of seizing one by the throat rendering him limp and powerless. (For these suggestions w. references to usage, s. Riggenbach; Michel; Hughes; Bruce; Delitzsch.) **πρὸς ὅν ἡμῖν ὁ λόγος** "w. whom our matter is," "w. whom our account is," i.e., "w. whom we have to deal," "w. whom our final reckoning has to be made" (Bruce). (For the meaning "w. reference to which our message applies," "which

word applies to us" as well as a discussion of other interpretations, s. Buchanan.)
■ **ἔχοντες** pres. act. part. to have, to possess. The part. 14
could be causal. **ἀρχιερεύς** high priest. **διεληλυθότα** perf. act. part. διέρχομαι to pass through, to go through. The perf. tense indicates that he has passed through the heavens and is still there. **κρατῶμεν** pres. act. subj. κρατέω to be in control of, to exercise power over, to hold to, to hold fast, followed by the gen.
ὁμολογία confession, profession. ■ **δυνάμενον** pres. mid. part. 15
συμπαθῆσαι aor. pass. inf. συμπαθέω to share the experience of someone, to sympathize w. someone. The word is not to be understood in a psychological sense, but rather in an existential sense. The exalted one suffers together w. the weakness of the one tempted (Michel). **ἀσθένεια** weakness. **πεπειρασμένον** perf. pass. part. πειράζω to tempt, to test, to try. The perf. tense emphasizes the completed state and continuing results. **ὁμοιότης** likeness. The word emphasizes exact correspondence
(s. Michel; TDNT). ■ **προσερχώμεθα** pres. mid. subj. 16
προσέρχομαι to come to, to draw near. The word was used in the LXX for the priestly approach to God in service (Westcott). The subj. is cohortative "let us come near." The pres. tense emphasizes that the privilege is always available. **θρόνος τῆς χάριτος** "throne of grace," i.e., a throne characterized by grace. **παρρησία** speaking all things, boldness, confidence, assurance (s. Heb. 3:6). **λάβωμεν** aor. act. subj. λαμβάνω to receive. Subjunctive used in a purpose clause. **ἔλεος** mercy (s. 1 Tim. 1:2). **εὕρωμεν** aor. act. subj. **εὔκαιρος** convenient, good time, well timed; i.e., at the right time (Delitzsch; s. also Michel; Preisigke; MM). **βοήθεια** help, help given to one in need (s. Heb. 2:18).

Ch. 5

■ **λαμβανόμενος** pres. pass. part. **καθίσταται** pres. pass. 1
ind. καθίστημι to constitute, to appoint. The pass. voice implies that he does not appoint himself (Hughes). The pres. tense is gnomic referring to that which is always true. **τὰ πρὸς τὸν θεόν** "in reference to things pertaining to God," "in reference to things in relation to God." **προσφέρῃ** pres. act. subj. προσφέρω to carry to, to offer. The word was used in a religious sense of bringing an offering or sacrifice to God. **δῶρον** gift. **θυσία** sacrifice. The expressions are best understood here as a general description of the offerings over which the high priest
officiated (Hughes). ■ **μετριοπαθεῖν** pres. act. inf. 2
μετριοπαθέω to moderate one's feelings, to have feelings in the right measure. The word was used in Aristotelian philosophical

tradition in the sense of moderating one's feelings or passions so as to avoid excesses either of enthusiasm or impassivity. The word indicates that an earthly high priest is not to pass over the sin of his fellow man without any regard at all; however, on the other hand he is not to allow himself to be caught up in his passion and pity for the sinner but he is rather to have a controlled feeling of sympathy (s. Michel; Buchanan; Hughes). **δυνάμενος** pres. mid. part. The part. is used to describe the character of one who is taken or appointed to be a high priest. **ἀγνοοῦσιν** pres. act. part. dat. pl. ἀγνοέω to be without understanding, to be ignorant. **πλανωμένος** pres. mid. part. πλανάω to go astray, to wander. The two part. used w. a single article refer to a single class or category of those sinning; i.e., those who erred through ignorance (N. Lightfoot; Montefiore; Westcott). **περίκειται** pres. pass. ind. περίκειμαι to be surrounded by, to be encompassed by. It is like a millstone around his neck (Mark 9:42; Luke 17:2) or like a chain lying around him (Acts 28:20)
3 (RWP). **ἀσθένεια** weakness. ■ **ὀφείλει** pres. act. ind. to be obligated "he must." The word speaks of moral obligation; i.e., "he is bound" in the very nature of things, in virtue of his constitution and of his office (Westcott). The pres. tense is gnomic indicating that which is always true (s. SMT, 8). **καθώς**
4 just as, as. **προσφέρειν** pres. act. inf., s.v.1. ■ **τιμή** honor. The word was used in Josephus to describe the "honor" of the office of high priest (Josephus, *Antiquities* III, 188f.; s. also Michel). **καλούμενος** pres. pass. part. καλέω. **καθώσπερ** just as. The author may have had in mind the leading sacerdotal families of Jerusalem in his day, who were not descendants of Aaron, but had sought for themselves the high priestly office and been elevated to it by Herod the Great. Such men, though approved by the state, were not approved by God (Hughes).
5 ■ **ἐδόξασεν** aor. act. ind. δοξάζω to glorify. **γενηθῆναι** aor. pass. inf. γίνομαι. The inf. may be epexegetical explaining the main verb; i.e., "Christ did not take for Himself the honor of becoming high priest" or it may be used to express result (s. IBG, 127). **ὁ λαλήσας** aor. act. part. λαλέω. **εἶ** pres. ind. 2nd per. sing. εἰμί. **γεγέννηκα** perf. act. ind. γεννάω to beget, to
6 become the father of. ■ **ἐν ἑτέρῳ** "in another place." **τάξις** rank,
7 order. ■ **δεήσις** prayer. **ἱκετηρία** supplication, petition. The word properly denotes an olive branch entwined w. wool borne by suppliants. The olive branch was the sign of the suppliant (Westcott; BAG; for the use of the word in the papyri, s. MM). **δάκρυον** tear. Later rabbinic piety laid stress on tears in regard to the three kinds of prayers; i.e., entreaty, crying, and tears. It

is said that entreaty is offered in a quiet voice, crying w. a raised voice, but tears are higher than all (Moffatt). **προσενέγκας** aor. act. part. προσφέρω to offer, s.v.1. **εἰσακουσθείς** aor. pass. part. εἰσακούω to hear, to answer, pass. to be heard. **ἀπό** "from." It is to be understood here in the sense of "arising from," "as the result of" (Hughes). **εὐλάβεια** godly fear. The word marks that careful and watchful reverence which pays regard to every circumstance in that which it has to deal (Westcott; s. also Michel; for various interpretations of the passage, s. Hughes; s.
also Bruce). ■ **καίπερ.** Used w. the part. "although." **ἔμαθεν** 8
aor. act. ind. μανθάνω to learn. **ἀφ' ὧν** = ἀπὸ τούτων ἅ "from these things which." **ἔπαθεν** aor. act. ind. πάσχω to suffer. **ὑπακοή** obedience. The article indicates the "particular obedience" which was required of him in the days of his flesh (EGT).
■ **τελειωθείς** aor. pass. part. τελειόω to complete, to perfect. 9
The part. could be temporal or causal. His perfection consisted in the retention of his integrity, in the face of every kind of assault on his integrity, and thereby the establishment of his integrity (Hughes; for a study of this word and its possible contextual backgrounds, s. Michel; TDNT; A. Wikgren, "Patterns of Perfection in the Epistle to the Hebrews," NTS, 6 [1960], 159–167). **ὑπακούουσιν** pres. act. part. ὑπακούω to obey, to be obedient. **αἴτιος** cause, reason, author. (For various examples of the word esp. from Philo, s. Bruce; N. Lightfoot; Westcott.)
■ **προσαγορευθείς** aor. pass. part. προσαγορεύω to desig- 10
nate, to greet, to salute, to hail. The word contains the idea of a formal and solemn ascription of a title (s. BAG; MM; EGT; Westcott).

■ **περὶ οὗ** "concerning whom," "concerning which." The 11
author refers to the priesthood of Christ; i.e., the order of Melchisedek (Hughes). **ἡμῖν** dat. pl. The dat. indicates the obligation signifying "the exposition which it is incumbent on us to undertake" (EGT). **δυσερμήνευτος** difficult to explain, difficult to interpret, hard to explain (s. Moffatt; Michel; EGT). **λέγειν** pres. act. inf. The inf. is used epexegetically to explain the adj. **νωθρός** dull, slow, sluggish. The word was used of the numbed limbs of a sick lion (EGT). In the papyri the corresponding verb is used of "sickness" (MM). **γεγόνατε** perf. act. ind. γίνομαι to become. It is not a question of what they are by nature, but of what they have become by default, the implication being that this was not the case w. them originally (Hughes). The perf. tense signifies the state or condition. **ταῖς ἀκοαῖς** dat. pl. dat.
of reference "in reference to hearing." ■ **ὀφείλοντες** pres. act. 12
part. to be obligated, one must. The part. is concessive "although

you are obligated." **χρείαν ἔχετε** "you have a need." It is followed by the gen. of the inf. indicating what is needful. **στοιχεῖα** pl. basic elements (s. Michel; TDNT). **ἀρχή** beginning. The gen. can be gen. of definition (Bruce) or descriptive gen.; i.e., "original elements." Here it denotes the foundational teaching (Spicq; s. also EGT). **τὰ λόγια τοῦ θεοῦ** "the oracles of God." The phrase might refer to the new revelation given by Christ to His apostles; but is seems more natural to refer it to the collected writings of the OT (Westcott). **γάλα** milk. The word can be compared to the rabbinical term "suckling" referring to young
13 students (EGT; Spicq; TDNT). **στερεός** solid. **τροφή** food. ■ **μετέχων** pres. act. part. to partake of, to partake, followed by the gen. **ἄπειρος** unskilled. It describes a person who lacks experience, is untried, or ignorant (Buchanan). **λόγος δικαιοσύνης** "word of righteousness." The phrase has been taken to refer to an infant's inability to speak correctly (Riggenbach) or to instruction concerning ethical righteousness (Westcott) or it is taken in the sense of the righteousness of Christ which is imputed to the believer (s. Hughes). **νήπιος** lit. "not
14 able to speak or talk," "infant" (RWP; Hughes). ■ **τέλειος** perfect, mature. It would refer to those who should assume adult responsibilities. The author is using terms of human development to describe the readers' development in faith (Buchanan; s. also v.6; for a parallel in the DSS, s. 1QS 1:10–11). **ἕξις** habit. It refers to a habit of body or mind indicating not the process but the result; i.e., the condition has been produced by past exercise and is then the habitual or normal condition, the disposition or character (EGT; Westcott; Spicq). **αἰσθητήριον** faculty. It means the faculties or senses of perception and is used here of spiritual sensitivity (Hughes). **γεγυμνασμένα** perf. pass. part. γυμνάζω to exercise, to train by exercise. **διάκρισις** distinguishing, deciding, making a judgment between two things. (For the force of the prep. in compound, s. MH, 303.)

Ch. 6

1 ■ **διό** therefore. **ἀφέντες** aor. act. part. ἀφίημι to leave. The part. could be means; i.e., "in that we leave." The "leaving" does not mean to despise or abandon the elementary doctrines. The point is that the beginning is not a stopping place; it is the door to progress and the spring board to achievement (Hughes). **τὸν . . . Χριστοῦ λόγον** "the word of the beginning of Christ." The gen. "of Christ" could be obj. gen.; i.e., the beginning teaching about Christ; or it could be subjective gen.; i.e., Christ's initial teachings (s. Buchanan; Hughes; J.C. Adams, "Exegesis of He-

brews 6:1f," NTS, 13 [July, 1967], 378–385). **τελειότης** perfection, maturity (s. Heb. 5:6, 14). **φερώμεθα** pres. pass. subj. φέρω
to carry, pass. to be carried. The subj. is cohortative "let us be
carried," and the pass. gives the thought of personal surrender
to an active influence (Westcott). It is not a matter of the learn-
ers being carried by their instructors, but of both being carried
forward together by God. It is a "divine pass." implying the
agency of God (Hughes; s. also BG, 76). **θεμέλιον** foundation,
basis. **καταβαλλόμενοι** pres. mid. part. καταβάλλω to cast
down, mid. to lay a foundation. **μετάνοια** change of mind,
repentence. **νεκρός** dead. ■ **βάπτισμα** washing. The pl. evi- 2
dently refers to the various washings to be found in Judaism.
(For this as well as evidence that the matters here refer primarily
to Judaism, s. J.C. Adams cited in v. 1; for various interpretations of the pl. of the word "baptisms," s. Hughes.) **διδαχῆς**
teaching. **ἐπίθεσις** placing upon, laying on. (For the Jewish
teaching regarding the laying on the hands, s. SB II, 647f.;
TDNT.) **ἀνάστασις** resurrection. **κρίμα** judgment. ■ 3
ποιήσομεν fut. act. ind. **ἐάνπερ** "if." The 2nd particle used w.
the conditional particle emphasizes that the action is in spite of
opposition; i.e., "if in spite of opposition God permits," "if indeed, if after all" (s. RG, 1154; BD, 237). **ἐπιτρέπῃ** pres. act.
subj. ἐπιτρέπω to allow, to permit. ■ **ἀδύνατος** impossible. 4
(For a study of this word in this connection, s. Spicq.) The adj.
is used w. the inf. which occurs in v.6. **ἅπαξ** once, once for all.
φωτισθέντας aor. pass. part. φωτίζω to enlighten, to illuminate. Illumination indicates that God gives the understanding
and the eyes of the person spiritual light (s. Michel; Hughes).
γευσαμένους aor. act. part. γεύομαι w. the gen. to taste of, to
taste. The verb expresses a real and conscious enjoyment of the
blessings apprehended in its true character (Westcott; s. also
Hughes). **δωρεά** gift. **ἐπουράνιος** heavenly (s. Eph. 1:3).
μέτοχος sharer, participant. **γενηθέντας** aor pass. part.
γίνομαι. ■ **ῥῆμα** that which is spoken, word. **μέλλοντος** pres. 5
act. part. μέλλω to be about to, coming (s. Heb. 1:5). ■ 6
παραπεσόντας aor. act. part. παραπίπτω to fall beside, to go
astray, to fall away. The part. could be conditional (s. Hughes).
ἀνακαινίζειν pres. act. inf. to renew again, to make new again.
εἰς "unto." The prep. gives the direction or the goal.
ἀνασταυροῦντας pres. act. part. ἀνασταυρόω to crucify
again. The part. is causal and indicates why it is impossible for
such people to repent and make a new beginning (Hughes;
Bruce). (For the force of the prep. in compound meaning
"again," s. MH, 295.) **ἑαυτοῖς** dat. pl., dat. of advantage "for

themselves." **παραδειγματίζοντας** pres. act. part.
παραδειγματίζω to expose publicly, to make a public example
of, to expose to disgrace (RWP; BAG). If the readers were to
return again to Judaism, there would be no possibility for them
to begin their spiritual life anew. This would require a recrucifix-
ion of Christ and a putting Him to open shame. For this reason
they must continue toward maturity despite the difficulties,
7 problems, and persecutions which attend their walk. ■ **πιοῦσα**
aor. act. part. **πίνω** to drink. **ἐρχόμενον** pres. mid. part.
ἔρχομαι. **ὑετός** rain. **τίκτουσα** pres. act. part. **τίκτω** to bear,
to bring forth, to produce. **βοτάνη** vegetation, green plants.
εὔθετος well-suited, conveniently placed, suitable, useable (s.
BAG). **διά** w. the acc. "because of," "on whose account." The
owners are intended or it refers to those whom the owners meant
to supply (EGT). **γεωργεῖται** pres. pass. ind. γεωργέω to cultivate. **μεταλαμβάνει** pres. act. ind. to receive w. someone, to
8 partake, to share in. ■ **ἐκφέρουσα** pres. act. part. **ἐκφέρω** to
carry out, to bring forth, to produce. The part. could be conditional "if it produces." **ἄκανθα** thorn. **τρίβολος** thistle, lit.
"three-pointed." (For the use of these terms in the LXX, s.
EGT.) **ἀδόκιμος** disapproved, rejected after examination (s. 1
Cor. 9:27). **κατάρα** curse. **ἐγγύς** near, "nigh unto a curse," for
in Gen. 3:17f. thorns and thistles are a consequent of the cursing
of the land for man's sake (Bruce). **καῦσις** burning.
9 ■ **πεπείσμεθα** perf. pass. ind. **πείθω** to persuade, pass. to
be persuaded, perf. to have confidence (s. Phil. 1:6). **κρείσσονα**
comp. pl. "better things." **ἐχόμενα** pres. mid. part. ἔχω to have,
mid. to hold one's self fast, to belong to, to accompany. The mid.
is used of inner belonging and close association; the "to" of
belonging and the "w." of association are expressed by the gen.
(BAG). **εἰ καί** "if also," "although." The words introduce a
10 concessive condition of the 1st class (RWP). ■ **ἐπιλαθέσθαι**
aor. mid. inf. ἐπιλανθάνομαι w. the gen. to forget. The inf. is
epexegetical explaining the word "unrighteous." **ἐνεδείξασθε**
aor. mid. ind. ἐκδείκνυμι to demonstrate. The prep. in compound suggests more complete demonstration than the simplest
—laying the "index" finger, as it were, on the object (MH, 305).
εἰς "for." This implies that their coming to the assistance of their
brethren is evidence of their willingness to identify themselves
w. the stigma attached to the name of Jesus, and thus of the
genuineness of their love for Him (Hughes). **διακονήσαντες**
aor. act. part. **διακονοῦντες** pres. act. part. to minister, to serve.
The pres. part. emphasizes the continuous action which was at
11 the pres. time going on. ■ **ἐπιθυμοῦμεν** pres. act. ind. to long

for, to yearn for, to have a strong desire (s. 1 Tim. 3:1). **ἕκαστος**
each one. **αὐτός** "the same." **σπουδή** earnestness, endeavor.
ἐνδείκνυσθαι pres. mid. inf., s.v.10. The inf. expresses the object of that which is desired. **πληροφορία** fullness, full assurance (s. Col. 2:2; 1 Thess. 1:5; MM; Michel). ■ **νωθρός** dull (s. 12
Heb. 5:11). **γένησθε** aor. mid. subj. γίνομαι. The subj. is used
in a neg. purpose clause. **μιμητής** imitator. **διά** w. the gen.
"through." **μακροθυμία** longsuffering, patience, patient endurance (s. Gal. 5:22; Rom. 2:4). **κληρονομούντων** pres. act. part.
κληρονομέω to inherit. **ἐπαγγελία** promise.
■ **ἐπαγγειλάμενος** aor. mid. part. ἐπαγγέλλομαι to 13
promise, to make a promise. The part. is temporal expressing
contemporaneous action "when God promised." **ἐπεί** since, because. **μείζων** greater. **ὀμόσαι** aor. act. inf. ὄμνυμι followed by
the prep. κατά w. the gen. to swear by (s. Heb. 3:11). The fact
that God swore by Himself indicates that He binds Himself to
His word by His eternal person (s. Cleon Rogers, "The Covenant
with Abraham and Its Historical Setting," Bib Sac, 127 [1970],
214–256; Michel; Buchanan). ■ **μήν** surely. **εὐλογῶν πρεσ.** 14
αξτ. παρτ. εὐλογέω to bless. **εὐλογήσω** fut. act. ind. The part.
and the finite verb are used as a translation of the Heb. inf. abs.
giving emphasis and certainty to the expression; i.e., "I shall
certainly bless you" (s. BG, 128; BD, 218). **πληθύνων** pres. act.
part. **πληθυνῶ** fut. act. ind. πληθύνω to increase, to multiply.
■ **μακροθυμήσας** aor. act. part. μακροθυμέω to endure pa- 15
tiently, to be longsuffering (s. Gal. 5:22). **ἐπέτυχεν** aor. act. ind.
ἐπιτυγχάνω w. the gen. to arrive at, to obtain. ■ **ἀντιλογία** 16
controversy, dispute, contradiction (s. EGT). **πέρας** confirming,
confirmation, legal guarantee. The word was a technical expression for a legal guarantee (s. BS, 104–109; TDNT; MM;
Hughes). ■ **ἐν ᾧ** "in which," "wherefore," "wherein," i.e., in this 17
method of appeal to remove all doubt and gainsaying (Westcott;
s. also EGT). **περισσότερον** adv. more abundantly, more con-
vincingly. It is probably best to take the adv. in its emphatic and
elative sense; i.e., "especially" (Hughes). **βουλόμενος** pres. mid.
part. βούλομαι to purpose, to will. **ἐπιδεῖξαι** aor. act. inf.
ἐπιδείκνυμι to point out, to demonstrate. The prep. in compound may be directive (MH, 312) or it may have the force of
"to show in addition" (RWP). **κληρονόμος** heir. **ἀμετάθετος**
not able to be removed, unchangeable, immutable, The word
belongs to the legal terminology of the time and signifies a ruling
or contract which is incapable of being set aside or annulled.
Here it indicates the irrevocability of God's purpose as expressed
in the promise and confirmed by the oath (Hughes).

ἐμεσίτευσεν aor. act. ind. μεσιτεύω to intervene, to act as a
mediator or sponsor or surety. Intransitively it is used to pledge
one's self as surety (RWP; s. also Riggenbach; Michel). **ὅρκος**
18 oath. ■ **πρᾶγμα** thing, matter. **ἀδύνατος** impossible.
ψεύσασθαι aor. mid. inf. ψεύδομαι to lie. **ἔχωμεν** pres. act.
subj. dependent on ἵνα. The subj. is used in a purpose clause.
καταφυγόντες aor. act. part. καταφεύγω to flee, to flee for
refuge. In the LXX (Deut. 4:42; 19:5; Josh. 20:9) for fleeing from
the avenger to the asylum of the cities of refuge (EGT).
κρατῆσαι aor. act. inf. κρατέω to hold fast, seize. The idea is
"to lay hold on and cling to that which has been taken" (Westcott). The inf. could express either purpose or result. The object
of the verb is in the gen. **προκειμένης** pres. mid. part.
19 πρόκειμαι to set before, to lie before. ■ **ἄγκυρα** anchor. The
term anchor was used in the Gr. Hellenistic world as the picture
for hope (s. Moffatt; EGT; Michel; RAC I, 440–443). **ἀσφαλής**
safe. The word indicates that which is outwardly safe (Michel).
βέβαιος firm, established, steadfast. The word indicates that
which is firm within itself (Michel). **εἰσερχομένην** pres. mid.
part. εἰσέρχομαι to go into. **ἐσώτερον** within, inside of.
καταπέτασμα curtain, veil. The reference is to the Holy of
20 Holies (Hughes; Michel). ■ **ὅπου** where. **πρόδρομος** one who
runs before, forerunner. The word was used esp. of the men or
troops which were sent to explore before the advance of an army
(Westcott; s. also Bruce; Spicq). **εἰσῆλθεν** aor. act. ind.
εἰσέρχομαι to go into. **τάξις** order. (For literature and a discussion of the priesthood of Melchisedek, s. Hughes; Bruce Demar-
est, *A History of Interpretation of Hebrews 7:1–10 from the
Reformation to the Present* [Tübingen: Mohr, 1976].)

Ch. 7

1 ■ **οὗτος** this one. **ὕψιστος** superl. highest, most high. "The
most high God" was not the title of some heathen deity, but the
same sovereign God whom Abraham worshiped (Hughes).
συναντήσας aor. act. part. συναντάω to meet.
ὑποστρέφοντι pres. act. part. ὑποστρέφω to return. The dat.
is used because the verb "to meet" takes its object in the dat.
κοπή slaughter, defeat (s. Bruce; EGT). **εὐλογήσας** aor. act.
2 part. εὐλογέω to bless (s. Eph. 1:3). ■ **ᾧ καί** "to whom also."
δεκάτη tenth. The offering of a tithe of the spoils to the gods
was a custom of antiquity (EGT). **ἐμέρισεν** aor. act. ind.
μερίζω to divide. **ἑρμηνευόμενος** pres. pass. part. ἑρμηνεύω to
interpret. **ἔπειτα** then. **Σαλήμ** Salem. The word refers to the
3 city of Jerusalem (s. Riggenbach; Bruce). ■ **ἀπάτωρ** without a

father. **ἀμήτωρ** without a mother. The words indicate that the father and mother were unknown (Riggenbach). In rabbinical writings such expressions could mean that the father and mother had died and the child was an orphan (SB III, 693). **ἀγενεαλόγητος** without genealogy. This would indicate that his genealogy was not known, which fact would have disqualified him for a Levitical priesthood (SB III, 693). The argument from silence plays an important part in rabbinical interpretation of Scripture where (for exegetical purposes) nothing must be regarded as having existed before the time of its first biblical mention (Bruce; SB III, 694). **μήτε . . . μήτε** "neither . . . nor." **ἀρχή** beginning. **ἔχων** pres. act. part. **ἀφωμοιωμένος** perf. pass. part. ἀφομοιάω to make like, to produce a facsimile or copy. The likeness is in the picture drawn in Genesis, not in the man himself (RWP). **μένει** pres. act. ind. to remain, to continue. **διηνεκής** without interruption, continually. In referring to a dynasty this word means that the family would never fail to have a male heir to rule (Buchanan).

■ **θεωρεῖτε** pres. act. imp. θεωρέω to see, to observe, to 4
consider. The word expresses the regard of attentive contemplation (Westcott). Although the form of the verb can be ind. or imp., the imp. would be stronger in this context (s. Hughes). **πηλίκος** how great. **δεκάτη** tenth, s.v.2. **ἔδωκεν** aor. act. ind. δίδωμι. **ἀκροθίνιον** (n. pl.) the top of the heap, spoils, the best part of the spoils. The Greeks after a victory gathered the spoils in a heap and the top or the best part of the heap was presented to the gods (EGT; s. also Riggenbach). **πατριάρχης** the one who ruled a tribe, patriarch. The definite article used w. the word contains the sense of "the great patriarch" or "our great patriarch" (Hughes). ■ **ἱερατεία** priesthood. The word emphasizes 5
the priestly office and service. The word ἱερωσύνη in v. 11 is originally more abstract and could be used to emphasize the worth or honor of the office (s. Michel; TDNT). **λαμβάνοντες** pres. act. part. to receive. **ἐντολή** command, commandment. **ἀποδεκατοῦν** pres. act. inf. to take a tenth from someone, to receive a tithe. The inf. is used epexegetically to explain the content of the command. **κατά** w. the acc. according to, in accordance w. the standard of. **νόμος** law. **καίπερ** although. **ἐξεληλυθότας** perf. act. part. ἐξέρχομαι to go out, to descend from. **ὀσφύς** waist, hip, loins. The Hebrews considered this to be the place of the reproductive organs and the expression "to go forth from someone's loins" means "to be someone's son or
descendant" (BAG; T). ■ **γενεαλογούμενος** pres. mid. part. 6
γενεαλογέομαι to trace one's genealogical descent, to have

one's genealogical descent from someone, to count or reckon someone's genealogy from another (s. EGT). **δεδεκάτωκεν** perf. act. ind. δεκατόω to take or receive the tithe. **ἔχοντα** pres. act. part. **ἐπαγγελία** promise. **εὐλόγηκεν** perf. act. ind., s.v.1. That this higher status is permanent may be indicated by the two perf. tenses here in v. 6 (Bruce). (For the so-called "perfect of allegory" used of a past but still relevant event, s. IBG, 15ff.)
7 ■ **χωρίς** w. the gen. "without." **ἀντιλογία** contradiction, opposition, quarrel (s. MM). **ἔλαττον** comp. lesser, inferior. **κρεῖττον** comp. better, superior. **εὐλογεῖται** pres. pass. ind.,
8 s.v.1. ■ **ἀποθνῄσκοντες** pres. act. part. ἀποθνῄσκω to die. The anarthrous part. is used as an attributive and emphasizes the character; i.e., "dying men," i.e., "mortal men" (s. RG, 1105f.; Hughes). **μαρτυρούμενος** pres. pass. part. μαρτυρέω to witness, pass. to be witnessed, to be reported (BS, 265; s. also BD,
9 164). **ζῇ** pres. act. ind. ζάω to live. ■ **ὡς ἔπος εἰπεῖν** "so to speak," an idiomatic expression found often in Philo. Here it could have the meaning "one might almost say" or "to use just the right word" (BAG). The phrase is used to limit a startling statement and the inf. could express conceived result (RWP) or it could be an example of the so-called "inf. abs." (MT, 136). **λαμβάνων** pres. act. part. λαμβάνω perf. pass. ind., pass. to
10 pay a tenth. ■ **ἦν** impf. εἰμί. **συνήντησεν** aor. act. ind. s.v.1.
11 ■ **τελείωσις** perfection, reaching the goal. The OT law and the Levitical system could not produce forgiveness or an eschatological completion or the holiness of heart demanded by God (s. Michel; TDNT). **ἱερωσύνη** priesthood, s.v.5. **αὐτῆς** "on the basis of it," i.e., "the Levitical priesthood," "in association w. it" (Hughes). **νενομοθέτηται** perf. pass. ind. νομοθετέομαι to enact a law, to furnish w. law (s. RWP; BAG). **ἀνίστασθαι** pres. mid. inf. ἀνίστημι to rise up. The mid. is used intransitively (RWP). If the form is taken as pass., the meaning of the verb is trans., i.e., "to be raised up" (s. BAG).
12 **λέγεσθαι** pres. pass. inf. ■ **μετατιθεμένης** pres. pass. part. μετατίθημι to change, to transfer. (For the idea of change involved in the prep. in compound, s. MH, 318.) The part. is used in a gen. abs. expressing either a conditional or temporal idea. **ἀνάγκη** necessity. **καί** also. **μετάθεσις** changing, transfer,
13 change. ■ **ἐπί** upon, concerning, w. reference to (EGT). **φύλη** tribe. **μετέσχηκεν** perf. act. ind. μετέχω w. the gen. to share w., to be a partaker of, to belong to. The choice of this word points to the voluntary assumption of humanity by the Lord. It is not said simply that He was born of another tribe: He was of His own will so born (Westcott; s. also Heb. 2:14). The perf. expresses a

condition of fact, both historic and official; beyond doubt it is
intended to accentuate the abs. incompatibility, resulting from
His birth, between Christ and the priesthood in terms of the
conditions of the validity prescribed by the old legislation
(Spicq; s. also Hughes). **προσέσχεν** perf. act. ind. *προσέχω* w.
the dat. to give attention to, to attend to, to serve at.
θυσιαστήριον the place of sacrifice, altar. ■ **πρόδηλος** before 14
all, obvious. It is an intensified adj. which means "it is perfectly
obvious" (Hughes). **ἀνατέταλκεν** perf. act. ind. *ἀνατέλλω* to
spring up, to arise. The word refers to rising as the sun, moon,
and stars arise, and is also used to describe the sprouting or
growing of plants, hair, and disease, and was used metaphorically where the imagery reflects the rising or growth of stellar
bodies or planets; the idea being that the subjects would arise or
had arisen to prominence or prosperity, and would increase in
prominence. For this reason the word easily applied to a king or
to the expected Messiah (Buchanan; s. also Michel). **εἰς** to, unto,
concerning. The prep. is applied to the direction of the thought
(EGT). **ἐλάλησεν** aor. act. ind. *λαλέω* to speak. ■ 15
περισσότερον comp. "more," especially." **κατάδηλος** quite
clear, evident. The prep. in compound is perfective. **ὁμοιότης**
likeness. **ἀνίσταται** pres. mid. or pass., s.v.11. ■ **σάρκινος** 16
fleshly. Adjectives w. this ending signify material, origin, or kind
(MH, 359). The enactment was fleshly inasmuch as it took to do
only w. the flesh. It caused the priesthood to be implicated w.
and dependent on fleshly descent (EGT; s. also Michel).
γέγονεν perf. act. ind. *γίνομαι*. **ἀκατάλυτος** not able to be
destroyed, indestructible. ■ **μαρτυρεῖται** pres. pass. ind. 17
μαρτυρέομαι to bear witness, to testify. The pass. may be the
divine or "theological pass." used to imply God as the subject
(s. BG, 76). **ὅτι** used to introduce direct discourse. ■ **ἀθέτησις** 18
setting aside, annulling, cancellation. The word was a legal term
used in the papyri for the cancellation or annulment of a legal
enactment. Here it has the idea "cancellation has taken place"
(s. BS, 228f.; Preisigke; MM; Hughes; Bruce). **προαγούσης**
pres. act. part. *προάγω* to go before, to precede. The part. is
used in an adjectival sense w. the meaning "former." **ἐντολή**
commandment. **ἀνωφελής** uselessness, profitlessness. The commandment was useless in that it had no ability to aid men to draw
near to God and was unable to effect the justification of sinners
before God (EGT; Hughes). ■ **ἐτελείωσιν** aor. act. ind. 19
τελειόω to perfect. to bring to perfection, to bring to the goal.
ἐπεισαγωγή bring in. The word was used in Josephus w. the
idea of "replacement" (Moffatt). The prep. in compound has the

idea of "in addition to," "over and beyond," i.e., "a bringing in in addition to" (Bruce). **κρείττων** comp. "better." The gen. "better hope" is obj. gen. **ἐγγίζομεν** pres. act. ind. to come near, to draw near. The pres. tense indicates that which is continually possible.

20 ■ **καθ᾽ὅσον** "according to how much," i.e., "inasmuch as." **ὁρκωμοσία** taking of an oath. **εἰσίν . . . γεγονόντες.** The perf. act. part. of γίνομαι is used in a periphrastic perf. act. construction. The periphrasis marks the possession as well as the impartment of the office: they have been made priests and they act as
21 priests (Westcott). ■ **διὰ τοῦ λέγοντος** "through the one who said." **ὤμοσεν** aor. act. ind. ὄμνυμι to swear, to take an oath (s. Heb. 6:13). **μεταμεληθήσεται** fut. pass. ind. μεταμέλομαι to be sorry, to repent out of sorrow, to have an "after" care (s.
22 EGT; Trench, *Synonyms*, 241; TDNT). ■ **κατὰ τοῦτο** "according to so much," "by so much." **κρείττονος** comp. "better." **ἔγγυος** surety, guarantee. The word means a bond, bail, collateral, or some kind of guarantee that a promise will be fulfilled. The word was used in the papyri in legal and promissory documents meaning "a guarantor" or "one who stands security." Jesus Himself is our security that there will be no annulment of this new and better covenant (s. Buchanan; Bruce; TDNT; Spicq; Michel; MM). **διαθήκη** contract, covenant, agreement, testament (s.
23 Michel; TDNT; CBB). ■ **πλείονες** comp. pl. of πολύς "many," "many in number," not many at one and the same time but many in succession (EGT). **εἰσίν . . . γεγονότες** (s.v.20). **διά** used w. the acc. of the inf. to express cause. **θανάτῳ** dat. sing., instrumental use of the dat. "by death." **κωλύεσθαι** pres. pass. inf. κωλύω to hinder, to prevent. The inf. is used w. the prep. to express cause "because they were prevented by death." **παραμένειν** pres. act. inf. to remain along side of, to continue, to remain in office or serve (Moffatt; for its use in the papyri, s. MM). The inf. is used epexegetically to explain that which was
24 prevented. ■ **μένειν** pres. act. inf. to remain, to continue. The pres. tense indicates the unending and continuing action or state. The inf. is used w. the prep. to express cause or reason. **ἀπαράβατος** not able to be passed on to another, intransmittable, nontransferable. The priesthood of Christ does not pass to another precisely because it is a perpetual priesthood (Hughes;
25 s. also Bruce; Moffatt). **ἱερωσύνη** priesthood. ■ **ὅθεν** therefore. **καί** also. **παντελής** complete. The phrase **εἰς τὸ παντελές** "unto completeness," can have a temporal sense "for all time" or it can have a qualitative sense and emphasize full completeness, i.e., "fully and completely," or it may be that both ideas are

contained and expressed in the phrase (s. Hughes; Michel). **προσερχομένους** pres. mid. part. προσέρχομαι w. the dat. to come to. The pres. tense emphasizes the continual activity. **πάντοτε** always. **ζῶν** pres. act. part. ζάω to live. The part. is causal "because He continually lives." **εἰς** w. the inf. is used to express purpose. **ἐντυγχάνειν** pres. act. inf. to make intercession, to intercede for another. It was sometimes used of bringing a petition before a king on behalf of another (s. 1 Tim. 2:1; EGT; Hughes; TDNT; MNTW, 54–56). Since rabbinical scholars assigned an intercessory function to the angels, it may be that the readers were tempted to worship angels as intercessors and therefore the writer makes it perfectly plain that Christ is the sole mediator and intercessor. To rely upon angels or saints or any other finite being for intercession is not only futile, but it also betrays a failure of confidence in the adequacy of Christ as our intercessor (Hughes).

■ **τοιοῦτος** such a one, "such a high priest." The word 26
refers to the previous indicating the one who is absolute in power and eternal in being (Westcott). **καί** indeed. The word emphasizes the thought; i.e., "such a high priest exactly befitted us" (Hughes; s. also Westcott). **ἔπρεπεν** impf. ind. act. πρέπω w. the dat. to be suited for, to be fit for. **ἀρχιερεύς** high priest. **ὅσιος** holy, pious (s. TDNT; CBB). **ἄκακος** without evil. The word describes the absence of all that is bad and wrong (Hughes). **ἀμίαντος** without defilement, stainless, untainted. The word implies not merely ritual purity, but real ethical cleanliness (RWP). **κεχωρισμένος** perf. pass. part. χωρίζω to separate. The separation is due to His perfect qualities; i.e., He is separated in that He is in a class separate from sinners. The perf. tense suggests that He is permanently separated from them (Hewitt). **ὑψηλότερος** comp. of ὑψηλός "higher," followed by the gen. of comparison. **γενόμενος** aor. mid. part. γίνομαι. The
part could express means or manner. ■ **καθ' ἡμέραν** "daily." 27
ἀνάγκη necessity. **πρότερον** first, first of all. The adv. is used for comparison between two things (RWP). **ἴδιος** one's own. **ἀναφέρειν** pres. act. inf. to bring up, to offer. The inf. is epexegetical explaining the necessity. **ἔπειτα** then; i.e., "after that." **ἐποίησεν** aor. act. ind. The aor. points here to the one time completed action. **ἐφάπαξ** once for all. **ἀνενέγκας** aor. act. part. ἀναφέρω to offer up, to sacrifice. The part could be temporal. ■ **καθίστησιν** pres. act. ind. to constitute, to appoint. The 28
pres. tense indicates that at the time when this epistle was being written the Levitical priesthood was still functioning, w. the implication that the Jerusalem temple was still standing

(Hughes). **ἀρχιερεῖς** acc. pl. in a double acc. construction; i.e., "appoint men as high priests." **ἔχοντας** pres. act. part. **ἀσθένεια** weakness. **ὁρκωμοσία** oath, taking of an oath, "oath taking" (Westcott). **μετά** w. the acc. "after." **υἱός** son. The lack of the article emphasizes the character or quality; i.e., one who is a son. **τετελειωμένον** perf. pass. part. τελειόω to perfect, to make perfect, to bring to the goal (s. Heb. 5:9).

Ch. 8

1 ■ **κεφάλαιον** pertaining to the head. The word can refer to the "sum" as of numbers added up from below to the head of the column where the result is set down and would have the meaning "summary," "synopsis" which is limited to the main points. The word however could also mean "the chief point" as of a copestone or capital of a pillar and thus have the meaning "main thing," "main point" (s. Buchanan; EGT; Michel; BAG; Westcott). **ἐπί** w. the dat. "in the matter of" (RWP). **λεγουμένος** pres. pass. part. "that which is being discussed," "the things being talked about." **τοιοῦτος** such a one. **ἐκάθισεν** aor. act. ind. καθίζω to take one's seat, to sit down. (For the concept of sitting at the right hand, s. Heb. 1:4; Eph. 1:20.) **ἐν δεξία** "on the right hand"; i.e., the place of honor. **μεγαλωσύνη** majesty.
2 ■ **τὰ ἅγια** n. gen. pl. "the holy things"; i.e., "the sanctuary" (s. Hughes; Michel). **λειτουργός** minister, one who ministers in religious matters (s. TDNT; Heb. 1:14). **σκηνή** tent, tabernacle. **ἀληθινός** true, genuine; i.e., the ideal or antitypical tabernacle. The word is used in the fourth gospel in contrast not to what is false, but to what is symbolical (EGT; for an extended discussion of this verse in relation to Heb. 9:11, s. Hughes 283–290). **ἔπηξεν** aor. act. ind. πήγνυμι to fix, to fasten as the pegs of a
3 tent, to pitch a tent (s. RWP). **κύριος** lord. ■ **εἰς** used w. the inf. to express purpose. **προσφέρειν** pres. act. inf. to bring to, to offer. The pres. tense emphasizes an action which was repeatedly done. **καθίσταται** pres. pass. ind. καθίστημι to appoint. **ὅθεν** wherefore. **ἀναγκαῖος** necessity, necessary. **ἔχειν** pres. act. inf. The so-called subject of the inf. in the acc. case is **τοῦτον** "this one," "this priest," and refers to Christ. **καί** "also." **προσενέγκῃ** aor. act. subj. προσφέρω The aor. tense emphasizes that Christ's offering was once for all and is consistent w. the author's repeated emphasis on the singularity of the sacrifice
4 which Christ offered (Bruce; Spicq; Hughes). ■ **ἦν** impf. ind. The ind. is used in a 2nd-class conditional sentence which expresses a contrary to fact statement. **ὄντων** pres. part. **εἰμί**. The part. is used in a gen. abs. construction and is causal. **προσφερόντων**

pres. act. part. s.v.3. **κατά** w. the acc. "according to," "according to the standard of." It was the law which regulated all that concerns the earthly priesthood and by this law He is excluded
from priestly office, not being of the tribe of Levi (EGT). ■ 5
οἵτινες "which one," i.e., those belonging to this class. The qualitative relative emphasizes the character of the Levitical priesthood (Westcott). **ὑπόδειγμα** pattern, copy. **σκιά** shadow. **λατρεύουσιν** pres. act. ind. to minister, to perform religious service. **τὰ ἐπουράνια** "the heavenly things" (s. Eph. 1:3). **κεχρημάταισται** perf. pass. ind. χρηματίζομαι to warn, to instruct. The word was used in the papyri of official pronouncements by magistrates and of a royal reply to a petition as well as an answer of an oracle. In the NT it is used of divine communications (AS; s. also BS, 122; MM). **μέλλων** pres. act. part. to be about to. The part. is used temporarily; i.e., "as he was about to." **ἐπιτελεῖν** pres. act. inf. to bring to completion. **ὅρα** pres. act. imp. to see. ὁράω pres. act. ind. to speak, to say. **ποιήσεις** fut. act. ind. The fut. used to express an imp. It's a fut. under Semitic influence and is a translation of the Heb. imp. (s. BG, 94). **τύπος** type, pattern. This was the stamp or impression struck from a die or seal; hence, a figure, draft, sketch, or pattern (EGT; s. also TDNT). **δειχθέντα** aor. pass. part. δείκνυμι to show. The pass. is the divine or theological pass. indicating God
as the One who did the action (s. Hughes; BG, 76). ■ **νῦν** now. 6
The particle is logical rather than temporal but the temporal factor is inevitably involved in the argument (Hughes). **διαφορώτερος** comp. διάφορος differing, excellent, comp. more excellent. **τέτυχεν** perf. act. ind. τυγχάνω to attain, to obtain. The perf. tense emphasizes the continual possession. The verb is followed by the gen. **λειτουργία** service, ministry, religious or sacred service (s. TDNT). **ὅσῳ** "by how much," instrumental case of the relat. (RWP). **καί** also. **κρείττων** better. **μεσίτης** mediator, arbitrator, go between (s. Michel; Bruce). **ἥτις** which. The antecedent of the relat. pron. is διαθήκη. This relat. properly indicates the class or kind to which an object belongs (RG, 727). **ἐπάγγελία** promise. **νενομοθέτηται** perf. pass. ind. νομοθετέω to legislate, to enact by law, to ordain by law. The perf. tense looks at the continuing result. (For this word, s. Hughes.)

■ **πρώτη** first; i.e., the first covenant. **ἄμεμπτος** blameless, 7
faultless. **δεύτερος** second. **ἐζητεῖτο** impf. pass. ind. ζητέω to seek. The verb is used in the second part of a contrary to fact conditional clause. **τόπος** place, room, occasion, followed by the
gen.; i.e., "room for . . . ," "occasion for . . . ." ■ **μέμφομενος** 8

pres. mid. part. μέμφομαι to blame, to find fault w. **αὐτούς** acc.
pl. "them"; i.e., the Israelites. **συντελέσω** fut. act. ind.
συντελέω to bring to completion, to accomplish, to establish.
9 **ἐπί** upon, w. ■ **κατά** according to. The second covenant was not
only to be a second one, but one of a different type (Westcott).
ἐπόιησα aor. act. ind. ποιέω. **ἐπιλαβομένου** aor. mid. part.
ἐπιλαμβάνομαι w. the gen. indicating the part affected (RWP)
to grasp, to take hold of. The part. is used in a gen. abs. construction indicating the time (BD, 218). **ἐξαγαγεῖν** aor. act. inf.
ἐξάγω to lead out. The inf. is used to express purpose.
ἐνέμειναν aor. act. ind. ἐμμένω to remain in, to continue in.
ἠμέλησα aor. act. ind. ἀμελέω to have no concern for, to
10 neglect (s. Heb. 2:3). ■ **αὕτη** "this." The pron. is used as the
subject of the verb to be supplied ἐστίν "this is . . . ."
διαθήσομαι fut. mid. ind. διατίθημι to make a covenant. Used
w. the dat. **διδούς** pres. act. part. δίδωμι. The part. could be
used temporarily or it could express the manner or means of
making the covenant; i.e., "I will make a covenant even by
putting . . ." (Westcott). **διάνοια** mind, understanding, intellect
(s. EGT; RWP). **ἐπί** w. the acc. "upon." **ἐπιγράψω** fut. act. ind.
ἐπιγράφω to write upon. **ἔσομαι** fut. mid. **εἰς** "to." The prep.
is used w. the verb "to be" to indicate the thought "to serve as."
Although this is a Hebraic use of the prep., there are also examples in Koine apart from a Semitic influence (s. LAE, 120f.; M,
11 71f.). ■ **διδάξωσιν** aor. act. subj. διδάσκω to teach. **πολίτης**
citizen, fellow citizen. **γνῶθι** aor. act. imp. γινώσκω to know.
ὅτι because. **εἰδήσουσιν** fut. perf. act. ind. οἶδα to know. (For
the fut. perf. form, s. RG, 361.) **μικρός** small. **μέγας** great. The
two adjectives are used in the superl. sense; i.e., "from the least
12 to the greatest." ■ **ἵλεως** gracious, merciful. **ἔσομαι** fut. mid.
ἀδικία unrighteousness. **μνησθῶ** aor. pass. subj.
13 μιμνήσκομαι to remember. ■ **πεπαλαίωκεν** perf. act. ind.
παλαιόω to declare or treat as old or obsolete, pass. to become
old or obsolete. The word was used in the papyri for a temple
and a wall which had become old and obsolete and needed
repairing (s. Preisigke II, 224; MM). **καινήν** new.
παλαιούμενον pres. pass. part. **γηράσκον** pres. act. part.
γηράσκω to grow old. The word refers to the decay of old age
(RWP). **ἐγγύς** near. **ἀφανισμός** disappearing, vanishing away.
The word is suggestive of utter destruction and abolition (EGT).

Ch. 9

1 ■ **εἶχε** impf. act. ind. ἔχω. **πρώτη** first. The word is to be
understood as modifying the unexpressed word "covenant"

(Hughes). **δικαίωμα** that which is demanded by righteousness,
regulation, ordinance (s. Westcott; Michel). **λατρεία** worship,
ministry, religious service. The word is to be understood as a gen.
sing. modifying the word "ordinance" rather than the acc. pl. (s.
Hughes; Riggenbach). **ἅγιον** holy place, sanctuary. **κοσμικός**
pertaining to the world, earthly. Here the word could mean
"mundane" or "material" (Bruce). ■ **σκηνή** tent, tabernacle. 2
κατεσκευάσθη aor. pass. ind. κατασκευάζω to outfit w. vessels, to equip, to prepare, to furnish (s. Heb. 3:3). **ᾗ** rel. pron. fem. dat. sing. "in which." **λυχνία** lampstand. It refers to the menorah which was placed at the south side of the holy place; it was made of gold, w. three branches springing from either side of the main stem; the main stem and all six branches each supported a flower-shaped lamp holder (Exod. 25:31ff.; 37:17ff.) (Bruce; s. also ND III, 707–718). **πρόθεσις** placing before, setting out. **τῶν ἄρτων** bread. The expression lit. means "the setting out of the bread (loaves)" i.e., "the bread set forth in two rows" (Lightfoot; s. also SB III, 719–728). **ἅγια** n. pl. The Holy Place (s.
Hughes). ■ **μετά** w. the acc. "after," "behind." **δεύτερος** sec- 3
ond. **καταπέτασμα** curtain, veil. **λεγομένη** pres. pass. part. **ἅγια ἁγίων** The Holy of Holies. The translation of the Heb.
idiom which is equivalent to a superl. (EGT). ■ **χρυσοῦς** golden. 4
ἔχουσα pres. act. part. **θυμιατήριον** altar of incense. The word has also been understood as being the "censer," or "incense shovel," and some have thought to connect the altar of incense to the Holy Place in a theological sense and point out a special doctrinal association between the altar of incense and the Holy of Holies. (For a discussion of this problem, s. Hughes; s. also SB III, 728ff.) **κιβωτός** box, chest, ark (s. EGT). **περικεκαλυμμένην** perf. pass. part. **περικαλύπτω** to cover, to cover on all sides. **πάντοθεν** all around. **χρυσίον** gold. **στάμνος** pitcher, jar. The rabbis believed that in the fut. Elijah would restore to Israel the container of manna, the flask of sprinkling water, and the jar of anointing oil (Buchanan). **ῥαβδος** stick, staff. **βλαστήσασα** aor. act. part. βλαστάνω to
sprout, to bud. **πλάξ** flat stone, tablet. ■ **ὑπεράνω** w. the gen. 5
"above." **χερουβίν** cherubim. The cherubim are the carriers of the divine glory and shekinah (Michel; s. also SB III, 168f.; TDNT). The cherubim were two figures, made of beaten gold, standing at either end of the mercy seat with which they were integratly connected, and facing inward toward each other, their wings stretched out and overarching the mercy seat (Exod. 25:17ff.) (Hughes). **κατασκιάζοντα** pres. act. part. κατασκιάζω to overshadow. **ἱλαστήριον** place of propitiation

(s. Rom. 3:25); mercy seat. The mercy seat was a slab of pure gold, two and one-half cubics long by one and a half cubics wide, which fit exactly over the top of the ark of the covenant (Hughes; s. also Bruce). **περὶ ὧν** "concerning which things." **κατὰ μέρος** "in detail," the distributive use of the prep. (RWP).
6 ■ **κατεσκευασμένων** perf. pass. part. gen. abs. used temporarily (s.v.2). **διὰ παντός** "through all," i.e., "continually." The phrase seems to express the continuous, unbroken permanence of a characteristic habit (Westcott). **εἰσίασιν** pres. act. ind. 3rd per. pl. εἴσειμι to go into. **λατρεία** religious service (s.v.1; s. also TDNT). **ἐπιτελοῦντες** pres. act. part. ἐπιτελέω to bring to conclusion, to complete, to fulfill, to perform. The verb is used by various writers for the accomplishing of religious
7 services (EGT). ■ **δευτέραν** second; i.e., the second tent or the "Holy of Holies." **ἅπαξ** once. **ἐνιαυτός** year, gen. of time; i.e., "once for each year" (RWP). **χωρίς** w. the gen. "without." **ὅ** rel. pron. n. sing. referring to the word "blood." **προσφέρει** pres. act. ind. to bring to, to offer, to offer a sacrifice, to sacrifice. The pres. tense is customary or iterat. indicating that which continually happened year after year. **ὑπέρ** w. the gen. "on behalf of." **ἀγνόημα** ignorances, sin of ignorance, error. The word refers to those sins which are committed inadvertently or in ignorance; i.e., unintentionally or through human frailty (Lev. 4:1f.; 5:17ff.), as distinct from those who sin in deliberate and rebellious defiance of God and His law (Hughes; s. also Michel; Moffatt; SB
8 III, 177f.). ■ **δηλοῦντος** pres. act. part. δηλόω to make clear. The part. is used as a gen. abs. **μήπω** not yet. **πεφανερῶσθαι** perf. pass. inf. φανερόω to make plain, to manifest. The inf. is used in indirect discourse explaining the part. of the gen. abs. **τῶν ἁγίων** sanctuary. Here the word is used to comprise the Holy Place and the Holy of Holies together (Bruce). **ἐχούσης** pres. part. gen. abs. **στάσις** standing. Used w. the previous part., the phrase means "retaining its status" (Bruce; s. also Westcott).
9 ■ **παραβολή** parable, symbol, figure (s. TDNT). **εἰς** "unto" (s. Riggenbach). **καιρός** time, time period. **ἐνεστηκότα** perf. act. part. ἐνίστημι to be present (s. Gal. 1:4). **καθ' ἥν** "according to which." The rel. pron. refers to the word "parable." It is in accordance w. the parabolic significance of the tabernacle and its arrangements, that gifts and sacrifices were offered which could purge only the flesh, not the conscience (EGT). **προσφέρονται** pres. pass. ind., s.v.7. The pres. tense implies that the temple ritual has not yet been discontinued (Hughes). **δυνάμεναι** pres. mid. part. **συνείδησις** conscience (s. Rom. 2:15; 1 Cor. 8:7). **τελειῶσαι** aor. act. inf. **τελειόω** to perfect (s. Heb. 5:9).

λατρεύοντα pres. act. part. λατρεύω to worship, to perform
religious services (s. TDNT). ■ **μόνον** only. **ἐπί** w. the dat. "in 10
the matter of" (RWP). **βρῶμα** food. **πόμα** drink. **διάφορος**
different. The expression "meats and drink" denotes food laws
in general (Bruce; s. also Moffatt). **βαπτισμός** washing (s. Heb.
6:2). **δικαίωμα** regulation, s.v.1. **μέχρι** w. the gen. "until."
διόρθωσις setting straight, restoring that which is out of line,
improvement, reformation, new order (Hughes; BAG).
ἐπικείμενα pres. mid. or pass. part. ἐπιτίθημι to lay upon, to
impose (RWP).

■ **παραγενόμενος** aor. mid. part. παραγίνομαι to come, 11
to appear (s. Hughes; s. also Westcott). **γενομένων** aor. mid.
part. γίνομαι to become, to be. **ἀγαθόν** good. **διά** w. the gen.
"through." The prep. is best understood not in the local sense,
but in the instrumental sense "by means of" (EGT). **μείζων**
(comp.) greater. **τελειότερος** (comp.) more perfect.
χειροποιήτος made w. hands. **κτίσις** creation. The gen. is gen.
of source or origin. ■ **τράγος** goat, male goat, he goat. **μόσχος** 12
calf. The goat was used for the sacrifice for the people and the
calf was used for the sacrifice for the high priest and his house
(s. Michel). **δέ** adversative "but." **ἴδιος** one's own, own.
εἰσῆλθεν aor. act. ind. εἰσέρχομαι to go in. **ἐφάπαξ** once for
all. The prep. in compound gives a directive strengthening (MH,
315). **ἅγια** sanctuary (s.v.8). **αἰώνιος** eternal. **λύτρωσις** redeeming, releasing by the payment of a price (s. Rom. 3:24;
Bruce; Hughes). **εὑράμενος** aor. mid. part. εὑρίσκω to find, to
obtain, to secure. The aor. part. means that Christ entered into
the heavenly sanctuary "after He had secured" an eternal redemption: the securing of our eternal redemption took place at
the cross and was followed by His entry into heaven (Hughes).
■ **ταῦρος** steer, young bull. **σποδός** ashes. **δάμαλις** young 13
female calf, heifer. **ῥαντίζουσα** pres. act. part. ῥαντίζω to sprinkle. The "ashes of a heifer" were those obtained by burning a red heifer outside the camp according to a specially prescribed process. The ashes were used to mix w. water, as necessity arose, to be sprinkled on persons who had become defiled by touching a corpse or being in a tent where there was a corpse, or by touching the slain in battle, or a bone from a corpse (Num. 19). This ceremonial impurity was regarded as a disqualification for intercourse w. men or God (Buchanan; Moffatt). **κεκοινωμένους** perf. pass. part. κοινόω to make common, to defile. The perf. part. looks at the state or condition. **ἁγιάζει** pres. act. ind. to sanctify, to set apart, to remove from the "common" or "profane" thus qualifying the person for again worship-

ing God (EGT). **πρός** w. the acc. "w. a view to," "for."
14 **καθαριεῖ** purity, cleanliness. ■ **πόσῳ** "by how much." **μᾶλλον**
more. (For this type of rabbinical argument, s. Rom. 5:9.) **προσήνεγειν** aor. act. ind. προσφέρω s.v.7. **ἄμωμος** unblemished, without blemish (s. Hughes; Eph. 1:4; Col. 1:22). The word was used of the Leviticus sacrifices but now it has an ethical significance and explains how the blood of Christ should not merely furnish ceremonial cleansing (EGT). **καθαριεῖ** fut. act. ind. καθαρίζω to cleanse. The word marks what the object is itself; i.e., "clean" ceremonially or morally (Westcott). The fut. tense is the logical fut. used in this type argument (Riggenbach; s. also Buchanan). The word was used in the papyri for religious cleansing (s. BS, 216f.). **λατρεύειν** pres. act. inf. to serve, to do religious service, to minister (s. AS, 226). The inf. is used w. the prep. and article to express purpose. **ζῶντι** pres. act. part. ζάω to live. The part. is used adjectivally and the dat. follows the verb "to serve." (For the use of the "ashes of a heifer" in relation to the death of Christ, s. Hughes 362ff.)
15 ■ **διὰ τοῦτο** "because of this." It refers to Christ's effectiveness in offering sacrifice and cleansing from sin so that the believer might worship the living God (Buchanan). **μεσίτης** mediator. **ὅπως** used w. the subj. to express purpose (s. MT, 105). **γενομένου** aor. mid. part. The part. is a gen. abs. expressing cause. **ἀπολύτρωσις** a releasing by the payment of a price, redemption (s. Rom. 3:25). **ἐπί** used w. the dat. "upon," here "by," "under." **παράβασις** transgression. The gen. case (ablative) expresses the idea of separation (s. Riggenbach). **λάβωσιν** aor. act. subj. λαμβάνω to receive. **κεκλημένοι** perf. pass. part. καλέω to call. The perf. tense indicates the completed state or condition. **κληρονομία** inheritance. The gen. is to be taken w. the word "promise" giving a further definition or content of the
16 promise (Westcott). ■ **ἀνάγκη** necessity. **φέρεσθαι** pres. pass. inf., pass. to be brought. The word is probably used here in the legal technical sense of "to be registered" or "to be publicly known" (s. Bruce; Michel; MM; TDNT). **διαθέμενος** pres. mid. part. διατίθημι to make a covenant, to make a testament. (For a detailed discussion of the meaning of the word "covenant"
17 here, s. Hughes; Bruce.) ■ **βέβαιος** firm, guaranteed. Used here in the legal sense "valid" (s. BAG; Riggenbach). **ἐπεὶ** since, because. **μήποτε** never. **ἰσχύει** pres. act. ind. to have strength, to be in force. (For the legal term, s. Michel; Riggenbach; Hughes.) **ζῇ** pres. act. ind., s.v.14. The pres. tenses here are
18 gnomic indicating that which is always true. ■ **ὅθεν** wherefore. **χωρίς** w. the gen. without. **ἐγκεκαίνισται** perf. pass. ind.

ἐγκαινίζω to renew, to inaugurate. The idea of the word is "to
introduce something new," "to initiate" w. the concepts of
"inauguration" and "dedication" being closely related (Hughes).
The perf. is used not in an aoristic sense, but rather to describe
what "stands written" in Scripture and is a marked feature of the
author's style (M, 142; s. also Michel; Riggenbach). ■ 19
λαληθείσης aor. pass. part. λαλέω. The part. is used as a gen.
abs. expressing time "after . . . ." **ἐντόλη** commandment. **κατά**
w. the acc. "according to." **λάβων** aor. act. part. λαμβάνω.
μόσχος calf. The Heb. term "oxen" used in Exod. 24:5 is applicable to bovine animals of any age (Hughes). The related word
is used in the Ugaritic language w. the meaning "young cow" (s.
Joseph Aistleitner, *Wörterbuch der Ugaritischen Sprache*, 259f.).
τράγος goat. The text here is unclear and many manuscripts
omit this word and the omission is probably the best reading (s.
Hughes; Bruce; s. also TC). **μετά** w. the gen. "with." **ἔριον** wool.
κόκκινος scarlet. **ὕσσωπος** hyssop, marjoram. The hyssop was
apparently tied w. the scarlet wool to a cedar wood stick, thus
forming a sprinkling implement which was dipped in the blood
diluted w. water. Although "water and scarlet wool and hyssop"
are not mentioned in the Exodus account, there is no reason why
this common method of sprinkling should not have been used by
Moses in the procedure described in Exod. 24 (Hughes; s. also
Delitzsch). **ἐρράντισεν** aor. act. ind. ῥαντίζω to sprinkle. ■ 20
ἐνετείλατο aor. mid. ind. ἐντέλλομαι to command. ■ **σκεῦος** 21
vessel. **λειτουργία** ministry, worship service. **τῷ αἵματι** dat. of
instrument "w. the blood." **ὁμοίως** adv. "likewise."
ἐρράντισεν cf. vs. 19. ■ **σχεδόν** almost. **καθαρίζεται** pres. 22
pass. ind., s.v.14. The pres. tense is gnomic indicating that which
is always true. **αἱματεκχυσία** blood shedding, shedding of
blood. The word may have been coined by the author, but is
related to the expression ἐκχεῖν αἷμα "to pour out blood" and
ἔκχυσις αἵματος "the pouring out of blood" which appear in
the LXX (s. Bruce; Michel). **γίνεται** pres. mid. ind. The pres.
tense is gnomic indicating that which is always true. **ἄφεσις**
releasing, forgiving, forgiveness. The expression here may have
been a proverbial expression since it occurs in the rabbinical
writings; i.e., "does not atonement come through the blood?" or
"surely atonement can be made only w. the blood" (Bruce; Buchanan).

■ **ἀνάγκη** necessity, necessary. **ὑποδείγμα** pattern, copy 23
(s. Heb. 8:5). **τούτοις** instrumental dat. "by these things," i.e.,
by these rites or by the different materials of cleansing depicted
from Heb. 9:19ff. (Hughes; Michel). **καθαρίζεσθαι** pres. pass.

inf. The inf. is epexegetical describing the "necessity." **τὰ ἐπουράνια** "the heavenly things." **κρείττων** comp. dat. pl.
24 "better." **παρά** used in the comp. sense "than." ■ **χειροποίητος** s.v.11. **εἰσῆλθεν** aor. act. ind., s.v.12. **ἅγιά** sanctuary, s.v.3. **ἀντίτυπον** copy, antitype. The word lit. means "answering to the type" and means here a counterpart of reality (Moffatt). **ἀληθινός** true, genuine. **ἐμφανισθῆναι** aor. pass. inf. ἐμφανίζω to make visible, pass. to become visible, to appear to someone. The prep. in compound is local; i.e., "to appear in the presence of." The inf. is used to express purpose. **πρόσωπον** face, presence. **ὑπὲρ ἡμῶν** "for us," "on our behalf." (For Christ's appearing in the presence of God, s. Hughes, 329–354,
25 esp. 349f.) ■ **προσφέρῃ** pres. act. subj., s.v.7. The subj. is used in a neg. purpose clause. The pres. tense emphasizes the continuous action and may be viewed here as iterat.; i.e., "to offer Himself over and over again." **ὥσπερ** as, just as. **κατ'ἐνιαυτόν** "yearly," the distributive use of the prep.; i.e., "year after year," "every year the same thing." **ἀλλότριος** belonging to another, not one's own. The blood provided by our High Priest for the atonement of mankind was human blood, and, moreover, His
26 own blood (Hughes). ■ **ἐπεί** since, since in that case (Westcott). The word is used to introduce causal clauses (s. MT, 318). **ἔδει** impf. act. ind. δεῖ it is necessary, impf. "it would have been necessary." The construction is a 2nd-class conditional clause (contrary to fact) w. the condition omitted in an eliptical construction; i.e., "since, if that were true, it would be necessary for Him to suffer often" (RWP; s. also RG, 963). **παθεῖν** aor. act. inf. πάσχω to suffer. The inf. is used to explain the necessity. **καταβολή** foundation. **ἅπαξ** once for all. **συντέλεια** completion, consummation (s. Heb. 5:9). **ἀθέτησις** putting away (s. Heb. 7:18). The prep. used w. the word indicates the aim, goal, or purpose. **πεφανέρωται** perf. pass. ind. φανερόω to appear. The verb indicates a public manifestation and appearance of Christ before the world (Michel). The perf. emphasizes the com-
27 pleted action w. continuing results. ■ **καθ'** "according to so much," i.e., "inasmuch as," "just as." **ἀπόκειται** pres. mid.-pass. ind. ἀπόκειμαι to lay away, to appoint. The pres. tense indicates a truth which is continually true. **ἀποθανεῖν** aor. act. inf. ἀποθνῄσκω to die. The inf. is used epexegetically explaining that which is appointed. The aor. tense points to the fact of death as a conclusive act. **μετά** w. the acc. "after." **κρίσις** judging, judgment. The rabbis taught that those born are appointed to die and those who die to live again and those who live again to be judged (s. Michel; Buchanan; M Aboth 4:11, 22).

■ **οὕτως** so. The comparison extends to both terms, the once 28
dying and the judgment. The results of Christ's life are settled.
In Christ's case the result is that He appears a second time
without sin unto salvation, the sin having been destroyed by His
death (EGT). **προσενεχθείς** aor. pass. part., s.v.7. The part. is
used temporarily "after . . . ." **ἀνενεγκεῖν** aor. act. inf.
ἀναφέρω to take up and carry away, to take away. The inf. is
used to express purpose. **ἐκ δευτέρου** "a second time." The
prep. is used temporarily (s. IBG, 72f.). **χωρίς** without; i.e.,
"without any further sin being laid upon Him," or "unburdened
further by any sin" (Delitzsch). **ὀφθήσεται** fut. pass. ind. ὁράω
to see, pass. to appear. **ἀπεκδεχομένοις** pres. mid. part.
ἀπεκδέχομαι to eagerly but patiently expect or await (s. Phil.
3:20). The word is used in the NT w. reference to a fut. manifestation of the glory of Christ (Westcott).

Ch. 10

■ **σκία** shadow. It refers to the outline or shadow cast by 1
the object which is the reality (s. Riggenbach; Michel). **ἔχων**
pres. act. part. The part. could be taken as causal. **μέλλων** pres.
act. part. to be about to. The part. is used as a substitutive "the fut. things," "the things about to come." **εἰκών** image. The image is the real object which cast the shadow that the law has (Buchanan; s. also Hughes; Michel). **πράγμα** that which is done, matter, thing; i.e., "the real object." It expresses the "good things which are coming" so far as they were embodied (Westcott). **κατ' ἐνιαυτόν** "yearly" (s. Heb. 9:25). **προσφέρουσιν** pres. act. ind. to bring a sacrifice, to offer. The pres. tense points to the continual repeated sacrifices. **εἰς τὸ διηνεκές** "continually," "without interruption" (s. Heb. 7:3). **προσερχομένους** pres. mid. part. προσέρχομαι to come to, to approach. The part. is used as a substitutive "those approaching," "those who continually draw near." **τελειῶσαι** aor. act. inf. τελειόω to
perfect, to complete, to bring to the goal (s. Heb. 5:9). ■ **ἐπεί** 2
"since," "for otherwise." Used in an elliptical construction of a contrary to fact conditional clause (s. Heb. 9:26; BD, 238f.). **ἐπαύσαντο** aor. mid. ind. παύομαι to cease. **προσφερόμεναι** pres. pass. part. The part. is used supplementarily to complete the action of the verb "to cease." This sentence should be taken as a question; i.e., "for if it were otherwise, would they have not ceased to be offered?" (s. Bruce). **διά** used w. the acc. of the articular inf. to express cause. **μηδείς** "not one," "no." The word is to be taken as negating the noun "conscience." **ἔτι** yet, any longer. Used in the neg. expression meaning "more," i.e., "no

more." **συνείδησις** conscience, consciousness. **λατρεύοντας**
pres. act. part. λατρεύω to worship. The part. is used as a substitutive and is the so-called "subject" of the inf. **ἅπαξ** once for
all. **κεκαθαρισμένους** perf. pass. part. καθαρίζω to cleanse.
The part. could be conditional or causal. The perf. tense suggests
3 a cleansing that is permanent (Hughes). ■ **ἐν αὐταῖς** "in these,"
i.e., "in the sacrifices." **ἀνάμνησις** remembering, reminder.
The word means "a calling to mind of sins" whereby men are put
4 in remembrance of them by a divine institution (Westcott). ■
ἀδύνατος impossible. **ταῦρος** steer, bull. **τράγος** goat, male
goat. **ἀφαιρεῖν** pres. act. inf. ἀφαιρέω to take away from, to
take away, to remove. The pres. tense points to a continual
action and emphasizes that which is always true.
5 ■ **διό** wherefore. **εἰσερχόμενος** pres. mid. part. The part.
is temporal "when He came." The words are considered prophetic, depicting beforehand the mind of Christ regarding OT
sacrifice, and His own mission (EGT). **λέγει** pres. act. ind.
Christ Himself speaks from Ps. 40:16–18 (Hewitt). **προσφορά**
offering. It refers to the Heb. "non-bloody offering" i.e., the
"meal offering" (EGT). **ἠθέλησας** aor. act. ind. θέλω.
κατηρτίσω aor. mid. ind. 2nd per. sing. καταρτίζω to prepare.
The words "a body you have prepared for me" were evidently
taken from the LXX and are an interpretative paraphrase of the
Heb. text. It could have been that the Gr. translators regarded
the Heb. words as an instance of "a part for the whole," i.e., the
"digging" or hollowing out of the ears is part of the total work
of fashioning a human body (Bruce). It may also have been that
the "ears" were taken as a symbol of obedience in that they were
the organ of reception of the divine will and the body was considered the organ of the fulfillment of the divine will (Riggenbach).
Perhaps there is an illusion to the custom of piercing a slave's
ears showing that he had voluntarily refused his liberty (s. Exod.
6 21:1–6; Deut. 15:17; but s. Hughes). ■ **ὁλοκαύτωμα** total or
whole offering, burnt offering. **περὶ ἁμαρτίας** "concerning
sin," i.e., sin offering. The phrase occurs frequently in Lev. to
denote sin offering (EGT). **εὐδόκησας** aor. act. ind. 2nd per.
7 sing. εὐδοκέω w. the acc. to be pleased w. ■ **ἥκω.** The verb has
the meaning of a perfect "I have come," "I am present" (s. BAG;
Westcott). **κεφαλίς** diminuative of the word "head" and is used
here w. the meaning "roll." (For various interpretations regarding the literal meaning of the word, s. Hughes; Michel.) The
words "the roll of the book" signify the books of Moses in which
the will of God and the way of obedience were written (Hughes).
γέγραπται perf. pass. ind. γράφω to write, perf. "it stands

written." The perf. signifies the legal binding authority of a document (s. MM). **περὶ ἐμοῦ** "concerning me." **ποιῆσαι** aor. act. inf. The inf. is used to express the purpose of His coming. Perhaps the gen. of the article used w. the inf. to express purpose indicates that which is closely connected w. the action as its
motive (s. Westcott, 342). **θέλημα** will. ■ **ἀνώτερον** adv. higher 8
up. Here it has the meaning "in the former part of the quotation" (EGT). **ὅτι.** Used to introduce a direct quotation and is the equivalent of quotation marks. **κατά** w. the acc. according to,
according to the standard of. ■ **εἴρηκεν** perf. act. ind. λέγω. The 9
perf. expresses completed action indicating what the speaker said stands henceforth on permanent record (Bruce). **ἀναιρεῖ** pres. act. ind. to lift up, to take away, to remove, to abolish. The word was used in classical Gr. of the destruction or abolition or repeal of laws, governments, customs, etc. (EGT; s. also Westcott; Michel). **πρῶτον** first. **δεύτερον** second. **στήσῃ** aor. act.
subj. ἵστημι to place, to establish. ■ **ἐν** "in," "by." The instru- 10
mental use of the prep. can also have a causal coloring (s. BD, 118). **ᾧ** rel. pron. "by which will," means "by the will of God thus fulfilled by Christ" (Bruce). **ἡγιασμένοι** perf. pass. part. ἁγιάζω to set apart, to sanctify. The part. is used in a perf. pass. periphrastic construction emphasizing the completed state or condition (s. RWP). **προσφορά** offering, s.v.5. **ἐφάπαξ** once for all. The prep. in compound gives a directive strengthening force (MH, 315). The word is found in the papyri where the context may suggest the meaning "at one time" (MM; s. also Preisigke).

■ **ἕστηκεν** perf. act. ind. ἵσταμι perf. to stand. The idea 11
of "standing" is that of a work still to be done, of service still to be rendered (Westcott). **καθ' ἡμέραν** daily. **λειτουργῶν** pres. act. part. λειτουργέω to perform religious service. The word was used in classical Gr. at Athens w. the meaning "to supply public offices at one's own cost," then generally "to serve the state," "to do a service." It was then used of service done by a priest and indicated the fulfillment of an office. The word has a definite representative character and corresponds to the function to be discharged (s. AS; NTW, 74f.; BS, 140; TDNT; Westcott, 230–233). The part. is used as a part. of manner. **αὐτός** "the same." **προσφέρων** pres. act. part., s.v.1. **αἵτινες** which, which one. The rel. pron. properly indicates the class or kind to which an object belongs (s. RG, 727). **οὐδέποτε** never. **περιελεῖν** aor. act. inf. περιαιρέω to take from around, to remove utterly (s.
RWP; Acts 27:20). The aor. tense expresses the finality. ■ 12
προσενέγκας aor. act. part. προσφέρω to sacrifice (s.v.1). The

part. is temporal "after ...." **εἰς τὸ διηνεκές** continually, unbroken, perpetually, forever (s. Heb. 7:3; AS). **ἐκάθισεν** aor. act. ind. καθίζω to take one's seat. **ἐν δεξιᾷ** "on the right" (s.
13 Eph. 1:20). ■ **τὸ λοιπόν** henceforth; i.e., "for the rest," "for the future"; i.e., all the remaining time till the end of the pres. world. The acc. is the acc. of the extent of time (Delitzsch; RWP). **ἐκδέχομενος** pres. mid. part. to await, to wait for. The prep. in compound has a perfective idea indicating that one is ready and prepared to deal with the situation when it arrives. It pictures the "going on w. the acc. of receiving till it comes" (MH, 310). **τεθῶσιν** aor. pass. subj. τίθημι to place, to put. The subj. is used
14 in a purpose and temporal clause (RWP). ■ **μιᾷ προσφορᾷ** "by one offering," dat. of instrument. **τετελείωκεν** perf. act. ind. τελειόω to complete, to perfect (s. Heb. 5:9). The perf. indicates a one time event w. a continuing result which is completed in the continual process depicted by the part. (s. Michel). **ἁγιαζομένους** pres. pass. part., s.v.10.
15 ■ **μαρτυρεῖ** pres. act. ind. to witness, to bear witness. For the writer of Heb. the truth of one kind of testimony required confirmation by another, in this case, by the testimony of the Scriptures. The testimony of the Scripture is the testimony of God (NTCW, 218, 221). **εἰρηκέναι** perf. act. inf. λέγω. The inf. is used w. the prep. expressing time "after ...." (For the signifi-
16 cance of the perf. tense, s.v.9.) ■ **αὕτη** this. The verb "is" must be supplied; i.e., "this is the covenant." **διαθήσομαι** fut. mid. ind. διατίθημι to make an agreement, to make a treaty, to make a covenant. **πρός** w. the acc. "with." **μετά** w. the acc. after. **διδούς** pres. act. part. δίδωμι. The part. could be temporal or it could express means or manner. **ἐπί** w. the acc. upon. **διάνοια** mind (s. Heb. 8:10). **ἐπιγράψω** fut. act. ind. ἐπιγράφω to write
17 upon. **αὐτοῦς** them; i.e., the laws. ■ **ἀνομία** lawlessness, iniquity. **μνησθήσομαι** fut. pass. ind. μιμνῄσκω w. the gen. to remember. The fut. is used here instead of the subj. of the LXX and of 8:12, because the writer emphasizes the extension of the forgetting to all futurity (EGT). **οὐ ....ἔτι** "no longer," "no
18 more." ■ **ὅπου** where. **ἄφεσις** forgiveness. **οὐκέτι** no longer. **περί** w. the gen. concerning, for.
19 ■ **ἔχοντες** pres. act. part. The part. is causal. **παρρησία** boldness, confidence, assurance (s. Heb. 3:6). **εἴσοδος** entrance. **τῶν ἁγίων** sanctuary. The expression designates the innermost sanctuary of the Holy of Holies into which, under the old dispensation, the people were forbidden to enter (Hughes). **ἐν** "by."
20 ■ **ἥν** rel. pron. "which" referring to the "entrance." **ἐνεκαίνισεν** aor. act. ind. ἐγκαινίζω to inaugurate, to dedicate.

The word is used in the LXX of the inauguration (dedication)
of the altar, the temple, the kingdom (1 Sam. 11:14), a house
(Deut. 20:5) (Westcott; s. also Heb. 9:18). **πρόσφατος** freshly
slaughtered, fresh, new, recent. The word indicates "fresh" not
only in the sense that it is a way which was before unknown, but
also as one that retains its freshness and cannot grow old (Westcott; Buchanan). **ζῶσαν** pres. act. part. ζάω to live. It is "living"
as a way which consists in fellowship w. a Person (Westcott; s.
also Michel). **καταπέτασμα** that which falls down, curtain,
veil. ■ **ἐπί** w. the acc. "over." ■ **προσερχώμεθα** pres. mid. subj. 21/22
προσέρχομαι to come to, to draw near (s. Heb. 4:16). The subj.
is cohortatory, "let us draw near." **πληροφορία** full assurance.
ῥεραντισμένοι perf. pass. part. ῥαντίζω to sprinkle, to cleanse.
The perf. tense indicates a completed state or condition.
λελουσμένοι perf. pass. part. λούω to wash. The part. express
not conditions of approach to God which are yet to be achieved,
but conditions already possessed (EGT). ■ **κατέχωμεν** pres. 23
act. subj. κατέχω to hold down, to hold fast. The subj. is cohortatory. **ὁμολογία** confession, agreement (s. ECC; TDNT).
ἀκλινῆ unwavering, not leaning (RWP). **ἐπαγγειλάμενος** aor.
mid. part. ἐπαγγέλλομαι to promise. ■ **κατανοῶμεν** pres. act. 24
subj. κατανοέω to place the mind down upon, to consider, to
consider thoughtfully (s. Heb. 3:1). The subj. is hortatory, "let
us . . . ." **παροξυσμός** irritating, inciting, stimulation (s. EGT;
RWP; Michel). ■ **ἐγκαταλείποντες** pres. act. part. to leave in 25
the lurch, to forsake. The part. is manner describing the main
verb "consider thoughtfully." **ἐπισυναγωγή** a gathering together, assembly. The pres. in compound indicates the common
responsibility (s. Michel). The term here should be understood
as simply the regular gathering together of Christian believers for
worship and exhortation in a particular place (Hughes). **ἔθος**
custom. **τισίν** dat. pl. The dat. may be possession "the custom
of some" or dat. of reference "the custom in reference to some."
παρακαλοῦντες pres. act. part. παρακαλέω to encourage, to
entreat. **τοσούτῳ** so much. Used in the expression **μᾶλλον ὅσῳ**
meaning "by so much more." It is a dat. or instrumental of
measure or degree, "by so much the more as" (RWP). **βλέπετε**
pres. act. ind. **ἐγγίζουσαν** pres. act. part. ἐγγίζω to draw near,
to come near.

■ **ἑκουσίως** adv. from ἑκούσιος willingly, voluntarily, de- 26
liberately, intentionally. **ἁμαρτανόντων** pres. act. part. gen.
abs. used to express a condition. **λαβεῖν** aor. act. inf. λαμβάνω.
The inf. is used w. the prep. in a temporal sense; i.e., "after . . . ."
ἐπίγνωσις knowledge, recognition. **ἀπολείπεται** pres. pass.

ind. ἀπολείπω to leave off, to leave behind, pass. to be left
behind, to remain. The concept of a "willful sin" without a
sacrifice is an OT teaching also reflected in Judaism (s. Num.
27 15:31; Michel; Moffatt; Hughes). ■ **φοβερός** fearful. **ἐκδοχή**
expectation. **ζῆλος** zeal. The phrase may be translated "zeal of
fire" or "fiery zeal" (Hughes). **ἐσθίειν** pres. act. inf. The inf. is
used w. the following part. to express the fut. **μέλλοντος** pres.
act. part. μέλλω to be about to. **ὑπεναντίος** one who opposes,
28 adversary. ■ **ἀθετήσας** pres. act. part. ἀθετέω to place aside,
to reject, to annul. **τίς** anyone. **χωρίς** without. **οἰκτιρμός** compassionate mercy, heartfelt mercy (s. Phil. 2:1; s. also TDNT).
δυσίν dat. "two." **τρίσιν** dat. "three." **ἀποθνήσκει** pres. act.
ind. The pres. tense is gnomic indicating that which is generally
29 true. ■ **πόσῳ** how much. The argument from the less to the
greater was common in rabbinical arguments (s. Moffatt; s. also
Rom. 5:9). **δοκεῖτε** pres. act. ind. to suppose. **χείρων** gen. of
comp. "worse." **ἀξιωθήσεται** fut. pass. ind. ἀξιόω to consider
worthy, to consider worthy of, followed by the gen. **τιμωρία**
punishment. **καταπατήσας** aor. act. part. καταπατέω to trample, to stomp upon. The word indicates to treat w. the utmost
contempt (Hughes). **κοινός** common, profane. It denotes the
opposite of "holy" (s. Michel). **ἡγησάμενος** aor. mid. part.
ἡγέομαι to consider, to count as. **ἡγιάσθη** aor. pass. ind.
ἁγιάζω to separate, to set apart for divine use, to sanctify.
ἐνυβρίσας aor. act. part. ἐνυβρίζω to treat w. utter contempt,
30 to arrogantly insult (s. TDNT; MNTW, 77–85). ■ **εἰπόντα** aor.
act. part. λέγω. **ἐκδίκησις** avenging, revenge. **ἀνταποδώσω**
fut. act. ind. ἀνταποδίδωμι to pay back. The prep. in compound indicates to pay back w. the same thing. **κρινεῖ** fut. act.
31 ind. κρίνω to judge. ■ **φοβερός** fearful. **ἐμπεσεῖν** aor. act. inf.
ἐμπίπτω to fall in, to fall into. The inf. is used as the subject of
the verb "to be" which is understood. **ζῶντος** pres. act. part.
ζάω to live.

32 ■ **ἀναμιμνῄσκεσθε** pres. mid. imp. to remind one's self, to
remember. **πρότερον** former, first. Since the distinction between comp. and superl. had been weakened in Koine, the
phrase may be translated "the first days," i.e., the time when
they first responded to the message of the gospel (Hughes).
φωτισθέντες aor. pass. part. φωτίζω to make light, to enlight-
en. **ἄθλησις** fighting, conflict, struggle. **ὑπεμείνατε** aor. act.
ind. ὑπομένω to remain under, to patiently bear, to patiently
33 and hopefully endure (s.v.36). **πάθημα** suffering. ■ **τοῦτο μέν
. . . τοῦτο δέ** "partly so" . . . "and partly so." The acc. w. gen.
reference is used w. the particles for contrast (RWP).

ὀνειδισμός reproach, revile, insult. **θλῖψις** pressure, trouble,
affliction. **θεατριζόμενοι** pres. pass. part. θεατρίζω to bring
upon the stage, to hold up to derision, to put to shame, to dispose
publicly. The meaning is that they had been held up to public
derision, scoffed and sneered at, accused of crime and vice,
unjustly suspected and denounced (s. RWP; BAG; Moffatt;
Michel). **κοινωνός** partner, sharer. **ἀναστρεφομένων** pres.
mid. part. ἀναστρέφομαι to conduct one's life, to be treated.
γενηθέντες aor. pass. part. γίνομαι. ■ **δέσμιος** prisoner. 34
συνεπαθήσατε aor. act. ind. συμπαθέω to suffer together, to
suffer w. someone. **ἁρπαγή** seizing, plundering. The word implies that their own property had been either confiscated by the
authorities or plundered in some mob riot (Moffatt).
ὑπάρχοντα possessions. **χαρά** joy. **προσεδέξασθε** aor. mid.
ind. προσδέχομαι to accept. **γινώσκοντες** pres. act. part.
ἔχειν pres. act. inf. The inf. is used in indirect discourse, i.e., the
object of the part. "knowing." **κρείττων** better. **ὕπαρξις** possession. **μένουσαν** pres. act. part. μένω to remain, to abide. ■ 35
ἀποβάλητε aor. act. subj. ἀποβάλλω to throw away. The aor.
subj. is used w. the neg. in a prohibitive sense implying that the
action is not yet existent and should not arise (MKG, 273).
παρρησία boldness, confidence (s. Heb. 3:6). **μισθαποδοσία**
payment, reward, recompense. ■ **ὑπομόνη** patient endurance. It 36
is the spirit which can bear things, not simply w. resignation, but
w. blazing hope; it is not the spirit which sits statically enduring
in one place, but the spirit which bears things because it knows
that these things are leading to a goal of glory (NTW, 60; s. also
TDNT; CBB). **ἔχω χρείαν** followed by the gen. "to have need
of something." **ποιήσαντες** aor. act. part. The part. is used
temporally, i.e., "after . . . ." **κομίσησθε** aor. mid. subj.
κομίζομαι to receive. The word indicates "to receive the fulfillment of promise" (Hughes). ■ **μικρόν ὅσον ὅσον** a very little, 37
i.e., "only for a very little while" (BD, 160). **ἐρχόμενος** pres.
mid. part. **ἥξει** fut. act. ind. ἥκω to come. **χρονίσει** fut. act. ind.
χρονίζω to delay. ■ **ζήσεται** fut. mid. ind. ζάω to live. 38
ὑποστείληται aor. mid. subj. ὑποστέλλομαι to draw one's
self back, to withdraw one's self, to shrink back. **εὐδοκεῖ** pres.
act. ind. to delight in, to have pleasure in. ■ **ὑποστολή** shrink- 39
ing, timidity. Used here in the expression "we do not belong to
those who are timid" (BAG). **ἀπώλεια** ruin, destruction.
περιποίησις possession. The term indicates what one makes
one's own, either by keeping or by gaining it (Hughes; s. also
Eph. 1:4).

Ch. 11

1 ■ **ἔστιν** pres. ind. The emphatic position of the word may suggest a "definition style" (s. Michel). **ἐλπιζομένων** pres. pass. part. **ὑπόστασις** assurance. The word has a number of connotations and usages, e.g., "essence," "substance" or "foundation," or "confident assurance" or "guarantee," "attestation," i.e., documents which attest or provide evidence of ownership. (For these meanings as well as other references, s. Hughes; Michel; TDNT; MM.) **πρᾶγμα** matter, thing. **ἔλεγχος** evidence, proof. The word was used in the papyri of legal proofs of an accusation
2 (s. MM; Preisigke; TDNT). **βλεπομένων** pres. pass. part. ■ **ἐν** "by." The prep. is used instrumentally. **ταύτῃ** "this," i.e., "face." **ἐμαρτυρήθησαν** aor. pass. ind. μαρτυρέω to bear witness. The pass. may be the so-called "theological passives" indicating that it is God who bears witness concerning the elders (s. BG, 76). **πρεσβύτερος** comp. πρέσβυς old, elder. These were the men and women of old who received the divine commendation for faith of this kind (Bruce).
3 ■ **πίστει** dat. sing. dat. of instrument "by faith." **νοοῦμεν** pres. act. ind. to understand. The word expresses a mental as distinguished from a sensuous perception (Westcott). **κατηρτίσθαι** perf. pass. inf. καταρτίζω to outfit, to perfect. The word expresses the manifoldness and the unity of all creation. The tense marks that the original lesson of creation remains for abiding use and application (Westcott). The word was used in Hellenistic literature to describe the act of creation and in this sense it has a solemn tone (Michel). The inf. is used in indirect discourse. **αἰών** age, world (s. TDNT). **ῥήματι** dat. sing. ῥῆμα that which is spoken, word. The dat. is instrumental dat. **φαινομένων** pres. mid. part. φαίνομαι to appear, to be visible. **βλεπόμενον** pres. pass. part. **γεγονέναι** perf. mid. inf. γίνομαι. The inf. is used here to express results (s. RG, 1003; BD, 207f.). The neg. should be taken w. the inf. and the translation would be "so that what is seen has not come into being from things which appear" (Hughes).
4 ■ **πλείων** better. **παρά** than. (For the prep. used in a comp. construction, s. Heb. 1:4.) **προσήνεγκεν** aor. act. ind. προσφέρω to bring to, to offer, to sacrifice. **ἐμαρτυρήθη** aor. pass. ind., s.v.2. **μαρτυροῦντος** pres. act. part. gen. sing. μαρτυρέω to testify, to bear witness. The part. is used in a gen. abs. construction. **ἐπί** concerning, w. respect to. (For the textual variation here, s. Bruce.) **ἀποθανών** aor. act. part. ἀποθνήσκω
5 to die. The part. could be concessive "although He died." ■ **μετετέθη** aor. pass. ind. μετατίθημι to change, to transpose, to

transfer, to remove from one place to another, to translate (s.
EGT). **μεμαρτύρηται** perf. pass. ind., s.v.2. **εὐαρεστηκέναι**
perf. act. inf. εὐαρεστέω to be well pleasing to. The inf. is used
in indirect discourse. ■ **χωρίς** without. **ἀδύνατος** impossible. 6
εὐαρεστῆσαι aor. act. inf., s.v.5. The inf. is used to explain what
is impossible. **πιστεῦσαι** aor. act. inf. The inf. is used to explain
that which is necessary. **δεῖ** pres. act. ind. "it is necessary." The
word speaks of the binding and logical necessity.
προσερχόμενον pres. mid. part. προσέρχομαι to come to, to
approach. **ἐκζητοῦσιν** pres. act. part. ἐκζητέω to search out, to
seek after. The prep. in compound always seems to denote that
the seeker "finds," or at least exhausts his powers of seeking
(MH, 310). **μισθαποδότης** one who gives a reward, one who
pays back a reward. ■ **χρηματισθείς** aor. pass. part. 7
χρηματίζομαι to give divine instruction, to warn (s. Heb. 8:5).
μηδέπω not yet. **βλεπομένων** pres. pass. part., s.v.1.
εὐλαβηθείς aor. pass. part. εὐλαβέομαι to take hold well or
carefully, to act circumspectly or w. reverence, to beware, to
reverence (RWP; AS; s. also Michel). **κατεσκεύασεν** aor. act.
ind. κατασκευάζω to construct, to outfit. **κιβωτός** ark.
κατέκρινεν aor. act. ind. κατακρίνω to pass. judgment against,
to condemn. **κατὰ πίστιν** "according to the standard of faith."
The prep. can also have the idea of "by virtue of," "on the
ground of," "in consequence of" (s. IBG, 59; EGT).
κληρονόμος heir.

■ **καλούμενος** pres. pass. part. καλέω to call. The part. 8
could be temporal "when he was called." **ὑπήκουσεν** aor. act.
ind. ὑπακούω to listen to, to obey. **ἐξελθεῖν** aor. act. inf.
ἐξέρχομαι to go out, to go forth from. The inf. is used to explain
the obedience. **ἤμελλεν** impf. act. ind. μέλλω to be about to.
The word is used w. the inf. to express the future and the impf.
w. the inf. expresses futurity or intention reckoned from a moment in the past (s. MKG, 307). **εἰς** "for." **κληρονομία** inheritance. **ἐξῆλθεν** aor. act. ind. **ἐπιστάμενος** pres. mid. part.
ἐπίσταμαι to know, to understand. **ποῦ** where. ■ **παρῴκησεν** 9
aor. act. ind. παροικέω to dwell alongside of, to be a foreigner
residing in a foreign country. Such foreigners had certain legal
rights even though they were considered to be only temporary
or foreign residents (s. TDNT; Michel; Eph. 2:19). **ἀλλότριος**
foreigner, stranger. **κατοικήσας** aor. act. part. κατοικέω to
reside, to dwell, to be at home. **συγκληρονόμος** fellow heir.
■ **ἐξεδέχετο** impf. mid. ind. ἐκδέχομαι to await expectantly. 10
The prep. in compound indicates "to be ready," "to be prepared
to deal w. the situation" (EGT). **θεμέλιος** foundation. **ἔχουσαν**

pres. act. part. ἔχω. **τεχνίτης** craftsman, artificer, designer, maker (s. Bruce; Michel; Hughes). **δημιουργός** public workman, constructer, maker. The first word refers to the plan and this word refers to the execution of it (s. Westcott; Bruce; Mich-
11 el). ■ **αὕτη** fem. sing. "herself." **καταβολή** casting down. Used as a t.t. for the sowing of a seed and used here in the idiom "to receive the sowing of the seed" to mean "to conceive." **σπέρμα** seed, sperm. **ἔλαβεν** aor. act. ind. λαμβάνω to receive. **παρά** beyond, past. **ἡλικία** age, i.e., "beyond the season of age" (s. RWP). **ἡγήσατο** aor. mid. ind. ἡγέομαι to consider, to reckon as, to count as. **ἐπαγγειλάμενον** aor. mid. part. ἐπαγγέλλω to promise. The part. is used here substitutively, i.e., "the one who
12 promised." ■ **διό** therefore. **ἑνός** gen. of εἷς "one." The idea is one who stands at the beginning of a long series. Abraham was known as "the One" (s. Michel; Delitzsch). **ἐγεννήθησαν** aor. pass. ind. γεννάω to bear, pass. to be born. (For the variant reading **ἐγενήθησαν** aor. pass. ind. γίνομαι to be, to become, s. Delitzsch; Bruce.) **νενεκρωμένον** perf. pass. part. νεκρόομαι to make dead, to treat as dead, to consider dead, "as good as dead" (RWP; Bruce). **καθώς** just as. **ἄστρον** star. **πλῆθος** quantity, number. The dat. is either locative "in number" or dat. of reference "in reference to quantity." **ἄμμος** sand. **παρά** w. the acc. "along," "along side of." **χεῖλος** lip, shore. **ἀναρίθμητος** unable to be counted, innumerable.
13 ■ **κατά** w. the acc. "according to," i.e., "in accordance w. the principle of faith" (Hughes). **ἀπέθανον** aor. act. ind. ἀποθνήσκω to die. **κομισάμενοι** aor. mid. part. κομίζω to receive, to obtain; i.e., "to obtain the fulfillment of the promise" (Michel). **πόρρωθεν** from afar, from a long distance away. **ἰδόντες** aor. act. part. ὁράω to see. **ἀσπασάμενοι** aor. mid. part. ἀσπάζομαι to greet. They hailed them from afar, as those on board ship descry friends on shore and wave a recognition (EGT), or they greet the fulfillment which is still far off as a wanderer who sees his home city arising on the horizon (Riggenbach). **ὁμολογήσαντες** aor. act. part. ὁμολογέω to agree, to confess. **ξένος** foreigner. **παρεπίδημος** one who makes his home alongside of, one from another country, pilgrim, one who stays for a while in a strange place. The word was used in the LXX and in the papyri for those who settled in a particular
14 district only for a time (s. MM; BS, 149; Preisigke; BAG). ■ **τοιοῦτος** such a one. **λέγοντες** pres. act. part. **ἐμφανίζω** pres. act. ind. to manifest, to show, to make clear. **πατρίδα** acc. sing. fatherland. **ἐπιζητοῦσιν** to seek after. The prep. in compound
15 indicates direction (EGT). ■ **ἐκείνης** gen. sing. "that one," i.e.,

the earthly country. The gen. is used after the verb.
ἐμνημόνευσον impf. ind. act. μνημονεύω to remember, to be
mindful of something. The ind. is used in a contrary to fact
conditional clause. ἐξέβησαν aor. act. ind. ἐκβαίνω to go out.
ἀνακάμψαι aor. act. inf. ἀνακάμπτω to bind back, to turn
back again. The inf. is used to explain the word "time," "opportunity." ■ νῦν now; i.e., "the truth is," "as it is" (Bruce). 16
ὀρέγονται pres. mid. ind. to desire, to stretch one's self out for,
to yearn for (RWP; s. also 1 Tim. 3:1). The verbs in the pres.
tense in this context indicate the continual habitual attitude of
life. ἐπουράνιος heavenly (s. Eph. 1:3). ἐπαισχύνεται pres.
mid. ind. to be ashamed. ἐπικαλεῖσθαι pres. mid.-pass. inf.
ἐπικαλέω to call upon, to name. If the verb is taken as mid., the
meaning is "God is not ashamed of them to call Himself their
God." If pass. "God is not ashamed of them to be called their
God." The inf. is epexegetical explaining the main verb.
ἡτοίμασεν aor. act. ind. ἑτοιμάζω to prepare, to make ready.
■ προσενήνοχεν perf. act. ind. προσφέρω to offer, to 17
offer as a sacrifice. The perf. indicates that this was an abiding
example (BD, 177). πειραζόμενος pres. pass. part. πειράζω to
try, to examine, to test. The pass. is "divine" pass. indicating that
"God tested Abraham" (Hughes; BG, 76). μονογενής unique,
only one of the kind, only (s. TDNT; CBB). ἀναδεξάμενος aor.
mid. part. ἀναδέχομαι to receive, to gladly receive. The idea
suggested here seems to be that of welcoming and cherishing a
divine charge which involves a noble responsibility (Westcott).
■ ἐλαλήθη aor. pass. ind. λαλέω. κληθήσεται fut. pass. ind. 18
καλέω. σπέρμα seed. ■ λογισάμενος aor. mid. part. 19
λογίζομαι to consider, to reckon. The verb is used by Paul in
the sense of to calculate or reckon up on the basis of firm evidence. The word denotes the inward conviction, persuasion, not
a more or less reliable opinion (Hughes). The part. could be used
to express the cause or reason and explains why Abraham had
the courage to sacrifice Isaac, although the action seemed certain to ruin the fulfillment of what God had promised him (Moffatt). ἐγείρειν pres. act. inf. δυνατός capable, able. ὅθεν wherefore. παραβολή parable, analogy, used here adverbially "figuratively speaking" (s. Hughes; s. also Michel; Westcott).
ἐκομίσατο aor. mid. ind., s.v.13. ■ περί concerning. μέλλοντα 20
pres. act. part. The part. is used as a substitutive; i.e., "future,
coming things." εὐλόγησεν aor. act. ind. ■ ἀποθνῄσκων pres. 21
act. part. The part. is used temporally and the pres. tense indicates that he was in the process of dying. ἕκαστος each one.
προσεκύνησεν aor. act. ind. προσκυνέω to worship. ἐπί w.

22 the acc. on, upon. **ἄκρον** top. **ῥάβδος** stick, staff. ■ **τελευτῶν**
pres. act. part. τελευτάω to come to the end, to expire, to die.
The part. is temporal and the pres. tense indicates that he was
in the process of dying. **ἔξοδος** way out, departure.
ἐμνημόνευσεν aor. act. ind., s.v.15. **ὀστοῦν** bones. **ἐνετείλατο**
aor. mid. ind. ἐντέλλομαι to instruct, to command.
23 ■ **γεννηθείς** aor. pass. part. γεννάω to bear, pass. to be
born. **ἐκρύβη** aor. pass. ind. κρύπτω to hide. **τρίμηνον** three
months, acc. of time "for three months." **πατέρες** fathers, parents. **διότι** because. **εἶδον** aor. act. ind. ὁράω to see. **ἀστεῖος**
beautiful. It describes an attractive comeliness that is uncom-
monly striking (Hughes; s. also Bruce). **ἐφοβήθησαν** aor. pass.
ind. φοβέομαι to be afraid, to fear. **διάταγμα** command, order.
24 ■ **γενόμενος** aor. mid. part. γίνομαι. **ἠρνήσατο** aor. mid. ind.
25 ἀρνέομαι to say no to, to deny, to refuse. ■ **μᾶλλον** rather.
ἑλόμενος aor. mid. part. αἱρέω to lift up, mid. to choose.
συγκακουχεῖσθαι pres. pass. inf. to suffer evil together, to
suffer w. someone. The inf. is used to explain the choosing.
πρόσκαιρος for a time, temporary, fleeting. **ἀπόλαυσις** enjoyment, pleasure. (For the use of the word in the papyri and in-
26 scriptions, s. MM; Preisigke.) ■ **μείζων** greater. **ἡγησάμενος**
aor. mid. part. ἡγέομαι to consider, to reckon. **θησαυρός** treasure, gen. of comparison. **ὀνειδισμός** reproach. **ἀπέβλεπεν**
impf. ind. act. ἀποβλέπω to look away from. Used w. the prep.
"to," to look to. The impf. emphasizes the continuous action in
the past time. The word was used of keeping one's attention
fixed upon something, as an artist fixes his attention on the
object or model that he is reproducing in painting or sculpture
27 (Bruce). **μισθαποδοσία** recompense, reward. ■ **κατέλιπεν**
aor. act. ind. καταλείπω to leave behind, to leave. **φοβηθείς**
aor. pass. part. φοβέομαι to be afraid, to fear. **θυμός** anger,
wrath (s. TDNT). **ὁ ἀόρατος** the one not able to be seen, "the
invisible one," i.e., God. **ὁρῶν** pres. act. part. to see.
ἐκαρτέρησεν aor. act. ind. καρτερέω to be strong, to hold out,
28 to endure. ■ **πεποίηκεν** perf. act. ind. ποιέω. The perf. tense
indicates that the celebration was the inauguration of a divine
institute (Spicq; s. also Westcott; Bruce). **πρόσχυσις** pouring,
sprinkling, followed by the obj. gen. **ὀλοθρεύων** pres. act. part.
ὀλοθρεύω to destroy. **πρωτότοκος** firstborn. **θίγῃ** aor. act.
subj. θιγγάνω to touch. The object of the verb is in the gen. The
29 subj. is used in a neg. purpose clause. ■ **διέβησαν** aor. act. ind.
διαβαίνω to go through, to pass through. **ἐρύθρός** red. **ξηρός**
dry. **πεῖρα** attempt, try. **λαβόντες** aor. act. part. λαμβάνω.
The part. is used temporally "when the Egyptians made an at-

tempt." **κατεπόθησαν** aor. pass. ind. καταπίνω to swallow
down, to engulf. The prep. in compound is intensive, i.e., "they
were totally engulfed," "overwhelmed" (Hughes). ■ **τεῖχος** 30
wall. **ἔπεσαν** aor. act. ind. **πίπτω** to fall. **κυκλωθέντα** aor.
pass. part. κυκλόω to encircle. ■ **πόρνη** prostitute, whore. 31
συναπώλετο aor. mid. ind. συναπόλλυμι to destroy together,
to be destroyed together. **ἀπειθήσασιν** aor. act. part. ἀπειθέω
to be disobedient. **δεξαμένη** aor. mid. part. δέχομαι to welcome, to receive. **κατάσκοπος** spy.

■ **ἐπιλείψει** fut. act. ind. ἐπιλείπω to fall upon, to fail. 32
διηγούμενον pres. mid. part. διηγέομαι to narrate, to tell
about, to carry a discussion through. The words are lit. "will
leave me telling about" (RWP). ■ **κατηγωνίσατο** aor. mid. ind. 33
κατηγωνίζομαι to struggle against, to overcome, to subdue.
The prep. in compound not only indicates the idea of "against,"
but indicates that the action is unfavorable to an object (MH,
316). **ἠργάσαντο** aor. mid. ind. ἐργάζομαι to work effectively.
The verb is used w. the noun "righteousness" in the LXX w. the
meaning "to practice justice" (Ps. 15:2) and is used of doing that
which is right in reference to personal integrity (Hughes).
ἐπέτυχον aor. act. ind. ἐπιτυγχάνω followed by the object in
the gen. to obtain, to receive. **ἔφραξαν** aor. act. ind. φράσσω
to fence in, to block up, to stop (s. RWP). ■ **ἔσβεσαν** aor. act. 34
ind. σβέννυμι to quench, to put out a fire. **ἔφυγον** aor. act. ind.
φεύγω to flee. The aor. is perfective indicating the success in
fleeing; i.e., "to escape." **στόμα** mouth, edge. **μάχαιρα** sword.
ἐδυναμώθησαν aor. pass. ind. δυναμόομαι to make strong, to
be strong. The aor. is ingressive; i.e., "to become strong," "they
became mighty." **ἀσθένεια** weakness. **ἐγενήθησαν** aor. pass.
ind. γίνομαι. **πόλεμος** war. **παρεμβολή** encampment, bar-
racks, armies in a battle line, army (RWP). **ἔκλιναν** aor. act. ind.
κλίνω to make to bend, to bow, to turn to flight (AS).
ἀλλότριος foreign. ■ **ἔλαβον** aor. act. ind. λαμβάνω. 35
ἀνάστασις resurrection. **ἐτυμπανίσθησαν** aor. pass. ind.
τυμπανίζω to torture. The root meaning of the word is "to
beat," "to strike," or "to pound." A related noun means a kettle
drum which has a skin stretched taut for striking. Those who
were tortured by some such means as this might either be beaten
directly or stretched over a wheel and whirled while being afflicted w. rods to break their limbs until they died (Buchanan; s.
also Westcott; Michel; BAG). **προσδεξάμενοι** aor. mid. part.
προσδέχομαι to accept, to receive. **ἀπολύτρωσις** release by
the payment of a price, release (s. Rom. 3:24). **κρείττων** better.
τύχωσιν aor. act. subj. τυγχάνω to receive, to obtain. ■ **ἕτερος** 36

other. **ἐμπαιγμός** mocking, heaping derision upon a person by
sarcastically imitating him. **μάστιξ** scourging, whipping w. a
scourge. **πεῖραν ἔλαβον** s.v.29. The expression "received the
trial" is the same idiom used in the LXX Deut. 28:56 to describe
a woman so delicate that she would not "risk" setting her foot
on ground. These "others" were not that delicate (Buchanan).
ἔτι δέ yea, moreover. The expression is commonly used to indi-
37 cate a climax (EGT). **δεσμός** bonds. **φυλακή** prison. ■
ἐλιθάσθησαν aor. pass. ind. λιθάζω to stone. **ἐπειράσθησαν**
aor. pass. ind. πειράζω to try, to tempt. (For the suspected
textual variation, s. Hughes; Riggenbach.) **ἐπρίσθησαν** aor.
pass. ind. πρίω to saw into. The tradition that the prophet Isaiah
suffered death by being sawed in two w. a wooden saw is also
found in writings as well as the Talmudic books and in the
pseudepigraphic Jewish work, *The Martyrdom of Isaiah*, in
which it is recounted that during this terrible ordeal "Isaiah
neither cried aloud nor wept, but his lips spoke w. the Holy Spirit
until he was sawn in two" (Hughes; s. also SB III, 747). **φόνος**
murder. The prep. is used here instrumentally, i.e., "by murder
of the sword." **ἀπέθανον** aor. act. ind. ἀποθνῄσκω to die.
περιῆλθον aor. act. ind. περιέρχομαι to go about. **μηλωτή**
sheepskin, used of the cloak worn by prophets (BAG). **αἴγειος**
of a goat. Adjectives w. this suf. have the meaning "of, or belonging to" (MH, 336). **δέρμα** skin; i.e., animal hide which was
processed. **ὑστερούμενοι** pres. mid. part. ὑστερέομαι to lack,
to suffer need. **θλιβόμενοι** pres. pass. part. θλίβω to put under
pressure, to cause distress, to afflict. **κακουχούμενοι** pres. pass.
38 part. κακουχέω to mishandle, to treat evilly, to ill treat. ■ **ἦν**
impf. εἰμί. **πλανώμενοι** pres. mid. part. πλανάομαι to wander,
to wander aimlessly, they wandered like lost sheep hunted by
wolves (RWP). **σπήλαιον** cave. **ὀπή** opening, hole, den. They
were outlawed as people who were unfit for civilized society; the
truth was that civilized society was unfit for them (Bruce). (For
an account of those who were persecuted who lived in caves and
dens and wandered about the mountains, s. I Maccabees 2:29–
38.)

39 ■ **μαρτυρηθέντες** aor. pass. part. μαρτυρέομαι to witness, pass. to be witnessed, to be attested by witness (s. Hughes;
Westcott). The part. is used concessively, i.e., "although . . . ."
40 **ἐκομίσαντο** aor.mid. ind., s.v.13. ■ **προβλεψαμένου** aor. mid.
part. προβλέπομαι to see before, to exercise forethought, to
foresee, to provide. The part. is used in a gen. abs. construction.
χώρις without. **τελειωθῶσιν** aor. pass. subj. τελειόω to bring
to the goal, to complete, to perfect (s. Heb. 5:9).

Ch. 12

■ **τοιγαροῦν** therefore then, a triple compound inferential 1
particle to draw a conclusion of emphasis making Heb. 12:1–3
the climax of the whole argument about the better promises
(RWP). **τοσοῦτος** such a one, so great. **ἔχοντες** pres. act. part.
ἔχω. The part. is used to express cause. **περικείμενον** pres. mid.
part. περίκειμαι to lie around, to spread around, to surround.
The competitors feel the crowd towering about above them
(Westcott). **νέφος** cloud. The picture of a cloud describing a
crowded group of people is a common classical figure and expresses not only the great number of people, but also the unity
of the crowd in their witness (Michel). **μάρτυς** witness. The
witness was to confirm and to attest to the truth of a matter (s.
NTCW; TDNT). **ὄγκος** bulk, mass, weight. An athlete would
strip for action both by the removal of superfluous flesh through
rigorous training and by the removal of all his clothes (Hughes).
ἀποθέμενοι pres. mid. part. ἀποτίθημι to lay aside from one's
self, to lay aside one's clothing. **εὐπερίστατος**. The word could
have a variety of meanings; e.g., (1) "easily avoided," (2) "ad-
mired"; lit. "well-surrounded," (3) "easily surrounding," "beset-
ting," (4) "dangerous"; lit. "having easy distress." The picture
here may be that of putting off a long heavy robe which would
be a hindrance in running. (For this word, s. MH, 282; Michel;
Westcott; MM; Hughes.) **ὑπομονή** patient endurance (s. Heb.
10:36). **τρέχωμεν** pres. act. subj. τρέχω to run, cohortative subj.
"let us run." **προκείμενον** pres. mid. part. πρόκειμαι to lie
before (s. Heb. 6:18). **ἀγών** struggle, contest, race. ■ 2
ἀφορῶντες pres. act. part. ἀφοράω to look away from one
thing and to concentrate on another, to look away to (cf. Heb.
10:36). **ἀρχηγός** pioneer, author (s. Heb. 2:10; s. also Michel;
Westcott). **τελειωτής** perfecter, one who brings to the goal (s.
Heb. 5:9). **ἀντί** for the sake of, because of. The prep. can also
have the idea of "exchange" or "substitution." (For a discussion
of the meaning of the prep. here, s. Hughes.) **προκειμένης** pres.
mid. part., s.v.1. **ὑπέμεινεν** aor. act. ind. ὑπομένω to patiently
endure (s. Heb. 11:26). **σταυρός** cross. **αἰσχύνη** shame, disgrace. **καταφρονήσας** aor. act. part. καταφρονέω followed by
the gen. to think down on something, to despise, to treat as
contemptible. **ἐν δέξιᾳ** on the right. **κεκάθικεν** perf. act. ind.
καθίζω to take one's seat, to sit down. The perf. tense indicates
that He is still there (s. Heb. 1:3; Eph. 1:20). ■ **ἀναλογίσασθε** 3
aor. mid. imp. ἀναλογίζομαι to reckon up, to count up, to
consider. The verb can also include the idea of meditation
(Michel). **τοιοῦτος** such a one. **ὑπομεμενηκότα** perf. act. part.,

s.v.2. The perf. part. suggests the abiding effect of Christ's redemptive suffering (Hughes). **ἁμαρτωλός** sinner. **εἰς** against. **ἀντιλογία** speaking against, hostility (s. Hughes). **κάμητε** aor. act. subj. κάμνω to grow weary, ingressive aor. to become weary. The subj. is used in a neg. purpose clause. **ἐκλυόμενοι** pres. pass. part. ἐκλύομαι to release, pass. to become weary or slack, to give out (s. BAG). The part. further describes the "weariness" of the main verb.

4 ■ **οὔπω** not yet. **μέχρις** w. the gen. unto, unto the point of.
ἀντικατέστητε aor. act. ind. ἀντικαθίστημι to stand in opposition against, in line of battle (RWP). **πρός** against.
ἀνταγωνιζόμενοι pres. mid. part. ἀνταγωνίζομαι to struggle
against. The metaphor is still that of the athletic contest, but now
5 shifts from the race track to the boxing ring (Hughes). ■
ἐκλέλησθε perf. mid. ind. ἐκλανθάνω to cause to forget, mid. to forget, to forget completely. The prep. in compound is perfective (s. MH, 311). **παράκλησις** encouragement, exhortation (s. Phil. 2:1). **διαλέγεται** pres. mid. ind. followed by the dat. to reason w., to converse w. The utterance of Scripture is treated as the voice of God conversing w. men (Westcott). **ὀλιγώρει** pres. act. imp. ὀλιγωρέω to think little of, to think lightly, to make light of something, to neglect (BAG; MM; Preisigke). **παιδεία** discipline, instructive discipline. In Judaism a father was required to provide for the instruction of his sons and daughters and to teach them good behavior. Whipping was accepted, along w. other disciplinary measures (JPFC II, 770f.; s. also
TDNT). **ἐκλύου** pres. pass. imp., s.v.3. **ἐλεγχόμενος** pres. pass.
6 part. ἐλέγχω to reprove. ■ **παιδεύει** pres. act. ind. **μαστιγοῖ**
to beat w. a whip, to scourge. (For the concept of suffering being
the chastisement or discipline from God, s. Michel; TDNT.)
7 **παραδέχεται** pres. mid. ind. to accept, to receive. ■ **ὑπομένετε**
pres. act. ind. to patiently endure (s. Heb. 10:36). **προσφέρομαι**
pres. mid. ind. to carry one's self toward, to deal w. someone.
8 ■ **μέτοχος** participant, partner. **γεγόνασιν** perf. act. ind.
γίνομαι. The perf. shows that the chastisement was personally accepted and permanent in its effects (Westcott). **ἄρα** therefore. **νόθος** illegitimate. The word not only indicates that the father is not sufficiently interested in them to inflict on them the discipline that fits his legitimate children (Moffatt), but it is also to be taken in the legal sense in which an illegitimate child does not
enjoy the inheritance rights and the rights to participate in
9 family worship (s. Spicq; Hughes). ■ **εἶτα** then, besides this
(Hughes). **εἴχομεν** impf. act. ind. ἔχω to have. The impf. is the customary impf. "we used to have" (RWP). **παιδευτής** one who

exercises discipline, one who instructs through discipline. The
acc. is a double acc., i.e., "fathers as ones who discipline."
ἐνετρεπόμεθα impf. mid. ind. ἐντρέπομαι to fear, to reverence. The impf. is customary impf. **ὑποταγησόμεθα** fut. mid.
ind. ὑποτάσσομαι to subject, to be in subjection, to be in
submission, to submit one's self. **ζήσομεν** fut. act. ind. ζάω to
live. ■ **ἐπί** w. the acc. for. The prep. indicates the purpose of a 10
few days and is a description for the whole earthly life (Michel).
δοκοῦν pres. act. part. acc. n. sing. to seem, to seem to be good,
"according to the thing seeming good to them" (RWP).
ἐπαίδευον impf. act. ind. **συμφέρον** pres. act. part. συμφέρω
to differ, to be better. The part. is used as a substitutive "that
which is best," "for our advantage" (EGT). **μεταλαβεῖν** aor.
act. inf. μεταλαμβάνω followed by the gen. to partake of, to
have a share in. The inf. is used w. the prep. to express purpose.
ἁγιότης holiness. ■ **πρὸς τὸ παρόν** "for the present." **δοκεῖ** 11
s.v.10. **λύπη** pain, sorrow. **ὕστερον** afterwards. **καρπός** fruit.
εἰρηνικός pertaining to peace, peaceful. **γεγυμνασμένοις** perf.
pass. part. γυμνάζω to exercise, to train. The perf. part. indicates the completed state or condition. **ἀποδίδωσιν** pres. act.
ind. to give back, to repay, to yield. (For rabbinical parallels
regarding the results of suffering, s. Bruce.)

■ **παρειμένας** perf. pass. part. παρίημι to let fall at the 12
side, to slacken, to weaken, pass. to be listless, drooping (BAG).
παραλελυμένα perf. pass. part. παραλύω to loosen on the
side, to dissolve, to paralyze, to undo, pass. to be weak, to be
lame (s. RWP; BAG). **γόνυ** knee. **ἀνορθώσατε** aor. act. imp.
ἀνορθόω to set up straight, to set upright or straighten again,
to revive (EGT). ■ **τροχία** track of a wheel, track made by the 13
feet of the runners. Here it could have the meaning "running
lane" and develop the athletic imagery (Hughes). **ὀρθος**
straight. **ποιεῖτε** pres. act. imp. **πούς** foot, dat. of advantage "for
your feet." **χωλός** lame. **ἐκτραπῇ** aor. mid. subj. ἐκτρέπομαι
to turn from, to turn aside. The word could have the idea of
turning aside in a race or it could be a medical figure of putting
a limb out of joint (Hughes; Westcott; Michel). **ἰαθῇ** aor. pass.
subj. ἰάομαι to heal, pass. to be healed. The subjs. are used here
to express purpose.

■ **διώκετε** pres. act. imp. διώκω to hunt, to follow after, to 14
pursue. **ἁγιασμός** holiness. In this epistle it is explained as a
drawing near to God w. a cleansed conscience (10:14, 22), a true
acceptance of Christ's sacrifice as bringing the worshiper into
fellowship w. God (EGT). **ὄψεται** fut. mid. ind. ὁράω to see.
■ **ἐπισκοποῦντες** pres. act. part. ἐπισκοπέω to watch over, to 15

watch out for. The word expresses the careful regard of those who occupy a position of responsibility (as a physician, or a superintendent) (Westcott). **ὑστερῶν** pres. act. part. ὑστερέω to lack, to come short, to fail. **ῥίζα** root. **πικρία** bitterness. The "root of bitterness" in Deut. 29:18 probably referred to anything that lead to idolatry and apostasy (Buchanan). **ἄνω** up. **φύουσα** pres. act. part. φύω to sprout, to spring up. **ἐνοχλῇ** pres. act. subj. ἐνοχλέω to trouble, to trouble w. a crowd, to annoy, to harass (s. Acts 15:19; RWP; Hughes). **μιανθῶσιν** aor. pass.
16 subj. μιαίνω to stain, to defile. ■ **πόρνος** immoral. **βέβηλος** profane, irreligious. **βρῶσις** food. **ἀπέδοτο** aor. mid. ind. ἀποδίδωμι to sell. **τὰ πρωτοτόκια** birthright, the privilege of
17 the firstborn son (s. TDNT). ■ **ἴστε** perf. act. ind. 2nd per. pl. οἶδα defective perf. w. a pres. meaning to know. **μετέπειτα** afterwards. **θέλων** pres. act. part. The part. is concessive. **κληρονομῆσαι** aor. act. inf. κληρονομέω to inherit. **ἀπεδοκιμάσθη** aor. pass. ind. ἀποδοκιμάζω to reject after examination, to reject completely. **μετάνοια** change of mind, repentance. **τόπος** room, place, opportunity. **εὗρεν** aor. act. ind. εὑρίσκω to find. **καίπερ** although. The particle is used in a clause of concession. **δάκρυον** tear. **ἐκζητήσας** aor. act. part. ἐκζητέω to seek out, to look for.
18 ■ **προσεληλύθατε** perf. act. ind. προσέρχομαι to come to, to draw near. **ψηλαφωμένῳ** pres. pass. part. ψηλαφάω to handle, to touch, i.e., to the mountain which may be touched (s. Hughes). **κεκαυμένῳ** perf. pass. part. καίω to burn. **πῦρ** fire. **γνόφος** darkness, blackness, thick darkness (Westcott). **ζόφος** darkness, deep gloom (AS). **θύελλα** storm, hurricane (RWP).
19 ■ **σάλπιγξ** trumpet. **ἦχος** sound. **ῥῆμα** word. **ἀκούσαντες** aor. act. part. **παρῃτήσαντο** aor. mid. ind. παραιτέομαι to beg, to ask for, to request. **προστεθῆναι** aor. pass. inf. προστίθημι to place to, to add to. The inf. is used in indirect
20 discourse. ■ **ἔφερον** impf. ind. act. φέρω to carry, to bear, to endure. **διαστελλόμενον** pres. act. part. διαστέλλω to command, to order. The pres. tense presents the command as ringing constantly in their ears (Westcott). **κάν** = **καὶ ἄν** "if even." **θηρίον** animal. **θίγῃ** aor. act. subj. θιγγάνω to touch, followed by the gen. **λιθοβοληθήσεται** fut. pass. ind. λιθοβολέω to
21 throw stones at, to stone. ■ **φοβερός** terrible, fearful. **ἦν** impf. εἰμί. **φανταζόμενον** pres. mid. part. φαντάζομαι to appear. **ἔκφοβος** terrified. The prep. in compound is perfective.
22 **ἔντρομος** trembling. ■ **προσεληλύθατε** perf. act. ind., s.v.18. **ζῶντος** pres. act. part. ζάω to live. **μυριάς** myriad, ten thousand. It indicates a number that cannot be counted, i.e., "tens of

thousands" (Hughes). **πανήγυρις** festive gathering. The word
indicated the great gathering for a festival occasion. In the OT
it was for the religious festivals. In the Gr. world it was a gathering for large athletic contests (Michel). ■ **πρωτότοκος** firstborn 23
(s. Heb. 11:28; TDNT; Col. 1:18). They are "firstborn ones"
enjoying the rights of firstborn sons, because of their union w.
Christ, the firstborn (Kent). **ἀπογεγραμμένων** perf. pass. part.
ἀπογράφω to write off, to enroll. **τετελειωμένων** perf. pass.
part. τελειόω to bring to the goal, to perfect (s. Heb. 5:9). ■ 24
μεσίτης mediator. **ῥαντισμός** sprinkling. **κρεῖττον** better.
λαλοῦντι pres. act. part. **παρά** used in a comparison "than."

■ **βλέπετε** pres. act. imp. βλέπω to see, to beware, to take 25
heed. **παραιτήσησθε** aor. mid. subj. to ask, to request, to
refuse, s.v.19. **λαλοῦντα** pres. act. part. **ἐξέφυγον** aor. act. ind.
ἐκφεύγω to flee from, to flee from successfully, to escape. The
prep. in compound is perfective and the aor. is complexive emphasizing the completion of the action. **παραιτησάμενοι** aor.
mid. part., s.v.19. **χρηματίζοντα** pres. act. part. to give divine
instruction, to warn (s. Heb. 8:5; 11:7). **ἀποστρεφόμενοι** pres.
mid. part. to turn away from, to turn from. ■ **ἐσάλευσεν** aor. 26
act. ind. σαλεύω to shake. **τότε** formerly, at that time.
ἐπήγγελται perf. mid. ind. ἐπαγγέλλομαι to promise. The
perf. tense indicates that the promise is still valid. **ἅπαξ** once,
"yet once more." **σείσω** fut. act. ind. σείω to shake, to cause
to tremble (s. Matt. 21:10). **μόνον** alone. ■ **δηλοῖ** pres. act. ind. 27
to make clear. **σαλευομένων** pres. pass. part., s.v.26.
μετάθεσις removing (s. Heb. 7:12). **πεποιημένων** perf. pass.
part. ποιέω. **μείνῃ** aor. act. subj. μένω to remain. ■ **ἀσάλευτος** 28
not able to be shaken, unshakeable. **παραλαμβάνοντες** pres.
act. part. παραλαμβάνω to receive. **ἔχωμεν** pres. act. subj.
used in the expression ἔχω χάριν to be grateful. The subj. is
hortatory "let us be grateful." **λατρεύωμεν** pres. act. subj.
λατρεύω to worship, to serve. **εὐαρέστως** well-pleasing.
εὐλάβεια reverence (s. Heb. 5:7). **δέος** awe. It is the apprehension of danger as in a forest (RWP). ■ **καταναλίσκον** pres. act. 29
part. καταναλίσκω to consume completely. The prep. in compound is perfective.

Ch. 13

■ **μενέτω** pres. act. imp. μένω to remain. The use of the 1
verb suggests that the bond had been in danger of being severed
(Westcott). ■ **φιλοξενία** entertaining of strangers, hospitality. 2
Since there were very few inns, the entertainment and showing
of hospitality to travelers was an important part of Jewish home

life (s. JPFC II, 762). **ἐπιλανθάνομαι** pres. mid. imp. followed
by the gen. to forget. The pres. imp. w. the neg. means "do not
go on being unmindful" of hospitality (Hughes). **ἔλαθόν** aor.
act. ind. λανθάνω to escape notice, to do something without
knowing it (s. BAG). **ξενίσαντες** aor. act. part. ξενίζω to entertain strangers, to show hospitality. The part. is used supplementary to the main verb giving the meaning "some escaped notice
3 when entertaining angels" (RWP). ■ **μιμνήσκεσθε** pres. mid.
imp. to remember followed by the gen. **συνδεδεμένοι** perf. pass.
part. συνδέω to bind together, pass. to be bound w. another, to
be a fellow prisoner. The perf. tense views the completed state
or condition. **κακουχουμένων** pres. pass. part. κακουχέω to
mishandle, to treat evilly (s. Heb. 11:37). **ὄντες** pres. part. εἰμί.
4 The part. is causal. ■ **τίμιος ἐν** honorable. **γάμος** marriage.
κοίτη bed, marriage bed, sexual intercourse. **ἀμίαντος** undefiled. **πόρνος** immoral. The word designates those persons
who indulge in sexual relationships outside the marriage bond,
both heterosexual and homosexual (Hughes). **μοῖχος** adulter-
ous. This word indicates those who are unfaithful to their marriage vows; thus, the two adjs. cover all who licentiously engage
in forbidden practices (Hughes). **κρινεῖ** fut. act. ind. to judge.
5 ■ **ἀφιλάργυρος** without a love for money. **τρόπος** manner,
manner of life, disposition, "let your turn of mind be free from
love of money, content w. what you have" (EGT). **ἀρκούμενοι**
pres. pass. part. ἀρκέομαι to have enough, pass. to be content.
παροῦσιν pres. part. πάρειμι to be present, to be at hand.
εἴρηκεν perf. act. ind. λέγω. The perf. indicates that the statement has been made and its authority continues. **ἀνῶ** aor. act.
subj. ἀνίημι to send up, to send back, to let go, to leave without
support (AS). **ἐγκαταλίπω** aor. subj. ἐγκαταλείπω to leave
6 someone in distress, to leave in the lurch, to desert. ■ **ὥστε** used
w. the inf. to introduce a result clause. **θαρροῦντας** pres. act.
part. θαρρέω to be courageous, to be bold, to be confident.
βοηθός helper, one who brings help in the time of need.
φοβηθήσομαι fut. mid. ind. φοβέομαι to be afraid. **ποιήσει**
fut. act. ind.

7 ■ **μνημονεύετε** pres. act. imp. to remember, to be mindful
of, followed by the gen. **ἡγουμένων** pres. mid. part. ἡγέομαι to
lead. **ἐλάλησαν** aor. act. ind. λαλέω. **ἀναθεωροῦντες** pres.
act. part. ἀναθεωρέω to look back upon, to scan closely (Moffatt), to look back carefully on (Hughes). **ἔκβασις** going out,
away out, end. The phrase can mean either "the end of one's life"
or more probably "the successful outcome or result of one's way
of life" (BAG). **ἀναστροφή** manner of life. **μιμεῖσθε** pres. mid.

imp. μεμέομαι to imitate. ■ **ἐχθές** yesterday. ■ **ποικίλος** vary- 8/9
ing, diverse. **ξένος** foreign, strange. **παραφέρεσθε** pres. pass.
imp. παραφέρομαι to carry along, to lead away. The pass.
would be permissive pass. **καλός** good. The words "it is" are to
be supplied. **βεβαιοῦσθαι** pres. pass. inf. βεβαιόομαι to make
firm, to confirm, to make stable. **βρῶμα** food. **ὠφελήθησαν**
aor. pass. ind. ὠφελέομαι to be profitable, to be useful.
περιπατοῦντες pres. act. part. περιπατέω to walk about, to
conduct one's life. ■ **θυσιαστήριον** altar, place of sacrifice. 10
φαγεῖν aor. act. inf. ἐσθίω to eat. The inf. is used epexegetically
explaining what is lawful. **ἐξουσία** that which is legal, lawful,
authority, prerogative. **σκηνή** tent, tabernacle. **λατρεύοντες**
pres. act. part. λατρεύω to serve religiously, to perform religious
service. ■ **εἰσφέρεται** pres. pass. ind. εἰσφέρω to bring in. **ζῷον** 11
living creature, animal. **κατακαίεται** pres. pass. ind. to burn, to
burn completely, to burn up. **ἔξω** outside. **παρεμβολή** camp.
■ **δίο** therefore, wherefore. **ἁγιάσῃ** aor. act. subj. ἁγιάζω to set 12
apart, to sanctify. **ἴδιος** one's own. **πύλη** gate. He refers to the
gate of the city of Jerusalem which, bounded by its walls, corresponds to the holy ground of the wilderness camp (Hughes).
ἔπαθεν aor. act. ind. πάσχω to suffer. The purpose of Christ's
suffering outside of the city gates is the sanctification of His
people. ■ **τοίνυν** therefore. The inferential particle draws a con- 13
clusion from the preceding. **ἐξερχώμεθα** pres. mid. subj.
ἐξέρχομαι. The subj. is hortatory "let us go out." The pres.
tense expresses vividly the immediate effort (Westcott). This
could be a call for the readers to refuse to go back into Judaism
(s. Hughes; Westcott). **ὀνειδισμός** reproach, insult. **φέροντες**
pres. act. part. φέρω to bear. ■ **μένουσαν** pres. act. part. μένω 14
to remain. **μέλλων** pres. act. part. to be about to, here "coming."
ἐπιζητοῦμεν pres. act. ind. to search for. ■ **ἀναφέρωμεν** pres. 15
act. subj. ἀναφέρω to bring up, to offer up. The subj. is cohortative "let us offer up." **αἴνεσις** praise. **διὰ παντός** "through all,"
"continually." A rabbinical tradition teaches that all the Mosaic
sacrifices would have an end except the thank offering, and all
prayers would cease except the prayer of thanksgiving (s.
Hughes; Michel; SB I, 246). **χεῖλος** lip. **ὁμολογούντων** pres.
act. part. ὁμολογέω to confess, to profess. The word carries the
idea of a proclamation (Michel) as well as the idea of praise (s.
MM). ■ **εὐποιΐα** good deed, doing good. **κοινωνία** fellowship, 16
sharing (s. Phil. 1:5). **ἐπιλανθάνεσθε** pres. mid. imp. to forget
something, followed by the gen. The pres. imp. w. the neg. is
used to forbid a habitual action. **εὐαρεστεῖται** pres. mid. ind.

to be well pleased w. The pres. tense indicates that which is
always true.
17 ■ **πείθεσθε** pres. mid. imp. to obey. **ἡγουμένοις** pres. mid.
part., s.v.7. **ὑπείκετε** pres. act. imp. to give in, to yield, to
submit. **ἀγρυπνοῦσιν** to be without sleep, to seek after sleep,
to be watchful (RWP). **ἀποδώσοντος.** The part. is fut. act. part.
and the expression means "to give an account," "to render account." **ποιῶσιν** pres. act. subj. ποιοῦσιν. **στενάζοντες** pres.
act. part. στενάζω to groan. **ἀλυσιτελής** unprofitable, harmful.
18 ■ **προσεύχεσθε** pres. mid. imp. to pray. **πειθόμεθα** pres.
mid. ind. to be persuaded, to have confidence, to be confident.
συνείδησις conscience (s. Rom. 2:15). **καλῶς** adv. good, clear.
θέλοντες pres. act. part. **ἀναστρέφεσθαι** pres. mid. inf. to
19 conduct one's life. ■ **περισσοτέρως** adv. more earnestly.
ποιῆσαι aor. act. inf. **τάχιον** comp. n. sing. The adj. is used as
an adv. "sooner." **ἀποκατασταθῶ** aor. pass. subj.
ἀποκαθίστημι to restore back again.
20 ■ **ἀναγαγών** aor. act. part. ἀνάγω to lead up, to bring
21 again. **ποιμήν** shepherd. **αἰώνιος** eternal. ■ **καταρτίσαι** aor.
act. opt. καταρτίζω to equip. The word includes the thoughts
of the harmonious combination of different powers, of the supply
of that which is defective, and of the amendment of that which
is faulty (Westcott). The opt. is used to express a wish for the
future (RWP). **ποιῆσαι** aor. act. inf. The inf. is used w. the prep.
to express purpose. **ποιῶν** pres. act. part. **εὐάρεστος** well-pleasing. **ἐνώπιον** before, in the presence of.
22 ■ **ἀνέχεσθε** pres. mid. imp. to hold one's self back from
(RWP), to endure, to bear w. **βραχύς** short. Used w. the prep.
w. the meaning "in few words" (Westcott). **ἐπέστειλα** aor. act.
23 ind. ἐπιστέλλω to send a letter to, to write. ■ **ἀπολελυμένον**
perf. pass. part. ἀπολύω to release. Although the word has a
variety of meanings, its most frequent sense in the NT is that of
releasing from custody persons who were under arrest or in
prison (Hughes). **τάχιον** soon. **ἔρχηται** pres. mid. subj.
ἔρχομαι. **ὄψομαι** fut. mid. ind. ὁράω.
24 ■ **ἀσπάσασθε** aor. mid. imp. ἀσπάζομαι to greet.
ἡγουμένους pres. mid. part., s.v.7.

JAMES

Ch. 1

φυλή tribe. **διασπορά** scattering, dispersion, diaspora. 1
The term indicates one who is living in a foreign country
(Mussner; Dibelius; s. 1 Peter 1:1). The term could refer to
Jewish Christians living outside of Palestine (Mayor; for a discussion of the word, s. also Ropes).
■ **ἡγήσασθε** aor. mid. imp. ἡγέομαι to consider, to deem 2
as, to reckon as. The object of the verb is placed first for emphasis (Mussner). The aor. is perhaps used because the writer is
thinking of each special case of temptation (Ropes; Mayor).
ὅταν w. the subj. "whenever." **πειρασμός** trial, temptation.
The word is used sometimes regarding outward trials and inward
temptations (Tasker; s. also Mayor; TDNT; CBB). **ποικίλος**
many colored, variegated, various, varied (s. 2 Tim. 3:6; Titus
3:2). ■ **γινώσκοντες** pres. act. part. The part. could be causal. 3
δοκίμιον trying, testing, proving. (For this active sense, s. May-
or.) The pass. sense has the idea of "approved after testing,"
"tested and approved," "the genuine part" (s. BS, 259ff.; IBG,
96; Ropes; Dibelius). ■ **τέλειον** perfection. Here James contin- 4
ues the OT idea of perfection as a right relationship to God
expressed in undivided obedience and unblemished life (Adamson). **ἐχέτω** pres. act. imp. **ἦτε** pres. subj. εἰμί. The subj. is used
to express purpose. **ὁλόκληρος** complete in all its parts, entire.
The word indicates the entirety of all of the Christian virtues (s.
Mussner). **λειπόμενοι** pres. mid. part. λείπομαι to be left behind, to lack. ■ **αἰτείτω** pres. act. imp. third-person sing. αἰτέω 5
to ask. **διδόντος** pres. act. part. **ἁπλῶς** adv. simply, uncondi-
tionally, without bargaining. The word could possibly have the
meaning here "generously," which would be derived from the
noun meaning "liberality," which comes from the idea of frankness and openheartedness (Mayor). Perhaps the best translation
here is "freely" (Adamson). **ὀνειδίζοντος** pres. act. part.
ὀνειδίζω to rebuke, to reprove, to reproach, to insult.
δοθήσεται fut. pass. ind. δίδωμι. The pass. would be the "divine pass." indicating that God is the giver (BG, 236). ■ **πίστις** 6
faith. Here it does not denote "constancy in the Christian reli-

gion" as in v.3. Here it means "confidence in prayer." It means
the petitioner's faith, his belief and trust, that God will heed his
prayer, and grant it or only in His superior wisdom deny it
(Adamson; s. also Ropes). (For the grammatical structure of the
conditional clause followed by the imp., s. Mussner; Beyer, 238.)
διακρινόμενος pres. mid. part. διακρίνομαι to divide, to be at
variance w. one's self, to waver, to doubt (Ropes). **ἔοικεν** pres.
act. ind. to be like, to resemble. **κλύδων** wave; i.e., "the surge
of the sea," "the billowing sea" (Ropes). **ἀνεμιζομένῳ** pres.
pass. part. ἀνεμίζω to drive w. the wind (Dibelius). **ῥιπιζομένῳ**
pres. pass. part. ῥιπίζω to fan, most often used of fanning a
7 flame (Mayor), here "to toss" (Dibelius). ■ **οἰέσθω** pres. mid.
imp. 3rd sing. οἴομαι to suppose. The word is often used in a
neg. sense indicating wrong judgment or conceit (Ropes).
8 **λήμψεται** fut. mid. ind. λαμβάνω to receive. ■ **ἀνήρ** male,
man. The word is used here in the sense of a "person" (Dibelius).
δίψυχος double-souled, double-minded, i.e., "w. soul divided
between faith and the world" (Ropes; s. also Adamson).
ἀκατάστατος not having stability, unsettled, unstable. Polybi-
us uses it both of political disturbance and of individual character
(Mayor). The word refers to "vacillating in all his activity and
conduct" (Dibelius).

9 ■ **καυχάσθω** pres. mid. imp. καυχάομαι to boast, to boast
over a privilege or possession. The word is used in the OT of
"any proud and exulting joy" (Ropes). **ταπεινός** low, low degree, humble position. The word is used in the LXX to translate
the Heb. word for "poor," "without possessions" (Dibelius).
ὕψος high, exaltation. It refers to the pres. spiritual status which,
by virtue of his relation to Christ, the Christian now enjoys
10 (Adamson). ■ **πλούσιος** rich. **ταπείνωσις** lowliness, humiliation. **ἄνθος** flower. **χόρτος** grass. **παρελεύσεται** fut. mid. ind.
παρέχομαι to pass along the side of, to pass away, to disappear
11 (Ropes). ■ **ἀνέτειλεν** aor. act. ind. ἀνατέλλω to rise up, to rise.
The aor. is gnomic indicating that which generally happens
(Ropes). **καύσων** burning heat. The word may refer to the blistering east wind called Sirocco (Mayor; Ropes; Adamson).
ἐξήρανεν aor. act. ind. ξηραίνω to dry, to dry out, to wither.
ἐξέπεσεν aor. act. ind. ἐκπίπτω to fall off. The word was used
in the LXX of flowers falling from the stem (Mayor). **εὐπρέπεια**
outward beauty. The word is used w. a suggestion of fitness to
the object and its relations, and so sometimes gains a notion of
stateliness or majesty (Ropes). **ἀπώλετο** aor. mid. ind.
ἀπόλλυμι to ruin, to come to ruin, to be destroyed. **πορεία**
way. The word could be used in the sense of "a business journey"

but here it is to be taken as a reference to the rich man's "whole"
way of life (Dibelius). **μαρανθήσεται** fut. pass. ind. μαραίνω
to wither, to waste away. The picture of the rich "withering"
continues the simile of the fading flower: the verb is picturesque
and may be used of the dying of a flower or the decaying of
plants like roses as well as ears of corn (Adamson; Ropes). The
reference is to the loss of riches and earthly prosperity, not to
eternal destiny (Ropes).

■ **μακάριος** blessed, happy (s. TDNT). The idea expressed 12
here is familiar in Judaism: "Happy is the man who can withstand the test, for there is none whom God does not prove"
(Adamson). **ὑπομένει** pres. act. ind. to endure, to patiently and
triumphantly endure, to show constancy under (Ropes). It is not
the patience which can sit down and bow its head and let things
descend upon it and passively endure until the storm is passed.
It is the spirit which can bear things, not simply w. resignation,
but w. blazing hope (NTW, 60). **δόκιμος** approved after testing
(s.v.3). **γενόμενος** aor. mid. part. γίνομαι. The part. is temporal
"after being approved" and not conditional (Dibelius; Ropes).
τῆς ζωῆς "of life." The crown spoken of here was a head wreath
or circlet which was the victor's prize in the Gr. games; it might
also be given to a man the public wished to honor and it was
worn in religious and secular feasts (Adamson; s. also Ropes;
TDNT). The gen. could be descriptive; i.e., "a living crown" in
contrast to the perishable crown or it could be an appositional
gen.; i.e., the crown is life. (For a discussion of the various
possibilities, s. Dibelius; s. also Mayor.) **ἐπηγγείλατο** aor. mid.
ind. ἐπαγγέλλομαι to promise. **ἀγαπῶσιν** pres. act. part.
ἀγαπάω to love. ■ **πειραζόμενος** pres. pass. part. πειράζω to 13
try, to tempt. Here the word is used meaning "temptation to sin"
(Ropes). **λεγέτω** pres. mid. imp. **ὅτι.** Used as quotation marks
to introduce a direct quotation. **ἀπὸ θεοῦ** "from God." The
prep. expresses the remoter rather than the nearer cause (May-
or). **ἀπείραστος** not able to be tempted, "invincible to assault
of evils" (Ropes; s. also Peter H. Davis, "The Meaning of *Apei-
rastos* in James I.13," NTS, 24 [March, 1978], 386–392). ■ 14
ἕκαστος each. **ἴδιος** one's own. **ἐπιθυμία** desire, strong desire
directed toward an object, lust. **ἐξελκόμενος** pres. pass. part.
ἐξέλκω to draw out, to draw away, to lure. **δελεαζόμενος** pres.
mid. part. δελεάζω to entice or catch by the use of bait. These
words were applied to the hunter or, esp., the fisherman who
lures his prey from its retreat and entices it by bait to his trap,
hook, or net (Ropes; s. also Adamson). In like manner the first
effect of lust is to draw the man out of his original repose, the

second to allure him to a definite bait (Mayor). (For the comparison of James' teaching regarding "lust," "desire" w. the Jewish
teaching regarding the "Evil Inclination," s. Mussner; s. also SB
15 IV, 466–483; PRJ, 17–35.) ■ **εἶτα** then. The word introduces the
practical result of the temptation arising from lust (Ropes). **συλλαβοῦσα** aor. act. part. συλλαμβάνω to become pregnant, to conceive. If the previous words refer to the enticement of a prostitute, then these words would picture the result of yielding to her seductive temptations (s. Mussner). The part. is temporal. **τίκτει** pres. act. ind. to give birth, to bear. **ἀποτελεσθεῖσα** aor. pass. part. ἀποτελέω to come to completion, to come to maturity, to be fully grown. The word connotes "completeness of parts and function . . . accompanying full growth as opposed to a rudimentary or otherwise incomplete state" (Adamson; Ropes). **ἀποκύει** pres. act. ind. to cease being pregnant, to give birth to. The word is frequently used of animals; otherwise it is a medical rather than literary word (Ropes). The prep. in compound denotes cessation (Mayor; s. also MH, 298).

16 ■ **πλανᾶσθε** pres. mid.-pass. imp. πλανάω to lead astray,
to deceive. The mid. or pass. could be permissive; i.e., "don't
17 allow yourselves to be deceived." **ἀγαπητός** beloved. ■ **δόσις**
giving. **δώρημα** that which is given, gift. **ἄνωθεν** from above. **καταβαῖνον** pres. act. part. καταβαίνω to come down. **πατήρ** father. **φῶτα** lights. The word generally refers to the light given to heavenly bodies and it describes God as the cosmic Father and Creator of the heavenly bodies (Mayor; Ropes; Dibelius). **ἔνι** = **ἔνεστι** pres. ind. ἔνειμι to be in, to be present (on this contracted form which may also be considered to be a strengthened form of the prep., s. BAG; BD, 49; MH, 306; RG, 313). It is not just the fact only which is negated but also the possibility (Mayor). **παραλλαγή** variation. It is used in Gr. for the setting of the teeth in a saw, or for stones set alternately, for a sequence of beacons or seasons and generally denotes some regularity or system in change (Adamson). **τροπή** turning. The gen. is a gen. of definition, "a variation consisting in turning." **ἀποσκίασμα** shadow. The word can mean the shadow cast by an object, as in an eclipse, or it can mean the act of overshadowing or it can have the meaning of a reflected image (Adamson; s. also Dibelius; Mayor; Ropes). God's benevolence is like a light which cannot be extinguished, eclipsed, or "shadowed out" in any way at all. Nothing can block God's light, interrupt the flow of His goodness, or put us "in shadow," so that we are out of the
18 reach of His "radiance" (Adamson). ■ **βουληθείς** aor. pass.

part. βούλομαι to counsel, to decide after counsel, to will. Here
it refers to the free sovereign, creative will, decision, decree of
God (Mussner; s. also TDNT). The part. is either temporal
"after deciding" or causal "because he decided." **ἀπεκύησεν**
aor. act. ind. ἀποκυέω = ἀποκύω to give birth, to bear (s.v.15).
Although the contract verb generally refers to the birth through
a woman, it is used here in reference to God giving birth (s.
Mussner; Adamson). **ἀπαρχή** first fruit. **κτίσμα** creation.
■ **ἴστε** 2nd per. pl. οἶδα defective perf. w. a pres. meaning. 19
ἔστω pres. imp. εἰμί. **ταχύς** quick, swift, fast. **ἀκοῦσαι** aor. act.
inf. The inf. w. the prep. can express purpose or result or it can
have the meaning "w. reference to hearing" (Ropes). **βραδύς**
slow. **λαλῆσαι** aor. act. inf. The inf. used w. the prep. and article
in the sense of "w. reference to" (Ropes). **ὀργή** anger, wrath. It
refers to the deep-seated anger (s. TDNT). ■ **θεοῦ**. Here the 20
gen., "God's righteousness," refers not to the righteousness that
is part of His character, but to the way of life, in deed and
thought, that He requires in us (Adamson; s. also Lenski).
ἐργάζεται pres. mid. ind. to work, to do, to practice (s. Ropes).
The pres. tense indicates that which is continually true. ■ **διό** 21
therefore. **ἀποθέμενοι** aor. mid. part. ἀποτίθημι to put off, to
strip off. It is a metaphor from the putting off of clothes (Mayor).
ῥυπαρία dirtiness, filthiness. The word was used of dirty clothes
and also referred to moral defilement (Mayor; Ropes).
περισσεία overabundance, excess. **κακία** evil, wickedness,
gen. of apposition. The phrase calls attention to the fact that
wickedness is in reality an excrescence on character, not a normal part of it (Ropes). **πραΰτης** meekness, mildness, gentleness.
It is the humble and gentle attitude which expresses itself in a
patient submissiveness to offense, free from malice and desire for
revenge. The word stands in contrast to the term "wrath" (s.
Mussner; Gal. 5:22; 2 Cor. 10:1; Matt. 5:5). **δέξασθε** aor. mid.
imp. δέχομαι to receive, to accept. **ἔμφυτος** implanted. It is the
word for an "implanting" not at birth but later in life. It is used
metaphorically to mean "sent into a man to be, or grow to be,
a part of his nature" (Adamson, 98–100). **δυνάμενον** pres. mid.
part. **σῶσαι** aor. act. inf. σῴζω to rescue, to save.
■ **γίνεσθε** pres. mid. imp. The pres. tense indicating con- 22
tinual action calls for a habit of life. **ποιητής** one who performs
an action, one who does something, doer. The expression would
be the same as the Semitic phrase "to do the law" meaning "to
observe the law" or "to fulfill the law." (For examples, s. Dibelius.) **ἀκροατής** one who hears. Both in the Jewish home as well
as in the education process and the synagogue worship, the

hearing of the law which was read aloud played an important
part in Jewish life (s. JPFC II, 800f.; 945–977; Dibelius). The
rabbis also stressed very strongly the necessity of keeping the
law (s. e.g. M Aboth 1, 17; for other examples, s. Mussner; SB
III, 84–88; 753). **παραλογιζόμενοι** pres. mid. part.
παραλογίζομαι to reason beside the point, to misjudge, to
miscalculate, to deceive one's self, to cheat in reckoning, to
23 deceive through fallacious reasoning (s. MM; MH, 319). ■
ἔοικεν pres. act. ind., s.v.6. **κατανοοῦντι** pres. act. part.
κατανοέω to put the mind down upon, to consider attentively,
to take note of, to look at (RWP; Ropes). **γένεσις** birth, origin,
natural, mortal. The word indicates the face which one received
at birth and the gen. is either gen. of attribute or perhaps of
source (s. Mussner; Adamson; Ropes). **ἔσοπτρον** mirror. Mirrors were generally highly polished metal (s. 1 Cor. 13:12; May-
24 or). ■ **κατενόησεν** aor. act. ind. κατανοέω (s.v.23).
ἀπελήλυθεν perf. act. ind. ἀπέρχομαι to go away. The force
of the perf. tense here is to express an immediate sequel, e.g., a
swift result (s. Adamson; Ropes). **εὐθέως** adv. immediately.
ἐπελάθετο aor. mid. ind. ἐπιλανθανομαι to forget. **ὁποῖος**
25 what sort of, what kind of. ■ **παρακύψας** aor. act. part.
παρακύπτω to stoop down and look into in order to see something exactly and to recognize (Mussner). Here it means "binding over the mirror in order to examine it more minutely,"
"hearing into it" (Mayor). **ἐλευθερία** freedom (s. Adams, 33f.).
The gen. is gen. of attribute (Mussner). **παραμείνας** pres. act.
part. παραμένω to stay beside, to remain, to continue (s. Phil.
1:25). **ἐπιλησμονή** forgetfulness. **γενόμενος** aor. mid. part.
s.v.12. **ἔργον** work. The gen. is a certain emphasis, "a doer who
does" (Ropes). **ποίησις** doing. **ἔσται** fut. εἰμί.
26 ■ **θρησκός** religious, pious. The word denotes the scrupulous observance of religious exercise—in action or words—sin-
cerely or hypocritically performed in the guise of devout religion. The word describes one who stands in awe of the gods, and
is tremendously scrupulous in what regards them (Adamson; s.
also Mayor; Ropes; TDNT). **χαλιναγωγῶν** pres. act. part.
χαλιναγωγέω to lead w. a bridle, to bridle. The picture is that
of a man putting the bridle in his own mouth, not in that of
another (RWP). **ἀπατῶν** pres. act. part. ἀπατάω to deceive.
μάταιος vain, empty, nonproductive, useless, dead (Mussner; s.
also TDNT). **θρησκεία** piety, religious worship. The word expresses the worship of God, religion, especially as it expresses
itself in religious service or cult (BAG; s. also MM; s. also the
27 adj. in this verse). ■ **ἀμίαντος** without defilement, undefiled,

free from contamination (AS). **ἐπισκέπτεσθαι** pres. mid. inf. to look upon, to visit, to provide help for. The word often was used for the visiting of the sick (Mayor; Ropes). **ὀρφανός** orphan. **χήρα** widow. (For the needs of the orphans and widows particularly in Judaism, s. Mussner; Mayor; JPFC II, 787ff.) **θλῖψις** stress, pressure, affliction. **ἄσπιλος** without a spot, unstained. **τηρεῖν** pres. act. inf. to observe, to keep, to guard. The inf. used in this v. are epexegetical explaining the nature of true piety or worship. **κόσμος** world, world system (s. TDNT; CBB).

Ch. 2

■ **προσωπολημψία** the receiving of one's face, partiality 1
(s. Rom. 2:11; Mayor). **ἔχετε** pres. act. imp. to have, to possess. **δόξα** glory. The gen. has been variously interpreted as having an objective, a subjective, or a qualitative force and has been connected to the various substitutives in the sentence. (For various
interpretations, s. Mayor; Adamson; Dibelius; Ropes.) ■ 2
εἰσέλθῃ aor. act. subj. εἰσέρχομαι to come into. **χρυσοδακτύλιος** w. a golden ring on the finger. It was common to wear rings in the ancient world either as a signet ring or as a piece of jewelry for adornment. Sometimes more than one ring was worn and the social status of a person could be noted by the quality of his ring (s. DGRA, 95–97; M, Kelim 11:8, 12:1). **ἐσθής** garment, clothes. **λαμπρός** shining. Some robes were said to have been made from silver which would glisten in the sunlight (s. Acts 12:21). The word here could refer to elegant and luxurious clothes or it may be used of fresh and clean clothes without reference to costliness (Ropes). **πτωχός** poor, abject poverty, poor as a beggar (s. NTW, 109–111; TDNT). **ῥυπαρός** filthy, dirty. The normal toga of the Romans was white, as was the robe of the Jews, and political candidates wore a brighter white which was produced by rubbing it with chalk. The white toga had to be cleaned, and when this was neglected, the Romans called it *sordida* and those who wore such garments were
called *sordidati* (s. DGRA, 1137; Mayor; Mussner). ■ 3
ἐπιβλέψητε aor. act. subj. ἐπιβλέπω to look upon, to direct one's attention to, to look w. attention or interest or respect or favor (Adamson). **φοροῦντα** pres. act. part. φορέω to carry, to wear, to wear clothes. **εἴπητε** aor. act. subj. λέγω. The subj. in this section are used in a third-class conditional clause assuming the possibility of the condition. **κάθου** pres. mid. imp. κάθημαι to sit. It has been supposed that the type of synagogue referred to here was one in which the cultic center was located close to the entrance and therefore the distinguished person is immedi-

ately provided w. a seat "here," while the poor man must either also take his seat near the sanctuary or else be satisfied w. a place to stand over "there" in that part of the building which is further from the entrance and the cultic center (s. Dibelius). **καλῶς** adv. "please," or it has the meaning "in a good place" (Adamson; s. also Matt. 23:6). **στῆθι** aor. act. imp. ἵστημι to stand, ingressive aor. "to take one's stand" (RWP). **ὑπό** w. the acc. under, down against, down beside (RWP). **ὑποπόδιον** footstool. This could have been something like that which was found in a synagogue of the 2nd or 3rd century. There was a stone bench running along the walls, w. a lower tier for the feet of those sitting
4 on the bench (s. Adamson). ■ **διεκρίθητε** aor. pass. ind. διακρίνομαι to judge between two, to face both ways, to be divided against one's self, to waiver, to distinguish. The verb has numerous meanings, here the best seems to be that of "to make a distinction," "to make differences." The neg. used in the question expects the answer yes and the words could be translated "You have made differences, haven't you?" w. the phrase "in (among) yourselves" meaning either distinctions between church members or the subjective opinion which one makes within himself (s. Mussner; Adamson; Dibelius; MM). **ἐγένεσθε** aor. mid. ind. γίνομαι. **διαλογισμός** reasoning. The word includes "purpose" as well as "deliberation" and the gen. is gen. of quality, "judges w. evil thoughts" (Ropes).
5 ■ **ἀκούσατε** aor. act. imp. **ἐξελέξατο** aor. mid. ind. ἐκλέγω to pick out, to choose out, mid. to choose for one's self. **τῷ κόσμῳ**. The dat. could be locative indicating the place "in the world" or it could be dat. of respect "those poor in respect to worldly goods" (Dibelius) or it could be an ethical dat. "poor in the opinion of the world"; i.e., "in the world's judgment" (Mayor; s. also BD, 103; MT, 239). **πλούσιος** rich, wealthy. **ἐν πίστει** "in faith." The phrase could mean "abounding in faith" (Mayor) or "in virtue of faith" or better "in the realm of faith" (Ropes; Adamson). **κληρονόμος** heir. **ἐπηγγείλατο** aor. mid. ind. ἐπαγγέλλομαι to promise. **ἀγαπῶσιν** pres. act. part.
6 ἀγαπάω to love. ■ **ἠτιμάσατε** aor. act. ind. ἀτιμάζω to treat without honor, to dishonor. **τὸν πτωχόν** "the poor." The article could point to a specific person or it is simply generic (Ropes). **καταδυναστεύουσιν** pres. act. ind. to exercise power against someone, to oppress. (For a description of the wealthy class as well as the middle class and poor class—to which the teachers of the law or the scribes often belonged—in Jerusalem at this time, s. JTJ, 87–119.) **ἕλκουσιν** pres. act. ind. to drag. **κριτήριον** place where cases are judged, tribunal, law court,

court of justice. ■ **βλασφημοῦσιν** pres. act. ind. to slander, to 7
blaspheme. **ἐπικληθέν** aor. pass. part. ἐπικαλέω to call upon,
pass. to be called upon, to be named. ■ **μέντοι** indeed. The 8
particle has both an adversative meaning "but," "nevertheless,"
"however," and an affirmative meaning "verily," "really" (s.
Ropes; Adamson). **τελεῖτε** pres. act. ind. to fulfill. **βασιλικός**
pertaining to a king, royal, sovereign, excellent, supreme. (For
various interpretations of this word, s. Adamson; Mayor; Ropes;
Dibelius.) **ἀγπήσεις** fut. act. ind. The fut. under Semitic influence is used as a "categorical imp." (BG, 94). **πλησίον** neighbor. ■ **προσωπολημπτεῖτε** pres. act. ind. to show partiality 9
(s.v.1). The ind. is used in a first-class condition assuming the
reality of the condition. **ἐργάζεσθε** pres. mid. ind. to work, to
do (s. James 1:20). **ἐλεγχόμενοι** pres. pass. part. ἐλέγχω to
convict, to convince w. overwhelming evidence. **παραβάτης**
transgressor, one who steps across a boundary (s. TDNT). ■ 10
ὅστις w. the subj. "whoever." (For this use w. the subj., s. RG,
956f.; BD, 192.) **τηρήσῃ** aor. act. subj. **τηρέω** to quard, to keep.
πταίσῃ aor. act. subj. πταίω to stumble, to trip. The "stumbling" means "to make a mistake, to go astray, to sin" (BAG).
ἐν ἑνί "in one point." The word is n. since "law" is not used of
single precepts (Ropes). **γέγονεν** perf. act. ind. γίνομαι. The
perf. tense indicates the continuing results of the action "he has
become guilty of all points" and ever remains so (Lenski).
ἔνοχος in the power of, guilty. Here the following gen. indicates
the authority or law against which one has transgressed (Dibelius; s. also Mayor). Stricter rabbis taught that the Torah even in
its separate statutes was immutable and indivisible (Adamson; s.
also SB III, 755). ■ **εἰπών** aor. act. part. λέγω. **μοιχεύσῃς** aor. 11
act. subj. μοιχεύω to commit adultery. **φονεύσῃς** aor. act. subj.
φονεύω to murder. (For **εἰ . . . οὐ**, s. M, 171. The sense of the
expression may be concessive; i.e., "although . . ." SMT, 179f.)
■ **λαλεῖτε** pres. act. imp. **ποιεῖτε** pres. act. imp. **ἐλευθερία** 12
freedom, liberty. The prep. here indicates the "state or condition
in which one does or suffers something"; i.e., "under the law of
liberty" (Ropes). **μέλλοντες** pres. act. part. μέλλω to be about
to. **κρίνεσθαι** pres. pass. inf. The part. w. the inf. has the meaning "those who are going to be judged by the law of liberty,"
signifying not just a fut. event, but a deliberate choice of the law
of liberty (and mercy) in preference to the old ruthless rigor of
the "Law" (Adamson). ■ **κρίσις** judgment. **ἀνέλεος** without 13
mercy, merciless (on the form s. Mayor; MM). **ποιήσαντι** aor.
act. part. **ἔλεος** mercy, pity. **κατακαυχᾶται** pres. mid. ind. to
boast against someone, to triumph over (s. Mayor; Dibelius;

Mussner). (For rabbinical parallels and Jewish emphasis on mercy and pity, s. Adamson; SB I, 203; Matt. 5:7.)
14 ■ **ὄφελος** profit. **λέγῃ** pres. act. subj. It is used in presenting this one's claim to be approved of men and of God (Ropes). **ἔργα** works. The word seems here to be a recognized term for "good works" (Ropes; s. also Mayor; Adamson, 34–38). **ἔχῃ** pres. act. subj. **ἡ πίστις** "the faith." The article could be the article of previous reference meaning "the previously mentioned faith," "*that* faith" (Mussner; BD, 131f.). The article could also be used to emphasize the particular faith of the one speaking; i.e., "*his* faith" (IBG, 111). **σῶσαι** aor. act. inf. σῴζω to rescue, to save. The aor. signifies "achieve salvation for him" (Adamson).
15 ■ **ἀδελφή** sister. **γυμνός** naked. The term does not necessarily imply absolute nakedness; it was used of a person wearing only an undertunic and means that someone was poorly clad (Mayor). **ὑπάρχωσιν** pres. act. subj. ὑπάρχω to exist, to be (s. 2 Cor. 12:16). **λειπόμενοι** pres. pass. part. λείπω to lack, pass. to be lacking (followed by the gen.). **ἐφήμερος** for the day. The phrase implies "food for the day" or "the day's supply of food"
16 (MM; for examples, s. also Dibelius). ■ **ὑπάγετε** pres. act. imp. ὑπάγω to go away, to depart. The expression "go in peace" is a Jewish expression meaning "good-by" and as an address to beggars; it may still be heard today in the streets of Jerusalem and it has the same effect. It signals the end of the encounter (s. Ropes; Adamson). **θερμαίνεσθε** pres. mid.-pass. imp. θερμαίνομαι to warm one' self, to be warm. The word was commonly used of the effect of warm clothes (Ropes). **χορτάζεσθε** pres. pass. imp. χορτάζω to feed until one is full, pass. to be filled. The word has the general meaning of satisfying hunger (Mayor; MM). **δῶτε** aor. act. subj. δίδωμι. **ἐπιτήδεια** pl. necessities, the necessities of the body, the necessaries of life
17 (RWP). ■ **οὕτως** likewise. This is used in making the application (Ropes). **καθ᾽ἑαυτήν** "in itself, in reference to itself, inwardly" (Dibelius; s. also Mayor; Adamson).
18 ■ **ἐρεῖ** fut. act. ind. λέγω. **δεῖξον** aor. act. imp. δείκνυμι to show. (For a discussion concerning the ones referred to here by the personal pron., s. Ropes; Adamson.) **δείξω** fut. act. ind.
19 ■ **δαιμόνιον** demon, evil spirits. **φρίσσουσιν** pres. act. ind. to bristle. It was used of the physical signs of terror, esp. of the hair standing on end. The word often expresses only a high degree of awe or terror (Mayor). The pres. tense indicates that which
20 is always true. ■ **γνῶναι** aor. act. inf. γινώσκω. **ἄνθρωπος** man. The term is used here in a derogatory sense. **κενός** empty, deficient. The word is used of a man who cannot be depended

upon, whose deeds do not correspond to his words; hence, of
boasters and imposters (Mayor). **ἀργός** inactive, barren, unprofitable, unproductive of salvation (Ropes). ■ **ἐδικαιώθη** aor. 21
pass. ind. δικαιόω to declare righteous, to pronounce to be in
the right, to justify (s. TDNT; Rom. 2:13; Bengel; Lenski).
ἀνενέγκας aor. act. part. ἀναφέρω to offer up, to sacrifice.
θυσιαστήριον place of sacrifice, altar. ■ **συνήργει** impf. ind. 22
act. συνεργέω to cooperate, to work together. **ἐτελειώθη** aor.
pass. ind. τελειόω to bring to completion, to bring to maturity,
to perfect, to consummate. As the tree is perfected by its fruits,
so faith by its works (Mayor). Works do not animate faith; but
faith produces works, and works perfect faith. Faith itself "is
perfected," i.e., is shown to be true, by works (Bengel). ■ 23
ἐπληρώθη aor. pass. ind. πληρόω to make full, to fulfill.
λέγουσα pres. act. part. **ἐπίστευσεν** aor. act. ind. **ἐλογίσθη**
aor. pass. ind. λογίζομαι to place to one's account, to reckon.
ἐκλήθη aor. pass. ind. καλέω. ■ **ἐξ ἔργων** "from works." 24
Though neither ignored nor belittled, faith is regarded as com-
plementing works, w. which it must be combined. The contrast
is between faith minus works, and works minus faith—not between faith and works (Adamson). **δικαιοῦται** pres. pass. ind.
■ **ὁμοίως** adv. "in like manner." **πόρνη** whore, prostitute. (For 25
the view that Rahab was one who provided lodging for strangers
or travelers, s. D.J. Wiseman, "Rahab of Jericho," TB, 14 [June,
1964], 8–11; for the Jewish views on Rahab, s. Adamson; SB I,
20–23.) **ὑποδεξαμένη** aor. mid. part. ὑποδέχομαι to receive,
to welcome. **ἐκβαλοῦσα** aor. act. part. ἐκβάλλω to throw out,
to send forth. The word is not used here in a bad sense, but it
simply emphasizes the difficulties of escape (Adamson). ■ **γάρ** 26
"for." The particle is used to introduce the supporting argument.
The relationship between vv. 25 and 26 is this: Rahab was justified by works; she could not have been justified in any other way,
for without works faith is dead. Therefore, the faith of Rahab is
presupposed (Dibelius). **πνεύματος** spirit, breath. The word refers to the "vital principle by which the body is animated"
(Ropes). A dead faith is like a corpse and therefore cannot save
(Mussner).

Ch. 3

■ **γίνεσθε** pres. mid. imp. γίνομαι to become. 1
διδάσκαλος teacher. The word is used perhaps in the rabbinical
sense of "rabbi" indicating one who had studied the law and its
application to life and was engaged in teaching others (s. TDNT;
Adamson; Herschel Shanks, "Is the Title 'Rabbi' Anachronistic

in the Gospels?" *Jewish Quarterly Review*, 53 [1963], 337–345). **εἰδότες** perf. act. part. οἶδα defective perf. w. the pres. meaning "to know." The part. is causal. **μείζων** comp. μέγας great, comp. greater. **κρίμα** judgment, results of a judicial decision, condemnation, sentence of punishment (Dibelius). The teacher's condemnation is greater than that of others because having, or professing to have, clear and full knowledge of duty, he is the more bound to obey it (Ropes). **λημψόμεθα** fut. mid. ind. λαμβάνω. James uses the first-per. pl. because he himself is a teacher in the church and knows that he must some day give
2 account to the divine Judge for his teaching (Mussner). ■
πολλά. The acc. can be acc. of general reference "in reference to many things" (s. RWP). **πταίει** pres. act. ind. to stumble, to offend (s. James 1:10). The pres. tense could be interat. indicating an action that occurs over and again. **οὗτος** this one. **χαλιναγωγῆσαι** aor. act. inf. χαλιναγωγέω to bridle (s.
3 James 1:26). ■ **ἵππος** horse. The gen. is dependent on the word
"bits" but is put first because it contains the new emphatic idea (Ropes). **χαλινός** bridle, bit. The word is used of the "bridle" proper (or "reins"), of the "bit," and, as perhaps here, of the whole bridle, including both (Ropes). (For a description of bridles and bits in the ancient world, s. DGRA, 548.) The word used here was also used of a particular type of rope connected w. sails of a ship (s. DGRA, 790). **πείθεσθαι** pres. mid. inf. to obey. The inf. is used w. the prep. to express purpose. **μετάγομεν** pres. act. ind. to change the direction, to guide (RWP). The pres. tense is used to express that which is always
4 true. ■ **τηλικοῦτος** so great. **ὄντα** pres. part. εἰμί. **ὑπό** w. the
gen. "by." The frequent use of the prep. in connection w. the word "wind" and similar words suggest that here it retains something of its local force, not simply "by," but "under" (Mayor). **ἄνεμος** wind. **σκληρός** harsh, stiff, strong (Ropes). **ἐλαυνόμενα** pres. pass. part. ἐλαύνω to drive. The word is used of wind or of sailors rowing or sailing a boat (AS). **μετάγεται** pres. pass. ind., s.v.3. **ἐλάχιστος.** The superl. of the adj. is used in an elative sense "very small" (BAG; s. also BD, 33). **πηδάλιον** rudder. The rudder of an ancient ship was like an oar w. a very broad blade and ships generally had two rudders which were placed on each side of the stern, not at the ship's extremity. Both rudders were managed by the same steersman to prevent confusion (s. DGRA, 788–789; Pliny, *Natural History*, VII, 57). **ὁρμή.** The word was used of the origin of motion either moral or physical. The word could mean here either the "pressure," or "touch" of the steersman or it could refer to the "impulse" of the

steersman (s. Mayor; TDNT; MM). **εὐθύνοντος** pres. act. part.
εὐθύνω to direct, to guide, to steer. **βούλεται** pres. mid. ind. to
decide, to will. (For examples of the use of the two figures of the
control of a horse and a ship, s. Dibelius; Ropes.) ■ **οὕτως** so, 5
thus. The word introduces the application of the examples.
γλῶσσα tongue. **μέλος** member. **μέγαλα** great, great things.
Sometimes the adj. is written in connection w. the following
verb: **αὐχεῖ** pres. act. ind. to boast. The phrase is used here in
the sense not of an empty boast, but of a justified, though
haughty, sense of importance (Ropes; Dibelius; Mussner).

ἡλίκος what size. In this context the n. has the meaning
"how small" and the fem. the meaning "how much," "how
large" (s. Ropes; Mayor). **ὕλη** woods, forest. It has been suggested that the word means "thicket" or "brush" (s. L.E. Elliott-
Binns, "The Meaning of **ὕλη** in James III.5," NTS 2 [1956],
48–50; s. also Dibelius). (For examples paralleling James' illustration of fire, s. Dibelius; Ropes.) **ἀνάπτει** pres. act. ind.
ἀνάπτω to set on fire, to ignite. ■ **κόσμος** world, here followed 6
by the gen. "world of injustice." (For the various interpretations
of this phrase, s. Mayor; Ropes; Dibelius.) **καθίσταται** pres.
mid. or pass. The pass. has the meaning "is constituted" and the
mid. the meaning "presents itself" (RWP; s. also Mayor).
σπιλοῦσα pres. act. part. σπιλόω to stain, to defile.
φλογίζουσα pres. act. part. φλογίζω to set in flames, to inflame,
to set on fire. **τροχός** wheel, cycle, circle. **γενέσεως** gen. sing.
γένεσις origin, birth. The phrase has been variously interpreted;
e.g., "the cycle of the coming" signifying little more than "life"
(Dibelius); i.e., "the whole circle of life" (Mussner). Others see
the phrase as eschatological signifying the course (of time) ordained by God for the present era, now in its last days, and the
phrase is translated "sets afire all that revolving time brings to
birth" (Adamson). (For examples, s. Ropes; Mayor; Dibelius; SB
I, 820.) **φλογιζομένη** pres. pass. part. **γέεννα** (Heb.) the valley
of Henna, Gehenna, hell. The valley of Henna just outside of
Jerusalem was the city garbage dump and is used as a picture of
hell, the place of punishment for the wicked (s. TDNT). ■ **φύσις** 7
nature. **θηριόν** wild animal. **πετεινά** (pl.) birds. **ἑρπετά** (pl.)
crawling animals, reptiles. **ἐνάλιον** sea creatures (s. Adamson).
δαμάζεται pres. pass. ind. δαμάζω to tame, gnomic pres. The
pres. points to the continual possibility of taming wild animals.
δεδάμασται perf. pass. ind. The perf. tense points to the completed action and the two tenses could be translated "is from
time to time, and has actually been, tamed" (Ropes). **τῇ φύσει.**
The dat. is used in the sense of "in subjection to" and the term

itself means "human kind" (Ropes). Both pagan and Heb. were proud of man's lordship over the animal world (Adamson).
8 **ἀνθρώπινος** human. ■ **δαμάσαι** aor. act. inf. **ακατάστατος** restless, unquiet, like the least tameable beasts (Mayor). **μεστός**
9 full. **ἰός** poison. **θανατηφόρος** death bearing. ■ **εὐλογοῦμεν** pres. act. ind. to bless. The pres. tense is customary indicating that which one usually does (s. Eph. 1:3). **καταρώμεθα** pres. mid. ind. to curse. **ὁμοίωσις** likeness. **γεγονότας** perf. act. part. The perf. tense looks at the completed action or state of man
10 being in the image of God. ■ **ἐξέρχεται** pres. mid. ind. to go out. **κατάρα** curse. **χρή** impersonal verb "it is necessary," "it ought to be." The necessity expressed by this word signifies a need or necessity resulting from time or circumstances or from the fitness of things (AS; T; Mayor). Here it denotes the incongruity for blessing and cursing to come out of the same mouth (RWP).
11 ■ **μήτι.** Used in a question which expects the answer "no" (s. Mussner). **πηγή** spring, fountain, well. The word is used w. the definite article and it is suggested that among country folk "the spring" or "the well" has a prominent individuality (Adamson). **ὀπή** opening. The word is used elsewhere of "a cleft in a rock" (Mayor; s. also Heb. 11:38). **βρύω** to gush forth. The word means "teem," "the full of bursting," and is ordinarily used of the swelling buds of plants and so figuratively of various kinds of fullness. Here the thought is of the gushing forth of the water (Ropes; s. also Mayor). **γλυκύς** sweet. **πικρός** bitter. The word here may denote a case where above the outlet good water has
12 suffered contamination from a salty source (Adamson). ■ **συκῆ** fig, fig tree. **ἐλαία** olive. **ποιῆσαι** aor. act. inf. to produce. **ἄμπελος** vine, grape vine. These three fruits, fig, olive, and grape, found in all the Near East, are particularly associated w. Palestine (Adamson). **ἁλυκός** salty.
13 ■ **σοφός** wise. The t.t. for the Teacher; in Jewish usage one who has a knowledge of practical, moral wisdom, resting on a knowledge of God (Ropes). In contrast the Gr. philosophical term meant "theoretical wisdom" (s. GPT, 179). **ἐπιστήμων** understanding. The word implies expert or professional knowledge (Tasker). The use of the interrogative is a Semitic construction which takes the place of a condition (s. Mayor; Mussner; Byer, 167). **δειξάτω** aor. act. imp. **δείκνυμι** to show, to demonstrate. **ἀναστροφή** manner of life, conduct. **πραΰτης** meekness, gentleness. It is the opposite of arrogance and indicates the humble and gentle attitude which expresses itself in a patient submissiveness to offense, free from malice and desire for re-
14 venge (s. Matt. 5:5; 2 Cor. 10:1; Gal. 5:6). ■ **ζῆλος** zeal. The idea

is of a fierce desire to promote one's own opinion to the exclusion of others (Ropes). **ἐριθεία** selfish ambition. The word really
means the vice of a leader of a party created for his own pride:
It is partly ambition, partly rivalry (Dibelius; s. also NTW, 39f.;
TDNT; Phil. 2:3). **κατακαυχᾶσθε** pres. mid. imp.
κατακαυχάομαι to boast against, to boast arrogantly. The word
is used sometimes w. the gen. to denote the triumph of one
principle over another. The prep. in compound is either intensive
or indicates an unfavorable action (Mayor; MH, 316). The pres.
imp. w. the neg. indicates either the stopping of an action in
progress or prohibits the habitual action. **ψεύδεσθε** pres. mid.
imp. ψεύδομαι to lie. ■ **σοφία** wisdom. **ἄνωθεν** from above. 15
κατερχομένη pres. mid. part. κατέρχομαι to come down.
ἐπίγειος earthly, on the earth (s. Adamson). **ψυχικός** natural;
i.e., pertaining to the natural life which men and animals alike
have, unspiritual (s. Ropes; Adamson). **δαιμονιώδης** demonic
(s. Adamson). ■ **ἀκαταστασία** disorder, disturbance, trouble, 16
instability. The word sometimes had political associations and
had the meaning "anarchy." Here it would refer to the "disorder" caused by those who w. their "false wisdom" trouble the
group of believers by demanding their own rights and exercising
a party spirit (s. Ropes; Adamson; Mussner). **φαῦλος** bad, foul,
vile. **πρᾶγμα** matter, thing. ■ **ἁγνός** pure. The word implies 17
sincere, moral and spiritual integrity (Adamson). **εἰρηνικός**
peaceable, loving, and promoting peace. **ἐπιεικής** gentle, reasonable in judging. The word signifies a humble patience, steadfastness which is able to submit to injustice, disgrace, and maltreatment without hatred and malice, trusting in God in spite of
all of it (s. Phil. 4:5; 2 Cor. 10:1; NTW, 38f.). **εὐπειθής** easily
persuaded, willing to yield, compliant. The opposite of the word
is "disobedient." The word is used of submission to military
discipline and for observance of legal and moral standards in
ordinary life; e.g., one who willingly submits to a fatherly will (s.
MM; Adamson; Mayor). **ἔλεος** merciful. **ἀδιάκριτος** undivided, unwavering, wholehearted w. reference to the evil situation
described in verses 9 and 10 (Ropes). **ἀνυπόκριτος** without
hypocrisy, unhypocritical. ■ **δικαιοσύνης.** The gen. could be 18
gen. of definition or apposition indicating that the fruit is righteousness (s. Mayor). Some view it as a subjective gen. or gen. of
source indicating that fruit is the product of righteousness and
the source of the fruit (Ropes). **σπείρεται** pres. pass. ind.
σπείρω to sow (s. Dibelius). **ποιοῦσιν** pres. act. part. dat. pl.
The dat. is either dat. of agency; i.e., "sown by those who do

peace" (Mussner) or it is dat. of advantage; i.e., "for peaceable people" (Dibelius; s. also Mayor).

Ch. 4

1 ■ **πόθεν** where, from where. **πόλεμος** war. **μάχη** battle, fight. The first word pictures the chronic state or campaign of war while the second word presents the separate conflicts or battles of the war (RWP). **ἐντεῦθεν** from here. It is used to indicate the reason or source (BAG). **ἡδονή** lust, pleasure. Although the word has a strong philosophical flavor (s. GPT, 75–78; TDNT), it is to be taken here in a practical and bad sense (Adamson; Mussner). **στρατευομένων** pres. mid. part. στρατεύομαι to carry on a campaign, to fight a military battle. **μέλος** member. Here the word "members" is used collectively
2 as the abode of the passions (Adamson). ■ **ἐπιθυμεῖτε** pres. act. ind. to desire, to long for. **φονεύετε** pres. act. ind. to murder. **ζηλοῦτε** pres. act. ind. to be zealous, to hotly desire, to possess, to covet (Ropes; s. also James 3:14). **ἐπιτυχεῖν** aor. act. inf. ἐπιτυγχάνω to obtain (s. Mayor). **μάχεσθε** pres. mid. ind. to fight a battle. **πολεμεῖτε** pres. act. ind. to wage war. **αἰτεῖσθαι** pres. mid. inf. to ask, to ask for one's self. (For a discussion of the significance of the mid. voice, s. Mayor; M, 160.) The inf.
3 is used w. the prep. to express cause. ■ **κακῶς** adv. evilly, wrongly. **δαπανήσητε** aor. act. subj. δαπανάω to spend, to spend freely. The object of the verb "to spend" is the means of securing enjoyment for which they pray; throughout the passage money is esp. in mind (Ropes). The subj. is used to express the purpose of the asking and at the same time indicates the reason
4 or cause for asking (Mussner). ■ **μοιχαλίς** adulteress, one who is unfaithful to the marriage vows. The term was a figure of speech particularly in the OT to indicate unfaithfulness to God and the practice of idolatry, here the false god being "world" (Adamson). **φιλία** friendship. The word involves the idea of loving as well as of being loved (Mayor). **ἔχθρα** enmity, active hostility. **τοῦ θεοῦ** obj. gen.; i.e., "hostility against God." **βουληθῇ** aor. pass. subj. βούλομαι to will, to want, to desire. The word has the connotation of preference or choosing one thing before another (Mussner; s. also TDNT). **καθίσταται** pres. pass. ind. to be constituted, to be rendered (s. RWP; James
5 3:6). ■ **δοκεῖτε** pres. act. ind. to suppose, to think. **κενῶς** adv. emptily; i.e., "without meaning all that it says" (Ropes). **γραφή** writing, Scripture. (For a discussion of the source of the quotation, s. Mayor; Ropes; Adamson.) **φθόνος** envy, malice, or envy arising out of ill will, jealousy (s. Mayor; Adamson; Trench, *Synonyms*, 34). **ἐπιποθεῖ** pres. act. ind. to strongly desire.

κατῴκισεν aor. act. ind. κατοικίζω to cause to dwell, to take
up one's dwelling. (For a discussion of the difficulties of this v.,
s. Adamson; S.S. Laws, "The Scripture Speaks in Vain; A Reconsideration of James IV. 5," NTS, 20 [1973–74], 220ff.) ■ 6
μείζων comp. μέγας greater. **ὑπερήφανος** haughty, one who
thinks above and beyond that which is proper, arrogant. The
word sometimes signifies the arrogant rich (Adamson; s. James
4:16; 5:1; s. also 1QH VI, 36; CD I, 15). **ἀντιτάσσεται** pres.
mid. ind. to stand against, to oppose. The pres. tense indicates
that which is always true. **ταπεινός** low, humble. ■ **ὑποτάγητε** 7
aor. pass. imp. ὑποτάσσομαι to submit, to align one's self
under the authority of another. **ἀντίστητε** aor. act. imp.
ἀνθίστημι to oppose, ingressive aor. to take one's stand
against. The aor. imp. call for urgent action (RWP). **διάβολος**
slanderer, devil. **φεύξεται** fut. mid. ind. φεύγω to flee. The use
of the imp. followed by the fut. forms a Semitical conditional
sentence; i.e., "when you take your stand against the devil, then
he will flee from you" (s. Byer, 253; Mussner). ■ **ἐγγίσατε** aor. 8
act. imp. ἐγγίζω to come near, to draw near. **ἐγγίσει** fut. act.
ind. (For the construction of an imp. followed by the fut. building
a type of conditional clause, s.v.7.) **καθαρίσατε** aor. act. imp.
καθαρίζω to cleanse, to purify. **ἁμαρτωλός** sinful, sinner.
ἁγνίσατε aor. act. imp. ἁγνίζω to purify, to make pure.
δίψυχος doubleminded (s. James 1:8). ■ **ταλαιπωρήσατε** aor. 9
act. imp. ταλαιπωρέω to undergo hardship, to endure misery.
Here it is used intransitively "be miserable, feel miserable" and
refers to the inner attitude of repentance (s. Mayor; Dibelius;
Mussner; Adamson). **πενθήσατε** aor. act. imp. πενθέω to
mourn. The word expresses a self-contained grief, never violent
in its manifestation (Ropes). The word is often connected w. the
term "weep" and it describes the mourning which cannot be
hidden. It describes not only a grief which brings an ache to the
heart, but also a grief which brings tears to the eyes (MNTW,
137; s. also Mussner). **κλαύσατε** aor. act. imp. κλαίω to cry,
to weep. **γέλως** laughter. The word indicates the leisurely laughter of gods and men in their pleasures. It is the laughter of a fool
who rejects God as the One who determines reality and believes
man to be an autonomous being (Mussner; s. also TDNT).
πένθος sorrow, mourning. **μετατραπήτω** aor. pass. imp. third-
per. sing. μετατρέπω to turn about, to turn into. The prep. in
compound has the idea of change (MH, 318). **κατήφεια** dejec-
tion, downcast, dismay. It describes the condition of one w. eyes
cast down like the publican in Luke 17:13 (Mayor; Adamson).
■ **ταπεινώθητε** aor. pass. imp. ταπεινόω to make low, to hum- 10

ble. The form is pass. but the meaning is reflex. "to humble one's self" (Adamson). **ὑψώσει** fut. act. ind. ὑψόω to exalt, to make high, to lift up. The use of the imp. followed by the fut. is a Semitic conditional construction (s. Beyer, 252f.).

11 ■ **καταλαλεῖτε** pres. act. imp. καταλαλέω to talk against, to defame, to speak evil of. It usually is applied to harsh words about the per. who is absent (Ropes). **καταλαλῶν** pres. act. part. **κρίνων** pres. act. part. κρίνω to judge. **ποιητής** one who performs an act, doer. The construction "doer of the law" means
12 "lawgiver" (Ropes). ■ **νομοθέτης** lawgiver, one who makes a law. **δυνάμενος** pres. mid. part. **σῶσαι** aor. act. inf. σῴζω to rescue, to save. **ἀπολέσαι** aor. act. inf. ἀπόλλυμι to destroy, to ruin. **ὁ πλησίον** the next one, neighbor.

13 ■ **ἄγε** pres. act. imp. ἄγω. The imp. is used as an interjection w. the meaning "come now," "see here" and is usually an insistent, here a somewhat brusque address (Mayor; Ropes). **λέγοντες** pres. act. part. **ἤ** "or." The word indicates the choice in planning. **αὔριον** tomorrow. **πορευσόμεθα** fut. mid. ind. πορεύομαι to travel, to go on a journey. The fut. tense indicates the certainty in the minds of those planning. There were three kinds of merchants, the old Hellenistic mariners; sea and caravan traders; and those who combined domestic w. foreign trade (Adamson). **εἰς τήνδε τὴν πόλιν** "into this city." The old demonstrative form "this" has the force of the particular as opposed to the general "we will go to this city," pointing it out on the map (Mayor). **ποιήσομεν** fut. act. ind. to do, to spend time. **ἐνιαυτός** year. **ἐμπορευσόμεθα** fut. mid. ind. ἐμπορεύομαι to conduct business, to carry on business as a merchant. **κερδήσομεν** fut. act. ind. κερδαίνω to make a profit,
14 to profit, to gain. ■ **ἐπίστασθε** pres. mid. ind. to know, to understand. **ποῖος** of what character; i.e., "is it secure or precarious?" (Ropes). **ἀτμίς** vapor, steam, smoke. The word was used of steam from a kettle or smoke which the wind carried away and graphically depicts the transience of life (Adamson; Mussner; Mayor). **φαινομένη** pres. mid. part. φαινομαι to appear, to appear visible. **ἔπειτα** then. **ἀφανιζομένη** pres. pass. part. ἀφανίζω to cause to vanish, to make to disappear, pass. to vanish, to disappear. Aristotle used the word of the migration of
15 birds (Mayor). ■ **ἀντὶ τοῦ λέγειν** "instead of you saying." The thought of v. 13 is resumed (Adamson; s. also Dibelius). **θελήσῃ** aor. act. subj. θέλω to will. **ζήσομεν** fut. act. ind. ζάω to live.
16 ■ **νῦν δέ** "but now," "but actually, in point of fact," in contrast to what they ought to do (Ropes). **καυχᾶσθε** pres. mid. ind. to boast, to glory. **ἀλαζονεία** bragging, pretentious, arrogant, arro-

gant words. The word refers to empty boasting which seeks to
impress men. It is extravagant claims which one cannot fulfill
(BAG; MNTW, 38–42; TDNT). **καύχησις** boasting. ■ **εἰδότι** 17
perf. act. part. οἶδα. **ποιοῦντι** pres. act. part. The dat. is dat. of
disadvantage and indicates that such a one is guilty of sin (May-
or).

Ch. 5

■ ἄγε "come now" (s. James 4:13). **πλούσιος** rich. 1
κλαύσατε aor. act. imp. **κλαίω** to cry, to weep. **ὀλολύζοντες**
pres. act. part. ὀλολύζω howl, to cry aloud. The word is used in
the LXX as the expression of violent grief (Mayor; Joel 1:5, 13;
Isa. 13:6; 14:31; 15:3; 16:7; Jer. 4:8; s. also Mussner; TDNT).
The part. is manner describing the crying. **ταλαιπωρία** misery.
ἐπερχομέναις pres. mid. part. ἐπέρχομαι to come upon. ■ 2
σέσηπεν perf. act. ind. σήπω to be rotten. The perf. tense
indicates the state or condition "is rotten" (Ropes). **ἱμάτιον**
garment. **σητόβρωτος** moth eaten. **γέγονεν** perf. act. ind.
γίνομαι. The perf. tenses are of prophetic anticipation rather
than "historical record" (Adamson). ■ **ἄργυρος** silver. 3
κατίωται perf. pass. ind. **κατιόομαι** to rust, to rust out, to rust
through. The prep. in compound is perfective "to rust through
down to the bottom" (RWP). **ἰός** poison, rust (s. Mayor). **ἔσται**
fut. εἰμί. **φάγεται** fut. mid. ind. ἐσθίω to eat. **πῦρ** fire.
ἐθησαυρίσατε aor. act. ind. **θησαυρίζω** to treasure up, to store
up. (For rabbinical and DSS parallels of fire being God's judgment, s. Mussner; SB IV, 866f.) ■ **μισθός** wage, pay. **ἐργάτης** 4
one who works, worker. **ἀμησάντων** aor. act. part. ἀμάω to
reap, to mow. **χῶραι** (pl.) fields. **ἀφυστερημένος** perf. pass.
part. ἀφυστερέω to be behind from, to fail of, to cause to
withdraw, to withhold. The verb indicates not just delay, but
complete default (Adamson; RWP). The perf. tense looks at the
completed state or condition. **ἀφ' ὑμῶν** "from you," "by you."
κράζει pres. act. ind. to cry out. The pres. tense indicates the
continual crying out. Both the OT (Lev. 19:13; Deut. 24:14) and
rabbinic teaching required that the workers be paid at the end
of the day and the withholding of wages is one of the four sins
which are said to cry to heaven (Mayor; s. also Adamson). **βοή**
cry. **θερισάντων** aor. act. part. θερίζω. to reap, to harvest. **οὖς,
ὠτός** ear. **σαβαώθ** (Heb.) armies, hosts. **εἰσελήλυθαν** perf.
act. ind. εἰσέρχομαι to come into. The perf. emphasizes that
the cries that come to the ears of the Lord remain, so that He
does not forget and they are not in vain. ■ **ἐτρυφήσατε** aor. act. 5
ind. **τρυφάω** to live in luxury. The word literally means "to

break down" and denotes soft luxury, not necessarily wanton vice (Ropes). The aor. is constantive and summarizes their total life (s. M, 109). **ἐσπαταλήσατε** aor. act. ind. σπαταλάω to give one's self to pleasure. The prominent idea is that of self-indulgence without distinct reference to squandering (Mayor; s. also 1 Tim. 5:6). **ἐθρέψατε** aor. act. ind. τρέφω to feed, to fatten,
6 to nourish. **σφαγή** slaughter. ■ **κατεδικάσατε** aor. act. ind. καταδικάζω to give a sentence against someone, to condemn. **ἐφονεύσατε** aor. act. ind. φονεύω to kill, to murder. **ἀντιτάσσεται** pres. mid. ind. to stand against, to oppose. The pres. tense brings the action before our eyes and makes us dwell upon this, as the central point, in contrast w. the accompanying circumstances (Mayor).
7 ■ **μακροθυμήσατε** aor. act. imp. μακροθυμέω to patiently endure. The word describes the attitude which can endure delay and bear suffering and never give in (NTW, 84; s. also TDNT; Gal. 5:22). **παρουσία** arrival, coming. **γεωργός** farmer. **ἐκδέχεται** pres. mid. ind. to wait for something. The pres. tense is gnomic indicating that which is common to farmers. **τίμιος** precious, valuable. **μακροθυμῶν** pres. act. part. **λάβῃ** aor. act. subj. λαμβάνω. **πρόϊμος** early. **ὄψιμος** late. The "early rain" normally begins in Palestine late October or early November, and is anxiously awaited because, being necessary for the germination of the seed, it is the signal for sowing. In the spring the maturing of the grain depends on the "late rain," light showers falling in April and May. Without these even heavy winter rains will not prevent failure of crops (Ropes; s. also Mussner; Mayor).
8 ■ **στηρίξατε** aor. act. imp. στηρίζω to strengthen, to make stable. **ἤγγικεν** perf. act. ind. ἐγγίζω to come near, to draw
9 near. ■ **στενάζετε** pres. act. imp. στενάζω to groan. The word denotes feeling which is internal and unexpressed (Mayor). The pres. imp. w. the neg. calls for the discontinuing of an action in progress or prohibits habitual action. **κριθῆτε** aor. act. subj. κρίνω to judge. The subj. is used in a neg. purpose clause.
10 **ἕστηκεν** perf. act. ind. ἵστημι to stand. ■ **ὑπόδειγμα** example. **λάβετε** aor. act. imp. λαμβάνω to take. **κακοπαθία** suffering hardship, suffering evil. **μακροθυμία** patient endurance (s.v.7).
11 **ἐλάλησαν** aor. act. ind. ■ **μακαρίζομεν** pres. act. ind. to consider happy, to consider blessed. The word refers to the prevelant habitual estimate of the worth of constancy (Ropes). **ὑπομείναντας** aor. act. part. ὑπομένω to remain under, to be patient in adverse circumstances (s. NTW, 60; TDNT; CBB; Heb. 10:36). **ἠκούσατε** aor. act. ind. ἀκούω to hear. **τέλος κυρίου** goal, purpose, outcome, result; i.e., "the conclusion

wrought by the Lord to his trouble" (Ropes; s. also Adamson). **εἴδετε** aor. act. ind. ὁράω to see. **πολύσπλαγχος** very kind, very pitiful, very sympathetic, extremely compassionate (s. Mayor; MNTW, 156f.; TDNT). **οἰκτίρμων** compassion.

■ **ὀμνύετε** pres. act. imp. ὀμνύω to swear. **ὅρκος** oath (s. 12
Matt. 5:33). **ἤτω** pres. imp. εἰμί. **πέσητε** aor. act. subj. πίπτω.
■ **κακοπαθεῖ** pres. act. ind. to suffer misfortune, to suffer 13
trouble. **προσευχέσθω** pres. mid. imp. προσεύχομαι to pray. **εὐθυμεῖ** to be happy, to feel good. **ψαλλέτω** pres. act. imp. ψάλλω to sing, to sing praises, to play on a harp (s. Adamson).
■ **ἀσθενέω** to be weak, to be sick. **προσκαλεσάσθω** aor. mid. 14
imp. προσκαλέω to call one along side, to summon. **προσευξάσθωσαν** aor. mid. imp. to pray. **ἀλείψαντες** aor. act. part. ἀλείφω to anoint. The word is used basically for an outward anointing of the body (s. TDNT). The aor. part. can express antecedent time; i.e., "after anointing pray," or contemporaneous time; i.e., "while anointing pray," or it can be used in the sense of an imp.; i.e., "anoint and pray" (Mussner; s. also BG, 129f.). **ἔλαιον** oil, olive oil. Oil was used as a curative by the ancients generally, including the rabbis (s. Adamson; TDNT;
Mayor; Ropes; SB IV, 533f.). ■ **εὐχή** prayer. **σώσει** fut. act. ind. 15
σῴζω to rescue, to save, to heal. Here the word has the idea "to restore to health" (Ropes). **ἐγερεῖ** fut. act. ind. **ἐγείρω** to raise. The word means "raise from the bed of sickness to health" (Ropes). **κἄν** = καὶ ἐάν. **ᾖ** pres. subj. εἰμί. **πεποιηκώς** perf. act. part. The perf. part. is used in a periphrastic perf. act. subj. in a condition of 3rd class which indicates the possibility of sin being related to the sickness (s. RWP). **ἀφεθήσεται** fut. pass. ind. ἀφίημι to forgive. The pass. is the so-called "theological or divine" pass. indicating that God is the One who forgives (s. BG,
76). ■ **ἐξομολογεῖσθε** pres. mid. imp. ἐξομολογέω to openly 16
agree to, to confess. The confession is to be not only to the elders but to "one another," i.e., probably to those they have wronged (Adamson). **προσεύχεσθε** pres. mid. imp. to pray. **ἰαθῆτε** aor. pass. subj. ἰάομαι to heal. The pass. is the theological pass. indicating that God is the One who heals (s.v.15). **ἰσχύει** pres. act. ind. to be strong, to be powerful, to have power, to be competent, to be able (BAG; s. also Phil. 4:13). **δέησις** request, prayer. **ἐνεργουμένη** pres. mid.-pass. part. ἐνεργέω to be effective, to produce (s. MNTW, 46; TDNT). (For a discussion of whether the form is mid. or pass. and the suggested translation, "the prayer of a righteous man is very powerful in its operation,"
s. Adamson 205–210; s. also Mayor; Ropes.) ■ **ὁμοιοπαθής** like 17
feelings, of similar feelings, circumstances, experiences w. the

same nature as someone (BAG). The word indicates that the power of Elijah's prayer did not lie in his supernatural greatness, but rather in his humanity and the prophet was only a human being like we are (s. Mussner). **βρέξαι** aor. act. inf. βρέχω to rain. The inf. is used in indirect discourse indicating the content of the prayer. **ἔβρεξεν** aor. act. ind. **ἐνιαυτός** year. **μήν** month.
18 ■ **ὑετός** rain. **ἔδωκεν** aor. act. ind. δίδωμι. **ἐβλάστησεν** aor. act. ind. βλαστάνω to sprout, to bring forth.
19 ■ **πλανηθῇ** aor. pass. subj. πλανάω to go astray. **ἐπιστρέψῃ** aor. act. subj. ἐπιστρέφω to turn around, to turn,
20 to convert. ■ **γινώσκετε** pres. act. imp. to know, to recognize. **ἐπιστρέψας** aor. act. part. **πλάνη** error. **καλύψει** fut. act. ind. καλύπτω to cover, to hide, to veil. **πλῆθος** a great number, multitude, many.

1 PETER

Ch. 1

ἀπόστολος apostle, an official representative who was 1
appointed and authorized by the one sending (s. TDNT; Best;
CBB; 1 Cor. 1:1). (For the omission of the article w. all of the
substitutives in this v. indicating a stereotype epistolary introduction, s. BD, 137.) **ἐκλεκτός** elect. Verbal adj. from the verb
meaning "to pick out, to select" (RWP). The word was used in
the papyri in our sense of the word "select" or "choice" (Beare).
παρεπίδημος one who lives alongside of, sojourner. The word
is used of those who are temporary residents, not permanent
settlers in the land; who have a deep attachment and a higher
allegiance in another sphere (Beare). The word emphasizes both
alien nationality and temporary residents (Stibbs; s. also Hort,
154–156; BS, 149; CBB; TDNT; TDOT under "Ger").
διασπορά dispersion, scattering, diaspora. The Jewish "diaspora" came about through deportation and through voluntary
moving to a foreign land. The people generally lived in their own
settlement or quarters in a foreign land and were still vitally
joined to the land of Palestine and the city of Jerusalem w. her
temple. There was always the hope for the eschatological regath-
ering of those who had been scattered. Peter uses the term for
believers who are scattered throughout the world yet have a
heavenly fatherland and a hope of one day being gathered into
this land (s. Goppelt; SB II, 490; TDNT; RAC III, 972–982;
JPFC I, 117–215). ■ **πρόγνωσις** knowing beforehand, fore- 2
knowledge. God's foreknowledge is much more than knowing
what will happen in the future; it includes, as it does in the
language of the LXX (e.g. Num. 16:5; Judges 9:6; Amos 3:2), His
effective choice (Kelly). **ἁγιασμός** holiness, sanctification.
πνεύματος gen. sing. The word could refer to the human spirit
but by the analogy of the other clauses, it refers to the Holy Spirit
(Hort). The gen. is subjective gen. indicating that the Spirit
produces the sanctification. **ὑπακοή** obedience. **ῥαντισμός**
sprinkling. It is probably a reference to Exodus 24:3–8 (Best).
πληθυνθείη aor. pass. opt. **πληθύνω** to multiply. The opt. is
used to express a wish or desire (s. MT, 120f.). Peter prays for

the multiplication of grace and peace that the trials through
which the Asiatic Christians are about to pass may result in a
manifold increase of grace and peace (Hort).
3 ■ **εὐλογητός** blessed (s. Eph. 1:3). **ἔλεος** mercy, pity, compassion (s. CBB; TDNT). **ἀναγεννήσας** aor. act. part.
ἀναγεννάω to regenerate, to cause to be born again. The idea
of a new beginning through a new birth w. the infusion of divine
life is an idea which was widespread in the ancient world. It was
an idea present in the mystery religions and also in Judaism. A
proselyte to Judaism was regarded as a newborn baby (s. Best;
RAC IX, 153–155; Schelkle; Goppelt; SB III, 763; for a parallel
in the DSS, s. 1QH3, 19–23). The part. gives the reason why
God is blessed (Schelkle). **ζῶσαν** pres. act. part. ζάω to live. Life
is a quality or characteristic of the hope here spoken of, not the
obj. of it (Hort). A living hope is one that is never extinguished
by untold circumstances, just as "living waters" are waters flow-
4 ing fresh from a perennial spring (Selwyn). ■ **κληρονομία** inheritance. The word can mean a property already received as
well as one that is expected. But in the present passage the
"inheritance" is kept for the believer, not on earth, but in heav-
en, and is another name for that salvation which is ready to be
revealed (Bigg; s. also Hort; Kelly). **ἄφθαρτος** imperishable, not
corruptible, not liable to pass away (Beare). It has been suggested
that the main idea of the word is "to injure, to spoil" and the
chief idea in mind is the ravaging of a land by a hostile army
(Hort). **ἀμάντος** unstained, undefiled. The thought here is being
unstained by evil (Beare). **ἀμάραντος** unfading. The word was
used of flowers and suggests a supernatural beauty which time
does not impair. The three verbal adjectives indicate that the
inheritance is "untouched by death," "unstained by evil,"
"unimpaired by time"; it is compounded of immortality, purity,
and beauty (Beare). **τετηρημένην** perf. pass. part. τηρέω to
guard, to keep, to take care of, to reserve. The perf. tense indicates the state or condition and underlines the fact that the
inheritance already exists and is being preserved for those who
5 are now being "guarded" (v.5) (Best). ■ **φρουρουμένους** pres.
pass. part. φρουρέω to guard, to watch over. The term is a
military term indicating the guarding done by soldiers and the
pres. tense emphasizes our need for continual protection in the
unending struggle of the soul. They are being guarded by God's
power and this is the guarantee of the final victory (Beare; s. also
Stibbs). **σωτηρία** salvation. The word indicates deliverance or
preservation bestowed by God, more specifically deliverance
from His wrath at the final judgment (Kelly). The term here

indicates "salvation" in its broadest sense (s. TDNT; CBB).
ἕτοιμος ready, prepared. **ἀποκαλυφθῆναι** aor. pass. inf.
ἀποκαλύπτω to unveil, to reveal. The pass. would be the "theological" or "divine" pass. indicating that God is the One who
does the action. The inf. is used to express purpose (s. BAG). **ἐν
καιρῷ ἐσχάτῳ** "in the last time." The word "time" indicates
the fit or appointed time or season for some particular thing,
whether it be a period or a moment (Bigg). The word "last"
means simply "last in order of time" (Bigg). ■ **ἐν ᾧ** "in which," 6
"in which circumstance," "wherefore." (For a discussion of the
antecedent of the rel. pron., s. Selwyn.) **ἀγαλλιᾶσθε** pres.
mid. ind. to rejoice, to be glad. This verb appears to be used
always w. the connotation of a "religious" joy, a joy which
springs from the contemplation of God or of the salvation which
comes from God (Beare; s. also TDNT; Hort; Kelly). **ὀλίγον** a
little, a little while, a short while (Kelly). **δέον** pres. act. part. δεῖ
it is necessary. The part. is used w. the conditional particle which
can be taken as a concessive sentence "although" (Beare), or it
can be taken as a first-class conditional clause which borders on
a causal sentence "since" (BD, 189; Kelly). **λυπηθέντες** aor.
pass. part. λυπέω to cause pain, to cause sorrow, to put to grief.
The word expresses not suffering but mental effect of suffering
(Hort). **ποικίλος** various, diversified, manifold, different kinds.
πειρασμός trial. The word here could mean the undeserved
sufferings from without (Bigg). ■ **δοκίμιον** tried, approved after 7
trial, genuineness. The genuine element in their faith was proven
by a process similar to that of metal refining and is found to be
something more precious than these precious metals (Selwyn; s.
also James 1:3; BS, 259f.). **πολυτιμότερος** comp. πολύτιμος
more precious, of greater price. **ἀπολλυμένου** pres. mid. part.
ἀπόλλυμι to destroy, to ruin, to perish. **πῦρ** fire.
δοκιμαζομένου pres. pass. part. δοκιμάζω to approve after
examination. **εὑρεθῇ** aor. pass. subj. εὑρίσκω. The subj. is used
to express purpose. **ἀποκάλυψις** unveiling, revelation. ■ 8
ἰδόντες aor. act. part. ὁράω to see. The part. is concessive
"although." The word here refers to physical sight or eye sight
(Selwyn). **ἀγαπᾶτε** pres. act. ind. The pres. tense indicates the
continual action. **ὁρῶντες** pres. act. part. The neg. used w. the
part. here is introduced as it were hypothetical, merely to bring
out the full force of "believing" (Hort; s. also Selwyn).
πιστεύοντες pres. act. part. **ἀνεκλάλητος** verbal adj. unspeakable, inexpressible, ineffable. The word contains the sense of a
divine mystery exceeding the powers of speech and thought
(Beare). **δεδοξασμένῃ** perf. pass. part. δοξάζω to glorify, pass.

to be glorified. Here the idea is "to be endowed w. glory from above" (Selwyn; for a study of the word s. esp. Selwyn, 253–258;
9 s. also TDNT; CBB). ■ **κομιζόμενοι** pres. mid. part. *κομίζω* mid. = to receive, to obtain. **ψυχαί** souls. This is not a special part of man's structure but is man as a whole; it is a Jewish rather than a Gr. or modern usage of the word (Best).
10 ■ **ἐξεζήτησαν** aor. act. ind. *ἐκζητέω* to seek out. The prep. in compound is intensive. **ἐξηρεύνησαν** aor. act. ind. *ἐξερευνάω* to search out. The prep. in compound is intensive. "Seeking out" is the more general term, "searching out" the minute and sedulous process of thought and investigation which subserve the seeking (Hort). The two verbs taken together give emphatic expression to the earnestness w. which enlightenment was sought (Beare; s. also MH, 310). **προφητεύσαντες** aor. act.
11 part. *προφητεύω* to speak for, to speak forth, to prophesy. ■ **ἐρευνῶντες** pres. act. part. *ἐρευνάω* to search. **ποῖος** what sort of. The indefinite pron. suggests a definite period, almost a date to be fixed, while this word suggests the general outward circumstances to be expected (Beare; s. also BD, 155). **ἐδήλου** impf. ind. act. *δηλόω* to make clear, to make plain. Though the word is often used of declarations through articulate language, it is still more often used of any indirect kind of communication (Hort). The impf. indicates continual action in the past time. **προμαρτυρόμενον** pres. mid. part. *προμαρτύρομαι* to testify beforehand (s. Selwyn). **τὰ εἰς Χριστὸν** "the sufferings to Christ," i.e., "the sufferings in store for Christ" (Kelly). It is quite possible that we have a reference to the words recorded in Luke 24:26–27 (Bigg). (For a discussion of the passages in 1 Peter which point to the words of Christ and support Petrine authorship of the epistle and the authenticity of the gospel passages, s. Robert H. Gundry, " 'Verba Christi' in I Peter: Their Implications Concerning the Authorship of I Peter and the Authenticity of the Gospel Tradition," NTS, 13 [July, 1967], 336–350; R.H. Gundry, "Further Verba on 'Verba Christi' in I Peter," *Biblica*, 55 [1974], 211–232.) **πάθημα** suffering. **δόξαι** glories, glorious
12 deeds, triumphs (Selwyn). ■ **ἀπεκαλύφθη** aor. pass. ind. *ἀποκαλύπτω* to reveal, to unveil (s. Selwyn, 250ff.). **διηκόνουν** impf. act. ind. *διακονέω* to serve, to minister to. The impf. tense points to the continual or customary action in the past. **ἀνηγγέλη** aor. act. ind. *ἀναγγέλλω* to report, to set forth, to tell, to declare, to proclaim (s. Selwyn; CBB). **εὐαγγελισαμένων** pres. mid. part. *εὐαγγελίζομαι* to proclaim good news, to evangelize, to preach the gospel. **ἀποσταλέντι** aor. pass. part. *ἀποστέλλω* to send, to send as an official au-

thoritative representative of the one sending (s. TDNT; CBB). **ἐπιθυμοῦσιν** pres. act. ind. to desire, to long for, to eagerly desire. The verb is fairly strong and consistent w. a longing not yet fulfilled (Kelly). The pres. tense indicates the continual action which did not reach a fulfillment. **ἄγγελοι** angels, heavenly messengers, heavenly beings. **παρακύψαι** aor. act. inf. παρακρύπτω to stretch forward the head, as esp. through a window or door, sometimes inward, more often outward. When used figuratively, it commonly implies a rapid and cursory glance. The word means "to bend down to look" and often suggests a fleeting glance; i.e., "to peep," "to catch a glimpse of" (Hort; Kelly).

■ **διό** therefore. This is the usual particle when an author 13
passes from statement to inference (Selwyn). **ἀναζωσάμενοι** aor. mid. part. ἀναζώννυμι to bind up, to gather up, to gird up. The word refers to the habit of the Orientals, who quickly gather up their loose robes w. a girdle or belt when in a hurry or starting on a journey. This is because the easterners' long flowing robes would impede physical activity unless tucked under the belt (RWP; Best). One writer describes tavern keepers who worked in front of their taverns w. their tunics belted high (DC, LXXII, 2). **ὀσφῦς** hip. **διάνοια** mind. The word refers to more than the mere intellectual faculties and indicates that which guides and directs conduct (Best). This is a call for the readers to be alert and ready in their whole spiritual and mental attitude (Kelly). **νήφοντες** pres. act. part. νήφω to be sober. In the NT the word generally denotes self-control and the clarity of mind which goes w. it (Kelly; s. also 2 Tim. 4:5; 1 Thess. 5:6, 8). **τελείως** adv. perfectly, unreservedly. The adv. is best taken w. the main verb "hope" (Selwyn). **ἐλπίσατε** aor. act. imp. to hope, to set one's hope upon something. **φερομένη** pres. pass. part. φέρω to carry, to bear, to bring. The pres. part. pictures the process, "that is being brought" (RWP). Although a pres. part. can have a fut. force, it is used here in keeping w. the writer's conviction that the object of their hope is already virtually within his readers' grasp (Kelly). **χάρις** grace. The word is used here in a concrete sense of the eschatological consummation (Beare).
ἀποκάλυψις s.v.7. ■ **ὑπακοή** obedience, s.v.2. 14
συσχηματιζόμενοι pres. mid. part. to form together, to conform (s. Rom. 12:2). The mid. voice is a direct mid. i.e., "do not fashion yourselves" (RWP). The mid. could also be a permissive mid., i.e., "do not allow yourselves to be fashioned." The part. is used to convey a command and conforms to the rabbinic Heb. practice of using part. to express rules of conduct and even

religious precepts (Kelly; for this use of the part., s. further David
Daube in Selwyn, 467–488; s. also GI, 165–168; MT Style,
128f.). **πρότερον** former, previous. **ἄγνοια** ignorance. (For a
discussion of this word, s. Hort.) **ἐπιθυμία** strong desire, lust.
15 ■ **καλέσαντα** aor. act. part. **ἅγιος** separate, marked off, holy.
The word indicates the display of the character of God whose
perfect attributes cause Him to be separated from His creation
(s. Kelly; CBB; TDNT). The adj. is a pred. adj. used in the clause
"just as the one who called you is holy." **ἀναστροφή** conduct,
active life. The word is used of public activity, life in relation to
others. Being holy as members of a holy people, they were to
show themselves holy in every kind of dealing w. other men
(Beare; Hort; s. also BS, 194). **γενήθητε** aor. pass. imp.
γίνομαι. The aor. may be taken as ingressive "began to be,"
16 "become" (Beare; RWP). ■ **διότι** therefore. **γέγραπται** perf.
pass. ind. "it stands written." The word was used of legal documents whose validity continued (s. MM). **ἔσεσθε** fut. ind. εἰμί.
The fut. here is volitive and is used like an imp. (RWP; s. also
BG, 94).
17 ■ **ἐπικαλεῖσθε** pres. mid. ind. to call, to call upon, to
invoke, to appeal to (s. Selwyn). **ἀπροσωπολήμπτως** adv. im-
partially, without showing respect or favoritism (s. Bigg).
κρίνοντα pres. act. part. **παροικία** temporary residency, temporary stay. The word denotes residence in a place without
taking out or being granted citizen rights (Kelly; s. also Hort; 1
Peter 1:1; TDNT). **ἀναστράφητε** aor. pass. imp. ἀναστρέφω
18 to conduct one's life (s.v.15). ■ **εἰδότες** perf. act. part. οἶδα. The
part. could be causal. Christian reverence rests upon the knowledge of redemption, four aspects of which are now enumerated:
(1) its cost in the death of Christ, (2) its transcendent origin, (3)
its certification in Christ's resurrection, (4) its fruit in the
church's faith and hope in God (Selwyn). **φθαρτός** subject to
decay, corruptible. **ἀργύριον** silver, instrumental dat. or dat. of
means (Beare). Silver and gold were used as money and slaves
were set free by silver and gold (BAG; RWP). **ἐλυτρώθητε** aor.
pass. ind. λυτρόω to release, to procure a release by a ransom,
to deliver by the payment of a price, to redeem. For the Jews the
picture of redemption would be God's deliverence from Egypt.
For the Gentiles it would be the picture of a slave whose freedom
was purchased w. a price (s. Hort; Beare; TDNT; CBB; GWHM,
70f.; APC; NTW, 76–83; LAE, 319–327; NTRJ, 268–284).
μάταιος vain, vanity. The idea is that which is lacking reality
(Beare). **πατροπαράδοτος** that which is passed on from fa-
19 thers, inherited. ■ **ἀμνός** lamb. **ἄμωμος** blameless. **ἄσπιλος**

spotless, without stain. Perhaps Peter has the Passover lamb in
mind (s. Hort). ■ **προεγνωσμένον** perf. pass. part. 20
προγινώσκω to know beforehand, to foreknow (s. 1 Peter 1:2).
καταβολή foundation. **φανερωθέντος** aor. pass. part.
φανερόω to make clear, to make plain, to manifest. **δι' ὑμᾶς**
"because of you," "for your sake." ■ **ἐγείραντα** aor. act. part. 21
ἐγείρω to raise up. **δόντα** aor. act. part. δίδωμι to give, to grant
that. The particle w. the inf. can express intended or contemplated results (Selwyn; s. also BD, 197). Since the book deals w. the believer's pilgrim life on the earth and persecution w. emphasis on faith and eschatological hope, it is felt that this clause is a sort of climax to the whole passage (s. William J. Dalton, " 'So That Your Faith May also Be Your Hope'," RH, 262–274; s. esp. 272f.). **ἡ πίστις ὑμῶν καὶ ἐλπίς** could be taken as the subject, "so that your faith and hope may be in God," or the word "hope" may be considered as the pred., "so that your faith may also be your hope in God" (Dalton, 272). **εἶναι** pres. inf. The inf. is used to express intended results.

■ **ἡγνικότες** perf. act. part. ἁγνίζω to make pure, to purify, 22
to cleanse. In the LXX the word generally has a ceremonial reference but it can also have the sense of moral purification. The perf. tense emphasizes the completed state or condition (s. Selwyn; Beare). **ὑπακοή** obedient. **τῆς ἀληθείας** obj. gen. **ἀνυπόκριτος** unhypocritical, without hypocrisy. **ἀγαπήσατε** aor. act. imp. **ἐκτενῶς** adv. earnestly. The fundamental idea is that of earnestness, zealousness (doing a thing not lightly and
perfunctorily, but as it were, w. straining) (Hort). ■ 23
ἀναγεγεννημένοι perf. pass. part. (s.v.3). **σπορά** seed. The contrast is between human seed which produces mortal human life and divine seed which produces eternal life (Best). **ἄφθαρτος** incorruptible (s.v.4). **ζῶντος** pres. act. part. (s.v.3).
μένοντος pres. act. part. μένω to remain. ■ **χόρτος** grass. 24
ἄνθος flower (s. James 1:10). **ἐξηράνθη** aor. pass. ind. ξηραίνω to dry up, pass. to be withered. **ἐξέπεσεν** aor. act. ind. ἐκπίπτω to fall off. The aor. vividly expresses the rapid blooming and
fading of herbage (Kelly). ■ **εὐαγγελισθέν** aor. pass. part. 25
(s.v.12).

Ch. 2

■ **ἀποθέμενοι** aor. mid. part. ἀποτίθημι to put off, to put 1
away. The part. shares the imp. force of the governing verb (Beare). The word is applied to any kind of rejection, esp. of what is in any way connected w. the person, body, or mind, whether clothing or hair (Hort). **κακία** wickedness. The word is an all-

inclusive term (Kelly). **δόλος** deceit. It comes from a verb meaning "to catch w. bait" (RWP). **ὑπόκρισις** hyprocrisy, pretense.
φθόνος envy. The verb was used often in secular Gr. to express
the envy which makes one man grudge another something which
he himself desires, but does not possess (CBB). **καταλαλιά**
speaking against someone. The verb means "to run down," "to
disparage," and was used by Aristophanes of a slave who "blabs"
2 his master's secrets (Selwyn; Bigg). ■ **ἀρτιγέννητος** recently
born, newborn. **βρέφος** baby, infant. The word is used of a baby
as long as it nurses at its mother's breast (Goppelt). **λογικός** that
which pertains to a word. There are three possible renderings of
this word: (1) "of the word," (2) "reasonable," "rational," (3)
"spiritual" (s. Best; TDNT). However, it seems hardly credita-
ble that he is not also consciously referring back to God's
"word," about which he was so concerned in 1:22–25 (Kelly).
ἄδολος without deceit, pure, unadulterated, uncontaminated.
The word is commonly used in this sense of corn, wheat, barley,
oil, wine, and farm products (Beare; Kelly; s. also MM). **γάλα**
milk. The many-breasted goddesses of the heathen religions who
were to sustain and nourish life were widespread in the ancient
world. The rabbis also compared the law to milk (s. Goppelt;
Beare; TDNT; Montefiore, 163f.; Selwyn; esp. 308; RAC II,
657–664). **ἐπιποθήσατε** aor. act. imp. ἐπιποθέω to long for,
to desire, to crave. The prep. in compound indicates intensive
desire directed toward an object (cf. Ps. 42:1). **αὐξηθῆτε** aor.
3 pass. subj. αὐξάνω to cause to grow, pass. to grow. ■
ἐγεύσασθε aor. mid. ind. γεύομαι to taste. The ind. is used in
a conditional sentence of the 1st class which accepts the reality
4 of the condition. **χρηστός** useful, good, gracious. ■
προσερχόμενοι pres. mid. part. προσέρχομαι to come to.
The pres. part. is used because stones keep coming one after
another (Bigg). **ζῶντα** pres. act. part. ζάω to live. (For the figure
of a "living stone," s. Beare; Selwyn.) **ἀποδεδοκιμασμένον**
perf. pass. part. ἀποδοκιμάζω to reject after examination, to
examine and deem useless. **παρὰ θεῷ** "by the side of God," and
He looks at it, in contrast w. the rejection "by men" (RWP).
ἐκλεκτός chosen, choice, select, elect (s. 1 Peter 1:1; Hort).
5 **ἔντιμος** precious, costly, expensive (s. Hort). ■ **αὐτοὶ ὡς λίθοι
ζῶντες** "you also are yourselves, like living stones" (s. Kelly;
Hort). **οἰκοδομεῖσθε** pres. pass. ind. οἰκοδομέω to build, to
erect a building. **πνευματικός** spiritual, pertaining to the Spirit,
"suited for the Spirit." **ἱεράτευμα** priesthood. **ἀνενέγκαι** aor.
act. inf. ἀναφέρω to bring up, to offer, to offer sacrifice.
πνευματικὰς θυσιάς "spiritual sacrifices." These are sacrifices

which consist of praise and thanksgiving, charity and mutual
sharing, and which are inspired by the Spirit (Kelly).
εὐπρόσδεκτος acceptable (s. Rom. 15:16). ■ **διότι** therefore. 6
περιέχει (impersonal) pres. act. ind. "it is included." The word
was used in the papyri concerning a will in the sense "in the will
as it stands written" (MM; s. also Beare). **γραφή** writing, Scripture. **τίθημι** pres. act. ind. to lay. **ἀκρογωνιαῖος λίθος** foundation stone, cornerstone, chief cornerstone. The word refers
either to a massive cornerstone placed at the upper corner of the
building in order to bind the walls firmly together, or it refers to
the key stone in the middle of an archway (Beare; s. also TDNT;
Eph. 2:20). **οὐ μή** "not at all." The two negatives form a strong
denial (s. M, 187ff.). **καταισχυνθῇ** aor. pass. subj. καταισχύνω
to put to shame. ■ **ἡ τιμή** "the honor." This honor includes their 7
privileged status here and now and also their triumph over their
mocking assailants and their salvation on the last day (Kelly).
(For a discussion of the grammatical difficulties and various
interpretations, s. Hort.) **τοῖς πιστεύουσιν** pres. act. part. "to
you who are believing." The part. is in apposition to the personal
pron. "you." The dat. is personal advantage or possession.
ἀπιστοῦσιν pres. act. part. ἀπιστέω to be unbelieving.
ἀπεδοκίμασαν aor. act. ind. ἀποδοκιμάζω to reject after examination (s.v.4). **οἰκοδομοῦντες** pres. act. part. **ἐγενήθη** aor.
pass. ind. γίνομαι. **γωνία** corner. ■ **πρόσκομμα** stumbling. 8
The "stone of stumbling" is the loose stone lying in the way,
against which the traveler "strikes" his foot (Hort).
προσκόπτουσιν pres. act. ind. to cut against, to stumble.
ἀπειθοῦντες pres. act. part. ἀπείθω to disobey. The word carries a strong sense of "to refuse to believe" (Kelly). **εἰς ὅ** "unto
which." **ἐτέθησαν** aor. pass. ind. τίθημι to place, to put, to
appoint.

■ **γένος** generation, race. **βασίλειος** kingly, royal. The 9
word could be taken as an adj. modifying "priesthood" or it can
be taken as a substitutive either w. the meaning "royal house,"
"palace," or "a group of kings" (Best; s. also Kelly; Goppelt; J.H.
Elliott, *The Elect and Holy. An Exegetical Examination of I
Peter 2:4–10* [Leiden: Brill, 1966]). **ἱεράτευμα** priesthood (s. E.
Best, "Spiritual Sacrifice: General Priesthood in the New Testament," *Interpretation* 14 [July, 1960], 273–299). **περιποίησις**
possession, private possession (s. Eph. 1:14). **ἀρετή** virtue, the
ability to do heroic deeds. When the word is applied to deity it
does not denote His virtues or intrinsic qualities but the manifestations of His power; i.e., His mighty and glorious deeds (s.
TDNT; Goppelt; Kelly; Hort; Beare; BS, 95f.; MM).

ἐξαγγείλητε aor. act. subj. ἐξαγγέλλω to tell out, to tell forth.
The word often has the additional force of declaring things unknown (Hort). In the LXX the word is used w. the sense of cultic
proclamation, or the rehearsal in adoring language of God's
righteousness and praises (Kelly). The subj. is used w. the particle to express purpose. **καλέσαντος** aor. act. part. The word
refers to the affective call of God. **θαυμαστός** wonderful, mar-
10 velous. ■ **ποτέ** then, at that time, formerly. **ἠλεημένοι** perf.
pass. part. ἐλεέω to be merciful, pass. to obtain mercy, to have
mercy and pity showed upon one. The perf. tense emphasizes the
completed state or condition. The contrast of the perf. tense w.
the following aor. tense stresses the contrast between the long
antecedent state and the single event of conversion which ended
it (Hort). **ἐλεηθέντες** aor. pass. part.
11 ■ **ἀγπητός** verbal adj. "love one," "beloved." **παρακαλῶ**
pres. act. ind. to urge, to encourage, to beseech (s. Rom. 12:1).
πάροικος alien. It denotes a man who lives in a foreign country
(Kelly; s. also 1 Peter 1:1). **παρεπίδημος** foreigner, stranger,
temporary sojourner. This word suggests a visitor making a brief
stay (Kelly; s. also 1 Peter 1:1). As long as we are in this world,
there should be in our lives as Christians a certain detachment
(Stibbs). **ἀπέχεσθαι** pres. mid. inf. to hold one's self away from,
to abstain. The inf. is used in indirect discourse after the main
verb. The object of the verb is in gen. indicating what one is not
to indulge in (s. Beare). **σαρκικός** fleshly, that which pertains
to the flesh; i.e., the impulses which belong to the selfish and
lower side of man's nature (Selwyn). (For the significance of the
suf., s. MH, 378f.) **ἐπιθυμία** strong desires, lust. **στρατεύονται**
pres. mid ind. to fight, to carry on a military campaign, to wage
12 war. The pres. tense emphasizes the continual warfare. ■
ἀναστροφή manner of life, conduct, behavior (s. 1 Peter 1:15).
ἔθνος nation, pl. heathen; i.e., those who have no knowledge of
the true God, "Gentiles." **ἔχοντες** pres. act. part. The pres. tense
indicates the continual possession and could have an imp. force
(Beare). **καταλαλοῦσιν** pres. act. ind. to speak against, to speak
evil of (s. Hort). **κακοποιός** evildoer. It denotes the doing of
mischief or injury, either to a specific person or other object, or
else absolutely. It is a wicked man who does evil in such a way
that he is liable to punishment from the magistrate (Hort; Bigg).
ἐποπτεύοντες pres. act. part. ἐποπτεύω to look upon, to observe, to be a spectator, to view carefully, to watch over a period
of time. The pres. tense indicates the covering of a longer period
of time and includes the observer's memory and reflection upon
the deeds. The thought is of spiritual insight which is to be

gained in the future "through the influence of" the "good works" (RWP; Selwyn; Beare). The part. could be temporal "when" or causal "because they observe." **δοξάσωσιν** aor. act. subj. δοξάζω to hold a high opinion of, to glorify. The subj. is used to express purpose. **ἐπισκοπή** visitation. The word is used in the OT either in the sense of a "visit" or in the sense of a visitation for blessing but here the visitation must be one of judgment (Hort; Best).

■ **ὑποτάγητε** aor. pass. imp. ὑποτάσσω to be in subjec- 13
tion, to submit one's self, to be subject to. **ἀνθρώπινος** human, that which is made by human beings, that which proceeds from men. (For the suf. of the word, s. MH, 378f.) **κτίσις** creation, institution. The word may refer to institutions which men have created (s. Best) or the word may refer to creations by God w. the previous adj. having the force "among men," so that the phrase means "to every (divine) institution among men" (Hort). **διὰ τὸν κύριον** "because of the Lord," "for the Lord's sake" (Kelly). **βασιλεύς** king, emperor (Beare). **ὑπερέχοντι** pres. act. part. ὑπερέχω to send out above, to have it over, to be supreme. The word refers to the head of public administration, not as a
deity (Beare). ■ **ἡγεμών** governor. The word has various appli- 14
cations but was specially applied about this time to governors of provinces whether appointed by the emperor or appointed by the senate (Hort; Best). **πεμπομένοις** pres. pass. part. πέμπω to send. **ἐκδίκησις** punishment, legal punishment, avenging (s. Bigg). **ἀγαθοποιός** doing good, upright, one who does right as
opposed to an evildoer (BAG). ■ **ἀγαθοποιοῦντας** pres. act. 15
part. ἀγαθοποιέω to do good, to do right. The part. further defines the will of God and gives the manner or means "by showing yourselves to be good subjects," "by active beneficence" (Beare). **φιμοῦν** pres. act. inf. φιμόω to muzzle, to put to silence, to gag, to restrain (Hort). **ἄφρων** foolish, without reason, those who are senseless in what they are prone to say about Christianity (Stibbs). **ἀγνωσία** ignorant. The word suggests culpable ignorance rather than mere lack of knowledge
(Best). ■ **ἐλεύθερος** free, freedman. To describe the ideal life in 16
terms of freedom meant much for the ancient world because of its clear distinction between the slave and the free man (Best). **ἐπικάλυμμα** that which covers over, veil, cloak. Here it has the significance of "pretext" (Hort). **ἔχοντες** pres. act. part.
ἐλευθερία freedom, liberty. ■ **τιμήσατε** aor. act. imp. τιμάω 17
to honor, constantive use of the imp. (RWP). **ἀδελφότης** brotherhood. The word has the concrete sense of a band of brothers (Hort; s. also RAC II, 631–640; TDNT; CBB). **ἀγαπᾶτε** pres.

act. imp. **φοβεῖσθε** pres. mid. imp. to fear, be afraid.
18 ■ **οἰκέτης** household servant. The word denotes household slaves, many of whom might be well-educated and hold responsible positions in their households (Best; s. also Goppelt; Philemon). The nom. w. the article is used as a voc. (Beare; s. also M, 70). **ὑποτασσόμενοι** pres. mid. part. The part. is used as an imp. (Selwyn; s. also Daube in Selwyn, 467–488). **παντί** used w. **φόβῳ** "in all fear." Not fear of the masters to whom they are subject, but fear of God. It is the spirit of reverence toward Him that induces respect and faithfulness to duty in the sphere of human relationships (Beare). **δεσπότης** master, ruler, one who has complete authority. **ἐπιεικής** mild, gentle (s. Phil. 4:5). **σκολιός** bent, crooked, severe, hard to deal w., harsh (Kelly;
19 Selwyn; s. also Phil. 2:15). ■ **χάρις** grace, thanks, excellence. The word is used here in the sense of that which is admirable, enhancing the esteem in which those who display it are held (Beare; s. also TDNT). **συνείδησις** conscience (s. Rom. 2:15; RAC X, 1025–1107). **ὑποφέρει** pres. act. ind. to bear up under, to endure, to put up w. (Kelly; s. also Goppelt). **λύπη** pain, sorrow. **πάσχων** pres. act. part. πάσχω to suffer. The part. could be temporal. Mere endurance is no cause for pride. Slaves, like school boys, sometimes vied w. one another in demonstrating the ability to endure corporal punishment without flinching. If the beating is deserved, there is no glory in bearing it; but to show patience in the face of injustice is true evidence of Chris-
20 tian character (Beare). **ἀδίκως** adv. unjustly. ■ **ποῖος** what kind of, what sort of. **κλέος** reputation, prestige, glory, credit (s. Kelly; Selwyn). **ἁμαρτάνοντες** pres. act. part. to sin, to do wrong (s. Bigg). **κολαφιζόμενοι** pres. pass. part. κολαφίζω to strike w. the fist, to beat, to treat roughly. Since the word was used of Christ and His suffering (s. Matt. 26:67; Mark 14:65), it could be that Peter is comparing the beating of a slave to the suffering which Christ endured (s. Selwyn; Schelkle; TDNT). **ὑπομενεῖτε** fut. act. ind. ὑπομένω to endure, to patiently endure. **ἀγαθοποιοῦντες** pres. act. part. to do good, to do that which is right. **πάσχοντες** pres. act. part. to suffer. The part. are
21 used temporally. ■ **τοῦτο** "this," i.e., the patient and cheerful endurance of maltreatment when you least deserve it (Kelly). **ἐκλήθητε** aor. pass. ind. καλέω to call. The pass. is the divine pass. indicating that it is God who calls. In calling us "to his eternal glory" (5:10), "out of darkness into his marvelous light" (2:9), God also calls us to do the exercise of this patient endurance of suffering that we have done nothing to deserve. In this very respect, Christ has given us a model of Christian conduct

(Beare). **ἔπαθεν** aor. act. ind. πάσχω to suffer. **ὑπολιμπάνων**
pres. act. part. ὑπολιμπάνω to leave behind. **ὑπογραμμός**
copy, example. The word is used in 2 Maccabees 2:28 of the
"outlines" of a sketch which the artist fills in w. details. It is also
used as the model of handwriting to be copied by the school boy,
then fig. of a model of conduct for imitation (Bigg; Beare).
ἐπακολουθήσητε aor. act. subj. ἐπακολουθέω to follow after,
to follow upon, to follow closely (RWP). The subj. is used to
express purpose (RWP) or the clause is epexegetical explaining
the "pattern" or "example" (Beare). **ἴχνος** footprint. In the pl.
it means the line of footprints. To follow a man's footprints is to
move in the direction he is going (Kelly). ■ **ἐποίησεν** aor. act. 22
ind. **εὑρέθη** aor. pass. ind. **δόλος** deceit (s.v.1). **στόμα** mouth.
■ **λοιδορούμενος** pres. pass. part. λοιδορέω to abuse, to revile, 23
to use vile and abusive language against someone, to heap abuse
upon someone (s. TDNT; T). The pres. part. indicates that this
was done over and over. **ἀντελοιδόρει** impf. act. ind.
ἀντιλοιδορέω to return abuse, to give back abusive language in
return. (For the prep. in compound indicating reciprocal action,
s. MH, 297.) The impf. is used for repeated incidences (RWP).
πάσχων pres. act. part. **ἠπείλει** impf. act. ind. ἀπειλέω to
threaten. The impf. is either inchoative; i.e., "he did not begin
to threaten," or it emphasizes the repeated action (RWP).
παρεδίδου impf. ind. act. παραδίδωμι to deliver over, to give
over to, to entrust, to commit. **κρίνοντι** pres. act. part. to judge.
δικαίως adv. righteously, according to justice. Christ accepted
without rebellion the unjust treatment meted out to Him, confident of vindication before God (Beare). ■ **αὐτός** Himself. 24
ἀνήνεγκεν aor. act. ind. ἀναφέρω to bear up, to bear away.
Peter stresses the redemptive significance of Jesus' death by his
use of OT sacrificial language (s. Best; Selwyn; Heb. 9:28; John
1:29). **ξύλον** wood, tree (s. TDNT; Gal. 3:13). **ἀπογενόμενοι**
aor. mid. part. ἀπογίνομαι to get away from, to die, to depart.
The word is followed by the dat. of reference; i.e., "to die in
reference to sin" (s. Selwyn; RWP). **ζήσωμεν** aor. act. subj. ζάω
to live. **μώλωψ** whelp, bruise, wound caused by blows. The word
denotes the weal or discolored swelling left by a blow from a fist
or whip. The word strictly means a cut which bleeds; he thinks
here of the lashing which draws blood (s. BAG; Kelly; Beare).
ἰάθητε aor. pass. ind. ἰάομαι to heal. ■ **ἦτε** impf. εἰμί. 25
πρόβατον sheep. **πλανώμενοι** pres. mid. part. πλανάω to
wander, to wander away, to go astray. The part. is used in periphrastic construction emphasizing the continual action in the
past "you were going astray" (s. Beare). **ἐπεστράφητε** aor. pass.

ind. ἐπιστρέφω to turn, to return. **ποιμήν** shepherd (s. TDNT). **ἐπίσκοπος** overseer, guardian, bishop (s. Best; Kelly; TDNT; CBB).

Ch. 3

1 ■ **ὁμοίως** adv. likewise, in like manner. **ὑποτασσόμεναι**
pres. mid. part. ὑποτάσσομαι to be in subjection, to subject one's self. **ἴδιος** one's own. **ἵνα** used w. the fut. (s. BD, 186–187). **ἀπειθοῦσιν** pres. act. ind. ἀπειθέω to be disobedient, to disobey (s. 1 Peter 2:8). The ind. is used in a first-class conditional clause which assumes the reality of the condition. **ἀναστροφή** conduct, behavior (s. 1 Peter 1:15). **κερδηθήσονται** fut. pass. ind. κερδαίνω to win, to gain. Here the verb means "to win over to a point of view" (Selwyn; s. also TDNT; Goppelt; David Daube, "Κερδαίνω As a Missionary Term," *Harvard Theologi-*
2 *cal Review* 40 [1947], 109–120). ■ **ἐποπτεύσαντες** aor. act.
part. ἐποπτεύω to look at, to observe (s. 1 Peter 2:12). **ἁγνός** pure, clean, chaste. Here it indicates the irreproachable conduct
3 of the wife (Kelly). ■ **ἔστω** pres. imp. εἰμί. **ἔξωθεν** outward.
ἐμπλοκή plaited, braiding. **θρίξ, τριχός** hair (s. 2 Tim. 2:4). **περίθεσις** placing around, wearing. **χρυσίον** gold, gold jewelry. (For references of writers in the ancient world who also spoke against the superficial preoccupation of women w. dress, jewelry, etc., s. Kelly; Goppelt; Selwyn, 432–439.) **ἔνδυσις** putting on.
4 **ἱμάτιον** garment, clothes. ■ **κρυπτός** hidden. **ἄφθαρτος** incor-
ruptible (s. 1 Peter 1:4). **πραΰς** meek, gentle. The word refers to the humble and gentle attitude which expresses itself in a patient submissiveness (s. Matt. 5:5; 2 Cor. 10:1; Gal. 5:23). **ἡσύχιος** quiet. **πνεῦμα** spirit, disposition (Selwyn). The gen. is
5 gen. of definition (Beare). **πολυτελής** very valuable, costly. ■
οὕτως so, thus, in this way. **ποτέ** at that time, formerly. **ἅγιαι** holy. **ἐλπίζουσαι** pres. act. part. fem. pl. to hope. **ἐκόσμουν** impf. act. ind. κοσμέω to adorn. The impf. indicates customary
6 action "they used to adorn themselves" (RWP). ■ **ὑπήκουσεν**
aor. act. ind. ὑπακούω to listen to, to obey. **καλοῦσα** pres. act. part. **ἐγενήθητε** aor. pass. ind. γίνομαι to become. The verb "become" insinuates that they were formerly pagans (Kelly). The aor. tense points to a one-time act (Goppelt). **ἀγαθοποιοῦσαι** pres. act. part. ἀγαθοποιέω to do good. **φοβούμεναι** pres. mid. part. φοβέομαι to be afraid, to have fear. The part. provide proof that they have become Sarah's children "in that you do good and are not a prey to terror" (Beare; Goppelt). **πτόησις** frightening, terrifying. The word means fluttering, excitement, perturbation of spirit, caused by

any passion, but more esp. by fear (Bigg). The acc. seems to be used as a cognate acc. (Beare).

■ **συνοικοῦντες** pres. act. part. συνοικέω to live together. 7
The part. is used as an imp. (s. Selwyn). **γνῶσις** understanding. Here it means Christian insight and tact, a conscious sensitivity to God's will (Kelly; s. also Beare). **ἀσθενέτερος** comp. ἀσθενής weak, comp. weaker. Here it may be "weaker" in the physical sense (s. Selwyn; Best; Beare). **σκεῦος** vessel, jar, instrument. The word may refer to the physical body (Selwyn; Schelkle). **γυναικεῖος** fem. female, woman. The n. adj. is used w. the article to denote an abstract noun (Selwyn). **ἀπονέμοντες** pres. act. part. ἀπονέμω to assign, to show, to pay. Used here in the sense of "to show honor to someone" (BAG). **συγκληρονόμος** fellow heir, joint heir, followed by the obj. gen. "fellow heirs of the grace of life," i.e., God's gracious gift of eternal life (Bigg). **ἐγκόπτεσθαι** pres. pass. inf. ἐγκόπτω to cut in on, to hinder (s. Rom. 15:22; Gal. 5:7; 1 Thess. 2:18; s. also TDNT; CBB). The inf. is used w. the prep. to express purpose (RWP). **προσευχαί** prayers.

■ **τὸ τέλος** used adverbially "finally." In this adverbial 8
sense the word always seems to introduce a fresh point and not simply to summarize what has gone before. Here it affects the transition from specific ethical duties to a general statement of Christian character (Selwyn). **ὁμόφρων** like-minded, i.e., of that inward unity of attitude in spiritual things which makes schism unthinkable (Beare). **συμπαθής** full of sympathy, sharing in feeling. The word denotes a readiness to enter into and share the feelings of others and to unite alike in sorrow and in joy (Kelly; Beare). **φιλάδελφος** love of brother, brotherly love (s. 1 Peter 1:22). **εὔσπλαγχνος** compassionate, compassionate tenderness (s. Eph. 4:32; TDNT; MNTW, 156f.). **ταπεινόφρων** humble
minded (s. Phil. 2:3; TDNT). ■ **ἀποδιδόντες** pres. act. part. 9
ἀποδίδωμι to give back, to pay back. The part. is used as an imp. **λοιδορία** railing, abuse (s. 1 Peter 2:23). **τοὐναντίον = τὸ ἐναντίον** on the contrary (s. RWP). **εὐλογοῦντες** pres. act. part. **ἐκλήθητε** aor. pass. ind. καλέω (s. 1 Peter 2:21). **κληρονομήσητε** aor. act. subj. κληρονομέω to inherit. The idea of an inheritance as a free gift which comes to the recipient
without his having to merit it remains present (Kelly). ■ **θέλων** 10
pres. act. part. **ἰδεῖν** aor. act. inf. ὁράω. **παυσάτω** aor. act. imp. παύω to cease, to stop. (For the change from the 2nd pers. imp. of the LXX to the 3rd pers., s. Selwyn.) **λαλῆσαι** aor. act. inf.
δόλος deceit, trickery (s. 1 Peter 2:1). ■ **ἐκκλινάτω** aor. act. 11
imp. 3rd pers. sing. ἐκκλίνω to turn from, to turn away from.

ποιησάτω aor. act. imp. **ζητησάτω** aor. act. imp. ζητέω to
seek. **διωξάτω** aor. act. imp. διώκω to hunt, to pursue. The
words enjoin the same active and persistent effort on behalf of
peace as enjoined in the beatitude in Matthew 5:9 (Selwyn).
12 ■ **οὖς**, ὠτός ear. **δέησις** request, prayer. **ποιοῦντας** pres. act.
part. The pres. tense emphasizes the continual doing of something.
13 ■ **καί** besides. The resumption is rapid after the quotation
from Psalm 34 and effects a swift and easy entrance into the new
theme (Selwyn). **κακώσων** fut. act. part. κακόω to do evil to
someone, to harm someone. The fut. part. has the idea "who is
going to harm you?" (s. Kelly). **ζηλωτής** zealot, enthusiast, one
who exercises zeal for an object (s. Selwyn; Best; Titus 2:14; Gal.
14 1:14). **γένησθε** aor. mid. subj. γίνομαι. ■ **πάσχοιτε** pres. act.
opt. πάσχω to suffer. The opt. is used in a condition of the 4th
class which implies that there is no certainty of fulfillment of the
condition "if perchance" (s. RWP; Best; BD, 195; BG, 111).
There is no contradiction w. this statement and 1 Peter 4:12ff.
and there is no evidence that the letter should be divided into
different writings. (For arguments against viewing 1 Peter 4:12ff.
as a separate writing, s. Kelly.) **μακάριος** happy, blessed, fortunate
(s. TDNT; BAG; CBB). **φοβηθῆτε** aor. pass. subj.
φοβέομαι to be afraid, to fear. The subj. w. the neg. is used to
form a prohibition. **ταραχθῆτε** aor. pass. subj. ταράσσω to
15 shake, to disturb, to trouble. ■ **ἁγιάσατε** aor. act. imp. ἁγιάζω
to sanctify; i.e., "to venerate and adore Him," thus dispelling all
fear of man (Beare). **ἕτοιμος** ready, prepared. **ἀεί** always.
ἀπολογία defense. The word was often used of the argument
for the defense in a court of law and though the word may have
the idea of a judicial interrogation in which one is called to
answer for the manner in which he has exercised his responsibility
(Beare), the word can also mean an informal explanation or
defense of one's position (s. 1 Cor. 9:3; 2 Cor. 7:11) and the word
would aptly describe giving an answer to the skeptical, abusive,
or derisive inquiries of ill-disposed neighbors (Kelly). **αἰτοῦντι**
pres. act. part. αἰτέω to ask. The pres. tense would be interat.;
i.e., "every time someone asks." **λόγος** account, a rational account
of (Selwyn). **ἐλπίς** hope. In this letter "hope" is used
16 almost as an equivalent for "faith" (s. 1 Peter 1:21; Best). ■
ἀλλά but, however. **πραΰτης** meekness, gentleness (s.v.4).
συνείδησις conscience (s. 1 Peter 2:19). **ἔχοντες** pres. act. part.
to have. The pres. tense can have the meaning "to possess," "to
maintain," and the part. is used as an imp. (Beare).
καταλαλεῖσθε pres. pass. ind. καταλαλέω to speak evil

against (s. 1 Peter 2:12). **καταισχυνθῶσιν** aor. pass. subj.
καταισχύνω to put to shame. Perhaps Peter was thinking of his
personal experience at Pentecost, when the Jews first scoffed
and were then pierced to the heart (Acts 2:13, 37) (Hart). The
subj. is used in a purpose clause. **ἐπηρεάζοντες** pres. act. part.
ἐπηρεάζω to threaten, to mistreat, to abuse, to insult, to treat
wrongfully, to deal despitefully w. someone. (For examples from
the papyri, s. MM.) **ἀναστροφή** behavior, conduct (s. 1 Peter
1:15). ■ **κρεῖττον** n. comp. ἀγαθός "better." **ἀγαθοποιοῦντας** 17
pres. act. part. to do good (s.v.6). The part. is acc. pl. agreeing
w. the subject of the inf. and is causal giving the reason for
suffering. **θέλοι** pres. act. opt. The opt. is used in a fourth-class
conditional clause (s.v.14). **κακοποιοῦντας** pres. act. part.
κακοποιέω to do evil, to do wrong. The part. is causal. (For
eschatological interpretation of this v. which views this v. as
referring to eschatological judgment, s. J.R. Michaels, "Es-
chatology in I Peter 3:17," NTS 13 [July, 1967], 394–401.) ■ **ὅτι** 18
καὶ Χριστός "because Christ also." This introduces a new
application of the imitation of Christ: we pass from the patient
Christ to the victorious Christ (Selwyn). **ἀπέθανεν** aor. act. ind.
ἀποθνῄσκω to die. (For the variant reading **ἔπαθεν** aor. act.
ind. πάσχω to suffer, s. TC, 692f.; Selwyn; Kelly; Goppelt.)
προσαγάγῃ aor. act. subj. προσάγω to lead or bring to, to
introduce, to provide access for, to bring about a right relationship. The word had various usages and could denote the bringing
of a person before a tribunal or presenting him at a royal court
or the ritual act of bringing sacrifice to God or the consecration
of persons to God's service (s. Kelly; TDNT; Eph. 2:18).
θανατωθείς aor. pass. part. θανατόω to put to death. **σαρκί**
dat. sing. "flesh." The expression refers to the reality of Christ's
physical death and the dat. is dat. of reference (Selwyn).
ζῳοποιηθείς aor. pass. part. ζωοποιέω to make alive. The expression "in reference to spirit" could refer either to the Holy
Spirit or to the spirit of Christ (s. Best). ■ **ἐν ᾧ** "in which." The 19
rel. pron. could refer to the word "spirit" or it can refer to the
state or circumstances; i.e., "in which state or circumstances"
(Selwyn; s. esp. Selwyn, 315f.; Reicke, 138; Best). **φυλακή** prison. **πορευθείς** aor. pass. part. πορεύομαι to go. **ἐκήρυξεν** aor.
act. ind. κηρύσσω to proclaim, to preach. (For various discussions and literature on this difficult passage, s. Goppelt; Best;
Selwyn, 314–362; Sherman E. Johnson, "The Preaching to the
Dead," JBL 79 [March, 1960], 48–51; Bo Reicke, *The Disobedient Spirits and Christian Baptism* [Copenhagen, 1946]; W.J.
Dalton, *Christ's Proclamation to the Spirits* [Rome, 1965].) ■ 20

ἀπειθήσασιν aor. act. part. to be disobedient (s. 1 Peter 2:8). **ἀπεξεδέχετο** impf. mid. ind. ἀπεκδέχομαι to earnestly and eagerly await w. expectancy, to wait out the time (Beare; s. also 1 Cor. 1:7; Gal. 5:5; Phil. 3:20). **μακροθυμία** longsuffering, patience (s. Rom. 2:4; Gal. 5:22). **κατασκευαζομένης** pres. pass. part. κατασκευάζω to make ready, to build, to construct. The part. is used as a gen. abs. expressing contemporaneous time. **κιβωτός** box, ark. **διεσώθησαν** aor. pass. ind. διασῴζω to save through, to bring safe through (RWP; s. also Acts 27:44). **δι᾽ ὕδατος** "through water." The prep. could be taken in a local sense; i.e., "they were brought to safety by passing through water" or it could be taken in an instrumental sense (s. Kelly).
21 ■ **ἀντίτυπος** n. adj. used as a noun (s. Goppelt), antitype. The word connotes the exactness of correspondence between the stamp and the die (Selwyn; MM; s. also Heb. 9:24). **σῴζει** pres. act. ind. to save, to rescue. The saving by baptism which Peter here mentions is only symbolic, not actual as Peter hastens to explain (RWP). Baptism is the occasion and sign of transition from an old way of life to another that is marked by a new ethic. In accepting baptism the person is affirming willingness to share in the known experience of baptized persons; i.e., the experience of suffering and being treated w. suspicion and hostility. This indicates that the main theme of 1 Peter is not baptism but rather suffering (s. David Hill, "On Suffering and Baptism in I Peter," Nov T 17 [July, 1976], 181–189; for those who would seek to make this v. the key to 1 Peter and view the book as a baptismal instructional sermon, s. Oscar S. Brooks, "I Peter 3:21—The Clue to the Literary Structure of the Epistle," Nov T 16 [October, 1974], 290–305; for Jewish parallels related to baptismal catechism for Jewish proselytes, s. NTRJ, 106–140.) **ἀπόθεσις** putting off, putting away. **ῥύπος** filth, dirt. **ἐπερώτημα** question, inquiry, pledge. In the papyri there is evidence that this word was a t.t. in making a contract and denotes the "pledge" or "undertaking" given by one of the parties in answer to formal questions addressed to him. The word then implies the registering of agreement to conditions or demands. Here the pledge is an expression of accent to certain conditions; i.e., it may imply a confession of faith as well as the willingness to accept the new duties (s. David Hill, "On Suffering and Baptism in I Peter," 187f.; Reicke; Kelly; MM). **δι᾽ ἀναστάσεως** "through the resurrection." Baptism is a symbolic picture of the resurrection of
22 Christ as well as our own spiritual renewal (RWP). ■ **δεξιά** right hand. (For the meaning of being "on the right hand," s. Eph. 1:20.) **ὑποταγέντων** aor. pass. part. ὑποτάσσω to subject, to

be in subjection. **ἐξουσίαι** authorities, powers. The designations "angels and principalities and powers" embrace all ranks of spiritual beings (Beare; s. also TDNT).

Ch. 4

■ **οὖν** therefore. This word introduces the main lesson to be 1
drawn from 1 Peter 3:18–22 (Bigg). **παθόντος** aor. act. part. πάσχω to suffer. The part. is used in a gen. abs. **ἔννοια** thought, principle, counsel, mind, resolve. The principle of thought and feeling here referred to is that of the dying life voluntarily accepted and put on as armor, and finding expression in the meek and courageous pursuit of the spiritual life (Selwyn; s. also Bigg; for the philosophical meaning of the word, s. GPT, 57). **ὁπλίσασθε** aor. mid. imp. ὁπλίζω to arm one's self w. weapons. The idea of the word is "put on as your armor" (Selwyn), "arm yourselves w. the same insight" (Goppelt). **ὁ παθών** aor. act. part. used here as a noun "the one who has suffered." **πέπαυται** perf. mid. ind. παύομαι to cease. The words seem to have been a proverbial expression related to Romans 6:7 and the suffering is taken to mean "dying" in the sense of "dying to sin" (Best; Beare; Stibbs). The perf. tense stresses the condition or
state. ■ **εἰς τό** "in order that." The words introduce a purpose 2
clause (RWP). **μηκέτι** no longer. **ἐπιθυμία** strong desire, lust, passion. **θελήματι** dat., sing. dat. of advantage indicating personal interest. These dat. could also express the rule by which man shapes his life (Bigg). **ἐπίλοιπος** remaining. **βιῶσαι** aor.
act. inf. βιόω to live. ■ **ἀρκετός** sufficient. The sense of the 3
word is "more than sufficient," "far too much" (Beare). The word may be used ironically w. the meaning "more than enough" (Kelly; s. also Goppelt). **παρεληλυθώς** perf. act. part. παρέρχομαι to go by, to pass by. One after another, the three perf. in this v. emphasize the thought that this past of theirs is a closed chapter; that part of the story is over and done w. (Beare). **βούλημα** will, wish. **κατειργάσθαι** perf. mid. inf. κατεργάζομαι to produce, to work, to accomplish. **πεπορευμένους** perf. mid. part. πορεύομαι to go. The word is used here in the Hebraic sense of "to walk," "to conduct one's life" (s. Bigg; Selwyn). **ἀσέλγεια** unbridled and unrestrained living. The word describes "the spirit which knows no restraints and which dares whatever caprice and wanton insolence suggest" (NTW 26; s. also TDNT; Gal. 5:19; Eph. 4:19). **ἐπιθυμία** lust, passion. **οἰνοφλυγία** wine bubbling up, drunkenness. The context shows that the word means "habitual drunkards" (s. RWP; Selwyn). **κῶμος** drunken party, reveling. The word orig-

inally referred to a band of friends who accompanied a victor in the games on his way home. They sang the rejoicings and his praises. But the word degenerated until it came to mean a "carousal," a band of drunken revellers, swaying and singing their way through the streets (NTW, 27). The public parties and revelings were associated w. the cult of certain gods, esp. Dionysus (Selwyn; s. also Eph. 5:18). **πότος** drinking, drinking parties. **ἀθέμιτος** abominable, unrighteous, lawless. **εἰδωλολατρία** worship of idols, idolatry. The prominence here is on sexual and
4 alcoholic excess w. the stress on idolatry (Kelly). ■ **ἐν ᾧ** "in which thing," "wherein," "in which manner of life" (Bigg). **ξενίζονται** pres. pass. ind. ξενίζω to entertain, to entertain strangers, to astonish, to surprise. The word has the idea of being surprised or entertained by the novelty of a thing or being surprised or upset at a new turn of events (Selwyn). The word also includes the thought of "take offense," as ignorant people often feel an unreasonable resentment at anything that does not fit into the pattern of life familiar to them. The matter of this resentful astonishment is expressed by the gen. abs. which follows (Beare). **συντρεχόντων** pres. act. part. συντρέχω to run together. The metaphor suggests the thought of joining in a mad race (Beare). The gen. abs. describes that which is considered to be thought strange. **ἀσωτία** wasteful, riotous living, dissipation (s. TDNT; Eph. 5:18). **ἀνάχυσις** pouring forth. The word was used of the rock pools filled up by the sea at high tide (Selwyn) or of a swamp which was formed by the pouring forth of waters. Here it has the act. verbal sense followed by the obj. gen.—"outpouring of profligacy"; w. the thought of the life of paganism as a feverish pursuit of evil, wherein men vie w. one another in pouring forth profligate living (Beare). **βλασφημοῦντες** pres. act. part. βλασφημέω to defame someone, to injure the reputation
5 of someone, to blaspheme (BAG). ■ **ἀποδώσουσιν** fut. act. ind. ἀποδίδωμι to pay back, to give account. **ἑτοίμως** adv. ready. **ἔχοντι** pres. act. part. The dat. indicates to whom account is rendered; i.e., "to the one who stands ready." (For this construction, s. Kelly; RWP; Acts 21:13.) **κρῖναι** aor. act. inf. κρίνω to judge. The inf. is epexegetical explaining the readiness. **ζῶντας** pres. act. part. ζάω to live. The phrase "the living and the dead"
6 means "all men" (Best). ■ **νεκροῖς** "to the dead." The reference may be to those who are spiritually dead, but it seems better to understand the term as referring to those to whom the gospel was preached during their earthly life and they have since died physically (Stibbs). **εὐηγγελίσθη** aor. pass. ind. εὐαγγελίζομαι to proclaim the good news, to evangelize, to

preach the gospel. **κριθῶσι** aor. pass. subj. The subj. is used in a purpose clause. **ζῶσι** pres. act. subj. ζάω to live. (For the omission of the moveable nu, s. Francis Thomas Gignac, *A Grammar of the Greek Papyri of the Roman and Byzantine Periods.* Vol. I Phonology [Milan, Italy: Cisalpano-Goliardica, 1976], 114f.) **κατὰ θεόν** "according to God." The phrase could mean either "in the eyes of God" (Kelly) or "in God's likeness," "as God lives," i.e., eternally (Selwyn).

■ **ἤγγικεν** perf. act. ind. ἐγγίζω to come near, perf. "to be 7
at hand." **σωφρονήσατε** aor. act. imp. σωφρονέω to be sound in mind. The word connotes the cool head and balanced mind to exercise self-control or moderation (Beare; Selwyn; GPT, 179f.; TDNT). **νήψατε** aor. act. imp. νήφω to be sober, to keep
a clear head (Kelly). ■ **πρὸ πάντων** "before all things," "above 8
all." **ἐκτενής** strenuous, intense (s. 1 Peter 1:22). **ἔχοντες** pres. act. part. **καλύπτει** pres. act. ind. to cover, to hide. The proverbial expression may be a quotation or adaptation of Proverbs 10:12 (Best; s. also Beare). The pres. tense is gnomic indicating
that which is constantly true. **πλῆθος** multitude. ■ **φιλόξενος** 9
hospitality, entertaining of strangers. The lack of a network of decent hotels for ordinary people had the results that readiness to provide board and lodging for friends and other suitably sponsored travelers was even more highly esteemed than it is today (Kelly; s. also 1 Tim. 3:2; and for Jewish parallels, s. SB III, 297; and in general RAC VIII, 1061–1123; TDNT). **γογγυσμός** murmuring, complaining, grumbling. The addition of these words has a sharp twang of realism about it. Then as now guests could overstay or otherwise abuse their host's welcome and a reminder that hospitality can be an exasperating chore, to be shouldered cheerfully if it is to be worthwhile, is in place (Kelly).
■ **ἕκαστος** each one. **καθώς** just as. **ἔλαβεν** aor. act. ind. 10
λαμβάνω to receive. **χάρισμα** gift, gracious gift, grace gift (s. 1 Cor. 1:7; TDNT; CBB). **διακονοῦντες** pres. act. part. to minister, to serve. **οἰκονόμος** steward. The word denotes a slave who was responsible for managing a man's property or household and for distributing their wages, food, etc. to its members (Kelly; s. also 1 Cor. 4:1; TDNT). **ποικίλος** many colored,
manifold, variegated (s. James 1:2; 1 Peter 1:6). ■ **λόγιον** utter- 11
ance, oracle. The word sometimes means "Scripture" and in classical Gr. it means any divine utterance (Selwyn). **ἰσχύς** strength, might. **χορηγεῖ** pres. act. ind. to supply. The word originally meant "to be in a chorus." Then it meant "to supply a chorus" and so produce a play at one's own risk. Finally it simply meant to furnish or supply anything (Selwyn; s. also Eph.

4:16). **δοξάζηται** pres. pass. subj. δοξάζω to glorify. The subj. is used to express purpose.
12 ■ **ἀγαπητός** one loved, beloved. **ξενίζεσθε** pres. pass. imp. (s.v.4). **πύρωσις** burning, fiery. The word was often used in the sense of a purifying or refining fire (s. Goppelt). **πειρασμός** trial, ordeal. **γινομένῃ** pres. mid. part. **ξένος** strange, foreign. **συμβαίνοντος** pres. act. part. συμβαίνω to happen, to occur.
13 ■ **καθό** "insofar; far as," "according to which thing" (RWP). **κοινωνεῖτε** pres. act. ind. to share in, to have fellowship. **πάθημα** suffering. **χαίρετε** pres. act. imp. χαίρω to be happy, to rejoice. The pres. tense calls for continual rejoicing. **χαρῆτε** aor. act. subj. χαίρω to rejoice. The subj. is used in a purpose clause. **ἀγαλλιώμενοι** pres. mid. part. ἀγαλλιάομαι to be exuberantly happy (s. 1 Peter 1:8). The part. w. the imp. is emphatic,
14 i.e., "rejoice w. rapture" (Selwyn). ■ **ὀνειδίζεσθε** pres. pass. ind. ὀνειδίζω to revile, to insult. The word is used in the LXX for reproaches heaped on God and His saints by the wicked and in the NT becomes associated w. the indignities and maltreatment which Christ had to endure (Kelly). **ἀναπαύεται** pres. mid.
15 ind. to give rest, to refresh. ■ **πασχέτω** pres. act. imp. 3rd sing. to suffer. **φονεύς** murderer. **κακοποιός** evildoer. **ἀλλοτριεπίσκοπος** one who looks after the affairs of another, agitator, mischief maker. (For this unusual word, s. Kelly; Best.)
16 ■ **αἰσχυνέσθω** pres. pass. imp. αἰσχύνομαι to put to shame,
17 pass. to be put to shame. **δοξαζέτω** pres. act. imp. (s.v.11). ■ **ἄρξασθαι** pres. mid. imp. ἄρχομαι to begin. The construction of the inf. is unusual and may be in apposition or epexegetical (RWP). **ἀπειθούντων** pres. act. part. ἀπειθέω to be disobedient
18 (s. 1 Peter 2:8). ■ **μόλις** w. difficulty, scarcely. The words do not imply doubt about the salvation of Christians, but emphasize the greatness of God's effort in saving them (Best). **σῴζεται** pres. pass. ind. **ἀσεβής** ungodly. **φανεῖται** fut. mid. ind. φαίνομαι
19 to appear. ■ **ὥστε** therefore, wherefore. The word sums up the thought of the entire paragraph (Beare). **καί** also. The word introduces a new thought: the certainty of divine justice being exercised is a call to a complete serenity of faith in God (Selwyn). **πάσχοντες** pres. act. part. **κτίστης** creator. **παρατιθέσθωσαν** pres. mid. imp. παρατίθημι to deliver over to, to entrust, to entrust for safe keeping. **ἀγαθοποιΐα** active well-doing (Kelly).

Ch. 5

1 ■ **παρακαλῶ** pres. act. ind. to beseech, to encourage (s. Rom. 12:1). **συμπρεσβύτερος** fellow elder. Here the word el-

der denotes the officials who acted as pastoral leaders of the
congregations (Kelly; s. also TDNT). **πάθημα** suffering.
μελλούσης pres. act. part. μέλλω to be about to.
ἀποκαλύπτεσθαι pres. pass. inf. ἀποκαλύπτω to reveal.
κοινωνός partner, sharer. ■ **ποιμάνατε** aor. act. imp. 2
ποιμαίνω to shepherd. The aor. may be ingressive "take up the
task of shepherding" (Beare). **ἀναγκαστῶς** forced, con-
strained. **ἑκουσίως** willingly. **αἰσχροκερδῶς** adv. shameful
gain. **προθύμως** zealously, eagerly. The word is extremely
strong and expresses enthusiasm and devoted zeal (Kelly). ■ 3
κατακυριεύοντες pres. act. part. κατακυριεύω to lord it over
someone, to domineer, to exercise complete control. The prep.
in compound indicates that the action is unfavorable to an object
(MH, 316). **κλῆρος** lot, charge. The word probably refers to the
flock or those who were put in charge of the flock (s. Best;
Beare). **τύπος** pattern, example. **γινόμενοι** pres. mid. part. ■ 4
φανερωθέντος aor. pass. part. φανερόομαι to appear.
ἀρχιποίμην chief shepherd, master shepherd. (For the use of
this term in the papyri, s. LAE, 100f.) **κομιεῖσθε** fut. mid. ind.
κομίζω to receive, to obtain. **ἀμαράντινος** unfading (s. 1 Peter
1:4).

■ **ὁμοίως** adv. likewise. **νεώτερος** comp. νέος new, young. 5
ὑποτάγητε aor. pass. imp. ὑποτάσσομαι to submit, to be in
subjection. **ταπεινοφροσύνη** lowly thinking, humility (s.
TDNT). **ἐγκομβώσασθε** aor. mid. imp. ἐγκομβόομαι to tie or
fasten something on one's self firmly w. a clasp, knot, or bow.
The word was also used of a slave who tied on an apron so that
the idea may be that of wearing humility as a slave's apron
(Selwyn; Beare). **ὑπερήφανος** showing one's self above others,
proud, arrogant (AS). **ἀντιτάσσεται** pres. mid. ind. to line up
against, to oppose, to resist. **ταπεινός** lowly, humble.

■ **ταπεινώθητε** aor. pass. imp. ταπεινόω to make low, to 6
humble, pass. to humble one's self, to be humble. **κραταιός**
strong, mighty (s. Eph. 1:19). **ὑψώσῃ** aor. act. subj. ὑψόω to
exalt, to lift up, to make high. ■ **ἐπιρίψαντες** aor. act. part. 7
ἐπιρρίπτω to throw something upon something else, e.g., to
throw clothes on an animal for riding (Luke 19:35) (BAG). The
part. is to be closely connected w. the imp. "humble yourselves"
showing that the true Christian attitude is not neg. self-abandon-
ment or resignation, but involves as the expression of one's
self-humbling the positive and trusting of one's self and one's
troubles to God (Kelly; s. also Ps. 45:22). **μέλει** pres. act. ind.
to have concern, to have care. Used impersonally w. the dat.
"there is constant care and concern to Him."

8 ■ **νήψατε** aor. act. imp. νήφω to be sober (s. 1 Peter 4:7).
γρηγορήσατε aor. act. imp. γρηγορέω to stay awake, to be
watchful, to be on the alert. The aor. imp. ring sharply: "be
alert!" "be awake!" Confidence in God must not lead to slack-
ness; the spiritual warfare which they wage demands vigilance
(Beare). **ἀντίδικος** legal adversary, opponent in a law suit. The
word then denotes an enemy in general (Kelly). **διάβολος** slanderer, devil. **λέων** lion. **ὠρυόμενος** pres. mid. part. ὠρύομαι
roar. The pres. tense pictures the continual roaring of Satan as
a lion. **περιπατεῖ** pres. act. ind. to walk about, to prowl around
(Kelly). **ζητῶν** pres. act. part. ζητέω to seek, to look for.
καταπιεῖν aor. act. inf. καταπίνω to swallow down, to eat up,
to devour. The word lit. means "to drink down" but it can be
9 used of an animal swallowing its prey (Jonah 2:1) (Kelly). ■
ἀντίστητε aor. act. imp. ἀνθίστημι to stand up against, to
withstand, to resist. The aor. could be ingressive, i.e., "take your
stand against" (s. James 4:7). **στερεός** compact, solid, firm,
stedfast (Selwyn; Kelly). **εἰδότες** perf. act. part. οἶδα.
ἀδελφότης brotherhood (s. 1 Peter 2:17; MM). **ἐπιτελεῖσθαι**
pres. mid. or pass. inf. ἐπιτελέω to complete, to perform, to lay
something upon someone (BAG), mid. the meaning can be "is
required," "to pay in full" (MT, 55) w. the idea of "knowing how
to pay the same tax of suffering" (Bigg). The mid. could also
have the meaning "to fulfill a religious duty," "to perform the
obligations of piety." The gen. "sufferings" would be a gen. of
definition and the meaning would be "to make the same fulfillment (of duty toward God) of sufferings" (Beare). If the pass. is
adopted the verb might be translated "knowing that the same tax
of suffering will be paid by your brotherhood" (s. Best). The inf.
10 is used as the object of the verb "to know." ■ **καλέσας** aor. act.
part. καλέω to call. **παθόντος** aor. act. part. πάσχω to suffer.
The part. is used temporally "after you have suffered."
καταρτίσει fut. act. ind. καταρτίζω to put in order, to mend,
to reestablish, to make whole. The word could be used in a
medical sense of "settling a broken bone" or of repairing and
refitting a damaged vessel (s. Selwyn; Beare; TDNT; Gal. 6:1).
στηρίξει fut. act. ind. στηρίξω to set up, to fix firmly, to
establish, to strengthen (s. BAG; MM). **σθενώσει** fut. act. ind.
σθενόω to strengthen, to make strong (s. Kelly; BAG).
θεμελιώσει fut. act. ind. θεμελιόω to make a foundation, to
provide a solid foundation, to ground firmly (Goppelt; Eph.
3:17).

12 ■ **λογίζομαι** to reckon, to count as, to regard. This does not
imply that others have doubted the ability of Silvanus but em-

phasizes Peter's confidence in his fidelity (Best). **ἔγραψα** aor.
act. ind. γράφω epistolary aor. "I am writing" (Beare).
παρακαλῶν pres. act. part. (s.v.1). **ἐπιμαρτυρῶν** pres. act.
part. ἐπιμαρτυρέω to testify, to affirm, to supply evidence that,
to confirm that fact by evidence (Selwyn; s. also Goppelt).
στῆτε aor. act. imp. ἵστημι to stand, ingressive aor. "take your
stand" (RWP). ■ **ἀσπάζεται** pres. mid. ind. to greet. 13
συνεκλεκτή fem. adj. "fellow elect." The fem. could refer to the
local church from which the letter was written (Kelly). **Μάρκος**
John Mark is intended who was not the real son but rather the
spiritual son of Peter (s. Best). ■ **ἀσπάσασθε** aor. mid. imp. 14
φίλημα kiss (s. 1 Cor. 16:20).

2 PETER

Ch. 1

1 ***ἰσότιμος*** w. the same honor. Here the word has the meaning "equal privilege" or "equally privileged," i.e., a faith which carries equal privileges (Mayor). ***ἡμῖν*** "w. us." The contrast could be between Jews and Gentiles who have equal privileges but the contrast is almost certainly between the apostles who had been eyewitnesses of the original revelation (cf. 1:16), and the Christians of the second or even third generation (Kelly; s. also Bigg). ***λαχοῦσιν*** aor. act. part. λαγχάνω to obtain by lot, to obtain. The word implies a gift of favor and God gives to all Christians equal privileges in His city (Bigg). ***πίστις*** faith. Here it is not the faith as a body of doctrine, but the faith or trust which brings a man salvation and is the God-given capacity to
2 trust Him (Green). ■ ***πληθυνθείη*** aor. pass. opt. πληθύνω to multiply, to increase, pass. to be multiplied, to grow, to increase as "may grace and peace be yours in ever greater measure" (BAG). The opt. is used to express a wish or desire (RWP; s. also 1 Peter 1:2). ***ἐπίγνωσις*** knowledge, knowledge which is directed toward a particular object which can imply a more detailed or fuller knowledge (s. Col. 1:9; Mayor, 171–174).

3 ■ ***θεῖος*** godly, divine. The term "divine power" in the gen. is the subject of the part. and was a phrase used for the term "God." A parallel expression is found in the decree of Stratonicea, an inscription in honor of Zeus and Hekate. (For this and its importance in relation to 2 Peter, s. BS, 360–368.) ***εὐσέβεια*** godliness, true religion which displays itself in reverence in the presence of that which is majestic and divine in worship and in a life of active obedience which befits that reverence (MNTW, 67ff.; TDNT; CBB; s. also 1 Tim. 2:2; 3:16). ***δεδωρημένης*** perf. mid. part. δωρέω to give as a gift, to grant, to bestow. The part. is used as a gen. abs. The perf. tense emphasizes the continuing nature of that which was given. ***καλέσαντος*** aor. act. part. καλέω to call. ***ἀρετή*** virtue, excellence, the display of divine power and divine acts (s. 1 Peter 2:9). The dat. case could be either instrumental "by" or dat. of advantage "to," "for" (s.
4 RWP). ■ ***δι᾽ ὧν*** "through which things." The antecedent of the

rel. pron. would be the words "glory and virtue" (Bigg). **τίμιος** honorable, precious, valuable. **μέγιστος** magnificent, elative superl. "very great." **ἐπάγγελμα** that which was promised, promised. **δεδώρηται** perf. mid. ind. (s.v.3). **γένησθε** aor. mid. subj. γίνομαι. The subj. is used to express purpose. **κοινωνός** partner, sharer, partaker (s. TDNT). **φύσις** nature. Peter does not mean that man is absorbed into deity but rather those who are partakers of Christ will be partakers of the glory that shall be revealed (s. Green; Kelly). **ἀποφυγόντες** aor. act. part. ἀποφεύγω to escape, to escape completely. **ἐπιθυμία** strong desire, lust, passion. **φθορά** corruption. The basic meaning of the word denotes primarily not a sudden destruction owing to external violence, but a dissolution brought on by means of
internal decay, i.e., "rottenness" (s. Mayor, 175–179). ■ 5
σπουδή haste, effort. **παρεισενέγκαντες** aor. act. part. παρεισφέρω to bring in alongside of. Used idiomatically w. the word "effort" to express the idea of bringing in every effort. We are to bring "into" this relationship "alongside" what God has done every ounce of determination we can muster (Green; s. also Bigg; Kelly; Mayor; BS, 361). **ἐπιχορηγήσατε** aor. act. imp. ἐπιχορηγέω to supply in addition to, to outfit the chorus w. additional (complete) supplies (RWP). The prep. in compound seems to have an accumulative force, "to add further supplies," "to provide more than was expected or could be demanded" (Mayor), "to give lavishly, w. generosity" (Kelly; for this graphic word, s. also 2 Cor. 9:10; Gal. 3:5; Col. 2:19; 1 Peter 4:11; Green; Bigg). **ἐν** "in." The since is: since you have faith, let it not be wanting in virtue, etc. (Huther). **πίστις** faith. Here it is to be understood subjectively of loyal adhesion to Christian teaching rather than of that teaching itself (Kelly). **ἀρετή** virtue, moral energy. In classical times the word meant the god-given power or ability to perform heroic deeds whether military deeds or athletic or artistic accomplishments or the conducting of one's life. The basic meaning of the word indicated the quality by which one stands out as being excellent. In respect to ethics Aristotle held that it was the right behavior or mean between two extremes. The Stoics connected it w. nature and taught that the essence of virtue was "living harmoniously w. nature" (s. Mayor; TDNT; GPT, 25; KP I, 530–531). **γνῶσις** knowing, knowledge.
■ **ἐγκράτεια** self-control, lit. "holding himself in" (RWP; s. also 6
Gal. 5:23). ■ **ταῦτα** "these things," i.e., "the possession of these 8
qualities and their continued increase" (Mayor). **πλεονάζοντα** pres. act. part. πλεονάζω to abound, to increase. In the classical writers the word is a term of disparagement, implying excess, to

be or to have more than enough, to exaggerate. But to fervent Christianity there can be no excess of good (Mayor). The pres. tense emphasizes the continual action. **ἀργός** not active, inactive, idle. **ἄκαρπος** not fruitful, unfruitful. **καθίστησιν** pres.
9 act. ind. to bring a person to a place, to make (s. Bigg). ■ **πάρεστιν** pres. act. ind. to be by, to be present. **τυφλός** blind. **μυωπάζων** pres. act. part. μυωπάζω to be short-sighted. The word refers to the involuntary contraction of the half-closed eyes of a short-sighted man and the word may be a correction or limitation of the idea of being blind (Mayor). On the other hand the meaning may be "shutting the eyes to the truth," the intention being to emphasize the responsibility of the believer (Kelly). **λήθη** forgetfulness. **λαβών** aor. act. part. λαμβάνω to take, to receive. Used in the expression "having received forgetfulness," i.e., "to forget." The part. could be causal "because he has forgot-
10 ten" (Bigg). **καθαρισμός** cleansing, purifying. **πάλαι** old. ■ **διό μᾶλλον** "wherefore the more" (Bigg). **σπουδάσατε** aor. act. imp. σπουδάζω to be in a hurry, to give diligence, to exert effort. The word stresses the urgency of his plea that they should determine to live for God (Green). **βέβαιος** firm, secure. Used w. the inf. in the sense of "to make firm," "to certify," "to confirm," "to attest." In the papyri the word was a t.t. for a legal guarantee (s. Mayor; BS, 107; TDNT; s. also 1 Cor. 1:6; Heb. 3:6). **κλῆσις** calling. **ἐκλογή** selection, election, choosing. **ποιεῖσθαι** pres. mid. inf. to do, to make. Used w. the adj. in the sense of "to make certain," "to give a guarantee." The holy life is the guarantee demonstrating the calling and election to others. The inf. is epexegetical or complementary explaining the verb "give diligence." **ποιοῦντες** pres. act. part. **οὐ μή** "never in any wise." **πταίσητε** aor. act. subj. **πταίω** to stumble. **ποτέ** ever,
11 never. ■ **πλουσίως** adv. richly. **ἐπιχορηγηθήσεται** fut. pass. ind. (s.v.5). **εἴσοδος** the way in, entrance.
12 ■ **μελλήσω** fut. act. ind. μέλλω to be about to, to be on the point of doing something. The verb is used w. the inf. to express the idea "I shall take care to remind you." This thought of the duty of reminding his readers appears again in verses 13 and 15, and in 3:1 (Mayor; s. also RWP). **ἀεί** always, ever. The word implies a prospect of frequent communication between him and them (Mayor). **καίπερ** "although." Used w. the part. to express concession. **εἰδότας** perf. act. part. **οἶδα** to know (s. ND, 344ff.). **ἐστηριγμένους** perf. pass. part. **στηρίζω** to set up, to formally establish, to strengthen. The perf. tense indicates the settled state or condition. The part. is used to express conces-
13 sion. **παρούσῃ** pres. act. part. (s.v.9). ■ **ἡγοῦμαι** pres. mid. ind.

to consider, to think. **ἐφ'ὅσον** "for as long as." **σκήνωμα** tent.
(For the concept of the "tent" picturing the body, s. 2 Cor. 5:1;
Mayor.) **διεγείρειν** pres. act. inf. to wake out of sleep, to stir up.
The prep. in compound is perfective "to stir up or wake up
thoroughly" (RWP; s. also Mayor). The inf. is used epexegetically to explain that which Peter considers to be "right."
ὑπόμνησις remembering, reminder. ■ **ταχινός** speedy, soon, 14
swiftly. The word here could mean either "suddenly" or "soon"
(Bigg). **ἀπόθεσις** putting off. The word could be used for the
idea of putting off clothing (s. Bigg; 1 Peter 3:21). **ἐδήλωσεν** aor.
act. ind. δηλόω to make clear, to make plain, to inform, to
reveal. The word is sometimes used of special revelations (1 Cor.
3:13; 1 Peter 1:11; s. also Kelly; TDNT). ■ **σπουδάσω** fut. act. 15
ind. (s.v.10). **καί** "even." Here he speaks of making provision for
them after his death (Mayor). **ἑκάστοτε** every time, on each
occasion, i.e., whenever there is need (Mayor). **ἔξοδος** departure, exodus. The word is used to indicate death (Bigg; s. also
Green). **ποιεῖσθαι** pres. mid. inf. to do, to make. Used w. the
noun "remembering" w. the meaning "to recall, to remember."
The inf. is used to complete the idea of the main verb "to make
an effort."

■ **σεσοφισμένοις** perf. pass. part. σοφίζω to make wise, 16
to be wise, to behave wisely, to cleverly contrive, to concoct
subtly, to reason out subtly (s. Mayor; Kelly; BAG). **μῦθος**
myth, fable. The word stood for mythical stories about gods, the
creation of the world, miraculous happenings, etc. (Kelly; s. also
CBB; TDNT; Bigg; Mayor; GPT, 120f.). Apparently the mockers of 3:3 spoke of the Christian hope of the glories to come as
resting on factitious prophecies (Mayor). **ἐξακολουθήσαντες**
aor. act. part. ἐξακολουθέω to follow after, to follow out, to rest
upon. (For the use of the verb in the papyri, s. MM.)
ἐγνωρίσαμεν aor. act. ind. γνωρίζω to make known.
παρουσία coming. The word was often used as a term for the
appearance of a god or the arrival of a king or ruler (s. Schelkle;
TDNT; 1 Thess. 2:19; 3:13). **ἐπόπτης** one who sees w. his eyes,
eyewitness. **γενηθέντες** aor. act. part. γίνομαι to become, to
be. **μεγαλειότης** majesty. The word means the majesty of the
divine and is used here to express the divine majesty as revealed
in the transfiguration of Jesus (Green). ■ **λαβών** aor. act. part. 17
(s.v.9). **τιμή** honor. Here the word denotes the exalted status
which the proclamation of sonship implies, while "glory" points
to the ethereal radiance of the transfigured Jesus, a radiance
which is a participation in that splendor of light which, according
to OT conceptions, belongs to God's very being (Kelly; s. also

Mayor). **ἐνεχθείσης** aor. pass. part. φέρω to bring, to bear. The word is used in the sense of "to make a word, speech, announcement, charge," and it is used of a divine proclamation, whether direct or indirect (BAG). **τοιόσδε** such, such as this, of this kind. The word refers to what follows and in the sense "so unique" (BAG). **μεγαλοπρεπής** magnificent, sublime, majestic. The word was used in the papyri as a term of honor and respect for political personalities. As preparations were made for the reception of a Roman senator in Egypt the instructions were "let him be received w. special magnificence" (MM; s. also Mayor). It was common for the Jews to use such statements when referring to God Himself (Schelkle). **ἀγαπητός** one who is loved, beloved. **εὐδόκησα** aor. act. ind. εὐδοκέω to be well-pleased, to be satisfied w. The word suggests the good pleasure of the Father
18 alighting and remaining on Jesus (Green). ■ **ἠκούσαμεν** aor.
act. ind. ἀκούω to hear. **ὄντες** pres. part. εἰμί. The part. is used
19 temporally "when we were on the holy mountain." ■
βεβαιότερος comp. "certain," "more certain," "more sure." (For this word, s.v.10.) Peter is saying that the holy Scriptures are more certain than experience. He is saying "if you don't believe me, go to the scriptures" (Green). **προφητικός** prophetical, that which pertains to the message of a prophet. The term "the prophetic word" was a current expression embracing the OT as a whole and not simply the prophets proper (Kelly). **καλῶς** adv. "well." **προσέχοντες** pres. act. part. προσέχω to hold the mind on something, to give heed to (RWP). The part. could be understood either as conditional "if you give heed" or it could express the manner or means of doing well "by giving heed to." **λύχνος** lamp. **φαίνοντι** pres. act. part. φαίνω to shine. The pres. tense emphasizes the continual shining. **αὐχμηρός** dry and parched, dirty, dark, murky. The word does not seem to imply absolute darkness, but dingy and dusky obscurity as contrasted w. "the brightness of Messiah's rising" (Isa. 60:3; Rom. 13:12) (Mayor; s. also RWP; MM). The word may also have the idea of dirty since that which is dirty is destitute of brightness and the thought may be that light shows up the dirt, and makes possible its removal (T; Green). **τόπος** place. The "darksome place" is the world as it at present exists, which in the NT is regularly characterized as darkness (Kelly). **ἕως οὗ** who "until," "until which time." The temporal conjuction w. the subj. is a usual construction for future time (RWP; s. also Mayor). **διαυγάσῃ** aor. act. subj. διαυγάζω to shine through, to dawn. The word is used of the first streaks of dawn breaking through the darkness (Mayor). **φωσφόρος** light bringing, light

bringer, the morning star, i.e., the planet Venus. The imagery lay
ready at hand, for the famous prophecy in Numbers 24:17 "there
shall come a star out of Jacob," was understood in Judaism as
pointing to the Messiah (Kelly) and the coming of the Messiah
is also compared to the dawn in Malachi 4:2 (Mayor). (For the
eschatological and messianic interpretation of Num. 24:17 in the
DDS, s. 1QM11, 6–7f.) In Greek and Roman times the term was
applied not only to the morning star (Venus), but also to royal
and divine persons (Green; s. also KP V, 1179–1180; MM).
ἀνατείλῃ aor. act. subj. ἀνατέλλω to rise, to arise (s. Matt.
5:45; James 1:11). ***ἐν ταῖς καρδίαις ὑμῶν*** "in your hearts."
This phrase could possibly be connected w. the part. of v. 20 w.
the meaning "knowing this first and foremost in your hearts . . ."
or the rising of the morning star in Christian hearts at the dawning of the day may mean the glow of anticipation in Christian
hearts when "the finds of the approaching Day are manifest to
Christians" (Green; s. also Mayor). ■ ***γινώσκοντες*** pres. act. 20
part. The part. could be causal or it continues the construction
of "you do well giving heed," and defines the spirit and feeling
w. which the Scriptures should be read, "recognizing this truth
first of all" (Mayor). ***πᾶσα*** all. Used w. the neg. in the sense of
"not even one" (BG, 151; s. also RG, 753). In the sing. the word
"all" without the article means "every" in a distributive sense,
i.e., "every single one" (s. BG, 61). ***προφητεία*** the message of
a prophet, prophecy (s.v. 19). ***γραφή*** writing, Scripture. Normally in the NT the word denotes the OT (Kelly). ***ἴδιος*** one's
own. It was the mark of a false prophet to speak "his own thing"
or "from himself" (Mayor). ***ἐπίλυσις*** releasing, solving, explaining, interpreting. The word almost comes to mean "inspiration" (Green; s. also Mayor; MM). The gen. (ablative) indicates
source. Peter is talking about the divine origin of Scripture, not
about its proper interpretation (Green). ***γίνεται*** pres. mid. ind.
to become. ■ ***ἠνέχθη*** aor. pass. ind. φέρω to bear. The word was 21
used of bearing or conveying or uttering a divine proclamation
and it could also have the sense of "to produce," "to bring forth"
(s. BAG; T). ***φερόμενοι*** pres. pass. part., pass. to be carried, to
be borne along. The word was used of a ship carried along by the
wind (s. Acts 27:15, 17) and the metaphor here is that the
prophets raised their sails and the Holy Spirit filled them and
carried their craft along in the direction He wished. Men spoke:
God spoke (Green). The part. expresses contemporaneous time.
ἐλάλησαν aor. act. ind. (For references to the inspiration of the
Scripture, s. 2 Tim. 3:16.)

Ch. 2

1 ■ **ἐγένοντο** aor. mid. ind. *γίνομαι* to become, to appear,
to arise. **καί** "also," "too," i.e., in addition to the holy men who
spoke the inspired Word of God there were also some in Israel
and now history was repeating itself (Green). **ψευδοπροφήτης**
false prophets. The compound in the word may either mean
falsely named, a "sham" or "counterfeit," or it may mean falsely
doing the work implied, i.e., "to speak falsely," and either meaning would suit the word, for to prophesy falsely in the narrow
sense was at any rate one of the marks of a pretended prophet
(Mayor). **ἔσονται** fut. *εἰμί*. **ψευδοδάσκαλος** false teacher (s.
the discussion in Mayor, CLXVII-CLXXX). **οἵτινες** who, i.e.,
who belong to a particular class or group. **παρεισάξουσιν** fut.
act. ind. *παρεισάγω* to bring into alongside of, to smuggle in.
The word may signify to bring in secretly w. the 1st prep. in
compound giving the idea of creeping along under some sort of
cover (Bigg; s. also Gal. 2:4). **αἵρεσις** heresy, false teaching.
ἀπώλεια destruction. **ἀγοράσοντα** aor. act. part. *ἀγοράζω* to
buy at the market place, to buy. **δεσπότης** lord, master, one who
holds authority over another. **ἀρνούμενοι** pres. mid. part.
ἀρνέομαι to say no to, to deny. The heretics were professing
Christians (RWP). **ἐπάγοντες** pres. act. part. *ἐπάγω* to bring
2 upon. **ταχινός** quick, sudden, soon. ■ **ἐξακολουθήσουσιν** fut.
act. ind. *ἐξακολουθέω* to follow, to follow after (s. 2 Peter 1:16).
αὐτῶν "their." The pron. refers to the false teachers, whose bad
example will be largely followed (Mayor). **ἀσέλγεια** unbridled
living. The pl. may denote either different forms, or repeated
habitual acts of lasciviousness (Bigg; s. also 1 Peter 4:3). **δι' οὓς**
"because of whom." The reference is clearly to the many back-
sliders (Kelly). **ὁδὸς τῆς ἀληθείας** "the way of truth." The
phrase refers to the teaching of the truth, the correct teaching,
the correct religion (Schelkle). Here the expression denotes the
Christian message and way of life which are inevitably brought
into discredit when their adherents identify themselves w. pat-
ently immoral courses (Kelly). **βλασφημηθήσεται** fut. pass.
ind. *βλασφημέω* to injure the reputation of someone, to
3 defame, to blaspheme. ■ **πλεονεξία** uncontrolled greed, insatiable greed (s. TDNT; NTW, 97; Rom. 1:29; 2 Cor. 9:5; Col. 3:5;
1 Thess. 2:5). **πλαστός** made up, factitious. The word was used
in the papyri of a "forged" contract (MM; s. also Mayor).
ἐμπορεύσονται fut. mid. ind. *ἐμπορεύομαι* to travel as a merchant, to travel on business, to carry on business, to trade in, to
cheat, to make a gain of, to exploit (Kelly; s. also Mayor). **κρίμα**
the decision of a judgment, verdict, condemnation, judgment.

ἔκπαλαι for a long time, from of old. **ἀργεῖ** pres. act. ind. not
working, to be idle. The judgment is not idle, but already active
in the punishment of other offenders, and gathering up for these
false teachers (Mayor). **νυστάζει** pres. act. ind. to nod, to sleep
(s. Matt. 25:5).
■ **ἁμαρτησάντων** aor. act. part. **ἐφείσατο** aor. mid. ind. 4
φείδομαι w. the gen. to spare. The ind. is used in a first-class
conditional clause which assumes the reality of the condition.
σιρός underground pit. The word is properly a pit for the storage
of grain but was used for a large bin for holding edible roots or
of a pit made for trapping a wolf (Mayor). **ζόφος** dark, darkness.
ταρταρώσας aor. act. part. **ταρταρόω** to confine in Tartarus.
Tartarus was the name in classical mythology for the subter-
ranean abyss in which rebellious gods and other such beings as
the Titans were punished. The word was, however, taken over
into Hellenistic Judaism and used in the book of Enoch (Enoch
20:2) in connection w. fallen angels. It is the angel Uriel who is
the rule of Tartarus (s. Kelly; Mayor; Bigg; KP V, 530–531).
παρέδωκεν aor. act. ind. **παραδίδωμι** to deliver over, to hand
over, to confine. **κρίσις** judging. **τηρουμένους** pres. pass. part.
τηρέω to keep, to guard. ■ **ἀρχαῖος** ancient. The gen. is used 5
as the object of the verb "to spare." **ὄγδοος** eighth, i.e., "Noah
w. seven others," "he being the eighth" (BD, 130). **δικαιοσύνη**
righteousness. The word denotes here the just or upright moral
behavior (Kelly). **κῆρυξ** preacher, herald (s. 1 Tim. 2:7).
ἐφύλαξεν aor. act. ind. φυλάσσω to guard, to watch over, to
protect. **κατακλυσμός** flood, deluge. **ἀσεβής** ungodly, impious (s. Rom. 4:5; 1 Tim. 1:9). **ἐπάξας** aor. act. part. ἐπάγω to
bring upon. The part. is used temporally expressing contemporaneous action. ■ **Σοδόμων καὶ Γομόρρας** gen. of apposition 6
(s. BD, 92; Mayor). **τεφρώσας** aor. act. part. **τεφρόω** to reduce
to ashes, or perhaps here better "to cover w. ashes" (s. Mayor).
The Roman historian Dio Cassius used the word to describe the
inner part of Mount Vesuvius which was constantly growing
brittle and "being reduced to ashes" so that the center section
in the course of time settled and became concave (Dio Cassius,
Roman History, LXVI, 21, 2). **καταστροφῇ** overturning, destruction, instrumental dat. **κατέκρινεν** aor. act. ind.
κατακρίνω to pronounce a verdict against someone, to sentence to punishment, to condemn. The verb continues the condition found in the first-class conditional clause beginning w. v. 4
(s. RWP). **ὑπόδειγμα** pattern, example. **μελλόντων** pres. act.
part. μέλλω to be about to. Used w. the inf. to form the fut.
ἀσεβεῖν pres. act. inf. to live ungodly, to be impious (s.v.5). (For

the variant reading "ungodly men" which would give the sense "unto ungodly men of things about to be," i.e., "of things in store for them," s. RWP; TC, 702.) **τεθεικώς** perf. act. part. *τίθημι* to place, to make, to constitute. The perf. tense emphasizes that
7 the example still has lasting validity. ■ **καταπονούμενον** pres. pass. part. *καταπονέω* to wear down through exhausting work, to trouble greatly. **ἄθεσμος** lawless. It pictures them as being rebels against the law not of Moses, but of nature and conscience (Bigg). **ἐν ἀσελγείᾳ** "in unbridled living" (s.v.2). The prepositional phrase indicates the sphere in which their conduct displayed itself. **ἀναστροφή** behavior, conduct (s. 1 Peter 1:15).
8 **ἐρρύσατο** aor. mid. ind. *ῥυομαι* to rescue. ■ **βλέμμα** sight. The word is generally subjective, where the eye reveals to outsiders the inner feeling of man. The idea would be "the righteousness of man showed itself in his shrinking from the sights and sounds which met him on every side": lit. "righteous in look and in hearing he tortured himself at their lawless deeds while he lived among them" (Mayor). **ἀκοή** hearing. **ἐγκατοικῶν** pres. act. part. *ἐγκατοικέω* to live or dwell among. The part. is used temporally describing contemporary action. **ἄνομος** lawless. **ἐβασάνιζεν** impf. ind. act. *βασανίζω* to torture, to torment. The impf. pictures the continual action of the past time. The rabbis generally viewed Lot as one who despised God and was given over to immorality (s. SB III, 769–771). Compare however the statements recorded in "the Genesis Apocryphon" (1QGENAP, XXI 5–7) "pasturing his herds he (Lot) reached Sodom and he bought himself a house in Sodom and settled in it. But I remained in the hill country of Bethel, and it grieved me that my nephew Lot had parted from me" (s. *Aramaic Text from Qumran* w. translations and annotations by B. Jongeling, C.J. Labuschagne, A.S. Van Der Voude [Leiden: E.J. Brill, 1976],
9 105). ■ **εὐσεβής** God-fearing, godly, devout (s. 2 Peter 1:3). **κολαζομένους** pres. pass. part. *κολάζω* to punish. The original sense of the word was "to cut short" and was used of "pruning" a tree and later took on the meaning "to correct" and then "to punish" and was also used of the punishment of slaves as well as divine punishment (s. BAG; MM; Kelly; s. also Acts 4:21).
10 ■ **μάλιστα** especially. **ὀπίσω** w. the gen. "after." The phrase "them that walk after the flesh" suggests sodomy (Green). **ἐπιθυμία** strong desire, lust, passion. **μιασμός** pollution. The gen. could be obj. gen. in the sense of "in their hankering after pollution," but if it is subjective, it would mean "in lust which pollutes" (Kelly). **πορευομένους** pres. mid. part. *πορεύομαι* to walk, to go. **κυριότης** lordship. **καταφρονοῦντας** pres. act.

part. καταφρονέω to think down upon, to despise. The false teachers despised the power and majesty of the Lord (Bigg).

ὁ τολμητής one who dares, one who is brazen, "headstrong daredevils," "shameless and headstrong." The word smacks of the reckless daring that defies God and man (Mayor; Green). **αὐθάδης** self-pleasing, arrogant. The word is used for an obstinate fellow who is determined to please himself at all costs (Green; RWP; s. also Titus 1:7). **δόξαι** "glorious ones." The word could refer to angelic beings, either those heavenly beings in God's service, or celestial beings, probably the fallen angels (Kelly). **τρέμουσιν** pres. act. ind. to tremble, to be afraid to. The verb is completed by the complementary part. rather than by an inf. (RWP). **βλασφημοῦντες** pres. act. part. to defame, to blaspheme. ■ **ὅπου** "where," "in a case in which," "whereas," "see- 11
ing that" (Mayor). **ἰσχύς** strength, indwelling strength (RWP; s. also Eph. 1:19). **μείζων** comp. μέγας great, comp. greater, superior. **ὄντες** pres. part. εἰμί. The part. is used concessively, i.e., "although." **φέρουσιν** pres. act. ind. to bear, to bring. The pres. tense emphasizes a continual attitude which is negated by the neg. particle. **βλάσφημος** defamation, railing, blaspheming.
■ **ἄλογος** without reason, irrational. They have physical, but not 12
intellectual life; they are no better than the brutes that perish (Bigg). **ζῷον** living creature, animal, beast. **γεγεννημένα** perf. pass. part. γεννάω to bear, pass. to be born. **φυσικός** natural, pertaining to nature, in accordance w. nature, here used in the sense of "mere creatures of instinct, born to be caught and killed" (BAG). **ἅλωσις** capture. **φθορά** corruption, destruction. The combination of the verb w. the noun makes it almost certain that destruction is meant (Bigg). **ἀγνοοῦσιν** to be without knowledge, to be ignorant. These have no more knowledge than brute beasts would have (Kelly). **φθαρήσονται** fut. pass. ind. φθείρω to corrupt, to decay, to destroy, to devastate (s. Mayor, 175ff.; s. also 2 Peter 1:4). ■ **ἀδικούμενοι** pres. mid. or pass. 13
part. ἀδικέω to commit injustice, to do wrong, mid. or pass. to suffer injustice, to be damaged, to be harmed (s. Kelly). The phrase "being defrauded of the wages of fraud" has been vindicated by an example from the papyri which reads "when this has been done [in the context, 'when a receipt has been given'], we shall not be defrauded" (Green). **μισθός** wage, recompense. **ἀδικία** unrighteousness, fraud. **ἡδονή** pleasure. In the NT the word always means sensual gratification (Bigg). **ἡγούμενοι** pres. mid. part. ἡγέομαι to consider, to reckon, to count. **τρυφή** indulgence, reveling. Daylight debauchery was frowned on even in degenerate Roman society (Green; s. also Kelly). Dio

Chrysostom represents Alexander the Great as feeling that other men "had all been well-nigh ruined in soul by luxury and idleness and were slaves of money and pleasure" (DC IV, 6). **σπίλος** spot, blot, a disfiguring spot (Bigg; s. also Eph. 5:27). **μῶμος** blemish. The accusation is one of riotous misbehavior at banquets, and since the correspondents participated in these, it would seem to be some kind of community celebration (Kelly). **ἐντρυφῶντες** pres. act. part. ἐντρυφάω to live in luxury, to revel. **ἀπάτη** deception. Perhaps the meaning here is in the sense of "dissipations" and the transition from "guile" or "deception" to "sinful pleasure" was natural and easy (Kelly). **συνευωχούμενοι** pres. mid. part. συνευωχέομαι to feed well, to feed abundantly, to eat together, to feast w. (s. RWP). The part. denotes the circumstances of the preceding action (Mayor).
14 ■ **ἔχοντες** pres. act. part. **μεστός** full. **μοιχαλίς** adultress. The connotation is probably more general and the meaning is "loose woman" (Kelly). **ἀκατάπαυστος** without succession, not pausing, "unable to stop" (RWP). **δελεάζοντες** pres. act. part. δελεάζω to trap by using bait, to ensnare. **ἀστήρικτος** without firmness, unstable. They lack a firm foundation in faith and discipline, and so are liable to be unsettled by scandalous conduct or erroneous teaching (Kelly; s. also Green). **γεγυμνασμένην** perf. pass. part. γυμνάζω to exercise, to do bodily exercise, to be familiar w. The gen. used after the part. denotes familiarity w. anything (Bigg). **κατάρα** curse. The Hebraic expression "children of curse" means "accursed creatures" (Kelly; s. also Bigg), i.e., "God's curse on them." These men rest under the curse of God, as do all who fail to trust in Christ who
15 bore man's curse (Green). ■ **καταλείποντες** pres. act. part. καταλείπω to leave off, to abandon. **εὐθύς** straight. Upright conduct is pictured in the Bible as a "straight path" (Kelly). **ἐπλανήθησαν** aor. pass. ind. πλανάω to go astray, to follow the wrong path. **ἐξακολουθήσαντες** aor. act. part. ἐξακολουθέω to follow after (s. 2 Peter 1:16). **ἀδικίας** unrighteousness, fraud. The gen. could be subjective or obj. gen., i.e., either reward prompted by fraud or reward which has fraud or unrighteousness as its object. **ἠγάπησεν** aor. act. ind. ἀγαπάω.
16 ■ **ἔλεγξις** rebuke. **ἔσχεν** aor. act. ind. ἔχω to have, aor. to get. **παρανομία** beyond the law, transgression. The word indicates not a general defiance of law, but rather a breech of a particular law (Mayor). **ὑποζύγιον** "being under a yoke." The term was used for a beast of burden, then specifically for a donkey (s. BS, 160f.). **ἄφωνος** not having a sound, speechless, dumb. **φθεγξάμενον** aor. mid. part. φθέγγομαι to make a sound, to

speak. The verb is esp. used of a portentous prophetic utterance
(Bigg). **ἐκώλυσεν** aor. act. ind. κωλύω to hinder. **παραφρονία**
beyond understanding, madness. It is being beside one's wits
(RWP). The idea of the v. is "he who was bribed by Balak to
curse Israel was rebuked for his own disobedience by the disobedience of the ass and thus hindered from receiving the promised
reward" (Mayor).
■ **πηγή** spring. **ἄνυδρος** waterless. **ὁμίχλη** fog, mist. 17
λαῖλαψ storm, squall (s. Mark 4:37; Luke 8:23). **ἐλαυνόμεναι**
perf. pass. part. ἐλαύνω to drive, to blow. **τετήρηται** perf. pass.
ind. ■ **ὑπέρογκος** swelling, inflated. The word means "unnatu- 18
rally swollen." They used big, ponderous words in their dis-
courses. Ostentatious verbosity was their weapon to ensnare the
unwary and licentiousness was the bait on their hook (Green).
ματαιότης vanity, futility. Their words amount to nothing of
significance w. the gen. being a descriptive gen. (Green).
φθεγγόμενοι pres. mid. part. (s.v. 16). **ὀλίγως** adv. The word
can mean either "very recently" or "in a small degree," i.e.,
"slightly," "a little" (Kelly; Mayor). **ἀποφεύγοντας** pres. act.
part. ἀποφεύγω to escape from. **πλάνη** error. The word stands
specifically for idolatry or paganism (Kelly; s. also TDNT).
ἀναστρεφομένους pres. mid. part. ἀναστρέφομαι to conduct
one's life, to live. ■ **ἐλευθερία** freedom, liberty. 19
ἐπαγγελλόμενοι pres. mid. part. ἐπαγγέλομαι to promise.
ὑπάρχοντες pres. act. part. ὑπάρχω to be, to exist. The word
denotes continuance of an antecedent state or condition (AS; s.
also 2 Cor. 12:16). **φθορά** corruption, destruction (s.v. 12).
ἥττηται perf. pass. ind. ἡττάομαι to be inferior, to be defeated,
to be overcome. **δεδούλωται** perf. pass. ind. to enslave. The
imagery derived directly from the ancient practice of enslaving
an enemy defeated in battle and so made prisoner (Kelly). ■ 20
ἀποφυγόντες aor. act. part. ἀποφεύγω to escape from.
μίασμα pollution. **ἐπίγνωσις** recognition, knowledge.
ἐμπλακέντες aor. pass. part. ἐμπλέκω to enweave, to entangle.
γέγονεν perf. act. ind. γίνομαι. **χείρων** (comp.) worse. ■ 21
κρείττων (comp.) better. **ἐπεγνωκέναι** perf. act. inf.
ἐπιγινώσκω to know (s. 2 Peter 1:3). The inf. is used epexegetically to explain that which is "better." **ἐπιγνοῦσιν** aor. act. part.
ἐπιγινώσκω. The dat. pl. agrees w. the pron. "for them"
(RWP). **ὑποστρέψαι** fut. act. inf. ὑποστρέφω to turn back.
παραδοθείσης aor. pass. part. παραδίδωμι to deliver over, to
commit. The word was almost a t.t. for the passing on of tradition
(s. TDNT). ■ **συμβέβηκεν** perf. act. ind. συμβαίνω to happen. 22
The dramatic perf. treats what is certain to befall as already

accomplished (Kelly). **παροιμία** proverb. **κύων** dog. **ἐπιστρέψας** aor. act. part. ἐπιστρέφω to turn to. **ἐξέραμα** that which is thrown out, vomit (s. Prov. 26:11). **ὗς** pig, hog. **λουσαμένη** aor. mid. part. λούομαι to wash one's self. The word means "having bathed itself in mud" (Bigg). **κυλισμός** wallowing. **βόρβορος** mud, mire, filth, slime (BAG). Epictetus says of those who refuse to keep themselves clean "go and talk to a pig, that he may wallow no more in mud!" (Epictetus, IV. XI. 29).

Ch. 3

1 ■ **δεύτερος** second. **διεγείρω** pres. act. ind. to awaken, to
stir up (s. 2 Peter 1:13). **ὑπόμνησις** remembering, reminder.
εἰλικρινής pure, unmixed, sincere. The word was used of things
unmixed, e.g., air as well as ethical purity (Mayor; s. Phil. 1:10).
διάνοια thinking, understanding. The phrase was used by Plato
to mean "pure reason," uncontaminated by the seductive influ-
2 ence of the senses (Green; s. also GPT, 37). ■ **μνησθῆναι** aor.
pass. inf. μιμνῄσκομαι to remind. The inf. is used to express
purpose, i.e., it states the purpose of his writing. The inf. could
also be taken as epexegetical defining the verb "to stir up" (May-
or). **προειρημένων** perf. pass. part. προλέγω to say before.
ἐντολή commandment. The construction of the gen. is not entirely clear, but probably could be translated "of the command-
3 ment of the Lord transmitted by the apostles" (BD, 93). ■
γινώσκοντες pres. act. part. The part. could be understood here
as having the force of an imp. (s. Mayor). **ἐλεύσονται** fut. mid.
ind. ἔρχομαι to come. **ἐμπαιγμονή** scoffing, making fun of
through mockery. **ἐμπαίκτης** one who makes fun through
mockery, mocker, scoffer. The phrase "mockers w. (in) mockery," i.e., "scoffers shall come w. scoffing" is a strong Hebraic
influence on the analogy of the Heb. inf. abs. (s. Bigg; MT, Style,
142f.). **ἐπιθυμία** strong desire, lust, passion. **πορευόμενοι** pres.
4 mid. part. πορεύομαι to walk, to come. ■ **λέγοντες** pres. act.
part. **ποῦ** "where?"; i.e., "what has become of?" This is a tradi-
tional formula for expressing skepticism (Kelly). **ἐπαγγελία**
promise. **παρουσία** coming (s. 2 Peter 1:16). **ἐκοιμήθησαν**
aor. pass. ind. κοιμάομαι to sleep, to fall asleep. The term is
used as a metaphor for dying (Kelly). **διαμένει** pres. act. ind. to
remain, to remain through, to continue. The pres. tense emphasizes the continual unbroken action. **ἀρχή** beginning. **κτίσις**
creation. They maintain that God's promise is unreliable, and
that God's universe is a stable, unchanging system where events
5 like the parousia just do not happen (Green). ■ **λανθάνει** pres.

act. ind. to escape notice of, to be hidden from, i.e., "for they shut their eyes to this fact that" (Mayor; s. RWP; Kelly). **θέλοντας** pres. act. part. The part. has here almost an adverbial sense (RWP). **ἦσαν** impf. εἰμί. **ἔκπαλαι** for a long time, long ago (s. 2 Peter 2:3). **συνεστῶσα** perf. act. part. συνίστημι to
consist (s. Col. 1:17). ■ **κατακλυσθείς** aor. pass. part. 6
κατακλύζω to surge over completely, to inundate, to flood (s. 2 Peter 2:5). **ἀπώλετο** aor. mid. ind. ἀπόλλυμι to ruin, to
destroy. ■ **νῦν** "now," "present." **τεθησαυρισμένοι** perf. pass. 7
part. θησαυρίζω to treasure up, to store up, to reserve. The sense of the metaphor here is "to set apart for," "destined for" (Mayor). The perf. tense emphasizes the completed state or condition. **πῦρ** fire. **τηρούμενοι** pres. pass. part. τηρέω to guard, to watch. **κρίσις** judging. **ἀπώλεια** ruin, destruction. **ἀσεβής** ungodly, impious (s. 2 Peter 2:5; Rom. 4:5; 1 Tim. 1:9).
■ **λανθανέτω** pres. act. imp. 3rd pers. sing. (s.v.5). **ἔτος** 8
year. ■ **βραδύνει** to be slow, to delay. (For examples in the 9
papyri, s. MM.) **βραδύτης** slowness, delay. **ἡγοῦνται** pres. mid. ind. to consider, to think, to count, i.e., as if delay sprang from impotence or unwillingness to perform (Bigg). **μακροθυμεῖ** pres. act. ind. to be longsuffering and patient. It is the Spirit which could take revenge if He liked, but utterly refuses to do so (s. NTW, 84; TDNT; Rom. 2:4). **βουλόμενος** pres. mid. part. βούλομαι to wish, to desire, to want. **ἀπολέσθαι** aor. mid. inf. ἀπόλλυμι to perish. **μετάνοια** change of thinking, repentence (s. Matt. 3:2). **χωρῆσαι** aor. act. inf. χωρέω to make room, to have room for. The apparent delay of God is rooted in the fact that His desire is that all have room, i.e., have opportunity for
repentence. ■ **ἥξει** fut. act. ind. ἥκω to come. The verb is placed 10
for strong emphasis at the beginning of the sentence (Kelly). **ῥοιζηδόν** adv. w. a hissing or crackling sound. The word is onomatopoeic, expressing the whizzing sound produced by rapid motion through the air and was used of shrill rushing sounds, the hissing of a snake, the whirr of a bird's wings, the hurtling of an arrow and is then used for the rushing movement itself or the accompanying crash or roar. Here probably the roaring of flame is meant (Bigg; Mayor). **παρελεύσονται** fut. mid. ind. παρέρχομαι to pass by, to go away, to pass away. **στοιχεῖον** "things arranged in a row," e.g., the letters of the alphabet, or the elements of nature. Here it clearly means physical elements (Bigg). It could refer to the elements of earth, air, fire, and water or the heavenly bodies such as sun, moon, and stars (Green), or it may refer to the atomic particles which are the basic structure of nature. **καυσούμενα** pres. mid. part. καυσόομαι to burn, to

melt. The word was employed by medical writers to express feverish heat. It may be intended to denote a conflagration arising from internal heat, such as a volcano (Mayor). **λυθήσεται** fut. pass. ind. λύω to loosen, to disintegrate. The word is used of breaking up a structure as in John 2:44, as well as of dissolving a compound into its elements (Mayor). **εὑρεθήσεται** fut. pass. ind. "will be found." The meaning here may be that the earth and man's achievements will be discovered and exposed to divine
11 judgment (s. Kelly; Mayor). ■ **λυομένων** pres. pass. part. The part. is used in a gen. abs. construction w. a causal meaning. The pres. tense is either the futuristic pres. or the process of dissolution is pictured (RWP). **ποταπός** what sort of, what kind of. In the context the word hints that great things are expected of the readers; "how outstandingly excellent" (Kelly). **δεῖ** used w. the acc. and the inf. "it is necessary." **ὑπάρχειν** pres. act. inf. to be, to exist as (s. 2 Peter 2:19). **ἀναστροφή** walk, life's practice, manner of living, way of life. **εὐσέβεια** godliness, a life of piety,
12 respect, and reverence (s. 1 Peter 1:3). ■ **προσδοκῶντας** pres. act. part. προσδοκάω to await expectantly, to look forward to. **σπεύδοντας** pres. act. part. σπεύδω to hasten, to accelerate, to desire, to be eager for (Mayor; s. also Kelly; Bigg). **δι' ἥν** "because of which." The destruction takes place because God's "day" has arrived (Green). **πυρούμενοι** pres. pass. part. πυρόω to set on fire, pass. to be on fire, to burn. **τήκεται** pres. pass. ind. τήκω to melt, to make liquid, pass. to be melted. The pres. tense
13 is futuristic (Bigg). ■ **ἐπάγγελμα** that which was promised, promise. **κατοικεῖ** pres. act. ind. to settle down, to dwell, to be at home at (s. Rev. 21:1).

14 ■ **ταῦτα** "these things," i.e., a freshly created heaven and earth where God's will is paramount (Kelly). **προσδοκῶντες** pres. act. part. to earnestly await, to expect (s.v.12). **σπουδάσατε** aor. act. imp. σπουδάζω to give diligence, to make an effort (s. 1 Peter 1:10). **ἄσπιλος** spotless. **ἀμώμητος** blameless. **αὐτῷ** "him." The dat. may be taken w. the adj., "spotless and blameless in His sight," or w. the inf. "to be found by Him" (Bigg). **εὑρεθῆναι** aor. pass. inf. The inf. is used to complete the verb "make an effort," "give diligence." **ἐν εἰρήνῃ** "in peace." This describes the state of reconciliation w. God
15 which the restored sinner enjoys (Kelly). ■ **μακροθυμία** long-suffering, patient endurance (s. Gal. 5:22; RAC IX, 254f.). **ἡγεῖσθε** pres. mid. imp. to consider, to count, followed by the double acc. **ὁ ἀγαπητὸς ἡμῶν ἀδελφός** "our beloved brother." The phrase refers not simply to a fellow Christian but in this case to a fellow apostle (Kelly). **δοθεῖσαν** aor. pass. part. **δίδωμι** to

give. The pass. is a theological or divine pass. indicating that God is the subject (s. BG, 76). **ἔγραψεν** aor. act. ind. Peter may be referring to Paul's letter to the Romans or he may be alluding
simply to Paul's constant teaching in all his letters (Green). ■ 16
λαλῶν pres. act. part. **δυσνόητος** difficult to understand, hard to understand. **ἀμαθής** untaught. The word brings out the moral value of teaching, of trained habits of reflection, of disciplined good sense (Bigg). **ἀστήρικτος** unstable (s. 2 Peter 2:14). **στρεβλοῦσιν** pres. act. ind. to twist, to torture. The fig. sense seems to flow from the notion of twisting or warping rather than that of torturing on the rack (Mayor). **λοιπός** rest. **γραφή** Scripture. Peter gives a very high place to Paul's writings. They are
placed alongside "the other scriptures" (Green). ■ 17
προγινώσκοντες pres. act. part. **προγινώσκω** to know beforehand, to know in advance. The part. could be causal. **φυλάσσεσθε** pres. mid. imp. **φυλάσσω** to guard, to keep watch, mid. to guard one's self. **ἄθεσμος** lawless (s. 2 Peter 2:7). **πλάνη** error. **συναπαχθέντες** aor. pass. part. **συναπάγω** to lead away together, to carry away together. **ἐκπέσητε** aor. act. subj. **ἐκπίπτω** to fall out of, to dislodge. The subj. is used in a neg. purpose clause. **στηριγμός** fixedness, firmness, steadfastness, firm stance. It connotes fixity as opposed to movement, and is used in conscience contrast to "unstable" above, to characteristic of the heretics and their dupes (II.14). Stability, or being firmly established in the faith, is clearly a quality which he
greatly esteems (Kelly). ■ **αὐξάνετε** pres. act. imp. **αὐξάνω** to 18
grow, to advance. **ἐν** "in." The prep. could express either the sphere of growth or the means by which one grows. **γνῶσις** knowledge.

1 JOHN

Ch. 1

1 **ἦν** impf. εἰμί. **ἀρχή** beginning. The "beginning" here could
refer to the beginning of creation or better, beginning in the abs.
sense and emphasizes the preexistence and divine character
(Schnackenburg; s. also Marshall). **ἀκηκόαμεν** perf. act. ind.
ἀκούω to hear. **ἑωράκαμεν** perf. act. ind. ὁράω to see. The
perf. tenses express an act in the past w. lasting results. It indicates that a revelation has been made in terms which men can
understand and the results are abiding (Marshall; Brooke; s. also
Abbott, 344). The 1st pers. pl. "we" could mean the writer of the
epistle and his companions, but it more probably means "we all,"
"we disciples of Christ" (Abbott, 311; s. esp. Schnackenburg,
52–58). **ἐθεασάμεθα** aor. mid. ind. θεάομαι to look at, to
behold. The verb expresses the calm, intent, continuous contemplation of an object which remains before the spectator (Westcott; s. also John 1:14). **ἐψηλάφησαν** aor. act. ind. ψηλαφάω
to grope or feel after in order to find, like a blind man or one who
is in the dark; hence, "to handle, to touch." The idea of searching
sometimes disappears altogether. Here it naturally suggests all
the evidence available for sense perception other than hearing
and sight (Brooke). **ζωή** life. The gen. could indicate the content
of the word or it could be gen. of quality and indicate "the living
word" or it could indicate the object; i.e., "the life-giving word"
2 (s. Stott; Marshall). ■ **ἐφανερώθη** aor. pass. ind. φανερόω to
make clear, to manifest, pass. to be revealed. The verb is used
of the revelation of the Lord at His first coming and indicates
the Incarnation (Westcott; Schnackenburg). **μαρτυροῦμεν**
pres. act. ind. μαρτυρέω to be a witness, to testify. The pres.
tense indicates the continuing abiding action or state.
ἀπαγγέλλομεν to report, to declare, to report w. reference to
the source from which a message comes (Brooke). The word "to
witness, to testify" is a word of experience and this word "to
declare" indicates the authority of commission (Stott) and both
words emphasize that the message rests on eyewitnesses (Bultmann). Verse 2 forms a parenthesis which the writer inserted to
make clear beyond all possibility of mistake that the life to which

John bears witness was revealed by God in the historical person
of Jesus (Marshall). ■ **ἀπαγγέλλομεν** pres. act. ind. This is the 3
main verb of the sentence which was started in v.1. **κοινωνία**
fellowship. The word indicates the setting aside of private interest and desires and the joining in w. another or others for common purposes (s. TDNT; CBB; RAC IX, 1100–1145). **ἔχητε**
pres. act. subj. The subj. is used to express purpose. ■ **ταῦτα** 4
"these things." The reference could be to the entire contents of
the letter (Brooke; Marshall) or it refers to the apostolic message
in vv. 1–3 (Westcott). **ᾖ** subj. **εἰμί. πεπληρωμένη** perf. pass.
part. **πληρόω** to fill, to fulfill, to make full. The part. is used as
a periphrastic perf. pass. subj. stressing the state of completion
in the purpose clause (RWP).

■ **ἀγγελία** report, message. The word may suggest that the 5
message contains a conception of God which men could not
have formed for themselves without His help. It is a "revelation
and not a discovery" (Brooke). **ἀναγγέλλομεν** pres. act. ind. to
announce. The prep. in compound has the additional idea of
bringing the tidings "up to" or "back" to the person receiving
them. It is the recipient who is prominent in this verb (Westcott).
■ **ἐάν** "if." The five conditional clauses introduced by this word 6
are followed by the aor. subj. or the pres. subj. In each case the
condition is a supposition which is possible "if this should happen" (s. Abbott, 371–374; Marshall). **εἴπωμεν** aor. act. subj.
λέγω "if we should say." In vv. 6, 8, 10, the phrase introduces
three statements of false doctrine (Abbott, 372). **περιπατῶμεν**
pres. act. subj. to walk about, to conduct one's life. The word is
comparable to the Heb. word "to walk" (s. TDOT) and is used
in the sense of the practical, ethical dealing (Schnackenburg).
■ **περιπατῶμεν** pres. act. subj. The conditional clauses in vv. 7
7, 9 introduce the hypothesis of pres. and continuous Christian
life, "on the supposition that we are walking or confessing"
(Abbott, 372). "Walking in the light" is the conscious and sus-
tained endeavor to live a life in conformity w. the revelation of
God, who is "light," esp. as that revelation has been made finally
and completely in Jesus Christ, and this is the necessary condition of fellowship (Brooke). **κοινωνία** fellowship (s.v.3).
ἀλλήλων (gen.) "w. one another." Although the phrase could
mean fellowship between God and man, John's general use indicates that he takes the fellowship of Christians as the visible sign
correlative of fellowship w. God (Westcott; Schnackenburg).
καθαρίζει pres. act. ind. to cleanse. The verbs suggest that God
does more than forgive; He erases the stain of sin and the pres.
tense shows that it is a continuous process (Stott). (For a study

of the term "blood" in the Scripture, s. APC, 108–124; A.M. Stibbs, *The Meaning of the Word "Blood" in Scripture* [London:
9 The Tyndale Press, 1962].) ■ **ὁμολογῶμεν** pres. act. subj. ὁμολογέω to say the same thing, to agree, to concede, to admit, to confess. (For a study of the word, s. ECC, 13–20; TDNT.) **δίκαιος** righteous, just. **ἀφῇ** aor. act. subj. ἀφίημι to release, to forgive (s. TDNT; CBB). The subj. clause expresses the way in which God expresses His faithfulness and justice and it is equivalent to an inf. of result (Marshall; s. also BD, 198). **καθαρίσῃ**
10 aor. act. subj. **ἀδικία** unrighteousness. ■ **ἡμαρτήκαμεν** perf. act. ind. ἁμαρτάνω to sin. **ψεύστης** one who lies, liar.

Ch. 2

1 ■ **τεκνίον** little child, small child. The dim. form is used expressing affection "dear child" (Marshall). **ἁμάρτητε** aor. act. subj. The aor. tense indicates the thought of a single act, not that of a state (Westcott). The subj. is used in a neg. purpose clause. **παράκλητος** helper. In rabbinical literature the word could indicate one who offers legal aid or one who intercedes on behalf of someone else. In the pres. context the word undoubtedly signifies an "advocate" or "counsel for the defense" in a legal context (Marshall; s. also Schnackenburg; Brooke; John 14:16).
2 ■ **ἱλασμός** satisfaction, propitiation. The idea is placating the wrath of God and the pres. passage would then be that Jesus propitiates God w. respect to our sins (Marshall; s. also Stott;
3 Rom. 3:25). ■ **ἐγνώκαμεν** perf. act. ind. γινώσκω. The tenses here are significant as we learn to perceive more and more clearly that our knowledge is genuine through its abiding results in a growing willingness to obey (Brooke). **ἐντολή** commandment. **τηρῶμεν** pres. act. subj. τηρέω to guard, to keep. The word has the idea of observing or holding something fast in memory (Schnackenburg). The subj. is used in a third-class con-
4 ditional clause which views the condition as a possibility. ■
5 **λέγων** pres. act. part. **ψεύστης** one who lies, liar. ■ **τηρῇ** pres. act. subj. The subj. is used w. the generalized rel. pron. w. the meaning "whoever keeps." **ἀληθῶς** adv. truly. **ἡ ἀγάπη τοῦ θεοῦ** "the love of God." The gen. could be subjective gen., i.e., "God's love for man" or it could be obj. gen., i.e., "man's love for God" or the gen. could be gen. of quality, i.e., "God's kind of love" (s. Marshall). (For the meaning of the term "love," s. 1 Cor. 13:1; Oda Wischmeyer, "Agape in der ausserchristlichen Antike," ZNW, 69 [1978], 212–238.) **τετελείωται** perf. pass. ind. τελειόω to bring to the goal, to perfect. True love for God is expressed not in sentimental language or mystical experience,

but in moral obedience. The proof of love is loyalty. Such love
is "perfected" (Stott). ■ **μένειν** pres. act. inf. to remain. The 6
pres. tense and the meaning of the verb indicate a continual being in Him. (For a study of this word, s. John 15:4; Schnackenburg, 105–110.) The inf. is used as indirect discourse after the part. "the one who says." **ὀφείλει** pres. act. ind. to be morally obligated "he ought to." **καθώς** just as. **ἐκεῖνος** "that one," i.e., Christ. **περιεπάτησεν** aor. act. ind. περιπατέω to walk, to conduct one's life (s. 1 John 1:6). The aor. tense sums up the total life of Jesus. **οὕτως** so, in like manner.
■ **ἀγαπητός** one who is loved, beloved. **καινός** new, novel, 7
new in kind (RWP; s. also Trench, *Synonyms*, 219–225; Schnackenburg). **παλαιός** old, ancient; i.e., old in time.
ἠκούσατε aor. act. ind. ἀκούω. ■ **ἀληθής** true, genuine. The 8
word expresses not only the truth of the logical content but it says that the newness of the commandment to love was actually manifested in Christ and in those who received the letter (Schnackenburg). **παράγεται** pres. mid. ind. παράγω to pass away. The pres. tense indicates that the process has already begun and the darkness is passing away (Brooke). **φῶς** light.
ἀληθινός true, genuine. ■ **μισῶν** pres. act. part. to hate. **ἄρτι** 9
now, at the pres. time. ■ **ἀγαπῶν** pres. act. part. "the one who 10
loves." **μένει** pres. act. ind. (s.v.6). ■ **περιπατεῖ** pres. act. ind. 11
to walk about, to conduct one's life. The pres. tense pictures the pres. continual action "he is walking about." **ὑπάγει** pres. act. ind. to go. The idea is not that of preceding to a definite point, but of leaving the pres. scene (Westcott). **ἐτύφλωσεν** aor. act.
ind. τυφλόω to make blind, to cause to be blind, to blind. ■ 12
γράφω pres. act. ind. The pres. tense could indicate the letter that John is now writing. (For a discussion of the views regarding the tenses of the verbs "to write," s. Marshall; Schnackenburg.) **ὅτι.** This particle used six times in vv. 12–14 could be causal "because," or they could indicate the content of that which John is writing, i.e., "that" (s. Schnackenburg; Marshall; Plummer). **ἀφέωνται** perf. pass. ind. ἀφίημι to release, to forgive. The perf. tense indicates that the sins have been and remain forgiven (Stott). The pass. could be the theological pass. indicating that God is the one who forgives the sins. **διά** w. the acc. "because
of." ■ **ἐγνώκατε** perf. act. ind. to know. The perf. indicates the 13
continuing results of the knowledge. **τόν ἀπ᾽ἀρχῆς** "the one who was from the beginning." **νεανίσκος** "young man." The word could indicate either one who is young in the faith or one who is physically young. **νενκήκατε** perf. act. ind. νικάω to bring about a victory, to achieve the victory, to conquer. The

perf. tense indicates the pres. consequence of a past event
14 (Stott). ■ **ἔγραψα** aor. act. ind. γράφω. The aor. could be epistolary aor. referring to the pres. letter or it could indicate a
previous writing (s.v.12). **μένει** pres. act. ind. to remain (s.v.6).
15 ■ **ἀγαπᾶτε** pres. act. imp. **κόσμος** world, world system.
The word can signify mankind organized in rebellion against
God (Marshall; s. also Schnackenburg, 133–137; TDNT). **ἡ
ἀγάπη τοῦ πατρός** "the love of the Father." The gen. could be
subj. gen., i.e., "the love from the Father" or it could be obj. gen.,
16 i.e., "the love for the Father." ■ **ἐπιθυμία** strong desire, lust,
passion. **ἀλαζονεία** pride, boasting arrogance. It means the
braggadocio which exaggerates what it possesses in order to
impress other people (Marshall; s. also MNTW, 38–42; Trench,
17 *Synonyms*, 98–102f.). ■ **παράγεται** pres. mid. ind. to pass
away, pres. tense "it is in the process of passing away" (s.v.8).
ποιῶν pres. act. part.
18 ■ **παιδίον** little child, dear child (s.v.1). **ἀντίχριστος**
Antichrist. The prep. could refer either to one who comes "instead of Christ" or one who "opposes" Christ. The lack of the
article stresses the category or quality (Schnackenburg; s. also
MT, 132). **ἔρχεται** pres. mid. ind. "he is coming." **γεγόνασιν**
perf. act. ind. γίνομαι, perf. "to have come to be," "to have
19 arisen" (Brooke). ■ **ἐξῆλθαν** aor. act. ind. ἐξέρχομαι.
μεμενήκεισαν plperf. ind. act. μένω to remain (s.v.6). The
plperf. expresses the continuance of the contingent results to the time of speaking (M, 148). The plperf. often lacks the augment in koine (BD, 36). The ind. is used in a contrary to fact conditional clause. **φανερωθῶσιν** aor. pass. subj. φανερόω to manifest, to bring to light, to reveal. The subj. is used in a purpose clause. John not only relates the fact of their departure from the fellowship, but discerns a purpose in it. The heretics went out of their own volition, but behind the secession was the divine purpose that they should be "made manifest." Their departing was their "unmasking." What is counterfeit cannot remain forever
20 hidden (Stott). ■ **καί** "and yet." The word has here an adversa-
tive force "but" (Marshall; BD, 227; Abbott, 135f.). **χρῖσμα**
anointing. The word, which expresses not the act of anointing
but that w. which it is performed, marks the connection of Chris-
21 tians w. their Head (Westcott; s. also TDNT; Marshall). ■
ἔγραψα aor. act. ind. epistolary aor. "I am writing." **ὅτι** "that."
22 ■ **ψεύστης** liar. **εἰ μή** "if not," "except." **ἀρνούμενος** pres. mid.
23 part. ἀρνέομαι to say no to, to deny. ■ **ὁμολογῶν** pres. mid.
24 part. ὁμολογέω to agree, to confess (s. 1 John 1:9). ■ **ἠκούσατε**
aor. act. ind. ἀκούω to hear, to hear and accept what has been

heard. **μενέτω** pres. act. imp. 3rd pers. sing. (s.v.6). **μείνῃ** aor.
act. subj. μένω. The subj. is used in a third-class conditional
clause which views the condition as possible (s. 1 John 1:6).
μενεῖτε fut. act. ind. It is significant that "remain" expresses a
continuing relationship (Marshall). ■ **ἐπαγγελία** announce- 25
ment, promise, pledge (s. BAG; Schnackenburg). **ἐπηγγείλατο**
aor. mid. ind. ἐπαγγέλλω to promise, to pledge, to pledge one's
self to do something.

■ **πλανώντων** pres. act. part. πλανάω to lead astray, to 26
deceive. The particle has a conative force, i.e., "trying to deceive" (Marshall). ■ **ἐλάβετε** aor. act. ind. λαμβάνω to receive, 27
to accept. **διδάσκῃ** pres. act. subj. The clause is used epexegetically to explain what the "need is." **ἐδίδαξεν** aor. act. ind.
μένετε pres. act. imp.

■ **φανερωθῇ** aor. pass. subj. (s.v.19). The subj. is used in a 28
third-class conditional clause and is a clear reference to the second coming of Christ which may be at any time (RWP). **σχῶμεν** aor. act. subj. ἔχω to have. The subj. is used in a purpose clause. **παρρησία** speaking everything, openness, boldness, confidence. The word originally meant openness in speaking and came from the political scene. It was soon taken over into the ethical area and was closely connected w. the concept of friendship. Philo used the word regarding a slave who had "openness," "confidence" w. his master when he had a good conscience. The person who has been cleansed from sin and continues in love also has "freedom of speech" w. his master who is also the ruler of the whole world (Schnackenburg; s. also TDNT; Heb. 3:6). **αἰσχυνθῶμεν** aor. pass. subj. αἰσχύνω to shame, pass. to be put to shame, to be made ashamed. **παρουσία**
presence, coming (s. 1 Thess. 1:19; 3:13). ■ **εἰδῆτε** perf. act. subj. 29
οἶδα. **γεγέννηται** perf. pass. ind. γεννάω to bear, pass. to be
borne. The child exhibits the parents' character because he
shares the parents' nature (Stott).

Ch. 3

■ **ἴδετε** aor. act. imp. ὁράω to see. The verb is followed by 1
an indirect statement as a means of arousing the readers' attention (Marshall). He invites his readers to contemplate the same truth as presented before them in an intellegent shape (Westcott). **ποταπός** what kind of. The word is used often of something of an admirable character (Brooke). The word means originally "of what country" and seems always to imply astonishment (Stott; Plummer). **δέδωκεν** perf. act. ind. δίδωμι to give. The word signifies an unearned gift. The perf. indicates that what

they had received is permanent and abiding (Brooke; s. also
Schnackenburg). **κληθωμεν** aor. pass. subj. καλέω to call, pass.
to be named. The subj. could be used here to express either
purpose (Westcott) or results (RWP). **ἔγνω** aor. act. ind.
2 γινώσκω. ■ **οὔπω** not yet. **ἐφανερώγη** aor. pass. ind.
φανερόω to make clear, to manifest, to reveal. **ἐσόμεθα** fut.
εἰμί. **φανερωθῇ** aor. pass. subj. The subject of the verb could be
either Jesus Himself or it could refer to "what we shall be" (s.
Marshall; Schnackenburg; Westcott). **ὅμοιοι** like. This likeness
of man redeemed and perfected to God is the likeness of the
creature reflecting the glory of the Creator (Westcott). **ὀψόμεθα**
fut. mid. ind. ὁράω to see. (For the ambiguous construction, s.
3 Marshall.) ■ **ἔχων** pres. act. part. to have, to possess. **ἁγνίζει**
pres. act. ind. to purify. The word originally had a cultic meaning
indicating to withdraw from the profane and to dedicate to God,
i.e., "to make ceremonially ready." The term, however, also took
on an ethical character (Schnackenburg; s. also TDNT). The
hope of appearing before the presence of God, and of seeing
Christ as He is, necessarily inspires its possessors w. the desire
of putting away every defilement which clouds the vision of God
(Brooke).
4 ■ **ποιῶν** pres. act. part. to do, to continue to do, to practice.
5 **ἀνομία** that which is without the law, lawlessness. ■ **ἄρῃ** aor.
act. subj. αἴρω to lift up, to take away, to remove completely.
6 The subj. is used in a purpose clause (s. John 1:29). ■ **μένων** pres.
act. part. μένω. **ἑώρακεν** perf. act. ind. ὁράω. The perf. would
indicate to see and to experience the continual results of having
seen. **ἔγνωκεν** perf. act. ind. γινώσκω to know. The verb "to
see" lays stress on the object, which appears and is grasped by
the mental vision; the verb "to know" stresses the subsequent
subjective apprehension of what is grasped in the vision, or it is
7 unfolded gradually in experience (Brooke). ■ **πλανάτω** pres.
8 act. imp. πλανάω to lead astray, to deceive. ■ **διάβολος** devil.
ἁμαρτάνει pres. act. ind. to sin. The pres. tense indicates continual, habitual action. **λύσῃ** aor. act. subj. λύω to loose, to
destroy. The word suggests destruction by undoing or dissolving
that which forms the bond of cohesion (Brooke). The subj. is
9 used in a purpose clause. ■ **γεγεννημένος** perf. pass. part.
γεννάω to bear, pass. to be borne (s. 1 John 2:29). **γεγέννηται**
perf. pass. ind. The perf. tense marks not only the single act of
birth, but the continuous presence of its efficacy (Westcott). The
v. indicates that it is the abiding influence of "His seed" within
everyone who is "born of God," which enables John to affirm
without fear of contradiction that "he cannot" go on living in

"sin." Indeed, "if he should thus continue in sin, it would indicate that he has never been born again" (Stott; for a discussion
of this v. w. various viewpoints presented, s. Marshall). ■ 10
φανερός clear, manifest, evident, conspicuous (s. MM).
■ **ἀγγελία** report, message (s. 1 John 1:5). **ἠκούσατε** aor. 11
act. ind. ἀκούω. **ἀγαπῶμεν** pres. act. subj. The subj. is used in a clause explaining the "message" (s. RWP). The pres. tense would indicate a continual, habitual attitude of love. **ἀλλήλους**
(acc. pl.) "one another." ■ **χάριν τίνος** "for the sake of what?" 12
"wherefore?" (RWP). **ἔσφαξεν** aor. act. ind. σφάζω to slaughter, to kill, to butcher, to murder. Although the word was used often of the slaying of animals particularly for sacrifice, this is not the sense here. It is used here of violent killing (s. Schnackenburg; Marshall; RWP). ■ **θαυμάζετε** pres. act. imp. θαυμάζω 13
to be amazed, to wonder, to marvel. The aor. tense would emphasize the immediate feeling aroused by a particular thought, or action (s. John 3:7). Here the pres. tense is used of the continuous feeling stirred up by the whole temper of men (Westcott; s. also Brooke). The verb is followed by the particle "if," "that"
(s. BD, 237). **μισεῖ** pres. act. ind. μισέω to hate. ■ 14
μεταβεβήκαμεν perf. act. ind. μεταβαίνω to pass over from one place to another, to transfer, to migrate (RWP). The perf. tense indicates the permanency of the step of salvation
(Schnackenburg). ■ **μισῶν** pres. act. part. **ἀνθρωποκτόνος** one 15
who kills a human being, murderer. **μένουσαν** pres. act. part.
fem. sing. ■ **ἐγνώκαμεν** perf. act. ind. (s.v.6). **ἔθηκεν** aor. act. 16
ind. τίθημι to place. Used here in the Semitic sense of "to lay down one's life," "to give one's life" (s. Marshall; Brooke; Bultmann; Gaugler). **ὀφείλομεν** pres. act. ind. to be morally obligated (s. 1 John 2:6). **θεῖναι** aor. act. inf. τίθημι. ■ **ἔχῃ** pres. act. 17
subj. to have, to possess. **βίος** life, i.e., things pertaining to life, "possessions," "wealth" (Houlden; s. also Schnackenburg). **θεωρῇ** pres. act. subj. θεωρέω to see. **ἔχοντα** pres. act. part. **κλείσῃ** aor. act. subj. κλείω to shut up, to lock. The word perhaps suggests that a barrier has been raised against the natural human feelings which the contemplation of such cases calls out (Brooke). **σπλάγχνον** the inward organs, tender mercy, strong compassion (s. Phil 2:1; TDNT; MNTW, 156). **ἡ ἀγάπη τοῦ θεοῦ** "the love of God," i.e., God's own love—which comes and dwells in the genuine believer, and is the source of the love in
the believing community (Houlden). **μένει** pres. act. ind. ■ 18
γλῶσσα tongue, language, speech, i.e., w. mere outward expression as opposed to the genuine movement of our whole being (Westcott).

19 ■ **γνωσόμεθα** fut. mid. ind. *γινώσκω*. **ἐκ τῆς ἀληθείας
ἐσμέν** "we are from the truth," i.e., "we draw the power of our
being from the Truth as its source" (Westcott). **πείσομεν** fut.
act. ind. *πείθω* to persuade, to convince, to reassure, to set at
rest, to appease (s. Marshall; Stott). **καρδία** heart. The word is
20 used here in the sense of "conscience" (s. Marshall). ■
καταγινώσκῃ pres. act. subj. *καταγινώσκω* to know something against someone, to condemn. **μείζων** comp. *μέγας* w. the
gen. "greater than." Our conscience is by no means infallible; its
condemnation may often be unjust. We can, therefore, appeal
from our conscience to God who is greater and more knowledge-
able. Indeed, He knows all things, including our secret motives
and deepest resolves, and it is implied, will be more merciful
21 toward us than our own heart (Stott). ■ **παρρησία** openness,
22 confidence, assurance (s. 1 John 2:28). ■ **αἰτῶμεν** pres. act. subj.
αἰτέω to ask, to request. **τηροῦμεν** pres. act. ind. to guard, to
keep, to obey. **ἀρεστός** verbal adj. pleasing, here "the things
23 pleasing." ■ **πιστεύσωμεν** aor. act. subj. The subj. is used in a
clause explaining what His commandment is. **ἔδωκεν** aor. act.
24 ind. *δίδωμι* to give. ■ **τηρῶν** pres. act. part. to observe, to hold,
to obey. **οὗ** rel. pron. gen. sing. The pron. is gen. because it is
attracted to the case of *πνεύματος*.

Ch. 4

1 ■ **ἀλλά** "but," "rather." **δοκιμάζετε** pres. act. imp.
δοκιμάζω to prove by trial, to test. **τὰ πνεύματα** "the spirits"
(s. 1 Cor. 12:10). (For a treatment of the word "spirit" in 1 John,
s. Schnackenburg, 209–215.) **ἐξεληλύθασιν** perf. act. ind.
ἐξέρχομαι to go out from. The perf. tense expresses the continuance of their agency as distinguished from the single fact of their
2 departure (Westcott). ■ **γίνώσκετε** pres. act. ind. The verb is to
be taken as ind. rather than imp. (Marshall). **ὁμολογεῖ** pres. act.
ind. to agree, to confess (s. 1 John 1:9; 2:22). **ἐληλυθότα** perf.
act. part. *ἔρχομαι* predicate acc. of the part. used after the verb
"to confess" (RWP; for this construction, s. also Stott; Marshall). The perf. tense indicates that the coming of Christ in the
flesh was well-known and that the effects of the Incarnation were
3 abiding (Schnackenburg; Brooke; McKay). ■ **ἀκηκόατε** perf.
act. ind. *ἀκούω*. **ἔρχεται** pres. mid. ind. The pres. tense here
4 also has a fut. implication. ■ **νενικήκατε** perf. act. ind. *νικάω*
to conquer, to be victorious. **μείζων** comp. *μέγας* "greater."
κόσμος world. In v. 3 the word means more the area inhabited
by man, but in v. 4 it refers rather to sinful mankind, while in
v. 5 the stress is more on the sinful principle found in such people

(Marshall; s. also TDNT). ■ **διὰ τοῦτο** "because of this." 5
ἀκούει pres. act. ind. followed by the gen. "to listen to," "to
hear." The world recognizes its own people and listens to a
message which originates in its own circle. This explains their
popularity (Stott). ■ **γινώσκων** pres. act. part. **πλάνη** error. 6
The word here can have the meaning "cause of error." (For this
and other parallels to the "spirits of truth and perversity" (s.
Marshall; Schnackenburg, 211f.; TDNT; CBB).

■ **ἀγαπῶμεν** pres. act. subj. cohortatory subj. "let us love." 7
ἀγαπῶν pres. act. part. **γεγέννηται** perf. pass. ind. γεννάω to
bear, pass. to be born. The perf. tense emphasizes the continuing
results of the new birth. ■ **ἔγνω** aor. act. ind. γινώσκω. (For the 8
term love and its relation to the person and nature of God, s.
Schnackenburg, 231–239; Marshall; 1 John 2:5.) ■ **ἐφανερώθη** 9
aor. pass. ind. to make clear, to make evident, to reveal. The
word conveys the thought of the manifestation of what was
previously hidden (Marshall). **μονογενής** only one of its kind,
single one, only, unique (s. Marshall; John 3:16). **ἀπέσταλκεν**
perf. act. ind. ἀποστέλλω to send, to send an official authoritative representative to do a specific task (s. TDNT). The perf.
indicates that God the Father sent Him and we now enjoy the
blessings of the mission (Westcott). **ζήσωμεν** aor. act. subj. ζάω
to live. The subj. is used in a purpose clause. ■ **ἀγάπη** love, i.e., 10
the quality of true love. True love is selfless (Brooke).
ἠγαπήκαμεν perf. act. ind. ἀγαπάω. The use of the perf. perhaps stresses that it is not our continuing love for God which
should be central, but the love which He revealed historically to
us in Jesus (Marshall). **ἀπέστειλεν** aor. act. ind. ἀποστέλλω.
The change from the perf. to the aor. stresses the historic manifestation of the love rather than the continuing effect of God's act
(Marshall). **ἱλασμός** satisfaction, propitiation (s. 1 John 2:2).
■ **ὀφείλομεν** pres. act. ind. to be morally obligated, to owe a 11
debt which must be paid, to have to do something, "we must,
ought" (s. 1 John 2:6). ■ **πώποτε** at any time, ever. **τεθέαται** 12
perf. mid. ind. θεάομαι to see, to behold (s. 1 John 1:1). Here
the thought is of the continuous beholding which answers to
abiding fellowship (Westcott). **ἀγαπῶμεν** pres. act. subj. The
subj. is used in a third-class conditional clause which views the
condition possible. **τετελειωμένη** perf. pass. part. τελειόω to
bring to completion, to bring to the goal, to perfect (s. 1 John
2:5).

■ **δέδωκεν** perf. act. ind. δίδωμι. The perf. emphasizes the 13
completed action w. the continuing results. ■ **τεθεάμεθα** perf. 14
mid. ind. (s.v.12). **ἀπέσταλκεν** perf. act. ind. (s.v.9). ■ 15

16 **ὁμολογήσῃ** aor. act. subj. (s.v.2). ■ **ἐγνώκαμεν** perf. act. ind.
γινώσκω. The perf. tense indicates "we have come to know and
still know" (Marshall). **πεπιστεύκαμεν** perf. act. ind. The perf.
indicates that the recognition of the love of God is considered
to be a lasting and settled conviction (Schnackenburg).
17 **μένων** pres. act. part. ■ **τετελείωται** perf. pass. ind.
(s.v.12). **παρρησία** openness, confidence, assurance (s. 1 John
2:28). **ἔχωμεν** pres. act. subj. The subj. is used either as in a
purpose clause or in apposition w. "in this" or w. the clause
"because," the latter of which would make this clause a paren-
18 thesis (RWP; s. also Westcott). **κρίσις** judging, judgment. ■
φόβος fear. **ἔξω** outside, out. **βάλλει** pres. act. ind. to cast out,
to drive out, to turn out of doors (RWP). **κόλασις** punishment.
The word indicates the disciplinary chastisement of the wrong-
doer (Westcott; s. also 2 Peter 2:9). **φοβούμενος** pres. mid. part.
19 φοβέομαι to be afraid, to have fear. ■ **ἀγαπῶμεν** pres. act. subj.
cohortatory subj. "let us love." **ἠγάπησεν** aor. act. ind. (s.v.10).
20 ■ **εἴπῃ** aor. act. subj. λέγω to say. The subj. is used in a third-
class conditional clause viewing the condition as a possibility.
μισῇ pres. act. subj. μισέω to hate. **ψεύστης** liar. **ἑώρακεν**
21 perf. act. ind. ὁράω to see. ■ **ἐντολή** command.

Ch. 5

1 ■ **ὅτι** "that." The particle introduces the content of what is
believed. **γεγέννηται** perf. pass. ind. γεννάω to bear, pass. to
be born (s. 1 John 2:29; RAC IX, 43–171). **ἀγαπῶν** pres. act.
part. **γεννήσαντα** aor. act. part. γεννάω. **γεγεννημένον** perf.
pass. part. This new birth, which brings us into believing recognition of the eternal Son, also involves us in a loving relationship
w. the Father and His other children and the part. here refers to
2 every child of God (Stott). ■ **ὅταν** used w. the subj. "whenever."
ἀγαπῶμεν pres. act. subj. **ποιῶμεν** pres. act. subj. The subj. are
used in an indefinite temporal clause (RWP; s. also Schnacken-
3 burg). ■ **τηρῶμεν** pres. act. subj. τηρέω to keep, to observe, to
obey. The subj. is used in an explanatory clause which defines
our love for God. **βαρύς** heavy, burdensome. The word suggests
4 the idea of a heavy and oppressive burden (Brooke). ■ **πᾶν τὸ
γεγεννημένον** "everyone who has been born" perf. pass. part.
n. sing. The n. phrase is possibly meant in a generalizing sense
or it is possible that the use is influenced by the fact that the Gr.
words for "child" are n. (Marshall). **νικᾷ** pres. act. ind. to conquer, to gain a victory, to overcome. **νικήσασα** aor. act. part.
The aor. could point to a definite act or fact (Brooke). **πίστις**
faith. "Our faith enables us to overcome the world." It acts as

a weapon of war, and its force consists in the fact that its content
is the true nature of Jesus (Houlden). ■ **νικῶν** pres. act. part. **εἰ** 5
μή "except," "if not."
■ **ἐλθών** aor. act. part. ἔρχομαι. **αἷμα** blood. Perhaps the 6
best explanation of the meaning of the term here is that it refers
to the bloody death upon the cross (s. Plummer; Westcott; Marshall; Brooke). **μαρτυροῦν** pres. act. part. μαρτευρέω to be a
witness, to testify. ■ **τρεῖς** three. **μαρτυροῦντες** pres. act. part. 7
(For a discussion of the textual problem in vv. 7 and 8, s. TC,
716–718.) ■ **μείζων** comp. μέγας "greater." In John 5:36 the 9
word indicates the greater credence, in 1 John 5:9 it indicates the
stronger, obligating power of the divine witness (Schnackenburg). **μεμαρτύρηκεν** perf. act. ind. μαρτυρέω to be a witness,
to bear witness, to testify. ■ **πιστεύων** pres. act. part. The verb 10
constructed w. the dat. usually expresses acceptance of the statement rather than surrender to the person (Brooke). **πεποίηκεν**
perf. act. ind. **πεπίστευκεν** perf. act. ind. The perf. tenses indicate the abiding affects. ■ **ἔδωκεν** aor. act. ind. δίδωμι. ■ **ἔχων** 11/12
pres. act. part. to have, to possess. The pres. tense of the verb
indicates continual possession (s. M, 110). The word is used to
describe our personal possession of the Father through confessing the Son (Stott).
■ **ἔγραψα** aor. act. ind. γράφω to write. The word could 13
be epistolary aor. referring to the whole epistle or it could refer
to the immediately preceding section either vv. 1–12 or vv. 5–12
(s. Marshall). **εἰδῆτε** perf. act. subj. οἶδα to know. The subj. is
used in a purpose clause. ■ **παρρησία** openness, confidence (s. 14
1 John 2:28). **ἐάν τι** "whatever," "if we ask anything." The
particle introduces a third-class conditional clause (RWP).
αἰτώμεθα pres. mid. ind. αἰτέω to ask, to request. **ἀκούει** pres.
act. ind. ■ **ἐάν** "if." The particle is used w. the ind. in a first-class 15
conditional clause and has almost a causal sense (s. BD, 189; MT
115f.; RWP). **αἴτημα** that which is asked, request. **ᾐτήκαμεν**
perf. act. ind. αἰτέω to ask, to request.
■ **ἴδῃ** aor. act. subj. ὁράω. The subj. is used in a third-class 16
conditional clause which views the condition as a possibility.
ἁμαρτάνοντα pres. act. part. (For a discussion of the "sin unto
death," s. Stott; Westcott; Marshall.) **αἰτήσει** fut. act. ind.
δώσει fut. act. ind. δίδωμι to give. **ἁμαρτάνουσιν** pres. act.
part. dat. pl. **ἐρωτήσῃ** aor. act. subj. ἐρωτάω to ask about, to
request information about (s. Westcott). ■ **ἀδικία** unrighteous- 17
ness.
■ **γεγεννημένος** perf. pass. part. (s.v.1). **γεννηθείς** aor. 18
pass. part. γεννάω (s.v.1). **πονηρός** evil, mean. The word refers

to active evil (s. TDNT; Trench, *Synonyms*, 315f.). **ἅπτεται**
pres. mid. ind. ἅπτω w. the gen. to touch. The verb means to
19 lay hold of someone in order to harm him (Marshall). ■ **ὅλος**
whole, total. **κεῖται** pres. mid. ind. of the defective verb κεῖμαι
20 to lie (RWP). ■ **ἥκει** pres. act. ind. "to have come." **δέδωκεν**
perf. act. ind. (s.v.11). **διάνοια** knowing, understanding. The
faculty of knowing or discerning seems to be what it expresses.
It is the ability to reason correctly and was used in Gr. philosophy of syllogistic reasoning (Brooke; Westcott; GPT, 37).
γινώσκωνεν pres. act. subj. The subj. is used in a purpose clause.
ἀληθινός true, genuine. **οὗτος** "this one." The pron. clearly
21 refers to Jesus (s. Marshall). ■ **φυλάξατε** aor. act. imp.
φυλάσσω to guard, to keep. The use of the act. w. the reflex.
may be regarded as emphasizing the duty of personal effort
(Westcott). **εἴδωλον** image, idol, false god. The presence of idols
in the ancient world is witnessed to not only by the geographical
description of Strabo and Pausanias, but also in literature, art,
theater, music, and the various archeological discoveries (s. Acts
17:16).

2 JOHN

Ch. 1

ἐκλεκτός verbal adj. ἐκλέγω to choose out, to select, elect, 1
chosen, choice (s. 1 Peter 1:1). The phrase “to the elect lady”
could refer to a specific person or it could be a personification
indicating some local church (Stott; s. also Westcott; Marshall).
τοῖς τέκνοις αὐτῆς “to her children.” This would refer to the
members of the church (Marshall). **ἐγνωκότες** perf. act. part.
γινώσκω. The perf. tense emphasizes the continuing results of
having known. ■ **ἀλήθεια** truth. Here the word refers to the 2
divine reality and signifies what is ultimately real, namely, God
Himself. Hence, it can refer to the expression of God in His
incarnate Son and in the Christian message (Schnackenburg;
Marshall). **μένουσαν** pres. act. part. μένω to remain. **ἔσται** fut.
εἰμί. ■ **ἔλεος** mercy (s. 1 Tim. 1:2). 3
■ **ἐχάρην** aor. pass. ind. χαίρω to rejoice, to be glad. The 4
aor. is not epistolary, but refers back to the time when the elder
met the members of the church (Marshall). **λιάν** greatly, very
much, very. **ὅτι** “that.” The word introduces not only the content of the rejoicing but also gives the reason for rejoicing (Bult-
man). **εὕρηκα** perf. act. ind. εὑρίσκω to find. The perf.
tense strongly suggests personal experience (Marshall).
περιπατοῦντας pres. act. part. περιπατέω to walk about, to
conduct one’s life. **καθώς** just as. The sentence introduced by
this word explains how the walk of these church members can
be called a “walk in the truth” (Schnackenburg). **ἐλάβομεν** aor.
act. ind. λαμβάνω to receive. ■ **ἐρωτῶ** pres. act. ind. to ask, to 5
request. **γράφων** pres. act. part. **καινός** new, new in quality (s.
1 John 2:7). **εἴχομεν** perf. act. ind. ἔχω to have. **ἀγαπῶμεν**
pres. act. subj. The subj. is used in a clause describing the content
of the request. ■ **ἀγάπη** love. Love means living according to 6
the Father’s commands (Marshall). **περιπατῶμεν** pres. act.
subj. (s.v.4). The subj. is used in a clause explaining what the
“commandment” is. **ἠκούσατε** aor. act. ind. ἀκούω. ■ **πλάνος** 7
deceiver, one who leads to wrong action and not only to wrong
opinion (Westcott). **ἐξῆλθον** aor. act. ind. ἐξέρχομαι to go out.
ὁμολογοῦντες pres. act. part. ὁμολογέω to agree to, to profess.

The verb is used w. the double acc. and has to do w. the messianic character of Jesus, and John uses the words in order to correct
faulty or inadequate messianic ideas current in his time (ECC,
8 105). **ἐρχόμενον** pres. mid. part. ■ **βλέπετε** pres. act. imp. to
see, to beware, to watch out. **ἀπολέσητε** aor. act. subj.
ἀπόλλυμι to lose, to suffer loss. **ἠργασάμεθα** aor. mid. ind.
ἐργάζομαι to work. **μισθός** pay. The metaphor seems to be
taken from the payment of labor since this word refers to a
workman's wage (Stott). **πλήρης** full, complete. **ἀπολάβητε**
aor. act. subj. ἀπολαμβάνω to take away, to receive. The word
9 was used in the papyri of "receiving" what is due (MM). ■
προάγων pres. act. part. προάγω to go before, to run ahead.
Perhaps this is a sarcastic reference to the way in which the false
teachers themselves proudly claim to be offering "advanced"
teaching; the elder claims that they have "advanced" beyond the
10 boundaries of true Christian belief (Marshall). ■ **λαμβάνετε**
pres. act. imp. to receive, to show hospitality to. It was common
in the ancient world to receive traveling teachers in the home
and offer them shelter and lodging. **χαίρειν** pres. act. inf. to give
greeting. The giving of greetings indicates entering in to fellowship w. the one greeted and to welcome a false teacher was to
express solidarity w. them (Schnackenburg; Marshall). The inf.
is used in indirect discourse as the object of the verb "to say."
λέγετε pres. act. ind. to speak, to say. Used here in connection
w. the inf. to mean "to give greeting." John's instruction may
relate not only to an official visit of false teachers, but to the
extending to them of an official welcome rather than merely
11 private hospitality (Stott). ■ **ὁ λέγων** pres. act. part. "the one
saying," "the one who says." **κοινωνεῖ** pres. act. ind. to have
fellowship, to share in (s. 1 John 1:3).
12 ■ **ἔχων** pres. act. part. The part. is used in a concessive
sense "although I have." **ἐβουλήθην** aor. pass. ind. βούλομαι
to will, to want to. **χάρτης** paper. The word was a leaf of papyrus
prepared for writing by cutting the pith into stripes and pasting
together (RWP). **μέλας** black, black ink. **γενέσθαι** aor. mid. inf.
γίνομαι. The inf. is used to present the content of the hope.
λαλῆσαι aor. act. inf. λαλέω. **πεπληρωμένη** perf. pass. part.
πληρόω to make full, to fulfill, to complete (s. 1 John 1:4).
13 ■ **ἀσπάζεται** pres. mid. ind. to greet.

3 JOHN

Ch. 1

ἀγαπητός verbal adj. one who is loved, beloved. The name 1
"Gaius" was a very prominent name in the Roman Empire and
occurs several times in the NT (e.g., Acts 19:29; 1 Cor. 1:4) (s.
Plummer; Brooke). We do not know who this Gaius was but it
is clear from the terms in which John writes that he occupied a
position of responsibility and leadership in the local church
(Stott).

■ **ἀγαπητέ** voc. **περὶ πάντων** "in all respects" (Marshall). 2
The phrase is to be taken w. the inf. "to prosper." The writer
prays for the prosperity of Gaius in all respects and the thought
may be of the public and social work of Gaius as well as his
personal health (Brooke; Westcott). **εὔχομαι** pres. mid. ind. to
pray, to wish (s. Marshall). **σέ** "you" acc. sing. used as the
"subject" or the inf. **εὐοδοῦσθαι** pres. pass. inf., pass. "to be lead
along a good road," i.e., "to get along well," "to prosper," "to
succeed" (BAG; s. also MM). The inf. is used in indirect discourse as object of the verb "to pray," "to wish." **ὑγιαίνειν** pres.
act. inf. to be well, to be in good health. It was a common
greeting and desire expressed in letters for the recipient to be in
good health (s. LAE, 187f.; Schnackenburg; MM; CBB; TDNT;
for the general concept of health and well-being in the ancient
world, s. RAC X, 902–945). **καθώς** "just as." The wish is that
Gaius' outward prosperity may correspond to the condition of
his soul (Schnackenburg). ■ **ἐχάρην** aor. pass. ind. χαίρω to be 3
happy, to rejoice, to be glad. **λίαν** very, exceedingly.
ἐρχομένων pres. mid. part. **μαρτυρούντων** pres. act. part. The
part. are causal but the temporal element of concurrent action
is also present. The pres. part. indicate repetition and show that
several visits had been paid to the elder, possibly by different
groups of Christians (Marshall). **ἀλήθεια** truth (s. 2 John 2).
περιπατεῖς pres. act. ind. to walk about, to conduct one's life.
The pres. tense indicates continual action. ■ **μειζότερος** comp. 4
of the comp. μείζων from μέγας. Used w. the gen. w. the
meaning "greater than." The koine has a number of the popular
new formations of double comp. and double superl. (s. BD, 33f.).

περιπατοῦντα pres. act. part. The pres. tense indicates the continual habitual conducting of one's life.

5 ■ **ἀγαπητέ** voc. **ἐργάσῃ** aor. mid. subj. 2nd pers. sing. ἐργάζομαι to work. The use of the rel. pron. "whatever" w. the subj. is indefinite and implies an unspecified number of ways or occasions of helping the brothers (Marshall; s. also Gal. 6:10; Col. 3:23). **ξένος** stranger. The fact that brethren who were strangers were helped is emphasized by the use of the acc. of general reference "and that too" (RWP; Westcott; Plummer).

6 ■ **ἐμαρτύρησαν** aor. act. ind. (s.v.3). The dat. is used to express the object of the witness, i.e., the thing to which one testifies. **ἐνώπιον** in the presence of. The absence of the article w. the word "church" denotes a meeting of the church at which the witness was borne (Brooke). **καλῶς** adv. well. **ποιήσεις** fut. act. ind. The expression "you will do well" is an idiom that means "please," "kindly," and was used often in the papyri to express a polite request (MM; Marshall). **προπέμψας** aor. act. part. προπέμπω to send forth, to send someone on their way. The sending of missionaries on their way involved providing for their journey—supplying them w. food and money to pay for their expenses, washing their clothes and generally helping them to travel as comfortably as possible (Marshall; s. also BAG; Acts 15:3; 1 Cor. 16:6, 11; 2 Cor. 1:16; Titus 3:13). (For a study regarding the support of wandering ministers and missionaries in the early church, s. Gerd Theissen, "Legitimation und Lebensunterhalt: Ein Beitrag zur Soziologie Urchristlicher Missionäre," NTS 21 [Jan., 1975], 192–221.) **ἀξίως** adv. followed by the gen. "worthily," "worthily of God," i.e., "worthily of their
7 dedication to the service of God" (Westcott). ■ **ἐξῆλθαν** aor. act. ind. ἐξέρχομαι to go out, i.e., to go out from the church (or from God) into the world, regarded as a field for evangelism (Marshall). **λαμβάνοντες** pres. act. part. The pres. tense indicates habitual and customary action. It was their custom to carry out the spirit of the commission to the Twelve and to the tradition established by Paul. They had, therefore, a special claim on hospitality and help of the churches in places through which they had to pass (Brooke; s. also Westcott). **ἐθνικός** pagan, heathen. That these missionaries were supported by fellow Christians stands in marked contrast both to the wandering philosophers of the day as well as the beggar priests of the Syrian goddess who went out on behalf of the goddess and returned triumphantly boasting that "each journey brought in seventy
8 bags" (LAE, 109; s. also Bultmann; Schnackenburg). ■ **ὀφείλομεν** pres. act. ind. to be morally obligated, to owe a debt.

ὑπολαμβάνειν pres. act. inf. to take up under in order to raise, to bear on high, to take up and carry away, to receive hospitality, to welcome, to support. The word is often used in the sense of "receiving" w. hospitality, and esp. of "supporting" (T; Brooke). Christians should finance Christian enterprises which the world will not, or should not be asked to, support. Indeed, Christians have an obligation to do so. They "must" support their brethren to whom the world should not be asked to contribute (Stott). **τοιοῦτος** such ones. **συνεργός** fellow-worker. As sharers in the truth themselves, they must prove to be fellow-workers in practice and are to work together w. the missionaries for the benefit of the truth (Marshall). **ἀλήθεια** truth. The dat. could mean either "fellow-workers w. the truth" or "on behalf of, for the truth" (s. Schnackenburg).

■ **ἔγραψα** aor. act. ind. γράφω. **φιλοπρωτεύων** pres. act. 9
part. φιλοπρωτεύω to be fond of the first position, to wish to be first, to like to be the leader. The word expresses ambition, the desire to have the first place in everything (BAG; Brooke). The pres. tense indicates the continual and habitual attitude. **ἐπιδέχεται** pres. mid. ind. to accept, to receive gladly. The word can mean either "to accept the authority of" or "to welcome." The pl. "us" will refer to the elder and his associates (Marshall).
The pres. tense again indicates a continuing attitude. ■ 10
ὑπομνήσω fut. act. ind. ὑπομιμνῄσκω to call to memory, to remind. **φλυαρῶν** pres. act. part. φλυαρέω to talk nonsense (about), to bring unjustified charges against. The word emphasizes the emptiness of the charges (s. BAG; MM; Brooke; 1 Tim. 5:13). **ἀρκούμενος** pres. mid. part. ἀρκέω to be enough, to be satisfied. **βουλομένους** pres. mid. part. βούλομαι to want to, to desire to. **κωλύει** pres. act. ind. to forbid. **ἐκβάλλει** pres. act. ind. to throw out, to put out. The verbs in the pres. tense here may be conative i.e., "he is trying to" (Westcott; but s. also Marshall; Schnackenburg).

■ **μιμοῦ** pres. mid. imp. μιμέομαι to mimic, to imitate. 11
ἀγαθοποιῶν pres. act. part. to do good. **κακοποιῶν** pres. act.
part. to do evil. **ἑώρακεν** perf. act. ind. ὁράω to see. ■ 12
μεμαρτύρηται perf. pass. ind. (s.v.3).

■ **γράψαι** aor. act. inf. The aor. expresses the writing of a 13
single letter containing what the writer felt obliged to say. The pres. inf. indicates the continuation of the pres. letter (Marshall). **μέλας** black, ink. The ink used was a writing fluid whose chief ingredient was soot or black carbon. It was mixed w. gum or oil for use on parchment, or w. a metallic substance for use on papyrus (ZPEB II, 279). **κάλαμος** reed, reed pen used for writ-

14 ing (Marshall; Brooke). ■ **εὐθέως** immediately, soon. **ἰδεῖν** aor.
act. inf. ὁράω to see. **στόμα** mouth. Here used in the expression
15 "face to face." **λαλήσομεν** fut. act. ind. λαλέω. ■ **ἀσπάζονται**
pres. mid. ind. **ἀσπάζου** pres. mid. imp. ἀσπάζομαι to greet.
(For the form of 2 and 3 John in relation to ancient letter writing, s. Robert W. Funk, "The Form and Structure of Second and Third John," JBL 86 [Dec., 1967], 424–430; s. also Joseph A. Fitzmyer, "Some Notes on Aramaic Epistolography," JBL 93 [June, 1974], 201–225.)

JUDE

Ch. 1

ἠγαπημένοις perf. pass. part. ἀγαπάω to love. The perf. 1
tense suggests that they were not only once but continued to be
the objects of God's love and care (Kelly). **τετηρημένοις** perf.
pass. part. τηρέω to keep safe, to guard, to watch over. The verb
used in a friendly sense means "to keep safe from harm," "to
preserve." The word expresses the watchful care given to someone (Mayor; T). The perf. tense emphasizes the continuing
watch care. **κλητός** verbal adj. "called." ■ **ἔλεος** mercy, pity (s. 2
1 Tim. 1:2). **πληθυνθείη** aor. pass. opt. πληθύνω to multiply,
to increase. The opt. is used to express a wish (s. 1 Peter 1:2).
■ **σπουδή** haste, diligence, effort, earnestness. **ποιούμενος** 3
pres. mid. part. to make, to do. The verb was used in connection w. a noun to build the verbal idea found in the noun (s. M, 159). **κοινός** common, that which all believers share commonly (s. 1 John 1:3). **ἀνάγκη** compulsion, necessity. **ἔσχον** aor. act. ind. ἔχω to have, aor. "to receive." (For the distinction between the pres. tense "to have" and the aor. tense "to get, to receive," s. M, 110; Kelly.) **γράψαι** aor. act. inf. The aor. contrasted w. the preceding pres. inf. implies that the new epistle had to be written at once and could not be prepared for at leisure, like the one he had previously contemplated (Mayor). The inf. is used epexegetically to explain the "necessity." **παρακαλῶν** pres. act. part. παρακαλέω to urge, to encourage, to beseech. It is the word used of speeches of leaders and of soldiers who urge each other on. It is the word used of words which sent fearful and timorous and hesitant soldiers and sailors courageously into battle (MNTW, 134; s. also Rom. 12:1). **ἐπαγωνίζεσθαι** pres. mid. inf. to struggle for, to contend for, to exercise great effort and exertion for something. The word was used of athletic contests and the struggle and effort of the athletes in their games (s. Kelly; 1 Cor. 9:24–27). The prep. in compound denotes direction (MH, 312) and the word following in the dat. denotes the cause on behalf of which one fights (Kelly). The inf. is used as the object of the verb "to exhort." **ἅπαξ** "once for all" (s. Mayor). **παραδοθείσῃ** aor. pass. part. παραδίδωμι to deliver over, to

hand down, to commit and entrust. The word is used for handing down authorized tradition in Israel (s. 1 Cor. 15:1–3; 2 Thess. 3:6), and Jude is therefore saying that the Christian apostolic tradition is normative for the people of God (Green). **πίστει** dat. sing. faith. The word here indicates the body of truth and the dat. is to be related to the verb "to struggle for" (s. Kelly).

4 ■ **παρεισεδύησαν** aor. act. ind. παρεισδύομαι to slip in along side of, secretly. (For this sinister and secretive word, s. Green; Gal. 2:4; 2 Peter 2:1.) **πάλαι** long ago. **προγεγραμμένοι** perf. pass. part. προγράφω to write down beforehand, to write down previously, i.e., "written before in God's book of judgment." The word is intended to show that they are already doomed to punishment as enemies of God (Mayor; s. also Kelly; SB II, 173). The perf. tense indicates the continuing authority of that which was written (s. MM). **κρίμα** that which was decided upon, judgment. **ἀσεβής** ungodly, impious (s. 2 Peter 2:5; 3:7). **μετατιθέντες** pres. act. part. to transpose, to change from one place to another, to transfer. The pres. tense could be conative, i.e., "they are trying to change." **ἀσέλγεια** unbridled living (s. 1 Peter 2:16; 2 Peter 2:19). **ἀρνούμενοι** pres. mid. part. ἀρνέομαι to say no to, to deny.

5 ■ **ὑπομνῆσαι** aor. act. inf. ὑπομιμνῄσκω to cause someone to remember, to remind. **εἰδότας** perf. act. part. οἶδα to know. The part. could be concessive "although you know" and this justifies the reminder. They only need to be reminded of truths already known, so that it is unnecessary to write at length (Mayor; s. also Schelkle). **λαός** people. The word is used without the article, i.e., "a people" indicating that not all the ones who left Egypt were believers (s. Green). **σώσας** aor. act. part. σῴζω to rescue, to deliver, to save. The part. is used temporally "after he saved." **τὸ δεύτερον** "the second time." The phrase could mean "the next time" or as an adverbial acc. "afterwards." Here the word marks a strong contrast and sharpens the point of the warning (Bigg; s. also Green; RWP; Kelly). **πιστεύσαντας** aor. act. part. **ἀπώλεσεν** aor. act. ind. ἀπόλλυμι to ruin, to destroy.

6 ■ **τηρήσαντας** aor. act. part. to keep, to guard. (s.v.1). **ἀρχή** dominion, office, authority. The word could indicate either the office of the angels or their domain, i.e., sphere of rule, or it could indicate the spiritual state in which they were created, i.e., they were made different from humanity but did not maintain this original state, rather they left their own habitation (s. Kelly; Mayor; Green). **ἀπολιπόντας** aor. act. part. ἀπολείπω to leave, to desert, to leave behind, to forsake. **οἰκητήριον** place of living, dwelling place. The ending of the word indicates the

place of action (s. MH, 343; RG, 154). **κρίσις** judging. **δεσμός**
band, bond, chain. **ἀΐδιος** eternal, everlasting. **ζόφος** darkness,
gloom (s. 2 Peter 2:7). **τετήρηκεν** perf. act. ind. to guard, to
keep. The word is used here in a neg. sense w. a punitive meaning, i.e., "to keep in custody" (s.v.1; Mayor). ■ **ὅμοιος** like, 7
similar. **τρόπος** manner. The phrase is a verbal acc. meaning
"likewise," "in like manner." **τούτοις** masc. dat. pl. "to these,"
"w. these." Since the word is masc., it cannot refer to the cities
"Sodom and Gomorrah" (Kelly) and evidently refers to the
"angels" of v. 6. It was a common understanding among many
of the Jewish rabbis that the beings referred to in Gen. 6 were
angelic beings (s. SB III, 780). **ἐκπορνεύσασαι** aor. act. part.
ἐκπορνεύω to indulge in excessive immorality. The prep. in
compound may be intensive (s. T) or it may suggest that this
immorality was "against the course of nature" (Green).
ἀπελθοῦσαι aor. act. part. ἀπέρχομαι to go after. **ὀπίσω**
behind, after. The participial phrase would emphasize their bent
and determination for unnatural sexual acts and the prep. in
compound indicates the turning aside from the right way (Huther). **πρόκεινται** pres. mid. ind. to lie before, to be exposed to
public view. The word was used of a corpse lying in state (BAG).
δεῖγμα example, sample. The word was used in the papyri of
samples of corn or wheat (MM). These are laid out before all as
a sample or warning of judgment (s. Bigg). **πῦρ** fire. **αἰώνιος**
eternal, everlasting. The pres. tense of the verb and the adj.
"everlasting" are intended to impress on readers that the appall-
ing effects of the catastrophe are still visible for all to see and
note w. dread (Kelly). **δίκη** punishment. Here it would indicate
a judicial sentence passed by a judge (s. MM). **ὑπέχουσαι** pres.
act. part. ὑπέχω to undergo, to suffer. The word was a legal t.t.
meaning "to undergo punishment" (BAG; s. also MM).

■ **ὁμοίως** adv. "likewise." This introduces the comparison 8
between examples that they knew about and the spiritual spies
about whom he is writing. **μέντοι** "notwithstanding," i.e., "in
spite of the dreadful fate of the three groups just mentioned"
(Kelly). **ἐνυπνιαζόμενοι** pres. mid. part. ἐνυπνιάζω to dream.
The word may indicate that in the false teachers' delusion and
their blindness, they take the real for the unreal and the unreal
for the real (Mayor) which would emphasize their false source
of revelation, but the word may also stress the fact that they are
asleep to God's judgment and entertained by the temporal allu-
sive and imaginary character of the pleasures of their lusts.
μιαίνουσιν pres. act. ind. to stain, to defile. The word often is
used of moral defilement or pollution (s. Kelly). The pres. tense

of the part. indicates a continual habitual action. **κυριότης** lordship, authority. The word indicates the majestic power that a lord uses in ruling (s. BAG). **ἀθετοῦσιν** pres. act. ind. to set aside, to do away w., to nullify, to not recognize as valid, to despise (s. Mayor; Gal. 2:21). **δόξαι** "glorious ones." The word refers here to angelic beings. They are the angels, whom they blaspheme by supposing that they had created the world in opposition to the will of the true God (Mayor; s. also Kelly). **βλασφημοῦσιν** pres. act. ind. to revile, to defame, to blas-
9 pheme. ■ **ἀρχάγγελος** archangel. The Jews considered Michael to be the highest among the angels and to be the representative of God (s. SB III, 831). **διάβολος** devil. **διακρινόμενος** pres. mid. part. διακρίνομαι to take issue w., to dispute (s. Acts 11:2; James 1:6). **διελέγετο** impf. mid. ind. διαλέγομαι to argue, to dispute. The impf. pictures the continuous action in the past time. **ἐτόλμησεν** aor. act. ind. τολμάω to dare. **ἐπενεγκεῖν** aor. act. inf. ἐπιφέρω to bring upon, to pronounce. **βλασφημιά** railing, blasphemy. Michael did not dare to pronounce a judgment of reproach upon Satan. **ἐπιτιμήσαι** aor. act. opt. ἐπιτιμάω to rebuke. This was a word of command used by Jesus that brought the hostile powers under control (s. Matt. 17:18).
10 The opt. is used in a wish. ■ **ὅσος** how much, how great, which things. **φυσικῶς** naturally, by instinct (s. 2 Peter 2:12). **ἄλογος** without reason, without rationality (s. 2 Peter 2:12). **ζῷον** living creature, animal (s. 2 Peter 2:12). **ἐπίστανται** pres. mid. ind. ἐπίσταμαι to understand. **φθείρονται** pres. pass. ind. φθείρω to corrupt, to ruin, to destroy. The natural antithesis here would have been "these things they admire and delight in." For this Jude substitutes by a stern irony "these things are their
11 ruin" (Mayor; for this word, s. 2 Peter 1:4; 2:12). ■ **οὐαί** "woe." The word is an imprecation of doom which is found in 1 Corinthians 9:16, frequently in the gospels, and repeatedly in 1 Enoch (esp. XCIV-C) (Kelly). **ἐπορεύθησαν** aor. pass. ind. πορεύομαι to go, to travel along. The word is used to indicate a manner of life. **πλάνη** error, wandering (s. 1 John 1:8). **μισθός** wage, reward, pay. The gen. is gen of price "for pay or gain." They were like Balaam greedy for money (Green). **ἐξεχύθησαν** aor. pass. ind. ἐκχέω to pour out. The pass. is used to express either the outward sweeping movement of a great crowd, or the surrender to an overwhelming motive on the part of an individual (Mayor). **ἀντιλογία** speaking against, hostility, rebellion. **ἀπώλοντο** aor. mid. ind. ἀπόλλυμι to perish. The aor. tense is a dramatic way of saying that their fate is already settled (Kelly). So in these three pen pictures from the OT we see three leading

characteristics of the errorists. Like Cain, they were devoid of love. Like Balaam, they were prepared in return for money to teach others that sin did not matter. Like Korah, they were careless of the ordinances of God and insubordinate to church
leaders (Green). ■ **οὗτοι εἰσιν** "these are." The same phrase 12
reoccurs in vv. 16 and 19 and begins an independent description of the false teachers in which sections of each statement is balanced by something said on the other side, which is introduced w. a conj. "but" (s. Green; Alford). **σπιλάς** spot (s. 2 Peter 2:13). The better meaning here is "hidden rocks." The word was used to denote rocks in the sea close to shore and covered w. water and so were dangerous to vessels (Kelly; s. also Mayor). **συνευωχούμενοι** pres. mid. part. συνευωχέομαι to come together to have a feast, to eat a feast together (s. 2 Peter 2:13). The meaning here is that at these meals the false teachers are liable to undermine the faith and decent comportment of their fellow Christians much as submerged reefs can wreck shipping (Kelly). **ἀφόβως** adv. without fear, fearless, without respect. **ποιμαίνοντες** pres. act. part. ποιμαίνω to shepherd, to care for as a shepherd. Here the sense is "to fatten, to indulge" (Mayor). **νεφέλη** cloud. **ἄνυδρος** waterless, without water. **παραφερόμεναι** pres. pass. part. παραφέρω to carry by. The picture here is that of clouds being blown by and passing on without bringing the long hoped for and refreshing rains. The suggestion is that the errorists are all show and no substance; they have nothing to give to those who are so foolish as to listen to them (Kelly). **φθινοπωρινός** belonging to late autumn. The word describes trees such as they are at the close of autumn, dry, leafless, w. bare branches w. all growth sapped at the approach of winter and without fruit (T; Kelly). **ἄκαρπος** without fruit, fruitless. Late autumn would be toward the end of the harvest and the picture here is that harvest had come and was almost gone but these trees had no fruit on them. They were worthless and disappointing. **δίς** twice. **ἀποθανόντα** aor. act. part. ἀποθνῄσκω to die, to be dead. The trees were "twice dead" in the sense of being sterile and then of being actually lifeless (Kelly). **ἐκριζωθέντα** aor. pass. part. ἐκριζόω to uproot. Such trees were commonly torn up by the roots and disposed of by burning, and the uprooting of trees is a favorite OT metaphor of
judgment (Ps. 53:5; Prov. 2:22) (Kelly; Green). ■ **κῦμα** wave. 13
ἄγριος untamed, wild. **ἐπαφρίζοντα** pres. act. part. ἐπαφρίζω to foam up, to cause to splash like foam. The word refers to the seaweed and other refuse borne on the crest of the waves and thrown up on the beach, to which are compared the overflowings

of ungodliness (Mayor; s. also Isa. 57:20). **αἰσχύνη** shame. **ἀστήρ** star. **πλανήτης** wandering. The figure of the "wandering star" is used in the Book of Enoch (s. Enoch 43, 44, 18, etc.) and describes shooting stars which fall out of the sky and are engulfed in darkness (Mayor; Green). **τετήρηται** perf. pass. ind. τηρέω (s.v.6).

14 ■ **ἐπροφήτευσεν** aor. act. ind. προφητεύω to deliver the message of a prophet, to speak forth, to prophesy. **ἕβδομός** the seventh. In Genesis 5:21 Enoch is listed as the seventh after Adam and is designated as the seventh from Adam in Enoch 60:8; 93:3; Jubilees 7:39 (s. Mayor; Green). **μυριάς** myriad, ten thousand. This refers to the angels who accompany God, esp. in
15 judgment (Kelly). ■ **ποιῆσαι** aor. act. inf. This verb is used w. the noun to form a verbal idea contained in the noun, i.e., lit. "to make judgment," "to do judgment" (s.v.3). The inf. is used to express purpose. **ἐλέγξαι** aor. act. inf. ἐλέγχω to convict. The inf. is used to express purpose. **ἀσέβεια** godless, irreverence (s.v.4). **ἠσέβησαν** aor. act. ind. ἀσεβέω to conduct an irreligious life, to be ungodly. **σκληρός** hard, harsh. The word conveys always a reproach and a grave one, it indicates a character of harsh inhumane and uncivil (Trench, *Synonyms*, 48). **ἐλάλησαν** aor. act. ind. **ἁμαρτωλός** sinful sinner. Jude's quotation from Enoch (Enoch 1:9) does not mean that the Book of Enoch was regarded as inspired or equal w. Scripture. An inspired man might well use contemporary ideas which were not contrary to revelation (Green, 49; for a study of the comparison between Enoch 1:9 and the quotation in Jude, s. Carroll D. Osborne, "The Christological Use of I Enoch I.9 in Jude 14, 15,"
16 NTS 23 [April, 1977], 334–341). ■ **γογγυστής** one who grumbles, one who murmurs and complains (s. 1 Cor. 10:10; Phil. 2:14). **μεμψίμοιρος** complaining of one's lot, to grumble about one's condition in life. The word was used to describe a standard Gr. character: "You're satisfied by nothing that befalls you; you complain at everything. You don't want what you have got; you long for what you haven't got. In winter you wish it were summer, and in summer that it were winter. You are like the sick folk, hard to please, and one who complains about his lot in life" (s. Green's quotation from Lucian, *Cynic*, XVII). The word indicates one who complained against God who has appointed each man his fate (TDNT; s. also MM). **ἐπιθυμία** strong desire, lust, passion. **πορευόμενοι** pres. mid. part. (s.v.11). **ὑπέρογκος** excessive size, puffed up, swollen. The word is generally used of great or even excessive size, and in later writers it is also used of "big" words, arrogant speech and demeanor (Mayor).

θαυμάζοντες pres. act. part. θαυμάζω to marvel, to wonder, to admire. The expression is used to translate the Heb. idiom "to take, or raise, a man's countenance," i.e., do honor or show favor to him. The formula had its origin in the oriental custom of making one to rise from the ground in token of welcome. This imagery soon disappeared and the expression meant "to show favoritism toward" or "to curry favor w." (Kelly). **ὠφέλεια** profit, gain, advantage. **χάριν** w. the gen. "on account of," "for the sake of."

■ **μνήσθητε** aor. pass. imp. μιμνῄσκομαι to remember, 17
to recall to memory. **προειρημένων** perf. pass. part. προλέγω
to say beforehand, to speak prior, to the events predicted, to
foretell (Kelly). The perf. tense indicates the lasting result of the
prediction. ■ **ἔλεγον** impf. ind. act. The impf. is customary 18
"they used to say," or it pictures the interat. action, i.e., "they
continued to say from time to time." **ἔσονται** fut. εἰμί.
ἐμπαίκτης one who makes fun by mocking, mocker, scoffer (s.
2 Peter 3:3). **ἀσέβεια** godlessness (s.v.4). ■ **ἀποδιορίζοντες** 19
pres. act. part. ἀποδιορίζω to make a boundary between someone and to separate from this one, to make a distinction, to make
a division, to cause division. The word would indicate to make
divisive distinctions between themselves and other people
(Green). It could also mean that by their ungodly living they
divide those in the assembly and some were being or about to
be taken by their error. **ψυχικός** worldly minded. The word
implies that these men follow their natural lusts and appetites
without restraint or control. **ἔχοντες** pres. act. part. ἔχω to have,
to possess. These do not have the Spirit of God and therefore live
unrestrained lives. ■ **ἐποικοδομοῦντες** pres. act. part. 20
ἐποικοδομέω to build up, to edify. The part. could express the
means or the manner of "guarding one's self" and expresses
contemporaneous time. **ἁγιώτατος** superl. most holy, holiest.
The superl. is used w. an elative force "very holy" (s. MT, 31).
The "most holy faith" would be the body of truth or faith which
has been once delivered to the saints (s.v.3) upon which one is
to build his life. **προσευχόμενοι** pres. mid. part. προσεύχομαι
to pray. The Christian must not only study the Scriptures if he
is to grow in the faith and be of use to others, but he must also
"pray in the Spirit" for the battle against false teaching is not
won by argument (Green). ■ **τηρήσατε** aor. act. imp. (s.v.1). 21
προσδεχόμενοι pres. mid. part. προσδέχομαι to earnestly
expect, to look forward to, to wait for. The part. expresses contemporary action and could be temporal, i.e., "while you are
awaiting." **τὸ ἔλεος** "the mercy." ■ **ἐλεᾶτε** pres. act. imp. 22

ἐλεάω to show pity, to be merciful. (For the textual problems in
vv. 22 and 23, s. TC, 727ff.) **διακρινομένους** pres. mid. part. to
dispute (s.v.9). The word may also have the meaning "to doubt,"
"to waiver," and the meaning might be "show pity on the waiv-
23 erers" (Green). ■ **σῴζετε** pres. act. imp. to rescue, to save.
ἁρπάζοντες pres. act. part. ἁρπάζω to seize, to snatch. The
figure of snatching them from fire may have been suggested by
the allusion to the punishment of Sodom and Gomorrah (Mayor). **μισοῦντες** pres. act. part. μισέω to hate. **ἐσπιλωμένον** perf. pass. part. σπιλόω to stain, to defile, to contaminate. The perf. tense emphasizes the state or result. **χιτών** the garment which was worn next to the body, i.e., undergarment. Then it referred to any garment. The idea seems to be that they are so corrupt that their very clothes are defiled (Green).

24 ■ **δυναμένῳ** pres. mid. part. "to the one who is able." **φυλάξαι** aor. act. inf. φυλάσσω to guard, to protect w. guards. The idea of protection and safety seems to be prominent here (s. T). **ἄπταιστος** without stumbling, not falling. The word is used of a horse which is sure-footed and does not stumble or of a good man who does not make moral lapses (Green). This would be the stumbling into the grievous sins of the spiritual spies. **στῆσαι** aor. act. inf. ἵστημι to place, to present. **κατενώπιον** "before the face of," i.e., "in the presence of." **ἄμωμος** without blame. **ἀγαλλίασις** rejoicing, exaltation. The word has special eschatological overtones denoting the jubilation of God's chosen people at His manifestation at the end (Kelly; s. also 1 Peter 1:6).

25 ■ **μεγαλωσύνη** greatness, majesty. **ἀμήν** truly, amen. The word regularly closes doxologies and sets a seal on this confident attribution of glory to the One to whom it belongs—the God who is able! (Green). (For general remarks regarding the Book of Jude, s. D.J. Rowston, "The Most Neglected Book in the New Testament," NTS 21 [July, 1975], 554–563.)

REVELATION

Ch. 1

ἀποκάλυψις unveiling, revealing, revelation (s. Hort; 1
Swete; 2 Thess. 1:7). The following gen. could be either obj., i.e.,
"a revelation of Jesus Christ" w. Him as the object or it could
be subjective gen. which fits better here, i.e., Jesus Christ is the
One who originates the revelation (s. Charles; Bousset). **ἔδωκεν**
aor. act. ind. *δίδωμι* to give. **δεῖξαι** aor. act. inf. *δείκνυμι* to
show. This word is characteristic of our author when it means
to communicate a divine revelation by means of visions
(Charles). **δεῖ** it is binding, it is necessary. The word denotes the
sure fulfillment of the purpose of God revealed by the prophets
(Swete). **γενέσθαι** aor. mid. inf. *γίνομαι* to happen, to come to
pass. **τάχος** quickly, suddenly, soon. The word indicates rapidi-
ty of execution (Walvoord). **ἐσήμανεν** aor. act. ind. *σημαίνω*
to signify. The word properly means strictly to show by some
sort of sign and it is esp. used of any intimation given by the gods
to men, particularly w. reference to the fut. (Hort). **ἀποστείλας**
aor. act. part. *ἀποστέλλω* to send, to send a commissioned
authoritative representative on a specific mission (s. TDNT).
■ **ἐμαρτύρησεν** aor. act. ind. *μαρτυρέω* to testify, to bear 2
witness. ■ **μακάριος** happy, blessed (s. Matt. 5:3). 3
ἀναγινώσκων pres. act. part. *ἀναγινώσκω* to read, to read
aloud. This is not the private student but the public reader
(Charles; s. also Swete). **ἀκούοντες** pres. act. part. nom. pl. "the
ones who hear." The public reading of Scripture was taken over
from Jewish practice (Mounce). **προφητεία** the message of a
prophet, prophecy. **τηροῦντες** pres. act. part. *τηρέω* to keep, to
observe. **γεγραμμένα** perf. pass. part. *γράφω*. The perf. tense
stresses the state or condition and often the authority of a legal
document (s. MM). **ἐγγύς** near.

■ **ἀπό** "from." The prep. is normally followed by the gen. 4
Here the names of God are to be treated as an indeclinable noun
and as an indeclinable noun are probably intended to be treated
as a paraphrase of the tetragrammaton, Y-H-W-H, "He who is"
(Ford; s. also Mounce; Swete). **ὤν** pres. act. part. *εἰμί*. **ἦν** impf.
εἰμί. **ἐρχόμενος** pres. mid. part. In the Gr. world similar titles

for the gods are found. In the song of the doves at Dodona we
read of "Zeus who was, Zeus who is, and Zeus who will be"
5 (Mounce). ■ **πρωτότοκος** firstborn (s. Col. 1:15). **ἄρχων** pres.
act. part. ἄρχω to be at the beginning, ruler, prince. The Resurrection carried w. it the potential lordship over all humanity and the words "the ruler of the kings of the earth" stand appropriately at the head of a book which represents the glorified Christ as presiding over the destinies of nations (Swete).

ἀγαπῶντι pres. act. part. **λύσαντι** aor. act. part. λύω to loose, to release. The aor. tense points to the completed act. **ἐν τῷ αἵματι** "by His blood." The prep. is instrumental (Ford) and the blood speaks of the sacrificed life which was the ransom or
6 payment for release (Swete; s. also 1 Peter 1:18–19). ■ **ἐποίησεν**
aor. act. ind. **ἀμήν** "amen." The word is acknowledgement of that which is valid. In the synagogue it is the response of the community to the prayers uttered by the leader (Ford).

7 ■ **νεφέλη** cloud. Not simply that He has a surrounding of clouds, but that He compels all the clouds into His retinue (Hort). It may be that the clouds are not the ordinary clouds of nature, but clouds in heaven seen in the vision around the throne of God. In any case the cloud in Heb. thought is commonly associated w. the divine presence (Exod. 13:21; 16:10; Matt. 17:5; Acts 1:9) (Mounce; s. also Dan. 7:13; Jastrow II, 1095; s. also 1QM 12:9). **ὄψεται** fut. mid. ind. ὁράω to see. **ἐξεκέντησαν** aor. act. ind. ἐκκεντέω to pierce. The word is used in John 19:37 and there they looked to Him in amazement; they will look to Him for forgiveness and salvation (Abbott, 247). In the gospel the main reference is to the crucifixion: whereas here it is eschatological (Charles). **κόψονται** fut. mid. ind. κόπτομαι to smite the chest in sorrow. **φυλή** tribe. **ναί** yes.

8 ■ **ἄλφα** "alpha," the first letter of the Gr. alphabet. **ὦ** "omega," the last letter of the Gr. alphabet. The phrase is seen to express not eternity only, but infinitude, the boundless life which embraces all while it transcends all (Swete). **ὤν** pres. act. part. **ἦν** impf. **ἐρχόμενος** pres. mid. part. (s.v.4). **παντοκράτωρ** the almighty, the omnipotent. The reference is more to God's supremacy over all things than to the related idea of divine omnipotence. The word was used in secular literature to describe the attributes of the gods and is probably used here in contrast to the Roman emperor's self-designation as *autokrator* (s. Mounce; Ford; TDNT).

9 ■ **συγκοινωνός** fellow partaker, one who shares together. **θλῖψις** pressure, trouble, tribulation (s. TDNT; Trench, *Synonyms*, 202). **ἐγενόμην** aor. mid. ind. **γίνομαι**. **νῆσος** island.

καλουμένῃ pres. pass. part. καλέω to call, to name. The island of Patmos was a small, rocky island about 16 sq. miles in the Aegean Sea some 40 miles southwest of Miletus. It was a penal settlement to which the Roman authorities sent offenders (Mounce; s. also LSC, 82–92; KP IV, 549; IBD III, 677; Caird).
■ **ἐν πνεύματι** "in the Spirit." The phrase denotes the prophet 10
under inspiration (Swete). **κυριακός** pertaining to the Lord, the Lord's Day. This could be a reference to "Sunday or it could be an eschatological reference to 'the Day of the Lord' so that the prophet was stationed as a spectator amid the very scenes of the great judgment itself" (Seiss; s. also W. Stott, "A Note on the Word KURIAKE in Revelation I.10," NTS 12 [Oct., 1965], 70–75; K.A. Strand, "Another Look at 'Lord's Day' in the Early Church and in Revelation I.10," NTS 13 [Jan., 1967], 174–181).
ἤκουσα aor. act. ind. ἀκούω. **ὀπίσω** behind. ■ **λεγούσης** pres. 11
act. part. fem. sing. The part. agrees w. the dependent gen. "trumpet," rather than the noun "voice," "sound" (Mounce). **γράψον** aor. act. imp. **πέμψον** aor. act. imp. πέμπω to send. (For writing and the sending of letters in the ancient world, s. LSC 1–49; RAC II, 564–585; KP II, 324–327; for Roman roads in the province of Asia, s. GAM 164–179.)

■ **ἐπέστρεψα** aor. act. ind. ἐπιστρέφω to turn around, to 12
turn toward. **ἐλάλει** impf. act. ind. λαλέω. The impf. emphasizes the continual action in the past time. **ἐπιστρέψας** aor. act. part. The part. is used temporally expressing either antecedent or contemporaneous action. **λυχνία** lampstand. The Mosaic lampstand for the Tabernacle, that which stood (one or more) in the later temples and in the vision of Zech. 6:2, had seven branches, but here we have seven distinct lampstands each w. its one light. Of course, it has nothing to do w. candlesticks but was a kind of lamp w. a wick and oil (Hort; s. also Mounce; Swete).
■ **μέσον** middle. **ὅμοιος** like. **ἐνδεδυμένον** perf. pass. part. 13
ἐνδύω to put on, pass. to be clothed. **ποδήρης** reaching to the foot. The word is used in Exodus 28:4 for the blue-purple outward robe of the high priest which reached down to his feet (Bousset; Mounce). The word is also used in Ezra 9:2 where it is applied to the man charged w. setting a mark upon some of the Jerusalemites before the destruction of the city. Of the two possible emphases, a priestly ministry and one of mercy in the face of impending judgment, the latter is more likely the choice since nowhere else in the book does Christ appear in a priestly capacity (Robert L. Thomas, "The Glorified Christ on Patmos," Bib Sac 122 [July, 1965], 243). **περιεζωσμένον** perf. pass. part. περιζώννυμι to be girded round about, to wear a wide belt

around one's self. **μαστός** breast. The ordinary girding for one actively engaged was "at the loins," but Josephus (Antiq. III.7.2) expressly tells us that the Levitical priests were girded higher up, about the breast—favoring a calmer more majestic movement. In like manner the angels who carry out the judgments of God have their breasts girded w. golden girdles (Rev. 15:6). **ζώνη** girdle. The girdle or wide belt is often contemplated as the symbol of
14 strength and activity (SCA; Swete). ■ **θρίξ, τριχός** hair. **λευκός** white. **ἔριον** wool. **χιών** snow. In Daniel 7:9 the Ancient of Days is described as having hair "like pure wool" and raiment "white as snow." The ascriptions of the titles and attributes of God to Christ is an indication of the exalted Christology of the Apocalypse. The hoary head was worthy of honor and conveyed the idea of wisdom and dignity (Lev. 19:32; Prov. 16:31) (Mounce). **φλόξ** flame. **πῦρ** fire. The "eyes as a flame of fire" indicated the penetrating glance which flashed w. quick intelligence and when need arose w. righteous wrath (Swete; s. also
15 SCA). ■ **χαλκολίβανον** gold ore, fine brass or bronze. The meaning of the word is somewhat uncertain but it is best understood as an alloy of gold or fine brass. In any case the shining bronze like feet portray strength and stability (Mounce; Swete; s. also BAG; Ford). **κάμινος** oven. **πεπυρωμένης** perf. pass. part. **πυρόω** to set on fire, to burn. The perf. tense emphasizes the completed state or results, i.e., "having been burned," "having been refined." The idea may be "glowing" and it would indicate that the metal is not only the finest and brightest, but
16 it is aglow as if still in the crucible (Swete). ■ **ἔχων** pres. act. part. **δεξιός** right. **ἀστήρ** star. **στόμα** mouth. **ῥομφαία** sword. This word is properly the long and heavy broad sword w. which the Thracians and other barbarous nations were armed and symbolizes the irresistible power of divine judgment (SCA; Mounce). **δίστομος** two-edged. **ὀξύς** sharp. **ἐκπορευομένη** pres. mid. part. **ἐκπορεύομαι** to go out. **ὄψις** appearance, outward appearance, face. In the context its primary reference is to the face but should not be limited to that alone (Mounce). **φαίνει** pres. act. ind. to shine "as the sun shines in His might" (Swete).
17 ■ **ἔπεσα** aor. act. ind. **πίπτω** to fall. **ἔθηκεν** aor. act. ind. **τίθημι** to place. **φοβοῦ** pres. mid. imp. **φοβέομαι** to be afraid. The pres. imp. w. the neg. indicates the stopping of an action in progress: "stop being afraid." **ἔσχατος** last. The expression "I am the first and the last" is the expression of absolute Godhead
18 (s. Isa. 41:4; 44:6; 48:12) (SCA; Ford). ■ **ζῶν** pres. act. part. **ζάω** to live. **κλείς** key. **ᾅδης** Hades, death, the place of the dead (TDNT; CBB; s. also SB IV, 1016–1065). To "have the keys of

death and of Hades" is to possess authority over their domain. The claim to possess potentially the key of death is made by Christ Himself in John 5:28; the Apocalypse connects the actual possession of the keys w. His victory over death. They are from
that moment in His keeping (Swete). ■ **εἶδες** aor. act. ind. ὁράω 19
to see. **εἰσίν** pres. ind. εἰμί to be. **μέλλει** pres. act. ind. to be about to. Used w. the inf. to express the fut. **γενέσθαι** aor. mid. inf. γίνομαι to become, to happen. This v. gives the threefold division of the Book of Revelation: "the things which you saw" refer to the vision of the glorified Christ, esp. vv. 11–18; "the things which are" refer to the letters to the churches in chapters 2 and 3; and "the things which will happen, come to pass after these things" refer to the events described in 4–22 (s. Lohse; Walvoord; Govett; Scott; Bousset; Robert L. Thomas, "John's
Apocalyptic Outline," Bib Sac 123 [Oct., 1966], 334–341). ■ 20
μυστήριον mystery.

Ch. 2

■ **γράψον** aor. act. imp. γράφω. **κρατῶν** pres. act. part. 1
κρατέω to have power over, to hold, to grasp, to hold fast (s. Ford). **ἀστήρ** star. **δεξιά** right. **περιπατῶν** pres. act. part. περιπατέω to walk about. The Lord patrols the ground and is ever on the spot when He is needed; His presence is not localized but coextensive w. the church (Swete). **μέσον** middle. **λυχνία**
lampstand (s. Rev. 1:12). **χρυσοῦς** golden. ■ **κόπος** laborious 2
work, toil. The word signifies not merely labor, but labor "unto weariness" (s. Hort; SCA; Trench, *Synonyms*, 378; s. also 1 Thess. 2:9). **βαστάσαι** aor. act. inf. βαστάζω to carry, to bear. **ἐπείρασας** aor. act. ind. πειράζω to try, to examine. **καὶ οὐκ εἰσίν** "and they are not." The words are a Hebraism for "not being" (Charles). **εὗρες** aor. act. ind. εὑρίσκω. **ψευδής** lying,
liars. ■ **ἐβάστασας** aor. act. ind. **κεκοπίακας** perf. act. ind. 3
κοπιάω to be weary, to work and labor to the point of weariness. The word implies strenuous and exhausting labor. Here it could be weary morally, i.e., to allow one's self to become weary (Hort; s. also SCA). The perf. tense looks at the continuing results of
the labor. ■ **ἀφῆκας** aor. act. ind. ἀφίημι to leave, to forsake. 4
■ **μνημόνευε** pres. act. imp. μνημονεύω to remember, to call 5
to remembrance. **πόθεν** from where. **πέπτωκας** perf. act. ind. πίπτω to fall. **μετανόησον** aor. act. imp. μετανοέω to change one's thinking, to think differently, to repent. The pres. imp., "repent," stands in contrast to the aor. imp., "repent," and suggests a continuing attitude over against a decisive break. "Bear in mind the loving relationships you once enjoyed and make a

clean break w. your present manner of life!" (Mounce).
ποίησον aor. act. imp. **σοί** "to you." The dat. could be taken
as dat. of disadvantage (Swete). **κινήσω** fut. act. ind. *κινέω* to
move. **τόπος** place. **μετανοήσῃς** aor. act. subj. *μετανοέω* The
subj. is used in a third-class conditional clause which assumes
6 that the condition is possible. ■ **μισεῖς** pres. act. ind. to hate.
(For a discussion of the identity of the Nicolaitans, s. Mounce;
7 Ford; Swete.) ■ **ἔχων** pres. act. part. **οὖς** ear. **ἀκουσάτω** aor.
act. imp. **νικῶντι** pres. act. part. *νικάω* to be victor, to gain a
victory, to be victorious. **δώσω** fut. act. ind. *δίδωμι*. **φαγεῖν**
aor. act. inf. *ἐσθίω* to eat. **ξύλον** tree. **παράδειος** paradise, a
Persian word meaning a park or enclosed garden. According to
rabbinical teaching there was a threefold paradise, i.e., the paradise of Adam where the tree of life stood; the paradise of the souls in heaven which was the abode of the redeemed between death and the Resurrection; the eschatological paradise where the souls of the righteous would be. The eschatological paradise was considered to be the paradise of Adam restored w. the tree of life (s. SB III, 792f.; IV, 1144–1165; Ford; s. also Luke 23:43).
8 ■ **ἔσχατος** last (s. Rev. 1:17). **ἐγένετο** aor. mid. ind.
γίνομαι. **ἔζησεν** aor. act. ind. *ζάω* to live. The purpose of this
statement is to fix attention upon the fact of the Resurrection.
As the Lord rose, so will His martyrs triumph over death
9 (Swete). ■ **θλῖψις** pressure, trouble, tribulation (s. Rev. 1:9).
πτωχεία poverty, extreme and abject poverty (s. 2 Cor. 8:9;
NTW, 109–111). **πλούσιος** rich, wealthy. **βλασφημία** slan-
10 der, railing, blasphemy. ■ **φοβοῦ** pres. mid. imp. *φοβέομαι* to
be afraid. **μέλλεις** pres. act. ind. to be about to. The word is used
w. the inf. to express the fut. **πάσχειν** pres. act. inf. to suffer.
βάλλειν pres. act. inf. to throw, to cast. **διάβολος** devil.
πειρασθῆτε aor. pass. subj. The prisons in the ancient world
were a place where the accused awaited sentencing which resulted either in execution or banishment (s. Mounce). **ἕξετε** fut.
act. ind. *ἔχω*. **γίνου** pres. mid. imp. *γίνομαι* to become, to
"prove thyself loyal and true, to the extent of being ready to die
11 for my sake" (Swete). **δώσω** fut. act. ind. (s.v.7). ■ **ἔχων** pres.
act. part. **ἀκουσάτω** aor. act. imp. (s.v.7). **ἀδικηθῇ** aor. pass.
subj. *ἀδικέω* to harm, to injure.
12 ■ **ἔχων** pres. act. part. **ῥομφαία** sword (s. Rev. 1:16).
13 **δίστομος** two-edged. **ὀξύς** sharp. ■ **κατοικεῖς** pres. act. ind. to
settle down, to live. **κρατεῖς** pres. act. ind. to hold, to grasp, to
hold fast (s.v.1). **ἠρνήσω** aor. act. ind. *ἀρνέομαι* to say no, to
14 deny. **ἀπεκτάνθη** aor. pass. ind. *ἀποκτείνω* to kill. ■
κρατοῦντας pres. act. part. to hold to. **ἐδίδασκεν** impf. ind.

act. **βαλεῖν** aor. act. inf. (s.v.10). **φαγεῖν** aor. act. inf. (s.v.7).
εἰδωλόθυτον sacrifices offered to idols, that which is slain for
a sacrifice (s. SCA). **πορνεῦσαι** aor. act. inf. πορνεύω to engage in sexual activities. The inf. are used after the verb "to
teach." ■ **οὕτως** so, thus. The application and parallel is now 15
drawn. The city of Pergamum was a stronghold of idolatry. It
was famous for the great altar of Zeus which had a frieze around
the base of the altar depicting the gods of Greece in victorious
combat against the giants of the earth (symbolizing the triumph
of civilization over barbarianism). The shrine of Asklepios, the
god of healing, attracted people from all over the world. Of
greatest import for the Christians living in Pergamum was the
fact that it was the official center in Asia for the imperial cult
(Mounce; s. also Charles; LSC, 281–315). **ὁμοίως** adv. in like
manner. ■ **μετανόησον** aor. act. imp. (s.v.5). **ταχύ** adv. quickly, 16
soon. **πολεμήσω** fut. act. ind. πολεμέω to wage war, to fight
against. ■ **ἀκουσάτω** aor. act. imp. **νικῶντι** pres. act. part. 17
δώσω fut. act. ind. (s.v.7). **μάννα** manna. **κεκρυμμένου** perf.
pass. part. κρύπτω to hide. It was a Jewish teaching that in the
messianic time the Messiah would send manna from heaven and
in the fut. age, manna would be the food of the righteous (SB,
793; s. also Mounce). In the context here the hidden manna
alludes to the proper and heavenly food in contrast to the unclean food supplied by the Balaamites. While the promise is
primarily eschatological, it is not without immediate application
for a persecuted people (Mounce). **ψῆφος** stone. **λευκός** white.
γεγραμμένον perf. pass. part. γράφω. **λαμβάνων** pres. act.
part. There were various usages of "a white stone" in the ancient
world. Perhaps in the context it is best to take the white stone
as a token which served for admission to a banquet. Many of
such tokens were little tablets of wood, metal, or stone and these
were distributed to the poor in Rome by the emperors to insure
a regular supply of corn. Or they were given to the victor at
games and to gladiators who won the admiration of the public
and had been allowed to retire from further combat. Here the
white stone as symbol of the triumph of faith would be considered to be a token for admission to the messianic feast (s.
Mounce; LSC, 303ff.).

■ **ἔχων** pres. act. part. **φλόξ** flame. **πῦρ** fire. 18
χαλκολίβανον (s. Rev. 1:15). ■ **διακονία** ministry. **πλείων** 19
comp. πολύς more than. **τῶν πρώτων** gen. of comparison "than
the first one." ■ **ἀφεῖς** pres. act. ind. ἄφημι to allow, to tolerate. 20
προφῆτις prophetess. **πλανᾷ** pres. act. ind. to lead astray, to
deceive. **πορνεῦσαι** aor. act. inf. (s.v.14). **φαγεῖν** aor. act. inf.

(s.v.7). **εἰδωλόθυτον** sacrifice offered to an idol (s.v.14). (For a good discussion of the woman "Jezebel" and an identification of her and her teachings, s. Mounce. She is viewed as a prominent woman claiming the gift of divine prophecy and leading many in pagan worship and pagan feasts which often led to sexual
21 promiscuity.) ■ **ἔδωκα** aor. act. ind. δίδωμι. **μετανοήσῃ** aor.
act. subj. The subj. is used in a purpose clause. **μετανοῆσαι** aor.
act. inf. **πορνεία** immorality. The word here means wanton
behavior including fornication (s. Joseph Jensen, "Does *Porneia*
Mean Fornication? A Critique of Bruce Malina," Nov T 20
22 [July, 1978], 168–184). ■ **κλίνη** bed. The bed is not a "funeral-
bier" or a "dining couch" of the guild feast, but a bed of sickness
or pain. Disease as a punishment for sin was an accepted view
(Mounce). **μοιχεύοντας** pres. act. part. μοιχεύω to commit
23 adultery. **μετανοήσουσιν** fut. act. ind. ■ **ἀποκτενῶ** fut. act.
ind. (s.v.13). **γνώσονται** fut. mid. ind. γινώσκω. **ἐρευνῶν**
pres. act. part. ἐρευνάω to search. The pres. tense indicates
habitual and continual action. **νεφρός** kidney. Kidneys were
regarded as the seat of the emotions, just as the heart was the
seat of the intelligence or the will. Hence, the speaker w. divine
omniscience will prove that no deceit or sophistry of any kind
24 can escape him (Ford). **δώσω** fut. act. ind. (s.v.7). ■ **λοιπός** rest,
remaining. **ἔγνωσαν** aor. act. ind. γινώσκω. **βάθος** deep,
25 depth. **βάρος** burden (s. Acts 15:28, 29). ■ **πλήν** except, only.
κρατήσατε aor. act. imp. (s.v.1). **ἄρχι οὗ** "until, until which
time." **ἥξω** fut. act. ind. ἥκω to come. Used in an indefinite
temporal clause and the form can be either fut. act. ind. or aor.
26 act. subj. (RWP). ■ **νικῶν** pres. act. part. (s.v.7). **τηρῶν** pres.
27 act. part. τηρέω to keep, to guard, to observe. ■ **ποιμανεῖ** fut.
act. ind. ποιμαίνω to shepherd. The word should be taken here
in the sense of wheeling the shepherd's staff or club to ward off
attacks of marauding beasts (Mounce). **ῥάβδος** stick, staff.
σιδηροῦς, ᾶ, οῦν iron. **σκεῦος** vessel. **κεραμικός** pottery,
earthenware. **συντρίβεται** pres. pass. ind. συντρίβω to crush
28 together, to smash. ■ **εἴληφα** perf. act. ind. λαμβάνω. **πρωΐνος**
morning, "morning star." In addition to authority over the nations the overcomer is promised the morning star. No completely satisfactory answer for this symbol has been offered (Mounce;
29 s. also his listing of various possibilities). ■ **ἀκουσάτω** aor. act.
imp. (s.v.7).

Ch. 3

1 ■ **γράψον** aor. act. imp. γράφω
ἔχων pres. act. part. **ἀστήρ** star. **ζῇς** pres. act. ind. to live.

As the city was rebuilt in the time of Alexander the Great, it was
dedicated to a local Asiatic goddess usually referred to as
Cybele, who was identified w. the Gr. Artemis. This patron deity
was believed to possess the special power of restoring the dead
to life (Mounce; s. also LSC, 363–365f.). ■ **γίνου** pres. mid. imp. 2
γρηγορῶν pres. act. part. γρηγορέω to be awake, to be watchful. Although the city of Sardis was considered to be a natural
citadel and incapable of capture, there were several times in the
city's history that the city fell because of self-confidence and
failure to watch. Perhaps the most famous incidence was when
Cyrus, king of Persia, captured the city as Croesus was king of
Sardis (s. Herodotus I, 84; LSC, 354–362; Mounce; C.J. Hemer,
"The Sardis Letter and the Croesus Tradition," NTS 19 [Oct.,
1972], 94–97). **στήρισον** aor. act. imp. στηρίζω to make firm,
to strengthen, to establish. **ἔμελλον** impf. act. ind. Used w. the
inf. to express the fut. The impf. w. the inf. expresses futurity or
intention reckoned from a moment in the past (MKG, 307).
ἀποθανεῖν aor. act. inf. ἀποθνήσκω to die. **εὕρηκα** perf. act.
ind. **πεπληρωμένα** perf. pass. part. πληρόω to fill, to be filled;
their works have not measured up to God's standard (RWP).
■ **μνημόνευε** pres. act. imp. μνημονεύω to remember. 3
εἴληφας perf. act. ind. λαμβάνω to receive. The word represents the faith as a trust and the perf. tense calls attention to the
abiding responsibility of the trust then received (Swete).
ἤκουσας aor. act. ind. ἀκούω to hear. The aor. looks back to
the moment when faith came by hearing (Swete). **τήρει** pres.
act. imp. τηρέω to keep, to watch, to guard. The pres. tense calls
for a continual watchful attitude. **μετανόησον** aor. act. imp.
μετανοέω to change one's thinking, to repent (s. Rev. 2:5).
γρηγορησῃς aor. act. subj. The subj. is used in a third-class
conditional clause which views the condition as a possibility.
ἥξω fut. act. ind. ἥκω to come (note the history of the city
alluded to in v. 2). **οὐ μή** "not in any wise." **γνῷς** aor. act. subj.
γινώσκω. **ποῖος** what kind of. The acc. here is acc. of time but
looks more at a point of time rather than a long duration (s. RG,
470f.; RWP; Mounce). ■ **ἐμόλυναν** aor. act. ind. μολύνω to 4
soil. The language recalls the inscription found in Asia Minor
which announced that soiled garments disqualified the worshiper and dishonored the god (Ford). It is also often noted that since
the manufacture and dying of woolen goods was a principle trade
in Sardis, an allusion to defiled garments would be immediately
recognized. It is unlikely, however, that any more than a general
reference to the danger of contaminating the Christian witness
by accommodation to the prevailing standards of a pagan city is

in mind (Mounce). **περιπατήσουσιν** fut. act. ind. περιπατέω
to walk about. **λευκός** white. The raiment here spoken of is the
heavenly raiment or it is the symbol of inner purity (Charles;
5 Ford). ■ **νικῶν** pres. act. part. νικάω to win a victory, to be
victorious, to overcome. **περιβαλεῖται** fut. mid. ind.
περιβάλλω to throw clothes around one's self, to clothe one's
self. **ἐξαλείψω** fut. act. ind. ἐξαλείφω to wipe out, to blot out.
In the OT the book of life was a register of all who held citizenship in the theocratic community of Israel. The idea was also
common in the secular world and all Gr. and Roman cities of
that time kept a list of citizens according to their class or tribe
in which new citizens were entered and from which degraded
citizens were expunged (Mounce; Ford; LSC, 385f.). The promise here is positive that these will not in any way have their
names blotted out. **ὁμολογήσω** fut. act. ind. ὁμολογέω to con-
6 fess, to acknowledge, to profess. ■ **ἀκουσάτω** aor. act. imp.
7 ■ **γράψον** aor. act. imp.
ἀληθινός true, genuine. **ἔχων** pres. act. part. **κλείς** key.
The "key of David" is a metaphorical expression indicating complete control over the royal household (Mounce; s. also Swete).
ἀνοίγων pres. act. part. ἀνοίγω to open. **κλείσει** fut. act. ind.
κλείω to shut, to lock. **κλείων** pres. act. part. (For a description
of keys and locks in the ancient world and how they worked and
how they were used as a symbol of power, s. OCD, 573; KP V,
8 18f.; TDNT.) ■ **δέδωκα** perf. act. ind. δίδωμι to give.
ἠνεῳγμένην perf. pass. part. ἀνοίγω to open. The perf. tense
indicates the continuing condition, i.e., "a door standing open."
The metaphor of the "open door" indicated the opportunity for
preaching the gospel (Swete; SCA; s. also 1 Cor. 16:9). **κλεῖσαι**
aor. act. inf. **ἐτήρησας** aor. act. ind. (s.v.3). **ἠρνήσω** aor. mid.
ind. ἀρνέομαι to say no, to deny. The aor. refer to some distinct
occasions in the past when, being put to the test, they had proved
9 themselves faithful to Him (SCA). ■ **διδῶ** pres. act. ind. A late
omega form for δίδωμι to give (s. RWP). **ποιήσω** fut. act. ind.
ἥξουσιν fut. act. ind. (s.v.3). **ἠγάπησα** aor. act. ind. ἀγαπάω.
10 ■ **ὑπομενή** remaining under, patient endurance. It is the spirit
which can bear things not simply w. resignation, but w. blazing
hope (NTW, 60; s. also TDNT; CBB; RAC IX, 255ff.). **τηρήσω**
fut. act. ind. **πειρασμός** testing, temptation. **μελλούσης** pres.
act. part. to be about to. The word is used w. the inf. to express
the fut. tense **οἰκουμένη** pres. pass. part. οἰκέω to live. The
word is used for the inhabited earth. **πειράσαι** aor. act. inf.
11 πειράζω to try. **κατοικοῦντας** pres. act. part. κατοικέω. ■
ταχύ quickly, soon. **κράτει** pres. act. imp. κρατέω to hold fast,

to grasp. **λάβῃ** aor. act. subj. λαμβάνω. The subj. is used in a
neg. purpose clause. ■ **νικῶν** pres. act. part. (s.v.5). **στῦλος** 12
pillar. The metaphor of being a pillar in a temple is current in most languages and conveys the idea of stability and permanence (Mounce). **ἐξέλθῃ** aor. act. subj. ἐξέρχομαι to go out. To a city that had experienced devastating earthquakes which caused people to flee into the countryside and to establish temporary dwellings there, the promise of permanence within the New Jerusalem would have a special meaning (Mounce; s. also LSC, 396f.). **γράψω** fut. act. ind. **καταβαίνουσα** pres. act. part.
καταβαίνω to come down. ■ **ἀκουσάτω** aor. act. imp. (s.v.6). 13
■ **γράψον** aor. act. imp. 14
ἀρχή beginning, first (s. Col. 1:18). ■ **ψυχρός** cold. **ζεστός** 15
boiling, hot. **ὄφελον**. Used to express a wish about the pres. "I
would that you were" (RWP). ■ **χλιαρός** warm, lukewarm. The 16
contrast here is between the hot medicinal waters of Hierapolis and the cold, pure waters of Colossae. Thus, the church in Laodicea was providing neither refreshment for its spiritual weary nor healing for the spiritual sick. It was totally ineffective and thus distasteful to the Lord (Mounce; s. also Ford). **μέλλω** pres. act. ind. to be about to. **ἐμέσαι** aor. act. inf. ἐμέω to vomit, to reject
w. disgust (s. RWP; SCA). ■ **ὅτι.** Used after the verb "you say" 17
to introduce direct speech and is equivalent to quotation marks. **πλούσιος** rich, wealthy. **πεπλούτηκα** perf. act. ind. πλουτέω to become rich, to be rich, i.e., my wealth is due to my own exertion (Swete). The city of Laodicea was known for its wealth (Ford; s. also LSC, 416ff.; Mounce). **ταλαίπωρος** miserable, wretched. **ἐλεεινός** pitiable, miserable. The word indicates one who is set forth as an object of extremest pity (SCA). **πτωχός** poor, extremely poor, poor as a beggar. **τυφλός** blind. Laodicea was widely known for its medical school and particularly famous for an eye salve made from "phrygian powder" mixed w. oil (Mounce; s. also LSC, 419f.; Ford). **γυμνός** naked. The city was famous for its garments of glossy black wool (Ford; LSC, 416).
■ **συμβουλεύω** pres. act. ind. to give counsel, to advise. 18
ἀγοράσαι aor. act. inf. ἀγυράζω to buy. **πεπυρωμένον** perf. pass. part. πυρόω to burn, pass. to be refined. **πλουτήσῃς** aor. act. subj. (s.v.17). **περιβάλῃ** aor. mid. subj. (s.v.5). **φανερωθῇ** aor. pass. subj. φανερόω to make known, to make clear, pass. to be manifest, to be revealed. **αἰσχύνη** shame. **γυμνότης** nakedness. In the biblical world nakedness was a symbol of judgment and humiliation (Mounce). **κολλύριον** eye salve. The phrygian powder was apparently applied to the eyes in the form of a doughy paste (Mounce). **ἐγχρῖσαι** aor. act. inf. ἐγχρίζω to

19 anoint w. salve. **βλέπῃς** pres. act. subj. ■ **φιλῶ** pres. act. subj.
φιλέω to be fond of, to love. **ζήλευε** pres. act. imp. to be zealous.
20 **μετανόησον** aor. act. imp. (s.v.3). ■ **ἕστηκα** perf. act. ind.
ἵστημι to place, perf. to stand. **κρούω** pres. act. ind. to knock.
The pres. tense indicates the continual knocking. **ἀκούσῃ** aor.
act. subj. The subj. is used in a third-class conditional clause
which assumes the condition to be possible. **ἀνοίξῃ** aor. act.
subj. (s.v.7). **εἰσελεύσομαι** fut. mid. ind. εἰσέρχομαι to come
in. **δειπνήσω** fut. act. ind. δειπνέω to eat, to eat a meal. The
word refers to the meal which came at the end of the day and
was the principal meal and the usual occasion for hospitality
21 (Swete). ■ **νικῶν** pres. act. part. (s.v.5). **δώσω** fut. act. ind.
δίδωμι to give. **καθίσαι** aor. act. inf. καθίζω to sit, to cause to
22 sit. **ἐνίκησα** aor. act. ind. **ἐκάθισα** aor. act. ind. ■ **ἔχων** pres.
act. part. **ἀκουσάτω** aor. act. imp. (s.v.6).

Ch. 4

1 ■ **εἶδον καὶ ἰδού** "I saw and behold." The words serve to
introduce a new vision of special importance (Swete; Charles).
ἠνεῳγμένη perf. pass. part. ἀνοίγω to open. The perf. tense
could suggest that the door had been opened and left that way
for John's arrival (Mounce). **ἤκουσα** aor. act. ind. ἀκούω.
λαλούσης pres. act. part. **ἀνάβα** aor. act. imp. ἀναβαίνω to
go up. **δείξω** fut. act. ind. δείκνυμι to show, to exhibit. **δεῖ** "it
is binding," "it is necessary." The vision that follows is an anticipation of a fut. which is yet to find its accomplishment and is a
prophecy of the things which will take place after "the things
which are" at the present time as described in Revelation 2–3
2 (s. Swete; Bousset; Rev. 1:19). ■ **εὐθέως** adv. "immediately."
ἐγενόμην aor. mid. ind. γίνομαι (s. Rev. 1:10). **ἔκειτο** impf.
mid. ind. κεῖμαι to lie, to stand. The verb is used as the pass.
of the verb "to place" (RWP; s. also Swete). **καθήμενος** pres.
mid. part. κάθημαι to sit. John is allowed to see the throne room
of the heavenly palace and his eye falls at first on the ruler's
throne, which kind was used by kings and judges as they presid-
ed. The one enthroned in heaven can then only be the king of
3 all kings who rules and judges the whole world (Lohse). ■
ὅμοιος like. **ὅρασις** appearance. **ἴασπις** jasper stone. Perhaps
this ancient stone was a translucent rock crystal or perhaps a
diamond, and it may suggest such qualities as majesty, holiness,
or purity (Mounce). **σάρδιον** sardius stone. This was a blood-
red stone named after Sardis near which it was found. The stone
may be interpreted as wrath or judgment (Mounce). **ἶρις** rainbow, rainbow colored. The word may indicate the halo of em-

erald which encircled the throne (Swete). **κυκλόθεν** w. the gen.
"encircling." **σμαράγδινος** made of emerald. If the rainbow
which surrounded the throne was a halo, then the emerald is
usually pictured as green; otherwise it is a colorless crystal which
would refract a rainbow of prismatic colors and would speak of
God's mercy (Mounce; s. also Ford). ■ **περιβεβλημένους** perf. 4
pass. part. περιβάλλω to throw around, pass. to be clothed.
λευκός white. **χρυσοῦς** golden. The 24 elders clothed in white
robes w. golden crowns could represent the church (Seiss; s. also
Walvoord; Scott). Others would interpret them as being an exalted angelic order who serve and adore God as an angelic priesthood (Mounce; Govett). ■ **ἐκπορεύονται** pres. mid. ind. to go 5
out from, to proceed from. **ἀστραπή** lightning. **βροντή** thunder. The thunderstorm is in Heb. poetry a familiar symbol of the
divine power and glory (Swete). **λαμπάς** torch. **πῦρ** fire.
καιόμεναι pres. pass. part. καίω to burn, pass. to be burning.
■ **ὑάλινος** made of glass. **κρύσταλλος** crystal. It was a pave- 6
ment of glass resembling an expanse of water which was clear as
rock crystal (Swete).

μέσον middle. **κύκλος** circle, encircling, around. It is an
adv. in the locative case used here as a prep. This seems to mean
that one of the four living creatures was on each of the four sides
of the throne, either stationary or moving rapidly around
(RWP). The exact location is a bit uncertain but "in the midst"
apparently means "in the immediate vicinity." Thus, they surround the throne as an inner circle (Mounce). **ζῷον** living creature. **γέμοντα** pres. act. part. γέμω to be full of. **ἔμπροσθεν** in
front. **ὄπισθεν** behind, in back of. ■ **λέων** lion. **μόσχος** a young 7
steer, calf. **ἔχων** pres. act. part. **ἀετός** eagle. The four forms
suggest whatever is noblest, strongest, wisest, and swiftest in the
animate nature (Swete). The beings here are heavenly creatures
which serve and worship God. **πετομένῳ** pres. mid. part.
πέτομαι to fly. ■ **ἀνά** each one, one by one, the distributive use 8
of the prep. (s. BAG). **πτέρυξ** wing. **ἔσωθεν** within.
ἀνάπαυσις ceasing, pause, rest. **παντοκράτωρ** almighty (s.
Rev. 1:8). **ἦν** impf. εἰμί. **ὤν** pres. part. εἰμί. **ἐρχόμενος** pres.
mid. part. ἔρχομαι. ■ **ὅταν** when, whenever. **δώσουσιν** fut. act. 9
ind. δίδωμι. **εὐχαριστία** thanksgiving. **ζῶντι** pres. act. part.
dat. sing. ζάω to live. ■ **πεσοῦνται** fut. mid. ind. πίπτω to fall, 10
to fall down. **προσκυνήσουσιν** fut. act. ind. προσκυνέω to
worship. **βαλοῦσιν** fut. act. ind. βάλλω to throw. ■ **λαβεῖν** aor. 11
act. inf. λαμβάνω. The inf. is used in explaining the adj.
"worthy." **ἔκτισας** aor. act. ind. κτίζω to create. **ἐκτίσθησαν**
aor. pass. ind.

Ch. 5

1 ■ **δεξιά** right. **καθημένου** pres. mid. part. κάθημαι to sit. **βιβλίον** book, scroll, document. This is a term used for writing material of papyrus, leather, skin, or parchment (Ford). **γεγραμμένον** perf. pass. part. The perf. tense indicates the completed action and was often used of legal authoritative documents whose authority continued (s. MM; TDNT). **ἔσωθεν** within. **ὄπισθεν** on the back. That the scroll is also written on the back indicates how extensive and comprehensive are the decrees of God (Mounce). **κατεσφραγισμένον** perf. pass. part. κατασφραγίζω to seal, to seal up, to seal completely and securely (Swete). **σφραγίς** seal. Seals were used as a stamping device in place of signatures to make a document valid. The impression was normally made on clay, wax, or some other soft material (Ford; s. also TDNT). According to Roman law a testament or will was sealed w. seven seals by seven witnesses (Bousset; s. also Emmet Russell, "A Roman Law Parallel to Rev. V," Bib Sac 115 [July, 1958], 258–264; s. also Buckland, 238f.). The book spoken of here seems to be the book of God's decrees and contains the full account of what God in His sovereign will has
2 determined as the destiny of the world (Mounce; Bousset). ■
κηρύσσοντα pres. act. part. proclaiming. **ἀνοῖξαι** aor. act. inf.
ἀνοίγω to open. **λῦσαι** aor. act. inf. λύω to loose, to remove.
3 ■ **ἐδύνατο** impf. mid. ind. **ὑποκάτω** down under, underneath.
4 ■ **ἔκλαιον** impf. act. ind. κλαίω to cry, to weep aloud, to wail.
The word is frequently used to mean professional mourning
5 (Ford). **εὑρέθη** aor. pass. ind. ■ **εἷς** one. **ἐνίκησεν** aor. act. ind.
νικάω to win a victory, to be victor, to overcome. **λέων** lion. The lion was an emblem of strength, majesty, courage, and menace as well as symbolic of intellectual excellence (Ford). **φυλή** tribe. **ῥίζα** root (s. Isa. 11:1). **ἀνοῖξαι** aor. act. inf. to open. The word is used of unrolling a book (Charles).

6 ■ **μέσον** in the middle (s. Rev. 4:6). **ζῷον** living creature. **ἀρνίον** lamb (s. John 1:29). This word for lamb is used exclusively of the resurrected and victorious Christ (Mounce). **ἑστηκός** perf. act. part. ἵστημι to stand. **ἐσφαγμένον** perf. pass. part. σφάζω to slaughter, to slaughter a sacrifice. The perf. indicates the lasting effects. The lamb has been offered, yet it stands erect and alive in the sight of heaven (Swete). **ἔχων** pres. act. part. **κέρας** horn. The horn is proverbially a symbol of courage, strength, and might (Ford). John sees a lamb w. seven horns and seven eyes, bearing the wounds of sacrificial slaughter, yet standing in readiness for action. In one brilliant stroke John portrays his central theme of NT revelation—victory through

sacrifice (Mounce). **ἀπεσταλμένοι** perf. pass. part.
ἀποστέλλω to send, to send as an official representative. The
verb has reference to the mission of the Spirit (Swete). ■ 7
εἴληφεν perf. act. ind. λαμβάνω to receive, to take. Rather than
being an aroistic perf. the perf. tense here is like a highly dramatic historical pres. (s. K.L. McKay, "Syntax in Exegesis," TB 23
[1972], 54). ■ **ἔλαβεν** aor. act. ind. λαμβάνω. **ἔπεσαν** aor. act. 8
ind. πίπτω to fall. **κιθάρα** harp. This is the general term for a
kind of harp or lyre (Ford; s. also 1 Cor. 14:7). **φιάλη** bowl. This
was a flat, shallow cup or bowl for drinking or libations
(Mounce). **χρυσοῦς** golden. **γεμούσας** aor. act. part. γέμω to
be full of. **θυμίαμα** incense. In Judaism the angels were considered to be the carrier of the prayers of men (s. SB III, 807f.).
Incense was used to produce fragrant perfumes and was used
both in secular life and liturgical life (Ford; s. also Matt. 2:11).
■ **ᾄδουσιν** pres. act. ind. to sing. ᾠδή song. The idea of a "new 9
song" grows out of the use of the expression in the Psalms. Every
new act of mercy calls forth a new song of gratitude and praise
(Mounce). In Judaism it was taught that Israel will first sing a
new song in the days of the Messiah as a song of praise for the
miracle of deliverance (SB III, 801). **ἄξιος** worthy. **λαβεῖν** aor.
act. inf. λαμβάνω to receive. The inf. is used to explain the adj.
"worthy." **ἐσφάγης** aor. pass. ind. σφάζω to slaughter (s.v.6).
ἠγόρασας aor. act. ind. ἀγοράζω to buy at the market place,
to redeem. **γλῶσσα** tongue, language. ■ **ἐποίησας** aor. act. ind. 10
βασιλεύσουσιν fut. act. ind. βασιλεύω to be a king, to rule
as king, to reign.

■ **ἤκουσα** aor. act. ind. ἀκούω. **κύκλῳ** dat. encircling, 11
round about. **ἦν** impf. ind. εἰμί. **ἀριθμός** number. Now it is the
innumerable host of angels who lift their voices in a great dox-
ology of praise. Their number is an apocalyptic symbol for
countless thousands (Mounce). ■ **ἰσχύς** strength, might (s. Eph. 12
1:19). **εὐλογία** praise (s. Bousset). ■ **κτίσμα** that which is 13
created, creation. **λέγοντας** pres. act. part. ■ **προσεκύνησαν** 14
aor. act. ind. προσκυνέω to worship.

Ch. 6

■ **ἤνοιξεν** aor. act. ind. ἀνοίγω to open, to break the seal. 1
With the opening of the first seal, the beginning of the seven-year tribulation period is described. The Jews considered this to be a time of unprecedented trouble and judgment which was to precede the messianic salvation. This was a time of judgment for Israel and for the whole world (s. Matt. 24:8; esp. SB IV, 858ff.). **ἀρνίον** lamb (s. Rev. 5:6). **σφραγίς** seal (s. Rev. 5:1). **ἤκουσα**

aor. act. ind. ἀκούω to hear. **ζῷον** living creature. **βροντή** thun-
2 der. **ἔρχου** pres. mid. imp. ■ **ἵππος** horse. The rabbis felt that the appearance of a white horse was a favorable sign. In the later rabbinic writings the coming of the Messiah was associated w. the sight of a horse. Perhaps war horses were associated w. the messianic woes, i.e., the suffering which would precede the advent of the Messiah (Ford). **λευκός** white. **καθήμενος** pres. mid. part. κάθημαι to sit. **ἔχων** pres. act. part. **τόξον** bow. The bow is not only the weapon of the Parthians, but, in general, a feared weapon of attack for all nations. It is a part of the typical cavalry equipment of all Oriental armies and the particular weapon of the king (s. Mathias Rissi, "The Rider on the White Horse," *Interpretation* 18 [Oct., 1964], 414). **ἐδόθη** aor. pass. ind. δίδωμι to give. **ἐξῆλθεν** aor. act. ind. ἐξέρχομαι to go out. **νικῶν** pres. act. part. νικάω to conquer. The part. is the manner of his going out and the pres. tense may be conative, i.e., "trying to conquer." **νικήσῃ** aor. act. subj. νικάω to be the victor, to overcome, to conquer. The subj. is used in a purpose clause. Although some have felt that the rider on the white horse is Christ Himself (Zane Hodges, "The First Horseman of the Apocalypse," Bib Sac 119 [Oct., 1962], 324–334), it is better to view this one as the Antichrist, i.e., the "man of sin" (s. Rissi, 407–418; s. also the discussion by Mounce; Walvoord; Ford).

4 ■ **πυρρός** fiery, red. The color represents bloodshed and sin (Ford). **λαβεῖν** aor. act. inf. λαμβάνω. The inf. is epexegetical explaining that which was given. **σφάξουσιν** fut. act. ind. σφάζω to slaughter. The fut. ind. is used here in an epexegetical explanatory purpose clause (RWP). (For the use here of the ind. rather than the subj., s. MT, 100.) **μάχαιρα** sword. This was the short Roman sword and is symbolic of violent death, war, and the power of the authorities to punish evildoers (Mounce; Ford).

5 ■ **μέλας** black. This color is symbolic of mourning or affliction or famine (Ford; Mounce). **ζυγός** scales. The beam of a pair
6 of scales (Swete). ■ **χοῖνιξ** quart. This was a dry measure of about a quart, i.e., approximately 1.92 pints. One of these rations was the daily ration of one man (Ford). **δηνάριον** denarius. This was a Roman silver coin equivalent to one day's wages. This indicated that enough wheat to feed one man for one day cost a full day's wages. The cost of wheat here is five to twelve times its normal price. Famine is indicated (Ford; s. also Mounce). **κριθή** barley. Barley was largely the food of the poor and was relatively cheaper than wheat (Swete). **ἔλαιον** oil, olive oil. **ἀδικήσῃς** aor. act. subj. ἀδικέω to injure, to do harm to. The

subj. w. the neg. is used to express a prohibition or neg. command.

■ **χλωρός** green, pale. The word means a yellowish green 8
but refers here to the color of a corpse or the blanched appearance of a person struck w. terror (Ford; Mounce). **ἐπάνω** upon,
on. **ᾅδης** Hades, the place of the dead, the underworld (s. Rev.
1:18). **ἠκολούθει** impf. ind. act. ἀκολουθέω to follow after, to
follow. **ἀποκτεῖναι** aor. act. inf. ἀποκτείνω to kill. The inf. is
used epexegetically to explain that which was given. **ῥομφαία**
sword. This was the sword w. the large blade (s. Rev. 1:16). The
word is used w. the prep. in an instrumental sense "w. the
sword." **λιμός** hunger. **θηρίον** wild animal, wild beast. Death by
wild beasts would be expected in a land decimated by war and
famine (Mounce).

■ **ὑποκάτω** under, underneath. **θυσιαστήριον** place of 9
offering, altar. **ἐσφαγμένων** perf. pass. part. σφάζω to slaughter, to slay. The souls of the slaughtered ones are seen "under
the altar" because in the Levitical rite the blood was poured out
at the foot of the altar (Swete). ■ **ἔκραξαν** aor. act. ind. κράζω 10
to scream out, to cry. **δεσπότης** lord, master, ruler, one who
exercises absolute authority. **ἀληθινός** true, genuine. **ἐκδικεῖς**
pres. act. ind. to avenge, to revenge, to execute vengeance.
κατοικούντων pres. act. part. κατοικέω to reside, to dwell.
■ **στολή** robe. The word refers to any stately robe and as long, 11
sweeping garments would have eminently this stateliness about
them, always or almost always it refers to a garment reaching to
the feet, or one train-like, sweeping the ground (Trench, *Synonyms*, 186). **ἐρρέθη** aor. pass. ind. λέγω. The pass. is the divine
or theological pass. indicating that God is the One who does the
action (s. BG, 76). **ἀναπαύσωνται** fut. mid. ind. ἀναπαύομαι
to cease, to pause, to rest. The fut. mid. used in the subfinal
clause is to be preferred rather than the aor. mid. subj. (RWP).
πληρωθῶσιν aor. pass. subj. πληρόω to fill, to fulfill.
σύνδουλος fellow slave. **μέλλοντες** pres. act. part. to be about
to. The verb is used w. the inf. to form the fut. tense.
ἀποκτέννεσθαι pres. pass. inf. ἀποκτέννω to kill.

■ **σεισμός** earthquake. Earthquakes were often used to 12
introduce God's judgment (s. Richard Buckham, "The Eschatological Earthquake in the Apocalypse of John," Nov T 19 [July,
1977], 224–233). **ἐγένετο** aor. mid. ind. γίνομαι to happen, to
occur, to be. **σάκκος** sackcloth. The was the rough cloth made
from the hair of a black goat and worn in times of mourning
(Mounce). **τρίχινος** made of hair. **σελήνη** moon. ■ **ἀστήρ** star. 13
ἔπεσαν aor. act. ind. πίπτω to fall. **συκῆ** fig tree. **βάλλει** pres.

act. ind. to throw, to cast. The pres. tense is gnomic picturing that which is always true. **ὄλυνθος** fig, unripe fig. The word means the green figs which appear in winter and of which, while some ripen, many fall off in the spring (Swete). **ἄνεμος** wind. **σειομένη** pres. pass. part. σείω to shake. The world and its well being depend on the faithfulness w. which the luminaries of heaven fulfill their parts. When the sun and moon and stars forsake this order, the end of the world is at hand (Charles).
14 ■ **ἀπεχωρίσθη** aor. pass. ind. ἀποχωρίζω to tear apart, to rip
apart. **βιβλίον** book, scroll, roll. **ἑλισσόμενον** pres. pass. part. ἑλίσσω to roll up. The figure is that of a papyrus rent into, whereupon the divided portions curl and form a roll on either side (Charles). **νῆσος** island. **ἐκινήθησαν** aor. pass. ind. κινέω
15 to move. ■ **μεγιστᾶνες** (pl.) magistrates, the civil officials in
authority (Swete). **χιλίαρχος** leaders of a thousand soldiers, tribune. The term was commonly used of the military tribune no matter how many he commanded. The word refers to the military authorities (Ford; Swete). **πλούσιος** rich, wealthy. **ἐλεύθερος** free, those who were no longer slaves. The seven conditions of life are named, covering the whole fabric of society from the emperor down to the meanest slave (Swete). **ἔκρυψαν**
16 aor. act. ind. κρύπτω to hide. **σπήλαιον** cave. ■ **πέσετε** aor.
act. imp. πίπτω to fall. **κρύψατε** aor. act. imp. **ὀργή** wrath, anger. The "wrath of the lamb" is a deliberate paradox by which John intends to goad his readers into theological alertness
17 (Caird). ■ **σταθῆναι** aor. pass. inf. ἵστημι to stand, to hold
one's ground (Swete).

Ch. 7

1 ■ **μετὰ τοῦτο εἶδον** "after this I saw." The phrase in-
troduces another part of the vision (s. Rev. 4:1). **ἑστῶτας** perf. act. part. ἵστημι perf. to stand. **γωνία** corner. **κρατοῦντα** pres. act. part. κρατέω to hold, to grasp, to have power over. **ἄνεμος** wind. **πνέῃ** pres. act. subj. πνέω to blow. The subj. is used in a neg. purpose clause (RWP). **μήτε** neither. The four winds as destructive agents of God are a regular feature in apocalyptic
2 literature (s. Mounce). ■ **ἀναβαίνοντα** pres. act. part.
ἀναβαίνω to come down. **ἀνατολή** rising, "the rising of the sun" indicates the east. **ἔχοντα** pres. act. part. **σφραγίς** seal. To the prophet's contemporaries "seal" would have connoted the branding of cattle and the tattooing of slaves and soldiers, esp. those in the service of the emperor who could be recognized by this mark if they deserted; the marking of a soldier or the member of a guild on the hand, brow, or neck to seal him as a religious devotee, i.e., a member of a sacred militia. The mark in this case

was a sign of consecration to the deity; it could refer to the mark prophets might have worn on their forehead, either painted or tattooed; or it could refer to the phylactery worn on the forehead and hand (s. Ford). The idea of the sealing would be to mark one's property and show ownership (Swete). **ζῶντος** pres. act. part. ζάω to live. **ἔκραξεν** aor. act. ind. κράζω to scream, to cry out. **οἷς ἐδόθη αὐτοῖς** "to whom it was given to them." This may reflect the Hebraic construction of the resumptive pron. (s. MH, 434f.; s. also W.F. Bakker, *Pronomen Abundans and Pronomen Coniunctum*, 41). **ἐδόθη** aor. pass. ind. δίδωμι. The theological or divine pass. indicating that God is the subject of the action. **ἀδικῆσαι** aor. act. inf. ἀδικέω to harm, to injure.
The inf. is used to explain that which was given. ■ **ἀδικήσητε** 3
aor. act. subj. The subj. is used w. the neg. to form a prohibition or neg. command. **σφραγίσωμεν** aor. act. subj. σφραγίζω to seal. The aor. subj. is used in a temporal clause of indefinite action for the fut. (RWP). **μέτωπον** between the eyes, forehead.
■ **ἤκουσα** aor. act. ind. ἀκούω to hear. **ἀριθμός** number. 4
ἐσφραγισμένων perf. pass. part. σφραγίζω. **φυλή** tribe.
■ **ἀριθμῆσαι** aor. act. inf. ἀριθμέω to count, pass. to be 9
counted. **ἐδύνατο** impf. ind. **γλῶσσα** tongue, speech. **ἀρνίον** lamb. **περιβεβλημένους** perf. pass. part. περιβάλλω to cast around, pass. to be clothed. **στολή** robe (s. Rev. 6:11). **λευκός** white. **φοῖνιξ** palm branch. The palm is a sign of festive joy. One inscription describes how the inhabitants of a city out of gratitude to the gods prescribed that thirty boys should daily sing prescribed hymns as they were "clothed in white and crowned w. a twig, likewise holding a twig in their hands" (BS, 370).
■ **καθημένῳ** pres. mid. part. κάθημαι to sit. ■ **εἱστήκεισαν** 10/11
plperf. act. ind. ἵστημι. The plperf. is used like an imperf. (RWP). **κύκλῳ** (dat.) encircling, in a circle, round about. **ζῷον** living creature. **ἔπεσαν** aor. act. ind. πίπτω to fall, to fall down.
προσεκύνησαν aor. act. ind προσκυνέω to worship. ■ 12
εὐχαριστία thanksgiving. **ἰσχύς** strength, might (s. Eph. 1:19).
■ **ἀπεκρίθη** aor. pass. ind. ἀποκρίνομαι to answer. **πόθεν** 13
from where, "where have they come from?" ■ **εἴρηκα** perf. act. 14
ind. λέγω. **ἐρχόμενοι** pres. mid. part. **θλῖψις** tribulation (s. Rev. 6:1). **ἔπλυναν** aor. act. ind. πλύνω to wash. **ἐλεύκαναν** aor. act. ind. λευκαίνω to whiten, to make white. The idea of making robes white by washing them in blood is a striking paradox. It is the sacrifice of the lamb upon the cross which supplies
white garments for the saints (Mounce). ■ **λατρεύουσιν** pres. 15
act. ind. to perform worshipful service (s. TDNT). **ναός** temple, sanctuary. **σκηνώσει** fut. act. ind. σκηνόω to live in a tent, to

16 tabernacle (s. John 1:14). ■ **πεινάσουσιν** fut. act. ind. πεινάω
to be hungry. **διψήσουσιν** fut. act. ind. διψάω to be thirsty.
πέσῃ aor. act. subj. πίπτω to fall. **καῦμα** burning, scorching.
17 ■ **μέσον** middle. Used in the phrase ἀνὰ μέσον w. the meaning
"between," "amongst" (Swete). **ποιμανεῖ** fut. act. ind.
ποιμαίνω to shepherd. **ὁδηγήσει** fut. act. ind. ὁδηγέω to lead
along the way, to guide, to lead. **πηγή** spring. The order in the
phrase emphasizes "life"—"to Life's water springs" (Swete).
ἐξαλείψει fut. act. ind. ἐξαλείφω to wipe away. **δάκρυον** tear,
i.e., "every single tear."

Ch. 8

1 ■ **ὅταν** "when." The temporal particle is not used here in
the indefinite sense "whenever" but as was common in the
Koine, writers used this particle w. the aor. ind. for a definite
occurrence (RG, 973). **ἤνοιξεν** aor. act. ind. ἀνοίγω to open,
to break a seal. **σφραγίς** seal. **ἐγένετο** aor. mid. ind. γίνομαι
to be. **σιγή** silence. **ἡμίωρον** half an hour. The silence is a
dramatic pause which makes even more impressive the judgment
about to fall upon the earth. Although a thirty-minute period is
a relatively short period, it would form an impressive break in
2 such a rapidly moving drama (Mounce; s. also Seiss). ■
ἑστήκασιν aor. act. ind. ἵστημι to stand. **ἐδόθησαν** aor. pass.
ind. δίδωμι to give. The theological pass. indicating that God is
the one who gives.

3 ■ **ἐστάθη** aor. pass. ind. ἵστημι to stand, ingressive aor.
"he took his place" (RWP). **θυσιαστήριον** place where sacrifices are made, altar. **ἔχων** pres. act. part. **λιβανωτός** golden
censer or fire pan. The word usually means incense but here it
appears to signify censer (Ford). **χρυσοῦς** golden. **ἐδόθη** aor.
pass. ind. (s.v.2). **θυμίαμα** incense (s. Rev. 5:8). **δώσει** fut. act.
ind. δίδωμι to give, to add. The fut. is used in a purpose clause
4 (s. MT, 100). ■ **ἀνέβη** aor. act. ind. ἀναβαίνω to go up.
καπνός smoke. The meeting of the incense and the hot coals
produces the fragrant smoke cloud, the symbol of divine accep-
5 tance (Swete). ■ **εἴληφεν** perf. act. ind. λαμβάνω. (For the use
of the perf., s. Rev. 5:7.) **ἐγέμισεν** aor. act. ind. γεμίζω to fill,
to make full of, to fill up. **πῦρ** fire. **ἔβαλεν** aor. act. ind. βάλλω
to throw. **ἐγένοντο** aor. mid. ind. (s.v.1). **βρονταί** thunder.
ἀστραπή lightning. **σεισμός** earthquake (s. Rev. 6:12).

6 ■ **ἔχοντες** pres. act. part. **ἡτοίμασαν** aor. act. ind.
ἑτοιμάζω to prepare. **σαλπίσωσιν** aor. act. subj. σαλπίζω to
blow the trumpet. (For various uses of trumpets in the OT and

in an eschatological sense, s. Ford.) The subj. is used to express
purpose.

■ **ἐσάλπισεν** aor. act. ind. **ἐγένετο** aor. mid. ind. (s.v.1). 7
χάλαζα hail. **μεμιγμένα** perf. pass. part. μείγνυμι to mix.
ἐβλήθη aor. pass. ind. βάλλω (s.v.5). The syntax of the v.
suggests that the blood-red storm appeared in heaven before it
was cast upon the earth (Mounce). **κατεκάη** aor. pass. ind.
κατακαίω to burn down, to burn up. The prep. in compound is
perfective. **χόρτος** grass. **χλωρός** green. It is only one-third of
the land and its vegetation that is devastated by fire. The fraction
would indicate that although God is bringing punishment upon
the earth, it is not as yet complete and final (Mounce).

■ **καιόμενον** pres. pass. part. **καίω** to set on fire, pass. to 8
be burning, to burn. ■ **ἀπέθανεν** aor. act. ind. ἀποθνῄσκω to 9
die. **διεφθάρησαν** aor. pass. ind. διαφθείρω to corrupt, to destroy. The prep. in compound is perfective.

■ **ἔπεσεν** aor. act. ind. **πίπτω** to fall. **ἀστήρ** star. **λαμπάς** 10
torch. **ποταμός** river. **πηγή** spring. Now the fresh water supply
is smitten (Swete). ■ **λέγεται** pres. pass. ind., pass. to be called. 11
ἄψινθος wormwood. It is called wormwood after the strong
bitter taste of the plant of that name. Wormwood symbolizes
God's punishment or bitterness, suffering and sorrow (Mounce;
s. also FFB, 198; ZPEB V, 969). **ἐπικράνθησαν** aor. pass. ind.
πικραίνω to make bitter, to cause to be bitter.

■ **ἐπλήγη** aor. pass. ind. πλήσσω to strike, to smite. 12
σελήνη moon. **σκοτισθῇ** aor. pass. subj. σκοτίζω to blacken,
to darken. **φάνῃ** aor. act. subj. φαίνομαι to shine. The subj.
moods are used in purpose clauses.

■ **ἤκουσα** aor. act. ind. ἀκούω to hear. **ἀετός** eagle. The 13
word may also be used for a vulture as well as an eagle which
in this context would symbolize impending doom. The vulture
hovers in mid heaven so as to be seen by all, and cries out in a
great voice so that none will fail to hear (Mounce). **πετομένου**
pres. mid. part. πέτομαι to fly. **μεσουράνημα** at the zenith, in
the meridian, i.e., "in mid heaven" (Ford; Swete).
κατοικοῦντας pres. act. part. κατοικέω to dwell, to inhabit, to
live. **μελλόντων** pres. mid. part. μέλλω to be about to. It is used
w. the inf. to express the fut. **σαλπίζειν** pres. act. inf. to blow
a trumpet.

Ch. 9

■ **ἐσάλπισεν** aor. act. ind. σαλπίζω to blow the trumpet. 1
ἀστήρ star. **πεπτωκότα** perf. act. part. πίπτω to fall. The perf.
is the dramatic perf. (s. Rev. 5:7; DM, 204; Mounce). **ἐδόθη** aor.
pass. ind. δίδωμι. The theological or divine pass. indicating that

God is the One who gives. **κλείς** key (s. Rev. 1:18; 3:7). **φρέαρ**
pit, well, shaft (s. Ford and esp. the references to the DSS; 1QS
9:16, 22; 10:19). **ἄβυσσος** bottomless, abyss, lit. "unfathomably
deep." It is a place of imprisonment for disobedient spirits (Ford;
2 s. also Swete; Charles). ■ **ἤνοιξεν** aor. act. ind. ἀνοίγω to open.
ἀνέβη aor. act. ind. ἀναβαίνω to go up, to ascend. **καπνός**
smoke. **κάμινος** furnace. **ἐσκοτώθη** aor. pass. ind. σκοτόω to
darken. As the smoke rises it blots out the sun and darkens the
3 atmosphere of the earth (Mounce). ■ **ἐξῆλθον** aor. act. ind.
ἐξέρχομαι to come out. **ἀκρίς** locust, grasshopper. Throughout
the OT the locust is a symbol of destruction. Bred in the desert,
they invade cultivated areas in search of food. They may travel
in a column of a hundred feet deep and up to four miles in length
leaving the land stripped bare of all vegetation (Mounce; s. also
FFB, 53; ZPEB III, 948–950). **σκορπίος** scorpion, a lobster-like
vermin some four or five inches long, it had a claw on the end
of the tail that secreted a poison when it struck. It should be
noted that the demonic locusts of the first Woe have the power
rather than the appearance of scorpions (Mounce; s. also FFB,
4 70; ZPEB V, 297). ■ **ἐρρέθη** aor. pass. ind. λέγω. **ἀδικήσουσιν**
fut. act. ind. ἀδικέω to injure, to harm. **χόρτος** grass. **χλωρός**
green. **εἰ μή** "except." **σφραγίς** seal. **μέτωπον** forehead (s.
5 Rev. 7:3f.). ■ **ἀποκτείνωσιν** pres. or aor. act. subj. ἀποκτείνω
to kill. **βασανισθήσονται** fut. pass. ind. βασανίζω to torment, to torture. **μήν** month. **βασανισμός** torturing, torture.
The word has the idea of punishment (Mounce). **ὅταν** w. the
6 subj. "whenever." **παίσῃ** aor. act. subj. παίω to strike. ■
ζητήσουσιν fut. act. ind. ζητέω to seek, to look for.
εὑρήσουσιν fut. act. ind. **ἐπιθυμήσουσιν** fut. act. ind.
ἐπιθυμέω to long for, to yearn after. **ἀποθανεῖν** aor. act. inf.
ἀποθνῄσκω to die. The inf. is used as the obj. of the verb "to
long for," "to desire." **φεύγει** pres. act. ind. The pres. tense
could perhaps be designated a "historical pres." in the fut., i.e.,
"death keeps fleeing from them."
7 ■ **ὁμοίωμα** likeness, shape (s. Swete). **ἵππος** horse.
ἡτοιμασμένοις perf. pass. part. ἑτοιμάζω to prepare, perf. to
8 be made ready. **πόλεμος** war. ■ **θρίξ, τριχός** hair. **ὀδούς** teeth.
9 **λέων** lion. **ἦσαν** impf. εἰμί. ■ **θώραξ** chest, breastplate.
σιδηροῦς iron, of iron, made of iron. The scaly backs and flanks
of the insects resembled coats of mail made of iron. The word
"of iron" points to the material of which such armor was ordinarily made, and at the same time indicates the hopelessness
of any effort to destroy assailants who were so protected
(Swete). **πτέρυξ** wing. **ἅρμα** wagon, chariot. **τρεχόντων** pres.

act. part. *τρέχω* to run. Pliny wrote "this plague (of locusts) is
interpreted as a sign of the wrath of the gods; for they are seen
of exceptional size, and also they fly w. such a noise of wings that
they are believed to be birds, and they obscure the sun, making
the nations gaze upward in anxiety lest they should settle over
all their lands" (Pliny, *Natural History*, XI.xxv.104). ■ **οὐρά** tail. 10
κέντρον goad for an ox, sting. **ἀδικῆσαι** aor. act. inf. to injure,
to harm. In Italy the swarms of locusts were so bad that a law
was passed that war should be made upon them three times a
year by crushing the eggs, then the grubs, and at last the fully
grown insects. The law had the penalty of a deserter for the man
who held back (Pliny, *Natural History*, XI.xxxv.105).

■ **ἀπῆλθεν** aor. act. ind. *ἀπέρχομαι* to go out, to go forth, 12
to go away.

■ **ἐσάλπισεν** aor. act. ind. (s.v.1). **ἤκουσα** aor. act. ind. 13
ἀκούω to hear. **μίαν** "one." Here it means a "single or solitary
voice" (Mounce). **κέρας** horn. The horns on the altar were the
symbol of God's power (Ford). **θυσιαστήριον** place where sacrifices are made, altar. **χρυσοῦς** golden. ■ **ἔχων** pres. act. part. 14
λῆσον aor. act. imp. *λύω* to loose, to release. **δεδεμένους** perf.
pass. part. *δέω* to bind. The perf. tense emphasizes the state or
condition. **ποταμός** river. ■ **ἐλύθησαν** aor. pass. ind. to release. 15
ἡτοιμασμένοι perf. pass. part. (s.v.7). **μήν** month. **ἐνιαυτός**
year. **ἀποκτείνωσιν** pres. or aor. subj. *ἀποκτείνω* to kill
(s.v.5). ■ **ἀριθμός** number. **στράτευμα** army. **ἱππικόν** per- 16
taining to a horse, horseman. The army consisted of cavalry
(Swete). ■ **ἵππος** horse. **ὅρασις** appearance, vision. 17
καθημένους pres. mid. part. *κάθημαι* to sit. **θώραξ** breastplate
(s.v.9). **πύρινος** fiery, made of fire (s. Swete). **ὑακίνθινος** hya-
cinth-colored, i.e., dark blue, a dusky blue color as of sulphurous
smoke (BAG; MM). **θειώδης** sulphur, sulphur-colored. Brimstone is what is known today as sulphur; hence, yellow. It is
difficult to determine whether the breastplates were of three
colors each or whether each breastplate was of a single color; i.e.,
some red, some blue, some yellow (Mounce). **λέων** lion. **στόμα**
mouth. **ἐκπορεύεται** pres. mid. ind. to go out, to come out. **πῦρ**
fire. **καπνός** smoke. **θεῖον** brimstone, sulphur. ■ **πληγή** stripe, 18
wound, calamity, plague (AS). **ἀπεκτάνθησαν** aor. pass. ind.
ἀποκτείνω to kill. **ἐκπορευομένου** pres. mid. part. ■ **οὐρά** tail. 19
ὄφις snake. **ἀδικοῦσιν** pres. act. ind. to injure, to harm.

■ **λοιπός** rest. **μετενόησαν** aor. act. ind. *μετανοέω* to 20
change one's mind, to change one's thinking, to repent,
προσκυνήσουσιν fut. act. ind. *προσκυνέω* to worship. The
fut. ind. could be used here to express result rather than purpose

(s. RG, 992). **εἴδωλον** idol, false god. **ἀργυροῦς** silver. **χαλκοῦς** brass. **λίθινος** made of stone. **ξύλινος** wooden, made
21 of wood. **περιπατεῖν** pres. act. inf. to walk about. ■ **φόνος** murder. **φαρμακεία** magic art, sorcery. The use of drugs either for divination or for healing (s. BAG; MM; Ford; Gal. 5:20). It is suggested that here the word has the special sense of magic spells inciting to illicit lust (EGT). Pliny describes the use of many superstitious and magical practices to bring about healing (*Natural History*, XXVIII) one being "that snake bites and scorpion stings are relieved by intercourse" (*Natural History*, XXVIII.x.44; for further remedies against snake bites and scorpion stings, s. XXVII.xlii. 149–155). **πορνεία** unlawful sexual intercourse, immorality (s. Rev. 2:21). **κλέμμα** stealing theft.

Ch. 10

1 ■ **καταβαίνοντα** pres. act. part. καταβαίνω to come down, to descend. **περιβεβλημένον** perf. pass. part. περιβάλλω to cast about, to be clothed, to be enveloped. This word is used of encircling or throwing an embankment around a city, or clothing someone, and in the context it indicates that the angel is encircled by a cloud (Ford). **νεφέλη** cloud (s. Rev. 1:7). **ἶρις** rainbow (s. Rev. 4:3). Here the word refers to the ordinary rainbow of many colors connected w. the cloud and due in this instance to the shining of the angel's face (Swete). **στῦλος** pillar. **πῦρ** fire. Some have taken "the other angel" described here as being Christ Himself (Seiss; Scott) but others see him as
2 an angelic being rather than Christ Himself (s. Mounce). ■ **ἔχων** pres. act. part. **βιβλαρίδιον** little book, a very small book. **ἠνεῳγμένον** perf. pass. part. ἀνοίγω to open. The perf. pass. part. indicates "having been opened and remaining so," i.e., "standing open." **ἔθηκεν** aor. act. ind. τίθημι to place, to put.
3 **δεξιός** right. **εὐθηκεν** left. ■ **ἔκραξεν** aor. act. ind. κράζω to scream, to cry out in a loud voice. **λέων** lion. **μυκᾶται** pres. mid. ind. μυκάομαι to roar. The word is used of a low, deep sound like the lowing of an ox or the growl of thunder and the word may have been preferred here to indicate that the voice of the angel had not only volume but depth, at once compelling attention and inspiring awe (Swete). **ἐλάλησαν** aor. act. ind. to
4 speak. **βροντή** thunder. ■ **ἤμελλον** impf. act. ind. μέλλω to be about to. The word is used w. the inf. to express fut. The impf. here is inchoative w. the meaning "I was on the point of beginning to write" (RWP). **ἤκουσα** aor. act. ind. ἀκούω to hear. **σφράγισον** aor. act. imp. σφραγίζω to seal, to seal up (s. Rev. 5:1). **γράψῃς** aor. act. subj. The subj. used w. the neg. is a

prohibition or a neg. command "do not start to write." ■ 5
ἑστῶτα perf. act. part. ἵστημι perf. to stand. **ἦρεν** aor. act. ind.
αἴρω to lift up. ■ **ὤμοσεν** aor. act. ind. ὄμνυμι to take an oath, 6
to swear. **ζῶντι** pres. act. part. ζάω to live. **ἔκτισεν** aor. act. ind.
κτίζω to create. **χρόνος** time. The word here means "delay,"
i.e., "there shall be delay no longer." Now nothing stands in the
way of the final dramatic period of human history (Mounce).
οὐκέτι no longer. **ἔσται** fut. εἰμί. ■ **ὅταν** w. the subj. "when- 7
ever." **μέλλῃ** pres. act. subj. The subj. is used in an indefinite
temporal clause. **σαλπίζειν** pres. act. inf. to blow the trumpet.
ἐτελέσθη aor. pass. ind. τελέω to bring to the goal, to complete,
to bring to completion. The proleptic use of the aor. This use of
the aor. occurs in vivacious speech of that which is annunicated
as a consequence of a condition, and is expressed as if it had
already come to pass, the condition being regarded as fulfilled.
The condition here would be the indefinite temporal clause
"whenever he sounds the trumpet" (s. BG, 84f.). **εὐηγγέλισεν**
aor. act. ind. εὐαγγελίζω to proclaim the good news, to deliver
good news (s. TDNT).

■ **λαλοῦσαν** pres. act. part. **ὕπαγε** pres. act. imp. "go 8
now." This is a Hebraic construction (s. Charles). **λάβε** aor. act.
imp. λαμβάνω. **βιβλίον** book, small book. ■ **ἀπῆλθα** aor. act. 9
ind. ἀπέρχομαι to go out, to go away from. John left his position by the door and went to the angel (RWP). **δοῦναι** aor. act.
inf. δίδωμι to give. The inf. is used in indirect discourse after the
verb "saying" and is used to express a command (s. RWP).
κατάφαγε aor. act. imp. κατεσθίω to eat down, to eat up
completely. **πικρανεῖ** fut. act. ind. πικραίνω to make bitter.
The imp. followed by the fut. tense is a Hebraic form of a conditional clause in which the fut. expresses the result of having filled
the command. (For this construction, s. Phil. 4:7; Beyer, 238–
255.) **κοιλία** stomach. **γλυκύς** sweet. **μέλι** honey. ■ **ἔλαβον** 10
aor. act. ind. λαμβάνω. **κατέφαγον** aor. act. ind. κατεσθίω.
ἦν impf. εἰμί. **ἔφαγον** aor. act. ind. ἐσθίω to eat. The effective
use of the aor., i.e., "after I had finished eating." **ἐπικράνθη** aor.
pass. ind., ingressive aor. "my stomach became bitter." The Seer,
if he would be admitted into a part of God's secret, must be
prepared for very mixed sensations; the first joy of fuller knowledge would be followed by sorrow deeper and more bitter than
those of ordinary men (Swete). ■ **λέγουσίν μοι** pres. act. ind. 11
"they say unto me." It is best to take the expression as an
indefinite pl. or the equivalent of the pass. "it was said"
(Mounce). **δεῖ** (followed by the acc. and the inf.) "it is binding,"
"it is necessary." **προφητεῦσαι** aor. act. inf. προφητεύω to

seek forth, to prophesy. The inf. is used to explain "what is necessary." **ἐπί** "about," "concerning" (Mounce; s. also John 12:16). **ἔθνος** nations. **γλῶσσα** tongue, speech, language.

Ch. 11

1 ■ **ἐδόθη** aor. pass. ind. δίδωμι. **κάλαμος** reed. This served for a surveyor's rule or measuring rod and it might have been the cane which grows along the Jordan valley and was known as the "giant reed" of Mediterranean lands. It grows in swampy areas and sometimes it may reach the height of twelve or even fifteen or twenty feet (Ford; s. also FFB, 171). **ῥάβδος** staff. **ἔγειρε** pres. act. imp. ἐγείρω to rise, to get up. **μέτρησον** aor. act. imp. μετρέω to measure. **ναός** temple, sanctuary. **θυσιαστήριον** place where offerings or sacrifices are made, altar.
2 **προσκυνοῦντας** pres. act. part. προσκυνέω to worship. ■ **αὐλή** court. **ἔξωθεν** outside. The outer court of the temple in Jerusalem is called the Court of the Gentiles (Ford). **ἔκβαλε** aor. act. imp. βάλλω to throw out, to cast out. The word is used here in the sense of "to exclude," i.e., exclude it from the sanctuary though the other courts are included (Swete). **μετρήσῃς** aor. act. subj. The neg. used w. the subj. indicates a prohibition or neg. command. **πατήσουσιν** fut. act. ind. πατέω to walk upon, to tread down, to trample. **μήν** month. The designation "forty-two months" is equal to three and one half years which is the half
3 of the seven-year tribulation period. ■ **δώσω** fut. act. ind. δίδωμι. **προφητεύσουσιν** fut. act. ind. προφητεύω to prophesy. The construction "I shall give and they shall prophesy" is a Hebraic construction meaning "I will commission (or give permission to) my two witnesses to prophesy" (Charles). **περιβεβλημένοι** perf. pass. part. περιβάλλω to throw about, to clothe. **σάκκος** sack, sackcloth. The fabric from which a sack is made is usually dark in color; hence, it is especially suited to be worn as a mourning garment (BAG). As latter-day prophets the two witnesses wear the rough garb of their ancient predecessors (Zech. 13:4). Their message is to call to repentance
4 (Mounce). ■ **ἐλαία** olive tree. **λυχνία** lampstand. **ἑστῶτες**
5 perf. act. part. ἵστημι to stand. ■ **ἀδικῆσαι** aor. act. inf. ἀδικέω to injure, to harm. **ἐκπορεύεται** pres. mid. ind. to go out, to come out of. The pres. tense would be interat. indicating that fire would come out of their mouth every time someone would seek to harm them. **κατεσθίει** pres. act. ind. to eat up, to consume completely. **θελήσῃ** aor. act. subj. **οὕτως** so, thus. **δεῖ** (w. the acc. and the inf.) "it is binding," "it is necessary."
6 **ἀποκτανθῆναι** aor. pass. inf. ἀποκτείνω to kill. ■ **κλεῖσαι**

aor. act. inf. κλείω to close, to shut up. The inf. is epexegetical
explaining the authority. **ὑετός** rain. **βρέχῃ** pres. act. subj.
βρέχω to rain. The subj. is used in a neg. purpose clause which
may also be considered a result clause. **στρέφειν** pres. act. inf.
to turn, to change. The inf. is used epexegetically explaining the
authority. **πατάξαι** aor. act. inf. πατάσσω to strike, to hit.
πληγή blow, plague. **ὁσάκις** as often as. Used w. the particle
ἐάν and the subj. to express an indefinite temporal clause "as
often as they will" (RWP). ■ **ὅταν** w. the subj. "whenever." 7
τελέσωσιν aor. act. subj. τελέω to complete, to finish. **θηρίον**
animal, wild animal. **ἀναβαῖνον** pres. mid. part. ἀναβαίνω to
go up, to ascend. **ἄβυσσος** bottomless pit, abyss (s. Rev. 9:1).
ποιήσει fut. act. ind. **πόλεμος** war. **νικήσει** fut. act. ind.
νικάω to gain the victory, to be victor, to overcome. **ἀποκτενεῖ**
fut. act. ind. ἀποκτείνω to kill. ■ **πτῶμα** that which is fallen, 8
corpse, dead body. **πλατεῖα** wide street, open street. **καλεῖται**
pres. pass. ind. **πνευματικῶς** spiritually, pertaining to the Spirit.
Perhaps the idea here is not "allegorically," but rather how the
Spirit of God interprets. **ὅπου** where. Here the word is used as
a pron. "the place where." **ἐσταυρώθη** aor. pass. ind. σταυρόω
to crucify. ■ **βλέπουσιν** pres. act. ind. **ἐκ τῶν λαῶν** "some of 9
the peoples." The expression is to be taken as a partitive gen.
(Mounce). **ἥμισυ** half. **ἀφίουσιν** pres. act. ind. to leave, to
allow. **τεθῆναι** aor. pass. inf. τίθημι to place, to put. **μνῆμα**
grave. ■ **κατοικοῦντες** pres. act. part. κατοικέω to reside, to 10
dwell. **εὐφραίνονται** pres. mid. ind. to rejoice, to be happy.
πέμψουσιν fut. act. ind. πέμπω to send. **ἀλλήλοις** dat. pl. "to
one another." **ἐβασάνισαν** aor. act. ind. βασανίζω to torment, to torture. ■ **εἰσῆλθεν** aor. act. ind. εἰσέρχομαι to come 11
into, to enter. **ἔστησαν** aor. act. ind. ἵστημι to stand.
ἐπέπεσεν aor. act. ind. ἐπιπίπτω to fall upon. **θεωροῦντας**
pres. act. part. θεωρέω to see, to behold, to watch. ■ **ἤκουσαν** 12
aor. act. ind. ἀκούω. **ἀνάβατε** aor. act. imp. ἀναβαίνω to come
up. **ἀνέβησαν** aor. act. ind. ἀναβαίνω to go up, to ascend.
νεφέλη cloud. **ἐθεώρησαν** aor. act. ind. ■ **ἐγένετο** aor. mid. 13
ind. γίνομαι to be, to become, to happen, to come about.
σεισμός earthquake. **ἔπεσεν** aor. act. ind. πίπτω.
ἀπεκτάνθησαν aor. pass. ind. ἀποκτείνω to kill. **ὀνόματα**
names, i.e., "people," "person." (For the use of the word in this
sense, s. BS, 196f.) **ἔμφοβος** afraid, scared. **ἔδωκαν** aor. act. ind.
δίδωμι to give.

■ **ἀπῆλθεν** aor. act. ind. ἀπέρχομαι to go away, to pass. 14
ταχύ quickly, soon.

■ **ἐσάλπισεν** aor. act. ind. σαλπίζω to blow the trumpet. 15

ἐγένοντο aor. mid. ind. (s.v.13). **χριστός** anointed, Messiah,
Christ. **βασιλεύσει** fut. act. ind. βασιλεύω to be king, to rule
16 as a king, to reign. ■ **καθήμενοι** pres. mid. part. κάθημαι to sit.
ἔπεσαν aor. act. ind. (s.v.13). **προσεκύνησαν** aor. act. ind.
17 προσκυνέω to worship. ■ **παντοκράτωρ** almighty (s. Rev.
1:8). **ὤν** pres. part. εἰμί. **ἦν** impf. εἰμί. **εἴληφας** perf. act. ind.
λαμβάνω. The perf. may indicate that God has taken the power
permanently (s. Mounce). **ἐβασίλευσας** aor. act. ind.
18 βασιλεύω. ■ **ὠργίσθησαν** aor. pass. ind. ὀργίζω to make
angry, pass. to be angry. **ὀργή** wrath, anger. **κριθῆναι** aor. pass.
inf. κρίνω to judge. **δοῦναι** aor. act. inf. δίδωμι. The inf. are
used to explain the word "time," "season." **μισθός** reward,
wage, pay. **φοβουμένοις** pres. mid. part. φοβέομαι to fear, to
have reverence for. **διαφθεῖραι** aor. act. inf. διαφθείρω to destroy, to corrupt. The prep. in compound is perfective, i.e., to
19 utterly destroy. ■ **ἠνοίγη** aor. pass. ind. ἀνοίγω to open. **ναός**
temple, sanctuary. **ὤφθη** aor. pass. ind. ὁράω to see, pass. to be
seen, to appear. **κιβωτός** box, ark. **διαθήκη** covenant. In the
OT the ark of the covenant was a symbol of the abiding presence
of God (Mounce). **ἀστραπή** lightning. **βροντή** thunder.
σεισμός earthquake (s. Rev. 6:12). **χάλαζα** hail.

Ch. 12

1 ■ **ὤφθη** aor. pass. ind. ὁράω to see, pass. to be seen, to
appear. **περιβεβλημένη** perf. pass. part. περιβάλλω to cast
about, to clothe, pass. to be clothed. **σελήνη** moon. **ὑποκάτω**
w. the gen. "under." **ἀστήρ** star. Of all the various interpretations of the woman here the most fitting is to view the woman
as representing the nation Israel. In the OT the image of a
woman is a classical symbol for Zion, Jerusalem, and Israel
(Ford; Scott; Bousset). The twelve stars may be an allusion to the
2 twelve tribes of Israel (s. Mounce). ■ **ἐν γαστρὶ ἔχουσα** "to
have something in the stomach," i.e., "to be pregnant." **κράζει**
pres. act. ind. to scream, to cry out w. a loud voice. **ὠδίνουσα**
pres. act. part. ὠδίνω to have birth pains, to be in labor.
βασανιζομένη pres. pass. part. βασανίζω to torment, to be in
pain. **τεκεῖν** aor. act. inf. τίκτω to bear a child, to give birth. The
3 inf. is used epexegetically explaining the pain. ■ **δράκων** dragon.
John does not leave us in doubt as to the identity of this monster:
he is "the old serpent, he that is called the devil and Satan" (v.
9; cf. 20:2) (Mounce). **πυρρός** fiery, red. **κέρας** horn. The horn
was a symbol of strength. **διάδημα** diadem, a royal crown. The
royal crown was a symbol of political authority and denotes
4 sovereignty (Swete). ■ **οὐρά** tail. **σύρει** pres. act. ind. to drag,

to sweep. **ἔβαλεν** aor. act. ind. βάλλω to throw. **ἕστηκεν** perf. act. ind. ἵστημι to stand. **μελλούσης** pres. act. part. μέλλω to be about to. Used w. the inf. to express the fut. tense. **ὅταν** w. the subj. whenever. **τέκῃ** aor. act. subj. τίκτω to give birth. **καταφάγῃ** aor. act. subj. κατεσθίω to eat up, to consume.
■ **ἔτεκεν** aor. act. ind. τίκτω. **ἄρσεν** male. **ποιμαίνειν** pres. 5
act. inf. to shepherd, to lead, to rule. The inf. is used in the construction expressing the fut. **ῥάβδος** staff. **σιδηροῦς** made of iron. **ἡρπάσθη** aor. pass. ind. ἁρπάζω to seize, to snatch, to
take away. ■ **ἔφυγεν** aor. act. ind. φεύγω to flee. 6
ἡτοιμασμένον perf. pass. part. ἑτοιμάζω to prepare. The perf. pass. indicates "to stand prepared," i.e., "that which has been prepared and now stands ready." **τρέφωσιν** pres. act. subj. τρέφω to nourish. The subj. is used in a purpose clause. The pl. may be impersonal and equivalent to a pass.

■ **ἐγένετο** aor. mid. ind. γίνομαι. **πόλεμος** war. 7
πολεμῆσαι aor. act. inf. πολεμέω to conduct war, to fight. The nom. used w. the inf. may be the result of a Hebraic construction
(s. Charles). **ἐπολέμησεν** aor. act. ind. ■ **ἴσχυσεν** aor. act. ind. 8
ἰσχύω to be strong, to be strong enough, to be able. The Dragon's supreme effort was not only a failure, but it resulted in his
final expulsion from heaven (Swete). **εὑρέθη** aor. pass. ind. ■ 9
ἐβλήθη aor. pass. ind. βάλλω. **ὄφις** snake. **ἀρχαῖος** old, ancient. **καλούμενος** pres. pass. part. **πλανῶν** pres. act. part. πλανάω to lead astray, to deceive. The pres. part. indicates a
continuous action which has become a habitual character. ■ 10
ἤκουσα aor. act. ind. ἀκούω. **κατήγωρ** one who brings a legal charge against another, accuser. **κατηγορῶν** pres. act. part.
κατηγορέω to bring a legal accusation, to accuse. ■ **ἐνίκησαν** 11
aor. act. ind. νικάω to be a victor, to overcome. **διά** w. the acc. "because of." The prep. here gives the ground, not the means of their victory (Mounce). **ἀρνίον** lamb. **ἠγάπησαν** aor. act. ind. ἀγαπάω. Their non-attachment to life was carried to the extent
of being ready to die for their faith (Swete). ■ **εὐφραίνεσθε** 12
pres. mid. imp. εὐφραίνομαι to rejoice, to be happy. **σκηνοῦντες** pres. act. part. σκηνόω to tabernacle, to live in a tent, to dwell. Here the word does not indicate a temporary residence, but emphasizes the presence of God (Mounce). **οὐαί** woe. The acc. which follows may be acc. of general reference instead of the normal dat. **κατέβη** aor. act. ind. καταβαίνω to go down, effective aor. "he did go down" (RWP). **ἔχων** pres. act. part. **θυμός** anger, burning anger (s. Trench, *Synonyms*, 131f.).
εἰδώς perf. act. part. οἶδα. The part. is causal. ■ **ἐδίωξεν** aor. 13
act. ind. διώκω to hunt, to pursue, to persecute. This would

indicate the tremendous persecution to be suffered by Israel in
14 the tribulation period. ■ **ἐδόθησαν** aor. pass. ind. δίδωμι. The
pass. would be the theological or divine pass. indicating that God
is the One who gives. **πτέρυξ** wing. **ἀετός** eagle. **πέτηται** pres.
mid. subj. πέτομαι to fly. The subj. is used in a purpose clause.
ἥμισυ half. The words indicate that the nation Israel will be
protected from total destruction for the last three and one half
15 years of the Tribulation. ■ **στόμα** mouth. **ὀπίσω** behind, after.
ποταμός river. **ποταμοφόρητος** to be carried by the river, to
be swept away by the river. **ποιήσῃ** aor. act. subj. The verb is
used in connection w. the noun to express the verbal action
contained in the noun. The subj. is used in a purpose clause.
ἐβοήθησεν aor. act. ind. βοηθέω to help. **ἤνοιξεν** aor. act. ind.
ἀνοίγω to open. **κατέπιεν** aor. act. ind. καταπίνω to swallow
17 down, to swallow up completely. ■ **ὠργίσθη** aor. pass. ind.
ὀργίζω to make angry, ingressive aor. "to become angry."
ἀπῆλθεν aor. act. ind. ἀπέρχομαι to go out, to go away from,
to depart. **ποιῆσαι** aor. act. inf. The inf. is used to express intent
or purpose. **λοιπός** rest. **σπέρμα** seed. **τηρούντων** pres. act.
18 part. τηρέω to watch, to keep, to observe. ■ **ἐστάθη** aor. pass.
ind. ἵστημι to stand. **ἄμμος** sand, beach.

Ch. 13

1 ■ **θάλασσα** sea. The sea is an apt symbol of the agitated
surface of unregenerated humanity and esp. of the seething caul-
dron of national and social life, out of which the great historical
movements of the world arise (Swete). **θηρίον** beast, monster.
This is the monstrous person in whom the political power of the
world is finally concentrated and represented and who is spoken
of in Daniel 7 and called "the man of sin" in 2 Thessalonians 2:3
(s. Walvoord; Seiss, ZPEB I, 180f.). **ἀναβαῖνον** pres. act. part.
ἀναβαίνω to go up, to arise, to ascend. **ἔχον** pres. act. part.
κέρας horn. **διάδημα** diadem, royal crown. These two figures
represent the mighty political power and also stand for kings and
their kingdom as in Daniel 7 (s. Walvoord). **βλασφημία** blas-
2 phemy. ■ **πάρδαλις** leopard. **ἄρκος** bear. **λέων** lion. This beast
combines the characteristics of Daniel's beasts in which the
leopard (or panther) indicates agility, cat-like vigilance, craft,
and fierce cruelty, and the feet of the bear indicate the slow
strength and power to crush. The lion blends massive strength
w. feline dexterity, following up a stealthy and perhaps unobserved policy of repression w. the sudden terrors of a hostile
edict (Swete). **ἔδωκεν** aor. act. ind. δίδωμι. **δράκων** dragon.
The great political leader receives his power directly from Satan.

■ **μίαν ἐκ τῶν κεφαλῶν** "one of his heads." This takes up the 3
narrative of v. 1 and the verb to be supplied is "and I saw"
(Swete). **ἐσφαγμένην** perf. pass. part. σφάζω to slay, to slaughter, to kill. The use of this word indicates that the deadly wound
was like the slaying of the Lamb (s. Bousset; Swete). **πληγή**
blow, wound. The following gen. is descriptive "death wound,"
"lethal wound" (Ford). **ἐθεραπεύθη** aor. pass. ind. θεραπεύω
to heal. Here we have the political death and resurrection of the
beast (Scott). **ἐθαυμάσθη** aor. pass. ind. θαυμάζω to cause
someone to wonder, to cause to marvel. **ὀπίσω** behind, after.
The pregnant use of the prep. means "all the earth wondered at
and followed after the beast" (RWP). ■ **προσεκύνησαν** aor. 4
act. ind. προσκυνέω to worship. **πολεμῆσαι** aor. act. inf.
πολεμέω to wage war, to fight against.

■ **ἐδόθη** aor. pass. ind. δίδωμι. **λαλοῦν** pres. act. part. 5
ποιῆσαι aor. act. inf. to do, i.e., to carry out his work. During
the forty-two months the beast actively carries out the will of the
dragon (Mounce; Swete). **μήν** month, acc. of time "for forty-two
months." ■ **ἤνοιξεν** aor. act. ind. ἀνοίγω to open. 6
βλασφημῆσαι aor. act. inf. βλασφημέω to ridicule, to slander, to blaspheme. **σκηνή** tent, habitation, dwelling place, tabernacle. To blaspheme the name of God is to speak evil of all that
He is and stands for. The name sums up the person. His tabernacle is His dwelling place (Mounce). **σκηνοῦντας** pres. act.
part. σκηνόω to live in a tent, to tabernacle, to dwell. ■ 7
πόλεμος war. **νικῆσαι** aor. act. inf. νικάω to win a victory, to
conquer, to overcome. ■ **προσκυνήσουσιν** fut. act. ind. to 8
worship. **αὐτόν** "him" The masc. pron. indicates that the beast
is a person. **κατοικοῦντες** pres. act. part. κατοικέω to live, to
dwell, to reside. **γέγραπται** perf. pass. ind. The perf. tense
indicates the continuing results and binding authority of that
which was written (s. MM). **βιβλίον** book, little book. **ἀρνίον**
lamb. **καταβολή** foundation, laying of a foundation. The "foundation of the world" refers to the creation of the visible order
(Mounce; s. also Eph. 1:4; 1 Peter 1:20).

■ **ἀκουσάτω** aor. act. imp. ■ **αἰχμαλωσία** one taken cap- 9/10
tive at spear point, captivity. **ὑπάγει** pres. act. ind. to go forth.
The pres. tense is gnomic indicating the statement of a general
truth. The proverbial style of the v. could be translated "if any
man leads into captivity, into captivity he goes." Thus, the v.
would stress that the enemies of God's people would be requited
for their persecution of believers in the same form they employed (captivity for captivity, sword for sword) (Mounce).
μάχαιρα sword. **ἀποκτενεῖ** fut. act. ind. ἀποκτείνω to kill. **δεῖ**

(w. the acc. and inf.) "it is binding," "it is necessary." **ἀποκτανθῆναι** aor. pass. inf. ἀποκτείνω to kill.

11 ■ **θηρίον** wild animal, beast, monster. The second beast
introduced is the religious leader or false prophet. **ἀναβαῖνον**
pres. act. part. to come up, to ascend (s.v.1). **κέρας** horn. **ὅμοιος**
like. **ἀρνίον** lamb. The second beast is a pseudochrist (Swete).
ἐλάλει impf. act. ind. The impf. pictures the customary action.
12 **δράκων** dragon (s.v.2). ■ **προσκυνήσουσιν** fut. act. ind.
(s.v.8). The false prophet who is a religious leader also inspired
of Satan causes the world to worship the man of sin who has set
himself up as God (s. 2 Thess. 2:4f.). **ἐθεραπεύθη** aor. pass. ind.
13 to heal (s.v.3). ■ **ποιῇ** pres. act. subj. to make, to cause. The subj.
could either be a purpose or result clause (RWP). **καταβαίνειν**
pres. act. inf. to come down. The inf. is used to complete the verb
14 "to make, to cause." ■ **πλανᾷ** pres. act. ind. to lead astray, to
deceive. **ἐδόθη** aor. pass. ind. (s.v.5). **ποιῆσαι** aor. act. inf.
15 (s.v.5). **εἰκων** image. **ἔζησεν** aor. act. ind. ζάω to live. ■ **δοῦναι**
aor. act. inf. δίδωμι. **λαλήσῃ** aor. act. subj. **ποιήσῃ** aor. act.
subj. The subj. are used in a purpose or result clause. The second
beast is given the power to animate the image of the first beast.
He gives to it the breath of life and the image speaks (Mounce).
προσκυνήσωσιν aor. act. subj. **προσκυνέω**. The subj. is used
in a third-class conditional clause which views the condition as
16 a possibility. **ἀποκτανθῶσιν** aor. pass. subj. (s.v.10). ■
πλούσιος rich, wealthy. **πτωχός** poor, poor as a beggar.
ἐλεύθερος free. **δῶσιν** aor. act. subj. δίδωμι. **χάραγμα** brand,
mark. (For various usages of the brand in the ancient world, s.
Mounce; BS, 242; LAE, 341f.; Ford; TDNT.) **δεξιός** right.
17 **μέτωπον** forehead. ■ **δύνηται** pres. act. subj. The subj. is in a
purpose clause or the clause is the obj. of the verb. **ἀγοράσαι**
aor. act. inf. ἀγοράζω to buy. **πωλῆσαι** aor. act. inf. πωλέω to
18 sell. **ἔχων** pres. act. part. **ἀριθμός** number. ■ **νοῦς** understanding, comprehension. **ψηφισάτω** aor. act. imp. ψηφίζω to count
up, to calculate, lit. to count w. pebbles, to reckon (s. MM; Luke
14:28).

Ch. 14

1 ■ **καὶ εἶδον, καὶ ἰδού** "and I saw and behold." The words introduce a new and dramatic part of the vision (s. Rev. 4:1; 6:2; Mounce). **ἀρνίον** lamb (s. Rev. 5:6). **ἑστός** perf. act. part. ἵστημι to stand. That the lamb is standing forms a contrast w. the beasts who are rising and indicates "being established," "standing firm," "holding one's own ground" (Ford). **ἔχουσαι** pres. act. part. **γεγραμμένον** perf. pass. part. to write, to in-

scribe. The perf. tense indicates the continuing result of the
authoritative writing. The seal consists in the name of God inscribed on the brow. This inscription declares that the person so
inscribed is God's own possession (Charles). The scene is an
obvious contrast to the beast of chapter 13 whose followers are
stamped w. his mark on the right hand or forehead (Mounce).
μέτωπον forehead, brow. ■ **ἤκουσα** aor. act. ind. ἀκούω. 2
βροντή thunder. **κιθαρῳδός** one who plays on a harp, harpist.
κιθαριζόντων pres. act. part. κιθαρίζω to play the harp.
κιθάρα harp (s. Rev. 5:8; 1 Cor. 14:7). ■ **ᾄδουσιν** pres. act. ind. 3
to sing. **ᾠδή** song (s. Rev. 5:9). **ζῷον** living creature. **ἐδύνατο**
impf. mid. ind. The impf. is used of unfulfilled action. **μαθεῖν**
aor. act. inf. μανθάνω to learn. **εἰ μή** "except." **ἠγορασμένοι**
perf. pass. part. ἀγοράζω to buy, to redeem, to purchase (s.
APC, 50f.; TDNT). ■ **ἐμολύνθησαν** aor. pass. ind. μολύνω to 4
defile, to soil, to stain. **παρθένος** virgin. It seems best to take
this description of chastity in a figurative sense indicating that
they have kept themselves pure from all defiling relationships w.
the pagan world system. They have resisted the seduction of the
great harlot, Rome, w. whom the kings of the earth have committed fornication (Mounce). **ἀκολουθοῦντες** pres. act. part. to
follow, to follow after, to be a disciple of someone. ἀκολουθέω
w. the subj. "wherever." **ὅπου ἄν** pres. act. subj. **ὑπάγῃ** to go
forth, to go. **ἠγοράσθησαν** aor. pass. ind. ἀγοράζω to buy at
the market place, to purchase, to redeem. **ἀπὸ ἀνθρώπων**
"from men," "from among men." The part. here denotes not
"separation," but "extraction" (Swete). **ἀπαρχή** firstfruit. In
the OT until the firstfruit of harvest or flock were offered to God
the rest of the crop could not be put to profane or secular use
(Ford; s. also Rom. 16:5; 1 Cor. 16:15). ■ **στόμα** mouth. **εὑρέθη** 5
aor. pass. ind. **ἄμωμος** unblemished. This is a Levitical sacrificial term meaning not spoiled by any flaw. If "unblemished"
continues the metaphor of the "firstfruit" it would refer to
"flock" rather than "crop," and Lamb (Ford).

■ **πετόμενον** pres. mid. part. πέτομαι to fly. 6
μεσουράνημα mid-heaven (s. Rev. 8:13). **ἔχοντα** pres. act.
part. **εὐαγγέλιον** good news, good tidings. It is not the gospel
of God's redeeming grace in Christ Jesus, but as the following
vv. show a summons to fear, honor, and worship the Creator
(Mounce). **εὐαγγελίσαι** aor. act. inf. εὐαγγελίζω to proclaim
good news. The inf. is used to express purpose or it could be also
epexegetical explaining that which the angel has (s. RWP;
Swete). **καθημένους** pres. mid. part. κάθημαι to sit. (For the
variant reading "the ones dwelling on the earth" rather than "the

ones sitting on the earth," s. Charles.) **ἔθνος** nation. **φυλή** tribe.
7 **γλῶσσα** tongue, language. ■ **λέγων** pres. act. part. **φοβήθητε**
aor. pass. imp. φοβέομαι to fear, to show reverence. **δότε** aor.
act. imp. δίδωμι to give. **κρίσις** judging, judgment.
προσκυνήσατε aor. act. imp. προσκυνέω to worship. The
eternal gospel calls upon men to fear and honor the Creator, for
the hour of judgment is at hand. God has revealed Himself in
nature so that men are without excuse (Mounce). **ποιήσαντι**
aor. act. part. to make, to create. **πηγή** spring.
8 ■ **ἠκολούθησεν** aor. act. ind. ἀκολουθέω to follow.
ἔπεσεν aor. act. ind. πίπτω to fall. The ancient Mesopotamian
city of Babylon had become the political and religious capital of
a world empire, renowned for its luxury and moral corruption.
Above all it was the great enemy of the people of God. For the
early church the city of Rome was a contemporary Babylon
(Mounce). **θυμός** anger, burning anger (s. Rev. 12:12). **πορνεία**
immorality, illicit sexual activity. **πεπότικεν** perf. act. ind.
ποτίζω to give to drink, to cause to drink. The drinking of the
wine indicates the intoxicating influence of Babylon's vices
(Ford).
9 ■ **θηρίον** wild beast, monster. **εἰκών** image. **χάραγμα**
10 brand, mark. ■ **πίεται** fut. mid. ind. πίνω to drink. The pron.
"he" in Gr. indicates that the pron. is there to emphasize "man,"
not to indicate another person. The author probably means that
one cannot drink one cup and not the other for both are linked;
the consequence of drinking Babylon's cup is the inescapable
necessity to receive the Lord's (Ford). **κεκερασμένου** perf.
pass. part. καρέννυμι to mix. The word was used of the preparation of wine by the addition of various spices and the word later
came to mean "properly prepared" (Mounce; s. also Charles).
ἄκρατος unmixed, undiluted, not diluted w. water. The words
mean that those who worship the image will drink the wine of
God's wrath poured out in full strength, untempered by the
mercy and grace of God (Mounce). **ποτήριον** cup. **ὀργή** wrath,
anger. This word refers more to the settled feeling of righteous
indignation whereas the word in v.8 and the first part of v. 10
refers to the white heat of God's anger (s. Mounce; Swete;
Trench, *Synonyms*, 131ff.). **βασανισθήσεται** fut. pass. ind.
11 βασανίζω to torment, to torture. ■ **καπνός** smoke.
βασανισμός torturing, pain, suffering. **ἀναβαίνει** pres. act.
ind. to go up, to ascend. The pres. tense connected w. the temporal designation "forever" indicates a continual unbroken action.
ἀνάπαυσις stopping, resting, ceasing, relief. The word was used
in the papyri w. the idea of relief from public duties and the word

contains the idea of temporary rest as a preparation for fut. toil (MM). The time indicator "day and night" is gen. of time indicating the kind of time within which something takes place (s. RG, 495; MT, 235; DM, 77; BD, 99f.). **προσκυνοῦντες** pres.
act. part. προσκυνέω. ■ **τηροῦντες** pres. act. part. τηρέω to 12
keep, to observe. **πίστις Ἰησοῦ** "faith of Jesus." The gen. is obj. gen., i.e., "faith in Jesus."

■ **ἤκουσα** aor. act. ind. **γράψον** aor. act. imp. **μακάριος** 13
happy, blessed. **ἀποθνῄσκοντες** pres. act. part. ἀποθνῄσκω to die. **ἵνα.** The word here passes into the meaning "in that" rather than "in order that" (Swete). **ἀναπαήσονται** fut. mid. ind. ἀναπαύομαι to have relief, to cease, to rest. **κόπος** toil, labor, hard work which produces weariness (s. Rev. 2:2).

■ **καὶ εἶδον, καὶ ἰδού** "and I saw and behold" (s.v.1). 14
νεφέλη cloud (s. Rev. 1:7). **λευκός** white. **καθήμενον** pres. mid. part. to sit. This is none other than the risen Christ (Mounce). **ἔχων** pres. act. part. **χρυσοῦς** golden. The golden crown or wreath indicated the type of crown or wreath given to a victor and this designates the Messiah as the One who has conquered and thereby won the right to act in judgment (Mounce; s. also Trench, *Synonyms*, 78–81; esp. CBB).
δρέπανον sickle. **ὀξύς** sharp. ■ **ἐξῆλθεν** aor. act. ind. 15
ἐξέρχομαι to come out. **ναός** temple, sanctuary. The angel that delivers the divine command to commence the harvest comes out from within the temple, that most holy place of the presence of God. Judgment upon sin is a necessary function of righteousness (Mounce). **κράζων** pres. act. part. κράζω to scream, to cry out w. a loud voice. **πέμψον** aor. act. imp. πέμπω to send, ingressive aor. "start at once." **θέρισον** aor. act. imp. θερίζω to harvest, ingressive aor. "begin at once." **θερίσαι** aor. act. inf. The inf. is epexegetical explaining the word "hour." The classical use of reaping to symbolize death and destruction is very common (s. EGT). **ἐξηράνθη** aor. pass. ind. ξηραίνω to dry, to be dry. Here the word indicates perfect ripeness (Swete). **θερισμός**
harvest. ■ **ἔβαλεν** aor. act. ind. βάλλω to cast. **ἐθερίσθη** aor. 16
pass. ind.

■ **θυσιαστήριον** altar. **ἐφώνησεν** aor. act. ind. φωνέω to 18
make a sound, to call out. **τρύγησον** aor. act. imp. τρυγάω to gather ripe fruit, esp. to pick grapes (BAG). **βότρυς** grapes, bunch of grapes. **ἄμπελος** grape vine. **ἤκμασαν** aor. act. ind. ἀκμάζω to be ripe, to be in the prime, to be at the peak (s. GEW
I, 53; Mounce). **σταφυλή** the ripe grape cluster (Swete). ■ 19
ἐτρυγήσεν aor. act. ind. (s.v. 18). **ληνός** trough, vat, wine press
(AS; s. also Matt. 21:33). ■ **ἐπατήθη** aor. pass. ind. πατέω to 20

walk, to walk on, to trample. In biblical days grapes were trampled by foot in a trough which had a duct leading to a lower basin where the juice collected. The treading of grapes was a familiar figure for the execution of divine wrath upon the enemies of God (Mounce; Isa. 63:3). **ἔξωθεν** w. the gen. "outside." **χαλινός** bridle. **ἵππος** horse. **στάδιον** stadion. A stadion measures about 670 feet so that the distance here would be approximately 184 miles (s. Mounce). When Jerusalem was taken by Titus, Josephus says that the Roman soldiers slew all they met w. and made the whole city run down w. blood to such a degree that the fire of many houses was quenched w. these men's blood (Govett; Josephus, *Jewish War*, VI, 406).

Ch. 15

1 ■ **ἄλλο** "another." The words "another sign" look back to 12:1 and 3 (Swete). **θαυμαστός** amazing, that which causes wonder. **ἔχοντας** pres. act. part. **πληγή** blow, wound, plague. **ἐτελέσθη** aor. pass. ind. *τελέω* to bring to conclusion, to complete.

2 ■ **ὑάλινος** glassy, crystal (s. Rev. 4:6). **μεμιγμένην** perf. pass. part. **μείγνυμι** to mix. **πῦρ** fire. **νικῶντας** pres. act. part. *νικάω* to gain a victory, to be victor, to overcome. **θηρίον** wild beast, monster. **εἰκών** image. **ἀριθμός** number. **ἑστῶτας** perf. act. part. *ἵστημι* to stand. This phrase could mean "standing on" or "standing by." This scene of the victors standing on the heavenly sea w. harps in their hands and praising God recalls Israel's song of triumph over Egypt on the shore of the Red Sea
3 (Charles). **κιθάρα** harp, lyre. ■ **ᾄδουσιν** pres. act. ind. to sing. **ᾠδή** song. **ἀρνίον** lamb. **παντοκράτωρ** almighty (s. Rev. 1:8).
4 ■ **φοβηθῇ** aor. pass. subj. *φοβέομαι* to fear, to show respect, to reverence. **δοξάσει** fut. act. ind. *δοξάζω* to glorify. **ὅσιος** undefiled by sin, free from wickedness, pure, holy (T; CBB; Trench, *Synonyms*, 328f.; TDNT). **ἥξουσιν** fut. act. ind. *ἥκω* to come. **προσκυνήσουσιν** fut. act. ind. *προσκυνέω* to worship. **δικαίωμα** righteous deed. This refers to the acts of God which meet His standards of faithfulness and loyalty to His person and word. It could refer also to God's judgments in a judicial sense (s. TDNT; Ford; Charles). **ἐφανερώθησαν** aor. pass. ind. *φανερόω* to make clear, to manifest, to reveal.

5 ■ **ἠνοίγη** aor. pass. ind. *ἀνοίγω* to open. **ναός** temple, sanctuary. **σκηνή** tent, tabernacle. The word refers to the dwell-
6 ing place of God. ■ **ἐξῆλθον** aor. act. ind. *ἐξέρχομαι* to go out, to come out. **ἐνδεδυμένοι** perf. pass. part. *ἐνδύω* to dress, to put on clothes, to be clothed. **λίνον** linen. **λαμπρός** shining. The

robes of linen, pure and shining, denote the noble and sacred nature of their office (Mounce). **περιεζωσμένοι** perf. pass. part. περιζώννυμι to be girded around, to wear a wide belt which held up the long flowing garments. **στῆθος** breast, chest. **ζώνη** wide belt, girdle. **χρυσοῦς.** The golden girdles are symbolic of
royal and priestly functions (Mounce; s. also Rev. 1:13). ■ **ζῷον** 7
living creature. **ἔδωκεν** aor. act. ind. δίδωμι. **φιάλη** bowl. This was a wide shallow bowl like a deep saucer (Mounce; T; NBD, 1310). **γεμούσας** pres. act. part. γέμω to be full, to be full of.
ζῶντος pres. act. part. ζάω to live. ■ **ἐγεμίσθη** aor. pass. ind. 8
γεμίζω to fill up, to make full. **καπνός** smoke. **ἐδύνατο** impf. mid. ind. **εἰσελθεῖν** aor. act. inf. εἰσέρχομαι to go into. **τελεσθῶσιν** aor. pass. subj. to complete. The subj. is used in an indefinite temporal clause.

Ch. 16

■ **ἤκουσα** aor. act. ind. ἀκούω to hear. **ναός** temple, sanc- 1
tuary. **ὑπάγετε** pres. act. imp. ὑπάγω to go forth. **ἐκχέετε** impf. act. ind. ἐκχέω to pour out, to empty out. **φιάλη** bowl. (s. Rev. 15:7). **θυμός** anger, burning, blistering anger (s. Rev. 14:8, 10).
■ **ἀπῆλθεν** aor. act. ind. ἀπέρχομαι to go forth, to go out. 2
ἐξέχεεν aor. act. ind. ἐκχέω. **ἐγένετο** aor. mid. ind. γίνομαι to become, to happen, to come to pass. **ἕλκος** sore, abscess, boil. This is the word used in the LXX of the boils w. which God smote the Egyptians (Ford; s. also Mounce). (For Pliny's description of the treatment of boils and carbuncles, s. Pliny, *Natural History*, XXX, 107–108.) **ἔχοντες** pres. act. part. **χάραγμα** brand, mark. **θηρίον** beast, monster. **εἰκών** image.
■ **ἀπέθανεν** aor. act. ind. ἀποθνήσκω to die. 3
■ **ποταμός** river. **πηγή** spring. ■ **ὤν** pres. part. εἰμί. **ἦν** 4/5
impf. εἰμί. **ὅσιος** pure, holy (s. Rev. 15:4). **ἔκρινας** aor. act. ind.
κρίνω to judge. ■ **δέδωκας** perf. act. ind. δίδωμι. **πεῖν** aor. act. 6
inf. πίνω to drink. The inf. is epexegetical after the verb "to give" (s. RWP). **ἄξιοί εἰσιν** "they are worthy," i.e., "it is what
they deserve" (Mounce). ■ **θυσιαστήριον** place of sacrifice, 7
altar. **ναί** "yes," "Yea." **παντοκράτωρ** almighty (s. Rev. 1:8). **ἀληθινός** true, genuine. **κρίσις** judging, judgment.
■ **ἐδόθη** aor. pass. ind. δίδωμι. The verb is used in the sense 8
of "he was given authority," "he was allowed." **καυματίσαι** aor. act. inf. καυματίζω to burn, to scorch (s. Ford; Swete). **ἐκαυματίσθησαν** aor. pass. ind. **καῦμα** heat, scorching. The cognate acc. retained w. a pass. verb (RWP). **ἐβλασφήμησαν** aor. act. ind. βλασφημέω to blaspheme. **πληγή** blow, wound, plague. **μετενόησαν** aor. act. ind. μετανοέω to change one's

mind, to change one's thinking, to repent. **δοῦναι** aor. act. inf. δίδωμι. The inf. is used to express actual or realized results.
10 ■ **ἐσκοτωμένη** perf. pass. part. σκοτόω to make dark, to darken. **ἐμασῶντο** perf. mid. ind. μασάομαι to chew, to gnaw. The word indicates that the pain caused by the scorching heat of the fourth plague and the malignant sores of the first was such that men chewed their tongues in agony. The phrase was used as an indication of intolerable pain (Swete; s. also Matt. 8:12). **γλῶσσα** tongue. **πόνος** pain, agony.
12 ■ **ἐξηράνθη** aor. pass. ind. ξηραίνω to dry, to dry up. **ἑτοιμασθῇ** aor. pass. subj. ἑτοιμάζω to prepare, to make ready. Subj. used in purpose clause. **ἀνατολή** rising, "rising of the sun,"
13 i.e., "the east" (s. Matt. 2:1). ■ **δράκων** dragon. **ψευδοπροφήτης** false prophet. **ἀκάθαρτος** impure, unclean. **βάτραχος** frog. The frog was classified as an unclean animal, an abomination (Lev. 11:10, 41) (Ford; s. also FFB, 33). The unclean spirits proceed from the "mouths" of the unholy triumvirate, suggesting the persuasive and deceptive propaganda which in the last days will lead men to an unconditional commitment
14 to the cause of evil (Mounce). ■ **ποιοῦντα** pres. act. part. to do, to perform. **ἐκπορεύεται** pres. mid. ind. to go out, to proceed from. **συναγαγεῖν** aor. act. inf. συνάγω to lead together, to gather together, to assemble. The inf. is used to express purpose.
15 **πόλεμος** war. ■ **κλέπτης** thief. **μακάριος** blessed, happy. **γρηγορῶν** pres. act. part. γρηγορέω to be awake, to watch. **τηρῶν** pres. act. part. to keep, to protect. **γυμνός** naked. **περιπατῇ** pres. act. subj. περιπατέω to walk about. As the priest kept watch in the temple an officer of the temple used to go around every watch w. a lighted torch before him and if any watch did not stand up and say to him "O officer of the Temple Mount, peace be to thee!" and it was manifest that he was asleep, he would beat him w. his staff, and he had the right to burn his raiment (M. Middoth 1:2). **βλέπωσιν** pres. act. subj. The pl. is used impersonally which gives the verb the force of a pass. "his shame is seen." **ἀσχημοσύνη** shamefulness, indecency. The word is probably a euphemism for "private parts" (Mounce;
16 BAG). ■ **συνήγαγεν** aor. act. ind. συνάγω to gather together, to lead together, to assemble. **καλούμενον** pres. pass. part.
17 ■ **ἀήρ** air. **ἐξῆλθεν** aor. act. ind. ἐξέρχομαι to go out, to come out of. **γέγονεν** perf. act. ind. γίνομαι. The perf. tense could be translated "it is done," "it has come to pass." The voice is esp. appropriate in this connection, since these plagues are "the last"; there remain no further manifestations of this kind
18 (Swete). ■ **ἀστραπή** lightning. **βροντή** thunder. **σεισμός**

earthquake. **οἷος** of such a kind. **ἀφ' οὗ** "from when."
τηλικοῦτος so large, so great (s. Rev. 6:12). ■ **μέρος** part, 19
section. **ἔπεσαν** aor. act. ind. πίπτω to fall. **ἐμνήσθη** aor. pass.
ind. μιμνῄσκω to remember, pass. to be remembered.
ποτήριον cup. **ὀργή** wrath, anger (s. Rev. 14:10). ■ **νῆσος** 20
island. **ἔφυγεν** aor. act. ind. φεύγω to flee. **εὑρέθησαν** aor.
pass. ind. ■ **χάλαζα** hail. **ταλαντιαῖος** talent. The talent varied 21
in weight among different peoples at different times. The range seems to be from about sixty pounds to something over a hundred (Mounce). **καταβαίνει** pres. act. ind. to go down, to descend. **σφόδρα** very much, extremely, greatly, very.

Ch. 17

■ **ἐχόντων** pres. act. part. **φιάλη** bowl (s. Rev. 15:7). 1
ἐλάλησεν aor. act. ind. **δεῦρο** "come here." **δείξω** fut. act. ind. δείκνυμι to show. **κρίμα** sentence, judgment. **πόρνη** prostitute, whore. In the OT and prophetic language prostitution or adultery was equal to idolatry and denoted religious apostasy (Ford; Mounce). The harlot here is Rome and denotes the corrupt apostate religious system headed by the false prophet who is the second beast of Revelation 13. **καθημένης** pres. mid. part. κάθημαι to sit. **ἐπὶ ὑδάτων πολλῶν** "upon many waters" (s.
Rev. 13:1). ■ **ἐπόρνευσαν** aor. act. ind. πορνεύω to engage in 2
immoral acts, to engage in unlawful sex. Again the picture is one of religious apostasy. **ἐμεθύσθησαν** aor. pass. ind. μεθύσκω to be drunk, pass. to be made drunk. The aor. could be ingressive, i.e., "to enter in the state of drunkenness," "get drunk." The figure indicates the intoxicating and controlling aspects of the false religion. **κατοικοῦντες** pres. act. part. κοτοικέω to live, to reside, to dwell. **πορνεία** immorality, unlawful sexual activity
(s. Rev. 2:21). ■ **ἀπήνεγκεν** aor. act. ind. ἀπρφέρω to carry 3
away. **θηρίον** wild animal, beast. **κόκκινος** scarlet, crimson. The color was popular in the Roman Empire and indicated luxurious and haughty splendor (EGT; TDNT). **γέμοντα** pres. act. part. γέμω to be full. **βλασφημία** blasphemy. **κέρας** horn. The picture is the close union of the political and religious powers of
the last days. ■ **ἦν** impf. εἰμί. **περιβεβλημένη** perf. pass. part. 4
περιβάλλω to cast about, to be clothed. **πορφυροῦς** purple. Purple was often used of royal garments and scarlet was a color of magnificence (Mounce). **κεχρυσωμένη** perf. pass. part. χρυσόω to inlay w. gold, to cover w. gold. **μαργαρίτης** pearl (s. 1 Tim. 2:9). **ποτήριον** cup. **χρυσοῦς** golden. **βδέλυγμα** that which stinks, abomination, that which is detestable. The word is used in the LXX of the moral and ceremonial impurity connect-

ed w. idolatrous practices (Mounce). **ἀκάθαρτος** impure, un-
5 clean. ■ **μέτωπον** forehead, brow. **γεγραμμένον** perf. pass.
6 part. to write, to inscribe. ■ **μεθύουσαν** pres. act. part. *μεθύω* to get drunk. The metaphor of getting drunk on the blood of the saints and the blood of the witnesses of Jesus portrays the wanton slaughter of a great number of believers along w. the intoxicating effect it produced upon the murderous harlot (Mounce). This depicts the tremendous persecution of true believers by the apostate religion of the last days.

ἐθάυμασσα aor. act. ind. *θαυμάζω* to be amazed, to won-
7 der. **θαῦμα** wonderment. ■ **ἐρῶ** fut. act. ind. *λέγω* to tell.
8 **βαστάζοντος** pres. act. part. *βαστάζω* to carry, to bear. ■ **ἦν καὶ οὐκ ἔστιν καὶ μέλλει ἀναβαίνειν** "who was and is not and is about to arise . . ." is perhaps an intentional antithesis to Revelation 1:4: "the one who was and is" (Swete). **μέλλει** pres. act. ind. to be about to. Used w. the inf. to express the fut. tense. **ἀναβαίνειν** pres. act. inf. to go up, to ascend. **ἄβυσσος** bottomless pit, abyss (s. Rev. 9:1; 11:7). **ἀπώλεια** destruction, ruin. **ὑπάγει** pres. act. ind. to go forth. **θυαμασθήσονται** fut. pass. ind. to be amazed, to wonder w. the amazement of a horrible surprise; the world will still wonder and admire (Swete). **γέγραπται** perf. pass. ind. **καταβολή** foundation (s. Eph. 1:4; Rev. 13:8). **βλεπόντων** pres. act. part. The part. is used temporarily "when they see." The gen. pl. agrees w. the gen. pl. of the rel. pron. (RWP). **παρέσται** fut. act. ind. *πάρειμι* to be
9 present. ■ **νοῦς** mind, understanding. The formula is a call to vigilance and close attention (Swete). **ὅπου** where. **βασιλεύς** king. The reference is either to seven world empires (Seiss) or it refers to seven emperors of the Roman Empire (s. Govett; s. also a discussion by Mounce; Ford). Others have viewed this as
10 various forms of government of the Roman Empire (Scott). ■ **ἔπεσαν** aor. act. ind. *πίπτω* to fall. **οὔπω** not yet. **ὅταν** w. the subj. "whenever." **ἔλθῃ** aor. act. subj. *ἔρχομαι*. The subj. is used in an indefinite temporal clause. **δεῖ** (w. the acc. and an inf.) "it is binding," "it is necessary." **μεῖναι** aor. act. inf. *μένω* to re-
11 main. ■ **ὄγδοός** eighth. The beast himself is an eighth king who is at the same time one of the seven. He is Antichrist, not simply another Roman emperor. His period of hegemony is the Great
12 Tribulation preceding the return of the Messiah (Mounce). ■ **ἔλαβον** aor. act. ind. *λαμβάνω*. The ten kings who are yet to receive their power refer to ten European kingdoms of a revived Roman Empire. The political beast of Revelation 13 will be one
13 of these leaders (s. Scott). ■ **γνώμη** opinion, purpose. The unity
14 of the ten appears in their support of the beast (Swete). ■ **ἀρνίον**

lamb. **πολεμήσουσιν** fut. act. ind. πολεμέω to wage war. **νικήσει** fut. act. ind. νικάω to gain the victory, to be victor, to overcome, to conquer. **κλητός** called. **ἐκλεκτός** chosen, elect.
■ **οὗ** where. **ὄχλος** crowd, multitudes. **ἔθνος** nation. 15
γλῶσσα tongue, language. The fourfold grouping stresses universality (Mounce). (For the figure of the "sea" representing
people and nations, s. Rev. 13:1.) ■ **μισήσουσιν** fut. act. ind. 16
μισέω to hate. **ἠρημωμένην** perf. pass. part. ἐρημόω to desolate, to make into a desert or desolate place. **ποιήσουσιν** fut. act. ind. **γυμνός** naked. **φάγονται** fut. mid. ind. ἐσθίω to eat. **κατακαύσουσιν** fut. act. ind. κατακαίω to burn down, to burn up, to completely destroy by fire. The political forces will turn
against the false religious system and completely destroy it. ■ 17
ἔδωκεν aor. act. ind. δίδωμι. **ποιῆσαι** aor. act. inf. **δοῦναι** aor. act. inf. δίδωμι. **τελεσθήσονται** fut. pass. ind. τελέω to bring to the goal, to complete.

Ch. 18

■ **μετὰ ταῦτα** "after these things." **καταβαίνοντα** pres. 1
act. part. καταβαίνω to come down, to descend. **ἔχοντα** pres. act. part. **ἐφωτίσθη** aor. pass. ind. φωτίζω to light up, to illuminate. So recently has he come from the Presence that in passing
he flings a broad belt of light across the dark earth (Swete). ■ 2
ἔκραξεν aor. act. ind. κράζω to scream, to cry out w. a loud voice. **ἔπεσεν** aor. act. ind. πίπτω to fall (s. Rev. 14:8; cf. also Isa. 21:9). The proleptic aor. are repeated like a solemn dirge or lament of the damned (RWP). **ἐγένετο** aor. mid. ind. γίνομαι. **κατοικητήριον** place of living, habitation. **φυλακή** prison, place of banishment. **ἀκάθαρτος** unclean. **ὄρνεον** bird.
μεμισημένου perf. pass. part. μισέω to hate. ■ **θυμός** anger, 3
wrath, burning anger (s. Rev. 14:8, 10). **πορνεία** immorality, unlawful sexual acts. The figure is also used for apostasy and idolatry (s. Rev. 17:1). **πέπωκαν** perf. act. ind. πίνω to drink. The perf. tense would indicate the continuing results. **ἐπόρνευσαν** aor. act. ind. πορνεύω to commit immorality. **ἔμπορος** merchant. **στρῆνος** strong, mighty, arrogant, complacent luxury. The noun along w. the verb contains the idea of "excessive luxury and self-indulgence w. accompanying arrogance and wanton exercise of strength" (Mounce; s. also GEW II, 890f.; Swete). **ἐπλούτησαν** aor. act. ind. πλουτέω to be wealthy, ingressive aor. "they became wealthy."
■ **ἤκουσα** aor. act. ind. ἀκούω. **ἐξέλθατε** aor. act. imp. 4
ἐξέρχομαι to come out, to depart from. **συγκοινωνήσητε** aor. act. subj. συγκοινωνέω to be a partner w., to be a copartner w.

(s. 1 John 1:3; 2 John 11). **πληγή** blow, wound, plague. **λάβητε** aor. act. subj. λαμβάνω. The subj. here are used in a neg. purpose clause. The neg. in an expression of apprehension is combined in classical Gr. w. the subj. if the anxiety is directed toward warding off something still dependent on the will (BD, 188).
5 ■ **ἐκολλήθησαν** aor. pass. ind. κολλάω to stick to, to join to. The idea here is "joined to one another till they reach heaven, till the ever growing mass rose sky high" (Swete). **ἐμνημόνευσεν** aor. act. ind. μνημονεύω to remember.
6 **ἀδίκημα** unrighteous act, injustice. ■ **ἀπόδοτε** aor. act. imp. ἀποδίδωμι to pay back. **διπλώσατε** aor. act. imp. διπλόω to double, to make double. **διπλοῦς** double. In this v. there is precise compensation: double punishment for double crimes (Ford). **ποτήριον** cup. **ἐκέρασεν** aor. act. ind. κεράννυμι to mix. **κεράσατε** aor. act. imp. κεράννυμι to mix a drink in
7 preparation for drinking (s. Rev. 14:10). ■ **ὅσος** "how much," "as much as" (s. AS). **ἐδόξασεν** aor. act. ind. δοξάζω to glorify. **ἐστρηνίασεν** aor. act. ind. στρηνιάω to live a proud and luxurious life (s.v.2). **τοσοῦτος** "so much," "so great." **δότε** aor. act. imp. δίδωμι. **βασανισμός** torture, torment, pain. **πένθος** mourning. **κάθημαι** pres. mid. ind. to sit, to sit established. **βασίλισσα** queen. **χήρα** widow. **οὐ μή** w. the subj. "not ever,"
8 "never in any wise." **ἴδω** aor. act. subj. ὁράω. ■ **ἥξουσιν** fut. act. ind. ἥκω to come. **θάνατος** death. **λιμός** hunger. **πῦρ** fire. **κατακαυθήσεται** fut. pass. ind. κατακαίω to burn down, to consume completely w. fire, to burn up. **κρίνας** aor. act. part. κρίνω to judge.
9 ■ **κλαύσουσιν** fut. act. ind. κλαίω to weep, to cry aloud. **κόψονται** fut. mid. ind. κόπτω to beat, to cut, mid. to beat upon one's self, to beat one's breast as an act of mourning, to mourn for someone (BAG). **πορνεύσαντες** aor. act. part. πορνεύω (s.v.3). **στρηνιάσαντες** aor. act. part. (s.v.3, 7). **ὅταν** w. the subj. when, whenever. **βλέπωσεν** pres. act. subj. **καπνός**
10 smoke. **πύρωσις** burning. ■ **μακρόθεν** from afar off. **ἑστηκότες** perf. act. part. ἵστημι to stand. **κρίσις** judging, judgment.
11 ■ **πενθοῦσιν** pres. act. ind. to mourn, to lament. **γόμος** ship's cargo, merchandise (s. MM). **ἀγοράζει** pres. act. ind. to
12 buy, to purchase. **οὐκέτι** no longer. ■ **ἄργυρος** silver. **τίμιος** costly, expensive. **μαργαρίτης** pearl (s. 1 Tim. 2:9). **βύσσινος** linen. **πορφύρα** purple. **σηρικόν** silk. **κόκκινον** scarlet. **ξύλον** wood. **θύϊνος** wood of a citrus tree. This wood which was imported from North Africa, where it grew freely in the neighborhood of the Atlas, was much prized for its veining, which in the

best specimens simulated the eyes of the peacock's tail or the
stripes of the tiger and spots of the panther or the seeds of the
parsley. At Rome citrus wood was much sought after for dining
tables, but it was also used for veneering and for small works of
art which were made out of the hard roots of the tree (Swete; s.
also Pliny, *Natural History*, XIII, 96–102; for a description of the
citron tree, s. also FFB, 190f.). **σκεῦος** vessel. **ἐλεφάντινος**
ivory. **τιμιώτατος** superl. used in the elative sense, "extremely
expensive." **χαλκός** brass. **σίδηρος** iron. **μάρμαρος** marble.
■ **κιννάμωμον** cinnamon. **ἄμωμον** spice. This was a plant from 13
India which was used as perfume (s. Pliny, *Natural History*, XII,
48). **θυμίαμα** incense. **μούρον** myrrh. **λίβανος** frankincense
(s. Matt. 2:11). **ἔλαιον** olive oil. **σεμίδαλις** fine flour. The fine
flour imported for the use of the wealthy (Swete). **κτῆνος** cattle.
πρόβατον sheep. **ἵππος** horse. **ῥέδη** chariot. A chariot which
came from Gaul and had four wheels (Swete; RWP). **σώματα**
bodies, human beings, slaves. ■ **ὀπώρα** fruit, the autumn fruit 14
ripe for ingathering (Swete). **ἐπιθυμία** strong desire, lust, passion. **ἀπῆλθεν** aor. act. ind. ἀπέρχομαι to go away, to pass.
λιπαρός oily, fat, costly, rich, luxury, sleek (BAG; Ford). The
word may refer to the rich and dainty food (Swete). **λαμπρός**
bright, shining. This may refer to the gay attire and costly furniture which were the fruits of Roman conquest and policy
(Swete). **ἀπώλετο** aor. mid. ind. **οὐκέτι** "no longer." **οὐ μή**
"not at all." **εὑρήσουσιν** fut. act. ind. to find. The impersonal
3rd pl. is equal to a pass. ■ **πλουτήσαντες** aor. act. part. 15
πλουτέω to be rich, to become rich. **στήσονται** fut. act. ind.
ἵστημι to stand. **κλαίοντες** pres. act. part. to weep, to weep
aloud. **πενθοῦντες** pres. act. part. to lament. ■ **περιβεβλημένη** 16
perf. pass. part. περιβάλλω to cast about, to clothe. **πορφυροῦν**
purple, purple garment. **κεχρυσωμένη** perf. pass. part. χρυσόω
to cover w. gold, to overlay w. gold, to decorate w. gold. ■ 17
ἠρημώθη aor. pass. ind. ἐρημόω to turn into a desert, to make
desolate, to devastate. **κυβερνήτης** one who guides a ship,
steersman, pilot. **τόπος** place. **πλέων** pres. act. part. πλέω to
travel w. a ship, to sail. "He who sails for (any) part" is the
merchantman who goes w. his goods, or the chance passenger
(Swete). **ναύτης** sailor. **ἐργάζονται** pres. mid. ind. to work, i.e.,
"those who gain their living by the sea" and it may refer to all
those who earn their living in connection w. the maritime industry (Mounce). **ἔστησαν** aor. act. ind. **ἵστημι** to stand. ■ 18
ἔκραζον impf. act. ind. The impf. could be inceptive "they began to cry out." **βλέποντες** pres. act. part. The part. could be
temporal "when they see" or it could be causal "because they

19 see." ■ **ἔβαλον** aor. act. ind. βάλλω to throw. **χοῦς** dirt.
20 **τιμιότης** costliness. ■ **εὐφραίνου** pres. mid. imp. εὐφραίνομαι
to rejoice. **ἔκρινεν** aor. act. ind. **κρίμα** judgment.
21 ■ **ἦρεν** aor. act. ind. αἴρω to lift up. **μύλινος** millstone.
ὁρμήματι rushing, instrumental dat. "w. a rushing," "like a
stone whizzing through the air" (Swete). The great millstone
does not fall but is violently hurled into the sea. This stresses
how suddenly and spectacularly the judgment of God will be
executed, not only upon an ancient city but ultimately upon the
entire anti-Christian world in its opposition to God (Mounce).
22 **βληθήσεται** fut. pass. ind. βάλλω. **εὑρεθῇ** aor. pass. subj. ■
κιθαρῳδός harp player. **μουσικός** pertaining to music, musi-
cian. The word means skilled in music and here it may refer
either to instrumentalists or vocalists (Swete). **αὐλήτης** flute
player. **σαλπιστής** trumpet player. **ἀκουσθῇ** aor. pass. subj.
Music was used in various aspects of life both for entertainment
and religion (s. Mounce; Swete). **τεχνίτης** skilled worker. It
may refer to an artist in metal, in stone, or even in textile fabrics
(Swete). **τέχνη** craft, skill. **μύλος** mill. The word is here apparently the mill, i.e., the whole apparatus as distinguished from the
millstone. The "sound of the mill" is best explained as the sound
23 made by the mill (Swete). ■ **λύχνος** lamp. **φάνῃ** aor. mid. subj.
φαίνομαι. **ἔμποροι** merchants. The word may refer to merchants who deal in foreign exports and imports (s. Mounce).
μεγιστᾶνες "the great ones." **φαρμακεία** use of drugs either
as medicine, poison, or magic (s. Gal. 5:20; Rev. 9:21).
ἐπλανήθησαν aor. pass. ind. πλανάω to lead astray, to de-
24 ceive. ■ **εὑρέθη** aor. pass. ind. **ἐσφαγμένων** perf. pass. part.
σαφάζω to slaughter, to kill.

Ch. 19

1 ■ **ἤκουσα** aor. act. ind. **ἀλληλουϊά** "Hallelujah," "praise
2 the Lord," "praise God" (Ford). ■ **ἀληθινός** true. **κρίσις** judging, judgment. **ἔκρινεν** aor. act. ind. κρίνω to judge. **πόρνη**
prostitute, whore. **ἔφθειρεν** aor. act. ind. φθείρω to corrupt.
πορνεία immorality, illicit sexual acts. **ἐξεδίκησεν** aor. act. ind.
3 ἐκδικέω to avenge. ■ **δεύτερον** a second time. **εἴρηκαν** perf.
act. ind. λέγω to say. **ἀναβαίνει** pres. act. ind. to go up, to
4 ascend. ■ **ἔπεσαν** aor. act. ind. πίπτω to fall, to fall down. **ζῷον**
living creature. **προσεκύνησαν** aor. act. ind. προσκυνέω to
worship. **καθημένῳ** pres. mid. part. κάθηναι to sit.
5 ■ **ἐξῆλθεν** aor. act. ind. ἐξέρχομαι to go out. **αἰνεῖτε** pres.
act. imp. αἰνέω to praise. **φοβούμενοι** pres. mid. part.
6 φοβέομαι to be afraid, to fear, to reverence (s. TDNT). ■

βροντή thunder. **ἐβασίλευσεν** aor. act. ind. βασιλεύω to be
king, to reign as a king, to rule. **παντοκράτωρ** almighty (s. Rev.
1:8). ■ **χαίρωμεν** pres. act. subj., hortatory subj. χαίρω "let us 7
rejoice." **ἀγαλλιῶμεν** pres. act. subj. ἀγαλλιάω to be glad, to
rejoice exuberantly (s. 1 Peter 1:8), hortatory subj. **δώσομεν** fut.
act. ind. δίδωμι. The variant reading would be aor. subj. and
would be grammatical parallel to the preceding subj. (s. TC,
762). **ἦλθεν** aor. act. ind. ἔρχομαι **γάμος** marriage. **ἀρνίον**
lamb. **ἡτοίμασεν** aor. act. ind. ἑτοιμάζω to prepare, to make
ready. (For references to wedding customs, s. Rev. 21:2.) ■ 8
ἐδόθη aor. pass. ind. δίδωωι to give, to allow. **περιβάληται**
aor. mid. subj. περιβάλλω to throw around, to be clothed.
βύσσινος linen. **λαμπρός** bright, shining. **δικαίωμα** righteous
deeds, acts of righteousness. The expression here is the sum of
the saintly acts of the members of Christ wrought in them by His
Holy Spirit which are regarded as making up the clothing of His
mystical body (Swete).

■ **γράψον** aor. act. imp. **μακάριος** happy, blessed. **δεῖπον** 9
banquet. (For an excellent description of both the preparation as
well as the different parts of a Jewish banquet, s. SB IV, 611–
639.) **κεκλημένοι** perf. pass. part. to call, to invite. It was not
only an honor to be invited to a wedding feast, but it was also
very impolite and discourteous to reject an invitation. **ἀληθινός**
true, genuine. ■ **προσκυνῆσαι** aor. act. inf. The inf. is used to 10
express intended purpose. **ὅρα** pres. act. imp. ὁράω to see. An
elliptical expression which understands the words "do not do it,"
i.e., "see that you do not do it" (s. RWP). **ἐχόντων** pres. act.
part. **Ἰησοῦ** "of Jesus," subjective gen., i.e., the witness which
was borne by Jesus. By His life and death Jesus has demonstrated to His followers what it means to bear a faithful witness
to the message revealed by God (Mounce). **προσκύνησον** aor.
act. imp. προσκυνέω. **προφητεία** prophecy. (For the meaning
of this expression, s. Mounce; Swete.)

■ **ἠνεῳγμένον** perf. pass. part. ἀνοίγω to open. The perf. 11
tense of the part. indicates "to have been opened and now stands
open." **ἵππος** horse. **λευκός** white. **καθήμενος** pres. mid. part.
καλούμενος pres. pass. part. **πολεμεῖ** pres. act. ind. to wage
war. The Messiah now returns to the earth as the conquering
king. ■ **φλόξ** flame. **πῦρ** fire (s. Rev. 1:14). **διάδημα** diadem, 12
the crown of royalty, a kingly crown. **ἔχων** pres. act. part. **ὄνομα**
name. The name was that which signified the character of the
person as well as the character of His kingly rule (s. TDNT).
Here the name no one knows would indicate the name that can
be known only when the apocaplyse is fulfilled and the name or

character which will then be revealed is "Jesus Christ his Lord"
13 (Ford). **γεγραμμένον** perf. pass. part. **εἰ μή** "except." ■
περιβεβλημένος perf. pass. part. (s.v.8). **βεβαμμένον** perf.
pass. part. βάπτω to dip. The perf. tense indicates a past completed action w. the continuance of the results or state. The
blood which stains the garment of the conquering Messiah is not
His own, but the blood of the enemy shed in conflict (Mounce).
κέκληται perf. pass. ind. καλέω to call, pass. to be named.
14 ■ **στράτευμα** army. **ἠκολούθει** impf. act. ind. ἀκολουθέω to
follow, to follow after. **ἐνδεδυμένοι** perf. pass. part. ἐνδύω to
15 put on clothes, pass. to be clothed. **βύσσινον** linen (s.v.8). ■
ἐκπορεύεται pres. mid. ind. to go out, to come out. **ῥομφαία**
sword, a large broad sword (s. Rev. 1:16). **ὀξύς** sharp. **πατάξῃ**
aor. act. subj. πατάσσω to smite. The subj. is used in a purpose
clause (Charles). **ποιμανεῖ** fut. act. ind. ποιμαίνω to shepherd,
to rule, to govern. **ῥαβδος** stick, staff, scepter. **σιδηροῦς** iron.
The Messiah's rod is a rod of iron; i.e., it is strong and unyielding
in its mission of judgment (Mounce). **πατεῖ** pres. act. ind. to
tread. **ληνός** trough, wine press. **θυμός** anger, burning anger.
ὀργή wrath, deep-settled, righteous wrath (s. Rev. 16:19).
16 **παντοκράτωρ** almighty (s. Rev. 1:8). ■ **μηρός** thigh. The inscription "king of kings, and lord of lords" was probably the
name written on that part of the garment which fell open across
the thigh (Mounce).
17 ■ **ἑστῶτα** perf. act. part. ἵστημι to stand. **ἔκραξεν** aor.
act. ind. κράζω to scream, to cry out w. a loud voice. **ὄρνεον**
bird. **πετομένοις** pres. mid. part. πέτομαι to fly.
μεσουράνημα mid heaven (s. Rev. 8:13). **δεῦτε** "come here."
συνάχθητε aor. pass. imp. συνάγω to gather together, to lead
together, to assemble. **δεῖπνον** feast, banquet. It is the supper of
18 God in the sense that God will provide it (Mounce). ■ **φάγητε**
aor. act. subj. ἐσθίω to eat. The subj. is used in a purpose clause.
σάρκας flesh, pl. "pieces of flesh" (RWP). **χιλίαρχος** commander of a thousand (s. Rev. 6:15; Mark 6:21). **καθημένων**
19 pres. mid. part. ■ **θηρίον** animal, beast. **στράτευμα** army.
συνηγμένα perf. pass. part. συνάγω to gather together, to
assemble. The perf. pass. part. indicates "to be assembled," "to
stand assembled." **ποιῆσαι** aor. act. inf. The inf. is used to
express purpose. **πόλεμος** war. The political leader described in
Revelation 13 as the first beast assembles his forces for war and
20 the battle takes place at Armageddon. ■ **ἐπιάσθη** aor. pass. ind.
πιάζω to seize, to take hold of. The word was used of arresting
someone and taking him into custody and it was used of catching
animals (BAG). **ψευδοπροφήτης** false prophet. The religious

leader who is the second beast of Revelation 13. **ποιήσας** aor. act. part. **ἐπλάνησεν** aor. act. ind. πλανάω to lead in the wrong way, to lead astray, to deceive. **λαβόντας** aor. act. part. λαμβάνω to receive, to take. **χάραγμα** brand, mark. **προσκυνοῦντας** pres. act. part., to worship. **εἰκών** image. **ζῶντες** pres. act. part. ζάω to live. **ἐβλήθησαν** aor. pass. ind. βάλλω to throw, to cast. **λίμνη** lake. **πῦρ** fire. **καιομένης** pres. pass. part. καίω to burn, pass. to be burning. **θεῖον** brimstone,
sulphur. ■ **ἀπεκτάνθησαν** aor. pass. ind. ἀποκτείνω to kill. 21
ῥομφαία sword (s.v.15; Rev. 1:16). **ἐξελθούσῃ** aor. act. part. ἐξέρχομαι to go out. **ἐχορτάσθησαν** aor. pass. ind. χορτάζω to feed, to fatten, pass. to be filled, to be satisfied. The supper of God is ready, and the vultures gorge themselves on the flesh of the wicked (Mounce).

Ch. 20

■ **καταβαίνοντα** pres. act. part. καταβαίνω to come 1
down, to descend. **ἔχοντα** pres. act. part. **κλείς** key. The key symbolized the authority over a place (s. Rev. 1:18; 3:7). **ἄβυσσος** bottomless pit, abyss (s. Rev. 9:1). The abyss stands here in sharp contrast w. the lake (19:20); the locked dungeon w. its black and bottomless depths form an antithesis to the open
shallow pool of fire (Swete). **ἄλυσις** chain. ■ **ἐκράτησεν** aor. 2
act. ind. κρατέω to exercise power, to take into custody (Mounce). **δράκων** dragon. **ὄφις** snake. **ἀρχαῖος** old, ancient. **ἔδησεν** aor. act. ind. δέω to bind. **ἔτος** year. The acc. "a thousand years" is acc. of time indicating the extent of time. ■ 3
ἔβαλεν aor. act. ind. βάλλω to cast. **ἔκλεισεν** aor. act. ind. κλείω to shut up, to lock. **ἐσφράγισεν** aor. act. ind. σφραγίζω to seal. The sealing would indicate the authoritative placing of a seal so that no one is allowed in or out (s. Matt. 27:66). The purpose of sealing the entrance to a prison was to prevent any attempt at escape or rescue passing unobserved (Swete). The activity of Satan is completely removed from the earth for a thousand years (s. Walvoord). **πλανήσῃ** aor. act. subj. πλανάω to lead astray, to deceive. The subj. could be used either in a purpose or a result clause. **τελεσθῇ** aor. pass. subj. τελέω to complete. **δεῖ** (w. the acc. and the inf.) "it is binding," "it is necessary." **λυθῆναι** aor. pass. inf. λύω to loose, to release. The release will be brief in comparison w. the captivity (Swete).
■ **ἐκάθισαν** aor. act. ind. καθίζω to take one's seat, to sit. 4
κρίμα judgment. **ἐδόθη** aor. pass. ind. δίδωμι to give, to grant. **πεπελεκισμένων** perf. pass. part. πελεκίζω to cut one's head off w. a double-edge ax, to behead. This ax was the instrument

of execution in the Roman republic (Mounce). **προσεκύνησαν**
aor. act. ind. προσκυνέω to worship. **θηρίον** beast. **εἰκών** image. **ἔλαβον** aor. act. ind. λαμβάνω. **χάραγμα** brand, mark.
μέτωπον forehead, brow. **ἔζησαν** aor. act. ind. ζάω to live.
ἐβασίλευσαν aor. act. ind. βασιλεύω to be king, to rule, to
reign. The aor. could be ingressive aor. "they began to reign."
5 ■ **λοιπός** rest. These were the wicked who did not have a part
6 in the first resurrection. ■ **μακάριος** happy, blessed. **ἔσονται**
fut. εἰμί. **βασιλεύσουσιν** fut. act. ind.
7 ■ **ὅταν** w. the subj. "when." **τελεσθῇ** aor. pass. subj. (s.v.3).
8 **λυθήσεται** fut. pass. ind. (s.v.3). ■ **ἐξελεύσεται** fut. mid. ind.
ἐξέρχομαι to go out. **πλανῆσαι** aor. act. inf. to lead astray, to
deceive. The inf. is used to express purpose. **γωνία** corner.
συναγαγεῖν aor. act. inf. συνάγω to lead together, to gather,
to assemble. The inf. is used to express purpose. **πόλεμος** war.
9 **ἀριθμός** number. **ἄμμος** sand. ■ **ἀνέβησαν** aor. act. ind.
ἀναβαίνω to go up, to ascend. **πλάτος** breadth. **ἐκύκλευσαν**
aor. act. ind. κυκλεύω to encircle. **παρεμβολή** camp. The word
signifies either a camp or an army on the march or engaged in
battle (Swete). **ἠγαπημένην** perf. pass. part. ἀγαπάω. **κατέβη**
aor. act. ind. καταβαίνω to come down. **πῦρ** fire. **κατέφαγεν**
aor. act. ind. κατεσθίω to eat up, to consume completely. The
10 prep. in compound is perfective. ■ **διάβολος** devil. **πλανῶν**
pres. act. part. The part. is used here as a noun "the deceiver,"
"the one who deceives them." **ἐβλήθη** aor. pass. ind. βάλλω to
cast, to throw. **λίμνη** lake. **θεῖον** brimstone, sulphur. **ὅπου**
where. Here it is used as a rel. pron. **ψευδοπροφήτης** false
prophet. **βασανισθήσονται** fut. pass. ind. βασανίζω to torment, to torture, to cause pain.
11 ■ **λευκός** white. The great white throne is the final judgment of the unbeliever and takes place after the thousand year
millennial reign of Christ and the judgment of Satan. The absolute purity of this supreme court is symbolized by the color of
the throne (Swete). **καθήμενον** pres. mid. part. κάθημαι to sit.
ἔφυγεν aor. act. ind. φεύγω to flee. Earth and heaven flee away
before the awesome grandeur of God seated upon the throne of
12 judgment (Mounce). **εὑρέθη** aor. pass. ind. ■ **ἑστῶτας** perf. act.
part. ἵστημι to stand. **βιβλίον** book. **ἠνοίχθησαν** aor. pass.
ind. ἀνοίγω to open. **ἐκρίθησαν** aor. pass. ind. κρίνω to judge.
γεγραμμένων perf. pass. part. The perf. tense indicates "that
which stands written." The sentence of the judge is not arbitrary;
it rests upon written evidence; the books which were opened
contain, as it seems, a record of the deeds of every human being
13 who came up for judgment (Swete). ■ **ἔδωκεν** aor. act. ind.

δίδωμι. ᾅδης Hades, the grave, the underworld as the place of
the dead. **ἕκαστος** each one. ■ **ἐβλήθησαν** aor. pass. ind. 14
(s.v.10). **λίμνη** lake. **πῦρ** fire.

Ch. 21

■ **ἀπῆλθαν** aor. act. ind. ἀπέρχομαι to go away, to depart, 1
to pass away. In rabbinical literature some taught that the world would be renovated and made new so that it would return to its original state after creation but would be cleansed from sin and evil. Others taught that the earth would return to the original chaos and would then be recreated w. a new cleansed existence and others taught that the world would be completely destroyed and the new heaven and new earth would be a totally new
creation (s. SB III, 842–847; Moore, *Judaism*, II, 338ff.). ■ 2
καταβαίνουσαν pres. act. part. καταβαίνω to come down, to descend. **ἡτοιμασμένη** perf. pass. part. ἑτοιμάζω to make ready, to prepare. The perf. pass. part. indicates "to have been prepared and to stand ready." **νύμφη** bride. **κεκοσμημένην** perf. pass. part. κοσμέω to make orderly, to put in order, to adorn, to decorate, to make beautiful or attractive (BAG). In preparation for the marriage and the arrival of the groom the bride was bathed and oiled, perfumed, her hair fixed, and was adorned w. her wedding garment. (For marriage preparations, s.
JPFC II, 752–760; SB I, 500–517; II, 373–399.) ■ **ἤκουσα** aor. 3
act. ind. ἀκούω. **σκηνή** tent, tabernacle. **σκηνώσει** fut. act. ind. σκηνόω to live in a tent, to tabernacle. The word indicates the abiding presence of God (s. Mounce). **ἔσονται** fut. εἰμί.
■ **ἐξαλείψει** fut. act. ind. ἐξαλείφω to wipe away, to wipe out. 4
δάκρυον tear, i.e., "every individual single tear." **πένθος** sorrow, mourning. **κραυγή** shouting, outcry, crying in grief or anxiety (MM). **πόνος** pain.

■ **καθήμενος** pres. mid. part. κάθημαι to sit. **γράψον** aor. 5
act. imp. ■ **γέγοναν** perf. act. ind. γίνομαι "they have come to 6
pass." Not only are the sayings mentioned in v. 5 faithful and true, but they have come to pass and their results continue on in the fut. **ἀρχή** beginning. **διψῶντι** pres. act. part. διψάω to thirst, to be thirsty. **δώσω** fut. act. ind. δίδωμι. **πηγή** spring, fountain. **δωρεάν** freely, without cost. In the arid climate of Palestine a spring of cool water would be a vivid symbol of
refreshment and satisfaction (Mounce). ■ **νικῶν** pres. act. part. 7
νικάω to be a victor, to conquer, to overcome. **κληρονομήσει**
fut. act. ind. κληρονομέω to inherit. ■ **δειλός** cowardly. 8
ἄπιστος unfaithful, unbelieving. **ἐβδελυγμένοις** perf. pass. part. βδελύσσω to pollute, to defile, to make detestable, to

commit abomination, perf. pass. part. "to be detestable." The word indicates persons whose very natures have been saturated w. the abominations which they practiced in their lifetime and the context suggests that in this case the abominations are not merely idolatrous acts, but the monstrous and unnatural vices of heathendom (Swete). **φονεύς** murderer. **πόρνος** immoral person, one who practices sexual immorality. **φαρμακός** one who mixes and uses drugs which were used either in sorcery or magic practices (s. Rev. 9:21; 18:23; Gal. 5:20). **εἰδωλολάτρης** one who worships idols, idolater. **μέρος** part. **λίμνη** lake. **καιομένῃ** pres. pass. part. καίομαι to burn, pass. to be burning. **πῦρ** fire. **θεῖον** brimstone, sulphur.
9 ■ **ἐχόντων** pres. act. part. **φιάλη** bowl. **γεμόντων** pres. act. part. γέμω to be full of. **πληγή** blow, wound, plague. **ἔσχατος** last. **ἐλάλησεν** aor. act. ind. to speak. **δεῦρο** "come here." **δείξω** fut. act. ind. δείκνυμι to show. **νύμφη** bride. **ἀρνίον**
10 lamb. ■ **ἀπήνεγκεν** aor. act. ind. ἀποφέρω to carry away. **ὑψηλός** high. **ἔδειξεν** aor. act. ind. δείκνυμι. **καταβαίνουσαν**
11 pres. act. part. (s.v.2). ■ **δόξα** glory, brilliance. The word refers to the shining radiance which comes from the presence and glory of God (s. Mounce; TDNT; CBB). **φωστήρ** radiance, luminary. The word means something in which light is concentrated and thence radiates (Swete). **τιμιώτατος** superl. τίμιος precious, costly. The elative use of the superl., "extremely expensive," "very expensive." **ἴασπις** jasper. In antiquity the designation jasper was used for any opaque precious stone. The point of comparison is the brilliance and sparkle of a gem and the reference could be to a diamond (Mounce). **κρυσταλλίζοντι** pres. act. part. κρυσταλλίζω to sparkle and shimmer like a crystal.
12 ■ **τεῖχος** wall. **μέγας** great, mighty. **ἐπιγεγραμμένα** perf. pass. part. ἐπιγραφω to write upon, to inscribe upon. **φυλή** tribe.
13 ■ **ἀνατολή** rising, east (s. Matt. 2:1). **βορρᾶς** north wind, north.
14 **νότος** south wind, south. **δυσμός** going down, west. ■ **θεμέλιος** foundation. Each foundation was probably a stout oblong block like the stones which may still be seen in the lower rows of the Herodian masonry at Jerusalem (Ford).
15 ■ **λαλῶν** pres. act. part. **μέτρον** measure. **κάλαμος** reed, rod (s. Rev. 11:1). **χρυσοῦς** golden. **μετρήσῃ** aor. act. subj.
16 μετρέω to measure. ■ **τετράγωνος** square, four corners. **κεῖται** pres. mid. ind. to lie. **μῆκος** length. **πλάτος** width. **ἐμέτρησεν** aor. act. ind. **στάδιον** stadion, furlong. A stadion is about 607 English feet; thus, the city would be about 1,400 miles in each
17 direction (Mounce). **ὕψος** height. **ἴσος** equal. ■ **πῆχυς** cubit. A cubit is roughly the length of a man's forearm and 144 cubits

would be 14 miles in height (Mounce). ■ **ἐνδώμησις** the act of 18
building into, "structure," building (Ford; s. also Mounce).
καθαρός pure, clean. **ὕαλος** glass. ■ **κεκοσμημένοι** perf. pass. 19
part. (s.v.2). **σάπφιρος** sapphire. This is a blue transparent precious stone (Ford). **χαλκηδών** agate, chalcedony. This gem is
taken to be of a green color (Charles; Ford; BAG). **σμάραγδος**
emerald. This is a bright green transparent precious stone, the
most valued variety of beryl (Ford). ■ **σαρδόνυξ** onyx, sard- 20
onyx. This was a layered stone of red and white. It was prized
for use in making cameos (Mounce). **σάρδιον** sardus, carnelian.
This was a blood-red stone and was commonly used for engrav-
ing (Mounce; Ford). **χρυσόλιθος** "gold stone," topaz, chryso-
lite. The ancients seemed to have used this term for the yellow
topaz (Ford; s. also Charles). **βήρυλλος** beryl. This was a green
stone ranging from transparent sea green to opaque blue (Ford;
Mounce). **τοπάζιον** topaz, a greenish yellow or gold. In ancient
times it was often used in the making of seals and gems (Ford;
s. also Mounce). **χρυσόπρασος** chrysoprase. This is an apple
green, finely grained hornstone, a variety of quartz, highly translucent (Ford). **ὑάκινθος** jacinth. It was a bluish purple stone and
similar to the modern sapphire (Mounce; s. BAG). **ἀμέθυστος**
amethyst, a variety of quartz, in color clear transparent purple
or bluish violet. It got its name from being regarded an antidote
for drunkenness (Mounce; s. also Ford). (For a brief description
of these stones, s. NBD, 631–634; Pliny, *Natural History*,
XXXVII; N. Hillyer, "Precious Stones in the Apocalypse," CBB
[English], III, 395–398.) ■ **μαργαρίτης** pearl. **ἀνά** "each one," 21
distributive use of the prep. **ἦν** impf. **εἰμί**. **πλατεῖα** street,
broad street. **διαυγής** transparent, clear.

■ **ναός** temple, sanctuary. **παντοκράτωρ** almighty (s. Rev. 22
1:8). ■ **σελήνη** moon. **φαίνωσιν** aor. act. subj. φαίνω to shine. 23
ἐφώτισεν aor. act. ind. φωτίζω to illuminate, to cause to shine,
to give light. **λύχνος** lamp. ■ **περιπατήσουσιν** fut. act. ind. 24
περιπατέω to walk about. **ἔθνος** nation. **φέρουσιν** pres. act.
ind. to carry, to bring. ■ **οὐ μή** "never in any wise." 25
κλεισθῶσιν aor. pass. subj. κλείω to close, to lock, to shut. The
gates would be closed for security at night (Ford). One is reminded of the Isaianic declaration concerning the restored
Jerusalem, "your gates shall be open continually" (Isa. 60:11)
(Mounce). **ἔσται** fut. (s.v.3). ■ **οἴσουσιν** fut. act. ind. φέρω. 26
■ **εἰσέλθῃ** aor. act. subj. εἰσέρχομαι to go in, to come in. 27
κοινός common, profane. **ποιῶν** pres. act. part. **βδέλυγμα** that
which is detestable, abomination. **εἰ μή** "except." **γεγραμμένοι**
perf. pass. part. **βιβλίον** book.

Ch. 22

1 ■ **ἔδειξεν** aor. act. ind. δείκνυμι to show. **ποταμός** river.
λαμπρός brilliant, bright. **κρύσταλλον** crystal.
ἐκπορευόμενον pres. mid. part. ἐκπορεύομαι to go out.
2 **ἀρνίον** lamb. ■ **πλατεῖα** wide street. Probably one is meant to
think of one main broad street in contrast to the narrow streets
in Eastern cities (Ford). **ἐντεῦθεν** "from here." **ἐκεῖθεν** "from
there." **ξύλον** tree. **ποιοῦν** pres. act. part. to make, to bear. **μήν**
month. **ἕκαστος** each. **ἀποδιδοῦν** pres. act. part. ἀποδίδωμι
3 to give, to render. **φύλλον** leaf. **θεραπεία** healing. ■ **κατάθεμα**
curse. The word may refer to that which is cursed (Swete).
ἔσται fut. εἰμί. **λατρεύσουσιν** fut. act. ind. λατρεύω to wor-
4 ship, to worship by serving. ■ **ὄψονται** fut. mid. ind. ὁράω to
5 see. **μέτωπον** forehead, brow. ■ **λύχνος** lamp. **φωτίσει** fut. act.
ind. φωτίζω to illuminate, to shine, to give light.
βασιλεύσουσιν fut. act. ind. βασιλεύω to be king, to rule as
king, to reign.
6 ■ **ἀληθινός** true, genuine. **ἀπέστειλεν** aor. act. ind.
ἀποστέλλω to send, to send as an official authoritative representative. **δεῖξαι** aor. act. inf. (s.v.1). The inf. is used to express
purpose. **δεῖ** "it is binding," "it is necessary." **γενέσθαι** aor.
mid. inf. γίνομαι to happen, be become, to come to pass. **τάχος**
7 quickly. The prepositional phrase is used adverbially. ■ **ταχύ**
quickly. **μακάριος** happy, blessed. **τηρῶν** pres. act. part. τηρέω
to keep, to observe. The pres. tense indicates a continual keeping. **βιβλίον** book.
8 ■ **κἀγὼ Ἰωάννης** "and I John." John now attests that he
has actually heard and seen all the things that are recorded in
the book (Mounce). **ἀκούων** pres. act. part. **βλέπων** pres. act.
part. **ἤκουσα** aor. act. ind. ἀκούω. **ἔβλεψα** aor. act. ind. **ἔπεσα**
aor. act. ind. πίπτω to fall down. **προσκυνῆσαι** aor. act. inf.
προσκυνέω to worship. The inf. is used to express purpose.
9 **δεικνύοντος** pres. act. part. ■ **ὅρα** pres. act. imp. (For this
construction and the meaning, s. Rev. 9:10.) **σύνδουλος** fellow
slave. **τηρούντων** pres. act. part. (s.v.7). **προσκύνησον** aor.
10 act. imp. προσκυνέω. ■ **σφραγίσῃς** aor. act. subj. σφραγίζω
to seal. (For the meaning of sealing, s. Rev. 5:1.) The neg. w. the
aor. subj. is used in a neg. command or a prohibition. **προφητεία**
11 prophecy. **ἐγγύς** near. ■ **ἀδικῶν** pres. act. part. ἀδικέω to do
injustice, to do unrighteousness. The part. used as a noun indicates he whose habit it is to do wrong, "the wrong doer," w.
special reference perhaps to the persecutor (Swete). **ἀδικησάτω**
aor. act. imp. **ῥυπαρός** dirty, filthy. **ῥυπανθήτω** aor. pass. imp.
ῥυπαίνω to soil, to make dirty, to defile (BAG). The filthy

disregard purity of life or even common decency. The aor. tenses here indicate the fixity of the state into which these have entered; there is henceforth no break in the downward course, which is indeed viewed as a single act (Swete). **ποιησάτω** aor. act. imp. ποιέω. **ἁγιασθήτω** aor. act. imp. ἁγιάζω to make holy, to sanctify, to set apart (s. CBB; TDNT; EWNT).

■ **ταχύ** adv. quickly. **μισθός** reward, wage, pay. 12
ἀποδοῦναι aor. act. inf. ἀποδίδωμι to give, to pay, to render.
The inf. is used to express purpose. ■ **ἔσχατος** last. **ἀρχή** begin- 13
ning (s. Rev. 1:8).

■ **πλύνοντες** pres. act. part. πλύνω to wash. **στολή** robe. 14
The word refers to a long flowing stately robe (s. Trench, *Synonyms*, 186; TDNT). **ἵνα** "that," "in order that." The word is used to introduce a purpose clause which is expressed first by the fut. ind. then by the aor. subj. (s. RWP). **ἔσται** fut. (s.v.3). **ξύλον** tree. **πυλών** gate. **εἰσέλθωσιν** aor. act. subj. εἰσέρχομαι to go
into. ■ **ἔξω** outside, without. **κύων, κυνός** dog (s. Phil. 3:2). 15
φαρμακός one who mixes drugs either for magic or for sorcery (s. Gal. 5:20; Rev. 9:21; 18:23). **πόρνος** immoral person, one who commits sexual acts of immorality. **φονεύς** murderer. **εἰδωλολάτρης** idol worshiper. **φιλῶν** pres. act. part. φιλέω to be fond of, to love. **ποιῶν** pres. act. part.

■ **ἔπεμψα** aor. act. ind. πέμπω to send. **μαρτυρῆσαι** aor. 16
act. inf. μαρτυρέω to witness, to testify (s. Trites). The inf. is used to express purpose. **ῥίζα** root (s. Rev. 5:5). **ἀστήρ** star. **λαμπρός** bright, shining, brilliant. **πρωϊνός** morning star,
Venus (s. 2 Peter 1:19). ■ **πνεῦμα** spirit. **νύμφη** bride. The 17
Spirit is the Holy Spirit and the bride is the church. It is the testimony of the church empowered by the Holy Spirit that constitutes the great evangelizing force of this age (Mounce). **ἔρχου** pres. mid. imp. **ἀκούων** pres. act. part. **εἰπάτω** aor. act. imp. λέγω. **διψῶν** pres. act. part. διψάω to be thirsty, to thirst. **ἐρχέσθω** pres. mid. imp. **θέλων** pres. act. part. **λαβέτω** aor. act. imp. λαμβάνω to take, to receive. **δωρεάν** without cause, freely, without charge.

■ **μαρτυρῶ** pres. act. ind. to bear witness, to testify (s.v.16). 18
The Speaker is still surely Jesus. Jesus has borne testimony throughout the Book by His angel, and now He bears it in person (Swete). **ἀκούοντι** pres. act. part. dat. sing. **προφητεία** prophecy. **βιβλίον** book. **ἐπιθῇ** aor. act. subj. ἐπιτίθημι to place upon, to place in addition, to add to. (For the meaning of the prep. in compound, s. MH, 312f.) The subj. is used in a third-class conditional clause which views the condition as a possibility. **ἐπιθήσει** fut. act. ind. ἐπιτίθημι. **πληγή** blow, wound,

plague. **γεγραμμένας** perf. pass. part. The perf. tense indicates
the continuing authority of that which was written (s. MM;
19 TDNT). ■ **ἀφέλῃ** aor. act. subj. ἀφαιρέω to take away, to take
away from, to deduct from. (For examples in the papyri, s. MM;
Preisigke.) **ἀφελεῖ** fut. act. ind. ἀφαιρέω. **μέρος** part. **ξύλον**
tree.

20 ■ **μαρτυρῶν** pres. act. part. (s.v.18). **ναί** yes, yea (s. Rev.
1:7). **ταχύ** adv. quickly, soon. **ἀμήν** amen (s. Rev. 1:7; EWNT).
ἔρχου pres. mid. imp.

21 ■ **χάρις** grace. The benediction is pronounced upon all who have listened to the book as it was read aloud in the churches of Asia (Mounce). Grace is the only ground on which any can stand for eternity (Govett). **μετὰ πάντων** "with all." Through clouds and sunshine, by night and by day, in all times and circumstances, His unfailing grace is their support and strength. It is grace from beginning to end, from otherwise hopeless ruin till complete redemption (Scott).